Branch Rickey

Branch Rickey

Baseball's Ferocious Gentleman

LEE LOWENFISH

University of Nebraska Press   Lincoln & London

Library of Congress
Cataloging-in-Publication Data
Lowenfish, Lee, 1942–
Branch Rickey: baseball's ferocious
gentleman / Lee Lowenfish.
p. cm.
Includes bibliographical references
and index.
ISBN-13: 978-0-8032-1103-2
(cloth: alk. paper)
ISBN-10: 0-8032-1103-1
(cloth: alk. paper)
1. Rickey, Branch, 1881–1965.
2. Baseball team owners—United
States—Biography. 3. Brooklyn
Dodgers (Baseball team)—
Presidents—Biography. I. Title.
GV865.R45L68 2007
796.357092—dc22
[B]
2006029860

To Caroline Rosenstone, for her understanding of the lonely craft of writing . . . and for her warm and loving spirit

Contents

Illustrations

Acknowledgments

Though the following story is by no means an authorized biography, family is one key to understanding Branch Rickey. Unfortunately, by the time I began working on this book in the late 1990s, both Branch and Jane, their son Branch Rickey Jr., and their daughters Sue Rickey Adams and Alice Rickey Jakle had passed away. However, I was able to visit their daughter Jane Rickey Jones and her husband, Robert Terry Jones, in Elmira, New York, in 1999. Bob Jones died shortly thereafter, but follow-up visits with Jane Rickey Jones at the home of her daughter Christine Young Jones in New York City added to my insights. Jane Rickey Jones died in January 2004 and is buried next to her husband in Arlington National Cemetery in Virginia.

I spent a memorable afternoon in the summer of 2000 with Mary Rickey Eckler at the home of her daughter Molly Eckler in Sebastapol, California. I will never forget being served lemonade in a silver pitcher that Leo Durocher had presented to Mary as a wedding gift in 1936. Later, I was able to meet Mary's other daughter, Jenne Eckler Pugh, at whose house in Philipsburg, Montana, Mary was living when she passed away at age ninety-two in November 2005. I have also profited from meeting Betty Rickey Wolfe, the one surviving Rickey offspring, and her daughter Emily Wolfe Phillips. Other Rickey grandchildren who contributed valuable memories and insights are Branch Rickey Jr.'s children Caroline Rickey Hughes, Nancy Rickey Keltner, and Branch Barrett Rickey; John Branch "J. B." and Christopher Jakle; and Elizabeth Adams Louis. I was able to find Beth Louis because of a fine story by sportswriter Tom Wheatley in the May 30, 2000, edition of the *St. Louis Post Dispatch*.

Branch Rickey's niece Julia Rickey Peebles, daughter of Frank Wanzer Rickey, and her husband, Jamie Peebles, provided wonderful stories and invaluable documentation. Late in my work, Donald Hughes, Branch Rickey's grandson-in-law, offered valuable insight and information. Lindsay Wolfe, Branch Rickey's former son-in-law, journeyed from Philadelphia to New York to give me a whole afternoon's worth of insight and stories. Conversations with Branch Rickey's grandnephew Richard Moulton, cousin Alice Moulton Barker, and grandnephew-in-law Charles Hurth Jr. enriched my portrait.

Robert Holm, a longtime administrator at Rickey's alma mater Ohio Wesleyan, was very helpful in providing information and encouragement. I was fortunate to meet and get to appreciate before they died two longtime Rickey men, scout Rex Bowen and front office assistant Bill Turner. Rex's wife, Hazel Stout Bowen, and his son and daughter-in-law Jack and Rita Drummond Bowen added additional insight and offered wonderful hospitality. I benefited from phone conversations with Tuga Clements Adams, widow of longtime Rickey assistant Robert Clements. Alan Cherry sent me many clippings about his colorful father-in-law, Pepper Martin. The honorable federal judge John S. Martin Jr., of the Southern District of New York, offered phone memories of when the Dodgers trained during World War II at the Bear Mountain Inn, which his father operated.

For their warm and informative letters, I offer my gratitude to E. J. "Buzzie" Bavasi, who worked with Rickey in Brooklyn; the late publicist and journalist Gene Karst, who worked with Rickey in St. Louis; and Lester Rodney, who covered baseball for the *Daily Worker* in the 1930s and 1940s. Thanks also to Professor Irwin Weil of the Slavic Studies department of Northwestern University for sharing a memoir of his father, Sidney Weil, owner of the Cincinnati Reds in the early 1930s, and the man who traded Leo Durocher to Branch Rickey's St. Louis Cardinals. (When I discovered that Slavic studies student Nina Shevchuk Murray, who helped edit this book with great skill, considers Irwin Weil a mentor and role model, I realized yet again how wide is the circle of rich relationships Branch Rickey created.) Phone conversations with Joe L. Brown, retired general manager of the Pittsburgh Pirates, and Bobby Bragan, former Brooklyn Dodgers catcher and Pirates manager, proved of lasting benefit. A phone interview with Mario Cuomo was very helpful. I was privileged to meet Rachel Robinson and Dorothy Reese in November 2005 at the unveiling in Brooklyn's Keyspan Park of the statue of their late husbands, Jackie Robinson and Harold "Pee Wee" Reese.

I appreciated the assistance via phone and in-person conversations, letters, and e-mails of the following people: retired Major League Baseball executives Vaughan "Bing" Devine, Robert Howsam, and Lee MacPhail; Continental League organizers Craig Cullinan Jr., now deceased, and Wheelock Whitney; Michael Roth, son of Branch Rickey's Brooklyn statistician Allan Roth; St. Louis Cardinals players Doug Clemens, Marty Marion, and Tim McCarver; Brooklyn Dodgers players Rex Barney, Ralph Branca, and Carl Erskine; Pittsburgh Pirates players Dick Hall, Ralph Kiner, Nellie King, and Frank J. Thomas; and Dodger broadcaster Vin Scully. Thanks too for the Brooklyn memories of Marty Adler, founder of the Brooklyn Dodgers Hall of Fame; prior Rickey biographer Murray Polner; and Bob Rosen, of the Elias Sports Bureau. Lynn, Tod, and Brian Parrott, the sons of Harold Parrott, provided stories and encouragement, as did Ruth Mann Stoecker, daughter of Arthur Mann.

Librarians and archivists are among the unacknowledged noblemen and noblewomen of our times. I am grateful to the staffs of the Columbia University Butler Library and the Forty-Second Street Branch of the New York Public Library, where I logged many microfilm and book reading hours. To Steve Gietschier, archivist of the *Sporting News*, who is a fine historian in his own right; Jane Westenfeld, of the Allegheny College library; Jason Stratman, of the Missouri Historical Society; Kay Schlichting, of the Ohio Wesleyan Beeghley Library; Karen Jania, of the University of Michigan's Bentley Historical Library; Jeffrey Flannery and the indefatigable and gracious Dave Kelly, of the Library of Congress; Tim Wiles, of the National Baseball Hall of Fame in Cooperstown, New York; and Mark Beckenbach and Bill Salyer, college sports information directors at Ohio Wesleyan and Allegheny, respectively, I thank you again. Stephanie Nordmann helped with research in St. Louis newspapers.

I give a round of applause for their swift help and encouragement to the following members of the Society for American Baseball Research: Evelyn Begley, Jim Kreuz, Richard D. Miller, Stephan Milman, Rod Nelson, and Steve Steinberg. Fellow baseball historians Brian Carroll, Richard Crepeau, Donald Dewey, Larry Hogan, Rick Huhn, Peter Laskowich, Larry Lester, Michael E. Lomax, Andy Mele, John Monteleone, Joseph Moore, Rob Ruck, Robert Shaffer, John C. Skipper, and Jules Tygiel answered questions and provided helpful leads. So did New York sportswriters Dave Anderson, Red Foley, Stan Isaacs, Roger Kahn, Herman Masin, the late Harold Rosenthal, Alan Schwarz, and George Vecsey, and Jay Weiner of Minneapolis. Helpful leads and inspiration were provided by writers Jim Brosnan, David Margolick, Danny Peary, and Sam Tanenhaus; Hall of Fame pitcher Robin Roberts; Chicago White Sox scout John Tumminia; SABR director John Zajc; and former Los Angeles Dodgers player and New York Mets manager Bobby Valentine. I want to salute the memory of Stan Lomax, a famed local New York radio broadcaster and former sportswriter who covered the Brooklyn Dodgers in their heyday. We did radio shows together on WBAI-Pacifica in New York in the 1980s, and while I never picked Stan's mind enough about Branch Rickey, he mentioned Rickey often enough to whet my appetite.

I owe a lasting debt to the late James R. Kearney, an old buddy from my years of graduate work in history in the 1960s at the University of Wisconsin–Madison. Raised a St. Louis Cardinals fan, Jim was the first one to put the bee in my bonnet about writing on Branch Rickey. Thanks also to James Odenkirk, a student of Jim Kearney at Arizona State University and emeritus professor at the same institution, who invited me to speak on Branch Rickey at the 1998 conference "Diamonds in the Desert." I want to acknowledge warmly Bill Kirwin, who invited me to speak at the 2001 "Spring Training" conference of *NINE: A Journal of Baseball History and Culture*, held in Tucson, Arizona, and who published a revised version of my speech on Branch Rickey in *NINE* (volume 11, number 1, 2002). Thanks also to Long Island University history professors Joseph Dorinson and Joram Warmund, who invited me to speak on Branch Rickey at the 1997 conference honoring the semicentennial of Jackie Robinson's arrival in the Major Leagues, and who included my work in their volume *Jackie Robinson: Race, Sports, and the American Dream* (M. E. Sharpe, 1998).

Portions of the manuscript were read and critiqued by Rick Huhn, Alan Kaufmann Jr., Caroline Rosenstone, and Charles "Tot" and Bonnie Woolston. Thanks to them all as well as to longtime friends and cheereruppers Ernie Accorsi, Billy Altman, Bill E. Collins and Catherine Kovach, Stephen Ernest Gould, Jane Jarvis, Gary, Jan, and Ted Meckler, Ken Moffett, Paul Staudohar, Walter Srebnick, and my wonderful companions at our monthly "Out to Lunch" club in New York City: Marty Appel, Evelyn Begley, Darrell Berger, Bob Costas, Robert Creamer, Stan Isaacs, Andy Jurinko, Ray Robinson, David Falkner Siff, and Al and Brian Silverman. The memory of founding lunch club members Michael Gershman and Larry Ritter continues to inspire and console.

I thank my family in California for their encouragement. Raised in New York in a solid National League family, my sister, Carol Norton, and I used to go to baseball games at the Polo Grounds and Ebbets Field, where the games of what we considered the real Major League were played. I think I played some role in my nephew Eric Norton's becoming a Mets fan. Warm greetings in baseball to him and his daughters, Lindsay, Kathryn, and Amy, and his wife, Jane DeAngelis Norton, who graciously drove me to my interview with Mary Rickey Eckler.

My warmest thanks are offered for the technical assistance provided to this largely computer-illiterate and too-often-paranoid-about-the-process fellow by Johanna Bresnick, Chris Reeves, and Amy Gilman Srebnick. The flow of this manuscript was abetted immeasurably by the stellar work of copyeditor Shana Harrington and of Nina Shevchuk Murray and Rob Taylor of the University of Nebraska Press. Of course, any errors that may appear in the pages ahead are my responsibility alone. I do hope, however, that there are far more hits and runs for the reader to savor.

Abbreviations

In the text baseball statistics are usually referred to by abbreviations that the sports lover will understand. For the general reader, here is an explanation of terms.

BA = batting average
BB = base(s) on balls or walks
H = hit(s)
HR = home run(s)
R = run(s)
RBI = run(s) batted in
SA = slugging average
SB = stolen base(s)
SO = strikeout(s)
2B = double(s)
3B = triple(s)

Branch Rickey

Prologue

On Saturday night November 13, 1965, nearly two hundred people gathered in the ballroom of the Daniel Boone Hotel in Columbia, Missouri. The weather outside was cold and dreary, but inside the mood was warmly expectant. Earlier in the day the Missouri Tigers had trounced the Oklahoma Sooners, 30–0, and accepted a bid to play in the New Orleans Sugar Bowl football game on New Year's Day. Now it was time to hear the featured speaker of the evening, eighty-three-year-old Branch Rickey, who had just been inducted into the Missouri Sports Hall of Fame.

To most people in the room, Branch Rickey was "Mr. Baseball," the man who had revolutionized the sport not once but three times. As the mastermind of the St. Louis Cardinals from 1917 to 1942, Branch Rickey had used his innovative farm system of developing players to turn a financially struggling franchise in the smallest metropolitan area in the National League into a juggernaut that often whipped the rich big-city boys in Chicago and New York. His signing of Jackie Robinson for the Brooklyn Dodgers after World War II not only was his second baseball revolution, obliterating with a stroke of his pen the so-called gentleman's agreement that had barred American players of color from competing in professional baseball, but also was a gesture of profound social importance that directly prefigured the national civil rights movement in the decade ahead. In the late 1950s Rickey made headlines again as the president of the Continental League, a proposed third Major League that, though it never lived to start a season, played an important role in a third baseball revolution, the expansion of the American and National Leagues.

Branch Rickey was a renowned orator, and the ballroom audience was eager to hear what he had to say. Few realized that he had made the trip from a hospital bed 125 miles away in St. Louis against the advice of his physicians. Branch Rickey had suffered two heart attacks in the past seven years, and the octogenarian now needed a cane to walk. His doctors had warned him that his heart was too weak for a long trip and for the exertion of public speaking, but Rickey was insistent. "Doctors evidently think that you can live forever," Rickey groused. "I've always believed that it is better to die ten minutes sooner than to live doing nothing."[1]

Despite the raw weather Rickey had attended the football game that afternoon. The lure of a Saturday on a campus was irresistible to Rickey, who, as a young man, had coached both football and baseball at his alma mater, Ohio Wesleyan, and had later coached baseball at the University of Michigan. He relished being in the presence of a crowd filled with ardent sports fans and ambitious young people. Rickey was currently leading a fund-raising drive for Ohio Wesleyan, and he couldn't wait to get out of the hospital to continue his work.

Another reason for Rickey's eagerness to attend the night's ceremonies was that George Sisler was a fellow inductee. Rickey first met Sisler in 1912 when the unassuming freshman southpaw pitcher walked into Rickey's Michigan varsity baseball practice and mowed down the upperclassmen with ease. Under Rickey's tutelage Sisler was gradually converted into a first baseman, and, upon his graduation three years later, he rejoined his coach, who was then managing the American League's St. Louis Browns. In 1939 Sisler would be enshrined in the first class elected to the National Baseball Hall of Fame in Cooperstown, New York. The first baseman also became one of Rickey's most trusted scouts, instructors, and friends. When learning that Sisler would be honored on the same stage, Rickey's mind was made up. "I wanted to come because of George," he said.[2] He added that he also wished to pay homage to the posthumous induction of J. G. Taylor Spink, the editor and publisher of the *Sporting News,* the influential St. Louis–based weekly that frequently had featured Rickey's ideas and accomplishments and had named him "Man of the Year" in 1936, 1942, and 1947.

After a warm introduction by St. Louis Cardinals broadcaster Harry

Caray, Branch Rickey hobbled to the rostrum. The audience murmured nervously at the sight of the bushy-browed Rickey's frail physical condition, but once they heard the cadences of Rickey's stentorian baritone—a voice *Time* magazine once likened to Lionel Barrymore playing Thaddeus Stevens—they settled back to be transported by his mesmerizing words.[3]

"I've been in the hospital so much I don't know whether I'm in or out," Rickey began. "I hate to leave anyone in suspense about something like that." Then, using the Socratic method, which had been second nature since his earliest days as a teacher, Rickey asked, "What's the matter with the old man? I'll tell you what's the matter." He explained that he had been hospitalized with a 105-degree fever of unknown origin. Days of tests had proved inconclusive, and he had promised the doctors that he would return for more tests after the night's talk. "You know, I actually believe that the medical profession can produce scientific men who are sufficiently sincere in thinking that they can extend human life in the flesh forever," Rickey declared.[4]

A vegetative life, however, without the struggle to put ideals into action, would never be worth living for Branch Rickey. Thus he was delighted to be speaking on the subject "Courage—Physical and Spiritual." He started by praising the successful performance of Missouri on the gridiron that afternoon. "In football, they call it guts," the onetime coach exclaimed. "Courage, we call it in literature."

Rickey then brought the audience back to a day in the 1920s when he was managing the St. Louis Cardinals and his first baseman Jim Bottomley exhibited rare physical courage. "Bottomley had a fine mind, not scholarly but a fine mind," Rickey recalled, his eyes watering at the memory of one of the first products of his farm system, the son of an Illinois coal miner, who had worked his way up from the Minor Leagues to St. Louis, where he played on three pennant winners and two World Series champions and ultimately won election to the Baseball Hall of Fame.

Rickey set the stage for the story. It was the bottom of the eighth inning of a tied game in St. Louis. Jim Bottomley was leading off and smashed a line drive down the right-field line. He hustled around first base and slid safely on an aching right hip into second with the potential tie-breaking run. Moments later, second baseman Rogers Hornsby, another future

Hall of Famer, singled Bottomley home with the deciding run in a big victory for the Cardinals. Bottomley's hip had been very sore, and he almost didn't play in the game, Rickey noted, but once the dedicated player went out on the field, he risked personal pain in service to his team. What was the moral of the story? Rickey asked. "He paid the price, he paid the price."[5]

The words might seem trite and superficially macho when spoken by ordinary coaches and nonathletic jock wannabes, but somehow when they came out of Branch Rickey's mouth, they carried the force of a genuinely spiritual as well as powerfully physical presence. Rickey's admirer the Reverend Billy Graham once said of him: "He was a rarity, a man's man and a Christian."[6]

"Now I want to talk about something even greater than physical courage," Rickey continued. "Spiritual courage." He was used to gruff, hard-boiled athletic types doubting the relevance of his biblical stories, but they were as real to him as the most secular tales of adventure swapped by his hunting and fishing buddies. Before he could read, Branch Rickey had learned over a thousand scriptural stories on the knee of his devout mother, Emily Brown Rickey.[7]

In his inimitable speaking style, part inspirational coach and part lay preacher, Rickey started to tell the story of Zaccheus from the book of Luke. "It just happens that this chap I'm telling you about, in my judgment, had the greatest amount of courage of any man in the Bible, more than David, Samson, or Paul," Rickey exclaimed. Ever the talent scout and evaluator, he described Zaccheus as "a little fellow. I don't think he could have been over five feet tall. Wealthy, he had embossed shirts and custom-made suits. He was dressed better than anyone around Jericho. He was a tax gatherer, hated by most people."[8] Zaccheus was one of Rickey's favorite biblical characters because he epitomized the kind of person who wasn't afraid to make a fool of himself by going up a tree, literally out on a limb, in search of the truth embodied by the word of Jesus. The passionate, retired executive believed that great baseball teams needed players like Zaccheus, hustling, never-say-die little fellows who knew how to overcome obstacles to win.[9]

This night, however, Rickey would not be able to further expound on the connection between biblical figures and baseball heroes. After an uncomfortably long pause, he staggered, grabbed the lectern, and gasped, "I don't believe I'm going to be able to speak any longer." Rickey collapsed into a chair next to his wife on the ballroom stage. Only the quick thinking of a doctor in the audience, who gave him mouth-to-mouth resuscitation, saved his life.[10] Unconscious, he was rushed to a hospital in Columbia, where he lingered in a coma for nearly a month. Jane Moulton Rickey, his childhood sweetheart and wife of nearly sixty years, maintained a constant bedside vigil, but he never regained consciousness. On December 9, 1965, Rickey's powerful heart ceased beating, eleven days shy of his eighty-fourth birthday.

At the funeral four days later at St. Louis's Grace Methodist Church, Reverend Ralph Sockman, a prominent New York City pastor, eulogized the soul and vision of Branch Rickey. "He was adventurous enough to explore new trails, and he was brotherly enough to bring others along with him," said his close friend, who had been a student at Ohio Wesleyan when Rickey was the baseball coach.[11] After the funeral Rickey's body was returned to his roots in Scioto County in southeastern Ohio, where it would be laid to rest alongside the graves of his parents and other members of the Rickey family.

As mourners gathered in a funeral home in Portsmouth, Scioto County's largest city, they were startled by the arrival of a group of huge black men. On tour one hundred miles away in Cincinnati, the Harlem Globetrotters basketball team had decided to pay their respects to the man whose signing of Jackie Robinson had set a national example for racial fairness. Satchel Paige, the legendary pitcher of the Negro Leagues who broke into Major League Baseball a year after Jackie Robinson, was part of the Globetrotters' traveling party. So was Frank Duncan, Jackie Robinson's manager on the Kansas City Monarchs when Robinson played in the Negro Leagues in 1945. "I can still picture them, one by one, offering condolences to Mrs. Rickey by the coffin," remembers Robert Holm, who was working with Rickey on the Ohio Wesleyan fund-raising drive. "And then as quickly as they appeared, they were gone."[12]

During Ralph Sockman's eulogy in St. Louis, the minister predicted that within twenty-five years Branch Rickey would be enshrined in the New York University Hall of Fame of Great Americans, joining the twelve

U.S. presidents already there. However, Sockman's prophecy has not been fulfilled. It is true that in 1967 Branch Rickey was posthumously inducted into the National Baseball Hall of Fame in Cooperstown, New York, and that since 1992 the Rotary Club of Denver has given an annual Branch Rickey Award to the Major League Baseball player most exemplifying Rickey's humanitarian and community-minded spirit. In 1999 an ABC-ESPN (American Broadcasting Company–Entertainment and Sports Programming Network) special also named him baseball's number one off-field "Influential." Yet the full measure of Branch Rickey's life and accomplishments has largely slipped from memory.

I believe there are several reasons for this neglect. Although the racial integration of the Brooklyn Dodgers in the late 1940s proved a financial and artistic success and made the team a perennial National League pennant contender, Rickey was driven out of Brooklyn after the 1950 season by his partner, Walter O'Malley, who felt he could dispense with Rickey's expensive services. Rickey was hired immediately by the Pittsburgh Pirates, but after five woeful seasons at the bottom of the National League, he was ousted from his position of authority. Rickey was not in the saddle to see the players he scouted and signed in the early 1950s—among them, Roberto Clemente, Elroy Face, Dick Groat, Bill Mazeroski, and Bob Skinner—bring Pittsburgh its first World Series title in thirty-five years, in 1960.

Neither did Rickey succeed in his attempt to establish the Continental League. The pressure of the proposed third league did force the Major Leagues to expand to ten teams and add the new cities of Houston and Minneapolis–St. Paul, but the pioneering executive believed that Major League Baseball needed more than unwieldy ten-team leagues to regain its rightful place as the true "national pastime" of the United States. Impelled by both a love of baseball and a remorseless Protestant ethic to resist idleness, Rickey returned to St. Louis after the 1962 season, accepting a position as senior consultant to St. Louis Cardinals owner August "Gussie" Busch Jr. It was a job that enabled Branch and Jane Rickey to return to a city where they had lived happily for nearly thirty years. However, younger men in the St. Louis organization resented Rickey's ill-defined authority, and he was forced to resign after the 1964 season despite the team's victory in the World Series.

Unfortunately, historical reputation is too often influenced by the last actions of a person's life, and the last fifteen years of Branch Rickey's baseball career were not marked by successes. Developments since his death have also tended to minimize his genuine earlier accomplishments. With the rise of an assertive Major League Baseball players' union, Major Leaguers were able in 1976 to earn the right of free agency after six years in the big leagues. With more than one team bidding for them, salaries leaped, and it became clear that players had been underpaid in the heyday of Branch Rickey.

The wily executive did not invent the "reserve system," which since the 1880s had kept professional baseball players bound indefinitely to one team. He did believe, though, that essentially it was a justified arrangement, and he certainly profited from the lack of a free market for players. Player frustrations at trying to negotiate a raise in salary with Rickey have produced memorable sayings. "He had a heart of gold and he kept it," said Brooklyn and Pittsburgh outfielder Gene Hermanski, while Enos "Country" Slaughter, the future Hall of Fame Cardinals outfielder, groused, "He was always going to the vault for a nickel's change."[13]

Since the 1960s many advocates of the black power movement in American society have also questioned the motives behind Rickey's trailblazing achievement in racial integration. The charge has been leveled that he signed Jackie Robinson primarily for economic advantage. "Jackie's nimble, Jackie's quick, Jackie makes the turnstiles click" went an oft-quoted ditty. As a hard-working, fervent believer in American capitalism, Rickey never denied that he was proud to be a successful baseball businessman who wanted to flourish both financially and morally. Yet, on a deeper cultural level, black power advocates and their white allies have criticized the integrationist zeal of both Branch Rickey and Jackie Robinson. In an erroneous oversimplification, these critics have dismissed Rickey as an overbearing faux emancipator and have charged that Jackie Robinson was too compliant to Rickey's wishes. As we shall see, by ridiculing Rickey's pontificating style, the impatient ideologues have ignored his moral substance and the genuine paternal relationship he built with Robinson the athlete and family man.

Another reason for Branch Rickey's relative eclipse in full historical memory is that at all his major stops in baseball, from St. Louis to Brooklyn to Pittsburgh, he could not help but get drawn into controversies with sportswriters. Probably because he had always yearned to be a college professor, he got into quibbles and more serious rifts with the writers, who could not understand his long-winded speaking style, which made him an easy target to lampoon. Rickey's sensitivity to press criticism was a major, if very human, flaw. He never could follow the wise if cynical advice to "Never offend the man who buys his ink by the barrel."[14]

Branch Rickey poses a formidable challenge to an aspiring biographer because, in the words of John Monteleone, the anthologist of *Branch Rickey's Little Blue Book: Sayings from Baseball's Last Wise Man,* he was "the man of ultimate paradoxes: a capitalist/moralist/competitor/do-gooder/visionary/reactionary all rolled into one."[15] It was said that as a salesman extraordinaire, he could sell a fur coat to a Hottentot and snow to an Eskimo. Frank Graham Jr., a young college graduate working for the Dodgers, remembered his first encounter with Rickey. "There was no break in the flow of words that fell in plangent tones from Rickey's lips. I cannot recall a word he said at the table, but who asks for syntax from the incantatory surge of the sea?"[16]

A minister friend once said of Branch Rickey that he wanted to know everything about you and then make you better. Lafayette "Fresco" Thompson, a former Major League infielder who worked for Rickey in Brooklyn, noted: "If the machinations of Rickey's mind had been observed through a super-powered fluoroscope showing the brain cells arriving at conclusions by serpentine excursions into labyrinthine passages, medical science might be amazed."[17]

To be sure, he could be difficult to work for. He kept long hours, always rushed at the last second to make travel connections, and throughout his life, in the words of Missouri baseball historian Roger Launius, displayed "streaks of petulance, moralism, and autocracy that either infuriated or endeared him to those he encountered."[18] Yet I believe that the rewards of working for and writing about Branch Rickey far exceed the limitations. It is past time to bring him back to life in the fullness of his passions and intellect.

I call this book *Branch Rickey: Baseball's Ferocious Gentleman* because Branch Rickey described his ideal baseball team as "a band of ferocious gentlemen," and in many ways he himself lived the life of a ferocious gentleman. He once said of one of his favorite players, Pepper Martin, the hustling Cardinals outfielder who dominated the 1931 World Series: "He will spend all day trying to beat you, and then stay up all night trying to make you well." In many ways Branch Rickey was a Pepper Martin of the baseball front office, who combined a lust for competition and excellence with genuine warmth, humor, and compassion.

In addition to his baseball achievements and the authenticity of his religious commitment, I want to explore the hitherto-untold story of Branch Rickey the family man, who brought his love of life, religion, competition, and community into the fiber of his household. Though he never forgot the piety and principle instilled by his religious parents on a struggling family farm in southern Ohio, he communicated an unquenchable joy in life. "You never knew fear around him," Mary Rickey Eckler, his oldest daughter, says, and "What fun he had in his life!" exclaims his second-oldest daughter Jane Rickey Jones.[19] So let us embark on the story of a man of astounding energy and radical individualism, a most unusual conservative revolutionary, as he first begins to make an impact on the wider world as a country schoolteacher at the turn of the twentieth century.

PART I

The Making of a Baseball Brain, 1899–1918

I try to be both a consistent ballplayer and a consistent Christian.
If I fail, it isn't the fault of the game or the religion, is it?

—*Branch Rickey to a Cleveland sportswriter, May 1906*

1

Diamond in the Rough

"Do you think you can run me out of my job?" schoolteacher Branch Rickey bellowed at a scowling student, squeezing hard on the defiant youngster's shoulder blades. "Well, you just can't do it. I need the money, I need the job, so sit down!" It was early in the fall of 1899, and the notoriously tough students in Turkey Creek in Scioto County were living up to their reputation as incorrigible and uneducable. The post office address of Turkey Creek might be Friendship, Ohio, but the name was quite ironic. The sons of Turkey Creek's loggers, farmers, and moonshiners had spat upon, physically attacked, and run the last two teachers out of town. Seventeen-year-old Branch Rickey thought he could meet the challenge of Turkey Creek's belligerent youngsters, but he was being tested early.

On Rickey's first day on the job, a long-haired, unkempt student, corn liquor on his breath, defied him by spitting at his feet. Sensing he needed to establish his authority quickly, Rickey ordered the slovenly student outside to settle the issue physically. Out of the classroom they strode, trailed by the other, amazed members of the class, who were eager to see how their audacious new teacher fared. Though Rickey was barely older than the defiant student, he beat him in a bloody fistfight. It would not be the last physical encounter Rickey engaged in with insubordinate students, but he was making the point that education mattered and, if necessary, was worth fighting about.[1]

Among the remarkable aspects of Rickey's first teaching job was that he had earned his teaching certificate without owning a high school diploma. Book learning and formal education were not especially valued in Rickey's home area of Scioto County. Most of the area residents were farmers who didn't believe that advanced schooling was needed for their children to work in the fields. Branch Rickey himself had been reluctant to leave home because his parents couldn't usually afford hired hands. He wanted to help his parents with the chores because his younger brother, Frank Wanzer, was scarcely ten and his older brother, Orla Edwin, was already licensed as a teacher.

Temperamentally, however, Branch Rickey was not cut out to be a farmer, much preferring to read and talk and argue. "He could sit down on a hoe faster than anyone I ever knew," Branch's mother, Emily Brown Rickey, liked to say with a twinkle in her eye.

Since he could earn $35 a month teaching in Turkey Creek, he persuaded himself that he could contribute to the household that way. So he invested in a fancy new bicycle and began commuting seventeen miles each way to Turkey Creek from Lucasville, where the Rickey family had moved in 1893 from Branch's birthplace a few miles away in Stockdale. He was licensed to teach orthography, reading, writing, arithmetic, geography, English grammar, U.S. history, physiology, and hygiene.[2]

Rickey had been hired by two young Scioto County school administrators, Frank Appel and James H. Finney, who saw him as a diamond in the rough, an especially passionate and intelligent young man who had college potential. Appel and Finney were both students at Ohio Wesleyan College in Delaware, twenty miles north of the state capital, Columbus, and they encouraged Rickey to follow in their footsteps. They were aware of his limited financial resources, but they hoped that the Turkey Creek teaching job would ultimately provide him enough money to afford his college tuition.

His mentors also liked Rickey's abilities as an athlete. He was a fierce football running back and a take-charge baseball catcher who was blessed with better than average running speed. In local games Rickey often caught Orla, a hard-throwing left-hander, and the battery of the two brothers was known with respect throughout Scioto and adjoining Ohio counties. In the spare time left after preparing classes, teaching, helping out on the farm, and playing sports, Branch Rickey boned up on the courses needed to enter college. Especially deficient in one of the requirements, Latin, Rickey walked miles for special tutoring in the subject.[3]

Rickey spent two years as a Turkey Creek teacher. Before the second year, Rickey had received an invitation to move to a less physically intimidating school in nearby Pike County at nearly double the salary. However, the Turkey Creek parents wanted to retain him, circulated a petition in his behalf, and offered him a slight increase in salary. Rickey felt obliged to stay when he saw "those Xs of poor people who wanted their children taught," he remembered a half century later to Arthur Mann, his first biographer.[4] Years later Rickey's father, Jacob Franklin Rickey, said that he considered the invitation to return to Turkey Creek for a second year of teaching his now-famous son's greatest achievement.[5]

Known in Scioto County as Frank Rickey, or "Uncle Frank," Branch Rickey's father worked hard on his vegetable farm, trying to eke out a living by growing potatoes, corn, and sorghum in the particularly barren soil of south-central Ohio. Whatever the economic privations of his hardscrabble existence, Uncle Frank was a well-respected and formidable personage in Scioto County. For a time, he served as a county commissioner—a Republican, of course, for it was said of Ohio at the turn of the twentieth century that Republicanism was as natural as snow for an Eskimo.[6] He was also a champion wrestler, well known in the region for his ability to pin men far larger than he was.

Rickey's father also liked to wrestle with God. Raised a Baptist, Frank Rickey, not long after Branch's birth, changed his church affiliation to the more tolerant form of Wesleyan Methodism, a religion that did not believe in heresy and that preached a doctrine of "think and let think." Yet his search for religious purity could be very demanding, and it led him to change churches many times and, when necessary, to establish his own.[7]

Religion played a significant role in the naming of Wesley Branch Rickey. A founder of Methodism was John Wesley, whose conversion in 1738 to a very personal form of Christianity at a meeting house on Aldersgate Street in London, England, became a seminal event in the history of the religion. The name Branch also had profound scriptural roots. One Rickey family Bible contained a handwritten note in which the word *branch* was capitalized in a passage from the Old Testament book of Isaiah, 11:1: "And there shall come forth a rod out of the stem of Jesse, and a Branch shall grow out of the roots." Branch's name might also have been inspired by the New Testament book of John, 15:2: "Every branch in Me that beareth not fruit He taketh away; and every branch that bears fruit He prunes, that it may bear more fruit."[8]

A devout belief in Jesus Christ as God's emissary on earth was thus a foundation in the household of Frank Rickey and his equally devout wife, Emily. Mary Rickey Eckler, the oldest of Branch Rickey's six children, recalls that whenever she visited her grandparents in Ohio, she felt the presence of God. She remembers how Frank would proclaim at grace before meals, "The Lord is the head of this house."[9]

Though Branch Rickey's parents were very pious and God fearing, their household was not a solemn one. Young Branch was encouraged to be an active, athletic boy and to have a mind of his own. He received no parental opposition when he decided to drop the name Wesley as a young teenager to avoid confusion with a cousin who had the same name and also because he simply preferred Branch to Wesley. He was encouraged to read good secular as well as religious books. In 1887, when Rickey was five years old, a fire at a bookstore in Portsmouth enabled Frank Rickey to buy for $2.25 twelve volumes that would become special treasures for his son's entire life. The bounty included Dante's *Inferno*, a collection of Washington Irving's short stories, a New Testament (which Jacob Franklin Rickey inscribed to his son), and a book of the illustrated drawings of Gustave Dore, a French etcher and painter who was also a lay Christian preacher. Dore's graphic representations of biblical struggles and his depictions of stormy and heavenly skies would remain permanently imbedded in Branch Rickey's consciousness.[10]

In addition to the anchor of religion in Branch Rickey's formative years, patriotism also played a major role. Young Branch was especially close to his paternal grandfather, Ephraim Wanzer Rickey, one of the larger landowners in Scioto County. Ephraim had been unable to fight in the Civil War because he had only one eye, so he became a horse trader who supplied steeds for the Union army and then later went into business for himself. Branch loved to listen to his grandfather's stories, and he took careful notice when Ephraim explained that the secret to good horse trading was "to know more about the other fellow's animal than your own."[11] It was a lesson Rickey would shrewdly apply when he got into baseball trading. In *The American Diamond*, Rickey's elegy to baseball written near the end of his life, he likened the authoritarian personality of his grandfather to American League president Byron Bancroft "Ban" Johnson. Both were men of strong determination and self-possession. Once they decided on a course of action, they would pound on a table and declare, "That's the way I think it is, and that's the way it is."[12]

As Branch Rickey entered his second year of teaching in Turkey Creek, he was beginning to look forward to attending college. Frank Rickey, however, was uncomfortable with the thought of his son moving on to the world of higher education. He told Branch that college was really for wealthy people, not for sons of farmers. He did not have to add that the temptation to sin and break away from the pieties and practices of solid Methodist religion would be ever present in the college atmosphere.

Emily Brown Rickey, known throughout Scioto County as Aunt Emma, shared her husband's fears of worldly temptations but she also had faith in her son's morality. Her reading of biblical stories to him had reinforced in young Branch the belief that there was a right way and a wrong way to live. Emily Rickey also believed in the value of secular learning, and she always encouraged Branch to develop his mind to the highest level. As far as she was concerned, there was no limit to what her son could achieve, not just individually but for the greater glory of the community and of God. She and her husband did not have to preach to Branch to imbue him with the living truth of John Wesley's precept, "Having, first, gained all you can, and, secondly, saved all you can, then give all you can."[13]

In addition to the total support of his mother, Branch Rickey had another reason to aspire to college and beyond. While he was teaching in Turkey Creek, his sweetheart, Jane Moulton, had entered Western College for Women in Oxford, Ohio, although she would shortly transfer to Ohio Wesleyan. Jane (born Jenne Moulton and often called Jen or Jennie until she adopted Jane after her marriage) was from the better side of the tracks in Lucasville, the fourth of six children of Chandler and Mary Cecilia Smith Moulton. Chan Moulton was one of the pillars of the small-town Lucasville community. The grandson of a Revolutionary War veteran from Vermont, he was a prominent merchant who ran the Lucasville general store and would be instrumental in bringing the

Ohio state fair to the town in 1904. Moulton, who served for years as a Republican member of the Ohio state legislature, was blessed with a serene temperament. "He takes everything easy and does not worry about anything," a contemporary marveled. "Job could have taken lessons of him and improved his book."[14]

It was expected that all the Moulton children, girls included, would go to college and marry respectably. Though the Moultons appreciated that Jane was smitten with Branch, they harbored grave doubts about whether he could support her in the manner they expected. He was an eager, affectionate young fellow, they conceded, but he hardly seemed a good marital catch. After all, he was a fellow of limited means who lived across the street from the Moulton general store.

Like all young people in love, Branch and Jane knew better. Branch always said that from the day he first laid eyes on Jane Moulton, she was "the only pebble on the beach." She was pretty and had nice legs, but she was also intelligent and athletic. She could outrun many of the boys in town and did so with an insouciant air. She was also a talented painter who, as a teenager, drew portraits of family members that have remained treasured heirlooms.

Branch and Jane understood each other intuitively, and as they grew older, their love and respect deepened. Having as great or perhaps even more of a sense of adventure than he did, she encouraged him to take both the West Point and Annapolis military service academy exams in the late 1890s. He scored very high on both tests but not quite well enough to receive an appointment. "I made almost nothing in history—didn't know what the thing was about," he told Arthur Mann years later.[15] It is also possible that a deficiency in the physical aptitude portion of the exams hurt his cause, which, of course, is ironic in that he would be a Major League Baseball player in a few years and would devote his professional life to trying to perfect the physical science of baseball. Although disappointed by his failure to enter one of the prestigious military academies, Branch Rickey vowed to make something of himself in the world of education. He wanted to succeed, and he wanted to win the hand of Jane Moulton.

Thus, for many reasons, it was a special day in the life of Branch Rickey when, in March 1901, with Turkey Creek's school closed for the year while farming duties resumed, he stepped down from the train in Delaware, Ohio, to begin his college studies at Ohio Wesleyan. Labeled a "conditional" student because of his lack of full academic credentials, Branch Rickey was the picture of the hayseed as he arrived on campus. Clad in ill-fitting clothes (hand-me-downs from brother Orla) and oversized shoes, he carried a battered straw suitcase in one hand and his baseball catching equipment in the other. He had his life savings of barely $60 in his pocket, but he had incalculable richness in the support of his friends.

Lucasville chums Clyde Brant and Ed Appel, school superintendent Frank Appel's younger brother, met Rickey at the train station in Delaware and took him to a rooming house. For 50 cents a week, he rented a room not much larger than a closet, with barely space for a bed and desk. The conditional freshman would make ends meet by rising before dawn to stoke the coal furnaces in several college buildings. Later, he augmented his earnings by waiting on college dining tables.

Adjustment to college life did not come immediately for Branch Rickey. His clunky, pigeon-toed gait and unmistakable country accent led to some uncomfortable moments. Early in his first semester, an experience in Latin class loomed as a potential disaster. When called upon by instructor John Groves to recite a passage from Cicero, Rickey stumbled over the correct conjugation of a Latin verb. Professor Groves asked a flustered Rickey, "What book did you study in high school?" "Yours, sir," Rickey hesitantly replied. The class broke up in gales of laughter, and Rickey reddened with embarrassment.

"See me after class, Mr. Rickey," Professor Groves said quietly. Rickey began to make plans to catch the next train back to Lucasville. Maybe his father was right, and college work was just too difficult for him. However, Professor Groves, like so many of the mentors Rickey encountered in his life, saw the obvious intelligence and eagerness to succeed in the conditional freshman. Groves suggested a special half-hour, 7:00 a.m. tutoring session in Latin for the next few weeks. Rickey jumped at the chance, and before long, Latin became one of his strongest subjects and undoubtedly influenced his eloquent, if long-winded, speaking style of the future.

Another early incident at Ohio Wesleyan became a guidepost in Rickey's education. It happened after one of the first student chapels of the school term. While walking down a hill on campus Rickey hesitantly asked a self-assured upperclassman, "Where do I go from here?" "Go anywhere you damned please," came the snarling reply. Having been raised in a home where swearing was frowned on, Rickey was taken a bit aback by his schoolmate's language and insolent tone. He didn't necessarily take the insult personally, but he remembered who had been so surly to him. When football practice started later in the fall, Rickey tackled the offending student hard enough that the fellow had to be carried off on a stretcher. Fortunately, there were no broken bones, and before long Rickey became fast friends with his teammate, whose advice he had taken to heart: he could go anywhere he pleased, and success was there for those who wanted it badly enough.[16]

Though Rickey was taking a full load of courses and working several jobs to pay for his tuition, he couldn't be kept from the athletic fields. The school provided limited equipment, so Rickey "sewed his own elbow pads on an ragged, unsightly sweater," baseball historian Richard D. Miller has noted.[17] Once again eliciting snickers for his dress, Rickey quickly quieted the scoffers by becoming a football standout. He scored the winning touchdown in Ohio Wesleyan's 10-6 victory over archrival Ohio State in Columbus, and area sportswriters voted him the starting halfback on the All-Ohio college team of 1901.

In the spring of 1902 Rickey was the starting catcher on the baseball team, a squad that finished with a 10-2 record and was awarded the informal All-Ohio college championship. He was thrilled that the core of Ohio Wesleyan's championship team came from his hometown of Lucasville: shortstop Ed Appel, third baseman Clyde Brant, and first baseman Ephraim Rickey, Rickey's cousin, who also later played Minor League Baseball.[18] Ohio Wesleyan's coach was Dan "Mickey" Daub, a former Major League pitcher who had won forty-four games in the 1890s (all but one for the Brooklyn "Bridegrooms," so nicknamed because of the many young newlyweds on the team). Daub put Branch Rickey in the leadoff spot, a rare position for a catcher but a testament to his speed and his igniting force at the top of the lineup.

Rickey showed plenty of pep and ginger behind home plate and loved the sensation of playing for his alma mater. During one contest a young hooligan ran off with the baseball, and for fifteen minutes the game was stopped as Rickey and his friend Ed Appel hotly pursued the culprit down to the Olentangy River. The thief swam away but left the ball in the water. The fiery catcher waded in and reclaimed it.[19]

The earnest and competitive young student-athlete was also making a name for himself on the Ohio Wesleyan football team. No one loved the school spirit embodied in college fight songs better than Branch Rickey, and he was thrilled when he inspired special verses for the annual big game against Ohio State:

> Speak to me, State, only speaky-spiky-spoky;
> Why are those tears on your cheeky-chiky-choky?
> You can't make first down against Rickey-Riky-Roky.
> Amen.[20]

Branch Rickey was enjoying living the life of sound body and sound mind on the Ohio Wesleyan campus, but his meager finances were a constant concern. In the summer of 1902 he accepted an offer to catch for the Portsmouth "Navvies," a semipro baseball team in his home area. He was paid $25 a week and was able to visit for the first time such southern cities as Knoxville, Louisville, Memphis, and Birmingham. Returning to campus in the fall, Rickey carried a huge course load of twenty-one credits so he could graduate in three and a half years. He continued to make ends meet by working his odd jobs, but he also found the time to play sports and to become an active member of the Mu chapter of the Delta Tau Delta fraternity on campus.

Unfortunately, after playing every minute of the first two football games in the 1902 Ohio Wesleyan season, Branch Rickey's college athletic career came to an abrupt halt. Newspaper articles throughout the area reported that Rickey must be ruled ineligible for all college sports because he had received pay to play baseball for the Portsmouth Navvies. He was now a professional, not an amateur, the articles charged. At a time when commercialized sports were seen by many critics as a blight and corruption on college campuses, the accusations were serious.

Rickey was summoned into the office of Ohio Wesleyan president James W. Bashford and shown the clippings. He was also handed a letter from Navvies owner Major Jack Andrews, who argued for Rickey's innocence. "Dear President, Whoever said I had paid Branch Rickey any money was a Goddamned liar. I never paid him a damn cent," Andrews wrote. President Bashford asked the earnest student for an explanation. "Major Andrews is not telling the truth, President," Rickey said. "I did accept pay, but I needed that money for school. I didn't know about the rule, but to tell the truth, Dr. Bashford, I would have played anyway."[21]

"I understand, Mr. Rickey," Bashford said quietly. However, the college president felt that since rules were rules, he had no choice but to declare Branch Rickey ineligible for the rest of his collegiate career. Bashford's ruling was disappointing for the student-athlete, but he realized that varsity athletic participation was only a secondary reason for his coming to college. His primary purpose was to obtain a good education and credentials for a future career in law. Preparing for law school would certainly make a good impression on Chandler Moulton, who Rickey ardently hoped would one day become his father-in-law.

Shortly thereafter, a great opportunity presented itself to the ambitious student. Baseball coach Dan Daub informed the school that he was not planning to coach again in the spring of 1903. For a replacement President Bashford immediately thought of Rickey, who was well liked and admired on the campus and had certainly been forthright in explaining his actions as a semipro player the previous summer. Rickey jumped at the chance. By coaching baseball he could stay involved with the sport, and the job also provided academic privileges. He could sit in on faculty meetings, even though he couldn't speak or vote. He relished the chance to become a part of both the coaching and teaching communities of Ohio Wesleyan.

The style of Rickey's two Ohio Wesleyan baseball teams would foreshadow his professional teams of the future. Following the lead of their young coach, they were highly competitive, passionate, and hustling teams. Though Rickey's first squad in 1903 went only 8-9-1, his 1904 team won 14 of 19 games, establishing a school record that lasted for more than eighty years.[22]

Rickey's first college coaching experience was also significant because one of his players was Charles "Tommy" Thomas from nearby Zanesville, Ohio, the only black player on the team and one of the few black students in the college. (Pictured in a photo of the 1903 team is a black mascot, who was also a student.)[23] An excellent athlete, Thomas had come to owu as an outfielder–first baseman, but after Rickey was ruled ineligible he moved him to catcher, thus making the black student-athlete the first of hundreds of players to switch positions under Branch Rickey's guidance.

In the two seasons Thomas played under Rickey, the coach was anguished by the racial slurs endured by his new catcher. When the owu was in Lexington to play the University of Kentucky in spring 1903, some of the Kentucky players and fans chanted, "Get that nigger off the field!" Twenty-one-year-old coach Branch Rickey raced across the field and confronted the Kentucky coach in the dugout. "We won't play without him!" Rickey declared. Many of the Kentucky fans, having come to see a game, sided with the Ohioans and started their own chant, "We want Thomas! We want Thomas!" After an hour's delay, the game began and was played without incident.[24] Thomas received similar rough treatment at West Virginia University, where he was the first black player ever to play on the school's diamond.[25]

During the 1904 season an incident occurred that Branch Rickey would cite frequently decades later as a key factor in his determination to break baseball's color ban and sign Jackie Robinson and other black players. Ohio Wesleyan journeyed to play Notre Dame University in South Bend, Indiana, but a hotel clerk would not allow Thomas to register with the rest of the team. Determined to keep his squad together, Rickey asked to see the hotel manager, while sending Barney Russell, the team equipment manager, to check on the availability of rooms at a local ymca. Already a passionate persuader at his young age, Rickey managed to convince the hotel personnel to put a cot in his room where Thomas could sleep.

The black player was grateful for his coach's support, but when they arrived in the room, Thomas broke down sobbing, scratching at his skin as if he wanted to forcibly remove the stain of its color. "I never felt so helpless in my life," Rickey remembered to Arthur Mann.[26] Though not yet well read on the subject of racial discrimination, Rickey instinctively empathized with Thomas's pain of rejection.

Rickey realized that, but for the color line, Thomas was a good enough athlete to have a chance at a professional baseball career.[27] (Rickey had also been impressed by another black athlete in Ohio, running back Charles Follis of Wooster College, who had scored four touchdowns against Ohio Wesleyan in 1903 and had been Rickey's teammate on the semipro Shelby Steamfitters football team.)[28] Together in his hotel room in South Bend, Rickey tried to console Thomas, telling him that a time would come when there would be equal opportunity for all, regardless of color. In the meantime he gave his hurting player a pep talk. "Come on, Tommy, snap out of it, buck up! We'll lick this one day," he said, "but we can't if you feel sorry for yourself."

The South Bend encounter between Rickey and Thomas has been re-told innumerable times and was undoubtedly embellished over the years by the master storyteller Branch Rickey. However, there is no doubt that the incident occurred and that Rickey and Thomas remained friends for the rest of their lives, sharing a mutual devotion to their alma mater, Ohio Wesleyan. In 1947 Thomas, who had become a dentist in Albuquerque, New Mexico, told writer Mark Harris the story of his visit to his former college coach in St. Louis "about the time when Dizzy Dean was in his prime." Rather than send him out to watch the game in the segregated section of Sportsman's Park, Thomas remembered that Rickey spent the time talking in his office, saying once again that one day the indignity of racial discrimination would not exist in a land founded on the idealism of the United States.[29]

Reflecting on the South Bend incident more than fifty years later, Rickey told black journalist Carl Rowan, "I later realized that in many cases a Negro could stay in a white hotel if he were a servant traveling with a white man and that so long as this relationship of master and servant was obvious, then it was perfectly all right with whites who otherwise would object to a Negro's staying in the hotel."[30]

In the summer of 1903 Branch Rickey resumed his professional baseball career, signing with a semipro team in Terre Haute, Indiana. However, on the recommendation of Billy Doyle, a onetime teammate on a Portsmouth town club, Rickey's contract was purchased by a team in LeMars, Iowa, which played in the faster Iowa-Dakota League. He hit .265, but his true worth was his catching and overall leadership, which contributed to LeMars's winning the league championship. After the 1903 season,

Rickey learned that Dallas, of the Texas League, an even higher classification Minor League, had purchased his contract for the 1904 season.

The school year of 1903–04, Rickey's last year as an Ohio Wesleyan undergraduate, was filled with many high points for the maturing farm boy. In athletics Rickey vigorously rooted on the 1903 Ohio Wesleyan football team as they provided some major thrills, most notably a victory over the big boys from Ohio State University in Columbus. He yearned to be out on the field with his teammates, but even if he had still been eligible to play, he could not have competed because he had broken his ankle in a Shelby Steamfitters game.

Academically, Rickey received his first full scholarship, enabling him to devote himself completely to study and coaching without the burden of menial jobs. When the 1904 spring term began, Rickey reached another milestone when he was seated in chapel for the first time with the regular Ohio Wesleyan senior class. Having lived up to his academic promise, he no longer carried the stigma of "conditional" student. He would graduate with his class in June 1904, having made good on his goal of completing the bachelor of literature degree in three and a half years. It was a thrilling moment for the young man who earlier had harbored grave doubts about his abilities as a college student. However, because he had not yet taken the required mathematics classes, Branch Rickey would have to wait longer to earn the bachelor of arts degree, a prerequisite for law school.

After graduation he was off to Dallas for another season as a baseball professional. Rickey hit only .261 for Dallas but stole 14 bases, scored 25 runs, and had 41 assists as a catcher, proof that he knew how to throw out opposing runners.[31] During Rickey's year in Dallas the gregarious catcher met a personable outfielder on the Houston team, Charley Barrett, who would become his closest friend among all his loyal baseball associates in the years ahead. Barrett never learned to hit the curve ball and did not reach the Major Leagues, but he was a speedy, aggressive player who loved the game. Barrett "had no newfangled ideas about baseball," Rickey later said about his good friend. "He knew that the main one was to get on and then around the bases."[32]

Rickey's 1904 performance in Dallas was rewarded when his contract was purchased before the end of the season by the Cincinnati Reds, the favorite team of his youth. As a rookie Rickey did not expect much playing time, but he absorbed the Major League atmosphere avidly. On Friday, August 26, 1904, he made his debut in an exhibition game at Rushville, Indiana. "He has a splendid whip and knows how to use it," wrote *Cincinnati Inquirer* sportswriter Ren Mulford of Rickey's performance. "His cheery voice was heard all through the contest."[33]

The next day, with Rickey watching from the bench, the Reds lost a tough home game to Boston. Afterward he handed his chest protector to first-string catcher Heinie Peitz. "You better take this," Rickey told his teammate. "I won't be here tomorrow." Sunday was his regular day of rest and worship, and Rickey assumed that Dallas owner Joe Gardner and field manager Charlie Moran had informed Cincinnati officials of his Sabbatarian convictions. However, Reds manager Joe Kelley, a crusty member of the tough, brawling championship Baltimore Orioles teams of the 1890s, knew nothing about Rickey's beliefs and contract stipulation. When he overheard Rickey's conversation with Peitz, Kelley barked, "This is a Sunday town; that's when the dough comes in to pay you fellows."[34] Kelley told Rickey that if he didn't play on Sunday, he should see Cincinnati owner August "Garry" Herrmann, receive his pay, and never return to the Reds.

Rickey was confused and concerned, but he was not going to bend his principles or yield his contractual rights. He also was not the only player unwilling to play Sunday baseball at a time when Cincinnati and St. Louis were in the small minority of cities allowing it. Famed New York Giants pitcher Christy Mathewson was the most noteworthy Sabbatarian early in his career (he later relented and played on Sunday), but several other Major Leaguers also did not play on the Sabbath. In the Sunday game Rickey refused to play, three Boston players also sat out for religious reasons, prompting the *Sporting News* to call the contest a "baseball farce" with "too many Sabbatarians" on the Boston team.[35]

Without any second thoughts Branch Rickey made the one-hundred-mile journey from Cincinnati to Lucasville for Sunday worship and rest with his family. He was consoled, as always, by his visits to his sweetheart, Jane Moulton, who was back in Lucasville, living with her parents after graduating from Ohio Wesleyan in 1903.

On Monday he returned to Cincinnati and headed to the imposing city hall office of Garry Herrmann, a onetime city water works commissioner who was a kingpin in the local Democratic political machine of "Boss" James Cox.[36] As he entered Herrmann's office Rickey saw the baseball mogul seated in a leather swivel chair more luxurious than any piece of furniture he had ever seen. After some hesitation because he felt one's religious beliefs and practices were private, Rickey defended his decision not to play on Sundays. He explained the deep religious commitment of his family and his plans to use professional baseball as a means of paying for his college and, ultimately, law school education. Rickey's side of the story was news to Herrmann, who listened sympathetically.

Like many others in authority at the beginning of young Branch Rickey's career, Garry Herrmann could not help but be impressed by the articulate, ambitious, and genuinely religious young man. Here was a raw rookie with only a few days in the Major Leagues, Herrmann thought, and he was willing to risk dismissal for his principles. "You go back to the team and tell Kelley I sent you," Herrmann declared. "Report every day except Sundays."[37] Pleased by the owner's support, Rickey returned to the Reds, only to find manager Kelley still adamantly opposed to his presence on the team. Though he did shine in an exhibition game victory, Rickey did not play in any games that counted in the standings.

Meanwhile, word of his refusal to play on Sunday became a big story in the Lucasville newspapers. Rickey's parents were upset that the stories in the sports pages made it seem as if their son was not playing at their request. Before he left on a road trip, Rickey wrote his "Dear Ones at Home" that he was "very sorry that the paper misrepresented somewhat" his views. It was one of the first times and, unfortunately, not the last time that the sportswriters made his refusal to play on Sunday a matter of something his "Ma" had demanded of him. "You need never feel that I will shift the burden of censure upon your shoulders," Rickey wrote. "My convictions are not for sale and no paltry sum of money can induce me to desert one of them."[38]

Early in September 1904, the unrelenting Joe Kelley prevailed on Garry Herrmann to give Rickey his release. Rickey was disappointed, hating to fail at anything, but he was shortly to start a new coaching and teaching job at Allegheny College in western Pennsylvania. Before he left for his new job, Rickey went into Herrmann's office to work out a settlement for his brief services for the Reds. The owner was again friendly, expressing regret that Rickey hadn't played in a regular season game, but he said that he couldn't interfere with field manager Kelley's prerogative. Expecting only payment for his expenses, Rickey was pleasantly surprised when Herrmann wrote him a check for over $300, which included a pro-rated monthly salary for the time he was on the Reds' roster.[39] It was the largest check Branch Rickey had ever received. On one hand he felt that he hadn't earned the salary because he hadn't played in any games, but on the other hand he needed the money and was very grateful.

After thanking the Cincinnati mogul for his generosity, Rickey headed home to Lucasville for a visit with his parents and a reunion with Jane Moulton. While in Lucasville Rickey realized what a stir the publicity about his not playing on Sunday had caused. He remembered years later to *New Yorker* writer Robert Rice that the town atheist was crowing about the trouble someone could get into if he believed too literally in scripture. "When [Rickey] heard the atheist's gloomy gibes, and when he heard his mother proudly defend him," Rice wrote, ". . . he resolved from then on not entering a baseball park on Sunday would for him have not only a religious significance but a symbolic personal significance as well; it would be a public gesture of solidarity with his mother."[40] The symbolism became very important to Branch Rickey, even if he never could adequately explain to most people, especially sportswriters, that it was a personal choice of his own and not something demanded by his mother. Emma Rickey's method of parenting was never by fiat but, rather, through example, reason, and love, a philosophy that Branch Rickey himself tried to live by.

After saying good-bye to the most important people in his life—his parents and his sweetheart— Branch Rickey set off for Allegheny College, a small Methodist institution in Meadville, Pennsylvania, located north of Pittsburgh and south of Erie, where he would serve as football and baseball coach and instructor in Shakespeare, English, and freshman history.

By the fall of 1904 college football had become a prominent spectator sport, even at small colleges like Allegheny, and Rickey was ready to make an impact on the campus. Taking advantage of the extra time to prepare because of his early departure from Cincinnati, Rickey gathered his Allegheny Gators football team for preseason training at the resort town of Conneaut Lake. In a foreshadowing of his future professional baseball spring trainings, he worked his players long and hard but always left time for relaxation and recreation. After a communal breakfast, a typical day started with rowing contests on the lake, followed by two hours of football drills. After lunch, the team swam and frolicked on the beach and then returned for more drills on fundamentals. At night Rickey gave the assembled squad a classroom lecture on football strategy.[41]

When the team returned to Meadville, the college community was enthusiastic about its prospects. Unfortunately, Rickey's Allegheny squad was no match for area powerhouse Penn State, who routed the undermanned visitors, 50–0. The *Campus*, the student newspaper, reported, "Saddest and most dejected of all was the coach, [who] had labored so hard and diligently to get the men into good playing form."[42] Yet Rickey bounced back quickly, and the next night addressed a campus rally. "Although we lost [at State], we don't want your sympathy. We want your support. Encourage the players by your presence on the foot ball [*sic*] field. Root, sing, do anything to help our team," he declared. Sounding the kind of stern note that would be a common theme in the exhortations throughout his career, Rickey told the student body, "Be loyal to your college. If you are loyal, you'll root; if you're not loyal, you had better go back to the farm and go to work."[43]

The student newspaper knew that it had a vivid subject in Rickey. One writer described Rickey, in what would soon be a familiar guise throughout his career, as "bent over a checker board, hard at work planning new plays for the [next] game."[44] In Rickey's first year as a coach, even though his team was outscored 268 to 67 points, Allegheny turned in a 5-5 record. "Every player and every scrub is a staunch friend of Coach Rickey," the *Campus* wrote, and all wanted him to return next season.[45]

In addition to the Allegheny campus community, local Meadville residents were taking notice of Branch Rickey and his feisty team. After one stirring victory, the *Daily Tribune Republican* exulted: "The determined . . . style of work by the local men made the spectators forget the disagreeable weather, and enthusiasm ran riot."[46] Rickey's lectures at the local Young Men's Christian Association on "The Evidence of Manliness on the Athletic Field" were also creating a buzz in Meadville.

Before the start of Rickey's first baseball season at Allegheny in the spring of 1905, the passionate young coach addressed the student body in chapel. "We do not expect to win many games for we have a team composed entirely of new men," Rickey said. "So much the more do we need your support. Had we a winning team we would not feel so much need of your help." He encouraged good rooting and the presence of the pep band at games, but he cautioned that booing and unsportsman-like behavior were not welcome. He explained that the team captain is best at handling any disputes on the field, and he urged the student body to cheer on the boys and give money to help the team meet its expenses. Rickey's prediction for his first and, as it turned out, only season as Allegheny baseball coach proved accurate as the team finished with a record of 3-7 with 1 tie.[47]

Rickey was consoled by the thought that a new adventure in professional baseball awaited him. Early in 1905 he learned that Chicago White Sox owner Charles Comiskey had purchased his contract from Dallas. Comiskey, a former Major League first baseman known for his excellent fielding, was already a dominant figure in the new American League, which, thanks to the strong leadership of president Ban Johnson, had established parity with the older National League in 1903.

In a sign of the twenty-three-year-old's athlete self-assuredness, Rickey asked Comiskey for contract provisions that forbade his playing on Sunday and allowed him to report late because of college duties. "He graciously accepted my terms," Rickey wrote in *The American Diamond* about his first dealings with the formidable Chicago mogul.[48] However, shortly after Rickey returned his signed contract, the owner changed his mind and decided that he needed a catcher who would play every day. Comiskey traded him to the St. Louis Browns for catcher Frank Roth.

Rickey reported to the Browns at the end of the Allegheny baseball season, beginning an association with a city that the country boy would come to love for the rest of his life. The Browns' manager was Jimmy McAleer, a former Major League outfielder who had been a key recruiter for Ban Johnson when the American League wanted to establish a St. Louis franchise.[49] McAleer was a native of Youngstown, Ohio, and as would happen often in his life ahead, Rickey found the home state connection a significant one in his relationships. The hard-boiled, forty-year-old McAleer called his scrappy, inquisitive, twenty-three-year-old catcher "Kid" and patiently answered the many questions about defensive and offensive strategy that bubbled out of his new backstop. Although the manager was glad at having his mind picked, sometimes the torrent of queries from curious Branch Rickey could grow overwhelming.

Rickey made an even more important connection in St. Louis with the team owner, Robert Lee Hedges. Hedges had risen to the top in American business after a modest start in life in a town outside of Kansas City. He lost his father and brothers at an early age, and his first job was as a clerk in an office of deeds in Missouri. Yet by age twenty-five Hedges had become a successful horse-and-buggy carriage manufacturer in Cincinnati. When he realized that the invention of the newfangled automobile threatened the future of his old-fashioned business, Hedges sold out at the top of the market, earning the notice of the J. P. Morgan banking house, which made him one of its midwestern representatives.[50]

It was Ban Johnson, based in Cincinnati, who brought Hedges into the American League, convincing him to move his Milwaukee Minor League franchise to St. Louis in 1902. Hedges was a man with many forward-looking ideas. He was the first owner to sponsor "Ladies Days," a promotion where women were admitted for free or minimal charge. He banned the sale of alcohol and hired security guards to control rowdy behavior at the ballpark. In 1908 Hedges would open at his home field, Sportsman's Park, the first steel-and-concrete grandstand in the Major Leagues.[51]

On June 14, 1905, Branch Rickey made his Major League debut for Hedges' St. Louis Browns. Entering a game in which the team was trailing Connie Mack's powerful Philadelphia Athletics, 8–1, Rickey handled Browns spitball pitcher Cy Morgan with ease and the A's scored no more runs in the game. Rickey was less impressive on offense. His first Major League at-bat came against George Edward "Rube" Waddell, the talented if eccentric Athletics southpaw, and he struck out on three pitches against the future Hall of Famer. In his two other at-bats Rickey struck out again and flied out.[52]

The glow from Rickey's first Major League competition quickly faded when he learned after the game that his mother had taken ill in Lucasville. Orla Rickey phoned his younger brother with an urgent plea to come home. The cause of Emily Rickey's illness was unknown, and the family was squabbling about what doctor to call. Rickey left immediately, with manager McAleer more sympathetic to Rickey's personal plight than Joe Kelley had been to Rickey's Sunday absence in Cincinnati. "You're only allowed one mother, kid," McAleer said. "Go on home, and stay as long as you are needed."[53]

Emma Rickey slowly recovered from her illness, her spirits obviously buoyed by the presence at home of a favorite son. While tending to his mother, Branch began to seriously study the books he would need for law school, reading by lamplight in a tiny room at the top of the stairs at the family home in Lucasville. However much he enjoyed playing baseball at the highest level, Branch Rickey still told himself that his future lay in law. Only then could he convince Chandler Moulton he was worthy of the hand of his daughter.

By mid-July 1905 Emma Rickey was sufficiently recovered for Branch to resume his playing career. Although the Browns were mired in the American League basement, manager McAleer advised Rickey that he wouldn't get enough playing time and told him that he would be best served playing every day in Dallas. The young catcher returned to the Texas League, where he picked up where he left off in 1904. He threw out more than half of the would-be base stealers and improved his batting average to .295, with 8 doubles and a home run among his 39 hits for a Dallas team that, while struggling when Rickey arrived, managed to finish at the respectable .500 mark.[54]

Minor League seasons traditionally ended by Labor Day, so Rickey was back at Allegheny by mid-September, preparing for his second season as coach and teacher. He soon received word that the Browns were so pleased with his Dallas showing that they wanted him back in 1906. Robert Hedges had been impressed by Branch Rickey, much as Rickey had been enthralled with Hedges as an admirable example of a self-made man and intelligent baseball capitalist. Buoyed by the news of his advancing baseball career, Rickey turned his attentions to the 1905 Allegheny football season with the hope of improving the school's surprise showing of the previous season.

Controversy swirled around the world of college football in fall 1905. Serious injuries were plaguing the sport, with almost 20 players killed and more than 150 injured in the 1905 season alone. The death of a Union College player from upstate New York in a game against New York University impelled President Theodore Roosevelt to summon to the White House the coaches of the big three universities in the East—Harvard, Princeton, and Yale. He warned them that they should control excess violence in their sport or else face possible national legislation.[55]

However, Roosevelt never took any action to regulate football's violence because he felt the sport could legislate itself and because his philosophy of "the strenuous life" left ample room for the importance of sports. A young Branch Rickey endorsed the Republican president's assertion: "In life, as in a football game, the principle to follow is: Hit the line hard; don't foul and don't shirk, but hit the line hard."[56]

At Allegheny, Rickey set a Rooseveltian tone for the upcoming 1905 football season in a speech at the college gymnasium about what was already one of his favorite subjects: courage. More than fifty years later an Allegheny graduate, Ray F. Turner, wrote that he never forgot the definition of courage that the coach had elucidated in his campus speech: "the drawing upon inner resources in emergencies and the giving of the last ounce of energy in any cause deemed worth while." Nor did Turner forget Rickey's concrete example of "a halfback who, battered, numbed, exhausted, called again, got up on his feet and summoning every drop of strength left in him . . . throws it into one more try."[57]

Rickey's intense passion for competition could provoke some satire. A whimsical student sportswriter "interviewed" Allegheny's tackling dummy during the 1905 season and came up with this "confidential" assessment of the college's earnest young coach. "I may tell you candidly that I regard that man Wesley Branch Rickey as endowed with a savage, barbaric nature unaffected by the advance of Christian civilization," the "dummy" opined. "When he digs at me with a nose-guard between his teeth and Sam Hill in his eye, there's no show for your Uncle Dudley. I just lie right down and bite dirt."[58]

Although Rickey's 1905 football team was slightly more competitive on the field than his 1904 squad, its record fell to 3-8. The team held the opposition to 215 points, an improvement on 1904, but scored only 66 points. Even more distressing for Branch Rickey than the poor won-lost record was the discovery that several of Allegheny's opponents had used "ringers," or ineligible players. Rickey, who believed in fair field with no favor, especially in a religiously oriented small college conference, was dismayed.

Rickey was also distraught when, during the season, one of the full-backs he most counted on, Marvin Orestus Bridges, was wooed away by league rival Washington and Jefferson. It was not uncommon in the formative years of so-called amateur college sports for a "tramp athlete," who was not enrolled in any classes, to sell his services under the table to the highest bidder. However, the idealistic Rickey's inability to keep Bridges from defecting left him thoroughly disillusioned. "He called no more chapel rallies, gave out no newspaper interviews and . . . held no more practice sessions," wrote college historian John Hanners.[59]

The tension between the amateur ideal of Victorian sportsmanship and the harsh reality of impoverished athletes was acutely felt by Branch Rickey throughout his life. After all, he had lost his college eligibility when he admitted to accepting money to play baseball, and he said that he would have done it again because he needed the money. How to reconcile the demands of commerce with the ideals of pure competition was a conundrum that would both plague and stimulate Branch Rickey's restless, fertile mind for the rest of his life. "Can you put the words 'Sport' and 'Professional' together?" he mused late in his life. "Is there moral turpitude in accepting money for display of physical skills?" On the other hand, Rickey never forgot what the University of Pennsylvania provost told him shortly after the New York Giants' great pitcher Christy Mathewson shut out the Philadelphia Athletics three times in the 1905 World Series. If Mathewson "qualifies in every respect with the college requirements for eligibility," the academic official told an impressionable young Rickey, he certainly should be allowed to pitch for the university.[60]

Christmas in 1905 brought more than the typical season of holiday joy for Branch Rickey. The year ahead promised many happy tidings. The St. Louis Browns wanted him back for the 1906 season, and his alma mater, Ohio Wesleyan, was prepared to hire him in the fall as athletic director; baseball, basketball, and football coach; and part-time law and literature instructor. Thus he no longer needed the jobs at Allegheny, a fortunate development because he was disillusioned with football, and baseball in 1906 would be limited to intramural status.[61] With salaries assured from two sources, professional baseball and the college, Branch Rickey felt financially secure enough to ask Jane's father formally for the hand of his daughter. Sensing that she had found her mate for life, Chandler Moulton consented to the marriage. The tacit agreement between Branch Rickey and his future father-in-law was that by the end of the 1907 season, the young catcher would retire from professional baseball and begin the study of law.

The happy young couple excitedly went to study the 1906 American League schedule to select a convenient day for their wedding. In late May, on the way home from their first eastern road trip of the season, the Browns would be playing in Cleveland. Branch and Jane decided that Friday June 1, 1906, would be an ideal wedding day for a ceremony in the Moultons' living room in Lucasville.

In March 1906 Rickey arrived in Texas for his first Major League spring training as a member of the St. Louis Browns. Owner Robert Hedges was glad to see Rickey, but manager Jimmy McAleer was not so pleased to have him back. Like Joe Kelley he was beginning to grouse about Rickey's planned Sunday absences and his overly religious outlook on life. Far away from his family and fiancée back in Ohio, Branch Rickey was again swept with waves of doubt about his future, wondering how long he could survive in baseball's excessively profane world. One fact was certain: he was not going to compromise his loyalty to his religion and his family. Rickey poured out his conflicted emotions in a letter to his parents.

"Honestly I'm just about ready to declare myself something besides a ball player. It is a sort of disgraceful profession. A few men make it so," he complained. "'Don't tell any one you are a ball player' if you want to meet good people. All ball players are wise on that point. I get more and more disgusted, and every time I have a good thought, I get more disgusted." Genuinely upset at the immoral behavior of a handful of ballplayers, Rickey expressed a revealing hope that his fiancée might help him choose a career other than baseball. "I think that Jen [Jane] will be able to persuade me very easily to something else," he wrote his parents. "I hope so—at any rate."[62]

Actually, Jane Moulton, who loved a man of enthusiasm, would be supportive of any route Branch chose for his life as long as he committed himself without reservation. She constantly encouraged him to better himself and to take chances, and she would be there for him and with him. "She held her own with Grandpa the way few women could have," granddaughter Nancy Rickey Keltner, daughter of Branch Rickey Jr., remembers. "It was a delight to watch."[63]

Yet the question of his deep religiosity still dogged Rickey wherever he traveled in the baseball world. In May 1906, not long before he left for his wedding day, a *Cleveland Press* sportswriter asked Rickey for comments on the provocative question "How do religion and pro baseball mix?" He was bothered once again by the invasion of privacy in such a query, but always loving to talk and express himself, Rickey tried to give a forthright answer.

"Why shouldn't they mix well? I try to be both a consistent ballplayer and a consistent Christian. If I fail, it isn't the fault of the game or the religion, is it? . . . [Religion] isn't a thing a fellow likes to talk about. My hometown is Portsmouth, Ohio, and my people are all Methodists. Sunday to me has always been a day apart. I can't help it. It was bred in me. You might almost call it a prejudice. So I won't play Sunday ball. I made them put it in my contract that I wouldn't have to. Instead, I go to church. I'm a member of the St. Louis YMCA and, whatever city I'm in, I generally find time to visit the local association. You see I'm doing the things I was brought up to believe in."

Rickey took pains to make it clear that he was speaking about only his personal preference, but he was such a mesmerizing speaker that his remarks were circulated widely and the *Campus*, the student newspaper at Allegheny College, reprinted them in full. He continued: "It doesn't necessarily follow that the other fellows have to believe as I do. That's why I'm sorry you put this proposition to me. I'm not a missionary and the boys on the team would have a right to resent it if I should have the nerve to try to convert them. The boys don't need conversion. They're good fellows, they have made me one of them, and I know of no reason why in such company a man can't play professional ball weekdays and be a consistent Christian all the week round."[64]

Shortly after the interview was published, the earnest, excitable young catcher took leave of the Browns in Cleveland and headed toward Lucasville and his wedding day. On his way home, however, he received a scare when he ate some poorly cooked oysters at a restaurant. He was felled with a case of ptomaine poisoning but recovered quickly. Nothing was to spoil the day he had dreamed about for years. When he arrived in Lucasville a day before the wedding, he was greeted at the train station by a horde of his well-wishing friends and a brass band welcoming home the conquering hero. Jane's friends were equally excited and playful about the coming big day; one of them may have even plotted to lock away Jane's bridal night dress at the local train station.[65]

On Friday, June 1, 1906, Branch Rickey and Jane Moulton were married in the stately living room of her parents, Chandler and Mary Moulton. Decorous music and contented sighs from the gathered assemblage filled the air. The next day the *St. Louis Post-Dispatch* reported the news about a player who, it described, "certainly for peculiarity, . . . is in a class by himself." The newspaper reported: "Mr. Rickey had taken unto himself a wife, . . . a Miss Jennie Moulton, daughter of State Senator Chandler Moulton." They were expected back in St. Louis "early next week."[66] The newlyweds weren't going to enjoy a long honeymoon, but they were in love and devoted to each other. However, as Jane Moulton Rickey would find out if she didn't realize already, her marriage would be interrupted by the baseball season.

2

From Catcher to Coach

"Whoa, young man, whoa!" Branch Rickey yelled to the young pitcher throwing to him in the Ohio Wesleyan field house. It was early in the new year of 1907, and the enthusiastic young baseball coach was helping his young team get into shape. However, he was due to resume his Major League playing career in the spring, and he was worried. A nagging pain in the shoulder of his throwing arm just wouldn't go away. Had he overdone demonstrating snap throws, his specialty for picking off napping base runners? He knew that he was hurting and needed to call off his indoor activities.

Rickey's pain seemed to go away with rest, and he had much to look forward to. At the end of 1906 he had earned his bachelor of arts degree from Ohio Wesleyan and was now eligible to begin preparatory law studies. The modest salaries from the athletic department and part-time teaching at the college came in handy for the young newlywed. So did the bonus of $320 that Robert Hedges had sent him as his share of the proceeds from the annual postseason Browns-Cardinals city series in St. Louis. Rickey could surely use the money, and he was flattered that the players, probably at the suggestion of Hedges, had voted him a share even though he didn't play because of his duties at the college.[1]

Rickey had ended the 1906 season with a rush, batting nearly .400 over the final weeks and helping the Browns finish over .500, with a 76-73 record. They almost made the first division, trailing the fourth-place Philadelphia Athletics by only four games. The Browns, though, were sixteen games behind the eventual World Series champions, the Chicago White Sox.

In the fall of 1906 Rickey had taken over an Ohio Wesleyan football team that had finished last in its conference in 1905, and he brought them home tied for second. Outmanned and outweighed by larger opponents, Rickey's Ohio Wesleyan squad used speed and quickness to outwit their opponents. After the season the *Bijou*, the campus yearbook, raved: "The bewildering mass of plays that were evolved from 'Rick's' fertile brain simply dumbfounded the 'dopesters' over the state and he got the credit he well deserved of being one of the brainiest coaches in Ohio."[2] The 1906–07 basketball team would win nine out of thirteen games, a good showing in a sport that had been taken up on campus only a few years earlier. Just ahead was a satisfying season for Rickey's 1907 baseball team, which won the conference title. As a proud and paternal athletic director, Rickey relished in the victories.

As the Major League season neared, Rickey was hoping to go out a winner. He intended to honor the agreement with Jane and her parents that 1907 would be his last year as a player, after which he would settle down to the serious study of law. Though Branch Rickey had come to like St. Louis, the city on the Mississippi River surrounded by countryside that made him feel that Ohio was not far away, he would not be resuming his career with the Browns. In December 1906 Robert Hedges, probably to satisfy manager Jimmy McAleer, who had grown tired of Rickey's Sunday absences, sold his contract to the New York Highlanders in a straight cash deal. New York manager Clark Griffith was looking for someone to catch his spitball pitcher, future Hall of Famer Jack Chesbro. Griffith had been impressed with the way Rickey handled Harry Howell, another hurler who moistened the ball.[3] Since Sunday baseball was still outlawed in New York, Griffith had no problem accepting Rickey's Sabbatarian contract terms.

Unfortunately, when Rickey tried to get his arm into playing shape before he left the campus, the pain in his shoulder returned. When he told his new manager about his lingering injury, Griffith paid for a visit to Hot Springs, Arkansas, in the hope that the hot baths of the resort town might nurse Rickey's sore arm back to health.[4] However, when Rickey reported to the Highlanders, he was still in pain. He languished on the bench and did not appear in a game until June 1, 1907, coincidentally his first wedding anniversary, when he went hitless in two appearances.

Rickey never got into either an offensive or defensive groove during the season, and on June 28, 1907, he would enter the record books in an ignominious way. During the Washington Senators' 16–5 rout of the Highlanders, 13 consecutive bases were stolen on the sore-armed catcher. On the first attempt his throw to second base was so wild that it landed in right field. Other tosses bounced in front of the second base bag, and the last bases were pilfered without Rickey even bothering to throw. Although the New York pitchers weren't good at holding runners on first base, and an umpire may have made a bad call on one steal of third base, it was clear that Rickey's ailing arm was the main factor in the embarrassing showing. The *Washington Post* chortled that the Senators "discovered that as a thrower Rickey was many chips shy, and they paused in their travels merely long enough to get breath."[5]

Griffith held Rickey out of action for the next few days, but the harsh and simple truth was that he no longer could throw at the level expected of a Major League catcher. He finished out the season playing a few games in left field and at first base, two positions that generally don't require a good throwing arm, and started his last game on September 7, 1907. Of course, he was disappointed that his performance had been so dismal. After a 1906 season in which he hit .285 and shone on defense, the numbers of 1907 showed that Rickey hit only .185 in 101 at-bats, the lowest average in the league for batters with more than a hundred official appearances.

Before the middle of September Rickey went into Clark Griffith's office to say good-bye, he thought, to professional baseball forever. He told the manager that he was going back to Ohio Wesleyan to resume his coaching and athletic director's duties and that he was planning on using his income to pay for night classes in law school. Griffith wished Rickey good luck in his new life but said that if he ever wanted to return to professional baseball, he should let him know and he would find a place for him. It was a significant gesture because, after winning 240 Major League games, Griffith was essentially retired as a pitcher and was embarking on a career in management and ownership that would stretch for almost fifty years (most of them with the Washington Senators).

In fall 1907 at Ohio Wesleyan, Branch Rickey's football team continued its good play. Nicknamed the Methodists or the Red and White, its record was 7-3. As in all his athletic assignments, Rickey formed lasting bonds with many players. "You taught us all to play hard, play clean, keep ourselves decent, use our brains and respect the other fellow," wrote Raymond Spahr decades later. Spahr, who had become a YMCA secretary, never forgot how his coach had been solicitous toward him, "a young country boy away from the home for the first time." He also recalled one of Rickey's "favorite 'pep talk' sayings of those days, "'We'll have no muckers on our teams.'"[6]

Rickey's plate at Ohio Wesleyan was overflowing. In addition to coaching football, basketball, and baseball, he was responsible as athletic director for administering all the other campus sports. There was substitute teaching in the basic elementary law class for the ailing professor John Groves, Rickey's first college Latin teacher. There were also Sunday Bible classes to teach at the town of Delaware's local YMCA, where Rickey was also augmenting his income as secretary. Most crucially for his future, there were night law school classes to attend at Ohio State University. A few times each week, Rickey made the forty-mile round trip to Columbus by electric railway. A schedule half as full would have overwhelmed almost anybody else, but Rickey was passionate about succeeding, and he always considered work a benediction, not a burden or a curse.

The Christmas holiday season of 1907 started with more than the usual joy and anticipation for Branch and Jane Rickey. They were eagerly awaiting in February the birth of their first child, whom Jane planned to deliver at the Moulton family home in Lucasville. However, shortly after the beginning of the new year, tragedy struck the young couple. As Jane's normal morning sickness during pregnancy worsened, the doctors grew concerned and tried to induce an early delivery. A baby girl was born prematurely in February 1908 and did not survive more than a day.[7]

As Branch wept at Jane's bedside, the Rickey and Moulton families offered solace to the young couple. Branch's mother had known the heartbreak of two lost babies between Orla and Branch, and she grieved empathetically with her daughter-in-law.[8] After the immediate shock and lingering sadness wore off, the doctors assured Jane that she was healthy enough to bear children in the future. Recovering quickly, she was soon back to her own vigorous pace as homemaker and helpmate to her passionate, hard-working, and fun-loving husband.

For the first time in five years there were no baseball road trips in 1908 to keep Branch away for months at a time, but he still obviously believed that idleness was the devil's workshop. As if being a college athletic director and coach, an organizer and inspirer of young Christian men at the YMCA, and an aspiring law student weren't enough, civic-minded Branch Rickey energetically threw himself into the Republican Party's 1908 presidential election campaign. William Howard Taft was the Grand Old Party's choice to succeed the retiring president Theodore Roosevelt. That Taft was a native son of Ohio made it all the more imperative for Rickey to lend his support.

Rickey also devoted his energies to the cause of the Anti-Saloon League. There was never any liquor in the Rickey household when Branch was growing up; nor did he and Jane keep any alcohol in their house during all the years of their married life. The waste of human potential and the destruction of family life were consequences of alcoholism that Branch Rickey learned about early in life and always abhorred. He knew that a lineal descendant on his mother's side had succumbed to the evils of drink and dissipation, had been disowned, and had died young.[9]

Yet Rickey's involvement in the 1908 Prohibition campaign may have occurred almost spontaneously. Walking down the street one evening with some of his football players after practice, Rickey noticed a crowd gathered around the railroad station. "A man was standing on a baggage truck making a speech to a considerable crowd around him," recalled Herman Shipps, one of Rickey's close friends at Ohio Wesleyan, years later. "Branch said, 'What's that fellow doin'?' Someone said, 'He's making a 'wet' speech.' Branch said, 'If you'll get a box over on the other corner I'll make a 'dry' speech."[10] Sure enough, the intense and loquacious Rickey began his counterargument, quickly drawing the crowd away from the "wet" advocate. Word of Rickey's eloquence spread quickly in the "dry" ranks, and before long Ohio anti-alcohol leaders were urging him to campaign in their behalf. When offered a small stipend for Sunday speeches plus expenses, Rickey could not say no.

He bought a used Maxwell automobile and sputtered his way through the state in behalf of the Rose Local Option Law, a bill that the Anti-Saloon League was advocating to enable local governments to vote out the sale and use of alcohol. On one trip to Chillicothe, formerly the state capital of Ohio, Rickey found no lodgings. Most of the hotels had adjoining bars and were not going to house a speaker intent on harming their economic interests. Fortunately, Rickey bumped into an old friend from Lucasville, Fred Hunter, who had played with him in the Texas League and was now bartending in town. Despite his job Hunter was a teetotaler and offered to share his lodgings with his old friend. Once again hometown roots paid off for Branch Rickey, who remained friendly with Hunter for the rest of his life, hiring him later as a scout and a Minor League manager.[11]

Characteristically, Rickey plunged into his Anti-Saloon League work with unbridled enthusiasm. A good friend of the Rickeys, Gertrude Hopping, described the fervor of his anti-alcohol crusade in a letter to her fiancé, Robert Murray Haig, Rickey's Ohio Wesleyan Delta Tau Delta fraternity brother. "Mr. Rick came puffing in, all fussed up by the temperance issue," Hopping wrote Haig, who later became an eminent Columbia University political economy professor. Despite Rickey's agitated state in behalf of the "dry" cause, Hopping noted the great affection between Branch and Jane. "It does me good to hear a woman talk about her husband as she does about him," Hopping wrote. "They certainly are in love with each other and after all, what else is necessary?"[12]

Branch Rickey's political activities proved fruitful. In November 1908 William Howard Taft was easily elected president over Democrat Alton Parker, and the Rose local option bill passed in several Ohio counties. On campus Rickey's Ohio Wesleyan football team, after a slow start, picked up the pace and finished at .500. Despite the long commute Rickey's law classes were going smoothly at Columbus, and he must have thought to himself that the journey was nothing compared to his thirty-four-mile round-trip commute by bicycle to his first teaching job in Turkey Creek. Branch Rickey's eye was firmly on the prize of law school—and a respectable living and good life for his wife and his future family.

Yet the pace of Rickey's vigorous work schedule was beginning to take its toll. He showed signs of fatigue in Lucasville during the 1908 Christmas season, when normally he was a human dynamo. His weight had dropped 30 pounds from the 175 pounds of his baseball-playing days. He resisted going to a doctor, but when blood appeared in his sputum after coughing, he had no choice. After a few days of tests Branch Rickey received the shocking news that he was suffering from tuberculosis, the dread disease of the day.

Tuberculosis was commonly referred to as "consumption," because from its inception in the lungs the illness consumed its victims with horrible suffering and ultimately death. In the early nineteenth century tuberculosis claimed more American lives than heart disease and cancer combined, and in the 1880s it was still responsible for one in seven deaths. Although German bacteriologist Robert Koch had isolated the tuberculosis bacillus in 1882, twenty years later the disease was still responsible for more than 10 percent of American deaths.[13]

Scarcely a year after Branch and Jane Rickey watched helplessly as their first baby died after only one day on earth, they now had to cope with the fear that a terrible disease might claim one of them prematurely. Though they were frightened their love gave them hope, and they resolved to find the best treatment possible. Again, one of Rickey's friends came to the rescue. Herbert Welch, who had become president of Ohio Wesleyan University in 1905 (and later would serve as the resident Methodist bishop in Korea and Japan), gave the anxious couple information about the Trudeau Adirondack Care sanatorium in Saranac Lake in upstate New York, where Welch's secretary had recently been treated.[14]

Rickey found inspiration in reading the story of Dr. Edward Livingston Trudeau, who had founded the first and most highly regarded sanatorium for the treatment of tuberculosis. Born in New York in 1848 and raised by his mother in Paris, France, Trudeau was the son of a doctor who served in the Confederate military during the Civil War. When young Edward returned to the United States after the war, he turned down an appointment to the United States Naval Academy in order to nurse his older brother, afflicted with tuberculosis. They slept in the same room with the windows closed because the conventional medical wisdom of the time was that fresh air would only make the sufferer's cough worse, but Trudeau's brother soon died.

Trudeau became a doctor, but in 1871, on his honeymoon in Paris, he himself contracted the disease. Three years later Dr. Edward Livingston Trudeau traveled to Saranac Lake, New York, essentially to die in a beautiful environment. "Why, Doctor, you don't weigh no more than a dried lambskin," a local Indian guide greeted him upon his arrival. Yet, by breathing the invigorating air and sleeping outside, Trudeau gradually regained his strength and soon became a permanent resident of the remote town in the Adirondack Mountains. By 1880, avid outdoorsman Branch Rickey read with great interest, the doctor felt healthy enough to establish a gun club, where he and like-minded men could share their love of hunting foxes and rabbits.[15]

Restored to reasonably vigorous health, Dr. Trudeau devoted the rest of his life to finding the best treatment and eventual cure for tuberculosis. With the help of such wealthy patrons as John D. Rockefeller, Russell Sage, and Edward Harriman, Trudeau established the Adirondack Care Sanatorium. In 1890 Trudeau first used Koch's tuberculin bacillus at the sanatorium, and by 1892 he was seeing eighty patients a year.[16] No means tests were required. If you were sick and were willing to make the rugged journey to the wilds of the Adirondacks, there was room for you. Trudeau established as the sanatorium's policy, "The worse you are, the less the bill."[17]

Armed with the knowledge that science and modern medicine could cure the disease, Branch Rickey settled up his affairs at Ohio Wesleyan before the end of the 1909 spring term. He had purchased an automobile to use for excursions with Jane, and also to keep him in the outdoors as much as possible because he was becoming well aware of the importance of breathing fresh air.[18] As he made preparations to leave for Saranac, he sold the car—but, he thought to himself, there would be other cars to buy and to enjoy when he returned from Saranac.

He and Jane headed back to Lucasville to say good-bye to their families. They were determined to lick the ailment, they bravely told the Rickey and Moulton clans, and Branch would be back soon, a healthy man. Privately, Jane Rickey was very worried, telling Gertrude Hopping that she didn't want to live if anything happened to Branch.[19]

Late in the spring of 1909 Branch and Jane Rickey set out on their anxious journey. Though he had been out of professional baseball for over a year, he had made enough of a name in the sports world that the *New York Times* of May 19, 1909, noted that "the well-known baseball player . . . has broken down in health and been compelled to go to Saranac Lake for a complete rest."[20] The newspaper mentioned Rickey's staggering work load as the reason for his illness.

After his first examination at the sanatorium, Branch Rickey received good news and bad news. He was listed as a Type Three case, the intermediate case of tuberculosis, which meant that the bacilli were limited to his lungs and had not spread deeper into his lymphatic system. The bad news was that his early treatment would require total rest for at least six weeks, which meant no talking, no exertion, and no heavy reading. In mid-June 1909 Gertrude Hopping wrote Robert Murray Haig that Jane Rickey had sent a postcard saying that "Branch was behaving fine—had to keep absolutely quiet. The blessed day." She added, "Think of Branch Rickey keeping quiet!"[21]

Resigning himself to what would be a difficult regimen for his hyperenergetic personality, Rickey became a good patient of his personal physician, Dr. Lawrason Brown. Like so many of the doctors who sought a cure for tuberculosis, Dr. Brown was himself a survivor of the disease. "They had left rich practices to live in an isolated country town where the streets were cleared by horse-drawn plows, and not one of them would have considered doing anything else," Elizabeth Mooney has written movingly about the dedication of the TB doctors in her book *In the Shadow of the White Plague.*[22] Formerly of the Johns Hopkins University in Baltimore, Lawrason Brown became not only a key associate of Dr. Trudeau but also the founder and editor of the *Journal of Outdoor Life,* which for decades would provide the latest remedies and inspirational messages for sufferers of diverse ailments. Its motto, "Buck up and cheer up," sounds like something that Branch Rickey might have said and often did say.[23]

In addition to the absolute rest and plentiful exposure to the bracing Adirondack air, Lawrason Brown prescribed one daily cough in the morning to bring up sputum for examination. Patients were implored not to cough more than once. "A man who coughs hard all day does as much work as a man who climbs a mountain," Dr. Brown warned. He oversaw a detailed and painstaking outdoor treatment in which druggists provided fever thermometers, sputum cups, and stone hot-water bottles, known as pigs, that kept the feet of patients warm as they lay outside during the long nights. Always an avid hunter and fisherman, Branch Rickey loved the outdoors and grew to like the invigorating aspects of sleeping outside. He came to see the wisdom of an aphorism in Dr. Brown's handbook, "What room suffices him who knows a porch?"[24]

By midsummer 1909 Branch Rickey was on the road to recovery. He had accepted the discipline of rest and outdoor sleeping and even, much against his principles, adopted the regimen of a glass of beer at dinner to help gain back his weight. More congenial aspects of his recovery diet were six glasses of milk daily (always a treat for Rickey), six raw eggs, cream soups, and another favorite, chocolate cake with icing. It wasn't exactly a pep song, but Rickey learned to like the lyrics of Dr. Brown's instructive ditty:

> Eat once for yourself,
> Eat once for the germs,
> Eat once to gain weight.[25]

When he was strong enough Rickey started occupational therapy. He made leather wallets and engaged in picture framing, activities at which he became adept, a pleasant development for him since work with his hands had never been his strong suit. No longer confined to his room or porch, Rickey relished the opportunity to mingle with the staff and some of the improving patients. Always an indefatigable game player, Rickey won a croquet tournament at the sanatorium and did his best to raise the spirits of some of the more seriously ill patients.[26]

Throughout his recuperation Branch was overjoyed at the presence of Jane, who was staying as nearby the sanatorium as health precautions allowed. As his condition improved Rickey rented a team of horses and a topless phaeton (a carriage drawn by four horses), and the young couple happily rode through the breathtakingly beautiful Adirondack countryside, where they renewed their eternal affections and mapped out their future plans. In late summer Rickey was elated to receive the news that his application to the University of Michigan Law School had been accepted. He was further gratified when he learned that Michigan would accept the night school credits he had already earned at Ohio State.

On the happy day late in the summer of 1909 when Branch Rickey was about to be discharged from the sanatorium, Dr. Lawrason Brown reminded him that he wasn't fully cured. Regular rest and continual exposure to outdoor air were absolutely necessary to keep the disease from recurring. "For other diseases, we may buy a cure," Brown warned. "Not consumptives. Patience and perseverance in leading a hygienic life are the only specifics for it." Dr. Brown's parting advice was wryly optimistic. "Get yourself a good chronic disease," he said. "Take good care of it and you'll outlive everyone else."[27]

With their worst fears behind them Jane and Branch Rickey entrained back to the Midwest to resume their normal lives. Jane would not be going to Ann Arbor immediately, returning instead to Lucasville to live with her family while Branch started school for the fall term of 1909. They would have joyous reunions at Thanksgiving and Christmas and would then set up home together in Ann Arbor before the spring term of 1910.

As Branch Rickey began his career as a Michigan law student, he felt confident about his chances for success. He had survived the horrors of his ailment, and he knew how to study now and how to maximize his time efficiently. The once-awkward, diffident student was becoming a powerful presence in the classroom and study hall, one headed for the *Law Review* and a place in the top 10 percent of his class. However, he also tried to follow the advice of his Saranac doctors, who implored him not to diffuse his energies and overwork himself. He continued to sleep outdoors as much as possible to strengthen his lungs and prevent a recurrence of the dread illness.

Rickey confined himself to the role of athletic spectator, but his partisanship was hard to contain. University of Michigan football had become very successful under the coaching of Fielding "Hurry-Up" Yost, who had coached Ohio Wesleyan in 1897, a few years before Rickey arrived as a student. Yost's one owu team tied Michigan at Ann Arbor, attracting the attention of the big university's athletic administration. After brief stops at the state universities in Nebraska and Kansas, Yost arrived at Michigan in 1901 and became an instant legend. It took two seasons before an opponent even scored on his team, and he compiled a 29-1-1 record in his first five seasons as Wolverines coach.[28]

Ann Arbor home football games elicited major outpourings of emotion from town and gown, but they often proved too taxing for the passionate Rickey. After one game in his first year on campus, he wrote Jane in Lucasville, "I'm not used to excitement and it nearly laid me out, gave me a high pulse and a fever. . . . I shall not go to all the games, I've decided."[29]

Of course, given his competitive nature, he would not be able to stay away from athletics for long. As a devoted Ohio Wesleyan alumnus, he somehow found the time to coach the school's 1909–10 basketball team to a 9-11 record.[30] But he was mainly concentrating on his law studies. Eager to catch up for time lost to his illness, Rickey successfully petitioned the Michigan administration for the right to take an almost unheard of twenty credits in the spring term of 1910. The man who had entered college as a conditional student without a high school diploma and graduated in three and a half years was now determined to finish one of the toughest and most prestigious law schools in the country in two years.

The spring term of 1910 would also be noteworthy for Branch Rickey in another way. He had been hired as the University of Michigan's new baseball coach. Lewis "Sport" McAllister, a versatile former Major League utility player who had ended his seven-year career with the Detroit Tigers, had resigned suddenly. Although he had compiled an enviable 58-17-1 record in his four seasons as Michigan coach, the Mississippi native was tired of coaching college players, who once were memorably described by former Major Leaguer and college coach Tony Lupien as "half-baked potatoes, not good enough to eat but too good to throw away."

When Branch Rickey learned of the baseball opening, he sprang into action. He wrote about sixty of his onetime associates in the college and professional baseball ranks, asking for letters of recommendation. Rickey carefully orchestrated the requests so that every day, two of the letters in his behalf arrived at the office of Michigan athletic director Philip Bartelme. The administrator did not know that a former Major League baseball player was on campus, but when he met the applicant, he was immediately impressed with his passion for the game and his principled views on the proper role of athletics on a college campus. Only a few years older than the law student, Bartelme warmed to Rickey's idealism because a growing number of college administrators were concerned about the rising influence of professionalized sports on campus, especially "King Football."

In 1908 the University of Michigan had become an independent, leaving the Western Conference (the forerunner of the Big Ten) to play a more national schedule, thus ignoring local midwestern rivalries. Not surprisingly, football coach Fielding Yost enthusiastically supported the move, since he himself was known for his fierce competitiveness and willingness to cut corners in the name of athletic excellence. (While an undergraduate at West Virginia University, Yost had played for Lafayette College under an assumed name in a game that broke the University of Pennsylvania's long winning streak.)[31]

College baseball was by no means as big or as economically profitable an exercise as college football, but Bartelme felt that Michigan needed a talented, respectable coach who knew the proper place of sports in the university. Eager to hire the earnest barrister-in-training, the administrator faced the hurdle of convincing law school dean Harry Hutchins that Rickey could handle his huge course load and coach a varsity team. After a two-hour, face-to-face meeting with the applicant, the dean reluctantly gave his consent on the condition that Rickey must be called on to answer questions every day in each of his law classes. The ambitious young man readily agreed, convinced that he had the energy and intelligence to perform well as both law student and baseball coach.

When Bartelme got the official word of the dean's approval, he called Rickey into his office with the good news. However, he made one earnest request of his new employee. "Stop sending me those darned letters!" he said, referring to the barrage of recommendations still being mailed by Rickey's friends.[32] He was mainly speaking tongue in cheek because the athletic director was already enamored with his new coach, and they would forge a lifelong association in college and professional sports and a lasting friendship.

In a revealing letter to his parents shortly after he won the coaching job, Branch Rickey gave the credit "to many good friends. It was really their victory for the odds were against me and *I* counted very little," he wrote. "My greatest joy is not the paltry job . . . but the fact of being known by men of such standing and character that their commendation places me above the pull and push of the other fellow." Rickey's letter also indicated his impatience at still being in school. "I want to get out and do something—some one thing and bend every effort," he wrote. "I may fizzle about for a while, but if I get a good grip on some *one* thing—and have a purpose— . . . I guess I'll do my best not to make God as ashamed of me as he has been these last few years." Despite the anxiety and insecurity indicated in the letter, Rickey's missive ended on an upbeat note. "Jen [Jane] will be here tomorrow," he exclaimed. "It makes me very happy to think of it."[33]

Branch and Jane did indeed have a warm and passionate reunion. She was thrilled that he looked healthy and was busy and successful at school. She took advantage of the opportunities afforded by the college environment by auditing classes in art and horticulture.[34]

The photographs of Branch Rickey as Michigan baseball coach portray a man of severe intensity and concentration, but he was also a very joyous man as he tried to convey to his players his zest for competition on the baseball field. Lew McAllister had left Rickey an inexperienced but eager team, and Rickey rolled up his sleeves and went to work at educating them in the art and science of baseball. He taught his charges the proper way to run and to bunt. He instructed the catchers in the right technique of removing the mask on pop-ups so as to not to trip over it while locating the ball. At Michigan he also came up with the idea for what has become one of the most commonly used defensive strategies in baseball, "the daylight play." Designed to keep runners from taking too big a lead off second base, the strategy involved the pitcher whirling to second base on a pick-off attempt when he saw "daylight" between an unsuspecting base runner and a shortstop breaking to cover the base.[35]

Always interested in helpful technical innovations, Rickey also came up with the idea of sliding pits filled with sand to teach the players how to slide on each leg. Rickey was less successful in creating a device to correct overstriding by hitters. He first tried placing a shot-putter's guard rail, borrowed from the track coach, in the front part of the batter's box so that the overzealous player would stumble on it if he took too long a stride. Too many sprained ankles ended that experiment. Rickey next tried tying rope around the ankles of a hitter, but the player's feeling of confinement doomed this experiment. He finally admitted with resignation, "You can't cure an overstrider."[36]

Rickey insisted, however, that sweat remained the best solvent for virtually every other problem in baseball. Although his first Michigan team in 1910 did not quite match McAllister's brilliant final-season record of 18-3, a 17-8 log was certainly a good one, and the team enjoyed great camaraderie, the hallmark of every Rickey squad. They bonded on a southern trip in which the team won four of the seven games against tough opposition. After games at home Rickey often bundled the team into his new state-of-the-art Chalmers convertible for excursions in Ann Arbor and the adjoining countryside. In words almost identical to what the Allegheny students had written about Rickey a few years earlier, the *Michiganensian*, the school yearbook, declared, "Coach was the hardest worker on the squad, kept everybody working to correct this or that mistake, and taught the game from the beginning to the end."[37]

Not only did Branch Rickey's first baseball season as Michigan coach end successfully, but he also continued to pile up good grades in law school. Although his prospects were looking up, he was still less than a year removed from his ordeal with tuberculosis. It was hard for him to accept slowing down, yet he knew that he couldn't keep up a tremendous work pace all year long. Realizing that mountain air was still the best environment for his permanent healing, he and Jane headed in June 1910 for a summer in the Rocky Mountains. During the day they hiked, fished, and explored the many nooks and crannies of the spectacular region. At night they enjoyed playing checkers, chess, and card games, including occasional hands of bridge with new friends.

At the end of the summer of 1910 the young couple returned to Ohio for a short visit with their families before returning to Ann Arbor and Branch's last year of law school. Once again he shone in the classroom. On the baseball diamond his 1911 baseball team didn't perform quite as well as the 1910 team, compiling a 16-10-1 record. Rickey's Wolverines committed too many errors, a foreshadowing of a problem on the teams he would manage in the Major Leagues. Yet, if the errors were ones of enthusiasm, he always forgave them, and his 1911 team did win three out of four games against Syracuse University, a national powerhouse.[38]

The word about Branch Rickey's coaching and baseball lecturing abilities was beginning to spread. Occasionally, on days off from the American League pennant race, Detroit Tigers players, scouts, and coaches came to Ann Arbor to sit in on Branch Rickey's practices and listen to his practical and inspirational instruction. At other times Rickey would take his players to Detroit to watch the gifted play of outfielders Ty Cobb and Sam Crawford, two future Hall of Famers, and other stalwarts on the Tigers, who had won the 1909 American League pennant, and though they lost a tough seven-game World Series to the Pittsburgh Pirates, remained a solid contender.

At the end of the 1911 season Rickey's Michigan team played two games against Keio University, the college champions of Japan. After a local Ann Arbor umpire persisted in making blatantly bad calls against the visitors, Rickey sided with the fans who were outraged at the arbiter's unfairness. He insisted that if the games were to continue, a new umpire must be found.[39]

Rickey also found the time to assist Coach Yost on the football field. After many home games Rickey would stay up Saturday nights with the passionate gridiron coach as he went over the day's plays and made plans for the next week's contest, often getting down on the floor to illustrate his ideas. Rickey always believed in learning strategy from the best, and there is no doubt that Yost was a master athletic mind, even if the son of a Confederate soldier was once called "an egomaniac and a rule-breaker, . . . in an era without many rules."[40]

Significantly, as much as Rickey enjoyed his varied experiences on the Michigan campus, he maintained his ties with St. Louis Browns owner Robert Hedges. Hedges remained an ardent admirer of the Michigan coach as an evaluator and a man, and the respect and affection were reciprocated by the young coach. The Browns owner wanted Rickey to scout amateur and semiprofessional players in Michigan, and his former catcher was glad to oblige. Rickey's frequent presence at noncollege games throughout Michigan led some sportswriters to dub him "The Mysterious Stranger."[41]

The greatest Michigan player Branch Rickey ever coached, George Sisler, would not arrive on the college baseball field until spring 1912. If the master plan that Rickey was ostensibly following had been realized, he would never have met George Sisler. Late in June 1911 Branch Rickey received his law degree with honors, fulfilling his pledge to finish the three-year law school program in two years. Still enthralled by his previous summer in the Rocky Mountains, he made plans to establish a law firm in Boise, the state capital of Idaho, with Frank Ebbert and Howard

Crow, two fellow Ohio Wesleyan graduates and Delta Tau Delta fraternity brothers, who also had recently passed the bar.

The mountain atmosphere of Boise was salutary for Rickey's health, but meaningful work was always the key component in his life. Very little business existed for the three young lawyers. Rickey had only one case, serving as a public defender for a grisly outlaw who had been charged with many crimes and who didn't even want an attorney. The criminal spat at his feet when he met him in the local jail, and Rickey might well have flashed back to his first surly students in Turkey Creek. This was not what the law was supposed to be about, he thought. "I never knew a man could be so guilty of so many crimes," Rickey reflected later about his one and only client in Idaho.[42]

Fortunately, Branch Rickey had not burned his bridges in Ann Arbor. Phil Bartelme had not hired a replacement for the 1912 season, perhaps sensing that Rickey might return. When Rickey asked the athletic director if the baseball position was still open, Bartelme said that indeed it was. Rickey's law firm partners encouraged him to return to his beloved Midwest. Business was simply not good in Idaho, and there was hardly enough work for two partners, let alone three.

Branch Rickey resumed his coaching duties in Michigan before the 1912 season started. He faced a major challenge because graduation had cost him his captain, catcher Jack Enzenroth, and the team showed inexperience in every part of the diamond. Then, one morning in late March, a tall, gangly, quiet left-handed pitcher appeared at the indoor practice session at Michigan's Waterman Gymnasium and wanted to know if he could try out for the team. He said that his name was George Sisler, and he was a freshman from Manchester, Ohio, studying mechanical engineering. "Oh, a freshman," Rickey said. "Too bad. You can't play this year. This inside work is only for the varsity."

The youngster carried himself with a quiet confidence that Rickey found rare and appealing in a young athlete. Yet when Sisler found out he wasn't eligible to play, he showed a trace of emotion. His shoulders sagged, and his disappointment was evident. Rickey's captain, Norman Hill, came over and told the coach that Sisler had set outstanding high school records in Ohio. Never liking to give bad news to anyone, Rickey consented to take a look at the freshman. Rickey asked if a catcher was available, and it just so happened that Russell Baer, another freshman and Sisler's high school battery mate, was standing nearby.

A one-minute workout was all Branch Rickey needed to appreciate what kind of jewel was sparkling on his coaching field. "This boy was something in grace and delivery from the very first pitch," Rickey wrote in *The American Diamond*. Although, as a freshman, Sisler could not play for the varsity, Rickey allowed him to work out with the team in the indoor drills. Restricted to throwing only fastballs, Sisler embarrassed the varsity with the speed and movement of his pitches. "He was a major league pitcher right then!" Rickey marveled.[43]

In the 1912 college season Sisler played for the freshman engineers and led them to the intramural title. In one seven-inning game against upperclassmen, he struck out twenty of the twenty-one batters. Despite his promise as a pitcher the young freshman was even more outstanding with a bat in his hand. A slender left-handed hitter, Sisler "was actually a threat to the [batting] cage pitchers," Rickey remembered in *The American Diamond*. "Such slashing and driving! Good pitches, bad pitches made no difference. . . . The whole squad seemed to prefer watching Sisler hit to hitting for themselves with Sisler pitching."[44]

As much as Branch Rickey admired George Sisler's athletic talents, he was even more drawn to Sisler's character and temperament. He would call him "the easiest to keep sweet" of all the players he developed. Undoubtedly, Rickey felt an affinity toward Sisler because he, too, was a product of small-town Protestant Ohio. The youngster hailed from Manchester, fourteen miles outside of Akron, a town so small that, like Branch Rickey's Lucasville, it had no fully accredited high school. At age fourteen George moved in with an older brother, Efbert, to attend high school in Akron. Before Sisler's senior year in high school, Efbert, only twenty-seven, died of tuberculosis and George found another family to live with in town.[45]

Sisler's baseball exploits led local sportswriters to dub him "the boy wonder," and professional scouts started to flock to his summer industrial league games. Sometime between Sisler's junior and senior years in high school, an amateur umpire, Jesse Goehler, acting in behalf of Lee Fohl, manager of the Akron team in the Ohio-Pennsylvania League, had offered a professional contract to the heralded prospect. Though

Sisler accepted no money he did sign the contract. The young player soon began to have second thoughts about his action and the impact it would have on his amateur eligibility. He was concerned that his father would be very upset that his son might forgo his education for the transitory pleasures of the sporting life. Catcher Russ Baer had been similarly tempted to sign a pro contract but opted instead to enroll at Michigan. Sisler decided to follow his high school friend's path. Since he had taken no money from a professional organization, and he was still under legal age, the youngster thought that his path was clear to a full college career.

What Sisler did not know was that his contract had been shifted from Akron to Columbus, Ohio, in the American Association and had been purchased in early 1912 for $5,000 by Pittsburgh Pirates owner Barney Dreyfuss. By the summer of 1912 the astute and powerful Dreyfuss was ready to make a raise a ruckus about forcing his property, George Sisler, to report to his owner. If Sisler did not report, he would be placed on the "permanently ineligible" list of professional baseball.[46]

The crisis was still a few months away for George Sisler and Branch Rickey, however. Sisler completed his freshman year without incident, and Rickey succeeded in leading a competitive Michigan varsity. Although the Wolverines' 1912 record slipped to 14-10-3, it was a typical Rickey team, playing with fire and passion, and no one exuded that competitive drive more fiercely than the coach. During some of the games Rickey had to remain in the dugout on crutches because of a broken ankle he had suffered while demonstrating techniques of sliding in practice. The temporary infirmity did not stop Branch Rickey, in one game at the University of Georgia, from hobbling angrily onto the field to take part in a melee at home plate after an opponent slid too recklessly into Michigan catcher Goodloe Rogers. Eyewitnesses relished the memory of Rickey lying at the bottom of the pile with one of his crutches pointed skyward. Legend has it that he walked away from the skirmish unaided, deciding that he didn't need the crutches after all.[47]

Meanwhile, during the season, an intriguing opportunity presented itself to Coach Rickey. Robert Hedges paid a visit to Ann Arbor, inquiring whether his former catcher was interested in becoming the business manager of the Kansas City Minor League team in the American

Association. Hedges continued to be impressed by Rickey's ability to see promise in young players. Having invested in the new steel-and-concrete grandstand at Sportsman's Park and wanting to taste the rare and intoxicating pleasure of winning a championship, Hedges was impatient for a winner in St. Louis. He thought that adding Rickey to his organization in Kansas City would be a major asset in his quest for a World Series title.

In the spring of 1912, however, Hedges's offer was one that Rickey could refuse. He still considered himself a tuberculosis survivor, and he and Jane were planning to head back to the healthy air of Idaho after the spring semester to rejoin his law partners. The Browns owner wouldn't leave Ann Arbor without some commitment of assistance from Rickey. The coach agreed that he would scout some players in the Rocky Mountain amateur and professional leagues and also consented to travel to the Pacific Coast to recommend some players from that area to the Browns.

As Branch Rickey said good-bye to his Michigan team and his friends at the end of the spring term of 1912, he thought it might be a permanent farewell. The law office of Crow, Ebbert, and Rickey was still open for business in Idaho, and there was no doubt that the mountain air did wonders for Rickey's health.

Before they left for their third straight summer in the breathtaking beauty of the Rocky Mountains, Jane had told Branch that she was pregnant again and that a successful delivery was forecast for the following February. Thoughts of starting a family cheered them both as they headed west for another summer of healthy outdoor living together.

Although the summer air of Idaho again proved a great tonic for Rickey's healing lungs, and while he enjoyed the baseball scouting he did for Robert Hedges, work for the firm of Crow, Ebbert, and Rickey was still scarce. There may also have been a little political tension in the office because Rickey and Ebbert were supporting the insurgent "Bull Moose" Progressive party of former president Theodore Roosevelt in the 1912 presidential election, while Crow was sticking with incumbent Republican president William Howard Taft.[48] (The Republican split would enable Democratic candidate Woodrow Wilson to win the presidency in November with less than 40 percent of the popular vote.)

Meanwhile, Rickey was keeping close watch on the George Sisler case, which had erupted into a cause célèbre in August 1912 when Barney Dreyfuss went public with his demand that George Sisler report to Pittsburgh. Dreyfuss's argument was simple: he had paid Bob Quinn's Columbus franchise $5,000 for Sisler's contract earlier in the year, and it was time to claim his property. Sisler's amateur eligibility at Michigan was, of course, no concern for Dreyfuss.

The sportswriters of Akron's *Beacon Journal* strongly backed the Pittsburgh owner. They warned Sisler that he risked being blacklisted if he refused to report to Pittsburgh. "Sisler has had many friends in this city, who were anxious to see him move to the front," the paper said, "but when he refused to report to Akron, and later to Columbus these same persons lost all interest in him. . . . [I]f he is wise he will report to the team which has purchased him."[49]

The young Michigan student-athlete was, of course, disturbed at the threat to his college eligibility, but he had many important people in his corner. His father, Cassius Sisler Sr. wrote the National Commission, the governing authority of Major League Baseball, explaining that his son was "a bashful, backward boy" who had been influenced by the flattery of the scout and had signed something that he did not "in any way understand." Judge George Codd, a trustee of the University of Michigan and a former mayor of Detroit, wrote the Commission that Sisler was a student in good standing who had every reason to return to and play for the university. Last but not least Branch Rickey submitted a stirring defense of Sisler's blamelessness. The coach attacked the machinations of the baseball people who were trying to coerce Sisler to play against his will. "Who is going to trust you," Rickey declared, "if you cajole minors into signing contracts and then declare them suspended, as you have tried to suspend Sisler, when they change their mind?"[50]

Baseball establishment supporters of Barney Dreyfuss were not impressed by Rickey's position. They retorted that in spite of the coach's moral and idealistic arguments, underage players were often signed to contracts. After tens of thousands of words were filed in the dispute, the Commission withheld judgment, in effect freeing the player to complete his college career. Barney Dreyfuss still claimed his rights to Sisler, and when the star player graduated in 1915, the case would arise once more. When Dreyfuss lost again it was the beginning of the end of the National

Commission as baseball's governing body. That Sisler wound up going to play for Branch Rickey and the St. Louis Browns only rubbed more salt in Dreyfuss's wounds.

Late in the summer of 1912, while still in the Rocky Mountains, Branch Rickey received another call from Robert Hedges. The owner was checking out a Minor League team in Salt Lake City, and he wanted to meet with Rickey to go over some plans for the future. Rickey was too embarrassed to say that his precarious finances made an out-of-pocket trip to Utah impossible, but Hedges, sensing Rickey's predicament, offered to provide round-trip train fare to Utah. When Rickey arrived the owner greeted him with a stunning new offer. He wanted someone to run not a Minor League team but the Major League St. Louis Browns. He offered Rickey $7,500 for his services as his assistant and business manager, a sum far larger than anything the ambitious young man had ever earned in college teaching and coaching. When Rickey told Hedges that he was committed to coach at Ann Arbor again in the spring of 1913, Hedges said that he could fulfill his commitment as long as he was prepared to move to St. Louis and start work permanently by June 1, 1913. With his partnership in Idaho all but dissolved, Rickey made the trip back to the Midwest with elation as well as concern.

For Rickey, baseball provided a tremendous sense of intellectual challenge and physical excitement, and now prospects for considerable financial reward, but it wasn't the respectable life of law that the Moultons expected of their son-in-law. Happily, Jane wanted what was most fulfilling for her husband, who by now had to realize that baseball was inexorably in his blood.

The Rickeys returned to Ann Arbor for a final year on the campus. Early in the new year of 1913, Jane traveled back to her family in Lucasville, preparing for the birth of their first child. A healthy baby daughter was born on February 3, 1913, and was named Mary Emily Rickey, after the two grandmothers, Mary Cecilia Smith Moulton and Emily Brown Rickey. Branch Rickey was ecstatic with the reality of parenthood and the prospect of soon adding more children to the family. After spending some time with his baby and overjoyed wife, Rickey headed back to Ann Arbor for his last baseball season in Michigan.

The year 1913 was the only one in which he would have the pleasure of coaching George Sisler in college. In his first year on the varsity, Sisler did not disappoint, hitting .445 and playing outstanding defense at first base. When an arm injury forced Sisler to cut down on his pitching, he was moved to left field for some of the games. The 1913 Wolverines had Rickey's best record at Michigan, 22-4-1.[51] In addition to Sisler's outstanding play, Michigan featured a scrappy, five foot five shortstop, John Lavan, nicknamed "Doc" because he was already attending medical school. In his one year at Michigan Lavan showed fine defensive prowess and enough offensive potential that by the summer of 1913 he was in the Major Leagues, playing shortstop for Branch Rickey's St. Louis Browns.

Before the end of that highly successful Michigan baseball season, Rickey delivered a heartfelt good-bye to his team and to others in the Ann Arbor community. Then he and Jane packed up baby Mary and their belongings and drove to Lucasville to visit with their families before it was time to head south to St. Louis. Rickey now faced the challenge of bringing a winner to the victory-starved city of St. Louis, which hadn't had a baseball championship since 1888. It wouldn't be easy, but he was beginning to believe that often in life, the best way was the hard way. He was ready to make the most of his opportunity to succeed.

3

Branch Rickey and the St. Louis Browns

Although Branch Rickey would never lead the St. Louis Browns out of the second division of the American League, the roots for his great innovations and triumphs in the next decade with the National League Cardinals were clearly planted in his work with the Browns under Robert Hedges. Hedges was delighted to have for the first time Rickey's undivided attention. Two Browns regulars in 1913, catcher Sam Agnew and pitcher Walter Leverenz, had been signed on tips from Rickey while he was an informal consultant, but other, more productive players had gotten away.[1]

Catcher Frank "Pancho" Snyder was a prime example. While coaching at Michigan, Rickey spotted Snyder as a teenager playing in his hometown of Flint. Rickey recommended him to Hedges, but the Browns dawdled in offering Snyder a contract. The rival Cardinals swooped in and signed the catcher, who went on to a sixteen-year career and played in four consecutive World Series with the Giants from 1921 to 1924. With Rickey now on board full-time, Hedges was confident that such slip-ups in the future wouldn't occur. (Rickey thought so much of Snyder's abilities as a leader as well as a player that after the catcher retired, he named him as manager of the Cardinals' Houston farm team.)[2]

There was only a skeletal staff of employees when Rickey arrived in St. Louis, but happily it included chief scout Charley Barrett. When Rickey accepted Hedges's offer to work full-time in professional baseball, knowing that Barrett was already on board was an important inducement. Barrett had continued his Minor League career while Rickey went on to the college life, but the two friends had remained in touch. Rickey loved Barrett's cheery personality and knowledge of inside baseball. The scout never married and may have been the first of the executive's close baseball associates to be teasingly dubbed a "matrimonial coward," but as a loyal friend and astute talent evaluator, Rickey trusted no one more than Charley Barrett.

When Robert Hedges first met Barrett in 1909, he, too, was immediately taken by his transparent good nature, easy ability at making friends, and baseball smarts. Recently retired as a player, Barrett was working as a sporting goods salesman and tried to interest Hedges in starting a downtown ticket office for the Browns. The owner wasn't interested in the idea, but he was impressed that the personable St. Louis native was very knowledgeable about the local talent in the amateur and semiprofessional ranks known as the "trolley leagues."

"How would you like to work for me?" Hedges asked. "Great," replied Barrett, who considered the owner's offer a dream come true. He wanted to stay close to baseball in any way. Selling sporting goods was just a way to keep involved in the game because a desk job never would have suited Barrett, who had left high school at age fourteen to help his family by working as a clerk and night messenger. In his first year on the job for Hedges in 1909, Barrett signed three future members of the Browns: catcher Bill Killefer, left-handed pitcher Earl Hamilton, and outfielder Gus Williams.[3]

After Rickey joined the Browns, he and Barrett became an indefatigable team. Fellow believers in hard work and attention to detail, each brought boundless enthusiasm to the job. Barrett tirelessly handwrote letters to coaches and prospects all over the South and the Midwest. He obtained team schedules and made sure that he attended many of the games. The scout's written evaluations and Rickey's own jottings on prospective players became the stuff of Rickey's soon-legendary, overstuffed black loose-leaf notebook, which the executive carried with him all the time. It contained a veritable Holy Grail of information about future Major Leaguers.

When his nonbaseball business schedule allowed, Hedges joined Rickey on some of his scouting trips. It cheered the young executive to have the companionship of his team's owner. Although Hedges would not stay in baseball long enough to see the idea come to fruition, the owner clearly wanted to develop a farm system in the Minor Leagues. When the idea to buy the Kansas City franchise he wanted Rickey to operate fell through, Hedges turned to Montgomery, Alabama, as a possible source of players. In 1912, a year before Rickey officially came on board (but possibly with his knowledge), Hedges loaned a few thousand dollars to four Montgomery businessmen to set up a Minor League team. It was Hedges's understanding that the Browns would have first claim on any player deemed ready for the Major Leagues. The St. Louis owner had been very pleased with the purchase of second baseman Derrill "Del" Pratt from Montgomery, who became a Browns regular in 1912.[4] He hoped to institutionalize the arrangement with the new owners of the Alabama team, but the businessmen had a falling out among themselves, and soon representatives of other Major League teams swooped into town, offering more money for players than Hedges was willing to pay. In January 1914 Hedges's plan took another serious hit when the National Commission, baseball's ruling triumvirate, declared invalid any so-called farming agreements.[5]

However, the indefatigable Branch Rickey knew that there were other ways to develop a contending team. As the summer of 1913 drew to a close, Rickey and Barrett prepared for Hedges a long list of Minor League players eligible to be drafted from teams that had not protected them. When the draft was held in early September 1913, Rickey astonished his brethren in the baseball business by claiming 30 of the 108 players ultimately selected by the sixteen Major League teams. The *Sporting News* marveled: "He should have enough strings out that the pulling in should by all the law of averages result in something worth while."[6]

Before the end of the 1913 season, as if Branch Rickey weren't busy enough, he found himself wearing another hat in the Browns organization. Hedges asked him to become field manager in addition to second vice president, business manager, and chief developer of talent. Rickey did not lobby for the additional job, but he agreed with Hedges that current manager George Stovall was not an ideal leader. Nearing the end of a career as a journeyman first baseman, Stovall was nicknamed "Firebrand"—and for good reason. Once, in a fit of temper, he threw a chair at his manager, and earlier in 1913 American League president Ban Johnson suspended Stovall for a week for kicking and spitting tobacco on umpire Charlie Ferguson.[7] The fiery manager's frustrations were building as the Browns were heading for a finish in the American League basement, thirty-nine games behind the eventual World Series champion Philadelphia Athletics. Stovall did not like college players, and when he released John Lavan, Rickey's former Michigan shortstop, the business manager agreed with the owner that it was time for a change in the dugout.[8]

Yet, when Hedges asked him to replace Stovall, Rickey hesitated. It was not necessarily the extra workload, but if he were to take on the daily duties of managing, he wanted a slice of ownership in the team. Uncomfortable with sportswriters' prying into what he felt was a private matter between the owner and him, Rickey did issue a forthright statement explaining his position. "I am asking the right to purchase a substantial stock of stock, we'll say, between 55 and 125 shares, and Mr. Hedges won't permit me," Rickey explained. "There is no serious estrangement between us, but I won't accept the manager's job until my terms are met."[9]

A few days after Labor Day 1913, Rickey did accept the manager's position without obtaining a coveted part ownership in the team. However, he did receive an increase in salary from the $7,500 he was already making, and perhaps also a bonus arrangement.[10] As part of his new manager's contract with Robert Hedges, Rickey would again abstain from appearing at the ballpark on Sunday. For the remainder of the 1913 season, third baseman Jimmy Austin, who had filled in for Stovall when the ex-manager was suspended, agreed to substitute on the Sabbath. Born in Wales, Austin didn't take up baseball until his late teenage years, but while being reared in Rickey country, Portsmouth, Ohio, he became an acolyte of the executive's hustling style of play. Although he didn't make the Majors until age thirty, he quickly became a fan favorite.[11] Under Rickey, with Austin subbing on the few Sundays left in the season, the Browns finished the 1913 season with a 5-6 record.

Before the start of the annual postseason city series against the Cardinals, Rickey sat down with Charley Barrett and Robert Hedges to evaluate the team's roster. Despite the last-place finish Rickey decided that all was not bleak on the team's horizon. The Browns possessed an outstanding player in fleet outfielder Burt Shotton, who led the American League in walks with 99 and was among the league leaders with 105 runs scored and 43 stolen bases. Shotton's fleetness of foot had earned him the nickname "Barney," after Barney Oldfield, a champion automobile race driver. In a 1915 All-Star team voted on by the players, Shotton's American League peers included him in an outfield with immortals Ty Cobb and Tris Speaker.[12]

Baseball intelligence was a big part of Shotton's success. He knew how to take advantage of his speed on the base paths and was a savvy defensive outfielder, especially adept at cutting down extra bases on hits. He liked playing for Rickey because he was the first manager in his career who thought players had minds and encouraged them to think on their own. Shotton and Rickey also hit it off personally, since Rickey always felt a special fondness for a hard-working, teetotaling, small-town Ohio boy. Shotton hailed from Brownhelm, twenty-eight miles west of Cleveland, and was the son of a farmer who later became a quarry engineer. In 1914 Burt Shotton became the Browns' "Sunday manager," but he disliked the term, preferring to call himself the team captain who followed Rickey's instructions on Sundays.[13]

Another stalwart on the 1913 Browns was second baseman Del Pratt, who hit .296 and drove in a team-leading 87 runs, 34 more than the second-leading RBI man on the team, outfielder Gus Williams. Pratt, who also led the league in put-outs, played with an aggressive fury that Rickey admired and had first observed in some memorable college games coaching the Michigan Wolverines against Pratt's Alabama Crimson Tide. Except for Pratt and Shotton, however, the Browns were wanting in many areas. They were weak on the pitching mound, where six foot six Carl Weilman was the American League's only twenty-game loser and George Baumgardner had lost nineteen games. Although in shortstop Bobby Wallace they had a future Hall of Famer, he was almost forty years old at the time and was used sparingly.[14] (Wallace was blessed with great hands and, like another shortstop in Branch Rickey's future, Leo Durocher, was also a gifted billiards player.)

The 1913 season had been a horrible one for the St. Louis Cardinals, who finished in last place too, giving more credence to a wicked canard circulating about local Major League Baseball: "First in booze, first in shoes, and last in the major leagues." Nonetheless, the Browns and the Cardinals were scheduled to play the annual postseason city series, games that had become a tradition in St. Louis and Chicago, the two midwestern cities that boasted teams in each Major League. In Chicago the contending Cubs and White Sox often drew twenty thousand or more to a postseason game, but, not surprisingly, postseason baseball attendance in St. Louis usually numbered in the hundreds.

The most significant development in the St. Louis city series occurred not on the field but in the clubhouse. It involved a dispute between deposed manager George Stovall and his successor, Branch Rickey. Still on the Browns roster as a first baseman, Stovall wanted to play in the postseason games. When Hedges fired Stovall as manager, he had wanted to release him as a player, but Rickey advised the owner that Stovall still had trade value and so should remain on the roster. However, well-founded rumors were circulating that Stovall was negotiating to be a manager in the Federal League and was also recruiting players from the established leagues to join the third league, which had begun play in 1913 as a Minor League but had now declared open war on the baseball establishment.

When Stovall tried to get in uniform for the city series games, he could not find it. Branch Rickey had hidden it, drawing criticism from some sportswriters, who felt the manager's behavior was petty and not becoming someone who was always encouraging Christian and gentlemanly behavior in his players.[15] The Browns' manager was unapologetic, however. By hiding Stovall's uniform, he was making it clear that he would not tolerate any rebellion against the existing baseball order. Although directly involved in the management of a professional baseball franchise for only a few months, Branch Rickey was already among the fiercest defenders of its prerogatives.

Denied a chance to play, Stovall left the ballpark in a huff, telling the sportswriters that he was going home to Los Angeles. He defiantly added that he might stop off in Kansas City to see about managing its Federal League team, which had recently been relocated from Indianapolis. Sure enough, Stovall soon signed to manage Kansas City for 1914. He leveled a parting shot at baseball's old guard, whom he felt treated players like pieces of furniture. "No white man ought to submit to be bartered like a broken-down plow horse," he declared.[16]

Branch Rickey did not believe that the Federal League would succeed. He felt that it lacked both quality players and experienced ownership, but he was aware that it posed an immediate threat locally. Before he had even begun his first full season as manager, both Rickey's Browns and the National League Cardinals were to be faced with third league competition in their small city, a metropolitan area that had the smallest population of any Major League franchise.

The Federal League owners had deep pockets and were intent on opening them. They promised to build new stadiums in six of their eight cities, and they enticed many Major Leaguers with offers of double or triple what they were currently earning. The Chicago Whales made the first big Federal League news in December 1913 when they signed manager Joe Tinker, the shortstop in the Cubs' famed double play combination of Tinker-to-Evers-to-Chance. Outfielder Max Flack, later a member of Rickey's Cardinals, also signed with the new Chicago team. The Whales were owned by Charles Weeghman, the wealthy owner of a chain of Chicago cafeterias, who made good on his promise to build a new ballpark on the north side of Chicago.

After playing the 1913 season at St. Louis University, the St. Louis team, known variously as the Terriers or the Sloufeds, moved into a new stadium in 1914.[17] Many pundits gave them a good chance of succeeding, since its opposition would be two teams that finished last in 1913 and rarely contended for a pennant. The main owner of the Sloufeds was millionaire ice manufacturer Philip DeCatesby Ball, who had made his fortune selling his product to brewers and meatpackers. A native of Keokuk, Iowa, Ball had worked at a variety of jobs, from railroad and construction worker to cowboy to Minor League baseball player, where his career prematurely ended when he was stabbed in the hand during a barroom brawl.[18]

Trying to make a splash with a big name, Ball signed pitcher Mordecai Centennial "Three-Finger" Brown, a future Hall of Famer, and named him the Terriers' player-manager. He also added former Athletics southpaw Eddie Plank, another aging future Hall of Famer. Among the promising outfielders on Phil Ball's roster were Jack Tobin, a local boy from St. Louis, and Armando Marsans, formerly with the Cincinnati Reds and one of the first Major Leaguers from Cuba. On paper many pundits thought that Ball's Federal team looked superior to the Hedges-Rickey Browns, who did not seem improved for 1914 and had already returned half of the thirty Minor Leaguers drafted in September 1913 to their original teams.[19]

Branch Rickey may have returned many of the Minor Leaguers, but he didn't come to St. Louis to fail. He had faith that the coaching methods he used at Michigan could be applied to improve and inspire Major Leaguers. Always an object of interest for curious writers in the press, Rickey consented to an interview with young local sportswriter Hunt Stromberg, which appeared in the January 1, 1914, issue of the *Sporting News*. The story was accompanied by a photograph of the manager, bent over on a St. Louis bench, staring intently at the playing field.[20]

Stromberg would go on to become a successful Hollywood producer, making several films in the *Thin Man* series and winning a 1938 Oscar for *The Great Ziegfeld*. However, in late 1913, the young writer was nervous about interviewing the intense new Browns manager, so first he handed him a typewritten list of twenty-five questions, which Rickey silently perused for about ten minutes. The questions were familiar to him by now, but he tried to answer them as honestly as he could: Concerning the omnipresent issue of the role of religion in baseball, Rickey said, "Going to church once a week has no connection whatever with the playing ability of any man," words very reminiscent to the ones he uttered to the Cleveland sportswriter in 1906. He added somewhat testily, "I wish you to know that I am not a religious and a church fanatic, as many have been led to believe. I have my own religious ideas and wish to conform [to] those ideas. The others may do as they see fit."[21]

As far as the usefulness of a college education in making a Major League baseball player, Rickey answered that there was no direct correlation but that "the kind of brains I have in mind play a big part." Stung by the charges leveled against him that he was too intellectual in his approach to baseball, Rickey said with rare publicly profane passion, "I want no theoretical baseball. . . . In plain words, to hell with that report." He added, "I know absolutely nothing regarding 'the law of averages.'" With the confidence of an expert, Rickey declared, "I played the game myself, . . . and I know the kind of baseball which produces winning teams."[22]

Miller Huggins, Rickey's Cardinals counterpart, was one critic of Rickey's theoretical ideas, and the two leaders engaged in some lively public jousting before both departed for spring training. The paths of Rickey and Huggins had briefly crossed in Cincinnati in August 1904 when Huggins was the starting second baseman and the new backup catcher arrived from Dallas, only to be told to leave by manager Joe Kelley when he wouldn't play on Sunday. Two years older than his rival, Huggins was also an Ohioan by birth, a Cincinnati native, and he, too, possessed a law degree but didn't practice. Unlike his counterpart, however, Huggins was still enjoying a successful Major League career, which would total thirteen seasons, split almost evenly between the Reds and the Cardinals. He finished with a respectable .265 career batting average and a very impressive 1002:312 walk-to-strikeout ratio. Listed at five foot six, Huggins was probably only five foot three, a size that earned him the nicknames in the press of the "Mighty Mite" and the "Midget Manager."

"I believe Manager Rickey has a lot of very good ideas, but I am not strong for theory," Huggins declared. He argued that the only way a Major Leaguer could be developed was by experience in actual games, not by overemphasis on practice drills. He took specific issue with Rickey's drilling players in the mechanics of sliding. "No ball player can learn these things sliding in pits," he scoffed. "How long do you think I would last if I was compelled to hit the dirt fifteen or twenty times every day? I am no longer a kid, and it would cripple me so badly that I would not be able to play ball for a month."[23]

Never one to walk away from an argument, Rickey countered: "Hitting alone will not win ball games. I want speed on my team and I also want every man on the squad to know how to slide. To attain speed, or at least to get more speed out of the men than has been the case in the past, I intend to have my players taught how to run. Few ball players know the slightest thing about sprinting, and this despite the fact that a great many of them have attended college." Rickey promised that in spring training, every one of his players would learn how to hook slide to each side of the base. They would also play handball, which would "brighten their eyes and make them alert. Handball is a great game and develops every muscle of the body." The idealistic manager insisted that the purpose of his curriculum was "to send a mighty clever ball club on the field. I don't say that we will win any pennants," he admitted. "No, far be it from me to mention anything of that kind, but I do think that my system of training will be laying the foundation for a pennant winner."[24]

Rickey also boldly predicted that, despite Miller Huggins's objections, the Cardinals would one day employ sliding pits and batting cages. Rickey had developed the latter in Michigan as a way of giving catchers more hitting practice. Receivers were generally considered poor hitters, Rickey reasoned, because they weren't given the chance to improve. By using a batting cage that had a wall in the back, catchers were freed from receiving duties and could work on their hitting.

Who was right? The man with long experience in the Major League trenches, Miller Huggins? Or the man of newfangled ideas and passionate theories, Branch Rickey? And could either or both establish local dominance over the Federal League Terriers? The proof would be in the pudding of competition in the upcoming season. Off the teams went to their respective 1914 spring training bases, the Browns to St. Petersburg, on the Florida Gulf Coast, and the Cardinals to Texas near San Antonio.

The Browns chose St. Petersburg because during the previous fall, promoter Al Lang, a future local Rotary Club president and town mayor, had impressed Robert Hedges and Branch Rickey with his presentation in behalf of the resort city on Tampa Bay. Lang, a native of Pittsburgh, had moved to Florida in 1911 and become friendly with Donald Beach, a graduate of Ohio Wesleyan and Rickey's Delta Tau Delta fraternity brother. Beach suggested that Lang look up Rickey and Hedges, and the Florida promoter and the St. Louis manager became fast friends. Besides a mutual love of baseball, Lang and Rickey were both endowed with exceptional stentorian capacities. It was said of Lang that he possessed "a voice that considers the distance from deep center field to home plate as whispering range."[25]

In 1914 St. Petersburg's facilities for baseball were barely developed. The Browns engaged in their morning workouts on a barren field in one part of town and then trekked over a rocky road for nearly two miles to another rudimentary facility, where they played intrasquad games or exhibitions against other Major League teams. Rickey hoped that the players might bond as they dealt with the inconvenient elements of their preseason preparation.

Rickey's first spring training as a Major League leader was not very different in tone and intensity than his preparations for baseball and football at Allegheny, Ohio Wesleyan, and Michigan. "I don't know very much about the game of baseball," he said on the first morning of practice, "but I intend to find out." His camp was well organized, of course. Everyone ate a 8:00 communal morning meal, followed by exercises in the sliding pits and on the running track. Afterward, batters worked in the batting cages, and those pitchers Rickey felt needed better control tried to improve by throwing to the pitching "strings," a typically innovative Rickey device that he had first experimented with at Michigan.

To form the pitching strings, two strong, upright poles were placed at either side of a home plate connected by two horizontal white cords. The lowest cord was strung at a level approximating a hitter's knees, and the highest cord was strung at approximately shoulder height. Both parallel cords stretched across the front tip of the plate, the point closest to the pitcher's mound. The cross stringing of both sets of cords resulted in the strike zone being outlined by a white cord rectangle. With a catcher crouching behind the plate, the pitcher was instructed to "hit the strings"—that is, to improve his control on the edges of the strike zone, the area known in modern parlance as the "black" of the seventeen-inch home plate. "Anybody can put a ball through the rectangle," Rickey declared, "but when you hit the strings, you've caught the edge of the plate."[26]

Rickey was trying to build the spirit of teamwork in his professional players. Turning a squad of individuals into a *team* of players was always his primary goal as a coach and manager. He wasn't hesitant about encouraging the college-style cheers and songs that he had heard at Ohio Wesleyan and Michigan. With the enthusiastic support of owner Robert Hedges, Rickey was continuing to scour the colleges for players, and he wasn't shy about bringing in Michigan players he had coached if he thought they could contribute. Catcher Jack Enzenroth, the captain of Rickey's first Wolverines team in 1910, would play three games for the 1914 Browns before leaving for Kansas City in the Federal League.

A far greater contributor to the 1914 Browns and future Rickey teams was shortstop John "Doc" Lavan, who starred for Rickey's last and greatest Michigan team in 1913. After finishing his collegiate career Lavan immediately arrived in St. Louis, but he suffered through a difficult rookie year, hitting a paltry .135 with 46 strikeouts in 163 at-bats. His fielding, however, drew raves from teammates and opponents alike. He exhibited an uncanny ability for completing double play throws from a remarkable number of angles. When former manager George Stovall released Lavan late in the 1913 season, Connie Mack quickly grabbed the collegian because the A's starting shortstop, Jack Barry, was injured. Lavan's defense helped the A's win the pennant and the World Series.[27] However, Rickey was able to re-obtain Lavan from Mack before the 1914 season. The shortstop would cut down on his strikeouts and continued to excel in the field.

When the Browns came home to St. Louis from Florida and beat the Cardinals in the preseason 1914 city series, the fans started to sit up and take notice. As the team got off to a good start in the pennant race, some of the scoffing local sportswriters began to revise their opinions about the Browns under their talkative and erudite new manager. They had to admit that the players were hustling and playing with passion.

Rickey was getting some favorable attention in the national press too. Former Minor League player Billy Evans, an astute Major League umpire and later a general manager in Cleveland and Detroit, praised Rickey's psychological methods in a piece in *Harper's Weekly* titled "The Somewhat Different Manager." Evans notes that when Rickey was hired, "his aspirations as a big league manager were treated more in the light of a joke."[28] With the Browns rising to the first division by early summer 1914, Evans wrote that Rickey's unusual style of passion, precision. and politeness was making baseball people take notice.

Evans gave an illustration of Rickey's method of arguing with an umpire while keeping himself from being ejected. "Mr. Umpire, you were wrong," Evans quoted Rickey. "The third baseman hasn't touched my player yet. You had a bad angle on the play. . . . It was only natural that my player should kick." Evans also praised the manager for taking the blame for mistakes, thereby shielding his players from public and press criticism. Evans lauded Rickey's psychological ploy of motivating a team that knew it wasn't a pennant contender by having "fired them with a desire to keep as far as possible from last place." When the Browns reached second place early in the season, Evans noted, Rickey simply called it seven places from last.[29]

The Browns' perch in the American League first division did not last.

After the team peaked in late June, their inexperience and lack of depth caused an inevitable decline. They still finished a strong fifth, 79-74, five games over .500 for the first time in the history of the franchise. Although the team trailed the pennant-winning Athletics by twenty-nine games, it was still a ten-game improvement over 1913.

Finishing over .500 was encouraging, but the Browns still trailed the fourth-place Tigers at the bottom of the first division by nine games. Detroit was led by fiery outfielder Ty Cobb, and, fittingly, one of the truisms in Branch Rickey's life as a competitor was "To be the best, you have to beat the best." Trying to manage against Ty Cobb proved an exasperating challenge for Rickey, but at least it provided him with ample fodder for his after-dinner speaking.

He loved to tell the story of how Cobb beat his Browns in an extra-inning game without the ball ever being hit. Rickey implored his pitcher not to walk lead-off man Cobb, but the future Hall of Famer did reach on a base on balls and promptly stole second base. When the catcher's throw trickled beyond second base, Cobb immediately headed for third. "That boy Cobb had reflex centers in his heels," Rickey exclaimed. "He did not have time to telegraph his brain." The third baseman was so intimidated by the Detroit star's reputation as a fierce slider that he missed the throw, and Cobb scored the winning run without the benefit of a hit or a pitch thrown to the next batter.

Rickey rushed out to protest to the umpire that Cobb's slide into third base had been illegal because he went for the ball and not the base. "He paid no attention to me—they have a habit of doing that," Rickey loved to add to this story, always drawing a big laugh from the audience. It was the umpire who had the last word in Rickey's tale of Ty Cobb's excellence. "Mr. Rickey, listen to me," the arbiter said, delivering the moral of the story. "Give the boy credit. He made his own breaks."[30]

Rickey was pleased that the Browns were no longer laughing stocks of the American League, but he would not be satisfied until they truly became pennant contenders. A believer in science and mathematics as well as spirit and soul, he was convinced that the ordinary method of evaluating baseball performance—batting average, runs batted in, and earned run average—was inadequate in judging the real worth of a player. Bad players on good teams might have better and more misleading statistics than good players on bad teams. One player might have an inflated RBI total because he had more opportunities on a good team than an equally good or better hitter would have on a bad team. Rickey knew that the object of the game was to score more runs than the opposition, and to do that you had to circle the bases speedily and efficiently.

From his earliest days running the Browns, Rickey pondered deeply the mystery of analyzing baseball statistics. With Robert Hedges's blessing, he hired a part-time employee, Travis Hoke, a young cub reporter for a St. Louis periodical, *Sport and Stage*, to chart every game with "base and out efficiency" in mind. Rickey gave Hoke a pad and a pencil and a box seat behind home plate and asked him to record the number of bases that each hitter advanced every runner. For instance, a single with no one on received one point, but a grand slam home run received ten points because the batter advanced four bases; the man on first, three; the man on second, two; and the man on third, one. Rickey's system also served as a double-entry mechanism because pitchers were penalized for the number of bases they gave up. Hoke became such a fixture at Browns home games that sportswriters frequently looked down from the press box and wondered just what the young man was writing on his pad. The young writer provided Rickey information until the end of the 1914 season, when he went on to become a nationally known writer.[31]

In 1914 Branch Rickey did not yet know what to make of all the "base and out" information Travis Hoke had provided him, but his idea prefigured by nearly seventy-five years the writing of modern-day analysts, so-called sabrmetricians like Bill James. For the earnest baseball executive, attention to detail was the key to success in any endeavor, and there was no item of information that he considered irrelevant until he passed it through his formidable intellect. (More than thirty years later in Brooklyn, Rickey hired statistician Allan Roth to a full-time position, charting every pitch of every game.)[32]

Miller Huggins's Cardinals also had a surprisingly successful 1914 season, bouncing up from the cellar to third place in the National League. The Cardinals gained over 50,000 fans for a total of 256,099, and the Browns drew 244,714, a loss of fewer than 6,000 from 1913.[33] It is hard to find accurate data on how many fans the Federal League Terriers drew, but they usually outdrew the established teams on weekends. Nationally, however, it was clear that the Federal League was hurting both established Major Leagues. By the end of 1914 the older leagues reported an alarming drop of almost 2 million in attendance, from 6,358,336 in 1913 to 4,454,988 in 1914.[34]

Yet the leaders of the Federal League were insisting that they would stay in business for a third season in 1915. They also intended to follow through on a federal antitrust suit against the established leagues. The trial was slated to begin on January 20, 1915, in the Chicago courtroom of federal judge Kenesaw Mountain Landis. In 1907 Landis had attracted national attention for levying a record-setting $29 million fine on Standard Oil company president John D. Rockefeller for antitrust violations in restraint of trade. Although an appeals court subsequently overturned Landis's verdict, his reputation as a friend of the little guy battling big business gave Federal League owners hope. Third league attorneys also drew encouragement from the passage in 1914 of the Clayton Anti-Trust Act by the United States Congress, which, as a supplement to the 1890 Sherman Anti-Trust Act, established a Federal Trade Commission to investigate trade irregularities and continued to levy triple damages on individuals or organizations ruled in violation of the law.

As the trial neared, Branch Rickey was spending part of the winter in Freeport, Texas, with Jane, his daughter, Mary, not quite two years old, and his young son, Branch Rickey Jr., born on January 31, 1914. Freeport offered a lot of good hunting and fishing, and it wasn't far from where the Browns planned to start spring training in 1915. Rickey didn't plan to attend the trial, feeling secure that the team's side of the case was in the good hands of attorney George Howard Williams, a Missouri state judge who had become one of Rickey's closest friends. Williams was part of a formidable team of lawyers for organized baseball, led by noted Philadelphia lawyer George Wharton Pepper.

On January 20, 1915, the antitrust trial began, and over six hundred spectators jammed Judge Landis's Chicago federal courtroom while hundreds more were turned away. Some players came to watch the proceedings, as did Terriers owner Phil Ball, who told a reporter that he had never met his rival St. Louis owners, Robert Hedges and the Cardinals'

Schuyler Britton. "I want to take a peek at some of the people I'm supposed to be dealing a punch at in the dark," Ball quipped.[35]

The Federal League introduced a ninety-two-page complaint charging that the existing Major Leagues had committed a conspiracy against
restraint of trade. Attorneys for the plaintiffs criticized the complicated
waiver and draft rules of baseball for limiting freedom of the players.
George Wharton Pepper, however, defended the status quo as serving
the needs of the players and the fans as well as the owners. Expressing
the viewpoint of Branch Rickey and the baseball establishment, Pepper
said of the Federal League rebels: "Their grievance is not that we prevent
them from finding young ball players on the 'lot' and developing them
through training in the various minor leagues as we do; they want to attain in one bound the advantage we have gained through ten years of
labor; they want to profit from the skill developed by our money."[36]

If the Federal League owners hoped that Landis's antiplutocracy stance
in his Rockefeller decision indicated that he would help their side, they
were quickly disabused. The third league plaintiffs had obviously ignored
that Landis was a huge baseball fan, often seen in box seats at Cubs and
White Sox games in Chicago. Early in the trial Landis made his true feelings known when he declared: "Both sides must understand that any blows
at the thing called baseball would be regarded by this court as a blow to
a national institution."[37] At another juncture in the trial he interrupted
an attorney's argument with an incredulous remark: "As a result of thirty
years of observation, I am shocked because you call baseball 'labor.'"[38] If
the established owners had any doubts as to where Landis's sympathies
lay, they breathed deep sighs of relief after hearing his ringing endorsement of the pure sporting aspect of the baseball business.

The hearing lasted for only two days, after which Landis said that he
would reserve judgment. The Federals hoped for a rapid and favorable
decision, but Landis waited and waited, his likely strategy from the outset.
The crucible of competition among the three big leagues would decide
the outcome, and by the end of the 1915 season, it was clear that the Federals as an eight-team competing Major League could not survive. Teams
in Buffalo and Pittsburgh barely made it to the end of the season, and the
Brooklyn franchise was moved to Newark following the death in the fall of
1915 of wealthy owner Robert Ward, founder of the Tip-Top Bakery.

The new owner of the Newark Feds was wealthy Sinclair Oil baron Harry T. Sinclair, who had the financial clout to make good on his proclamation that the league would continue. Sinclair even talked of moving his Newark team to New York, where he claimed that he would build a stadium in Flushing Meadows in Queens (at a location where, nearly fifty years later, Shea Stadium was indeed built.) Actually, Sinclair was mainly maneuvering for a good position in the end game of the Federal League, which he obtained by becoming the broker for the third league players wanting to return to the established leagues once their short-lived circuit dissolved in December 1915.[39]

Judge Landis's delay in rendering a decision in the Federal League antitrust suit pleased Branch Rickey, who never thought that the Federals would succeed. Yet the omens for the Browns' 1915 season from the very first days of spring training in Texas were not good. Rickey was stricken with a bad case of grippe, and Charley Barrett contracted malaria. Once the season started, the team stumbled out of the gate and never got untracked. It was becoming clear to Rickey that the Browns lacked the depth of talent and pitching skill to improve on their promising 1914 season.

However, Rickey was not giving up, and early in the season he persuaded Robert Hedges to spend $30,000 to purchase the contract of two high Minor League players, catcher Hank Severeid and pitcher Grover Lowdermilk. Severeid would go on to enjoy a fifteen-year Major League career as a backup catcher and a .289 hitter, who appeared in the World Series for the 1925 Washington Senators and caught all seven games for the 1926 New York Yankees in their World Series loss to Rickey's Cardinals. On the other hand, despite his mellifluous name, Grover Lowdermilk would win only twenty-three games in his Major League career.

Branch Rickey didn't expect a pennant in 1915, and he said so frankly to the sportswriters. Yet he was disappointed at the lackluster performance of his team, which was headed back into the second division with ninety-one losses. Losing games always devastated Branch Rickey, and he reminded himself of an adage, which he would repeat throughout his life, to maintain his optimistic outlook: "Never grow accustomed to the emotions of continuous defeat."

During the summer of 1915, while in Washington DC for a series against the Senators, Rickey addressed a Bible class at a YMCA. On an afternoon so hot that the minister who introduced him told the audience to "take off your coats and be as comfortable as if you were in the bleachers," Rickey expounded on one of his favorite themes. "There's no such thing as 'luck,'" he declared. "Our lives are peculiarly within our own making, so that when you hear a fellow talking about the 'kick' of someone else and his own misfortune, you know that he has not taken advantage of all of his opportunity." Always trying to make explicit the connection between a baseball game and the competition in life, Rickey insisted, "A fellow makes his own breaks, as it is paying attention to the things we do after we hit the ball that usually determines the result."[40]

Rickey invoked a favorite metaphor—that the "scoreboard of life" and the scoreboard of a game are virtually the same thing. "Any slight change in the operation of those plays [in a game] might change the score entirely," he said. "So it is in life. All of us can look back and see where we could have done differently, with the result that things would now be different." Instead of moaning about lost chances in the past, Rickey urged the young Christians to focus on the present with intelligence, good mechanics, and indifference to glamour. "We should give more attention to the means and details that make the record rather than how it will look after the making," he advised.[41]

The one highlight of the Browns' dismal 1915 season was the arrival in late June of George Sisler, Rickey's first and greatest collegiate find. After graduating from Michigan with a degree in mechanical engineering, Sisler would become one of the rare players who didn't spend a day in the Minor Leagues prior to his Major League debut. However, there would be a few uneasy moments before the reunion of mentor and protégé was made official. Pittsburgh Pirates owner Barney Dreyfuss still considered Sisler his property. On the eve of the first baseman's graduation, the mogul reminded the National Commission that its decision in 1912 only allowed Sisler to maintain his college eligibility, but now it was time for baseball's ruling body to definitively rule on who owned his professional rights.

Rickey, of course, was well aware of the budding controversy and was in close touch with the star player and the university's legal authorities. At the start of Sisler's senior year at Michigan in the fall of 1914, his lawyer George B. Codd wrote a strong letter to the Commission, insisting that the player, at the end of his collegiate eligibility, should be declared a free agent, thus able to sign with any Major League team. Codd strongly hinted that an antitrust, triple-damage law suit would be in the offing if baseball ruled otherwise.[42] Rickey fully agreed with Codd's position, a striking example of how Rickey's belief in individual excellence allowed him to support antitrust protection for a worthy person like Sisler while his distrust of the unauthorized collective action of the Federal League made him vigorously oppose their antitrust case. (It also explains why he vigorously opposed the Players Fraternity, a fledging Major League baseball players union that made some inroads during the Federal League war, dismissing it as "a good name abused.")

Most baseball owners, however, thought that Dreyfuss had a legitimate claim to Sisler because the Pittsburgh mogul, one of their inner circle, had paid $5,000 for the promising player's contract three years earlier. However, American League president Ban Johnson, still the most influential member of baseball's ruling triumvirate, said that he was not in the business of courting damage suits. The Commission denied Dreyfuss's claim to exclusive rights to George Sisler.

Dreyfuss was still within his rights to try to sign the future star, and he made an offer of a $1,000 signing bonus plus a $700 a month salary for the remaining months of the 1915 season, a total package of $5,200. Branch Rickey countered with a much larger signing bonus for Sisler, $5,000, and a lower salary of $400 a month, a total package of $7,400. Rickey also omitted the controversial ten-day clause from Sisler's contract, the one-sided arrangement whereby a team could release a player on ten days' notice but the athlete was bound indefinitely. Rickey's exclusion of this clause for the exceptional Sisler was another revealing sign that for a player of great promise, the executive would eliminate the most oppressive aspects of the baseball contract. It was an offer that Sisler could not and did not refuse.[43]

Barney Dreyfuss was not a gracious loser. He was infuriated that Ban Johnson had probably swayed the votes of the two National Leaguers on the National Commission, league president John K. Tener and Cincinnati Reds owner Garry Herrmann. When the Pittsburgh owner found out that Rickey had signed Sisler for a total amount similar to what he had offered, he brought a charge of "tampering" to the Commission. However, in June 1916, baseball's ruling body closed the Sisler case forever by saying that the first baseman could remain a member of the Browns.[44] A furious Dreyfuss was all the more convinced that baseball needed a better ruling body, and thus the Sisler case hastened the coming demise of the National Commission. Looking back in *The American Diamond*, however, Rickey lavished praise on Ban Johnson for making the absolutely right decision in the Sisler case. "He stood viciously pat on the free agency of the player," Rickey wrote, "because of the nonconforming with a deadline date for the promulgation of a contract signed long since by a seventeen-high school boy."[45]

Never having any second thoughts that his claim to George Sisler was rightful and mutually desired, manager Branch Rickey warmly welcomed the former Michigan star to the Browns. On June 28, 1915, Sisler made his Major League debut, pitching three shutout innings in relief against the first-place White Sox and stroking his first Major League hit. A day before the Fourth of July, the Federal League Terriers drew nearly ten thousand fans for a preholiday game. On the same afternoon fewer than a thousand people came to see the St. Louis Browns, but those who did saw George Sisler make his debut as a Major League starting pitcher, hurling the first game of a doubleheader against Cleveland. Sisler rewarded the home crowd with a complete-game, 3–1 victory. He nervously walked nine batters but also struck out nine. After the game his former Michigan coach confidently told the press, "I consider this boy the 'find' of the season, and I venture to say that he won't pass on an average of two batters per game from now on."[46]

Sisler completed the 1915 season with a very respectable pitching log, a 4-4 record and a 2.83 ERA. Included in his wins was a 1–0 victory over the Senators' future Hall of Fame right-hander Walter Johnson. Sisler's control, however, was not as good as Rickey predicted. He finished the year with 38 walks and 41 strikeouts. Before the end of Sisler's rookie season, Branch Rickey decided that having his sizzling bat and adept glove in the lineup every day made the most sense for the young player's career. Though Sisler's final 1915 offensive numbers of a .285 BA, 3 HR, and 29 RBI were not overly impressive, it would be the last time Sisler hit under .300 until near the end of his career in 1926. He would hit over .400 in 1920 and 1922, and when he hit .420 in 1920, he collected 257 hits, a record that stood until 2004 when the Seattle Mariners' Ichiro Suzuki broke it with 264. Sisler finished with the outstanding career numbers of a .340 BA, tied for fifteenth on the all-time list; a .468 SA; and 2,812 H, all good enough for Hall of Fame enshrinement in 1939. His additional gifts as a base runner and defensive first baseman led the self-centered, hypercritical Ty Cobb to admit that Sisler was "the nearest thing to a perfect ballplayer."[47]

When Branch Rickey sat down with Charley Barrett and Robert Hedges the day after the 1915 season mercifully ended, the atmosphere was gloomy. With ninety-one losses the Browns had finished thirty-nine and a half games behind the pennant-winning (and ultimately world champion) Boston Red Sox, and twenty-two and a half games behind the last team in the first division, the fourth-place Washington Senators. The Browns finished sixth only because Cleveland lost 95 games and the Philadelphia Athletics, the defending league champions, had plummeted to the basement with a staggering 109 losses. Rickey sympathized with the plight of Connie Mack, who had traded away most of his stars after they had been swept in the 1914 World Series by the "miracle" Boston Braves, who rose from last place on the Fourth of July to win the world title.

An embittered Mack had suggested publicly that many of his 1914 players were distracted by thoughts of lucrative Federal League contracts, which he said contributed to their poor play against the Braves. There was no way that Mack was going to meet the salary demands of his stars, so he traded them away and waited to rebuild with less expensive players (ultimately returning to the World Series for three years in a row, from 1929 to 1931). How the excesses of greedy ballplayers afflicted his respected colleague Connie Mack was an instructive lesson for Branch Rickey, and he never forgot it. Silently, he vowed such a misfortune would never happen to him.

The news got worse for Branch Rickey in the fall of 1915 when he learned that Robert Hedges wanted to sell the Browns. Rickey was not going to be a miracle worker, Hedges had decided, and there did not seem to be any light in the second-division tunnel the Browns had again fallen into. Attendance took a plunge to 150,358 in 1915, a loss of almost 100,000 fans from 1914.[48] It was, by far, the worst year in Robert Hedges's ten-year-plus tenure as owner.

The Cardinals also plummeted in 1915 after a hopeful 1914. Although they lost fewer than four thousand fans from their total of 1914, the team finished tied for last place with the Cincinnati Reds, with ninety-three losses.[49] Only Phil Ball's Terriers had a good season on the field, missing the Federal League pennant by percentage points. (They won and lost one more game than the champion Chicago Whales.) Although none of the St. Louis teams did well in drawing more fans, Ball was as eager to stay in baseball as Hedges was now anxious to get out. Shortly, a willing buyer and a willing seller got together.

The sale of the Browns to Phil Ball was announced shortly before Christmas 1915. It was part of the overall peace settlement that ended the Federal League war. Judge Landis's strategy of inaction had worked. Most of the Federal League owners were in a peace-making mood by the end of the season, and yet two of their brethren, Phil Ball and Charles Weeghman, made out very nicely, as they were welcomed into the established baseball monopoly. Rumors had been circulating that Ball was to purchase the Cardinals, but he entered the American League by buying the Browns. Weeghman, of the Chicago Whales, bought the National League Cubs from Charles Murphy.

In selling to Ball, Robert Hedges turned a handsome profit of $400,000 on his initial investment of 1901, but not before some protracted negotiations. A generous owner, Hedges had advanced a lot of money to certain players, but Ball wanted to make sure that he had no liability because of Hedges's prior debts. The parting words of the outgoing Browns owner to the baseball world moved Branch Rickey deeply. "The biggest danger in baseball is the presence of so much money behind certain clubs," Hedges warned. "There are in both big leagues men who can buy winners. If they allow that ability to run to extremes, the game will suffer greatly. The weak fellows have no chance against men who can bid up to the skies for players."[50]

One of Hedges's last benevolent gestures to his admired associate Branch Rickey was presenting him with the security of a long-term, iron-clad contract. Thus Phil Ball, when he came in to take over the Browns in

January 1916, could not fire Rickey. However, the new Browns owner did not have to work closely with Rickey either or particularly like him. "So you're the goddamned Prohibitionist!" were Ball's first words to Rickey when they met for the first time in the team's offices.[51] Never comfortable being in a subordinate position, Rickey would have to deal with a boss who not only was domineering but for whom profanity was second nature.

Not surprisingly, Ball brought in his own people to run the Browns. He replaced Rickey as field manager with Fielder Jones, who had almost won the 1915 Federal League pennant for the Terriers (and had led the 1906 Chicago White Sox, the so-called "hitless wonders," to an unexpected World Series victory over the crosstown Cubs, winners of 116 regular season games). Unlike Hedges, Ball had no interest in Rickey's ideas of developing players on Minor League farms and teaching them the best techniques of the game. Accordingly, during the 1916 season, Rickey felt frustrated and underutilized. He mainly devoted himself to finding Minor League placements for the ex-Terriers who didn't make the Browns while continuing to scout young players, the work he always loved.

Before the start of the 1916 season, Rickey said good-bye to a young employee of the Browns, Roscoe Hillenkoetter, who had been a fifteen-year-old office boy when Rickey came to work for Robert Hedges. The youngster, a St. Louis native, loved being around baseball, but as Rickey got to know him better, he realized that the boy had abilities that would enable him to go far in the world beyond clerical work. When Roscoe told Rickey that he was wavering at the opportunity to apply to the Naval Academy because he liked baseball too much, Rickey exploded. "Young man, you must take that exam," he declared.

Perhaps thinking of his own disappointment at not scoring high enough on his military academy exams, Rickey added rhetorically (because he found it difficult to terminate anybody), "I will fire you if you don't take the test." The young man did take the qualifying exam, passed it, and rose to vice admiral in the United States Navy. Wounded at Pearl Harbor, he organized an intelligence network for Admiral Chester W. Nimitz in the Pacific war theater, and in 1947 he became the third director of the Central Intelligence Agency. He died in 1982 and is buried in Arlington National Cemetery.[52]

Before Hillenkoetter left for Annapolis, Rickey asked the future midshipman to recommend a replacement. The youngster suggested a thirteen-year-old peanut and soda vendor, William Orville DeWitt, who seemed to have a talent for organization, enthusiasm, and hard work. Young DeWitt was summoned for an interview with Rickey, who, as always, subjected the prospective employee to a barrage of questions about his family, religious background, schooling, and political party preference—everything, presumably, but marital status. The youngster, who came from a background of limited means, impressed the executive and was soon hired, beginning an association and friendship with a man more than twenty years his senior that would last for the rest of their lives.

Although Rickey was, as usual, showing his special knack for finding hard-working and loyal associates, he was still frustrated by his subordinate position on the 1916 Browns. He confided to his friend attorney George Williams that working for Phil Ball was "the most trying and unpleasant relationship I have experienced."[53] He was glad to see George Sisler emerging as a major star, but he wanted to be more involved in finding new stars and shaping a baseball organization to his own liking. George Sisler's biographer Rick Huhn has written perceptively about Rickey's professional life in 1916: "Like a good soldier, Rickey performed his duties, but with one eye open for greener pastures."[54]

Because he was no longer field manager, Rickey's salary had been cut by perhaps a third, but he worked on as best he could. On August 6, 1916, a third child was born into the Rickey household, Jane Elizabeth Ainsworth Rickey, and supporting his growing family was a driving mission of Rickey's life. By the end of the 1916 season, in which the Browns finished five games over .500 but still in the second division, Rickey was actively exploring other opportunities in baseball. Connie Mack, still struggling in his Philadelphia rebuilding program, expressed a desire to hire Rickey, but he did not have the money to pay the annual salary of at least $10,000 that Rickey expected.

A prospective position with Clark Griffith in Washington nearly came to fruition. Griffith was negotiating to increase his ownership of the Senators to 50 percent. He told his former Highlanders catcher that if Rickey could come up with a $50,000 down payment, he would offer him a quarter share of the team and the presidency. "To me, the Washington position seems a good one," Rickey wrote George Williams. "I want to be in it in a big way. I can get on with Griffith and I can help his management immediately. We can make money."[55] Wanting to retain the bright innovator's services for the American League, Charles Comiskey and Ban Johnson expressed interest in helping Rickey to raise the money. They were as pleased that Rickey brought George Sisler to the American League as Barney Dreyfuss was enraged that Pittsburgh and the National League lost out on the budding star.

Early in 1917 an opportunity in St. Louis ended all speculation about Rickey's possible departure to greener and less profane pastures than Phil Ball's Browns. The long-rumored sale of the Cardinals was finally about to transpire. Mrs. Helene Britton, who had inherited the team in 1911 from her childless uncle Stanley Robison, was tired of losing games and losing money. She was also weary of her marriage to Schuyler Britton. After an attempt at reconciliation failed, Mrs. Britton, nicknamed "Lady Bee" in the sporting press, filed for divorce and announced her intention to sell. She was willing to divest herself of the Cardinals at less than market value.[56]

There was a great fear in St. Louis that the nearly bankrupt Cardinals franchise might be moved to another city. Civic-minded citizens sprung into action, offering to buy shares of the team to keep it in St. Louis, but the ball club needed a chief executive. The civic group asked a panel of seven sportswriters and editors to provide on slips of paper the names of people to lead the Cardinals out of the wilderness. All seven suggested the same man, Branch Rickey.

John B. Sheridan, a leading St. Louis sportswriter who also coached a local teenage baseball team, summed up much of the St. Louis sporting community's feeling about Branch Rickey. "He is a trifle too good, too religious, too strict, too Puritanical," Sheridan wrote, "yet Rickey has done pretty close to my idea of what a young American should do." After attending Rickey's recent speech to the chamber of commerce on the subject "Baseball as an Aid to Business," the writer marveled, "I have never heard a more convincing pleader than Branch Rickey."[57]

Of course, the chance to stay in St. Louis with his growing family and make a winner out of the Cardinals excited the young family man and baseball partisan. He was even more thrilled when the civic group offered him a chance to buy into ownership. The job offer was truly a dream come true, a position of executive influence in Major League Baseball in a city and region he and his family had come to love and call home. When presented with the offer to run the Cardinals, Rickey immediately got in touch with his parents in Lucasville, Ohio. Although he was loath to ask his cash-poor parents for any financial help, he did mention that a $5,000 loan would help him buy his stake in the team. It didn't take much convincing of Frank and Emily Rickey. Rickey's mother especially had the utmost faith in the good works and endeavors of her son. She and her husband quickly made plans to mortgage their farm to enable their son to fulfill his dream. With the remainder of the funds available to him, the future president of the St. Louis Cardinals made a down payment on a three-story, twelve-room house on tree-lined Bartmer Avenue in a comfortable and respectable St. Louis neighborhood, where he would shortly move his growing family.[58]

There was one snag, though, before the deal could be finalized. Branch Rickey was still under contract to Phil Ball. Normally, front office people did not stand in the way of baseball executives advancing to a better position. When Ball first heard of the Cardinals' interest in his associate, he even told Rickey that he might help him get a better deal by offering more money to drive up the National League's team price.

But in March 1917 Ban Johnson undoubtedly stepped up the pressure on Phil Ball to try to keep Rickey in the American League. Since Ball and Johnson had suspicions that Rickey was already beginning to sign players for the Cardinals without having formally resigned, the Browns owner hired high-priced lawyers and went to court and obtained a temporary injunction preventing Rickey from leaving. The idealistic executive was incensed, fearful that a great opportunity could be snatched from him. There was no way that Rickey would return to work for Ball, but the equally stubborn Browns owner was not in a mood to relent.

Finally, on the eve of the 1917 baseball season, a compromise was reached, allowing both sides to claim victory. Ball was granted an unusual "permanent twenty-four–hour injunction" against Rickey.[59] In effect, the ruling meant that at 6:00 p.m. on April 6, 1917, Branch Rickey was free to join the St. Louis Cardinals as their president and chief architect. Earlier in the day President Woodrow Wilson had received the overwhelming approval of the United States Senate to take the United States into World War I. Before the so-called "war to end all wars" ended in November 1918, Branch Rickey, a rising master in the baseball wars, would be an actual participant in the military war.

4

"War Overshadows Everything"

In coming to the Cardinals as president, Branch Rickey found himself in the potentially awkward situation of working with field manager Miller Huggins. Hired in 1913 by the former owners Schuyler and Helene Britton, Huggins maintained a professional but not intimate relationship with Rickey. Back before the 1914 season, the two men had tilted in the press about the pros and cons of theories in baseball. Yet at the start of the 1917 season, both had enjoyed enough success in building competitive teams that they were widely considered in the baseball world as leaders of potential champions.

The stickiest point in their fledgling relationship was that Huggins had lost out on his own bid to become part of a new ownership syndicate. In partnership with his chief scout, Bob Connery, Huggins thought he had the inside track because he was a personal favorite of Helene Britton. However, his main money man, millionaire Julius Fleishmann, of the yeast-making family, was based in Cincinnati. James C. Jones, Mrs. Britton's attorney, convinced his client to accept a smaller bid from the local syndicate to ensure that the Cardinals remained in St. Louis. Huggins was thus faced in the 1917 season with a predicament similar to Rickey's with the Browns in 1916. He had an iron-clad contract ensuring employment for at least the coming season, but he realized that the new ownership might understandably have their own people in mind to hire.[1]

On the surface Huggins and Rickey got along well, and the Cardinals showed promise during the early stages of the 1917 pennant race. After winning the preseason city series from the Browns three games to none, with one tie, they opened on the road and returned home with a winning record. More than fourteen thousand fans greeted them for their home opener at Cardinal Field (the new name for Robison Field, named for Helene Britton's father and uncle, Frank and Stanley Robison). The assemblage went home happy as spitballer Bill Doak beat the Reds, 5–1.

A hope for contention was beginning to flower among St. Louis rooters, who sometimes were referred to in the press as "Cardinal Idealists," in reference to the slogan that James C. Jones, the new chairman of the Cardinals board, had devised for the new ownership. "The Cardinal Idea is twofold in purpose," Jones explained in an advertisement shortly before the season began. "To give the City of St. Louis a pennant-winning baseball team [and] to 'CARDINAL-IZE' the boys of St. Louis ." Jones pledged "to employ the best baseball brains" and "to employ the best boy developing brains" to make the "Cardinal Idea" work. "If it is only fifty per cent efficient it will give to St. Louis the best ball team that it has had in fifteen years—And do more to develop its boy life than anything that has been attempted in a decade."[2] There is no direct evidence, but it is possible that idealistic Branch Rickey provided some of the inspiration for the "Cardinal Idea" prospectus.

Happy that the team remained in St. Louis, the local press rallied behind the new ownership group, writing many positive stories about the "Cardinal Idea" and community-minded fan ownership of the team. Board chairman James C. Jones was especially willing to try out new ideas to attract fans. During the preseason city series, Jones introduced free scorecards and "noiseless" soda pop vendors to provide fewer distractions for fans watching the game.[3]

Another member of the new syndicate, insurance executive W. E. Billheimer, came up with the idea of the "Knothole Gang." Billheimer suggested that every stockholder who had invested $25 or more in the team should give away a free pass to a youngster of his choice. The idea would be a real test of the compatibility of the ideal and the practical because National League rules required that a visiting team get 18 percent of every paid admission at a ballpark. The cash-strapped Cardinal owners were thus not only subsidizing the free youngsters but contributing a sizable slice of the ticket cost to their fellow owners in the National League.

The program did not catch on immediately. Only a couple hundred youths came to the first Knothole Gang promotions in April, mainly because the wealthy stockholders did not know many impoverished young fans. Drawing on his wide knowledge of the YMCA and other youth programs, Branch Rickey urged a widening of the program to include less-advantaged youngsters. His only stipulations were that the parents approved of their children going to the games and that no school classes were missed.[4]

Once school was out in the summer, participation in the program blossomed as an estimated thirty thousand young fans flocked to the ballpark to cheer on their local heroes.[5] A special Knothole Gang outfield entrance gate was erected, and a few times during the season, pregame parades featuring youths from communities in and around St. Louis were staged, a tradition that continues into the twenty-first century and has contributed to the enduring success of the St. Louis Cardinals franchise.

Unfortunately, rowdiness marred some of the 1917 Knothole Gang days. Unruly fans hurled soda pop bottles at opposing players and umpires. Upset at the breach in ballpark decorum, Branch Rickey told sportswriters of a plan to maintain peace. "I intend today to place plainclothes men in all the stands, to gather evidence against bottle throwers, who will be prosecuted to the limit," Rickey announced in July. However, he opposed stopping all soda sales. "No, sir, fans get thirsty and must have their soda," he said. But he insisted that the spectators must behave like "gentlemen and sportsmen, not ruffians and partisans."[6]

The concerned team president also took issue with his own board chairman, James C. Jones, for condoning the fans who shouted "Robber!" at umpires for making bad calls. "Authority must be treated respectfully, especially by impressionable boys," Rickey cautioned. He warned that if the incidents continued, he would call off the Knothole Gang for a day, and then a week, and then permanently if good manners were not restored.[7] Early on in his new job Branch Rickey was making it clear that he expected players and fans, as well as himself, to behave like ferocious gentlemen.

On the playing field the 1917 Cardinals experienced an unexpectedly successful season. After having finished last in 1916, Miller Huggins brought the Cardinals into third place in 1917 with a respectable 82-70 record. They trailed the pennant-winning Giants by fifteen games, and the second-place Philadelphia Phillies by five games, but it was a year of hope for the team, and the fans responded. Attendance increased by almost 100,000 to more than 289,000, a far cry, of course, from the crowds in the bigger cities, where the New York Giants led the National League with over 500,000 fans, and the Chicago White Sox led all of baseball with almost 685,000.[8] Still, the Cardinals' increased fandom was definitely promising.

The Cardinals had three reliable, workhorse pitchers, veterans Bill Doak and Leon "Red" Ames, and the young Lee Meadows, the first Major League player to wear glasses in a game.[9] Doak led the team in innings pitched (285) and wins (16), although he also lost 20. Despite missing a month at the start of the season due to a car accident, Leon Ames returned to win fifteen games, as did bespectacled Lee Meadows. The Cardinals also had a promising outfielder in Jack Smith, who contributed a .297 BA, 3 HR, and 34 RBI, and a versatile second baseman in Jack "Dots" Miller, whose offensive statistics were mediocre—.248 BA, 2 HR, and 45 RBI—but whose leadership skills on and off the field were invaluable.

The rising star in the St. Louis firmament was undoubtedly Rogers Hornsby, a hard-hitting shortstop from Winters, Texas, a cattle-raising town outside of Fort Worth. When Hornsby was signed in 1915 by Miller Huggins's scout Bob Connery, the nineteen-year-old weighed only 135 pounds. After he played a few games for St. Louis at the end of 1915, the manager looked at the promising but scrawny rookie and suggested he might need some "farming," that is, more experience in the Minor Leagues. Hornsby took Huggins's advice literally, and in the off-season of 1915–16, the young Texan bulked up on steak and milk, returning in 1916 with twenty pounds of new muscle. He was on his way to stardom and a future Hall of Fame ranking as quite possibly the greatest right-handed hitter of all time.

In 1917, at age twenty-one, Hornsby led the National League in slugging, with a .484 SA, and in triples, with 17. He finished second in the batting race to Cincinnati's outfielder Edd Roush, hitting .327 with 8 HR and 66 RBI. By 1917 Hornsby was also on his way to becoming a matinee idol, attracting many squealing, doting female fans to the ballpark, who threw him perfumed handkerchiefs and made other enticing offers in person or by mail.

Despite the good showing of the Cardinals in making the first division, Branch Rickey knew that his team was not yet a real contender because it lacked consistent pitching and defense as well as a good bench. As the season progressed, it also became clear to him that whatever the future might hold for the Cardinals, Miller Huggins would not be a part of it. Huggins's guaranteed contract, negotiated with prior owner Helene Britton, was expiring at the end of the season, and stymied in his attempt at ownership, Huggins definitely wanted more guarantees in his next contract than the assurance of job security and a regular paycheck. Rickey was evidently willing to give Huggins a percentage of the proceeds in future club profitability, an agreement similar to the one he already enjoyed, but negotiations stalled on the amount of salary. Huggins wanted the status of at least $10,000 a year, and Rickey was reportedly offering $2,000 less.[10]

When American League president Ban Johnson entered the picture, the stalemate was transformed into an opportunity for Huggins. Still angry at the loss of Rickey to the hated National League, Johnson plotted with the new owners of the Yankees, Colonels Tillinghast Huston and Jacob Ruppert, to bring the Cardinals manager to the American League as a replacement for manager "Wild" Bill Donovan. The Yankees were on their way to a sixth-place finish in 1917, eleven games under .500 and twenty-eight games behind the eventual world champion White Sox. They continued to play second fiddle to the perennially contending Giants, who not only lorded their dominance over their poor cousin but also were their landlord at the Polo Grounds.

In the middle of the 1917 season, Johnson arranged for Huggins to meet secretly in New York with Yankees president Ruppert. Johnson offered Huggins a piece of personal advice before he departed. He told the diminutive manager to take his jaunty cap off before the interview. "Ruppert thinks you're a jockey as it is!" Johnson snapped. On the train to New York, Huggins unexpectedly ran into Rickey, who was traveling to a special National League meeting called to explain John McGraw's recent suspension for punching New York sportswriter Sid Mercer. Rickey didn't discuss why Huggins was traveling to Gotham, but he had an inkling as to the reason. When a bareheaded Huggins met Ruppert for his interview, he made a good impression on the beer baron/owner. At the end of October 1917, Huggins was introduced as the new manager of the Yankees, reportedly set to earn double his St. Louis salary.[11]

Branch Rickey was now faced with the first major challenge of his Cardinal presidency: hiring a new manager for his improved but still financially precarious team. Rickey told the press that he had no one in particular in mind. Some St. Louis sportswriters built up a case for Jack "Dots" Miller as player-manager. Respecting Miller's leadership abilities, Rickey thought that the second baseman was a definite possibility. However, Miller was called to military duty late in 1917. (Miller returned to play in 1919 but had contracted tuberculosis and would die at Saranac Lake in 1923.) When Rickey traveled to Chicago and was reported to be visiting the city's prestigious university, a rumor spread that the young executive was planning to bring an idealistic college coach into the ranks of the hard-bitten pros, but the story proved unfounded.

At the end of 1917, after a drawn-out negotiating process, Branch Rickey decided on Minor League manager Jack Hendricks as the Cardinals' skipper for 1918. Like Rickey and Huggins, the Chicago-born Hendricks possessed a law degree and experience as a player, though his Major League career as an outfielder consisted of only forty-two games for the Giants, Chicago Nationals, and Washington Senators early in the twentieth century. Hendricks's reputation was based on his managing since 1905 of the successful Indianapolis franchise in the American Association, owned by James McGill.

Rickey's delay in hiring Hendricks was most likely due to the Minor League manager's connection with McGill, who had at one time been a business associate of James Gilmore, a wealthy insurance man and former president of the defunct Federal League. An archconservative on the sanctity of the baseball reserve system, Rickey was suspicious of anyone who had even an indirect association with the disbanded Federal League. He was also concerned that Hendricks had not been forthcoming in describing his contract commitments with McGill that might require compensation to the Indianapolis owner for Hendricks's services. "I will not pay anything to anybody for the right to sign Mr. Hendricks," Rickey said bluntly. When asked by sportswriter John E. Wray (known as

Ed Wray) if he was considering managing the team himself, Rickey replied, "That is not in my mind. It may prove to be a necessity, but we are not considering that now."[12]

Ultimately, probably because he could not find another suitable candidate, Rickey signed Hendricks at the end of December 1917. However, in the photograph of the obligatory handshake accompanying news accounts of the signing, Rickey's somewhat suspicious gaze and arm's-length distance from his new manager strongly suggest that he had doubts about his new employee before he even started on the job.[13] Although terms were not disclosed, Hendricks perhaps received a two-year contract but no share of the team profits, given the precariousness of the Cardinals' financial condition. Mrs. Helene Britton had given the James C. Jones syndicate a local discount to buy the team, but there were still major payments to make to her and a perilously thin team treasury to draw on for those.

As the 1918 baseball season neared, the uncertainty of the outcome of the world war added to the Cardinals' ongoing economic problems. The team would lose more than a half dozen players to the military before the end of the season. Nearly a hundred Major Leaguers would give up baseball in 1918 for military duty, among them such Rickey signings for the Browns as left-handed pitcher Ernest Koob and shortstop John "Doc" Lavan, Rickey's Michigan shortstop in 1913, who would become a lieutenant surgeon in a naval unit in France. Intensely patriotic, Rickey applauded the decisions of the players to serve their country. "War overshadows everything" was a mantra he often uttered. Privately, he was already thinking of ways of serving the nation directly himself.

For the time being the hard-working executive focused his attention on trying to put a contending Cardinals team on the field. There remained precious little money in the team treasury, and another $40,000 payment was due to Mrs. Britton before the start of the season. In what would become almost an annual off-season ritual in St. Louis, pressure began building on Rickey to trade Rogers Hornsby, the Cardinals' one undeniable asset. Former Federal League owner Charles Weeghman, the new owner of the Chicago Cubs, was aware of St. Louis's cash-strapped situation, and he lusted for the budding star from Texas. Two weeks before Christmas 1917, Weeghman made a big splash by trading for the Philadelphia Phillies' high-powered battery of pitcher Grover Cleveland Alexander and catcher Bill Killefer. Obtaining future Hall of Famer Alexander was a major coup because from 1915 to 1917 the great pitcher had won thirty or more games, an unprecedented and probably unbreakable record. Weeghman wanted next to give Chicago fans another big Christmas present, offering reportedly more than $50,000 in cash and perhaps a few players to obtain Hornsby.

Rickey adamantly refused to consider trading Hornsby, realizing the huge potential in the young Texan who at age twenty-one hadn't even begun to enter his physical prime. Rickey understood the value of off-season publicity in the so-called hot stove league, but he was blunt about the not-for-sale tag on Hornsby. The combative Cardinals president gave a very logical argument for holding on to his budding star. No players could replace Hornsby effectively, and the cash he might receive would ultimately be consumed; he then would be left "with no cash and no Hornsby." While in New York for a February 1918 National League meeting, Rickey made local sports page headlines by "verbally pounding" Charles Weeghman for his willingness to spend extravagant amounts of money for players.[14] Rickey warned that team morale was guaranteed to suffer if a few players were paid far more than the majority of the team.

Back in St. Louis, the Cardinal franchise's money crunch was getting tighter. The team's board of directors made public a letter to stockholders, which implored them to increase their contributions to the club treasury. "The 'Cardinal Idea' is that we shall have a major league club, ownership in which is widely distributed among public-spirited citizens, to the end that it may be utilized for the better manly development of OUR BOYS," chairman of the board, banker Benjamin G. Brinkman, wrote. The letter stressed that Hornsby "was RETAINED, not sold for the tempting offers made, because the management is determined to give St. Louis a PENNANT WINNER, and we believe proved players should not be disposed of for mere monetary considerations."[15]

Unfortunately, the response to the call for more money was meager. Less than two-fifths of the next installment on the purchase price was raised, and a $50,000 payment was due on May 1.[16] Yet Branch Rickey, ever ready to accept a challenge and throw himself into the task with unflagging energy, vowed to improve the team. He knew that the key to the success of the Cardinals would be in the quality of the players he assembled around Hornsby, and in the scouts and instructors he hired to find and develop those players.

Rickey was elated to have Charley Barrett back at his side. After 1916, with Rickey's future under Phil Ball uncertain, Barrett had left the Browns for the Tigers, but when Rickey took over the Cardinals Barrett couldn't wait to come back to work with his revered friend, even if he had to supply pads and pencils for the small, barren team office in downtown St. Louis's Railway Exchange Building and would have to go without a salary check for the first three months on the job.[17] Other able scouts soon coming on board were Joe Sugden, Rickey's former teammate in Cincinnati, and Charley "Pop" Kelchner, the baseball coach at Lebanon Valley College in Pennsylvania. All members of the staff were eager to work alongside the master baseball and psychological mind of Branch Rickey and were indifferent to the low pay and the long hours.

In building a championship team Rickey's preference was always for finding hungry young players with a high ceiling for improvement. Rickey was enough of a showman, however, to realize that fans cannot wait forever for a winner. They want and need visible stars to root for in the present. Before the start of spring training in 1918, Rickey considered signing "Wahoo" Sam Crawford, the recently released Detroit Tigers outfielder. For years Crawford had played in the shadow of tempestuous Ty Cobb and now needed only 36 hits to reach the rarefied zone of 3,000 career hits.

Though the pursuit of personal milestones was nowhere as great a news story as it is in the twenty-first century's 24/7 world of all news, all trivia, all the time, Rickey undoubtedly saw the value of Crawford's quest as a gate attraction. He also greatly admired the outfielding skills of the Wahoo, Nebraska native, even if he had inevitably slowed down at age thirty-eight. Rickey was concerned that the Giants had corralled 280 more outfield putouts in 1917 than the Cardinals, and he was always seeking ways to improve defense. "We would like to have Crawford," Rickey said, "and if he will come at a reasonable salary, we may be able to find a place for him." However, when he learned of Crawford's asking price, the executive called it "ludicrous. He expects a great deal more than we feel justified in paying."[18] (Getting no other offers, Crawford retired with 2,964 career hits; he was elected into the Hall of Fame in 1957.)

Early in March 1918 Branch Rickey began his first spring training as Cardinals president in Hot Wells, Texas, a modest spa resort not far from San Antonio. Rickey announced beforehand that no player would be welcome in camp without having signed a contract. However, some potentially key contributors to the 1918 Cardinals were holding out for more money. Outfielder Jack Smith was at home in California, rumored to be enlisting in the Navy. The most significant holdout was Rogers Hornsby, who expected to be paid a salary worthy of the star of the team, if not the entire National League. The young Texan reportedly wanted an $8,500 salary, while Rickey was rumored to have offered $3,000 less.

Sportswriters generally enjoy holdout stories because they provide something to write about during the long training period when no meaningful games are played. However, with the world war raging and the future of the baseball season unclear, even those writers generally sympathetic to the players took management's side. Ed Wray, for instance, warned Hornsby that he was mistaken to think that the big-city owners in Chicago and New York should be used to up his ante in St. Louis. The player should understand that the "European war is on and the federal [league] war off," he opined in the *Post-Dispatch*.[19]

Priding himself on being able to talk any player into the fold to the mutual satisfaction of team and athlete, Rickey made a trip to Texas to negotiate face to face with his star. It was becoming common for the team president to pay a personal visit to a player's home to get a sense of the home life of the athlete and to employ his salesman's charm to get the player's signature on the dotted line. Rickey journeyed outside Fort Worth to meet Hornsby and his mother, Mary Rogers Hornsby, who had been widowed when Rogers was only two years old. Deeply attached to his own mother, Rickey was pleased to see that the young player was truly devoted to his mother, because he could be so difficult in other aspects of his life. "As the French say, [Hornsby is] deficient in the social relation," John Sheridan once neatly summed up the star player's truculence.[20]

Although in the future Hornsby would insist on contract dealings with management people other than Rickey, he agreed to terms during the team president's house call. "Hornsby signed. Delighted with his contract and said he was mighty glad he was not traded to Chicago," an exuberant Rickey wired the office in St Louis. "Club did not sacrifice principle or chance of prosperity, therefore contract pleased me also."[21] Hornsby reportedly received a two-year contract at $4,000 a year, including a clause that gave him the right to approve any sale or trade. It was another example of Branch Rickey giving a special star like Hornsby or George Sisler considerations that an ordinary player would never receive.

In spring training new manager Jack Hendricks began two-a-day sessions, hoping to whip the Cardinals into contenders in the coming season. However, the omens for the season were not good. Jack Smith never came to Texas at all, and though he agreed to terms just before the start of the regular season in April, the outfielder left in June to join the Navy. Hornsby delayed his arrival, quickly making it known that he did not like Jack Hendricks's style of managing. The temperamental Texan was one of those players who dislike meaningless exhibition games because they aren't being paid and could suffer a serious injury. He readied himself for the season at his own pace, turning a deaf ear to his new manager's ideas on preparation. Hornsby simply refused to play in many of the games as the Cardinals barnstormed their way back to St. Louis for the opening of the regular season.

He did play in the preseason city series against the Browns but was held hitless as the Browns beat the Cardinals, four games to none. Browns manager Fielder Jones even went public with an article on how Hornsby, who stood far back in the batter's box, could be pitched to successfully low and outside.[22] (Jones, a gifted but volatile leader, would not finish the year, quitting abruptly in midseason and retiring permanently from baseball.)

Once the regular season started it became clear that the Cardinals were nowhere near the competitive team that Miller Huggins had managed to third place in 1917. They quickly fell under .500 and never got above it all season, finishing last in the National League, twenty-seven games under .500 and thirty-three games behind the pennant-winning Chicago Cubs. The three hitters counted on for carrying the offensive load—Hornsby and outfielders Jack Smith and Walton Cruise—all got off to bad starts, perhaps because all had been involved in protracted contract disputes. By Memorial Day Hornsby was hitting only .270 and was plagued by a chronically sore ankle as well as injuries to his groin, a shoulder, and a thumb.

Hornsby was out of the lineup for days at a time, prompting Hendricks to suspect that Hornsby was "jaking" it, that is, faking an injury, always the most serious charge that can be brought against any athlete. Hornsby scoffed at the accusation and was openly contemptuous of Hendricks, calling him a Minor League "boob" manager. During one game the headstrong star refused to slide into home plate and was tagged out. "I'm too good a ball player to be sliding for a tailend team," he snorted.[23]

Rickey almost always sided with management against players in matters of team discipline, and he knew how stubborn and ornery Hornsby could be. However, Rickey was determined to keep Hornsby, even if the Cardinals were not yet a contending team. They needed more players to build around him, most urgently in the outfield. However, reinforcements were not easy to find because the wartime military draft had deeply cut into Minor League personnel. Charley Barrett told Rickey that he had never seen such a lack of talent on the lower levels.[24]

Refusing to "grow accustomed to the emotions of continuous defeat," Rickey constantly shuffled players to and from the Minor Leagues and suggested lineup changes to Hendricks almost every day. Before the end of June 1918, only four players from the St. Louis opening day lineup remained on the team. Complicating matters was the continuing financial struggle. Another $40,000 payment was due in May to Mrs. Britton, and the board of directors had to ask for two delays until they could come up with the money.

Rumors abounded that the team was for sale, which prompted denials from two of the club directors, automobile magnate W. G. "Fuzzy" Anderson and banker Ben Brinkman. However, the silence of chairman James C. Jones, who had organized the syndicate based on community ownership and the "Cardinal Idea," alarmed many followers of team fortunes. The team continued to sponsor the Knothole Gang and stage "Ladies Day," when girls and women got in for free or a nominal charge, but the disappointing results on the field led to reduced attendance. Because of World War I the season would be cut short on Labor Day, but even so the Cardinals suffered an alarming loss of fans in 1918. Only 111,000 paid their way into Cardinal Park, a loss of nearly 180,000 from 1917.[25]

In an atmosphere of economic uncertainty and disheartening defeat on the field, Rickey still forged ahead on his scouting trips, as did his trusted assistants, Joe Sugden and Charley Barrett. You never knew when you might find the cornerstone of a future contender, Rickey optimistically reminded himself and his associates. After getting cross-checking confirmation from Barrett and Sugden, Rickey announced in mid-June 1918 the acquisition of outfielder Austin McHenry from Milwaukee, of the American Association, in exchange for two Minor League pitchers and journeyman outfielder Marty Kavanagh. Rickey's evaluating skills told him that the twenty-three-year-old McHenry would become a far better player than the twenty-seven-year-old Kavanagh.

Austin McHenry was the kind of earnest Ohio farm boy who was closest to Rickey's heart. The son of a country doctor, he was born in 1894 in Wrightsville in Adams County, adjacent to Scioto County in southern Ohio. After playing high school and semipro ball, McHenry turned professional in Portsmouth in the Ohio State League in 1915. After two successful seasons in the lower Minors, Cincinnati purchased his contract for $2,500. The Reds, however, obviously didn't evaluate McHenry highly because they returned him to the Minors, where Rickey, Barrett, and Sugden all concurred about the promise of the young outfielder.

McHenry's numbers from his eighty games played for the Cardinals in 1918 were unexceptional, a .261 BA, 32 HR, and 29 RBI. But his defense was sensational, and he quickly became a fan favorite. McHenry made his in-season residence near Cardinal Field, and "Fireman" became one of his nicknames in 1919 when late one night, he smelled smoke at the rickety old ballpark and alerted the fire department to the danger. He even joined the fire fighters in helping to douse the flames.[26]

The uncertainty caused by World War I played a major role in the 1918 season. In June secretary of war Newton Baker issued a domestic "Work or Fight" order, and many baseball players scurried to find domestic wartime work or enlist. Rogers Hornsby took leave of the Cardinals in early July and returned to Texas, hoping to get a draft deferment as "the sole support of an invalid mother and sister." The War Department was not impressed, and Hornsby became the first Major League player to be told bluntly by the authorities, "Work or fight."[27]

After committing himself to join a shipyard in Wilmington, Delaware (where his main function would be to play on the factory baseball team), the blunt ballplayer returned to St. Louis in late July, where he wound up hitting .281 with only 5 HR and 60 RBI, the last time he hit under .300 until near the end of his career.

So many stars and journeyman Major Leaguers had left for the war effort that the 1918 baseball season was bound to be shortened. A matter of such magnitude should have been decided swiftly by the National Commission with the consent of the sixteen Major League owners. In July 1918 American League president Ban Johnson suggested August 20 for the closing date of the regular season, with the World Series to be completed by Labor Day. In the past Johnson had usually gotten his way on the Commission. By the summer of 1918, however, his power as the dominant leader in baseball was waning. His influence on Commission chairman Garry Herrmann, the Cincinnati Reds owner, had long irritated other National League owners, especially Barney Dreyfuss, who was still fuming at the loss of George Sisler to the Browns.

Among American League owners, Connie Mack, once one of Johnson's most loyal supporters, had recently demonstrated the erosion in Johnson's powers when he had gone to court successfully to keep pitcher Scott Perry, whose services had been awarded to the Boston Braves.[28] Any position of Johnson's power was now almost guaranteed to be opposed on principle by the majority of baseball owners. Thus eleven of the sixteen owners were reported to be against an early end to the season.

Branch Rickey agreed with Ban Johnson that the season should be cut short. The Cardinals president wondered if there should even be a World Series, with many stars and key players already drafted by the military. He made a suggestion that the owners schedule thirty postseason games to be played by "draft-proof" Major Leaguers, but the idea was quickly dismissed.[29] Rickey had only one vote, and he represented an impoverished, hardly influential franchise in league meetings, so his views at this early moment in his career carried little weight.

The Major Leagues dallied on its decision past mid-August even as attendance was falling into the low hundreds at many games, and virtually all Minor Leagues would not complete a full schedule.[30] Ultimately, the Major League moguls decided to end the season on August 31, with the

World Series to begin in the National League ballpark on September 5. The Series would feature the Boston Red Sox, led by a pitcher and occasional outfielder named Babe Ruth, versus the Chicago Cubs, led by the National League's winningest pitcher, Jim "Hippo" Vaughn, who won twenty games.

When it came time for the World Series, Branch Rickey's thoughts would not be exclusively on baseball. He told a St. Louis sportswriter that he'd like to see some of the games in Chicago but that the decision was out of his hands. At age thirty-six, Branch Rickey had decided to enlist in the American military to serve the world war effort in Europe. "War overshadows everything," Branch Rickey fervently believed, and now it was time to act on his principles.

Many in the baseball world assumed that Rickey might limit his work to YMCA duties. For instance, recently retired shortstop Johnny Evers (who had become famous as the shortstop in the Cubs' rhythmic double play combination of Tinker to Evers to Chance) had been hired as the athletic director for the Knights of Columbus in France. However, Rickey intended to serve more actively.

The die had been cast earlier in the summer of 1918 when Rickey met in New York with Percy D. Haughton, the Harvard football coach, who was in his third (and last) year as president of the Boston Braves. Haughton had enjoyed far less success in baseball than in football, discovering that his gridiron-style exhortations to the players did not easily translate to success on the diamond. At their meeting Houghton told Rickey that he was planning to enlist in the new Chemical Warfare Service that the United States Army was establishing to counteract the German poison gas offensive. The military was looking for men from outside their ranks, Haughton explained, who could mastermind surprise attacks on the enemy. At age forty-two the intense Bostonian was six years older than Rickey, so when he asked if Rickey were interested in serving, the patriotic Cardinals president could not refuse.[31]

Rickey's decision to go to war was announced in late August 1918, and during his last days on the job in St. Louis, Major Branch Rickey came to work in his military uniform.[32] Yet, to choose to go to war, Branch Rickey would have to weather a crisis in his family. Jane Rickey understood and supported her husband's patriotism, but risking his life in war with a wife and four little ones at home, including the baby, Alice, born on July 31, 1918, was another question. "How could Branch consider taking the risk of leaving so large a family without a breadwinner?" Jane thought to herself. She even contemplated leaving her husband and returning to Lucasville permanently if he insisted on going to war.[33]

However, Rickey's mind was made up when one day, on his way to work, he passed a sign on a downtown storefront that read, "Closing up after six months in business. I am going to war."[34] Like Percy Haughton, the store owner was a few years older than Rickey, and the simplicity of the sign convinced the patriotic executive that he had no choice but to enlist. "War overshadows everything," he must have repeated to himself again and again.

The reaction of the Cardinals' board of directors was mixed. Some applauded his patriotism and inspiring commitment. Attorney George Howard Williams, a member of the board and Rickey's close friend, wanted to join him in the war. Always ready to do anything for a friend, Rickey immediately sent a telegram to the military authorities in Washington in Williams's behalf, but the request came too late and he was informed that there were no more openings in the Chemical Warfare Service.[35] George Williams would have to stay stateside and support the war effort vicariously.

Other team officials were worried about losing Rickey's services, most notably board chairman James C. Jones. He was concerned about both the physical risk to Rickey and the further deterioration of the franchise without its vigorous president. However, Rickey's mind was made up. The board accepted his resignation effective at the end of the regular season, August 31 in the war-shortened year. It was implied, though, that his contract would be resumed upon his return from the hostilities.

Jane Rickey reluctantly accepted her husband's decision, knowing that once her husband was set on an objective, there was nothing further to be said. Plans were made for Jane to drive back to Lucasville, Ohio, where she and the children and sister Mabel would stay for the duration with her widowed mother, Mary Moulton. Rickey drove back to Ohio with trusted aides Bill DeWitt, who had become his personal secretary, and Charley Barrett.

As Rickey said his tearful good-byes in Lucasville shortly after Labor Day, he was terribly conflicted. His family, his religion, and his Ohio roots gave him his reasons for being and had instilled the values of God, community, and loyalty in him. Yet he was leaving it all now, taking a chance that he would never see family or Ohio or baseball again. Still, he felt that he had no choice. The patriotic call of duty to his country outweighed his deep love of family.

The United States was threatened by an enemy that may have been near defeat, Rickey understood, but that clearly was prepared to fight to the end. The hindsight of history tells us that the armistice that ended "the war to end all wars" was scarcely two months in the future, November 11, 1918. Of course, the people living in the summer of 1918 did not know that outcome. The forecasts of brutal closing battles ahead proved grimly accurate. Germans were firing on the outskirts of Paris as Rickey prepared to leave for Europe, and the French and Allied counterattack in the Somme was by no means a guaranteed success.

Major Branch Rickey arrived in Washington in mid-September to receive official orders. Soon he was headed for Hoboken, New Jersey, where he sailed to France on a top secret voyage aboard the battleship *President Grant.* Rickey was pleased to learn that he had been placed in a unit that included Captains Ty Cobb and Christy Mathewson. (George Sisler also enlisted in the same service but applied too late to serve time in Europe.)[36]

Three days into the weeklong voyage to Europe, the dreaded influenza bug swept through the ship. The epidemic that would kill more people than the war itself—22 million before its end in 1919—would claim more than a hundred servicemen on Rickey's ship alone, all buried at sea. Rickey was one of the ailing soldiers. He grew delirious and was placed on an upper deck of the ship, kept away from his fellow servicemen. Fortunately, when examined by the ship doctor, the diagnosis was pneumonia, not influenza. "And you're going to get well," the physician cheered him.[37]

Rickey was obviously relieved but was still so weak upon arrival at the French seaport of Brest that he had to be brought to shore on a stretcher (a story he didn't share with Jane until years later). Rickey was fearful that the pneumonia might mean that his dormant tuberculosis had returned and that he would be shipped home without ever having served. One of Rickey's major reasons, beyond pure patriotism, for going to war was that he was convinced that he could never be certain that he had truly licked tuberculosis until he subjected himself to the demands of a military mission.

Fortunately, Rickey got a clean bill of health upon his arrival in France and was cleared for duty. "I am on my way to my schooling station—very close to the front, but a safe distance," he wrote Cardinals treasurer Hiram W. Mason. "Within about six weeks I expect to be in the game as a player—no longer a spectator." He confided: "My legs are very weak and my right one won't carry me only about a block at a time—then a rest. It seems like fate was against me, but if you knew how fatal this influenza-pneumonia has been, you would understand how very fortunate I have been."[38]

In what turned out to be the last weeks of World War I, Major Rickey's regiment saw considerable action. The unit, which included Captains Ty Cobb and Christy Mathewson, hauled heavy Livens projectors, filled with chlorine gas and TNT, and Stokes mortars, filled with gas and thermite and smoke, and participated in more than 150 operations supporting tanks and infantry.[39]

With renewed energy Rickey led his men in forays during the day and socialized in the tents with them at night. Ty Cobb proved as ornery in military uniform as he was on the baseball field, but time spent with Christy Mathewson was far more pleasurable. Rickey spent many evenings chatting and relaxing in the tents with the former star New York Giants pitcher, who had become manager of the Reds. They passed some of the time playing checkers. The St. Louis executive considered himself an able checker shark, but Mathewson was a master, and Rickey could never beat him; once in a while, he could play him to a draw. Although it has been said that Mathewson caught his fatal tuberculosis during the war, neither the legendary pitcher nor the ferocious gentleman believed it. They felt that he was too physically vital during his war experiences to have been incubating the dread disease. "Matty took part in an impromptu broad jump contest in our group, and outleaped everyone . . . by a comfortable margin," Rickey remembered in *The American Diamond.*[40]

Rickey also spent time socializing with the lower ranks. If war served any value, Rickey soberly thought, it was in bringing a feeling of community and sense of duty to all men in battle. As he had done in Saranac Lake with the recovering tuberculosis patients, Rickey pepped up the spirits of the wounded, playing chess or checkers with them and generally trying to imbue them with his optimism for life. He relished the opportunity to help twenty noncommissioned officers who had been sent to the chemical warfare unit try to obtain a higher officer's rating. Many had been seriously wounded, but he helped them to prepare for taking the officers' exams. Before he was ready to return stateside in December 1918, the twenty soldiers, all of whom were now commissioned, gave Rickey a dinner in the barracks in his honor and presented him with some of their combat souvenirs.[41]

A relieved and happy Branch Rickey returned to New York on December 23, 1918, and arrived in Lucasville the day after Christmas. Jane and the children embraced him, overjoyed to have the breadwinner back, safe and sound. It didn't matter that Christmas was a little late this year, Branch Rickey thought. It was a heartwarming celebration, and he felt tremendous consolation, surrounded by his immediate and extended family and his colorful and cantankerous neighbors and friends in Scioto County.

Early in the new year of 1919, it was time to return to St. Louis with a new addition to the family. Mary Moulton, Jane's widowed mother, was going to join the family. In addition to Jane and Branch and their four young children, there was Mabel Moulton, Jane's older sister, and Clara, a maid whom persuasive Branch Rickey had lured down from Ann Arbor.[42]

When he returned to work at the Cardinals' barren office in the downtown Railway Exchange Building, Branch Rickey knew that the team's financial situation was worse than when he left. The immediate future might look gloomy, but sometime in the near future, he was confident that he would make a success of his baseball organization. He was prepared to employ all his native intelligence, work ethic, passion, and horse-trading guile in pursuit of the cause.

PART II

The St. Louis Prime of Branch Rickey, 1919–1942

This compulsion to succeed was to be a life-long characteristic of
Rickey and, according to the wife of a Cardinal farm club manager, the need
to prove himself worthy of Jennie's [Jane's] hand was a significant
driving force, even thirty years after their marriage.

—Donald Ray Andersen, "Branch Rickey and the
St. Louis Cardinal Farm System: The Growth of An Idea"

He really leads a double life—one with his conscience and the other with the
employer who pays him one of the top salaries in baseball. . . . Perhaps the most
moral man in private life in the sports field, Rickey is an ardent
churchman, a volunteer, non-professional missionary.

—Stanley Frank, New York Post

5

—

Necessity Is the Mother of Invention

"Hurry up with the rug, Charley," Branch Rickey implored Charley Barrett as they carried one of Jane Rickey's priceless heirlooms to the car parked outside the Cardinals' team office in downtown St. Louis. "Mother will be home from her trip tonight, and I won't hear the end of it if that rug isn't back in the living room." It was not the first time that Branch Rickey had temporarily borrowed some of his wife's family treasures to give an aura of respectability to the Cardinals' barren office. He had pulled the ploy before he went to war, and he was resorting to the ruse again in 1919 because the team was still in perilous financial condition.

Branch Rickey was going to have to use every resource of cunning and energy at his disposal to make the Cardinals a competitive team. Although he still dreamed of building a successful Major League organization from players signed inexpensively as amateurs and developed and groomed on his own Minor League teams, Rickey was faced with the reality that the Cardinals were a cellar-dwelling outfit with limited hopes of rising in the standings. He needed more players ready for the Major Leagues. He resented being at the mercy of Minor League owners charging inflated prices for their players, but he had little choice. With the aid of his coconspirator Charley Barrett, Rickey would every now and then put on a show in his office, placing a luxurious rug on the floor and one of Jane's stately settee sofas across from his desk, to convince owners of Minor League teams that the Cardinals were a respectable, prosperous concern that would make good on its payments.

It was in these cleverly manufactured settings that Rickey purchased two Minor Leaguers who started making major contributions to the Cardinals in 1920: first baseman Jacques "Jack" Fournier, who had previous Major League experience with the White Sox, and pitcher Jess Haines, a small-town Ohioan from near Dayton who would win 210 games and a place in the baseball Hall of Fame.[1] As events turned out, Haines would be Branch Rickey's last Minor League purchase of a player during his next twenty-three years at the Cardinals' helm. Of course, the executive had no such foreknowledge early in 1919. He knew only that he faced a formidable challenge in bringing the Cardinals out of the National League cellar and toward respectability, and he was ready to go to work.

As he prepared for his first spring training of the postwar years, Rickey was reluctantly wearing the dual mantle of team president and field manager. Incumbent manager Jack Hendricks wanted to return, but Rickey had never been sold on Hendricks's abilities and Rogers Hornsby had made it clear that he did not want to play again under a man he had called a Minor League "boob" manager. Rickey didn't want it thought that Hornsby was dictating the choice, but the executive was distressed at the personality clash between Hendricks and the prickly Hornsby, who Rickey would say was "the hardest to keep sweet" of all the players he managed. However, Rickey never doubted that the talented Texan had the ambition and talent to become a great star, if handled properly.

With little time to search for a new manager, James C. Jones, chairman of the Cardinals' board of directors, implored Rickey to accept the job, making a convincing argument that the club treasury would be saved about $10,000 if a new man did not have to be hired. With some misgivings team president Branch Rickey took on the additional duties of field manager.

A trip to a warm weather site for spring training was out of the question. The organization was so strapped for cash that it couldn't afford two sets of uniforms, home and away. The Cardinals would have to make do with one set of threadbare togs, dutifully patched up by a tailor friend of the earnest executive. Thanks to Rickey's many contacts in college athletics, he was able to secure use of the campus facilities of Washington University of St. Louis for his preseason program. He rented rooms in a local hotel, where the players were quartered together, building early on what Rickey hoped would be the kind of camaraderie and solidarity a winning team needs. They dressed for practice in the hotel and, clad in uniforms and carrying spikes, took the trolley to the university's gymnasium; if weather permitted, they would also work out at the outdoor Francis Field.

Rickey was pleased that the newspapers were giving more coverage to the Cardinals, preparing for the season in St. Louis, than to the Browns, who were training in San Antonio, Texas. The ardent new manager drew press attention for some of his new training innovations. He led the players in preworkout calisthenics and came up with the idea of having the pitchers get into shape by shagging fly balls in the outfield.[2]

The downside of the newspaper coverage was that his strapping young athletes attracted plenty of attention from awestruck males and ogling females. There was such an overflow of fans at one of the Francis Field workouts that Rickey ordered the closing of intrasquad games to spectators.[3] He was wary of excessive adulation of his players, believing that the fans would have plenty of time to root for and idolize their heroes once the regular season began. Until then Rickey scheduled many exhibition games, most of them played on the road in neighboring small towns and cities. The Cardinals returned to St. Louis for the preseason city series against the Browns, which the American Leaguers won, five games to three, with Rickey's former star George Sisler outshining his new star Rogers Hornsby.

On the eve of the 1919 season the indefatigable executive sat down with Charley Barrett and assessed his roster. There was some promise in the outfield with Jack Smith back from the Navy. Rickey was hoping that Smith could regain the form of his 1917 season, in which he put up the promising numbers of .297 BA, .398 SA, and 25 SB. He also had high hopes for the Ohio farm boy Austin McHenry, who had gotten his feet wet in sixty games in 1918. Rickey loved McHenry's work ethic and ambition, and he made him a special project. Team coaches spent hours in the morning hitting the young outfielder fly balls to improve his defensive skills. (McHenry possessed a great outfield arm, and in a future city series he would throw out the fleet George Sisler at home plate.) They also threw endless rounds of batting practice to help the Ohioan learn to hit to all fields.

Rickey hoped that some of his off-season trades would also bolster the

Cardinals' chances in 1919. From the Phillies he obtained catcher Bill Dillhoefer, a Cleveland, Ohio, boy (inevitably nicknamed "Pickles") who had started his professional career playing with McHenry in Portsmouth. He also acquired from the Washington Senators two of his favorite pepper pots, shortstop John "Doc" Lavan and outfielder Burt "Barney" Shotton. Both Shotton and Lavan, who was already a practicing physician and surgeon in St. Louis, had played for Rickey's Browns, but after the executive left for the Cardinals, they grew discontented with hard-headed owner Phil Ball. During the 1917 season, Lavan and second baseman Del Pratt even sued Ball for slander when he accused them publicly of not giving full effort in games against Ty Cobb and the Tigers.[4] Although it is doubtful that Rickey, the staunch advocate of management, liked the idea of the lawsuit, Lavan and Pratt did eventually win a cash settlement from the outspoken Browns owner. The Cardinals president was convinced that under his tutelage Lavan would play well, and so would Burt Shotton.

On the 1919 pitching staff Rickey was counting on two gritty players from Pennsylvania coal mine country, five foot nine left-hander "Wee" Willie Sherdel and lanky six foot one spitballing right-hander Bill Doak. Sherdel, at 155 pounds, was among the lightest players in baseball, but his guile would make him a durable Major League pitcher for over fifteen years, and a winner of 165 games. Doak was already a veteran of six full seasons with the Cardinals and would win 170 games in a sixteen-year career. A savvy competitor, he devised a special pitcher's glove—the Bill Doak model, with a pocket between the thumb and index finger—that remained a popular Major Leaguer's glove for years after his retirement from the game in 1929.[5]

The most valued asset of the Cardinals remained, by far, infielder Rogers Hornsby. With Jack Hendricks out as manager, Rickey expected a big year from the emerging star. Off the field the manager and the player might be a study in contrasts: Rickey, the moral, intellectual, talkative preacher-teacher, and Hornsby, the self-absorbed, racetrack-addicted narcissist who, in baseball historian Lee Allen's memorable phrase, was "as subtle as a belch."[6] However, when it came to commitment to excellence in baseball, Rickey and Hornsby were birds of the same feather. The budding superstar was so addicted to his craft of hitting a baseball that he refused to go to movies because it might harm his eyesight, and he once described his off-season activities: "I stare out the window and wait for spring."[7]

Hornsby's hard work at refining his skills became one of the great success stories passed down by Branch Rickey to his staff. In a March 2000 interview Rex Bowen, who joined Rickey as a scout in St. Louis in the 1930s and worked with him in Brooklyn and Pittsburgh, remembered the tale of Hornsby's development.

> As a young player, Rogers Hornsby pulled everything foul down the third base line. Mr. Rickey took him out every morning for ten days in a row. He made Hornsby hit every ball to the right of the pitcher. Hornsby almost broke his thumb on a bat, working so hard to improve. But he finally got to the point where he could hit the ball easily to the right of the pitcher, regardless of where the pitch was thrown. Ultimately, Rogers Hornsby's best alley for hitting was right center field.[8]

In 1919 Hornsby was on the cusp of becoming a great power hitter as well as a great hitter for average. Freed from the nagging injuries and the military duty that had limited his 1918 season to 115 games, Hornsby would produce a .318 BA and a .430 SA in 1919. His 71 RBI tied him for second in the league with Cincinnati's Edd Roush, two behind Brooklyn's outfielder Henry "Hy" Myers. Beginning in 1920 Hornsby would win six batting and slugging championships in a row. From 1920 to 1922 he would win three Triple Crown awards, leading the National League in hitting average, home runs, and runs batted in. An astounding .424 average lay ahead in 1924. From 1921 to 1925 his *average* season consisted of 29 HR, 140 RBI, and a .402 BA.

Hornsby usually hit the ball so hard that tough, fearless Major League infielders were afraid for their lives. In Ogden Nash's "Lineup for Yesterday: An ABC of Baseball Immortals," the popular poet noted that after a pitch to "Rog," the hurler had better "dodge."[9]

Rickey still hadn't decided on Hornsby's best position on defense. He shuttled him from shortstop to third base to second base and even briefly to left field, before in 1920 finally settling on second base as Hornsby's permanent position. Although Hornsby always had problems with pop-ups (St. Louis sportswriter Roy Stockton joked that it was "because he never hit them"), he was superb at turning the double play because he played a shallow second base. As a pure craftsman with the bat, he was on his way to becoming a legend among his peers. Catcher Clyde Sukeforth, another longtime Rickey loyalist who played against Hornsby, observed, "There was no disagreement when he was in the batting cage. When he stepped in to hit, all he had was admirers."[10]

In spite of Hornsby's growing prowess, the 1919 season was a disappointing one for Branch Rickey and the Cardinals. The team played hard and hustled, as Rickey's teams always did, and the manager tried to educate and inspire the players with pregame blackboard talks and exhortations from the dugout. He continued to believe that professional athletes could be inspired by college-type encouragement, and he even encouraged some players to learn the Ohio Wesleyan fight song. However, despite all his pep talks and boundless energy, the Cardinals were never a factor in the 1919 pennant race, nor did they make a move toward the respectability of the first division. They started the season 10-22, won 7 in a row, and then fell back again, finishing in seventh place with a 54-83 record, forty and a half games behind the pennant-winning Cincinnati Reds. Inevitably, attendance lagged. The Cardinals drew only 167,059 at home, an improvement of more than 50,000 over the war-shortened 1918 season, but the team averaged fewer than 2,500 spectators at Cardinal Field.[11]

Although Rickey and the Cardinals were not participants in the pennant race, 1919 was an exciting year in Major League Baseball. The Chicago White Sox nosed out the Cleveland Indians by three and a half games for the American League pennant, while the Cincinnati Reds won the 1919 National League flag by nine games over the New York Giants. The Major League schedule was limited to 140 games in 1919 because the owners were unsure how many fans would return in the first postwar year. It turned out that the moguls were too cautious in their expectations because total Major League attendance more than doubled in 1919, totaling 6,532,439, compared to 3,080,126 fans in 1918.[12]

After the season there was an ownership change in Chicago, a development that Branch Rickey watched closely. Charles Weeghman, the wealthy restaurateur who bought the Cubs after the demise of his Federal League Chicago Whales franchise, was ready to exit the baseball scene. His team finished a poor third in 1919, twenty-one games behind the Reds, just a year after winning the pennant in 1918. In many ways Weeghman never recovered from losing the 1918 World Series to the Boston Red Sox. He watched helplessly as his big purchase of pitcher Grover Cleveland Alexander from the Phillies turned useless when he was called up for military duty after only three starts. Weeghman had been one of those owners who thought he could buy pennants, but he had failed to pry Hornsby from the Cardinals, and Branch Rickey made the point publicly many times that the influence of unadulterated wealth in baseball was not conducive to good competitive sport. In 1920 Weeghman sold the Cubs to chewing gum millionaire William Wrigley, who six years later would rename the northside Chicago ballpark Weeghman had built Wrigley Field.

The New York Giants now became Rogers Hornsby's most eager suitor. Manager John McGraw thought that obtaining the productive hitter from the Cardinals would put his team back to the top of the standings. The Giants had won six pennants since McGraw arrived in New York in 1903 but hadn't raised a banner since 1917. Early in 1919 McGraw was gratified when the Giants' new owner, stockbroker Charles Stoneham, rewarded him with a slice of ownership. Almost immediately, the two New York leaders plotted strategy on how to pry the valuable Hornsby away from Rickey's impoverished Cardinals.

Charles Stoneham was a man used to having his own way in business. By day he was an active player in the New York stock and curb exchanges and was also involved in the so-called bucket shops, where he took people's money to invest in certain securities but could change his mind and put the money in speculative issues more to his liking.[13] At night Stoneham was a man about town, spending freely and gambling as only a New York high roller could.

In midsummer 1919, when the Giants thought they still could catch the Reds, Stoneham and McGraw invited Branch Rickey to a tavern after a Cardinals-Giants game in New York. The Giants moguls thought that they had a proposal the Cardinals president could not refuse. After the exchange of a few pleasantries and Rickey's polite refusal to have a drink, the New Yorkers made their offer. "I'll give you $175,000 cash for Mr. Hornsby, Major Rickey," Stoneham said, addressing the St. Louis executive as "Major" in deference to his military rank in the recently concluded war. Stoneham's offer was for the precise amount of the St. Louis team's indebtedness to former Cardinals owner Mrs. Helene Britton. "I'm not interested in trading Mr. Hornsby, Mr. Stoneham," Rickey politely answered.

Stoneham raised the ante, but Rickey continued to refuse. Used to having his way in business, Stoneham thought he had finally come up with an irresistible proposal. "Major, I'll give you $300,000 and if we win the pennant with Hornsby, I'll give you a bonus of $50,000," Stoneham said. "But you can't do that," Rickey protested. "Why not, Major?" Stoneham asked. "Because I still have a lot of games to play with the New York Giants," Rickey explained. "It wouldn't be right if it was to our advantage to have you win."

McGraw interjected, "Branch, how can you face your stockholders if they learn you have turned down this amount of money?" The St. Louis executive paused. The grandson of horse trader Ephraim Rickey loved the competitive challenge of the baseball marketplace, even though he knew he was not yet dealing from a position of strength. "Maybe I will consider dealing Mr. Hornsby if you offer me a new player of yours, Mr. Frank Frisch," Rickey said. "In fact, I'll offer $50,000 for him."[14]

In June 1919 infielder Frisch had leaped directly to the Giants from the campus of Fordham University in the Bronx borough of New York. Frisch was a great all-around athlete, a good enough 155-pound halfback to be named to the second team of Walter Camp's All-American football squad. Although the inexperienced rookie, who had no Minor League experience, would hit only .224 in 190 at-bats in 1919, he would soon emerge as "The Fordham Flash" on his way to a Hall of Fame career. Branch Rickey's keen evaluative sense had already drawn a bead on Frisch, but Charles Stoneham guffawed at the suggestion of selling Frisch to Rickey. "You haven't got $50,000. You haven't a quarter," Stoneham snorted at Rickey as he and John McGraw exited the tavern.[15]

During the game the next day at the Polo Grounds, according to a story that Rickey loved to tell years later, an errant toss from shortstop John Lavan hit Hornsby on the head, knocking the second baseman unconscious. "Three hundred and fifty thousand dollars suddenly mobilized out there on the turf at the Polo Grounds," Rickey recalled, re-creating the anxiety he experienced as Hornsby lay motionless on the ground. "There were large silver dollars. They had arms and legs and wings and faces that mocked at me," Rickey elaborated, with characteristic dramatic flourish. "They did squads right and squads left, and right oblique and left oblique. They turned cartwheels, and as they rushed on their way out, toward the exits and over the fences, each one laughed at me."[16]

Fortunately, Hornsby's injury was minor, and he continued to perform well in St. Louis. Without the Cardinals' star, the Giants did not laugh in 1919 as the Reds went on to win the pennant and the tainted World Series over the Chicago White Sox (who had several players, known to history as the "Black Sox," conspiring with gamblers to fix the games). Stoneham and McGraw grew more eager to obtain the second baseman, a desire that intensified when Babe Ruth was purchased by the New York Yankees from the Boston Red Sox after the 1919 season. The Giants wanted Hornsby not only for his current prowess as a player but also for his potential as a drawing card to counteract Babe Ruth's growing popularity. Ruth would hit fifty-four home runs in 1920 for the Yankees, more than virtually every *team* in the Major Leagues. Yet McGraw believed that Hornsby was a far more versatile and dangerous threat at the plate than Ruth. He often said, "I am three times more worried about Hornsby at the plate than Ruth."

Faced with the artistic and financial challenge from the Yankees, McGraw in 1920 tried another maneuver to pry the star player away from the Cardinals. He offered not only significant cash but five players to bolster Rickey's thin roster. He may have even suggested a lineup with the five ex-Giants in it. Rickey still said no, realizing that a quarter for five nickels was not a good baseball trade.

Thus the Cardinals held on to their budding star and were to benefit from his prodigious talents through their first world championship season of 1926. Rickey kept his great chip on the playing field and was gratified at the amount of money other owners were willing to shell out for his standout player. As a baseball businessman, Rickey surmised correctly that if the Cardinals had an asset for which wealthy owners like Charles Stoneham and Charles Weeghman were willing to spend tens of thousands of dollars, potential investors would soon see that the Cardinals were definitely a money-making property.

Branch Rickey still believed that the essence of lasting success in baseball rested in finding and patiently developing his own players. He and Charley Barrett continued to beat the bushes for new talent, prompting a *St. Louis Globe-Democrat* cartoonist to draw the executive carrying a large bag and a pointed stick. "Branch Rickey on a scouting trip 'policing up' the back woods for new material," the caption read.[17] During the summer of 1919 Rickey opened the doors of Cardinal Field for the team's first tryout camp. Hundreds of eager amateurs came at their own expense from all over the Midwest and South to work out under the keen eyes of Rickey and his staff.

One hopeful who came from the St. Louis suburb of Creve Coeur was the kind of energetic, hustling, confident ballplayer Rickey always favored. His name was Clarence "Heinie" Mueller, and his first meeting with the Cardinals leader became the stuff of legend. Brought into the team offices by Charley Barrett, Rickey asked Mueller how he would describe himself as a hitter. "Better than Babe Ruth!" the confident youngster replied. "How would you describe your running speed, young man?" Rickey asked. "Faster than Ty Cobb, Mr. Rickey," Mueller answered. "Judas Priest!" Rickey exclaimed. "I don't know about Judas Priest, Mr. Rickey," came Mueller's unadorned reply. "I never saw him play."[18]

Another raw recruit came from the southern Illinois mining town of Nokomis and was so poorly dressed that his feet were sticking out of his shoes. Early in his career the *Sporting News* identified the player only as "J. Bottomly [*sic*]," but he quickly caught the eye of Barrett and Rickey. They were prepared to like him because Bottomley (the correct spelling) had handwritten a polite but obviously confident letter: "I am nineteen years old and I love to play ball." It was a letter that Charley Barrett kept as a souvenir for the rest of his life.[19] Jim Bottomley was a coal miner's son whose younger brother had been killed in a cave-in after serving in World War I.[20] Working as a blacksmith's apprentice, Bottomley played semipro ball in the mining area, and Barrett spotted his sweet, left-handed-hitting stroke, which reminded the scout of Charley Grimm, a product of the St. Louis Irish neighborhood sandlots known as the "Kerry Patch," who was briefly a Cardinal before he was let go in 1918.

Barrett and Rickey saw the potential in the almost comically awkward athlete. Signed for a small bonus, Bottomley struggled in his early months as a pro, but in August 1922 he arrived in the Majors as a reserve first baseman. By 1923 Bottomley established himself as a Cardinals regular for the next ten years. He finished with career numbers of a .310 BA and .510 AB and was elected into the baseball Hall of Fame in 1974. Aware of the mental stresses in the game of baseball, Bottomley once observed that the best way to stay on an even keel is for a team not to get involved in many streaks. If you won 3 and lost 1, and won 2 and lost 1, Bottomley suggested, you would have one hundred wins and a successful season.[21]

Another signing from the first tryout camp at Cardinal Field was outfielder Ray Blades, whom Rickey and Barrett had followed from his days as a teenaged pitcher in Mount Vernon, Illinois, just outside St. Louis. Converted to an outfielder to utilize his great fleetness of foot, Blades would become a regular in the Cardinals outfield from 1924 to 1926, and a consistent .300 hitter. Unfortunately, his career was shortened when he broke his leg on a wire fence at Brooklyn's Ebbets Field, chasing down a line drive.[22] Once his playing days ended he became a loyal Rickey coach in both St. Louis and Brooklyn and managed the Cardinals in 1939 and part of 1940. A devoted exponent of Branch Rickey's hustling brand of baseball, Blades once observed that the most tired player on any baseball team should be the right fielder because he backs up the most plays.[23]

In January 1920 a momentous restructuring of the Cardinals front office occurred. It was obvious by now that the "Cardinal Idea" of community ownership was not working. Very few local investors had stepped forward to bail the Cardinals out with cash. If the team were to survive in St. Louis and ultimately prosper, deeper pockets and probably fewer hands were needed. On January 12, 1920, the *St. Louis Post-Dispatch* introduced an unfamiliar name to its sports page readers under the headline "Rickey to Remain Manager, But Names Samuel Breadon As Cards' Next President."[24]

Samuel Breadon (pronounced Bray-den) was the prosperous owner of the Western Automobile Company, a firm that specialized in the sale of luxury Pierce-Arrow cars. Breadon had been only a minor stockholder of the syndicate that purchased the Cardinals from Mrs. Helene Britton in 1917, participating mainly as an act of civic obligation at the suggestion of Warren C. "Fuzzy" Anderson, his auto business partner, who was a big baseball fan.

Born in 1876 in the tough, decidedly unbohemian part of Greenwich Village in New York City, Breadon was one of eight children of an Irish immigrant drayman who died in his midforties from overwork. Young Samuel dropped out of school after the fourth grade to help his family make ends meet. By the turn of the twentieth century, Sam Breadon was working as a clerk in a Wall Street office at $125 a month.[25]

Yet the thought of a lifetime of indoor work counting other people's money did not appeal to him. When two New York neighborhood friends, Gus and Oscar Halsey, encouraged him to move to St. Louis, where they were working as garage mechanics, Breadon pulled up his stakes and headed west. He liked the idea of starting at the bottom of an infant but potentially lucrative industry. "I didn't know a thing about automobiles," Breadon said later. "However, the customers who came . . . looked upon me as the expert from New York."[26]

The ambitious Breadon soon decided to go into business for himself, a decision that led the Halsey brothers to fire him. Though the ambitious ex–New Yorker went through some hard times starting out on his own (even living in his new garage for a while), he was making friends with wealthy customers who brought their cars in for service. He made a good impression on one customer, pharmaceutical magnate Marion Lambert, who was impressed when the ambitious young man wouldn't accept a tip for his services.[27] Breadon wanted to rise into management, and shortly thereafter Lambert asked Breadon to become an executive in his new business, the Western Automobile Company. The former New Yorker rose quickly in the firm, at first selling the basic-model Ford cars. Lambert soon sold out his interests to Breadon, and by 1917 Breadon and his partner, Fuzzy Anderson, had branched out into sharing a lucrative distributorship of Pierce-Arrow automobiles.[28]

After he attended a baseball dinner during the 1917 season, Breadon discovered that he enjoyed hobnobbing with the vigorous athletes, especially rising star Rogers Hornsby. He increased his investment from a couple hundred dollars to more than $2,000 worth of Cardinals stock. By 1919 it was clear that the Cardinals were facing a serious economic crisis, with few shareholders willing to increase their investment. An exception was Fuzzy Anderson, who confided to his automobile partner that since he had more than $15,000 tied up in the Cardinals, he could not get out now. He asked Breadon to raise his stake, and his partner consented, loaning more than $18,000 to the struggling franchise as well as buying more stock. Given his greater financial involvement, Breadon was named to the board of directors by chairman James C. Jones.[29]

At a crucial late 1919 meeting Jones asked Breadon to become president of the team. Jones was also the lawyer for former owner Mrs. Helene Britton, who was still owed about $175,000, the final portion of the purchase price. Breadon accepted the new position on the condition that the number of people on the board of directors be reduced from twenty-five to a more manageable number, preferably five. "I learned early the idea of fan ownership is the bunk," Breadon explained. "You wouldn't think of running the average business that way, and baseball isn't so much different from other businesses."[30] Ultimately, the new team president accepted a reduction of board members to seven.

Fuzzy Anderson, holder of the second biggest chunk of Cardinals stock, felt he was entitled to a vice presidency, but Breadon balked at sharing the power. A miffed Anderson decided to sell out completely and leave baseball. With the aid of a loan from Breadon, Branch Rickey bought Anderson's stock, which amounted to less than 20 percent of the total shares.[31] The "Cardinal Idea" of community ownership was now officially dead.

One of Breadon's first acts as team president was to offer Anderson's vice presidency to Branch Rickey. He accepted the position, and it was more than just balm for Rickey's ego because he had been removed as president. Keeping a front office title was also important because the National League had recently passed regulations preventing field managers from sitting in on league councils. As vice president and the executive in charge of the baseball side of the Cardinals, Rickey would still be able to keep his finger on the pulse of the other franchises in the Major and Minor Leagues. It seems that board chairman Jones encouraged Rickey to give up his field manager's job to devote himself entirely to player development, but Rickey wanted to finish the job he had started.

Thus began, early in 1920, the formation of what would become for over twenty years one of baseball's oddest and most successful couples, taciturn Sam Breadon and loquacious Branch Rickey. Under their arrangement there was no doubt that Breadon was the boss who controlled the purse strings and Rickey was the employee who engineered the baseball transactions. However, unlike many baseball owners who get so intoxicated with their power that they think they understand the mechanics of the game itself, Breadon deferred completely to Branch Rickey on the nuts and bolts of player development. He respected Rickey's intelligence as a baseball evaluator and enthusiastically endorsed the idea of a farm system.

Even more frugal than Rickey, Breadon liked the idea of signing players cheaply and watching them develop until they were ready "to ripen into money." The phrase was Rickey's, but the idea was very palatable to Breadon, who, as a businessman, easily grasped the basic principle of the farm system: buy raw talent inexpensively, watch it develop under the best managers, coaches, and instructors, and patiently wait to reap the profit from the finished product while trading away the surplus players for cash and maybe other prospects. No longer would the Cardinals have to be at the mercy of a "handshake" agreement with Minor League owners for rights to Minor League players. Too often in the past the Minor League businessman had violated the arrangement the moment a higher bid came in. Rickey told a sympathetic Breadon that the last straw had come when Charley Barrett was in Texas, expecting to sign key players, only to be outbid because rival owners believed that if the astute scout wanted a player he must be a good investment. At that moment Rickey wired his trusted scout: "Pack up and come home—we'll develop our own players."[32]

To be sure, the Breadon-Rickey relationship did provide a stark contrast between personalities. Breadon was the Irish Catholic product of the mean streets of New York who never lost his "dese, dem, dose" New York accent and who talked about his goal of reaching "foist" place. He loved good Irish whiskey and singing in barbershop quartets, often in the company of sportswriters, who nicknamed him "Singin' Sam." Rickey, on the other hand, was the teetotaling Protestant whose favorite songs were pep songs and hymns and who tended to harbor suspicions of sportswriters and certainly could not glad-hand them.

Yet, as a baseball business team starting in 1920, Breadon and Rickey would soon transform baseball. Breadon made a financial commitment early on in his team presidency by approving the purchase of a majority interest in a Minor League franchise in Fort Smith, Arkansas, in the class C Western Association. Shortly thereafter he bought majority interest in the Houston Buffaloes Minor League team in the higher-classification Texas League. Houston's first manager under the aegis of the Cardinals was Al Bridwell, a former Major League infielder who had been Rickey's teammate on the 1902 Portsmouth Navvies in 1902 (the semipro experience that had cost the Ohio Wesleyan student-athlete his college eligibility). The Houston business manager was Fred Ankenman, who would become another loyal Rickey associate.[33]

Early in 1921 Breadon met Syracuse businessman Walter Landgraf at an after-hours encounter at a baseball convention. Before long the Cardinals had an affiliation with the upstate New York franchise in the International League. Rickey was hoping that his friendship with Tom Watkins, a Memphis, Tennessee, businessman, would enable the Cardinals to bring a farm team to that southern city, but he deferred to president Breadon's choice.[34]

Breadon was able to finance the start of the farm system by two master business strokes. First, he decided that Cardinal Field was too dilapidated. Its seven-thousand-seat grandstand was a fire hazard, and authorities feared it could ignite at any time from a stray cigarette ash. "I never sleep on Saturday night for fear that stand will collapse on Sunday when you get a doubleheader crowd into it," a St. Louis building commissioner had recently warned the Cardinals' new president.[35]

Breadon was able to abandon Cardinal Field because he talked St. Louis Browns owner Phil Ball into allowing his team to become Ball's tenant at the newer Sportsman's Park, a few blocks away. Always a hard man to do business with, Ball was ultimately amenable to the arrangement because he was afraid that Breadon might build a new ballpark on land he had recently purchased at an abandoned St. Louis quarry.[36] On July 1, 1920, the Cardinals played the first of many eventful games over the next forty-five years at Sportsman's Park. The milestone coincided with the annual Tuberculosis Day promotion at the ballpark. Though there was no mention of Branch Rickey's battle with the disease at the ballpark, nor did he want it noted, privately he may well have said a prayer of gratitude for his recovery from the dread illness.

Breadon's second act of business acumen was to tear down the decrepit Cardinal Field grandstand, and in two shrewd maneuvers, he sold most of the land rights for $200,000 to the St. Louis Board of Education, which erected Beaumont High School on the site. He sold the rest of the land rights for $75,000 to the St. Louis local transit company, which built a streetcar line. Once the paupers of the National League, the Cardinals were on the road to economic security.[37]

As the farm system grew and prospered, the press on occasion referred to Breadon and Rickey as "David Harum," a reference to the title character in Edward Westcott's popular 1898 novel of the same name about a country banker and trader who made a success in business by applying knowledge not usually learned in books. Breadon also was called "Lucky Sam" for the golden touch in his business deals, but Rickey scoffed at the nickname. It was not until much later that Rickey was widely associated with the saying "Luck is the residue of design." In the early 1920s Branch Rickey did not feel that luck had anything to do with Sam Breadon's business acumen. He was thrilled at his new boss's talent for making the most of a good opportunity.

On the playing field in 1920, the first year of the Breadon-Rickey front office team opened with a good omen. Instead of the discomforts of preparing for the season in wintry St. Louis, the Cardinals established spring training in the more hospitable climate of Brownsville, Texas, near the Mexican border. The funds for the training season were provided by Adolph Diez, a wealthy St. Louis manufacturer of leather supplies and one of the local angels who had saved the Cardinals from relocation in the dire days of 1917.[38]

John McGraw's Giants and Connie Mack's Athletics were training in nearby Texas towns, and one of the great experiences of Branch Rickey's Cardinals' managerial career would be barnstorming north with these legendary managers. He spent many valuable evenings in Pullman cars, picking their minds of baseball knowledge. Like Rickey, Connie Mack believed in developing intelligent, college-educated players, but he was also able to handle some of baseball's more colorful eccentrics, such as pitcher Rube Waddell. Rickey admired Mack's ability to patiently instruct players in the finer points of the game without embarrassing them in front of their peers.

"He was a pedagogue, a kindly instructor," Rickey warmly remembered his colleague years later. Mack was the first man in baseball to hold pregame meetings to prepare his players for the challenges in the game ahead, and Rickey adopted the same method. "I found it the best way to bring separated forces together," Rickey reflected. "Some players don't like it, but there is no substitute."[39] (It was perhaps during these nightly talks with Mack that the St. Louis leader got the idea of managing in street clothes, like his Philadelphia friend and rival, a practice that Rickey first adopted in 1920.)

Rickey also admired John McGraw's managing ability. He could handle the college man like Christy Mathewson and the raw recruit equally well, all in the service of team unity. Like Rickey, McGraw was always interested in converting players from different positions, whether it was pitchers to regular players, outfielders to infielders, or vice versa, depending on what caught his keen, evaluative eyes. Although McGraw liked and respected his St. Louis counterpart, he was less impressed than Connie Mack with the manager's intense, intellectual approach to the game. The tough-talking McGraw scoffed at Rickey's keeping a detailed scoreboard on the bench. "Doesn't he know what happened in the game?" the Giants manager groused. He also publicly pooh-poohed the idea of a farm system. When famed National League umpire Bill Klem came back raving about the baseball being taught at Rickey's extensive spring tryout camps, McGraw scoffed, "It will never work."[40] He discouraged his team's owner, Charles Stoneham, from even thinking about wasting money on a development system. Only after McGraw's death in 1934 did the Giants begin to make plans for a Rickey-style farm program.

Despite John McGraw's skepticism 1920 proved an encouraging year for the Cardinals. The team climbed to a tie for fifth with the Cubs and finished only four games under .500, a 21-game improvement over 1919 (although 14 more games were played as the Major Leagues returned to the 154-game schedule). Rogers Hornsby had his first monster year, leading the league in five categories: .370 BA; .559 SA; 250 H; 44 2B, and 94 RBI. Austin McHenry showed steady improvement with a .282 BA, .423 SA, and led the Cardinals with 10 HR (Hornsby hit 9). McHenry was getting more at-bats and experience, which augured well for the future.

He was also becoming a great fan of the Knothole Gang youngsters, who cheered him on from their left-field seats.

Rickey's last Minor League cash player purchases also justified their promise. First baseman Jack Fournier hit .306 with a .438 SA, 3 HR, and 61 RBI. Although new addition pitcher Jess Haines was a twenty-game loser, he led the league in starts and game appearances, and his ERA was a respectable 2.98. Bill Doak was 20-12 with a team-best 2.53 ERA. Willie Sherdel improved to a 11-10 record, and Ferdie Schupp, who came over in a trade with the Giants that Rickey and McGraw did agree on (for catcher Frank "Pancho" Snyder), went 16-13. Rickey had great hopes for the left-handed Schupp, who had gone 21-7 for New York in 1917 and won a game in the World Series, the highest achievement Rickey believed a pitcher could possess. The manager donned catching gear to work on Schupp's stuff in practice, but the pitcher's wartime injuries never really healed.[41] After his respectable 1920 season in St. Louis, Schupp soon faded from the Major League scene.

What probably kept the Cardinals from making the first division was a laxity in defensive baseball. The team led the league in errors by a wide margin, 17 more than the closest competitor in the dubious category. Shortstop John Lavan, second baseman Rogers Hornsby, and third baseman Milt Stock all led the league in errors at their positions. Undoubtedly, many of those miscues were "the errors of enthusiasm" that Rickey always excused, but they surely played a role in keeping the team under .500. Nonetheless, fans could see improvement in the team. The Cardinals drew more than 326,836 fans, almost twice as many as 1919.[42] As a loyal National League supporter, Rickey was disappointed when the Brooklyn Dodgers, the surprise winner of the 1920 pennant, lost the World Series to the Cleveland Indians.

The Browns, the Cardinals' landlord at Sportsman's Park, also showed improvement in 1920 as they climbed into fourth place, although they were one game under .500 at 76-77. Rickey's great discovery George Sisler hit .407 with 19 HR, 122 RBI, and a league-leading 140 assists as a first baseman. The Browns remained the larger draw in St. Louis, attracting 419,311 fans, but the Cardinals were gaining on them.[43]

After the 1920 season the Cardinals, minus Rogers Hornsby, played what was supposed to be a five-game series against the St. Louis Giants, a team that had just completed its first season in the Negro National League. The segregated circuit was the brainchild of Andrew "Rube" Foster of Chicago, a onetime great pitcher and an excellent entrepreneur. Third baseman Milton Stock managed the Cardinals in the series, though it is likely that Branch Rickey attended some of the games. He certainly marveled at the skills of the St. Louis Giants center fielder Oscar Charleston, the so-called "black Ty Cobb," who led his team to victory in the first game. Jess Haines and Ferd Schupp turned the tables in the next two games, pitching shutout victories, but because of a dispute over gate receipts that ultimately landed in the courts, with the black Giants evidently winning a court verdict a few years later, there were only three games played in the postseason series.[44]

For spring training in 1921 the Cardinals continued to make their camp in Texas, but Rickey decided to move away from the border town of Brownsville, probably because he did not want the players unnecessarily tempted by nocturnal distractions.[45] He based the team in the more remote area of Orange, Texas. An overflow crowd flocked to the ballpark early in the exhibition season to see Babe Ruth and the Yankees play Rogers Hornsby and the Cardinals. On the slow trip home to St. Louis for the start of the season, Rickey was pleased once again to have John McGraw and Connie Mack as his traveling companions.

Yet, in Branch Rickey's endlessly churning brain and often troubled soul, he continued to harbor doubts as to his career choice. Before he left for spring training in Texas, he had been offered a chance to return to the University of Michigan, which was looking for an athletic director after Phil Bartelme resigned to pursue business opportunities in Florida. Bartelme, who had hired Rickey as baseball coach over ten years earlier, recommended him as a man who could lead a highly competitive collegiate sports program within the framework of the university's educational mission.

Rickey's letter of January 27, 1921, to James Murfin, chairman of the Board of Regents of the University of Michigan, revealed his ongoing inner struggle. "I dislike the 'give and take' of professional baseball and I dislike some of its associations. I love college work as you know," he wrote Murfin. However, as in all the times ahead in his career, Rickey could not break away from the alluring and lucrative game. "I regret, indeed, that it is impossible to permit you to recommend me to the Board of Regents," he concluded. "It is a matter of doing the thing you start to do and I must make a great ball club, successful artistically and financially in a town where there is every handicap under the sun against my making good on account of some of my personal beliefs and practices for which I have no apology."[46] Approaching age forty, with a wife, a mother-in-law, a sister-in-law, a son, and three daughters to support (and with two more children to come, in 1922 and 1924), Rickey was casting his lot with St. Louis and making a success of the Cardinals.

6

Years of Contention and Frustration

As Branch Rickey began spring training in Texas with the Cardinals in 1921, a new era in baseball's governance was beginning. Federal judge Kenesaw Mountain Landis had just taken over as the first commissioner of baseball. Although Major League baseball attendance in 1919 and 1920 had grown faster than the national population and would continue to rise throughout the 1920s, it was clear that the three-man National Commission could no longer govern the sport adequately. Individual owners had been carping at the Commission's decisions for years, and the death knell came in September 1920 when eight Chicago White Sox players admitted to local legal authorities that they were involved with or aware of the plot to fix the 1919 World Series.

The baseball owners could not take the chance that the public would believe the entire sport was infested with unsavory influences, so they turned to Landis, the man whose judicial inaction in the Federal League antitrust case pleased the baseball establishment. Realizing that the owners needed him more than he needed them, Landis exacted extraordinary concessions from the baseball moguls. He made them pledge never to criticize him in public, however much they might disagree with his rulings. He also insisted on a clause in his contract that gave the commissioner the sole power to determine "conduct detrimental to baseball."

Landis served notice early on that he wouldn't hesitate to exercise his authority as commissioner, wielding his powers as if his title indeed meant that he represented a public utility. In August 1921 he banned the eight "Black Sox" from baseball for life, even though they had been acquitted of criminal wrongdoing in a local Chicago court. "Regardless of the decisions of juries," Landis decreed, "no player that undertakes or promises to throw a ball game; no player that sits in a conference with a bunch of crooked players and gamblers where the ways and means of throwing games are planned and discussed and does not promptly tell his club about it, will ever play professional baseball."[1]

Branch Rickey was very much in accord with Judge Landis's desire to protect baseball from the influence of gamblers, but he was always wary of too much power in any one individual's hands. In light of the forthcoming battles between Landis and Rickey in the next twenty years over the rapid growth of the Cardinals' farm system, it seems fitting that Landis's first ruling as commissioner went against Rickey's claim to a Minor League first baseman, Phil Todt. Todt, a young product of the St. Louis sandlots had been signed by the Cardinals and assigned to a Sherman, Texas, Minor League team and later shifted to another club's roster in Houston. Todt never played a game for either Texas franchise but when, a year or so later, St. Louis Browns owner Phil Ball offered Todt a contract, Branch Rickey protested to the National Commission, claiming exclusive rights to the player. The three-man body disbanded before it heard the case, but in Landis's first ruling as commissioner, on February 22, 1921, he awarded Todt to the Browns because Rickey had "covered up"—that is, not disclosed his ownership of—Todt's contract on the two Texas teams.[2] (Todt never played for the Browns, though he did have a eight-year journeyman's career, mainly with the Red Sox.)

Rickey was not pleased with Landis's decision, but the ruling affected only one player. With the full support of Sam Breadon, Rickey and Charley Barrett were busy signing dozens of other young players and finding Minor League team owners interested in giving them places to develop. Under the new National Agreement of 1921, which incorporated the creation of a commissioner's office into organized baseball's rules, changes in the complex system of Major League–Minor League relationships were instituted, most of which helped to accelerate Rickey's developmental program. In 1919 the higher Minor Leagues, upset at the low prices Major League teams were offering, had banded together and refused to allow the Majors to draft their players. By 1920, however, the high Minors realized that they needed the Majors as a market, and in the 1921 agreement the draft was reinstated with the high Minors gaining an increase in the price paid by the Majors and draft exemptions for a few of their players.[3]

There were no stipulations in the new agreement, however, concerning the control of and rights to the hundreds of players in the lower Minor Leagues. Branch Rickey was thus free to continue to sign and develop the raw youngsters, his major source of pride and joy, without interference. In addition to the high Minor League teams the Cardinals already were affiliated with in Syracuse and Houston, and the lower Minor League club at Fort Smith, they soon added lower level farm clubs at St. Joseph, Missouri, Danville, Illinois, and Topeka, Kansas. By the end of the 1920s they owned eight teams and had working agreements with several others. At the peak of the Cardinals' farm system in the late 1930s, they would have control of more than seven hundred players and interests in over thirty clubs, including one in every Class D League, the lowest classification, except one in Canada.[4]

As the St. Louis farm system began to blossom in the Minor Leagues, 1921 also proved to be a year of hope on the Major League level. For the first time in Rickey's managerial career, one of his teams finished in the first division. The 1921 Cardinals finished a strong third with an 87-66 record, only seven games behind the Giants, the eventual world champions, and just three games behind the second-place Pirates. They stayed in the race until the Giants got hot in late August and won twenty-nine of their last forty games. Rickey was envious of the ability of John McGraw's team to pull away at the key late summer moments of the season, and he was more than ever determined to build a team of his own that one day would show the same great late speed at the end of the pennant race marathon.

The Cardinals had many individual heroes in 1921. Rogers Hornsby had another spectacular offensive year, leading the league with a .397 BA and 126 RBI, and his 21 HR were second only to league leader, Giants first baseman George "Highpockets" Kelly. Austin McHenry came into his own, raising his average to .350 with 17 HR and 102 RBI. Bill Doak was 15-6 and led the league with a 2.59 ERA. (Rickey's earnest attempt to convert Doak into a first baseman had mercifully ended.) Recovering from his twenty-loss season of 1920, Jess Haines compiled an 18-12 record. Defensively, the Cardinals had also improved. Hornsby cut his errors down to 25; however, shortstop John Lavan would lead the league in miscues with 49.

It was an exciting summer for all St. Louis baseball fans. The Browns made a strong run for the pennant until the Yankees broke open the race in late summer. George Sisler's average dropped from .407 to .371, but he still drove in 104 runs. Attendance at Sportsman's Park picked up in the warmer weather for both teams, and the feared side effects of the Black Sox scandal never materialized. The Cardinals added almost 60,000 new fans, attracting 384,773 in attendance for the 1921 season, outdrawing the Browns, who brought in 355,978.[5]

Branch Rickey was pleased when the National League retained the world championship as the Giants became the first team since the World Series started in 1903 to win the title after losing the first two games. Babe Ruth missed two games and nearly a third because of a leg injury; his absence certainly helped the Giants' cause, but John McGraw continued to say that Hornsby worried him at the plate three times more than Babe Ruth did.

After the best year in the combined baseball history of the Browns and the Cardinals, expectations were high for both St. Louis teams in 1922. However, in what would be a bad omen for a year marked by tragedy, terrible news greeted the Cardinals as they gathered in Orange, Texas, for spring training. On February 23 twenty-seven-year-old reserve catcher Bill "Pickles" Dillhoefer died in St. Louis from complications after an operation to repair an injury he suffered in a collision at home plate. The medical report listed pneumonia, typhoid fever, and gall bladder dysfunctions as all contributing to the untimely death of the young catcher.[6]

Dillhoefer was a capable defensive catcher and a popular teammate, and his spirited play reminded many fans of Browns third baseman Jimmy Austin, Rickey's first "Sunday manager." Both men played the game with an enthusiasm that transcended statistics in terms of value to a team. Branch Rickey was moved to tears by the passing of someone so young and in his prime. Along with Charley Barrett and pitcher Bill Sherdel, Rickey led a delegation of mourners to Mobile, Alabama, where Dillhoefer was laid to rest. Also attending the funeral was Cardinals third baseman Milton Stock, who had been the best man at Dillhoefer's wedding.[7]

When Rickey returned to spring training, he greeted Sam Breadon,

who was now a regular visitor to camp. Enjoying the privileges of ownership, Breadon donned a uniform and often sat on the bench during practices and exhibition games. Breadon was in very good physical shape—to
office workers it always sounded as if he were taking the steps to his office at Sportsman's Park two at a time—and enjoyed mingling with the
players.[8] A photo taken during spring training 1922 suggests the distant
dynamics of the Breadon-Rickey relationship. On a bench overlooking
the practice field, Breadon sits on one end, wearing a Cardinals uniform
and a touring cap, a proud look on his face as his legs dangle down. Next
to him but facing away is Rickey, clad in a union suit and a fedora hat, his
mind evidently focused on removing lint from the trousers of bow-tied
team secretary Clarence Lloyd, who is seated on Rickey's other side.[9]

Breadon was undoubtedly relishing his time in the sun with the players, but Rickey was less sanguine about the coming year. In another of the
frank observations Rickey made to sportswriters, he told J. Roy Stockton,
a rising star on the *St. Louis Post-Dispatch*, that he was worried about overconfidence on his 1922 team. Observing the early spring workouts, he
told Stockton: "Watch the man who drops out after the first turn around
the park. Is it some recruit fighting for a job? No, you can gamble its
some star, a regular sure of his job, satisfied that he will be ready when
the season starts." Rickey warned of the complacency in batting practice
by veterans, who lost interest if a pitch came close to their heads. "If he
were a recruit, he would dodge the pitch, pick up his bat and want to
knock the next one down the pitcher's throat to show him he was not
scared by that close one near his head," the manager declared. He went
on to denounce his "smug-faced regulars, sure of their jobs, satisfied that
they have a job and are great ballplayers." The attitude of self-satisfac-
tion, he warned, "may lose a pennant for us."[10]

Rickey's sharp words about overconfidence were probably intended
as a kind of reverse psychology because the Cardinals got off in 1922
to their best start since Rickey became manager. After winning the preseason city series over the Browns before enthusiastic crowds of more
than twenty thousand a game, the team was near the top of the National
League through May. Fans were flocking to Sportsman's Park, even in
the colder spring weather. As summer neared, boosters were becoming
excited about a team that looked like a solid pennant contender. Mati-

nee idol Rogers Hornsby was heading toward winning his first Triple Crown; he would finish the season with a .401 BA (his first time over .400), 42 HR, and 152 RBI.

Austin McHenry looked ready for another big year, hitting over .300 and slugging nearly .500 through early June. He was showing the stellar form of 1921 that had prompted John McGraw, before the start of the 1922 season, to offer the Cardinals a reported $50,000 for his contract.[11] McHenry continued to be the favorite of the Knothole Gang youngsters in the Sportsman's Park left-field bleachers, who nicknamed him "The Airedale" because of his fleetness of foot and his tenacity. They composed a special cheer for him, "Ooooooooh Mack!," making a snapping sound on the name "Mack."[12]

Sometime in June, however, McHenry began to slump. He not only was suffering at the plate but was unsteady on the bases and in the field. He seemed to lose track of fly balls, letting many fall behind him that he normally would catch easily. Both McHenry and Rickey were worried, with the outfielder fearing that he was going blind. The executive sent the player home to southern Ohio for rest and consultation with his doctor-father. When McHenry returned in late July Rickey sensed that his prized outfielder was still ill. Sent home again, McHenry was diagnosed by doctors in Cincinnati as having a brain tumor. They operated but could not remove all the diseased tissue. "I'm afraid it is three and two on me in the bottom of the ninth," the ill-fated outfielder wrote his manager from the hospital. "I must hit the next one out."[13]

Alas, it was too late to save McHenry's life. He returned to his home in Adams County, Ohio, where he died in Mt. Areb on November 27, 1922. Like Bill Dillhoefer, he was only twenty-seven years old. He left behind a wife and two little girls. McHenry's teammates Jess Haines and Burt Shotton joined Rickey at the funeral, the largest in the history of the little town of Blue Creek, near Jefferson Township in Adams County. "The sorrow at the loss of a great ball player is overshadowed by the loss of a dear friend," a grieving Rickey said.[14] (In the last interview Sam Breadon gave before his death in May 1949, the Cardinals owner told *St. Louis Post-Dispatch* sportswriter Bob Broeg that if McHenry had lived, his career might have been as outstanding as Hall of Famer Stan Musial's twenty years later.)[15]

Despite the loss of the popular and productive Austin McHenry, the Cardinals battled on throughout the 1922 season. The Browns were also contending in the American League, making 1922 the best year for St. Louis Major League Baseball since the turn of the century. Deep into July both the Cardinals and the Browns were in first place, the first time both of St. Louis's Major League teams led their leagues so late in the season.[16]

Then the bugaboo of big bucks and Big Apple entitlement reared its ugly head. In late July both wealthy New York teams, the Giants and the Yankees, made key acquisitions from tail-end teams in their respective leagues. The Giants traded for pitcher Hugh McQuillan from the Boston Braves, and the Yankees obtained infielder Joe Dugan from the Boston Red Sox. Many fans and non–New York managements cried foul, not the least of whom was Branch Rickey. Addressing a St. Louis Rotary Club luncheon, the ferocious gentleman raised a rhetorical question for Commissioner Landis. "How can those teams without unlimited resources in their deposit boxes have a chance to compete fairly?" he roared.[17] Many other owners in both leagues agreed that one-sided transactions late in the season were detrimental to what in later years would be called "competitive balance" within leagues.

Commissioner Landis decided to stay out of the controversy. Still relatively new to the job, Landis issued a statement (which the commissioner's office would repeat many times in the years ahead) regarding controversial baseball matters. "It is a league matter," he said simply. However, the uproar was large enough within baseball that beginning with the 1923 season, June 15 was added to baseball's regulations as a trading deadline. All player trades after June 15 would now be first subject to waivers—that is, no player in either league could be traded without every team in the league having a chance to obtain the player, with the league's lowest-standing team having the first chance at selection.[18] (June 15 would become a well-remembered date on the baseball calendar for more than seventy years, until the mid-1990s, when it was moved ahead to July 31.)

Shortly after the controversial trades of McQuillan and Dugan were completed, another bombshell with potentially more serious repercussions hit Major League Baseball. New York Giants pitcher Phil Douglas was expelled from the game for life, and Branch Rickey inadvertently became a key figure in this bizarre and tragic episode.

Douglas was a gifted right-handed pitcher who had won two games for the Giants in the 1921 World Series, pitching twenty-six innings to a sparkling 2.08 ERA. He was a much better pitcher than his 93-93 career record indicated, but he came with off-field baggage. He was an alcoholic who hailed from the backwoods of Georgia and Alabama. Nicknamed "Shufflin' Phil," the pitcher had been traded four times, but John McGraw had managed alcoholics before. Alcoholic pitcher Arthur "Bugs" Raymond had contributed to contending Giants teams from 1909 to 1911, and McGraw thought he could handle another pitcher who battled with the bottle. Just in case, however, the Giants manager hired a "keeper," former Major League pitcher Jesse Burkett, to keep an eye on Douglas's off-field activities.

In late July 1922 the disturbing story unfolded. After the Giants lost to the Cardinals in New York, McGraw chewed out Douglas in front of the whole team for throwing too many strikes to the fearsome Rogers Hornsby. At the batting cage before the next day's game, a visibly upset and angry Phil Douglas complained to Hornsby and St. Louis outfielder Leslie Mann, a former teammate. McGraw was persecuting him, Douglas said, and he would love to play for the Cardinals.[19]

In his next start against the Pirates, Douglas was knocked out early, and eluding his keeper Jesse Burkett, he disappeared on a binge for two days. When the pitcher was located at a friend's apartment, a furious John McGraw had Douglas committed to a Manhattan sanitarium, where he was sedated and submitted to an excruciating drying-out procedure. Discharged a few days later, he was shocked to discover when he returned to the Giants that his stay at the sanitarium had been docked from his paycheck. In an angry and obviously not too coherent state, he drafted a letter on August 7, 1922, to Leslie Mann.

"I want to leave here, but I want some inducement," the distraught pitcher wrote. "I don't want this guy [McGraw] to win the pennant, and I feel if I stay here I will win it for him," Douglas went on. "So you see the fellows, and if you want to send a man over here with the goods I will leave for home on the next train." Douglas concluded the letter with the confused, conspiratorial statement: "Nobody will ever know. I will go down to a fishing camp and stay there. I am asking you this way so there can't be any trouble to anyone."[20]

The troubled pitcher told a Giants clubhouse boy to send the letter to Mann special delivery to wherever the Cardinals were playing, which happened to be Boston. When the St. Louis outfielder received the letter, he was stunned. A more unlikely target for a possible bribe offer could hardly be imagined. Leslie Mann was as straight a shooter as existed in baseball. He was active in YMCA activities, had coached several sports for many college teams, and had also served as a troop director of athletics in World War I.[21]

For twenty-four hours a concerned and conflicted Leslie Mann thought about what to do with Douglas's letter. He finally showed it to his manager, Branch Rickey, who described the letter as "a hot potato—in fact, dynamite," Rickey told sportswriter John Lardner more than thirty years later. "I told him he could not afford to do anything but send it to Landis at once."[22]

Commissioner Landis had come to baseball, of course, on a mission to eradicate all taints of gambling and suspect behavior by the players. His reaction when he learned about the letter was swift and predictable. So was manager John McGraw's. Douglas was going to be permanently expelled from baseball. In Pittsburgh on August 16, 1922, where the Giants were playing a series against the Pirates, McGraw informed the press that Phil Douglas "will never play another game in organized baseball." He added: "I have ordered that his name be stricken from the hotel register." Landis called Douglas's letter "tragic and deplorable. I might use even more forceful terms if so many people hadn't already criticized me for using strong language."[23]

Despite the loss of Phil Douglas, the Giants pulled away from the rest of the National League, winning the 1922 pennant by seven games over the Reds. The Pirates and Cardinals tied for third place with 85-69 records, eight games behind the pennant-winners. Pitcher Hugh McQuillan, the controversial late July acquisition, contributed six victories down the stretch for the Giants.

In the American League consistent Joe Dugan batted .286 for the Yankees (six points over his career average) and helped the New Yorkers to their second consecutive pennant. The St. Louis Browns battled them into the final weekend of the season, falling one game short of their first American League pennant. If George Sisler had been healthy at the end of the 1922 season, the outcome might have been different, St. Louis fans lamented.[24] Of course, Rickey was pulling for his talented protégé, but Sisler's sinus ailment, which would cost him the entire 1923 season, was beginning to curtail his great career. However, he still wound up the 1922 season setting an all-time American League record with a batting average of .420.

In the 1922 World Series Branch Rickey again took satisfaction that the Giants upheld the pride of the National League by beating the Yankees four games to none. Giants pitchers held Babe Ruth to 2 hits in 17 at-bats, and their hitters outscored their Yankees counterparts, 18–11. However, it was the Giants' last hurrah as a dynasty. In 1923 Yankee Stadium would open and no longer would the American Leaguers be lowly tenants at the Polo Grounds. The Yankees celebrated their new freedom by finally beating the Giants in the 1923 World Series, and the tide in New York baseball began to turn turning toward the American League.

Not long after the end of the 1922 World Series, Branch Rickey sat down with his staff for an annual review of the year past and the year ahead. Although the cherished goal of a pennant had still eluded the Cardinals, everyone agreed that progress was being made. It had clearly been the most exciting season in St. Louis baseball history, with both the Browns and the Cardinals legitimate contenders. Befitting a team that stayed in the pennant race until the last days of the season, the Browns set an attendance record, drawing 712,918 fans. The Cardinals also set a franchise record, with 536,998 fans, an improvement of more than 150,000 over 1921.[25]

As for individual seasons, in addition to Hornsby's Triple Crown year, the Cardinals received good offensive production from two players who later would become trusted coaches for Branch Rickey. Third baseman Milt Stock hit .305 with 5 HR and 79 RBI, and left fielder Joe Schultz hit .314 with 2 HR and 64 RBI. The pitching staff had five double-digit winners, led by thirty-four-year-old Jeff Pfeffer's nineteen wins. Impressed by Pfeffer's having played on two pennant winners for the Dodgers, in 1916 and 1920, Rickey had traded for him in 1921, sending pitcher Ferdie Schupp and shortstop Hal Janvrin to Brooklyn. Pfeffer never won in double digits again, but when he left Major League Baseball after 1924, he possessed an impressive career record of 158-112 and a 2.77 ERA. Steady Bill Sherdel was the second-biggest winner on the 1922 staff, with 17 wins, followed by veterans Jess Haines and Bill Doak, with 11 victories apiece.

Rickey was increasingly in demand as a speaker in St. Louis at church gatherings, service clubs, and youth organizations. The ardent supporter of the Knothole Gang concept rarely turned down an opportunity to address young people, and local newspapers knew that Rickey always made for good copy. Shortly before Thanksgiving 1922 the *St. Louis Globe-Democrat* sent a reporter to cover Rickey's talk to a Boy Scouts dinner.

"Boy Scouting teaches boys to be self-reliant and to have a lot of ginger and pep," Rickey said. He stressed, though, that people must learn to be patient and to accept the confounding mysteries in development. "You can't raise boys like race horses and know in advance what they will be," he cautioned. "Your boy may be a famous doctor or he may be a footpad, according to the way his thoughts run now." As always, he hammered home the connection between spirited play in baseball and success in life. "You should not raise boys to be on the defensive," he insisted. "They should be of the aggressive type—the type that is willing to do the great things of life." The key element for Rickey was concentration at all times. "Sometimes a bad play in the first inning means defeat in the ninth," he warned. "It is the first inning for the boys in St. Louis now and it is up to the men of St. Louis that the ninth bring success," he concluded in the kind of peroration that would soon lead Bill Corum, a Missouri-bred, New York–based sportswriter to fondly dub Rickey "The Great Rotarian."[26]

As always, the Christmas season was a joyous, bustling time in the Rickey household. There was a new member of the family, Sue Moulton Rickey, who had been born in March 1922 when the paterfamilias was in spring training in Texas. He was now the proud father of four daughters and one son as well as the supporter of his mother-in-law and sister-in-law.

The earnest breadwinner brought home good economic news at holiday time. Sam Breadon had been very pleased with the Cardinals' progress in both the Major and Minor Leagues and had offered Rickey a long-term contract to stay as vice president and business manager. The team president was elated that the team stock, just a few years earlier a subject of charity and selling for as little as $3.50 a share, was now paying a dividend of $2.50 a share at a price well over $50 and still rising. In November 1922 Breadon had bought out the shares of board chairman James C. Jones and now owned approximately two-thirds of the team stock; vice president Rickey possessed most of the other 20 percent.[27]

Convinced that the Cardinals were soon headed to a championship, Breadon had actually wanted to tie up Rickey contractually for ten years. Although flattered by the offer, Rickey had misgivings about committing ten years of his life so far in advance. He loved baseball as a sport and competitive challenge, but he still recoiled at its often profane climate. Rickey negotiated his five-year deal with the provision that in all years when the team showed an operating profit, he would gain a percentage—as much as 10 percent—of all the sales of the Cardinals' Minor and Major League players.[28]

Rickey was very pleased with the new contract and its handsome "emolument," as he liked to call financial reward for work.[29] Giving his children a comfortable and rewarding life without the fear of privation he had grown up with was a driving motivation of Branch Rickey's life. Thus his work ethic would not slacken with his new security but would only increase. "This compulsion to succeed was to be a life-long characteristic of Rickey," scholar Donald Andersen, whose father managed for Rickey in the Minor Leagues, has written.[30]

Early in January 1923 Sam Breadon called a press conference to officially announce that he had just signed Branch Rickey to a five-year contract. Although Rickey was pleased to receive the vote of confidence, his pessimistic Protestant side was not sanguine about the chances of the coming 1923 edition of the Cardinals. "It hasn't a chance to get much of anywhere unless pitchers, infielders, outfielders and maybe a catcher are developed," Rickey warned the St. Louis community at the very press conference when Breadon happily announced his signing.[31]

Always focusing on youth, Rickey was hopeful about the development of his young players in the Minor Leagues, who might soon be ready to challenge his regulars. Competition for jobs within an organization was a healthy thing, Branch Rickey believed, and if the young players showed that they were hungrier and had higher ceilings than the veterans, Rickey was ready to swap age for youth. Aging was inexorable, Rickey understood, and he was always observant of its irreversible signs. A player might squint at the fine print in his contract, indicating his eyesight was slipping, or another might take his shoes off in the dugout, hinting that his feet were aching. Very few revealing details were missed by the eagle-eyed executive. Already forming in his mind was one of his most widely quoted axioms: "It is better to trade a player a year too early than a year too late."

To prove his point Rickey pulled off a major trade just before the start of 1923 spring training. He swapped thirty-year-old first baseman Jack Fournier to the Brooklyn Dodgers for center fielder Henry "Hi" Myers. The trade was made to make room for young Jim Bottomley, who had not yet turned twenty-three. Although Hi Myers was more than three years older than Fournier, Rickey envisioned him as an outfield replacement for the late Austin McHenry. The executive liked that his new player was fast and aggressive, having led the league in triples twice, and had World Series experience with the 1916 and 1920 Brooklyn National League champions. It also didn't hurt that Myers had good small-town Ohio roots, hailing from East Liverpool.

However, shortly after the Fournier-Myers trade was announced, Rickey took ill during a function at a local business club. He was rushed to a hospital, where acute appendicitis was diagnosed and immediate surgery was recommended. "Can't we postpone the operation?" Rickey pleaded. "There is not going to be a debate, Mr. Rickey," the physicians replied. "You have no choice."

Rickey reluctantly complied. Not for the first or last time, doctors told him to cut down on his enormous workload to reduce the stress on his bodily systems. Of course, he didn't listen. While still hospitalized Rickey booked himself on a train to Houston. He simply could not miss the crucial farm team meeting. "His physician even went so far as to advise that he would not be responsible for his condition if the trip was attempted," *Sporting News* writer L. H. Addington noted a few years later. "But the desire to be doing things and to gather up the stray threads was uppermost and Rickey went. . . . He is still alive to tell the tale."[32]

After presiding over the Houston meeting, Rickey headed for spring training, based now in Bradenton, near Sarasota, on the west coast of Florida. He rarely had an idle moment, overseeing the instruction sessions in the morning, the intrasquad games in the afternoon, and the special tutorials in pitching and hitting for those prospects that needed it. During one of his visits to observe the progress of the Minor Leaguers, he heard a sound that all baseball people live for: the unmistakable thwacking of rare home run power coming from a baseball bat.

"Who is hitting the ball?" Rickey asked scout-instructor Joe Sugden, with coach Burt Shotton standing nearby. "That's a pitcher, Charles Hafey, Mr. Rickey," Sugden said. "You mean he was a pitcher," Rickey declared. The Cardinals mastermind told the scouts to tell Hafey to throw away his pitcher's toe plate and get himself an outfielder's glove and plenty of bats.

Rickey had made another, almost instantaneous conversion of a player. He expected Hafey, who would become known as Chick Hafey, to struggle at first in developing into an everyday player, but learning through trial and error and hard work was what Rickey's development system was all about. Hafey would arrive in the big leagues late in 1924 and become a regular in 1927. He wound up as a career .317 hitter and .526 slugger and was elected to the Hall of Fame in 1971, two years before his death. Rickey always maintained that had Hafey enjoyed "normal eyesight and good health," he could have surpassed Rogers Hornsby as the greatest right-handed hitter of all time. However, his eyes were so bad that teammates noticed he had trouble reading the departure blackboards at train stations.[33]

As Rickey plotted more improvements for 1923, he knew that the pitching staff needed bolstering. He had long been enamored of tall pitchers with long fingers who could manipulate the ball in cunning and successful ways. He decided to sign a pitcher who fit that description, six foot two, 235-pound, thirty-four-year-old veteran right-hander Fred Toney. (Toney was best known for the ten-inning no-hitter he pitched for the Reds in 1917, beating the Cubs' Jim "Hippo" Vaughn, who pitched a nine-inning no-hitter himself before losing the game in the tenth.) In 1920 Toney had won twenty-one games for the Giants, and in 1921 he won eighteen and started two games in the World Series, but he didn't get out of the second inning in either appearance. Although the Giants beat the Yankees in the Series, Toney was treated roughly by some sports-writers, who branded him the "goat" of the competition.[34]

In July 1922 Toney had ostensibly retired from baseball rather than report to the Boston Braves as part of the controversial Hugh McQuillan deal. Rickey thought he could motivate Toney to another World Series, where he would erase the blemishes of his past failures and prove John McGraw wrong for trading him away.[35] The pitcher, however, was known as a difficult player to manage. He would openly criticize his teammates for fielding lapses, never a good way to build team cohesion. Reared in the backwoods of Tennessee, he preferred the country to the city and moved to the sound of his own drummer. He was occasionally photo-graphed with his pet greyhounds and also kept a bear as a pet in his home in the country. New York sportswriter William McGeehan once memorably described him as "The Man Who Walks Like A Bear."[36]

Branch Rickey loved the quirks in individuals, especially in country boys, and he signed Toney without concern for his most controversial off-field baggage. During World War I Toney had refused to register for the military draft, claiming a wife and child as dependents. It was soon discovered that he was neither living with his wife nor paying any child support. His local draft board filed charges, and the press went up in arms against Toney as a war shirker, but no successful criminal action was ever undertaken against him.[37]

Moreover, when Branch Rickey wanted someone for his baseball team, he was not going to be deterred by the person's questionable past. His feeling was, of course, ironic, given that Rickey himself was ultrapatriotic and had served in World War I. However, as far as the St. Louis leader was concerned, Toney had committed no crime and his pitching skills could help the Cardinals.

The signing of Toney drew the criticism of St. Louis sports columnist John B. Sheridan, who wondered why Rickey wanted a "draft dodger" for his pitching staff. "I suppose it is the survival of the fittest in baseball," Sheridan wrote, describing the sport as "a queer, queer world or rather queer people in it. And Major Wesley Branch Rickey is one of the queer-est of the queer."[38] Yet Rickey stuck to his guns, and Toney pitched for the 1923 Cardinals. In his last season in the Major Leagues, he would compile an 11-12 record with a 3.84 ERA, a little below the team and league average. (He retired with a 131-102 lifetime record and an excellent career ERA of 2.69.)

As the Cardinals gathered in Bradenton, Florida, for the start of 1923 spring training, expectations were growing for a successful season. For the first time in recent memory, St. Louis sportswriters picked the Cardinals to finish in the first division and maybe rise even higher. The fans shared similar hopes, and Rickey announced an innovation that he thought would help the St. Louis rooters to better follow their heroes. For the first time in baseball history, the Cardinals were placing uniform numbers on the sleeves of the players to better identify them to the fans. Similar numerals had been in use for ten years in college football, but as usual in a baseball business resistant to change, the innovation was not welcomed by many of the press, the players, and the fans, and virtually all of the scorecard vendors were opposed. Bowing reluctantly to the protests, Rickey scrapped the idea of sleeve numbers, though by the early 1930s, all teams used uniforms with numbers on the back.[39]

Another change had already been implemented that was much more successful. The front of the St. Louis uniform was now graced by two cardinals resting on a baseball bat. Not long after Rickey returned from World War I, he had attended a St. Louis women's club luncheon and was captivated by a drawing of redbirds on a napkin. He recommended that the team adopt the logo, and it has become one of baseball's most beloved and enduring.[40]

The Cardinals got off to a bright start in the 1923 season, giving the fans hope that the good 1922 season had not been a mirage. Though Rogers Hornsby was in and out of the lineup with knee and ankle injuries, George "Specs" Toporcer, the first position player to wear eyeglasses in the Major Leagues, was proving an adequate temporary replacement at second base.[41] By late June the Cardinals were within four games of the defending league champion Giants. Jim Bottomley was emerging as a star, on his way to an outstanding season with a .371 BA, 8 HR, and 94 RBI. The fans quickly adopted the shy, unassuming player as a new hero to replace the traded Jack Fournier. Dubbed by some in the press as "the prize package" of the 1923 season, the *Sporting News* noted that Bottomley's stirring exploits thrilled his home region. It was said that radio sets were installed in half the homes in Central Illinois, just to get the results of Cardinal games and to learn from the broadcasts what Bottomley had or had not done on the field.

Although Fournier was not missed, Hi Myers, for whom he was traded, did not turn out to be an adequate replacement for Austin McHenry. At thirty-four he was past his prime, playing in only ninety-six games. He did hit .300, but in only 330 at-bats, scoring a mere 29 runs with 48 RBI. He soon vanished from the Major League scene. By contrast, in the four seasons Fournier played for Brooklyn, he hit 82 home runs and in 1923 he hit .351 and in 1925 he hit .350 respectively.

Hi Myers's poor performance was just one of the problems that began to cast doubt on Rickey's stewardship of the team. By midseason the Cardinals were exhibiting a disturbing trend of playing much better on the road than at home. They fell behind the leaders of the league, the Giants, Reds, Pirates, and Cubs, who would finish in that order in the 1923 pennant race, neatly separated by four games. Whispers turned to open comment that Branch Rickey was perhaps too intellectual a manager to lead a team of less cerebral athletes.[42] His incessant lineup and batting order shifts discomfited many players, and he was a picture of nervousness in the dugout, wearing his pants out on the bench sliding from one end to the other. Rickey also wasn't present at every game, taking leave of the team at times to scout young players. He handed over the managerial reins to his loyal lieutenant Burt Shotton, who had retired as an active player in 1922.

The low point of the season for Branch Rickey came in late August 1923 during a four-game series against the league-leading Giants in New York. All the games turned out to be close, one-run contests, but St. Louis lost three out of four. During one game the score was tied in the late innings, and Rogers Hornsby was on third base with one out. The count was 3-1 on the batter, and the star second baseman yelled encouragement to the hitter to drive him home. Branch Rickey, managing in the dugout in street clothes, flashed the "take" sign to the third base coach, probably Burt Shotton, and the batter took a second strike. Hornsby threw up his hands in disgust, publicly showing up his manager, a definite violation of baseball etiquette. Hornsby never scored, and the Cardinals lost the game.

In the clubhouse shower after the game, the frustrated star loudly complained to catcher Ed Ainsmith that Rickey did not want to win badly enough and used too many college "projects" as pitchers.[43] Rickey, still irritated at his star for his insolent actions on the field, overheard Hornsby's critique. Tempers flared, and when the second baseman called him many unprintable names, the ferocious gentleman swung wildly at him with the kind of anger he once had displayed at a Turkey Creek miscreant. The disgruntled star shoved his manager away, but the enraged Rickey ran at him again. Loyal, quick-thinking Burt Shotton pulled him away, sparing his out-of-shape mentor from possible serious injury at the hands of the well-conditioned athlete.[44]

If the altercation had occurred during the 24/7 coverage of sports today, the mind boggles at the kind of coverage a player-manager fight would have attracted. In the sportswriting world of the 1920s, however, there was little desire to make headlines out of intramural feuds. "What happens here, stays here" was a familiar sentiment in baseball clubhouses, and thus no immediate word appeared in the newspapers about the confrontation. Rickey kept Hornsby in the lineup as the Cardinals continued on a long twenty-game road trip that ended, after a Labor Day game in Chicago, with an exhibition game in Galesburg, Illinois, on the way home to St. Louis.

Shortly after the Cardinals began a home stand, Hornsby, claiming he had a skin rash, took himself out of the lineup. The news of the fight in New York began to filter into the newspapers. John Sheridan added to his criticism of Rickey, asking, "What is the advantage of a college education, if our leading college men are to settle things as angry wolves settle them?"[45] Hiram Mason, the team's road secretary, tried to downplay the situation and said that he wasn't going to discuss "dirt." But a St. Louis sportswriter rejoined, "Fans do chew over such morsels."[46]

When Hornsby refused to play for the rest of the September, many close observers of the St. Louis sports scene were wondering whether Hornsby's lingering ailment was just his way of getting revenge on Rickey. Dr. Robert Hyland, the devoted volunteer Cardinals team physician, had informed management that Hornsby's skin infection was not serious enough to keep him out of the lineup.[47]

Rumors of a possible postseason trade began to resurface. Local insurance executive Robert W. Newman, a friend of Hornsby, escalated the controversy by telling sportswriters that the second baseman needed a trade to a team that would appreciate him more. Sam Breadon and Rickey were indignant that an outsider would dare tell them what to do, though it was a sign of Hornsby's growing sense of his special status in baseball that he was not afraid of having outside agents lobby for him. When asked for a comment on the Rickey-Hornsby altercation, Breadon downplayed it. "It all came about in the heat of battle," the team president said, adding quickly, "Hornsby is not for sale or trade."[48]

Showing management solidarity, Breadon publicly lauded Rickey's "ability as a baseball man" and sternly added that Hornsby, as the highest-paid player in the National League (and second in baseball only to Babe Ruth), should play whenever he was physically able. In the last week of the season Breadon announced that the idle Hornsby would be fined $500, in addition to being docked his salary for the rest of the season, beginning on September 8, the day he benched himself.[49]

In a statement just before the end of the season to Ed Wray of the *Post-Dispatch*, Rickey declared that Hornsby "will NOT be sold by this club but will play here or nowhere in the major leagues. That is absolute." The executive tried to explain his actions in New York. "I am not a 'fighting manager,'" he said. "However, I am not sorry I resented the vile and unspeakable language used by Hornsby," adding that there are "some things that even peace-loving people will not put up with."[50]

Because of the time missed due to injuries and suspension, Hornsby played in only 107 games in 1923, but he still finished the season with impressive statistics, leading the league with a .384 BA and a .627 SA. Although the Cardinals as a team finished with a winning 79-74 record, they were a distant fifth, sixteen games behind the Giants. They also won eight fewer games than the 1922 team. Not surprisingly, the season was not a financial success. Attendance dropped to 338,551, a disturbing loss of almost 200,000 fans from 1922.[51]

Despite the denials from St. Louis management, Hornsby trade rumors reemerged as the 1923 off-season began. William Wrigley of the Cubs put in a bid and, of course, so did John McGraw and Charles Stoneham of the Giants. Rickey remained convinced that Hornsby was an untouchable asset, but the team's slippage in the standings disturbed the executive greatly. The stress of being both the major domo of the grow-ing Cardinals organization and the field manager was beginning to take its toll. He wondered whether handling the two jobs was too much. He considered asking Breadon to hire Burt Shotton as the field manager for 1924.

Shotton was willing to do almost anything for the man he called "Rick." Although the retired outfielder's devoted fealty to his friend made him the subject of ridicule among anti-Rickey factions in St. Louis, most promi-nently the one led by Rogers Hornsby, he was a respected baseball man whose advice on managing and motivating players occasionally made the pages of such prominent journals as the monthly magazine *Baseball*. Shot-ton wasn't flashy or highly quotable, but the aggressive, teetotaling base-ball lifer spoke for Rickey when he said such things as "The only thing a manager can really do is to know his men" and "I don't like losing games in cocktail lounges."[52] Breadon, however, agreed with Hornsby that Shot-ton was too closely associated with his mentor to make much difference as a manager. The owner decided to keep Rickey in both jobs.

As Rickey gathered his staff for the annual postseason review of 1923, he thought that there was promise ahead despite the mediocre Major League record in 1923. Farm system products were beginning to blos-som in St. Louis. In his first full year of 1923, Jim Bottomley had hit a robust .371 with 94 RBI and a .535 SA. Howard Freigau, a graduate of Ohio Wesleyan, had been a surprise contributor at shortstop, replacing Rickey's former University of Michigan player John Lavan. Rickey was pleased that other farm system products, among them shortstop Lester Bell and center fielder Taylor Douthit, made their debuts in the last week of the season and looked like comers.

As for the pitchers, Rickey had high hopes for collegian John Stuart, a former standout at Ohio State University, who compiled a 9-5 won-loss record and who, one afternoon in July, started and won both games of a doubleheader against the Boston Braves. Rickey still preferred expe-rienced moundsmen, and he drew solace from the good records of vet-eran pitchers Jess Haines, who won twenty games for the first time, and Bill Sherdel, who collected fifteen wins. Rickey thought that there was no reason they couldn't keep up the good work the next year.

On the eve of the 1924 season, however, St. Louis sportswriting pundits were wary of making positive predictions after the disappointment of 1923. Their caution turned out to be wise because the Cardinals were never in the 1924 pennant race. They plummeted to a very poor sixth place, at twenty-four games under .500 and twenty-eight and a half games behind the pennant-winning Giants. A punchless outfield and inconsistent pitching were major weaknesses that even one of the most remarkable individual seasons in baseball history could not overcome. Rogers Hornsby, putting out of his mind on the field any lingering dissatisfaction with his manager Branch Rickey, hit .424 (still a National League record), with 25 HR and 94 RBI. He led the league in seven categories: 227 H, 121 R, 373 TB (total bases), 43 DB, .696 SA, and 89 BB.

Yet Hornsby's heroics did nothing to move the Cardinals up in the standings. Nor did one remarkable game of Jim Bottomley's in Brooklyn in September 1924, in which he collected a record-setting 12 RBI. Home attendance fell to 272,885, a decrease of nearly 70,000 from 1923, and an alarming loss of more than a quarter million spectators from the team record in 1922.[53]

After the season Sam Breadon and St. Louis fans suffered another indignity when Rogers Hornsby lost out on the Most Valuable Player award to Dodgers pitcher Clarence Arthur "Dazzy" Vance. Vance won twenty-eight games and led the league with 262 strikeouts for a Brooklyn team that finished only one game behind the Giants, who won the pennant for the fourth straight year. Breadon was enraged that Hornsby did not win the award, but a good case could be made that Vance was more valuable to a contending team.

Branch Rickey was less concerned about individual awards than with bringing the team back into contention in the face of mounting criticism. During 1925 spring training at Stockton, California, rumors again swirled that Sam Breadon wanted Rickey to step down, and one report had the owner making a special trip to the West Coast for Rickey's resignation.[54] However, the business and field manager wanted to finish the job he started. If he must hand over the managerial reins, he again wanted to give them to Burt Shotton, but neither Sam Breadon nor his temperamental star Rogers Hornsby seriously considered that possibility.

Although he was losing patience, Sam Breadon was willing for now to give Rickey one more chance. Like all owners he wanted the thrill of winning a title, and the sooner the better. He had invested good money in the farm system, and it was running smoothly now that all the local Minor League owners saw eye to eye with the St. Louis office. There had been some nervous moments when future stars Jim Bottomley and Chick Hafey had almost been sold to wealthier teams until Breadon was willing to increase his price.[55] With the problems ironed out below, Breadon now wanted results on the top, with Branch Rickey delivering the pennant to him and the fans of St. Louis.

Rickey started the 1925 season, his sixth straight at the Cardinals' managerial helm, with characteristic enthusiasm and hope, but the team started off badly. By the end of May the Cardinals were already deep in the second division with a 13-25 record. Advance sales for a post–Memorial Day home stand in St. Louis were almost nonexistent, and the team was mired in a seven-game losing streak. Sam Breadon decided that he couldn't wait any longer to make a change.

He took a night train to Pittsburgh to relieve his manager of his duties. Having no advance warning of his coming dismissal, the news stunned Rickey, who felt thoroughly humiliated. "Sam, you are ruining me," he cried. "In time, Branch, you will see that I am doing you a great favor," Breadon responded. "You can now devote yourself fully to player development and scouting." Aware that Breadon's mind was made up, Rickey hoped again to have Burt Shotton replace him, but Breadon told his ex-manager that he had convinced Rogers Hornsby to take the job of player-manager.

Hornsby had accepted with some reluctance, given his boundless concentration on his own game and his gruff impatience with bad baseball by others. Breadon reminded the second baseman that three star players were already holding both jobs in the American League: Ty Cobb on the Tigers, Tris Speaker on the Indians, and George Sisler on the Browns. Hornsby soon had another reason for accepting the job. In an act of emotional petulance Rickey blurted to Breadon upon news of his firing: "If I am not good enough to manage the team, Sam, then I don't want to have stock in it, either." Breadon calmly replied that he could find buyers for Rickey's shares. It turned out that Hornsby was interested, and just as Breadon had loaned money to Rickey in 1920 to buy out his automobile partner, Fuzzy Anderson, the owner arranged a loan for Hornsby to purchase Rickey's stock.[56] No longer the field manager of the Cardinals, Branch Rickey went to Forbes Field, told the players the news about his replacement, and urged them to play hard for their new manager.

On the train ride from Pittsburgh to St. Louis, Branch Rickey, fighting shame and anger, agonized about whether he should stay in baseball after being so summarily dismissed as manager. He hated failure and, as he so often expressed it, would "never grow accustomed to the emotions of continuous defeat." Upon his arrival in St. Louis's Union Station, he was greeted by Frank Ruppenthal, a St. Louis businessman and sports aficionado, who knew that the executive would need cheering up. "You were feelin [*sic*] so down," Ruppenthal remembered years later in a letter to Rickey. "I patted you on the knee, and told you cheer up' [*sic*] That you were still the biggest man in baseball and some day you would be baseball's TOP MAN. . . . With a big smile you gave me a big thank you, and tight handshake."[57]

When Rickey returned to his house, Jane Rickey was as supportive as ever of her husband and his struggles. She listened empathetically to his story of the "brutal" manner of Breadon's firing him, but she urged him not to act hastily. "Remember, Branch, what your grandfather used to say about getting your belly rest before you act on anything," she counseled. Many of Rickey's friends stopped by his house to boost his morale. A police inspector in St. Louis suggested that he would make a good chief of police and that, if Branch were interested, he would make inquiries in his behalf.[58]

Yet, as always in his eventful and passionate life, whenever there was a possibility of choosing another path outside baseball, Branch Rickey didn't take it. Baseball was too deep in his blood. He loved the game and its challenges, and for supporting a large family, his work in baseball afforded him a very good standard of living. St. Louis was feeling more and more like home to Branch and Jane Rickey. He and Jane had made many friends in the business, religious, and academic communities. There were now six children in his family, with Elizabeth Ann "Betty" Rickey having been born in March 1924, when he was away in spring training. All six of his children would attend the Burroughs private school, where Rickey soon would become a member of the board of trustees. It was a happy and fulfilling life he was leading in St. Louis, and he wanted to maintain it.

Another family situation affected Rickey's calculation of the future. His younger brother, Frank Wanzer Rickey, was shortly to stand trial in Detroit, Michigan, for murder. As a federal prohibition law enforcement officer working in Michigan, the younger Rickey had killed a man in the line of duty. The government was convinced that he would be exonerated, but Branch had feared for his brother's safety ever since he started his dangerous new job.

Almost seven years younger than Branch, Frank Rickey was a genuinely free spirit who loved hunting and fishing and all kinds of outdoor adventure. He had started college at Ohio Wesleyan, but sitting in a classroom was too hard for him to take. He went back home to Scioto County, where he went into the grocery business and also performed local police work.[59]

In the early 1920s Frank Rickey became a federal marshal in the prohibition enforcement wing of the U.S. Treasury Department. On January 16, 1920, the Eighteenth Amendment to the Constitution of the United States had been enacted when the thirty-sixth state legislature in the nation approved the Volstead Act, which made it a crime to make, transport, sell, or consume alcohol. Raised in a family of teetotalers, Frank Rickey believed in the "dry" cause and became an effective law enforcer.

At times the younger Rickey was a partner of Izzy Einstein, the colorful, nationally known, three-hundred-pound prohibition agent based in New York. In July 1923 Izzy Einstein and Frank Rickey received newspaper notice about a raid in Mount Clemens, a Michigan resort town north of Detroit. Posing as a southern "colonel" in dire need of drink to soothe his rheumatism, Frank Rickey spent a week gaining the confidence of the wealthy Michigan tipplers, and then he and Einstein blew their cover and arrested the violators of the federal law.[60]

Branch Rickey shared his brother's convictions that alcohol was a very dangerous substance, and he never kept intoxicating beverages in his home. Yet, as a man very involved in the secular world, Branch doubted whether the Volstead Act could be successfully enforced. From his vantage point in the baseball business, Rickey knew about the often-irresistible lure of drink among players and owners. For instance, Cincinnati Reds owner Garry Herrmann was known to travel in a luxury train equipped with a full supply of bootleg liquor, and in April 1925, during the Reds' first road series of the season with the Cardinals, he had been arrested outside St. Louis's Statler Hotel for drinking illegal alcohol. When served with a summons Herrmann feigned disbelief that the liquid he was drinking contained alcohol.[61]

Although Rickey personally favored abstinence from drink, he was growing increasingly aware that the Prohibition law wasn't working. He realized that respectable people, in their zeal to obtain alcohol, would enlist the aid of the underworld and thus, ironically, were abetting the rise of crime syndicates. The executive was beginning to believe that Prohibition was causing more problems than drink itself. With his brother facing trial for murder, Rickey did not have to be reminded that the work of a prohibition marshal was extremely dangerous. In the worst-case scenario, Rickey feared that his brother might be killed in the line of duty and that he would have to support his brother's seven children.[62]

In the summer of 1925, not long after Sam Breadon replaced Branch Rickey as field manager, his brother's trial began in Detroit. Members of Frank Rickey's family journeyed northward from Ohio to give him support in the courtroom, but before the ordeal ended the family would suffer another huge scare. Julia Rickey, Frank's twelve-year-old daughter, was nearly kidnapped outside the hotel where the family was staying. As she was preparing to cross the street to buy fruit, she heard a voice, saying, "Hey, little girl, I'll help you," Julia Rickey Peebles remembered in a 1999 interview. After taking one look at the stranger calling to her, she quickly ran back to the safety of the hotel lobby, foiling a kidnapping attempt by one of the bootleggers who wanted to avenge their crony's death. For the rest of Frank Rickey's family's stay in Detroit, Julia did not venture outside alone.[63]

As the government predicted, Frank Rickey was quickly acquitted in the murder trial, but Branch was determined to find his brother a safer occupation. He thought that his younger brother, a congenial and gregarious man who knew how to evaluate baseball talent, would make an excellent scout. Of course, Rickey could have the kind of influence to hire his brother only if he stayed on in the Cardinals' front office. By the end of 1925 Branch Rickey received the go-ahead from Sam Breadon to add his brother to his staff. To the great relief of his brother, Frank Rickey no longer needed to work at his dangerous job in Prohibition enforcement.[64]

Frank Rickey went on to be a specialist in southern scouting for the Cardinals and was directly involved in the signing of such future St. Louis stars as Marty Marion, Johnny Mize, Terry Moore, and Ernie White. Almost every one of the 1942 championship Cardinals, the so-called "St. Louis Swifties," would be scouted by Frank Wanzer Rickey. Before joining his brother in Brooklyn in the mid-1940s, Frank Rickey would also scout for the New York Giants.[65]

Meanwhile, the Cardinals finished with a rush under new manager Hornsby in 1925. Gone from the dugout was the intense Rickey, who even his strongest supporters conceded might have been too nervous and agitated for the good of the players. One of Hornsby's first acts as manager was to throw away the blackboard Rickey used for chalk talks before the game. "That was for that Ohio Wee-zel-an bastard, Rickey," Hornsby snorted.[66] In terms reminiscent of Miller Huggins's critique of Rickey in 1914, Hornsby declared, "It's base hits that win ballgames, not smart ideas." The new manager also announced that Rickey's pregame meetings were a thing of the past. He would trust the instincts of his players to play the game hard and smart. The Cardinals finished 64-51 under Hornsby, and 77-76 overall, good for fourth place, eighteen games behind the Pittsburgh Pirates, who won the World Series in a thrilling seven-game battle with the Washington Senators.

Although the wounds from what he always called his "brutal" firing by Breadon healed very slowly, Branch Rickey was gradually accepting the wisdom of losing the field managerial position. With his brother safely in tow in the hard but infinitely safer work of baseball scouting, the executive could look forward to a 1926 season, when he hoped at last the groundwork he had established in the farm system would pay off with a pennant in St. Louis.

7

That Championship Season

At the first meeting of the 1926 Cardinals in spring training just outside of San Antonio, Texas, player-manager Rogers Hornsby proclaimed, "We are going to win the pennant, and anyone who doesn't believe it can go right home now." He added that he didn't want any "second division" ballplayers around, meaning players not alert enough to know how to win games consistently. His training regimen, however, was less intensive than former manager Branch Rickey's had been. There was only one practice session, from 11:00 a.m. to 3:00 p.m., and there were no morning and evening lectures. Gone too was Branch Rickey's blackboard for his chalk talks in the clubhouse.[1]

Hornsby did take the preseason exhibition games seriously because he wanted the team to get into the habit of winning. "No game is unimportant," he declared. "The more of 'em you win, the better, regardless of the conditions." The team responded with a 22-1 record in southern exhibition games. Because of bad weather in St. Louis, they lost the only game played in the preseason series with the Browns, but twenty-three thousand fans showed up to demonstrate faith in the team's prospects and cheer on the popular player-manager.[2]

Meanwhile, though Branch Rickey would never forget his firing as manager, he realized that he had no choice but to accept Sam Breadon's edict because hiring and firing Major League managers was to be the Cardinals owner's prerogative for the remainder of their relationship. Freed from the necessity of being in the dugout, Rickey threw himself into overseeing the development of the farm system from the lowest to the highest levels.

He was grateful that Breadon continued to finance the expansion of Rickey's scouting and development program. In the summer of 1925 the Cardinals had begun to sponsor on-site tryout camps. No longer did players have to pay their way to St. Louis to show their wares; now the Cardinals came to them. The first camp was in Danville, Illinois, and hundreds of hopefuls came from all over the Midwest and South to show their stuff in front of Rickey's scouts and instructors. By 1927 Danville was also used as a spring training and instructional camp for raw Minor Leaguers, prompting the *Sporting News* to headline with awe, "Where Did Rickey Dig Them All Up?"[3] In 1928 a second tryout camp would open in Shawnee, Oklahoma, and there were more ahead in the 1930s. At his core Branch Rickey was always a teacher, and selecting and developing raw recruits into finished products was probably his most satisfying achievement.

For his 1926 manager at the highest level of the farm system, Syracuse in the International League, Rickey named loyal Burt Shotton. The executive knew that Hornsby wanted no part of Shotton, who the temperamental Texan felt was too much of an acolyte of the deposed field manager. However, Rickey thought that Shotton's managerial abilities were excellent, and he always tried to help further his career. In 1928 his influence helped Shotton to become the Philadelphia Phillies' manager, and, as we shall see later, Rickey would call on him in an emergency in Brooklyn in 1947.

For president of the Syracuse franchise, Rickey installed Warren Crandall Giles, who had been working as general manager of the Cardinals' St. Josephs, Missouri, affiliate. Giles was promoted in part for alerting Rickey in 1924 that promising outfielder Taylor Lee "Flyhawk" Douthit (pronounced "DOUBT-it") had not been protected from the Minor League draft. Rickey quickly rectified the error, saving a coming star St. Louis center fielder from the clutches of other teams.[4] (With Rickey's endorsement, Giles later went on to be a general manager in Cincinnati and, ultimately, president of the National League.)

In St. Louis the wisdom of Breadon's managerial shift from Rickey to Hornsby was borne out when the Cardinals, in 1926, went on to win their first pennant and world championship in the twentieth century. The team would have the lowest winning percentage of any pennant winner to date, .570 with only 89 wins, but they prevailed over the defending world champion Pittsburgh Pirates and the Cincinnati Reds in a thrilling pennant race. The pleasure was more than doubled when the Cardinals conquered the Yankees in a dramatic seven-game World Series that wasn't decided until the very last pitch at Yankee Stadium.

Even though he wasn't on the field to enjoy the triumph, and even though his name had largely vanished from the sports pages, Branch Rickey's hand was unmistakable on the 1926 championship Cardinals. With the aid of Charley Barrett and other scouts, the farm system was directly responsible for fifteen members of the twenty-five-man roster. Although Jim Bottomley's batting average fell to .299, his 120 RBI led the league. Player-manager Rogers Hornsby was nagged by injuries, including painful thigh carbuncles that sent him to the hospital in July, and his batting average fell off to .317, but he still scored 96 runs and drove in 93. Once the pennant was in sight, he was a fiery leader by example. Shifted from shortstop to third base, Lester Bell had a career year, hitting .325 with 100 RBI. The Harrisburg, Pennsylvania, native was another diamond in the rough discovered by Charley Barrett, who predicted that Bell would develop into an offensive force in the infield comparable to Hornsby. Bell even adopted the player-manager's practice of standing deep in the batter's box, and in 1926, though never again, Bell was a feared and productive player.

Shortstop Tom Thevenow was another unheralded player, the kind of gritty small-town Midwesterner—born in Centralia, Illinois, raised in Madison, Indiana—whom Charley Barrett excelled in finding. In 1926 Thevenow hit only .256 but drove in 63 runs, many of them big ones. He played in every game, providing the stellar infield defense that every championship team must have. In a testimony to his range in the field, he amassed a remarkable 155 more assists than any other shortstop in the league. Baseball people always evaluate outfielders in terms of their ability at getting a "jump" on fly balls, but Thevenow insisted that infielders must have the same kind of skill. Thevenow would be an unlikely 1926 World Series offensive hero, hitting .417 with 10 hits and playing spectacular defense.

The 1926 Cardinals outfield was a classic product of Rickey scouting, conversion, and development. Starting the season in left field was pepper pot Ray Blades, the onetime semipro pitcher and infielder whom Rickey converted into an outfielder. When Blades broke his leg during the 1926 season, the growing depth of the Cardinals organization was demonstrated when Chick Hafey, another ex-pitcher converted by Rickey, stepped in. His numbers weren't outstanding—he hit .271 with 4 HR and 38 RBI—but he went 7 for 22 as a pinch hitter. After the season, at the suggestion of team physician Dr. Robert Hyland, Hafey started to wear eyeglasses and emerged in the next few years as one of the most feared power hitters in the National League.

The success of center fielder Taylor Douthit was another testimony to the extent of Branch Rickey's dragnet. A 1923 agriculture graduate of the University of California at Berkeley, Douthit had been signed on the recommendation of Berkeley Latin American history professor Charles C. Chapman. In 1921 Chapman, having read about Rickey's interest in college-educated players, wrote the executive a letter, asking, "Why is baseball so lax in scouting west coast talent?"[5] Always eager to encourage bright people with good ideas, Rickey immediately followed through on the professor's tip about Douthit, and later on another one about Berkeley boy Chick Hafey. Douthit advanced steadily through the Cardinals farm system and became an aggressive .300 singles hitter and a far-ranging outfielder, earning the nickname "The Flyhawk" for his outstanding defensive skills.

(Charles Chapman was typical of the kind of idealistic scout attracted to Rickey. Chapman liked to tell prospective players to accept low pay in the Minor Leagues for at least a year "for the immense advantage to be obtained in human experience and happy memories." Rickey hired Chapman as a part-time scout, but in 1932, the polymathic professor—who knew several languages; had four advanced degrees, including one from Harvard Law school; and had played college and semipro baseball in Japan as well as the United States—accepted a more lucrative position as a scout with the Cincinnati Reds.[6] Just before he died in 1941, Chapman coauthored a book with catcher Hank Severeid, whom Rickey had signed for the St. Louis Browns. The book was titled *Play Ball! Advice to Young Ballplayers.*)

The final piece in the 1926 outfield puzzle was completed by right fielder Billy Southworth, who was obtained from the Giants just before the June 15 trading deadline in an even-up swap for Clarence "Heinie" Mueller. John McGraw thought he had pulled a fast one on Branch Rickey because Mueller was almost six years younger than Southworth. As it turned out, Mueller didn't take to his new surroundings in New York, nor could he adjust to manager McGraw's irritable temperament. Mueller batted only .249 as a Giant in 1926, and his career petered out by 1929. On the other hand the thirty-three-year-old Southworth flourished in his new St. Louis home. His total 1926 numbers of .317, 11 HR, and 71 RBI told only part of the story of his contributions to the team. He also played good defense in right field and hit a big home run in the pennant-clinching game in late September.

Completing the everyday lineup for the 1926 Cardinals was catcher Bob O'Farrell, whom Rickey had obtained in May 1925 shortly before his firing as manager. It was one of Rickey's better trades because it cost St. Louis only the well-traveled catcher Miguel "Mike" Gonzalez (who coined the memorable description of a weak-hitting player, "Good field, no hit") and shortstop Howard Freigau. In another sign of the lack of sentiment in making key baseball deals that Branch Rickey insisted was necessary, Freigau was an Ohio Wesleyan alumnus but at the time Rickey felt that he was less valuable to the Cardinals than O'Farrell. (Freigau would meet a tragic end, dying in 1932 at age twenty-nine in a drowning accident in Chattanooga, Tennessee.)[7] O'Farrell was not yet thirty but had been a Major Leaguer for almost ten years. In 1926 St. Louis's new catcher would hit .293 with 30 2B, 63 R, and 68 RBI and would handle the pitching staff with aplomb. Highly regarded as a team leader, O'Farrell would be selected by the sportswriters as the 1926 National League Most Valuable Player.

The 1926 pitching staff was led by young Flint Rhem, a rangy six foot two right-hander who, in his second full Major League season, won twenty games and lost only seven. He hailed from Rhems, South Carolina, a small town named after his socially prominent family. Two other pitchers making major contributions to the 1926 Cardinals were the durable veterans Jess Haines, who was 13-4, and Bill Sherdel, who was 16-12.

However, the Cardinal pitching staff did not become truly formidable until the acquisition in late June of right-hander Grover Cleveland Alexander. The Chicago Cubs had placed the thirty-nine-year-old Alexander on waivers after he had compiled a disappointing 3-3 record. Joe McCarthy, the Cubs' rookie manager, thought that the aging right-hander was finished as a winning pitcher, and he was not in the mood to put up with Alexander's well-known alcoholic binges off the field.

Rogers Hornsby, though, thought that Alexander had plenty left in his tank, and so did his coach, Bill Killefer. Killefer had been Alexander's catcher in the pitcher's glory years in Philadelphia, when he led the 1915 Phillies to their first World Series and won thirty games three years in a row. Killefer, nicknamed "Reindeer" for his lumbering running style, was a good friend and hunting buddy of Alexander, and the man who bestowed on the pitcher his famous nickname "Ol' Pete." During a hunting trip, the story went, Alexander fell backward off a log and landed in a bog filled with alkali peat and mud. Probably a more accurate explanation of the nickname comes from Ol' Pete being used as a term for Prohibition alcohol.[8]

Both Hornsby and Killefer believed that all Alexander needed was a change in scenery, away from the withering stares of his rookie manager, who had never even played in the Major Leagues. As for the pitcher's off-field problems, Hornsby was adamant that a player's private life was his private life. He felt it was nobody's business what happened away from the ballpark as long as the player reported on time and competed hard. Hornsby grew very indignant when his own penchant for horse and dog track betting became a big issue management raised against him.

By a stroke of fate, when Alexander's name appeared on the waiver wire, Branch Rickey was out of the office visiting farm clubs. We will never know how he would have responded to the chance to sign Alexander. Though Rickey fully agreed with Hornsby that a ballplayer's private life was his own business, Rickey knew of no good that could come from imbibing alcohol recklessly and he was always fearful of alcoholic players seeking company in their search for the strong waters. On the other hand, Rickey liked veteran pitchers and he might have approved the signing.

In any event, by the 1926 season, it wasn't Branch Rickey's decision to sign or not sign Grover Cleveland Alexander. The power in Major League decision making had shifted to Rogers Hornsby, who had the ear of Sam Breadon. Rickey was just the "business manager," as Hornsby called him with no little contempt. Breadon was telling everyone that

Hornsby was "a John McGraw in the making," and the Cardinals player-manager quickly convinced the owner that Alexander would be a bargain at the $4,000 waiver price.

In a dramatic twist Alexander's first start for the Cardinals was in St. Louis against the Cubs on June 27, 1926. Taking advantage of the newly double-decked stands at Sportsman's Park, more than thirty-seven thousand fans, the largest crowd in St. Louis baseball history, watched Alexander tantalize his former team and win a 3-2, complete-game victory.[9] For the rest of the regular season, Alexander would compile a 9-7 record with two saves and an ERA under three runs a game. Further immortality was awaiting him in the World Series.

Even with the addition of Grover Cleveland Alexander, the Cardinals were locked in one of the tightest races in National League history with the Cubs, Pirates, and Reds. Barely over .500 for the first half of the season, the Cardinals caught fire in late July and went into first place in mid-August after winning three out of four games from the archrival Giants (who, in 1926, would finish weakly in fifth place). However, a Cardinals loss the next day saw the Reds climb back on top. Then the Pirates made a move to first, and for the rest of the month baseball fans were treated to a roller coaster ride of a pennant race. When the Pirates came to St. Louis for a critical five-game series at the end of August, more than 113,000 fans flocked to Sportsman's Park, and the Monday crowd of nearly 30,000 broke a weekday St. Louis record.[10] A pattern was being established for Cardinals attendance in St. Louis: mediocre crowds early in the season, even on opening day, and frenzied, large crowds late in the year as the pennant race neared its climax.

When the Cardinals moved back into first place on Labor Day, it was the first time in twentieth-century history that they had led the league so late in the season. Yet the schedule maker was not being kind to St. Louis. The team embarked on a long road trip that would keep them on the road until the end of September. Still, the Cardinals were in a good groove now, and Hornsby was primed to lead by example, and push the squad for the final burst to the finish line. He didn't care that the Cardinals would have to win in their rivals' backyards. Great teams meet great challenges, he believed, and behind the scenes Branch Rickey applauded the player-manager's assessment of the situation.

When Hornsby took a closer look at the road schedule, however, he grew concerned. He noted that before a big late-season series with the Giants in New York, the Cardinals had scheduled a Minor League exhibition game in New Haven, Connecticut. There were also two games for the team to play in Syracuse and Buffalo. Under Rickey and Breadon the Cardinals led all of professional baseball in exhibition games. Breadon saw them as extra revenue producers, and Rickey saw them as a way to build community interest in small towns and also as a means to keep players out of extracurricular trouble. Hornsby saw them as unnecessary inconveniences when he was trying to guide the team to a pennant.

He pleaded with Breadon to cancel the game in New Haven. He reminded his owner that he had guaranteed a pennant in spring training, but now he needed his help in getting the players needed rest. Breadon said that he would look into the matter, but he knew the likelihood of a cancellation was remote. New Haven business manager George Weiss had already sold over $500 worth of tickets to the exhibition game. Weiss, in the early years of a brilliant career that would take him to the Yankees in 1932 as their first farm system director (and ultimately as the general manager of the longest-running dynasty in baseball history), reminded Breadon that the game was played in years when the Cardinals were not a good draw. "Now that you are up, and you are the attraction, you'll have to keep your end," Weiss said.[11]

Breadon broke the bad news to Hornsby in Pittsburgh, where the owner was traveling with the team for part of the long September road trip. His timing was unfortunate, telling the manager in the clubhouse after a tough loss. If Branch Rickey had been consulted, he would have advised Breadon to choose a calmer time to talk to his manager. Rickey believed that the clubhouse was the field manager's domain, and he made it a point rarely to enter that sanctuary after he was fired as manager. Outsiders, Rickey believed, even the team president, should not invade that turf unless expressly invited.

When the owner told Hornsby that the team had to play the New Haven game, the temperamental Texan exploded in waves of profanity and told Breadon where he could shove his exhibition game. When he cooled off slightly, Hornsby said, "All right, but I won't send the first team! Now get the hell out of my clubhouse!"[12] "My clubhouse?!"

Breadon thought to himself. "What nerve!" And out into the late afternoon the irate, insulted team president stalked. Breadon was not used to taking that language from anybody, let alone an employee, no matter how well paid and idolized. He stewed silently and did not forget the rude outburst of his manager.

When Rickey learned of Breadon's unfortunate confrontation with Hornsby, he winced. He hoped, though, that the passage of time and the ultimate success of the team would change the owner's mind. After all, Rickey had endured a fistfight with Hornsby just three years earlier but hadn't lost his respect for him as a player and a leader who one day soon should be a champion.

The Cardinals played all the exhibition games as planned in September, but without Hornsby and many of the regulars. In a sign of his complete self-assurance, instead of going to New Haven the manager took several of his players to Yankee Stadium to watch their likely opponents in the World Series. Hornsby was photographed atop the Yankees dugout, in street clothes, sitting with Babe Ruth, the only player in baseball higher paid than the Cardinals star.[13]

In spite of the tedious September travel schedule and the controversial exhibition games, the Cardinals slowly took command in the pennant race. The pitching of Cincinnati, managed by Jack Hendricks, Rickey's unsuccessful Cardinals manager in 1918, crumbled down the stretch, and they lost five in a row at a crucial juncture. Meanwhile, the Cardinals fattened up on the bottom-feeding Philadelphia Phillies, winning six in a row and scoring more than sixty runs in the process.

As a result they needed only one victory in New York to clinch the pennant. Some of the Cardinals stayed over in Philadelphia to watch Gene Tunney wrest the heavyweight crown from Jack Dempsey and then entrained to meet the once-mighty Giants, now also-rans. The afternoon of Friday, September 24, 1926, was particularly sweet for Cardinals right fielder Billy Southworth. The former New York Giant hit an eighth-inning home run to lead the Cardinals to a come-from-behind, pennant-clinching, 6–4 victory. Flint Rhem won his twentieth game and Bill Sherdel got the save. In a deliriously happy clubhouse afterward, Jim Bottomley hugged Hornsby, exclaiming, "You told us in spring training that we would win it, Rog, and we did win it!"[14]

Pandemonium erupted in St. Louis when news of the pennant came over loudspeakers broadcasting an account of the game to throngs gathered in city streets. Nine hours of unfettered celebration commenced with dancing in the streets and confetti streaming down many thoroughfares, including in front of the Railway Exchange Building, where the Cardinals had their offices in the first impoverished days of the Rickey regime before they moved to roomier quarters at Sportsman's Park. Some delirious fans held up a homemade banner: "Hornsby For President—All Other Cardinals Cabinet Members."[15]

Branch Rickey celebrated his first pennant quietly at home. He felt very happy for the loyal fans and the city of St. Louis. He allowed himself a feeling of accomplishment, even though part of him still wished that he could have managed the team to victory. He did not take offense when Hornsby, in a ghostwritten *Post-Dispatch* story, said that he didn't "want to criticize anybody" but the Cardinals won because they played aggressive baseball while having the fewest signs in the league.[16]

Rickey made no plans to go to New York for the opening two games of the World Series. He would listen on the radio and help out in the ticket office as the Cardinals faced one of the dilemmas of their success, the task of disappointing thousands of fans clamoring for a limited number of World Series tickets. While Rickey would content himself to stay in St. Louis and attend only the middle three games of the Series at home, Rogers Hornsby never left New York after clinching the pennant against the Giants. The man who was nicknamed "Rajah" and who could have been elected president, if Missouri had its say, was taking his share of regal liberties. Seeing no need to play in the meaningless final home games of the regular season, he remained in the big city. He would greet the team when they returned for practices prior to the first game at Yankee Stadium.

Another sign of Hornsby's self-possession was his decision not to return immediately to Texas for the funeral of his mother. The day after the end of the regular season, Mary Dallas Rogers Hornsby, age sixty-two, died after a long illness. She lived long enough to see her son win the pennant, and her last message to him reportedly was to not rush home but go and win the World Series.[17] Though he was criticized in some quarters for not returning home immediately, his status as a local Texas hero was such that the funeral was delayed until after the World Series.

The 1926 World Series was destined to be one of the most dramatic confrontations in baseball history, a battle of East and West, of biggest city versus smallest metropolitan area in Major League Baseball, and a contest between two potentates of the diamond, the Sultan of Swat, Babe Ruth, versus the Rajah, Rogers Hornsby. A plethora of ghostwriters had a field day writing columns for Ruth, Hornsby, Yankees (and former Cardinals) manager Miller Huggins, Giants manager John McGraw, and Grover Cleveland Alexander. "Cardinals a Great Club, But We'll Win If We're Playing up to Form," headlined a pre-Series prediction by Babe Ruth.[18] The Yankees, returning to postseason competition for the first time since 1923, were installed as a slight favorite by most oddsmakers, who were impressed with the power hitting of Babe Ruth and the new regular first baseman Lou Gehrig as well as with the three double-digit winning pitchers, Herb Pennock, Waite Hoyt, and Urban Shocker.

Game one of the World Series was a thrilling pitchers' duel between left-handers Herb Pennock and Bill Sherdel. The Yankees won, 2–1, with Lou Gehrig's sixth-inning single scoring Babe Ruth with what proved to be the game-winning blow. The Cardinals evened the Series the next afternoon, 6–2, as Grover Cleveland Alexander threw a complete-game four-hitter, retiring the last twenty-one Yankees in a row. Bill Southworth's three-run homer broke a 2–2 tie in the top of the seventh inning. The largest crowd in World Series history, 63,600 fans, passed through the turnstiles.[19]

Another sign of Rogers Hornsby's remarkable clout in the championship year of 1926 was revealed when he was able to dictate the manner of the Cardinals' return trip to St. Louis. Commissioner Landis thought he had a deal for the New York Central Railroad to serve as the exclusive carrier for the pennant-winning teams. Hornsby, however, had made his own plans for the Cardinals to travel in an exclusive Pennsylvania Railroad car. "Your job is to run the World Series and not tell the players how to travel," Hornsby informed Landis with his customary bluntness.[20]

After the Cardinals' train pulled into St. Louis Union Station the next afternoon, the team was escorted to a massive parade down Washington Avenue. Some of the crowd got rowdy, mussing Hornsby's hair and bumping the hat off the head of Jeannette Pennington Hornsby, the manager's second wife, bringing tears to her eyes and those of their little boy, Billy Hornsby, but, fortunately, no real harm was done to anyone.[21]

Game three was a great triumph for veteran Jess Haines, the last player Branch Rickey had bought as a nearly finished Minor League product in 1919. Haines not only shut out the Yankees, 4–0, he also hit a two-run home run to aid his cause. The ecstasy in St. Louis was short-lived, however, because the next day—before a record crowd of 38,825, squeezed into every possible nook and cranny of Sportsman's Park—Babe Ruth administered a sobering dose of Yankees power by becoming the first man in World Series history to hit three home runs in a game. The New Yorkers dominated the middle innings, winning 10–5, to even the Series at two games each.

The crucial game five would be the last one played in St. Louis in 1926. Although the Cardinals had been an excellent road team, it was not likely that they could win two in a row in New York if they lost this one. Another record crowd, 39,552 strong, jammed Sportsman's Park, but the rematch between first-game starters Herb Pennock and Bill Sherdel produced the same result. The Yankees won an extra-inning thriller, 3–2, with rookie second baseman Tony Lazzeri hitting a sacrifice fly in the top of the tenth inning to drive in the winning run.

St. Louis fans exited the ballpark slowly, even mournfully, feeling that the championship had eluded them. On the train ride to New York, the players were anything but defeatist. "Pete gets the ball in the next game, and I can't think of anyone better to pitch a game we have to win," Hornsby said confidently. Staying at home to listen to the last games of the Series on the radio, Branch Rickey felt a similar confidence in his veteran pitcher.

In a promising omen of the glory to come, the Cardinals' special Pennsylvania railroad train made the trip back to New York in record time, breaking the old record by three hours and surpassing the swift time the Yankees' New York Central train had made on its trip to St. Louis.[22]

When it was time for game six at Yankee Stadium, Grover Cleveland Alexander did not let St. Louis down. The Cardinals set the tone immediately in game six by scoring three runs in the first inning, and the aging right-hander took it from there. He pitched another complete-game victory as the Cardinals won in a 10–2 romp. Lester Bell was the hitting star, with 3 hits and 4 RBI.

The stage was now set for a climactic game seven of the World Series, but the weatherman didn't want to cooperate. Sunday, October 10, 1926, dawned wet, chilly, and rainy in New York City. Many of the St. Louis players, staying in the Alamac, the team hotel on Manhattan's Upper West Side, expected the game would be rained out, but Commissioner Landis called with the word, "Get to the ballpark, boys. We're playing!" Many fans also had assumed that the game would be postponed; only 38,093 attended what would become one of the most dramatic games in World Series history, a fitting end to a very dramatic 1926 season.

Jess Haines was seeking to repeat his game two victory, pitted against Waite Hoyt, the Yankees' game four winner. New York took a 1–0 lead in the bottom of the third on Babe Ruth's fourth home run of the Series. Like all good teams the Cardinals immediately answered the New York run with three of their own, aided by errors by shortstop Mark Koenig and left fielder Bob Meusel. Haines gave up a run in the bottom of the sixth, but he still held a 3–2 lead.

In the bottom of the seventh inning, the New York crowd got its hopes up as center fielder Earle Combs led off with a single. Mark Koenig sacrificed him to second, and Babe Ruth was walked intentionally, his eleventh walk in the Series. Bob Meusel, given a chance to redeem himself for his error, hit into force play at second. With two out Haines got ahead of Lou Gehrig 0-2 but then walked him. The bases were loaded for Tony Lazzeri, the rookie second baseman who had slugged an impressive .462 in the regular season but who had also led the American League in strikeouts.

Rogers Hornsby asked for time and walked to the mound. He looked at Haines's fingertips, which were bleeding profusely from a blister that the knuckleballer had irritated. Though the veteran right-hander wanted to stay in the game, Hornsby slapped him on the back and signaled to the bullpen. Flint Rhem and Bill Sherdel were warming up, but Hornsby wanted someone else, a pitcher sitting bent over on the bullpen bench, wearing a heavy warmup jacket on the damp, cold afternoon. He wanted Grover Cleveland Alexander, winner of game six the day before, who had celebrated his victory with an evening of drink. Even if he weren't hungover, as legend claims, Alexander certainly wasn't warmed up and ready to pitch. Still, Hornsby had great faith in the rugged Nebraskan, who had told him that he would be available if needed for game seven.

Alexander lumbered slowly toward the mound, his undersized cap askew on his head, acting as if he didn't have a care in the world. Hornsby greeted him near second base and looked into his eyes to see if they were functioning and game ready. "The bases are loaded with two out, Pete," Hornsby said. "Lazzeri's up." "Well, I guess there is no place to put him, Skip," Alexander said. "Give me the ball. I struck him out the other day, and I'll strike him out again."

Back in St. Louis Branch Rickey was listening to the game on the radio with Jane, the children, and his sister-in-law and mother-in-law. In the fourth inning, to his utter exasperation, the radio went on the blink, but fortunately his next-door neighbors, Gene Mudd and his family, were home and he rushed over to listen to the rest of the game with them. Although Rickey's worried, inquisitive mind envisioned "trouble ahead, trouble ahead" in almost any situation, he liked the odds of a savvy veteran pitcher over an aggressive, overeager rookie batter. "Wait and see, Jane," Rickey predicted to his wife. "Alexander will take it nice and easy and get impatient Lazzeri out."

Alexander did retire Lazzeri, but not before one heart-palpitating moment. Working slowly and carefully Alexander threw a high outside fastball for ball one. His next pitch was down the middle for strike one. His third pitch tried to jam Lazzeri, but the rookie lined it into the left-field corner. Eyewitness accounts and imaginative memories disagree on how close the smash was to becoming a grand slam home run. Either it went inches foul at the last moment, or it was foul all the way by a few feet, which Alexander always insisted was the case. He told sportswriter Roy Stockton a week after the game that the pitch could only have been hit foul and thus was expressly designed to frustrate the hitter.[23]

The count was now 1-2, advantage Alexander. On the next pitch Lazzeri swung and missed at a low outside curveball off the plate. The inning was over with the Cardinals still leading, 3–2. St. Louis was finished scoring for the day, but Alexander breezed through the bottom of the eighth inning, and in the bottom of the ninth he quickly retired the first two Yankees.

Only Babe Ruth stood in the way of the Cardinals' first World Series championship. The count went to 3-2 on Ruth. Alexander tried another of his low and outside curves, but home plate umpire George Hildebrand called it ball four. Alexander groaned and mildly protested to Hildebrand, who indicated that the pitch missed only by inches. "If it was that close," the pitcher sighed, "I'd think you would have given an old geezer like me the break."[24]

His mild complaint over, Alexander bowed his neck and went back to business. Bob Meusel, the Yankees' cleanup hitter, again had a chance to redeem himself for his damaging error. (As a first-year regular Lou Gehrig was batting not yet fourth but fifth in the lineup.) After Alexander's first pitch to Meusel, Babe Ruth startled everybody by taking off to second base on a delayed steal. Catcher Bob O'Farrell was not fooled, and he fired the ball to Hornsby, who tagged out the sliding slugger to end the Series in an anticlimactic but totally satisfying way for the Cardinals.

When the news of the victory was brought to St. Louis via telegraph tickers and outdoor radio speakers, more than a hundred thousand fans ran into the street to celebrate the victory. The world championship thrilled every segment of St. Louis society, where the big news in October usually centered on the upper crust's "Veiled Prophet" ball. "Flappers and gray-haired men, demure grandmothers and women with babes in arms, college sheiks and men with the marks of human toil upon their clothes all rubbed shoulders," a special correspondent for the *New York Times* reported.[25] A local advertising company boasted that no longer would St. Louis have to serve as the butt of jokes about being first in booze and shoes but last in the league. "Every man, woman and child in St. Louis tingles with a brand-new pride," the ad firm proclaimed.[26]

The *St. Louis Post-Dispatch* gave exultant editorial praise to the pitching hero of the Series, grizzled thirty-nine-year-old "Old Pete" Alexander, who thrilled middle-aged males everywhere. "Gounod was 80 when he wrote the opera 'Faust,' 'Pop' Hindenburg was 65 when he won the battle of Tannenburg, Russell Sage was 45 when he crawled down from a bookkeeper's stool and began his financial career," the editorialist exulted.[27]

Forty-four-year-old Branch Rickey celebrated with his family and his neighbor Gene Mudd's family. "What a corking victory!" he roared. Not only had his team become world champions, but they had whipped both the New York Giants (and other National League foes) and the New York

Yankees in the same year. His largely homegrown team had vindicated his faith in the process of patient farm system development.

Rickey received a rare compliment in the press from Roy Stockton of the *St. Louis Post-Dispatch*, who praised Rickey's farm system idea and its philosophy that "no matter how green a young player might be, there was a place to plant him."[28] New York sportswriter Damon Runyon also tipped his cap to Rickey and Charley Barrett for the success of their "chain store idea" that enabled the Cardinals to develop their own players instead of paying "fancy prices for ball players." Like many followers of baseball, Runyon remembered when the St. Louis franchise was so poor "it had enough trouble paying its laundry bills."[29]

A triumphant parade in downtown St. Louis was followed by many other celebrations. Two days after the game seven triumph, Rickey and Breadon joined other team officials and about two hundred local boosters to pay homage to chief scout Charley Barrett at a St. Louis luncheon. Barrett was notoriously shy about public speaking, and all he did at the function was wave and display his winning smile throughout the festivities. Barrett's reticence was legendary. He once was honored by the St. Louis Catholic Holy Name Society for his contributions in keeping youth involved with baseball instead of turning to delinquency. When the gathering begged him for some words, the scout reluctantly got up and said, "Aw, I can't make no goddam speech," and sat down, never again to be invited to the event.[30]

A few days later Rickey himself was honored by over four hundred of his friends and admirers at a testimonial dinner. He was touched by the outpouring of gratitude from people in many walks of life who knew that his behind-the-scenes organizational work was a major reason for the Cardinals' success. Among those who paid homage to the ferocious gentleman were Robert Hedges, the former Browns owner; James C. Jones, the former chairman of the board of the Cardinals; Herbert S. Hadley, the chancellor of Washington University of St. Louis; and Walter Weisenburger, a St. Louis businessman and future president of the National Association of Manufacturers.[31]

Scarcely a month after the Cardinals were crowned champions of the baseball world, what should have been an off-season of delight and contentment in St. Louis was thrown into crisis. Sam Breadon had not forgiven or forgotten what Rogers Hornsby had told him he could do with his September exhibition game in New Haven. On the train ride back to St. Louis after winning the pennant, Breadon had even asked coach Bill Killefer if he were interested in managing the Cardinals next year, but Killefer refused out of loyalty to his close friend.[32]

Branch Rickey insisted for the rest of his life that if he had the control and power in St. Louis in 1926, he never would have traded Hornsby. Despite the sourness of his personality and his self-absorption, Hornsby was a proven commodity. Still barely thirty years old, he was not yet on the decline, as far as the astute executive was concerned. He had played hurt in 1926 and provided a good example to the rest of the team. With a full year's experience as player-manager under his belt, Rickey envisioned that the future for the Cardinals under Hornsby was secure.

Breadon's mind was made up, however, and in a fortuitous development John McGraw was now ready to include Frank Frisch in a trade for Hornsby. The Giants had missed the World Series two years in a row, and McGraw was dissatisfied with being an also-ran. The Giants' decline certainly could not be blamed on Frisch, who had fulfilled all the promise that McGraw (and Rickey) had seen in him as a rookie in 1919, a player who would never play an inning of Minor League Baseball.

Frisch was a perennial .300 hitter, always among the National League leaders in runs scored, hits, and stolen bases. He almost always put the ball in play, only once striking out more than twenty-five times a year in what would be a nineteen-year career. He had become a fine defensive second baseman, using his great speed and competitiveness to overcome the technical shortcoming of his "bad hands."

Frisch was available in a trade because McGraw was feuding with him. In one midsummer loss to the Cardinals in the 1926 season, McGraw was infuriated when he thought that Frisch had missed coverage on a hit-and-run play and ran to second base instead of keeping his position. Opportunistic Tom Thevenow singled through the vacated second-base hole, and the Cards went on to win. McGraw chewed Frisch out after the game, never a good idea after a defeat, and Frisch bolted the team for a few days.[33] The act of insubordination grated on the frustrated New York manager, who was watching helplessly as the Giants slid to a second division finish for the first time since 1915. Frisch wasn't as persona non grata to McGraw as Hornsby had become to Breadon—Frisch did return to the Giants and complete the 1926 season—but McGraw hated losing and becoming second best in a New York where he had ruled the roost for years.

As we have seen, McGraw and owner Charles Stoneham had long coveted Hornsby, who was now the world champion and had beaten Babe Ruth's Yankees. The Giants brass were unconcerned that Hornsby obviously lacked the charisma and infectious charm of the Bambino. "Even his longest hits seem somehow of no great consequence," writer Heywood Broun noted perceptively. "A Hornsby homer contains less of human fervor than a strikeout by Babe Ruth."[34] Yet the Giants front office still thought his acquisition could take away some of the attention on Ruth and the Yankees. The wheels were thus set in motion for the blockbuster deal.

In early December 1926 baseball's annual meetings convened in New York City. The halls of the Roosevelt Hotel were filled with rumors of the imminent trade, and whenever Breadon was seen huddling with Stoneham, it was assumed that the final nail in Hornsby's Cardinals coffin was being hammered. However, when the St. Louis owner returned to St. Louis, the second baseman was still a Cardinal. St. Louis fans did not believe that the popular player might actually be leaving. To momentarily ease the ruffled emotions of the fans, Breadon announced that he would try to negotiate a contract settlement with Hornsby face to face, as he had done in prior seasons. The second baseman had not received a new contract after he became manager, and he was rumored to be wanting a three-year deal worth $150,000.

Breadon's meeting with Hornsby proved to be a short one. The owner expressed no interest in offering a three-year contract but told him he could have a $50,000, one-year contract, take it or leave it. He also included in the contract offer a provision that would bar the second baseman from betting on horses during the season. He also told him to keep his opinions of Branch Rickey's meddling with the team to himself. In short, Breadon wanted him to leave. The owner later admitted, "I was so determined to get rid of Hornsby that I was afraid he might accept my one-year offer."[35]

The trade was now inevitable, and the final details were worked out on the highest level of ownership between Charles Stoneham and Sam Breadon, with neither John McGraw nor Branch Rickey involved in the final details. Rickey did tell Breadon to obtain a pitcher in addition to Frisch because Hornsby was a more versatile and accomplished offensive player than his counterpart (though two years older). Thirty-one-year-old journeyman right-hander Jimmy Ring was included in the deal, a pitcher with a sub-.500 career record who once had won eighteen games for the Phillies and had pitched for the Reds in the 1919 World Series. However, plagued by wildness throughout his career, Ring would never win a game for St. Louis.

The trade was announced on December 20, 1926, and the reaction in St. Louis made for a most unpleasant Christmas for Sam Breadon. Fans flooded the Cardinals office switchboard with protests. Nasty calls, even death threats, were telephoned to Breadon's home, and black crepe paper was placed over his front door. Angry fans called for a boycott of Breadon's Pierce-Arrow automobile business. Mark Steinberg, Hornsby's stockbroker, resigned from the Cardinals' board of directors. *St. Louis Star* sports editor James M. Gould vowed never to cover another Cardinals game (and didn't for ten years, it was said). The St. Louis Chamber of Commerce passed a resolution asking Commissioner Landis to intercede to block the trade.[36]

Breadon was stunned by the intensity of the protest, but he had made up his mind. The man who, when he got into baseball, said, "Fan ownership is the bunk," wasn't going to back down. His reaction to the chamber of commerce denunciation was to resign from the organization.

Then a serendipitous bit of timing diffused some of the uproar. On the same day as the announcement of the Hornsby-Frisch trade, a story broke about baseball heroes Ty Cobb and Tris Speaker betting on baseball during the 1919 season, the same year as the World Series scandal. Pitcher Hubert "Dutch" Leonard, a teammate of Cobb on the Tigers, made the accusations, claiming he had letters to prove his charges. Commissioner Landis immediately summoned Leonard to a hearing, and the national sportswriters had another huge controversy to write about. Indirectly, the Leonard charges reduced some of the outrage against the Hornsby trade because of the second baseman's penchant for betting on the horses and his acquaintanceship with many gamblers and high-stakes rollers.

The Cobb-Speaker case proved a tempest in a teapot. Landis decided that Leonard had grudges against the two baseball greats and thus revenge was a motive. After his investigation Landis decided that whatever money had exchanged hands in the games in question occurred after the pennant race was decided and was a reward for players whose hits had helped some teams to finish higher in the standings. Cobb and Speaker were cleared to continue in baseball, and Landis, upset that old scandals before his arrival in baseball kept reappearing, moaned, "Won't these God damn things that happened before I came into baseball ever stop coming up?"[37]

Another factor in dissipating some of the local St. Louis outrage against the trade was the naming of popular catcher Bob O'Farrell as player-manager for 1927. O'Farrell's dual role was announced early in the new year of 1927 at a press conference in which Branch Rickey was conspicuously present. Rickey was almost never quoted or written about in the sports pages of 1926, and his appearance was Breadon's way of showing the solidarity of Cardinals management.

Suddenly, more alarm swept through St. Louis baseball circles. Frank Frisch, the newest Cardinal, was reported to be in Saranac Lake in upstate New York, perhaps undergoing treatment for the same dread tuberculosis that had claimed Dots Miller in 1923 and Christy Mathewson in October 1925, and where Branch Rickey himself had recuperated in 1909. Skittish St. Louisans worried that the replacement for Hornsby might be damaged goods before he even played a game for the Cardinals.

Happily, the rumor turned out to be false. Frisch was in upstate New York, but not at Saranac Lake; rather, he was nine miles away in Lake Placid, another town in the Adirondack Mountains, working out with close friends who were Olympic bobsledders and skaters.[38] To make sure that the rumors about Frisch's ill health were false, Branch Rickey invited his new second baseman down to Syracuse, where the executive was making plans for the upcoming season of the Cardinals' International League farm team. Rickey always liked to meet players in the off-season, to get more acquainted with them personally, and if there so happened to be a contract in his briefcase, he just might find the time to get a player's signature.

The St. Louis vice president liked what he saw in meeting his new player. He was impressed that Frisch was working out with Olympic athletes, a promising sign of his commitment to good physical condition. He sensed that the infielder was ready to accept the challenge of replacing a legend like Hornsby and that he would not place undue pressure on himself by trying to imitate the departed star.

As Branch Rickey sized up Frisch at their first meeting, he sensed that his new second baseman would warm to the challenge of a new team and would be primed to show that John McGraw had made a mistake trading him. After a little haggling on terms Frisch soon returned a signed two-year contract to the Cardinals office in St. Louis. Before the end of February 1927, he would arrive in Avon Park, Florida, near Bradenton, for his first spring training as a St. Louis Cardinal. The team would be trying to accomplish the difficult feat of repeating as champions. It was a new challenge for Branch Rickey, but one that he welcomed and relished.

8

—

The Near-dynastic Years and a Place in *Who's Who*

When the Cardinals convened in Avon Park, Florida, for spring training in 1927, all eyes were on Frank Frisch as he tried to fill the formidable shoes of the departed Rogers Hornsby. Branch Rickey was pleased to observe that Frisch fit in easily. His winter workout regimen left him in far better physical shape than most of his teammates, and he seemed relaxed. He was looking forward to playing for rookie manager Bob O'Farrell, who would provide a welcome relief from the constant carping of his former manager John McGraw. Despite the loss of Hornsby, the pundits picked the Cardinals to be in the hunt for a repeat championship, with their main challengers to be the Cubs, Giants, and Pirates.

Sam Breadon, Branch Rickey, and the whole Cardinal organization wanted to put Rogers Hornsby's great contributions to the team behind them and look to the future. However, one major obstacle remained before the Cardinals' deck could be cleared of the temperamental star. He still owned the nearly 1,200 shares of team stock that he had purchased from Rickey after Breadon replaced his petulant associate as manager in 1925. There was no way that the National League would allow a player on one team, the Giants, to own stock in a rival team, the Cardinals. League president John Heydler made the point firmly and was backed by all the league owners.

Not surprisingly, given the bitterness between Breadon and Hornsby, the two men couldn't agree on a price for Hornsby's stock. Hornsby had paid $45 a share in 1925, but given the great profitability of the Cardinals in the World Series year of 1926, he was now demanding $115 per share. Breadon scoffed, telling Hornsby's people that there was no way he was going to receive any more than $85 a share. A long, potentially embarrassing impasse loomed. "I'd rather get into a ring with Dempsey than argue with Hornsby," Breadon moaned.[1]

Outsiders tried to get into the action. Entertainer Al Jolson, a big baseball fan who had befriended Hornsby on the sports and entertainment scene, reportedly made an attempt to buy Hornsby's stock, but the offer was not sufficient.[2] As the opening of the 1927 season neared, Giants management started to talk defiantly. "There is no rule in the league's constitution or by-laws to keep Hornsby from playing with the Giants," a team official said. "Heydler can't invent new rules."[3] The league president insisted, however, that Hornsby must sell his St. Louis stock before he could suit up for New York.

Hornsby was reportedly holding out for a slice of the Cardinals' Houston franchise in the Texas League, which was becoming a lucrative investment. Giants treasurer Leo Bondy tried to mediate, visiting the star player in his hotel before the start of the season. It proved a sobering experience for the team official. "While I was talking, I never was so uncomfortable in my life," Bondy told *New York Sun* sportswriter Frank Graham. "And when I had finished, he said, 'Why don't you mind your own business?'"[4] Finally, on the eve of opening day in mid-April 1927, a compromise was reached. Breadon's seven National League partners chipped in an equal amount to pay for the difference between the price offered by Breadon and the price wanted by Hornsby, which reportedly had been reduced to $105 a share.[5] The season could start without the specter of the player's alleged conflict of interest.

The 1927 season proved a rousing success for the Cardinals in every aspect except winning the pennant. The 1926 attendance record was surpassed by more than 80,000 fans, as 749,340 flocked to Sportsman's Park.[6] Frank Frisch had one of the greatest statistical years of any second baseman in history: a .337 BA, .472 SA, 208 H, 112 R, 31 2B, 11 3B, 10 HR, 78 RBI, and his 48 stolen bases led the National League. His walk-strike-out ratio of 48:10 was excellent. In the field Frisch successfully handled 1,037 chances and shattered the all-time assist record for a second baseman, with 641.[7] Although he committed 22 errors, his .979 fielding percentage led the league.

As always, statistics told only part of the story. Frisch was a dervish on the base paths, challenging outfielders' arms and always looking to take the extra base. He loved to go from first to third on singles to left field, and more than once he scored from second on long sacrifice flies to the outfield.

At first Frisch had not welcomed the trade, having never lived outside of New York City. He was the son of a wealthy, German-born linen importer, who was not very thrilled that Frank chose to make his living in sports. "You send your boys to college, and they play feet ball and baseball," the elder Frisch had grumbled.[8] The disappointed father had at least been able to pass down to his son refined tastes, ranging from opera to gardening to fine cigars, and happily, Frank Frisch found that he could indulge in some of these tastes in his new home city. St. Louis sportswriter Bob Broeg would write memorably about the Cardinals' new star: "He was an intellectual roughneck who knew the difference between Richard Wagner and Honus Wagner, but he was above all a leader."[9]

Rogers Hornsby also did well with his new team. In fact, he statistically outshone Frisch, with a .361 BA, a .586 SA, 26 HR, and 125 RBI, and he led the league with 133 R and 86 BB. With John McGraw ailing at times during the season, Hornsby substituted as manager for thirty-two games and did well, with a 22-10 record. Just before summer Hornsby made his first trip to St. Louis as a member of the Giants. His local fans honored him with a "Rogers Hornsby Day," but Frisch outplayed him in a Cardinals victory. The next day, Sunday, June 18, 1927, provided another festive occasion, when the 1926 championship flag was hoisted up the Sportsman's Park center-field flagpole. Doing the honors was Charles A. Lindbergh, who had just returned from his historic solo flight across the Atlantic to Paris in a plane called *The Spirit of St. Louis*.[10]

At the end of the season the Cardinals finished half a game head of the Giants, both teams winning ninety-two games, but the Pirates won the pennant with a 94-60 record. Twenty-four-year-old Pittsburgh outfielder Paul Waner, a future Hall of Famer, led the league in four categories, with a .380 BA, 237 H, 131 RBI, and 17 3B. In such a close race it is hard to pin down the precise reasons that prevented the Cardinals from repeating as league champions. It wasn't the pitching that let St. Louis down, as Jess Haines won twenty-four games; Grover Cleveland Alexander, twenty-one; and Bill Sherdel, seventeen. Flint Rhem, however, fell off to 10-12, with a 4.41 ERA in only twenty-seven games. Still, the staff as a whole led the league in shutouts and was third in team ERA.

Offensively, though, there was a decline from 1926. Although Jim Bottomley had a big year, with a .303 BA, 19 HR, and 104 RBI, Lester Bell's numbers fell at the other corner of the diamond. The third baseman slumped to .259, 9 HR, and 65 RBI, and outfielders Taylor Douthit and Bill Southworth didn't match their outputs of the previous season. Chick Hafey led the league with a .590 SA, but because of his ongoing sinusitis problem, he was limited to 103 games. Although the team led the league in stolen bases, the 1927 Cardinals scored only 754 runs, 63 fewer than the Pirates and the Giants.

Even more importantly, the Cardinals were weakened at two key positions of the diamond: catcher and shortstop. Because of a sore arm, player-manager Bob O'Farrell was limited to sixty-one games, and neither Frank "Pancho" Snyder nor John Schulte could make up for the loss of the reigning National League MVP. The most crippling loss was shortstop Tom Thevenow, who broke his leg in June in an automobile accident. He played in only fifty-three games, and the team had no adequate replacement for the gifted infielder. Heinie Schuble was found wanting, and veteran Walter "Rabbit" Maranville, one of the heroes of the 1914 "Miracle" Boston Braves world champions, arrived from Rochester too late in the season to have an impact, playing in only nine games.

A future Hall of Famer, Maranville had been demoted to the Minor Leagues in part because of an ongoing battle with alcoholism. Branch Rickey and Charley Barrett loved the baseball smarts of the wispy, colorful native of Springfield, Massachusetts, who at five feet five inches tall was one of the smallest players in baseball. Convinced that the shortstop had his drinking under control, Rickey was glad to welcome the diminutive shortstop back to the Major Leagues, where he would shine for the 1928 Cardinals.[11] ("Never take a backward step on that diamond," Maranville once summed up his baseball philosophy, and a hometown protégé, Leo Durocher, would soon follow his advice.)

It certainly wasn't a consolation for finishing second, but if the Cardinals had managed to win a second straight pennant in 1927, they most likely would have had to play their World Series home games in another city. On September 29, 1927, a vicious tornado swept through St. Louis, killing eighty people, injuring more than five hundred, and causing $10 million in property damage. The pavilion roof at Sportsman's Park was blown off, the center-field flagpole fell onto the field, and many of the seats in the newly expanded upper deck were ripped apart.[12] It would have been very unlikely that repairs could have been made in time for the World Series.

Branch Rickey and the Cardinals were reduced to rooting on the National League as spectators in the 1927 World Series, which found the Yankees in a vengeful mood. Determined to show the nation that their loss to the Cardinals in 1926 was an aberration, they dismissed the Pirates in four straight games, overwhelming and perhaps intimidating their opponents. The 1927 Yankees juggernaut made the Cardinals aware that the Bronx Bombers were going to be formidable rivals for baseball supremacy in the foreseeable future.

Still, Branch Rickey and Sam Breadon could draw great consolation from the experience of 1927. On the Major League level the Cardinals put together superior consecutive years for the first time in their history. Frank Frisch's performance vindicated the Hornsby trade and made Sam Breadon feel forever grateful to the "Fordham Flash." The fans rewarded the owner with a record attendance of nearly 750,000. After the successful replacement of Hornsby by Frisch, Breadon remarked: "I never again was afraid to dispose of a player, regardless of his ability or popularity. I knew after that year that what the fans want is a winner, and that a popular player is quickly forgotten by one who is equally popular."[13]

The Cardinals were now clearly established as the number one team in the hearts and minds of St. Louis fans. The year 1927 was George Sisler's last as a St. Louis Browns first baseman. Many of his statistics were still respectable. He hit .327 with 97 RBI, and his 27 stolen bases led the league. However, his long ball power was gone. He hit only 7 home runs, and his slugging average fell to .430. The Browns had little else, and they finished a poor seventh, thirty-five games under .500. In one of the great ironies of St. Louis baseball history, Phil Ball had double-decked Sportsman's Park in 1926, feeling that the Browns would take advantage of the increased seating, but it was the Cardinals, Ball's tenants, who took advantage of the bigger ballpark. The Browns drew only 247,879, and were to be permanently demoted to second-class status in St. Louis.[14]

Yet, near the midpoint of the 1927 season, Branch Rickey had still not signed the new five-year contract Sam Breadon offered him to continue in his lucrative posts as vice president and business manager. Although Breadon's unexpected firing of Rickey as field manager was more than two years in the past, Rickey still bore resentment over his dismissal. He wondered if one day the owner would do the same thing to him in his current position. The college life continued to appeal to the voracious polymath, who, in the last years of his field managing career, had developed an interest in reading history as a way of putting team losses in perspective.[15] When a feeler came from a Big Ten university (perhaps Northwestern, outside of Chicago) to serve as athletic director, Rickey pondered the possibility.[16]

However, as always, Rickey could not leave the competitive baseball life and his comfortable lifestyle. He signed on for another five years, a contract that would pay him $65,000 annually plus a 10 percent bonus on all Major and Minor League transactions. In 1928, the first year of his new contract, Rickey reportedly took home $95,000.[17] As a fervent believer in the American system of capitalist individualism, he felt that he deserved his "emolument" because both the parent Cardinals and the Minor League farm clubs—the "subsidiaries," as he liked to call them— were all operating successfully.[18]

On the Minor League level the Cardinals directly owned eight farm teams and had working agreements with more than a dozen others. Most were either pennant winners or first-division contenders. To keep the talent flow coming, Rickey was pleased that Sam Breadon had given his approval to start in the summer of 1928 a second amateur tryout camp in Shawnee, Oklahoma. It would be at Shawnee, two years later, that the farm system founder would have his memorable first encounter with a brash, teenaged pitcher who had taken a leave from the Army to attend. Slated to throw only an inning, the cocky youngster from the Ozark Mountains of Arkansas struck out the side on nine pitches. Rickey gave the signal for the youngster to throw another inning, and once again no batter came close to a hit. A contract was immediately offered to the youngster with only a third-grade education who, to escape the cotton fields, had joined the Army under legal age. His name was Jay Hanna Dean, but soon he would be almost universally known as Dizzy Dean.

Dean started his rise to the Majors at the St. Louis farm club in St. Joseph, Missouri, where his roommate was Forrest Twogood, a left-handed pitcher from the University of Iowa, the same school that produced Cardinals infielder Roscoe "Wattie" Holm. Twogood, who also played varsity basketball and football, sometimes served as Rickey's chauffeur, since the executive always preferred others to do the driving. "He talked baseball and talked sense," remembered the versatile athlete, who went on to become the basketball coach at the University of Southern California. "He said baseball was a game of penalties and inches."[19] (Working in the shadow of UCLA's legendary John Wooden, Twogood had thirteen winning seasons in sixteen years at USC, and a Final Four appearance in 1954.)

With the security of his new five-year contract, Branch Rickey was able to add more trusted and able people to his staff. He had already brought on board his brother Frank Rickey as a scout. William DeWitt had advanced from personal to administrative secretary. After, at Rickey's insistence, earning his law degree through night school work, he would become the team treasurer in 1935. DeWitt's work ethic matched his mentor's. One story in Cardinals lore describes an occasion when the two men, to save precious time, had a hole drilled in the walls between bathroom stalls in the team offices to enable them to continue working while nature called.

Rickey often hired individuals who were not just talented and devoted but also needed a break. When a friend was in need, it was not Rickey's style to say, "Let me know if I can help you." Rather, his proactive and paternal way of operating was to tell the person, "I need you. Can you come today, or tomorrow at the latest?" For example, Blake Harper had operated the Cardinals' first farm team in Fort Smith, Arkansas, but when the franchise was sold to new owners, Rickey brought Harper to St. Louis to become the director of concessions at Sportsman's Park.[20] Later, when the Great Depression caused the failure of a Florida bank managed by his Delta Tau Delta fraternity brother Donald Beach, Rickey hired him as the auditor of the Cardinals' American Association franchise in Columbus, Ohio.[21] When business losses in Florida set back Phil Bartelme, Rickey brought him into St. Louis as an office administrator. In 1936, when Sacramento became a Cardinals franchise in the Pacific

Coast League, Rickey selected Bartelme, who had hired him at Michigan and served briefly as president of the Cardinals' Syracuse affiliate, to lead the new team.[22]

The only discordant note in Branch Rickey's baseball life in St. Louis remained his testy relationship with many sportswriters. At a local sportswriters dinner, probably late in 1927, a disturbance broke out. He had not been initially invited to the dinner because bootleg booze would be flowing and most of the writers thought the "blue nose" would not approve. Wanting to show management solidarity, however, Sam Breadon had insisted that Rickey be invited.

On his way to another holiday party, the combative executive arrived in a tuxedo only to be soon confronted by Ed Wray, a *St. Louis Post-Dispatch* sports columnist, who was also tuxedo-clad. Usually a polite and dignified man, Wray had imbibed a goodly share of the evening's illicit libations and he took issue with Rickey's telling reporters at times, "I never lie." "What about the time you put Bill Doak on waivers and said that you didn't?" Wray demanded, referring to the veteran Cardinals pitcher who, in 1924, had been traded to Brooklyn. Rickey always believed that waivers were purely a management prerogative, and it was none of the business of the sportswriters until actual transactions were made. He denied, though, that he lied about the Doak situation. Wray was in no mood or condition to let the matter drop and continued to insist that Rickey did lie. Leveling such a damnable accusation at Branch Rickey was like waving a red flag in front of a bull. Before long the executive and the writer were shouting at each other, taking their tuxedo jackets off and preparing to settle their dispute by physical means. Other writers joined the fray, including one of Rickey's stronger supporters in St. Louis, Sid Keener of the *St. Louis Times*. Ultimately, cooler heads prevailed, but reportedly it was the last St. Louis sportswriters' dinner held for twenty years.[23]

The year 1928 proved to be another successful National League season for the Cardinals. A record number of 761,574 fans flocked to Sportsman's Park, establishing a mark that would stand until 1946.[24] The team was being led by its fourth manager in three years because, after the 1927 season, Bill McKechnie had been selected by Sam Breadon to replace player-manager Bob O'Farrell. The owner felt that O'Farrell had not been the kind of leader he expected in 1927, even though the Cardinals won three more games than the 1926 world champions and stayed in the pennant race until the last weekend of the season. McKechnie had served as O'Farrell's coach in 1927, so he knew the personnel. He also had a good managerial pedigree, having piloted the Pittsburgh Pirates to victory over the Washington Senators in the 1925 World Series.

As usual, the hiring and firing of Major League managers was Sam Breadon's prerogative, with minimal input from Branch Rickey. Although Rickey did not believe in change for change's sake, especially when dealing with the psychology of a baseball club that required the delicate balancing of many different temperaments, he did agree with Breadon that Bill McKechnie was a fine manager and, happily, also an exemplary religious person. The son of devout Scottish Presbyterian immigrants, McKechnie had been raised in the Pittsburgh suburb of Wilkinsburg and sang in the choir of his local church.[25] Inevitably, the sportswriters bestowed upon McKechnie the nickname of "Deacon."

McKechnie's 1928 Cardinals displayed an admirable balance of pitching and hitting. Veteran hurlers Jess Haines and Bill Sherdel were both twenty-game winners, Grover Cleveland Alexander had enough left in his forty-one-year-old right arm to contribute sixteen victories, and Flint Rhem pitched in with eleven. Offensively, Jim Bottomley had a career year, leading the league with 31 HR and 136 RBI to go with a .325 BA, numbers that helped earn him the league MVP Award. Although Frank Frisch's batting average fell 37 points to .300, his 10 HR matched his 1927 total, and his 88 RBI were 10 more than in 1927. Defensively, even though he didn't come close to matching his all-time record of 647 assists in 1927, he once again led the league in fielding average. Frisch's excellent play continued to make Cardinals fans nearly forget about his predecessor, the legendary Rogers Hornsby.

At shortstop, with Tom Thevenow not yet recovered from his broken ankle, Rabbit Maranville performed capably in more than a hundred games. At third base Andy High, another product of the St. Louis sandlots brought to Branch Rickey's attention by Charley Barrett, performed creditably. High was obtained from the Braves in a trade for Lester Bell, who never lived up to his Hornsby-like promise of 1926. Farm system graduate Wattie Holm also contributed at the so-called hot corner, where quick reactions to hard-hit balls were a prerequisite. (The versatile Holm had played center field in the last three games of the 1926 World Series because of an injury to Taylor Douthit.)

The 1928 outfield was sparked by two farm system products, center fielder Taylor Douthit and left fielder Chick Hafey. Douthit lived up to his nickname of "Flyhawk" by establishing a Major League record for put-outs.[26] He played in every game, scored 111 runs, and hit .295. Chick Hafey put together the second of his five great years in a row, with a .337 BA, a .604 SA, 27 HR, 111 RBI, and 101 R. Right field was shared by Wally Roettger and George Harper. Roettger, another player found on the St. Louis sandlots by Charley Barrett, was a very productive platoon player in 1928, with a .337 BA and 44 RBI in 261 at-bats. Barrett also recommended Wally Roettger's older brother, Oscar, who was not as talented as Wally and who played only parts of four years in the Majors. (After Oscar Roettger retired Branch Rickey hired him as a uniform maker for the Cardinals; a third brother, Harold, later became a key front office administrator for Rickey in Brooklyn and Pittsburgh.)[27]

Also bolstering right field for the 1928 Cardinals was thirty-six-year-old outfielder George Harper, who was obtained from the Giants for catcher Bob O'Farrell shortly before the June 15 trading deadline. The Cardinals had hoped that O'Farrell would have a big year now that he was relieved of his managing duties, but he hit only .200 for St. Louis before the trade. Harper went on to hit .305 with 17 HR and 58 RBI in his three and a half months as a Cardinal. Just as Billy Southworth had done two years earlier, Harper had a big game against his old team in late September 1928, hitting three home runs at the Polo Grounds just prior to their clinching the pennant. Like the 1926 champions, the Cardinals won the title on the road. Two fifteen-inning victories, one of them a complete game by Bill Sherdel, contributed mightily.[28]

The 1928 Cardinals won ninety-five games, nosing out the Giants by two games and the Cubs by four. They showed great closing speed, a trademark of Rickey-organized teams, winning thirty-one of their last forty-five games. The Cardinals entered the World Series as the favorite to beat the Yankees for the second time in three years, primarily because of disabling injuries to southpaw Herb Pennock, who had won two games against the Cardinals in 1926, and to center fielder Earle Combs.

However, Babe Ruth, Lou Gehrig, and other New Yorkers in the Murderers Row hadn't forgotten their narrow 1926 loss. They exacted total revenge by sweeping the Cardinals in four games, duplicating their rout of the Pirates in 1927. As in 1926 Yankee right-hander Waite Hoyt beat Cardinal southpaw Bill Sherdel in game one, 4–1, at Yankee Stadium. The Yankees exacted sweet revenge on Grover Cleveland Alexander in game two, routing him with eight runs in the first three innings on their way to a 9-3 win behind George Pipgras.

When the Series traveled to St. Louis, it was more of the same as the Yankees routed Jess Haines and won 7–3 behind Tom Zachary. They won the championship the next day by the same score, 7–3, with Waite Hoyt yet again outpitching Bill Sherdel. Game four was closer than the final score might indicate, as the Cardinals led, 2–1, in the top of the seventh inning. With two out and two on, Babe Ruth was up and Sherdel had the count in his favor at 0-2. With the slugger seemingly distracted, chatting with home plate umpire Cy Pfirman, the crafty southpaw tried to quick pitch the Bambino. But the arbiter disallowed it, and despite a vociferous argument put up by beleaguered manager Bill McKechnie, Pfirman ordered Sherdel to throw another pitch to Ruth. Like all great players Ruth took advantage of the second chance and blasted the next pitch far out of Sportsman's Park for his second home run of the day. To add icing to the victory, Ruth hit a third home run in the ninth inning.

All four Yankee victories were complete-game wins for the starting pitcher, and Babe Ruth and Lou Gehrig lived up to their reputations by blasting three and four home runs, respectively. In all, Gehrig was 6 for 11, and Ruth an extraordinary 10 for 16, in the four-game sweep. A sidebar to the 1928 Series was the appearance of rookie Leo Durocher as a defensive replacement late in the games for ailing second baseman Tony Lazzeri. Already known as "Leo the Lip" for his brassy, cocky attitude, Durocher sassed the St. Louis players and local fans with glee as the Yankees rolled on to victory. "The pesky flea of a rookie infielder . . . rode the opposition unmercifully," baseball writer Frederick Lieb wrote about the smooth-fielding youngster from the wrong side of the tracks in Springfield, Massachusetts, who was destined within five years to have a major role in the Branch Rickey story.[29]

The Yankees were undoubtedly the better team in 1928, but an odd piece of strategy irked St. Louis fans and owner Sam Breadon. Unlike Rogers Hornsby in 1926, who had his pitchers tread carefully with Ruth and walk him twelve times, Bill McKechnie inexplicably elected to have his pitchers confront the Bambino, walking him only once. Lou Gehrig, batting after Ruth, was an emerging threat too, but the Cardinals paid the price with Ruth's massive success. Breadon was so livid after the Series that he ordered a flip-flop of managers for 1929. McKechnie was assigned to Rochester, which had just replaced Syracuse as the Cardinals' top affiliate in the International League. Billy Southworth, who had managed the farm club in upstate New York to a 1928 pennant in his first year as skipper, became the new St. Louis manager.

As always, Branch Rickey had no input into Breadon's managerial merry-go-round, but he was at least glad that McKechnie had a position for the next year, even if only in the Minor Leagues. Such peremptory treatment by a boss after winning a pennant was hardly the way Branch Rickey would operate, but it was not his decision. Rickey himself was not pleased with the Cardinals' performance in the World Series, yet he knew when to tip his cap to the opponents.

Except for the World Series disappointment, Branch Rickey counted his blessings in 1928. Not only had his baseball organization brought home many laurels, he also received his share of personal recognition. Throughout 1928 he served as president of the St. Louis branch of the Optimists Club. He certainly was an ideal spokesperson for an organization whose tenets included "to talk health, happiness and prosperity to every person you meet" and "to think only of the best, to work only for the best, and expect only the best."[30]

In June 1928 McKendree College in Lebanon, Illinois, awarded Rickey an honorary degree. Originally called Lebanon Seminary, McKendree was founded in 1828, making it the oldest college in the state of Illinois. Its name had been changed late in the nineteenth century to honor William McKendree, the first American-born bishop of the Methodist Church. Because of his own deep, lineal connection to the Methodist Church, Rickey was very moved by the honor.[31]

Politically, 1928 brought another satisfying triumph for staunch Republican Branch Rickey. In November Herbert Clark Hoover was elected to the presidency of the United States. He won in a landslide victory over the Democratic candidate, New York State governor Alfred E. Smith, the first Catholic ever to vie for the White House. Continuing the Republican control of the White House that began with Warren Harding in 1921, Herbert Hoover possessed, in Branch Rickey's opinion, the finest attributes of an American leader, a man who combined belief in capitalist enterprise with a genuine sense of social service.

One criticism of Hoover was that he wasn't a charismatic figure or a good speaker, but for Rickey, his words perfectly articulated the American ideal. "As a result of our distinctly American system our country has become the land of opportunity to those born without inheritance, not merely because of the wealth of its resources and industry, but because of this freedom of initiative and enterprise," Hoover declared in one of his last speeches before he won the presidency. "Business progressiveness is dependent on competition," Hoover continued. "New methods and new ideas are the outgrowth of a spirit of adventure of individual initiative and individual enterprise." Rickey positively glowed when Hoover used a baseball metaphor at the end of his speech. The candidate declared that the role of government in our system should be "as an umpire instead of a player in the economic game."[32]

Hoover's resume was outstanding, Rickey thought: internationally acclaimed mining engineer; President Woodrow Wilson's European relief administrator after World War I; most recently, secretary of commerce under President Calvin Coolidge; and, in 1927, administrator of the program that brought relief to hundreds of thousands of victims of the Mississippi River flood.[33] Although Rickey would not come to know Hoover personally until after he left the presidency, he was already inspired by the trajectory and achievement in Hoover's life and work.

Born in Iowa in 1874, Hoover—like Rickey—was a product of the rural Midwest. The future president's boyhood was shortened when he was orphaned at age ten and moved in with relatives in Oregon. A man of great intellect, if stolid demeanor, he attended Stanford University in Palo Alto, California, where in addition to developing his outstanding skills as a mining engineer he was treasurer of the campus football team.[34] Late in his life Hoover, who died in 1964, wrote a book, *On Growing Up*, about his early years in Iowa. "I grew up on sand-lot baseball, swimming holes, and fishing with worms," he recalled. In one chapter, "Advice to an Eighth Grader," Hoover drew up a list that Branch Rickey couldn't have improved on. "1. Work hard in school hours to get some indestructible things stored in your head. 2. Play every chance you get— including fishing. 3. Keep the rules of sport."[35]

As Branch Rickey enjoyed the Christmas season in 1928, he had a lot to celebrate and to look forward to. Professionally, his Cardinals were a thriving, almost envied organization; politically, his hero Herbert Hoover was about to take the reins of the country; and domestically, the Rickey family was heading for a new adventure in a new home. For years Branch and Jane Rickey had felt their twelve-room, three-story house in St. Louis was inadequate for the needs and desires of six children; Jane's mother and sister; a maid, Clara; and a cook, Aldine, whom master salesman Branch Rickey had retained with the promise of a bonus if she stayed for ten years.[36] The Rickeys yearned for a place in the country where everyone could have more room and live closer to nature.

After scouring the real estate pages in the newspapers and asking for tips from their friends, Branch and Jane Rickey fell in love with a twenty-three-acre property in the St. Louis County township of Clayton. Located over fifteen miles from Sportsman's Park, their prospective new home was part of a new development called Country Life Acres, and the attractions were many. The main house was a big Tudor-style mansion, with a smaller cottage nearby. The buildings were surrounded by cherry and apple orchards, a grape arbor, and ample fertile soil for Jane to create a copious vegetable garden. A small lake with an island reachable by a small bridge would allow the children to explore and indulge their sense of fantasy and adventure. For the grown-up child, the ferocious gentleman Branch Rickey, nearby wild turkeys and pheasants afforded many opportunities to pursue his treasured hobby of hunting small game.[37]

Enraptured by the possibilities of the new place, Branch and Jane Rickey made plans to move the family early in the summer of 1929. The Rickey offspring could hardly wait. All six children were taking on distinctive personalities. Mary, the oldest, who turned sixteen on February 3, 1929, looked very much like her mother and seemed to have inherited both Jane's prettiness and playfulness. Branch Jr., whom everybody called "Boy" because none of the girls could pronounce the name Branch easily, was a bright, boisterous, and adventurous young man. Born on January 31, 1914, the same day, incidentally, on which Jackie Robinson was born in 1919, Branch Jr. was becoming an adept wrestler, like his grandfather Jacob Frank Rickey. The younger Rickey would make the varsity at Ohio Wesleyan, as would his own son, Branch Barrett Rickey, thirty years later.

Jane Elizabeth Ainsworth Rickey, born on August 6, 1916, was a budding young artist, who was particularly enamored of her father's life in athletics. She remembers once accompanying him to an Ohio State-Michigan football game, and he got so excited after a "corking" good first half that, forgetting that she was still on his arm, he stormed into the Michigan locker room at halftime. "I saw some huge arms and legs in there before I was escorted out," Jane Rickey Jones recalls.[38]

The fourth Rickey child, Alice Mabel, who turned eleven on July 31, 1929, was the most precocious, having started school at age four. The family joke was that the real reason for her early matriculation was that it was the only way to bring a little peace and quiet to the household. The move to the country would also enable the younger girls, seven-year-old Sue and five-year-old Betty, to have their own rooms and their own space to explore and grow into.

There would be more room, too, for Branch Rickey's mother-in-law and sister-in-law. Jane's loyal sister, Mabel Moulton, a petite woman with a size two and a half foot, never married and was not talkative, but she was an excellent interior decorator and gladly took care of most of the baby-sitting activities.[39] Jane's mother, the widowed Mary Moulton, was a formidable, strong-minded presence in the family hearth. Her family, originally from Vermont, settled in southern Ohio in the first part of the nineteenth century. She had memories of families leaving in covered wagons, heading west in search of California gold, but she was content in moving no farther west than Missouri. She would live to be ninety-nine, a "mulier fortis" (a strong woman") as Branch Rickey described her, a very proper matriarch, an excellent seamstress, and bred in the proprieties of Victorian America.[40]

Like her daughter Jane, Mary Moulton understood how important baseball was to Branch Rickey as both a cause and a means to provide a good life for the family. Her satisfaction with him as a provider deeply pleased the paterfamilias, even if she didn't understand baseball. One day in the prime of Rogers Hornsby, Branch Rickey coaxed her to the ballpark to see the Cardinals. It turned out that Hornsby won the game with a bottom-of-the-ninth, grand slam home run, causing wild jubilation in the stands. When asked that evening what she thought about her experience, Mary Moulton replied, "The game was all right, but the place was full of crazy people."[41] A serious but not solemn woman, Mary Moulton knew how to twit her son-in-law and keep him from taking himself too seriously. Many nights at the dinner table, Branch's daughter Jane Rickey Jones recalls, her grandmother would start the conversation with a tart salvo, "Well, Branch, who did you get angry with today?"[42]

As excited and satisfied as Branch Rickey was about developments in his family life in 1929, his year in baseball was a major disappointment. Nothing seemed to go right, from the first days of spring training in Bradenton, Florida, until the Cardinals limped home at the end of the season with a 78-74 record, in fourth place, a distant twenty games behind the pennant-winning Chicago Cubs.

New manager Billy Southworth was earnest and pennant-minded, but he got off on the wrong foot by sending a letter to the players suggesting that they don't drive separately to spring training in Florida but instead travel together as a team. Rickey always liked the idea of forging team camaraderie early on, but the new manager had forgotten that ballplayers cherished their freedom of movement in the off-season. He failed to realize that during the long months of a baseball season, the players spend more time with one another than with their own families. Most of them wanted to report to Florida in their own way and were not going to be dissuaded by a thirty-five-year-old rookie manager.[43]

Another factor in the disappointing season for the Cardinals was that age was creeping up on the team, especially for the pitching staff. Grover Cleveland Alexander began the 1929 season needing 9 victories to surpass Christy Mathewson's 372 as the winningest pitcher in National League history. (Cy Young's 511 wins, compiled in both leagues, and Walter Johnson's 414 victories, all in the uniform of the Washington Senators of the American League, were the unreachable top two.) Breaking individual records was not as big a headline-grabbing story as it would be decades later in Major League Baseball, but the record was one that Alexander, Breadon, Rickey, and the Cardinals fans wanted broken.

The ancient hurler did reach 373 in 1929, winning nine games and losing eight with a respectable but hardly Alexandrian ERA of 3.89. But, as with rookie manager Joe McCarthy in Chicago in 1926, Alexander chafed under the rule of rookie skipper Southworth. The pitcher's drinking binges continued, and in midseason Sam Breadon sent him home to Nebraska. (After the 1929 season the Phillies re-obtained Alexander for two journeymen, but the ill-fated right-hander would never win another game in the Major Leagues; when Mathewson was awarded another victory in 1944, Alexander had to share the record.)

(Branch Rickey was saddened by Alexander's demise. His compassionate Christian heart empathized with a pitcher who had a serious drinking problem, compounded by epilepsy and the shellshock he had suffered during World War One. "He was a kindly, well-intentioned individual," Rickey wrote of Alexander in *The American Diamond.* "He deserved the sympathy and understanding of players, managers, owners, writers, and the public generally, for he so sincerely wanted to quit drinking." Rickey embellished the point with a moving memory of Alexander "walking about restlessly in my room in the Auditorium Hotel in Chicago in 1927, grasping an imaginary bottle against his chest." Alexander told Rickey: "When I take a drink, it just seems I can't let it go. I keep on and take it all." Rickey noted that a few days later, Alexander took the second of two Narcosan treatments, hoping to end his addiction. Rickey sadly concluded, "I never knew him to have an enemy—only one, himself.")[44]

The other graybeards on the 1929 Cardinals staff, Jess Haines and Bill Sherdel, completed the season with thirteen and ten wins, respectively, but their earned run averages ballooned to well over five runs a game. Jim Bottomley and Chick Hafey had big years offensively, and Frank Frisch had another consistent year at the plate—.336 BA, 5 HR, and 74 RBI—and sparkled again in the field. Frisch teamed well with the new shortstop, twenty-three-year-old Charley Gelbert, who had the kind of background and heritage that Rickey thought exemplary for a future Major Leaguer.

Gelbert had starred in football and baseball at Lafayette College in Easton, Pennsylvania, and was named to one of the last of Walter Camp's

All-American teams. The shortstop came highly recommended by Charles "Pop" Kelchner, the scout who earlier had sent Cliff Heathcote to the Cardinals. A native of the coal mining area of Scranton, Pennsylvania, Gelbert's father, Charles Saladin Gelbert, had been an All-American football end at the University of Pennsylvania in the 1890s.[45] Young Gelbert showed great promise in the field, leading the National League in assists in 1929. He also led in errors, but undoubtedly many were the "errors of enthusiasm" Branch Rickey always forgave in the name of adventure. His offense was promising as he hit .262 with a .367 SA, and he had a positive walk-strikeout ratio of 51:46. The new catcher was Jimmy Wilson, obtained in a trade with the Phillies. He led all National League catchers in assists and put-outs while hitting a solid .325 with 4 HR and 71 RBI.

Yet the team never jelled under the intense new manager. Southworth's final gaffe in his first season at the helm was to raid the hotel rooms of his players during an East Coast road trip, mistakenly thinking that he would break up a big party. Instead, Southworth discovered that most of his men were sleeping.[46] Late in July Sam Breadon, always quick with the managerial trigger finger, decided that Southworth was too inexperienced to lead a Major League team. He ordered a reversal of his impetuous post-1928 World Series decision, summoning Bill McKechnie back from Rochester and shipping Southworth back to the Minor League team. The move did not make much difference, as the team under McKechnie went only 34-29 and was consigned to fourth place.

The Cubs won the 1929 pennant with Rogers Hornsby, who was playing for his fourth team in four years, winning the MVP with another stellar offensive year. He led the league with a .679 SA and 154 R and also compiled a .380 BA, 39 HR, and 149 RBI. His teammate slugging outfielder Hack Wilson hit .345 and tied Hornsby for the team lead, with 39 homers. Wilson, nicknamed "Hack" because his five foot five, two-hundred-pound physique reminded a sportswriter of the wrestler George Hackenschmidt, was another hard-drinking ballplayer, who had worn out his welcome in an earlier stint with John McGraw's Giants. (In 1930 Wilson would set a National League home run record of 56, and his 190 RBI is a record that still stands in the early twenty-first century.)

During the 1929 World Series Branch Rickey was again forced into the role of spectator as he rooted for the National League Cubs against the American League champions, Connie Mack's Athletics. However, Philadelphia prevailed, beating Chicago in five games, limiting Rogers Hornsby to 5 hits in 21 at-bats, with only 1 RBI. At the end of 1929 venerable Connie Mack, born three years before the American Civil War ended, was voted the highest honor in his city, the Edward Bok Prize. Named after the editor of *Ladies Home Journal*, the prize was awarded to the person who contributed the most in 1929 to the wider Philadelphia community.[47] Although disappointed at their loss, the Cubs could take solace in setting a single-season Major League attendance record of 1,485,166.[48]

Shortly after the World Series ended, Sam Breadon responded to the Cardinals' disappointing season by naming yet another manager, coach Charles "Gabby" Street, who had led the team to one victory in 1929 while it awaited the return of Bill McKechnie from Rochester. The forty-seven-year old Street was a thirty-year veteran of professional baseball, 80 percent of which he had spent in the Minor Leagues. A journeyman catcher who hit .208 in fewer than one thousand at-bats in an eight-year Major League career, Street's major claim to fame was that he was the regular battery mate of the Washington Senators legendary pitcher Walter Johnson and once tried to catch a baseball that the future Hall of Famer threw down from the Washington Monument.

Street was also nicknamed "Old Sarge" because he saw military action in the Argonne forest of France late in World War I. Branch Rickey considered Street's war service an obvious plus on his resume, but once again the switching of managers was Sam Breadon's decision, with limited input from his chief business associate. Rickey may have preferred to retain McKechnie, but he was happy that the deacon from Pittsburgh was offered the security of a five-year contract to manage the Boston Braves.[49]

As the Cardinals convened in late February 1930 for the beginning of spring training near Bradenton at Avon Park, Florida, the baseball pundits did not foresee that the team would rebound from their disappointing 1929 season. The consensus was that St. Louis would at best bring up the rear of the first division of the eight-team National League.

There were also danger signs on the economic horizon. The stock market had crashed resoundingly scarcely two weeks after the end of the 1929 World Series. Major baseball figures John McGraw and Connie Mack suffered financial losses from which they would never recover; Branch Rickey took a beating in some of his portfolio, especially in his wholly owned stock in Air Reduction, a company that specialized in making oxygen for use in industrial and medical businesses.[50] He kept his losses to himself, for there was no way that he was not going to keep his family from enjoying their new life in the beautiful countryside. He remained confident that the latest economic downturn would be like others in the past, simply a passing disturbance in an otherwise sound and solid American capitalist system.

Only the clairvoyant could have predicted the lasting calamity of the Great Depression. The history of American capitalism had been one of boom and bust cycles, and recovery had always seemed to happen. As he arrived at spring training Branch Rickey was still very much sold on the future of the country. When shortly before the start of the 1930 baseball season, President Hoover said, "We have now passed the worst," Rickey agreed with the president's assessment.[51]

As he always was at the dawn of spring training, the Cardinals' mastermind was excited about the coming season of 1930. He thought that the National League pennant race would be, as usual, a dogfight among the perennial contenders. The Giants would be tough with three future Hall of Famers: first baseman Bill Terry, right fielder Mel Ott, and left-handed pitcher Carl Hubbell, master of the screwball, a pitch Rickey called "the reverse curve." The Cubs still had Hornsby and Hack Wilson and another future Hall of Famer, spunky catcher Gabby Hartnett. When Hartnett was photographed with bootleg liquor king Al Capone at Wrigley Field after the mobster got out of prison, Commissioner Landis was livid. "I go to his place of business," Hartnett replied. "Why shouldn't he come to mine?"[52]

The Pirates and the Dodgers also could not be discounted as contenders, but Rickey was confident that the Cardinals would conquer them all. He liked his solid infield of Jim Bottomley, Frank Frisch, Charley Gelbert, and Andy High. The slugger Chick Hafey and Taylor Douthit were still in their prime in the outfield, and Rickey was pleased at the way catcher Jim Wilson handled his pitchers. It remained to be seen if new manager Gabby Street could instill the will to win in the fine individual components of the squad and make it into an indomitable team. Rickey had cautious hopes that if the team stayed close into the summer, it might have the finishing kick that propelled all successful pennant winners.

The 1930 National League pennant race was very competitive, but the Cardinals could not seem to develop any winning momentum. As late as August 10 they lagged in fourth place, just two games over .500, and eleven games behind the league-leading Dodgers. Then, as Branch Rickey always wished his teams would do, they went into overdrive. They went 23-9 in August, and a remarkable 17-1 in September, finishing at 92-62 and nosing the Cubs out by two games, the Giants by five, and the collapsed Dodgers by six games.[53]

A dramatic mid-September doubleheader sweep in Brooklyn catapulted the Cardinals into first place to stay, but the triumph did not occur without some off-the-field drama. Flint Rhem was the scheduled starter for the first game, but he was nowhere to be found. Rhem, a budding alcoholic who, alas, had become one of Grover Cleveland Alexander's off-hours buddies, had gone off on one of his binges and would turn up two days later, claiming he had been kidnapped, drugged, and driven off to New Jersey.[54]

Southpaw "Wild" Bill Hallahan, who would lead the National League in both walks and strikeouts in 1930 and 1931, was named by manager Street to start in Rhem's place, but the night before the start of the crucial series, the pitcher caught his right hand in a taxicab door. Two of his fingers were seriously bruised, but he sucked it up—and paid the price, as Rickey would say. Hallahan won one of the most dramatic pennant race games in baseball history, a 1–0, ten-inning victory over Dazzy Vance, a future Hall of Fame right-hander.

Vance carried a no-hitter into the seventh inning, and Hallahan allowed no hits until the eighth inning. In the top of the tenth inning, pinch hitter Andy High drove in the only run of the game. In the second game of the doubleheader, the Cardinals showed championship mettle by coming from behind and scoring five runs in the last two innings to win, 5–3. They remained in first place for the rest of the season, clinching their third pennant in five years in front of a packed Sportsman's Park house on the last Friday of the regular season.

As always in a baseball season, varied factors explained the Cardinals' triumph. The year 1930 featured the liveliest ball in National League history, a response to Babe Ruth's home run heroics in the American League. The Cardinals as a team batted .314 in 1930, but they were only third in the league, behind the Pirates and the Cubs. The entire infield batted over .300, with Frisch and Bottomley having their consistently solid years and second-year man Charley Gelbert coming into his own at age twenty-four with a .304 BA, 11 HR, 71 RBI, and 92 R. Earl "Sparky" Adams played the most games at third base, with Andy High and Jake Flowers in reserve roles.

At five feet four inches tall, Adams was the smallest man in the Major Leagues, but he made up for his lack of power at a traditional power position by leading the league in fielding average. Rickey felt gratified by Adams's emergence because he had been signed by the Cardinals in the early 1920s, another Charlie Barrett discovery, and overcame by effort and moxie the handicaps of his short stature. In fact, when Rickey first glimpsed Adams at a spring training camp, the executive thought he was the bat boy.[55]

The 1930 Cardinals were also aided by outfielder George Watkins, who would set a Major League rookie record by hitting .373. Having toiled for several seasons in the St. Louis Minor League system, the thirty-year-old Watkins was old for a rookie, but he made up for lost time by belting 17 HR with 87 RBI and 85 R. He was occasionally subbed for by Ray Blades, who, near the end of his career, still hit .401 in only 101 at-bats. Nagged by chronic sinus problems, Chick Hafey was limited to 446 at-bats but made the most of them, with a .336 BA, 26 HR, and 107 RBI. Taylor Douthit led the league in put-outs in center field and contributed offensively with a .303 BA, 7 HR, and 93 RBI.

Starting catcher Jim Wilson was on his way to another solid season until he was injured. Backup catcher Gus Mancuso filled the void admirably by hitting .366 and playing well defensively. Rickey made no public comment about the irony of Mancuso's good performance because the catcher was only on the roster at the insistence of Commissioner Landis, who had voided Mancuso's option to Rochester before the start of the season. The commissioner ruled that Mancuso had been farmed out one time too many. Rickey bristled at the decision, claiming it was an "edict" and not justified by the rules, but he had no choice but to keep the receiver on the roster.[56] He had to be glad, though, that manager Street could use the catcher effectively.

Bill Hallahan led the pitching staff with fifteen victories, many of them big games like the key game in Brooklyn in September. Although Branch Rickey was not pleased at Hallahan's wildness, he admired the southpaw's competitive stubbornness on the mound. He obviously did not give in to the hitters, and he displayed the kind of confident spirit that Branch Rickey considered a priceless asset.

Although Flint Rhem's time to shine would soon be over, he won twelve games but pitched only 140 innings. Right-hander Sylvester "Syl" Johnson, another Californian recommended to Rickey by scout-professor Charles C. Chapman, also won twelve games.[57] After pitching for the Detroit Tigers in the early 1920s, Johnson languished in the Minors until Charley Barrett spotted him one season, toiling along with a 3-17 record. The clever scout saw something salvageable in the man with horrible won-lost statistics, and before long he was helping the Cardinals to win a pennant.[58] Thirty-seven-year-old knuckleballer Jess Haines won thirteen games and, in a sentimental touch, was the winning pitcher in the pennant-clinching game in St. Louis against the Pirates on the last Friday of the regular season.

Perhaps the greatest addition to the pitching staff came just before the June 15 trading deadline when spitballer Burleigh Grimes, a future Hall of Famer, was obtained from the Pirates in a trade for veteran Cardinals hurlers Bill Sherdel and Fred Frankhouse. Grimes was the last of the "grandfathered" spitball pitchers, hurlers allowed to throw the pitch after it was ruled illegal in the early 1920s. He was another of the grizzled veteran pitchers, like Jess Haines and the retired Fred Toney, that Branch Rickey loved and felt that every pennant winner needed.

When the Cardinals struggled in the first part of the season, St. Louis fans stayed away, keeping with the city's pattern of mediocre attendance for mediocre performance but packed houses for championship-caliber teams. During the great pennant push in September, fans flocked to Sportsman's Park, and by the end of the year the Cardinals' home attendance jumped more than 100,000, to 508,501, despite 1930 being the first full year of economic depression.[59]

Even though the pennant had already been clinched, a near-sellout crowd came to celebrate on the last Sunday of the regular season. The game provided an augury of the future with the debut of Dizzy Dean, not yet twenty years old, who had won twenty-six games in the Minor Leagues, rocketing from class A St. Joseph, Missouri, in the Western League to double-A Houston in the Texas League. All the cocky pitcher did in his Major League debut was pitch a 3-1 complete-game victory and drive in a run with a bunt single into left field. After Dean's first victory, manager Gabby Street offered a prophecy on the future on the new pitcher. "I think he's going to be a great one," Street told St. Louis mayor Victor Miller. "But I'm afraid we'll never know from one minute to the next what he's going to do or say."[60]

Dean, of course, was ineligible for the World Series, but the rest of the Cardinals entrained to Philadelphia for their first World Series against the Athletics. The contest featured an intriguing match-up between teams assembled by the two brainiest minds in baseball, Connie Mack and Branch Rickey. As in the Cardinals' two previous World Series appearances, Rickey did not join Sam Breadon's road entourage but stayed at home, content to listen to the radio. He was eager to see how his home-bred Cardinals would match wits with his respected foe Connie Mack. Both teams were made up of players schooled in baseball fundamentals, but most pundits thought the power and pitching of the reigning world champion A's would prevail.

President Herbert Hoover took a train trip to Philadelphia to throw out the first ball for game one. Connie Mack considered Hoover the A's good luck charm because his team had never lost while the president attended. Listening back home in St. Louis, Rickey might well have uttered a wry chuckle at the irony of his idol Herbert Hoover rooting against his Cardinals.

Despite their role as underdogs, the Cardinals believed they could repeat their 1926 triumph; however, the first two games of the 1930 World Series in Philadelphia left the St. Louis faithful gloomy. The A's came from behind to win a close game one, 5–2, as Lefty Grove outpitched Burleigh Grimes. Game two featured an early rout of Flint Rhem and George Earnshaw's easy 6-1 victory. Catcher Mickey Cochrane homered in each game for the Athletics. It was a somber group of Cardinals that entrained for St. Louis for the middle three games of the series. Trying to rally the troops, manager Gabby Street predicted that the Cardinals would play better after some home cooking.

In game three, Bill Hallahan showed why he was not just "Wild" Bill anymore. After escaping a first-inning jam, he shut out the A's, 5–0, scattering 7 hits and 5 walks. Taylor Douthit hit the only home run. The next day 39,946 fans, the largest baseball crowd in St. Louis history, greeted their heroes for game four, and Jess Haines evened up the Series by outdueling Lefty Grove, 3–1.[61] The thirty-seven-year-old right-hander did not allow a hit after the third inning.

The pivotal game five was a gripping, scoreless pitchers' duel between Burleigh Grimes and George "Rube" Walberg. It lasted until the ninth inning when Jimmy Foxx hit a 2-run home run to give the Athletics a 2–0 victory. The Cardinals never got a base runner to third base off Walberg and Lefty Grove, who pitched the last two innings to gain the victory.

After a day off for train travel back to Philadelphia, game six proved anticlimactic. Already down by two runs in the second inning, Bill Hallahan had to leave the game with a blister on his pitching hand. Neither his relievers nor the Cardinals hitters could do much to stave off a 7–1 defeat. The Athletics had now won two World Championships in a row, and the Cardinals had lost their second World Series in three years.

At least, unlike in 1928, when the Yankees swept them convincingly, the 1930 Cardinals put up a good fight. They displayed fine veteran pitching but simply could not hit the Philadelphia moundsmen. Jim Bottomley and Taylor Douthit had only three hits between them, and Frank Frisch was 5 for 24 and didn't score or drive in a run. The loss of the World Series disappointed Branch Rickey, but he knew that the Athletics were a deeper, more well-rounded team. Losing to Connie Mack made the defeat a little more palatable. Even Sam Breadon didn't take the defeat too hard, bringing Gabby Street back to manage for 1931.

As the off-season began, Branch Rickey could look back at a 1930 season filled with great professional and personal accomplishment. After largely fading from the sports pages after his dismissal as field manager in 1925, he was now becoming a household name in St. Louis. On November 9, 1930, the Sunday magazine section of the *Post-Dispatch* profiled him as an "Interesting St. Louisan." Rickey admitted publicly, perhaps for the first time, that Rogers Hornsby had been a better manager than he was. The players "were too eager, too highly keyed," he told writer Keith Kernan. "They brooded over their mistakes, took small failures too much to heart—because I did." Kernan noted perceptively that many people in baseball resented Rickey's popularity with the intelligentsia and people in other walks of life, and many were "inclined to ridicule his efforts to produce . . . some of the idealism of amateur athletics." The executive conceded that some of his "exalted notions . . . have had to be considerably modified; professional baseball is a commercial enterprise and has to be dealt with as such."[62]

Rickey was becoming hot copy. L. H. Addington contributed a profile to the *Sporting News* that described him as "the man who lives for work."[63] *New York Times* sports columnist John Kieran devoted a long section of a *Saturday Evening Post* story on the business of baseball to an appraisal of Rickey's growing farm system empire. Kieran liked to lampoon the executive as the "non-alcoholic Rickey" (a reference to the popular spiked drink, the lime rickey), but he presented a lively description of how the passionate and dramatic executive appraised the prospects working their way up his Minor League ladder.

"What about John Doe of Laurel?" Kieran asked. "19 years old, left-handed hitting first baseman. Hits curves. Can't go to his left for grounders. We'll use him in a trade to get an outfielder for Rochester next season," Rickey answered. "What about Richard Roe of Shawnee?" Kieran inquired. "High school boy; 6'2". Laid up two months last year—bad tonsils, must have 'em out—righthanded pitcher; good fast ball; no change-up; curve just a wrinkle; three years away."[64]

Undoubtedly, the notice that gave Rickey his greatest satisfaction of the year was when he appeared as an entry in the 1930 edition of *Who's Who in America*, his first time in the volume. The man who, when he started out in life, thought that having a secretary would mean his greatest success was now worthy of honor in the highest realms of society. Rickey's entry in *Who's Who* gives a revealing insight into his self-image. For profession he listed "athletics, lecturer, lawyer." Among the clubs that he belonged to, he listed the Optimists and the Public Question club. (The latter was a group that debated leading political and social issues of the day and included among its members Wiley T. Rutledge, a dean and professor at Washington University of St. Louis law school who in October 1942 was nominated by President Franklin D. Roosevelt to the United States Supreme Court.)[65] Under the heading "Achievements," Rickey wrote as his last entry, "Organizer of 'Knot-Hole Gang' for boy baseball fans."[66]

The tireless baseball executive thus had much to be grateful for in 1930. Not only had the Cardinals been champions of the National League three times in the last five years, but the farm teams were almost always near the top of their Minor League circuits. When the time came for the annual December meetings of the Minor Leagues, held in 1930 in Montreal, Canada, he decided it was time to respond publicly to Commissioner Landis's continuing attacks on his farm system. Rickey's impassioned speech to the Minor League conclave would serve as a prelude to a very satisfying season in 1931.

9

—

Another Championship Season and Then Decline

The Cardinals delegation that arrived in Montreal for the annual December 1930 Minor League meetings numbered thirteen, the team's largest contingent ever. It was led by Sam Breadon, Branch Rickey, and manager Gabby Street, and it included many Minor League officials. Rickey would thus have plenty of moral support as he rose to speak out against the chief opponent of his farm system, Commissioner Kenesaw Mountain Landis. The presence of his supportive associates pleased the Cardinals' mastermind because, temperamentally, he did not enjoy public confrontation. To be sure, he loved to talk and to argue, but only to win his points by debate and not by head-on collision. By December 1930, however, he saw the need, if not the urgency, to take on Landis publicly.

The economic depression was deepening in baseball as well as the rest of the country. Although still confident that President Hoover and his credo of American individualism would straighten the ship of state, Rickey had to admit that Hoover's optimism of early 1930 that "the worst was over" was not proving correct. The ranks of employed workers and the value of national capital were less than 50 percent of what they were before the great stock market crash of October 1929, and signs of improvement were scarce. The declines in Missouri, the area that Rickey knew best, were even worse than the national averages.[1]

The economic depression had not yet affected Major League Baseball, as attendance in 1930 soared to 10,132,262 customers, the first time that more than 10 million fans passed through big league turnstiles.[2] However, it would not be until after World War II that the combined attendance of the Major Leagues would again exceed 10 million. The Minor Leagues were already in deep trouble, and Branch Rickey addressed this precipitous decline at the outset of his speech in Montreal.

"Three Class D leagues, two in B, and one in A, may not open this coming year. Thirteen leagues have closed down since 1926. Not one of the thirteen that failed has had major-league affiliation," Rickey observed, pausing to look directly at his antagonist Commissioner Landis, who was sitting in the front row.[3]

"The farm system is not an ideal system," Rickey admitted, "but when people are hungry, they eat food which may or may not be ideally cooked and served." After using the food metaphor, Rickey switched to a health analogy in defending his Minor League system. "It is all right to have a physician, who will feel your pulse and look at you and say you are a sick man, I think you are going to die," Rickey said. "He offers you no medicine, none at all. He gives you no change of climate. He just says you are sick, he's awfully sorry."

Gathering steam in his oratory, Rickey, the tuberculosis survivor, continued with the medical metaphor. "Then along comes somebody else who says you've got epizootic and he can cure epizootic and he doesn't have to cut off the epi," he went on. "He doesn't have to take out an eye. He can make you live. Here's pill number one and here's pill number two, and when you get through with one, you can take number two." Pausing for another glance at Landis, Rickey thundered, "In no way should it be said, 'You can't give him those pills! You can't give him anything!'" With the audience of Minor League executives in the palm of his hand, Rickey built up to a powerful conclusion. "Without the minor leagues, baseball can get nowhere," he roared. "When the majors get to the point where they think they do not have to consider the status of the minors, then a great danger exists to the structure of baseball." He ended his speech with a classic Rickey peroration. "Baseball is bigger than any one club," he declared. "I owe much to this game. It is bigger than I am. It is bigger than any one man!"[4]

Landis did not respond to Rickey's speech. For the first time in years the commissioner made no statement whatsoever about the farm systems of the Cardinals and other Major League organizations. Landis decided that the time was not ripe for another attack on the "chain gangs," as

Rickey's critics had dubbed his operation. The reality of Minor League disarray and disintegration was too serious to ignore, and even Landis for the moment decided to back off on his criticism.

Far from curtailing his farm system, Branch Rickey was always thinking of ways to expand it, increasing the opportunities for players to learn the game and for communities to enjoy what he felt was the best sport ever invented. He was thus receptive when one morning early in 1931, he received a long-distance call from Chicago. A vigorous-sounding man introduced himself on the phone as Larry MacPhail, the new operator of the Columbus, Ohio, franchise in the American Association. MacPhail informed Rickey that he had recently purchased the team from Sidney Weil, owner of the Cincinnati Reds. He said that Weil and Walter Jones, who was in the glass business in Chicago, had suggested that he call to see if the Cardinals were interested in affiliating with his new operation.[5]

Rickey was immediately interested because MacPhail had mentioned the names of two people of substance and achievement, and the ties of personal friendship counted for everything in the world of Branch Rickey. Walter Jones was a fellow Ohio Wesleyan graduate, and Sidney Weil was not only a National League colleague but also a man as deeply involved in the Reform Jewish philanthropic activities in Cincinnati as Rickey was in similar Methodist programs in St. Louis.[6]

Always eager to entice enthusiastic, intelligent new blood into baseball, Rickey scheduled an appointment with MacPhail for three o'clock, presumably the next day. He assumed that his eager caller would take the train from Chicago to St. Louis. Larry MacPhail, however, had been waiting for an opportunity to get into baseball for years, and he couldn't wait one day. He dashed to the airport, took the first plane to St. Louis, and knocked on Rickey's door at three o'clock on the same day.[7]

Leland Stanford MacPhail was most definitely a man of action. He was born in Cass, Michigan, on February 3, 1890, the son of a general store owner who parlayed a safe deposit service for his customers to ownership of twenty-one banks in Michigan small towns.[8] Named for a good friend of his mother—railroad mogul Leland Stanford, who founded the private university in California—Larry MacPhail was accepted at age sixteen into the U.S. Naval Academy. However, his parents convinced him that he was too young for the assignment, so he enrolled at Beloit College in Wisconsin, where he played on the baseball team and became one of the more vociferous members of the debate team. After graduation he entered the University of Michigan law school, Rickey's alma mater, but with thoughts of going into the foreign service, he transferred to George Washington University in the nation's capital.[9]

After working for two law firms in the Midwest and becoming president of a Nashville department store at age twenty-five, MacPhail enlisted as a private in the Army in World War I. He saw action, was gassed and wounded, and rose to the rank of captain. At the end of the war he got involved in a plot to kidnap imprisoned German Kaiser Wilhelm in Holland and bring him to American justice. Foiled in his efforts, and narrowly missing a court-martial, MacPhail did manage to pilfer an imperial Hohenzollern ashtray, which he kept as a trophy in his office. After the war he settled in Columbus, Ohio, and used his legal and entrepreneurial skills in many businesses. Before depression woes forced severe cutbacks, MacPhail had been administering a hospital in Columbus.[10]

Sports remained MacPhail's abiding love. To keep his finger in the athletic pie, MacPhail had served as a Big Ten college football referee, where he may have been the first official to use hand signals to indicate what penalties had been committed. The chance to operate a baseball team was a dream come true for Larry MacPhail, explaining why he couldn't wait a day to make his case to Rickey.[11]

Rickey was immediately impressed with the energy, ambition, and intelligence of MacPhail. Within an hour of their first meeting, he introduced the red-headed dynamo to Sam Breadon, and before the day was done the St. Louis Cardinals had a new affiliate in the American Association, the Columbus Redbirds. Offered a choice between a straight commission of $10,000 or a two-year contract and the club presidency, MacPhail chose the latter.[12]

He immediately went to work turning around a franchise that had not won a pennant since 1906. He used the method he would follow in all his later stops in baseball. He painted the ballpark, hired brightly attired and courteous ushers, staged all kind of pregame promotions from vaudeville acts to fashion shows, and put a scrappy, competitive team on the field. In his first season in 1931, as the economic depression ravaged the nation and most baseball attendance lagged appreciably,

MacPhail's Columbus Redbirds increased its fan support by over 50 percent. Attendance would boom even more the next year when, on June 3, 1932, a new seventeen-thousand-seat stadium opened before a capacity crowd, including special guests Branch Rickey, Sam Breadon, Commissioner Landis, and National League president John Heydler. MacPhail arranged for the first Columbus radio broadcast of the game, another innovation he would stress in every city where he worked. Later, in June 1932, an overflow crowd witnessed the first night game in Columbus, a prelude to what the energetic entrepreneur innovated three years later in Cincinnati.[13] As we shall soon see, MacPhail did not stay with the Columbus Redbirds long enough to enjoy their winning the 1933 pennant, but he certainly made Columbus a successful addition to the Cardinals' growing farm system.

Before the start of the 1931 season, Branch Rickey made another significant hiring for the organization when he signed twenty-four-year-old Eugene Karst as the first team publicist in baseball history. The two Major Leagues each employed a publicity person to assist in general promotion, but no individual team had ever hired one person to promote its fortunes. Karst won the job as the result of a typed, three-page, single-spaced letter he wrote Rickey shortly before Thanksgiving 1930. He emphasized that he was a local boy, a graduate of both the Knothole Gang and St. Louis University, and had interned on the St. Louis morning newspaper, the *Globe Democrat*, and had also been published in the national magazine *Baseball*.

"I believe in Baseball and I believe in Publicity," Karst had written. He suggested that his newspaper background made him the ideal person to provide stories about the Cardinals to the hinterlands where St. Louis fans were starved for information. Karst stressed that he was a genuine journalist, not a press agent with an ax to grind. He argued that a good publicity man would attract cash customers to all the teams in the growing Cardinals farm system. Perhaps the clinching argument for Branch Rickey was when Karst wrote: "Chain-store baseball, as it is called, is often disliked by the fans of the smaller circuits, and a publicity man could help overcome this antipathy."[14]

Early in the new year of 1931, Rickey, impressed by Karst's letter, invited the young man to an interview at the Cardinals' offices in Sportsman's Park. After opening pleasantries the ferocious gentleman asked him, "Can you take the third degree?" Seventy years later the journalist recalled vividly the torrent of questions Rickey directed to him: "Was I married or single? Did I have a girl? Did I go to church? Which church? When was the last time? Did I drink or smoke? How many brothers and sisters in my family? [Karst was in the middle of ten children, five girls and five boys.] My father's occupation? Any divorces in the family? My hobbies? Was I Republican or Democrat? Could I drive a car? Could I type or take shorthand?"[15]

For over an hour Rickey interviewed—grilled, if you will—the young man, and at the end he told him that if Sam Breadon agreed, Karst would be placed on the payroll at $150 a month. The sooner he could start work, the better. Karst was ushered in to meet Breadon, and after a brief meeting the Cardinals president approved the hiring of Gene Karst, bestowing the title "Director of Information" on the team's newest employee.[16]

For the next four eventful seasons Karst was to be publicist for his favorite hometown team and an occasional bridge partner and chauffeur of Branch Rickey. On the job for barely a couple of weeks, Karst drew the assignment of driving the executive to 1931 spring training in Bradenton, Florida. "Rickey often dozed while I was driving, sometimes leaning to his right to my shoulder and I would have to push him back towards his seat," Karst remembers. But it was a special excitement to work with an older man who had such a youthful relish for life. "Often I did not know our destination when I left my office," Karst recalls, noting that when Rickey said, "Let's go!" he said it with an irresistible passion.

Karst adds that he learned a lot about psychology during his years working with Rickey. One season the young publicist wrote a series of glowing reports about the bright prospects in the St. Louis farm system and prepared to distribute thousands of copies of his handiwork to newspapers in the towns where the Cardinals had affiliates. But when Rickey read Karst's copy, he immediately ordered it destroyed. He feared a negative reaction among the Major League Cardinals if there were too much publicity circulated about Minor Leaguers eager to take their jobs.[17]

One afternoon under the broiling Florida sun, one frustrated player asked for a meeting with Branch Rickey and then presented the classic disgruntled baseball player's complaint, "Play me or trade me." Normally, Rickey and most baseball executives were unmoved by such a request, but the Cardinals mastermind sensed that there was something different about this player. He seemed so genuine and earnest in his ambition. His name was John Leonard Roosevelt Martin, soon to be known to the fans as Pepper Martin and "The Wild Horse of the Osage." Rickey would call him his favorite among the many extraordinary players he developed. "He is as was," Rickey said. "He is a child of nature and never pretends to be anything he isn't."

Signed in 1924 on Charley Barrett's recommendation off the roster of a class D Minor League team in Greenville, Texas, Martin had worked his way up the Cardinals ladder but felt stymied that his Major League resume to date consisted of only thirteen at-bats in 1928 and one plate appearance in 1930. Almost twenty-seven years old, Martin was champing at the bit, begging Rickey for a chance to earn a regular Major League job. "I am glad that you want to play every day, John," Rickey said sympathetically, addressing Martin, as he usually did all his players, by his given Christian name. "I wouldn't want someone on my team who didn't want to play regularly."

Rickey advised Martin to be patient. "Keep your head up, John, and be ready to play whenever called upon," Rickey counseled. "Every year is different and you never know when your opportunity will arise. Just be prepared to seize it when it arrives." Martin listened intently, being one of those players who loved to hear the baseball brain orate. Yet, as spring training commenced in 1931, Martin thought ruefully, it seemed that the outfield of Chick Hafey in left, Taylor "Flyhawk" Douthit in center, and George Watkins, coming off a .373 rookie season, was fairly well set (even if Hafey, as was his custom, was holding out for a higher salary).

A greater controversy was developing in shaping the pitching staff. Dizzy Dean fully expected to make the rotation after winning twenty-five games in the Minors in 1930 as well as winning in his Major League debut on the last day of the regular season. However, Gabby Street's prediction of the unpredictability of the future star was proving truer than maybe even Street expected. In training camp Dean started to tell everyone about how great he was going to be in the big leagues and how superior he was to the veterans already on the team. Rookies were supposed to be seen and not heard, but the exuberant Dean did not care about that propriety. He infuriated manager Street by appearing late for spring training drills and then having the audacity to proclaim publicly, "Let some of the other clucks work out for the staff; nobody can beat me."[18]

Although he always offered at least subtle input, Branch Rickey usually left the final roster choices to his manager. Rickey understood that Dizzy Dean was a special case, a raw, gifted talent who exuded enormous confidence. Not many players had ever called Branch Rickey "Branch" at their first meeting, and Rickey pointedly addressed the lad in conversation as "Mr. Dean" until the pitcher got the point of who was the boss. Still, Rickey always liked adventurous and aggressive players, especially those with a high ceiling for achievement.

Rickey enjoyed most of Dean's antics, such as making up different names for different reporters so each one would have a new story. Rickey usually addressed Dizzy as Jerome, for Jerome Herman Dean, but the pitcher's given name was probably Jay Hanna Dean, supposedly because his impoverished mother named him after the wealthy financiers Jay Gould and Mark Hanna. The name that best described Dean for Rickey, though, was "a very unpredictable boy," which he felt summed up the unschooled sharecropper's son with a great zest for life and a very live arm.

During the off-season of 1930–31, Rickey, ever the paterfamilias, had decided that Dean needed some social grooming. He arranged for Oliver French, the business manager of the St. Joseph, Missouri, farm club where Dean had won seventeen games in 1930, to house the pitcher for the winter. "Keep an eye on the boy and make sure he doesn't get into trouble," Rickey counseled his loyal farm assistant. To keep his pitching arm in shape, the imaginative Dean invented a game in which he threw coals at the furnace in Oliver French's basement. If the coals went in the furnace, Dean called them strikes; if he missed, they were hits. "When the house got unbearably hot, we knew Dizzy had set another strikeout record," French informed Rickey.[19]

The promising pitcher was already a celebrity in St. Joseph, and automobile dealers and other businessmen were more than willing to provide him with cars, and even a Piper cub airplane. Dizzy somehow managed to avoid crashes, although he had several close calls. He was always asking for more spending money, but Rickey gave French strict orders to keep the pitcher on a strict allowance. Dean became so disconsolate that French drove him to St. Louis for a head-to-head meeting with the boss at his new, luxurious country home. Dean, the sharecropper's son, was, of course, awed by Rickey's baronial house and its lush surroundings. He expected that a man who could afford such a manor would easily increase his allowance, but all he received was a lecture on the birds and the bees and the importance of sexual abstinence. "Golly, Oliver, when he first begin talkin' about the facts of life," Dean afterward told French, "I thought for sure he meant money!"[20]

Not surprisingly, Rickey's lecture on sex had little impact. Shortly after Dean's return to St. Joseph, he became infatuated with a young high school girl and sent her expensive silk pajamas as a Christmas present. The outraged parents ordered their daughter to return the gift as "inappropriate." Heartbroken at his romantic loss, Dean wrote Rickey a letter asking for advice. Rickey telephoned Dean with the paternal advice, "Ballplayers should marry, but I mean the right marriage." As he often did Rickey then offered Dean a $500 bonus, but only if he married well. The pitcher seemed confused, and when word reached Oliver French that a boyfriend of one of Dizzy's amours was gunning for him, it was decided to dispatch the promising hurler to an early start in Bradenton spring training.[21]

However, Dean's dismissive attitude toward his teammates was disturbing to both manager Gabby Street and Branch Rickey. When the pitcher continued to be late for spring training drills and persisted in calling his teammates "clucks," management decided that a full year in Houston couldn't hurt the hurler who, after all, had just turned twenty. As it turned out Dean had a great 1931 in the Texas League, going 26-10, and he also met Patricia Nash, a bank teller eight years older than he was. In 1932 he was both a Major Leaguer and a happy husband.

Instead of Dizzy Dean, the prize rookie on the 1931 Cardinals pitching staff became Paul Derringer. A husky six foot three, 205-pound native of Springfield, Kentucky, Derringer had been spotted by Rickey's brother Frank Rickey, and Charley Barrett confirmed that Derringer had the goods. When word came that Cy Slapnicka, Cleveland's top scout (who later signed Bob Feller), was also trying to sign him, Rickey convinced Sam Breadon to rush in extra cash to sign the burly right-hander.[22]

Derringer had spent five years in the Cardinals farm system before arriving in 1931. The first truly successful pitcher developed since Rickey took over the organization, Derringer went 18-8 in his rookie year, finishing only one victory behind his teammate Bill Hallahan's league-leading nineteen wins. Burleigh Grimes contributed seventeen wins in his first (and only) full season as a Cardinal, and Flint Rhem, in his last full season with the Cardinals, chipped in with eleven. The 1931 Cardinals would win 101 games, the first National League team to reach the rare 100-win plateau since the Giants in 1917. They led every weekend of the season and ultimately beat the Giants by twelve games, with the Cubs and Dodgers rounding out the first division.

At the June 15 trading deadline Pepper Martin got his big break as Rickey decided to make a change in the outfield. Chick Hafey's holdout for more money had lasted into the middle of May, allowing Martin more playing time. It was becoming clear that George Watkins would not come close to his high rookie average of .373, as he fell off to .288. (All averages were down in 1931, a year when baseball moguls decided to use a less lively baseball after the excessive offensive output of 1930 increased players' salary demands, which all the owners in the deepening economic depression, of course, opposed.)[23]

Rickey, however, felt that Watkins still had value as a reserve player. His merciless, evaluative eye focused instead on the subtly declining talents of Taylor "Flyhawk" Douthit. He was still a .300 hitter, but his number of doubles was declining and he wasn't as fast in running down balls in the outfield. Rickey feared that Douthit might become prone to hitting into more double plays, and at age thirty, he was starting on the downslide of his career. His veteran's salary of $14,000 was also significantly higher than Pepper Martin's $4,500 a year.[24]

Douthit was aware that Pepper Martin needed a position to play, but he didn't want it to be his place. On June 14, 1931, the day before the trade deadline, Douthit did all he could to show that he still belonged on the Cardinals by lashing eight hits in a Sunday doubleheader against the Reds. He ran the bases with aplomb and made several adept catches in the outfield. However, when Douthit was summoned the next morning into Rickey's office, his worst fears were confirmed. He had been traded to Cincinnati for outfielder Wally Roettger, a St. Louis native who had played with the Cardinals in the late 1920s and was hitting .345 for the Reds (fourteen points higher than Douthit) at the time of the trade. When Douthit got the bad news, "there were tears in his eyes as he said goodbye to office workers," publicist Gene Karst remembered.[25]

Pepper Martin took full advantage of the Douthit trade, claiming center field as his own and compiling fine statistics in 1931: .300 BA, .467 SA, 7 HR, 75 RBI, 68 R, 32 2B, and 8 3B. He also showed his versatility by playing fifteen games at third base, but Martin's contributions were far more than could be measured in numbers alone. His headfirst slides into bases symbolized an overwhelming desire to win, and he became the poster boy for a 1931 team that was not to be denied.

Many memorable days highlighted the glorious season of the 1931 Cardinals. On July 12 a Sunday doubleheader against the Chicago Cubs drew an astounding 45,715 fans. It was a promotional day, and farmers and town folk from all over the Midwest gathered to see the Cardinals against their fiercest rival. The first game started an hour late to allow the fans to get to their seats. Obviously, there were going to be more fans than seats because the maximum seating capacity at Sportsman's Park in 1931 was 33,000. The umpires decided that the extra fans would have to be placed in the outfield with a rope separating them from the rest of the diamond. A special ground rule was introduced for the occasion: any ball hit over the rope but not into the stands was declared a double. The Cubs won the first game, 7-5, with both teams combining for nine doubles. The Cardinals came back to earn a split, 17-13, in a game that featured twenty-three doubles. The day after, Gene Karst, whose publicity work had been responsible for much of the attendance, asked Sam Breadon for a share in the proceeds. The young employee was not surprised when the frugal owner said no, but he did give him a $50 bonus for his efforts.[26]

When the Cardinals swept the Giants in a late August doubleheader at the Polo Grounds, their lead became eight and a half games, and they were never seriously threatened in September. The biggest drama at the end of the 1931 regular National League season was the closest batting race in league history. Two St. Louis teammates, Chick Hafey and Jim Bottomley, were competing with Giants first baseman Bill Terry and Phillies outfielder Chuck Klein. (If you consider that Klein had once been a Cardinals farm hand, freed by Commissioner Landis, three of the top four National League hitters in 1931 were St. Louis farm system products.)[27] The batting title race went down to the very last day of the season with Hafey and Terry tied at .349. Hafey won the title with a three thousandth of a point edge, .3489, to Terry's .3486. Bottomley finished at .3482, with Klein at .337.

More league honors came for the Cardinals when Frank Frisch won the 1931 National League Most Valuable Player Award. His numbers were not personal bests, in part because of the deader baseball, but Frisch's .311 BA, 94 R, 88 RBI, and league-leading 28 SB were adequate enough offensively. Defensive whiz Charley Gelbert at shortstop and Frisch formed an excellent double play combination.

The 1931 World Series featured a rematch of the Cardinals and the Athletics, who were trying for an unprecedented "three-peat," a third World Series title in a row. The A's were a strong 2–1 favorite because they had won 107 games, a team record, and featured the American League's batting champion, Al Simmons at .390, and its most dominant pitcher, Robert "Lefty" Grove, who compiled a remarkable 31-4 record. Mack's Philadelphia juggernaut retained most of the cast that had dismissed the Cardinals in six games in 1930, including first baseman Jimmy Foxx, catcher Mickey Cochrane, and two other able pitchers, George Earnshaw and George "Rube" Walberg.

However, the Athletics would be surprised by the grittiness of the Cardinals, especially that displayed by their new center fielder, Pepper Martin. Before game one of the Series Branch Rickey broke with his custom of avoiding the clubhouse. He gave an impassioned speech to the team, drawing on his vast reservoir of oratorical skills and competitive fire. He reminded the Cardinals of their loss in 1930 and noted that the National League had not won a Series since the Cardinals beat the Yankees in 1926. There was now a great opportunity for vindication, Rickey declared, winding up his speech with the passionate exclamation, "The greatest attribute of a winning ball player is a desire to win that dominates."[28] After hearing the ferocious gentleman's oration in the clubhouse, Pepper Martin had to be restrained from running immediately onto the field of battle.

An opponent's starting pitcher, however, can deflate the inspirational words of even a Branch Rickey, and Lefty Grove did exactly that in game one of the 1931 World Series. He won easily over Paul Derringer, 6–2, but in an omen of good things to come, Pepper Martin had a double and two singles. Martin's teammates collected nine more hits off Grove, chipping away at his supposed invincibility. Connie Mack was beginning to sense that he had been eerily prophetic in his pre-Series premonition that "Martin is the kind of ballplayer who can take over a whole Series. He's the kind of aggressive, unpredictable kid who could be the hero or the goat."[29]

In game two Martin continued his offensive heroics by singling twice and stealing second each time on the supposedly impregnable Mickey Cochrane. The swift center fielder scored the only two runs in St. Louis's Series-evening 2–0 victory. Bill Hallahan hurled a 3-hit shutout, living up to his growing reputation as a big game pitcher. The southpaw continued to walk almost as many as he struck out, but he always was on top of his game in the so-called "pinches," when you had no margin for error and you simply had to make your pitch and not the one the hitter wanted. Rickey beamed at Hallahan's success because he was the sort of team-oriented, community-minded person for whom he always wished good things. (After his retirement Hallahan, the son of a Binghamton, New York, railroad man and brother of a local alderman and fireman, returned to his home area and served as a county auditor.)[30]

Normally, after the second game of the World Series, there was one travel day, but since the second game was played on a Friday, there would be two days off because Sunday baseball was still forbidden in Philadelphia. Branch Rickey took advantage of the extra day off by scheduling a gala party at his house in the country. It was a joyous celebration with more than a hundred guests invited from his wide circle of friends and acquaintances. The attendees included major and Minor League baseball associates, neighbors, clergy of many faiths, actor-comedian Joe E. Brown (a huge baseball fan), and iconoclastic, atheistic lawyer Clarence Darrow.[31]

Rickey and Darrow were not exactly friends but were certainly admiring acquaintances who had much in common despite their obvious differences on religion. Both had been raised in rural Ohio, where playing baseball had been one of their great recreational delights. Both loved books and ideas and shared a passionate desire to talk and argue about them. They were free of racial prejudice, and Rickey undoubtedly applauded Darrow's defense of Ossian Sweet, a black Detroit physician who had been charged with murder in 1925 for defending his home from a mob of bigots.[32] At some time in the mid-1920s Rickey had chaired a debate on atheism versus religion between Darrow and Methodist bishop Donald Hughes, Rickey's Ohio Wesleyan classmate and Delta Tau Delta fraternity brother.

There is a possibility that Rickey himself once thought of publicly debating Darrow, probably not long after July 1925, when the brilliant lawyer ridiculed the biblical fundamentalism of William Jennings Bryan, the former Democratic presidential candidate, at the trial of John Scopes for teaching evolution in the public schools of Tennessee. The humanity and the divinity of Jesus Christ were unbending reeds of Branch Rickey's faith, but he thought he was enough of a rationalist and freethinker to not fall into the trap of literal fundamentalism that Bryan had gotten into squaring off against Darrow. Rickey believed in both science and Jesus Christ, and he loved to argue the case for the coexistence of both. He had hanging in his Cardinals office a framed motto of William Henry Drummond, the late-nineteenth-century Scottish theologian and scientist: "He who will not reason is a bigot; he who cannot reason is a fool; and he who dares not to reason is a slave."[33]

A Rickey debate with Darrow never happened, though he certainly was intrigued by the idea and kiddingly suggested that he could pack the room with his friends. It was probably Jane Rickey who told her husband that Darrow was too proficient a debater to tangle with in public.[34]

When the World Series resumed in Philadelphia, Pepper Martin was still riding a hot streak. In game three he contributed two more hits and a stolen base off the rattled Mickey Cochrane, as Burleigh Grimes mastered the A's on two hits, 5–2. The only Philadelphia runs came on Al Simmons's bottom-of-the-ninth home run, which merely made the final score more respectable. The thirty-eight-year-old Grimes, who retired with an exceptional .248 batting average for a pitcher, also chipped in with two hits, winning his first World Series game since he had pitched for the Brooklyn Dodgers in 1920.

The only disturbing moment in game three for Branch Rickey was hearing boos in the Philadelphia crowd during the radio broadcast. "We want beer! We want beer!" came the muffled cries, a response to the arrival of President Herbert Hoover at the game. As Rickey heard the voices of the alcohol-deprived fans demanding an end to Prohibition, he may well have thought to himself: "Herbert Hoover can't win on this one. I think he knows the Prohibition law isn't working, but too many Republicans still favor it." (Not that the staunch individualist Branch Rickey accepted public opinion polls as gospel, but he was aware that the results were showing that opponents of the law outnumbered the "drys" three to one.)[35] However, he was very pleased that Hoover had shown his true colors as a baseball fan by making the trip to Philadelphia to see the game. For the first three years of his troubled presidency, Hoover would get a copy of the baseball schedule, mark down the dates of the World Series, and plan to attend at least one of the games (but in 1932 he stayed away from the Yankees-Cubs Series).[36]

Game four showed that the Athletics were not giving up on achieving their unprecedented "three-peat." George Earnshaw hurled a two-hit, 5–0 shutout over Sylvester Johnson and the Cardinals. Predictably, Pepper Martin got the only St. Louis hits, but the Series was now knotted at two games apiece. In the pivotal game five it was Martin again who set the tone by smashing three hits, including a two-run home run, as Bill Hallahan beat the former Yankees right-hander Waite Hoyt, 5–1. The happy Cardinals took the train back to St. Louis, knowing that they needed only one more victory to win their second World Series in the last five years.

The legend of Pepper Martin was growing. His clutch-hitting and irrepressible joy was a godsend not only to his teammates and St. Louis fans but to an entire American nation, which was uneasily realizing that the current economic depression was not a normal one and that hard times might be here indefinitely. Martin's intensely joyous style of play made people forget momentarily the fears of the day and the ongoing depression. Instead, they identified with his joy in competition and his playing as if there were no tomorrow.

What made Pepper Martin even more appealing to Branch Rickey was that the fiery Cardinal was a devout Christian who was active in his Baptist church in Oklahoma. "Learning to play good baseball is a lot like learning how to live a good life," Pepper Martin would later explain in *Guideposts*, the self-help Christian magazine on whose board Rickey served. "In baseball, you've got to know the fundamentals—sliding, running, hitting, fielding. In life you need more basic fundamentals—belief in God, the Bible, prayer, love of people."[37]

The infectious enthusiasm and glorious play of Pepper Martin was one area where Branch Rickey and Commissioner Kenesaw Mountain Landis were in agreement. On the train back to St. Louis for game six, Landis asked Martin, "Would you like to trade places with me?" In a famous retort Martin quipped, "If we exchange salaries, that will be fine."

In game six of the 1931 World Series Philadelphia again bounced back from a loss. The A's broke open a scoreless tie in the fourth inning, scoring four runs on only two hits off Paul Derringer. Four walks and an error helped to undo St. Louis, who fell quietly to Lefty Grove's five-hit complete game, 8–1.

Game seven for the world championship of baseball presented the St. Louis Cardinals with their first opportunity to win a World Series at home, and they were up to the challenge. They scored four runs in the first three innings off George Earnshaw, the last two coming on a George Watkins home run. Burleigh Grimes shut out the Cardinals until there were two outs in the ninth inning. After a Jimmy Foxx home run brought the A's within two runs, Bill Hallahan came out of the bullpen to get Max Bishop to fly to center field to give the Cardinals a 4–2 victory and the Series trophy.

It was fitting that Pepper Martin caught the last out of the World Series because his hustle and great performance had put an indelible mark on the Series. Although he didn't get a hit in either game six or game seven, he reached base on walks, and his aggressiveness caused a run-scoring wild pitch at a key moment in the seventh game. Martin's twelve hits in one Series remained a Series record until the Yankees' Bobby Richardson tied it in the 1960 Series. So did Martin's five stolen bases remain in the books until Lou Brock stole seven bases for the Cardinals in the 1967 Series.

Connie Mack was as gracious in defeat as Branch Rickey had been the year before when Philadelphia had won. "Their speed and that Martin fellow were too much for us," Mack said. John McGraw, commenting on the Series for one of the newspaper syndicates, echoed the sentiment, saying that the Cardinals' aggressiveness had caught the Athletics off guard.[38] *St. Louis Post-Dispatch* bard L. C. Davis composed a poem in honor of Pepper Martin for his regular "Sport Salad" column. Since the World Series hero and soon-to-be-voted Athlete of the Year by the Associated Press had been born on February 29, 1904, Davis called his poem "Leap Year Kid":

> Hero of the Redbird clan
> Six years old but what a man!
> When you reach maturity
> What a player you will be.[39]

The year 1931 was a triumph for the entire Cardinals organization. Not only had the St. Louis team won both the pennant and the World Series, but the farm system was awash with Minor League champions and prospective stars for the Major League team. Always interested in keeping the competitive fires stoked in his aspiring farm hands, Rickey announced that he was planning a round-robin tournament in Minor League spring training in which farm hands from Columbus, Rochester, and Houston would compete for a silver trophy.[40]

Financially, the St. Louis organization did well in a year when Major League Baseball as a whole lost almost 900,000 fans from its 1930 total. The Cardinals added 100,000 customers, drawing 608,535 fans in 1931.[41] Although the other Major League franchises reported a combined loss of $130,000 in 1931, the Cardinals had another good year in the ledger books. A reported profit of $230,000 in 1930 increased to $345,000 in 1931.[42] An interesting sidelight, though, was that after drawing nearly 40,000 for each of the first three home games in the 1931 World Series, only 20,805 turned out for the seventh game. The small crowd puzzled Sam Breadon, and as we shall soon see, disappointing fan support would disturb the chief owner even more in the next few years.

As spring training in 1932 commenced, Rickey concentrated as always on keeping the profit margin alive for Sam Breadon while trying to field a competitive team at the top of the National League. With the surplus of talent in the farm system, Rickey realized that room for Dizzy Dean would have to be made in 1932 after the pitcher's outstanding twenty-eight-victory season in Houston. Following his now-embedded dictum of trading a player a year too soon rather than a year too late, Rickey dealt World Series hero Burleigh Grimes to the Cubs for slugger Hack Wilson and the marginal pitcher Arthur "Bud" Teachout. Rickey would always chortle about this transaction because Hack Wilson, another player plagued by alcoholism, was nearing the end of the career. He would never play a game for the Cardinals, yet Rickey was able to receive $45,000 from the Dodgers for Wilson's contract in the winter of 1931.[43]

With slugger Joe Medwick ripening in Houston, Rickey decided that he had endured enough of Chick Hafey's holdouts, so he traded Hafey to Cincinnati for two journeymen—pitcher Benny Frey and outfielder–first baseman Harvey Hendrick—and the ever-helpful cash, or "boot," as he called it, that he put to good use in the farm system. For 1932 he planned to ease in first baseman Jim "Rip" Collins, who Rickey felt, after eight years in the farm system, should soon be ready to take over from Jim Bottomley. (It wouldn't be until after the 1932 season, though, that he would trade Bottomley to the Cubs for outfielder Estel Crabtree, from Crabtree, Ohio, near Rickey's Scioto County, and pitcher Owen "Ownie" Carroll.) Rickey even started thinking publicly about promoting infielder Burgess Whitehead, an articulate graduate of the University of North Carolina (who wore his Phi Beta Kappa key around his neck), as a potential replacement for Frank Frisch at second base.[44]

Although he knew that there were no guarantees of success in baseball, and that every season was different, Branch Rickey could not have expected the precipitous decline in the Cardinals' fortunes in 1932. They plummeted twenty-nine games from their 101-win season to wind up in an ignominious tie for sixth with the Giants, whose legendary manager John McGraw retired in midseason. The Cardinals' twenty-nine-game-slide to a 72-82 record was the sharpest decline of any league champion in baseball history.

There were many reasons for the Cardinals' failure in 1932. Frank Frisch went to the Orient on an All-Star tour after the World Series. He didn't return until shortly before spring training and was not in the best of health. Frisch's batting average fell to .292 with only 60 RBI and 59 R, far below his peak years. His 18 stolen bases ranked him third in the league, but the spark was gone in 1932.

Pepper Martin began the off-season earning $1,500 a week as a vaudeville entertainer, twirling a rope and telling stories. However, he quickly realized that he was not an entertainer and much preferred an off-season devoted to his usual hobbies of hunting and fishing. Martin invested most of his World Series winner's share of $4,484 in eighty acres of land west of Oklahoma City. A child of nature, Martin loved to sleep outdoors, but some time before spring training he contracted a serious skin rash, probably caused by insect bites that became infected.[45] In 1932 he played in only eighty-five games and slumped to a .238 BA, 4 HR, and 34 RBI.

In his first season in the Major Leagues Dizzy Dean led the St. Louis mound staff with eighteen wins and a league-leading 286 innings pitched, but he also lost fifteen games. Paul Derringer was only 11-14; the only other winning pitcher on the staff was Bill Hallahan, with a 12-5 record, but the aging southpaw threw only 176 innings. Although Rip Collins performed well as a rookie first baseman, with a .279 BA, 21 HR, and 91 RBI, "Sunny" Jim Bottomley's presence was less cheerful now that his playing time was cut in half. Chick Hafey's veteran presence may also have been missed on the field and in the clubhouse.

The fans reacted to a poor team, predictably, by staying away in droves. The loss of more than 325,000 fans brought attendance down to 279,219, the lowest since Branch Rickey's last full season as field manager in 1924. With the economic depression deepening, total Major League attendance plummeted to under 7 million fans, a loss of more than 1.5 million from 1931's total of 8,467,107.[46]

The Cardinals never were a factor in the 1932 season, as Joe McCarthy's Cubs rose to the top, winning the pennant by four games over the Pirates. However, it was Chicago's fate to meet the revived Yankees in the 1932 World Series. Branch Rickey was a somewhat embarrassed spectator, rooting for the National League in Chicago as the New Yorkers swept away the Cubs in four straight games. It was the Series of Babe Ruth's legendary "called shot" home run at Wrigley Field in the final game of the sweep. Like most fans in attendance at game four, Rickey was not sure if Babe Ruth really did point to the right-field bleachers, where he rocketed Charlie Root's 0-2 pitch, or just to the Cubs dugout to tell them that he had one more pitch to unload on the beleaguered pitcher. Whatever the real story, the outcome was another humiliating

National League loss to the Yankees, making their third sweep of the World Series in six years.

There was much belt-tightening in Major League Baseball in 1932. Team rosters were reduced to twenty-three players, and Sam Breadon lobbied unsuccessfully for a further cut to twenty. The Cardinals president also failed in convincing his colleagues to approve night baseball for the next year. "It makes every day a Sunday," was the slogan Breadon preached, and he cited the ten thousand fans who came out in St. Louis in August 1932 to see Grover Cleveland Alexander pitch for the touring House of David team in an exhibition game against the Cardinals.[47] For the first time since 1926, Breadon did not declare a team dividend, and a lean year in 1933 was forecast for both baseball and the national economy. Branch Rickey's take-home pay, as high as $95,000 in 1928, slipped to less than $35,000 in 1932; even Commissioner Landis agreed to take a cut in salary, from $65,000 a year to $40,000.[48]

November 1932 brought both bad political and bad baseball news to Branch Rickey. His Republican idol Herbert Hoover was routed by Franklin Delano Roosevelt in the presidential election. The loss was not unexpected, given the extent of the depression, with millions of people unemployed and many living in makeshift housing dubbed "Hoovervilles." Hoover also was hurt when early in 1932 he gave the order to General Douglas MacArthur to open fire in Washington on World War One veterans demanding their bonuses.

Branch Rickey did not know much about Franklin Roosevelt except that he was a cousin of former president Theodore Roosevelt and had served as President Woodrow Wilson's assistant secretary of the navy in World War I. Those were good credentials, Rickey conceded, but since Franklin Roosevelt was a former Democratic governor of New York, who drew considerable support from big-city machines the idealistic, individualistic executive did not trust, Rickey was skeptical about Roosevelt's ability to keep the free enterprise system working to the satisfaction of traditional Republicans.

Shortly before Thanksgiving in 1932 Branch Rickey received bad baseball news from Pennsylvania. Cardinals shortstop Charlie Gelbert had accidentally shot himself in the leg during a hunting trip. The prognosis for the career of the twenty-six-year-old was guarded at best. The injury to the area above his ankle was severe enough that amputation was at first feared, and he definitely would not be available for the 1933 season.[49]

Branch Rickey understood that having a consistent shortstop was an essential component of any championship team, but the organization did not have a likely replacement for Gelbert. Rickey invited thirty-seven-year-old Rogers Hornsby, who had worn out his welcome with the Cubs, to spring training in 1933. Sam Breadon was willing to forgive Hornsby's insolence in 1926 that had precipitated his trade, especially since the former St. Louis star might still have some gate value as a drawing card in the deepening depression. Rickey suggested to Frank Frisch that perhaps he could move to shortstop, with Hornsby taking over second base. When Commissioner Landis tried to put restrictions on Hornsby because of his continuing racetrack associations, Rickey insisted to Landis that his second baseman had a right to a job and that the Cardinals had every right to sign him.[50]

However, the aging Frisch and Hornsby simply could not do the job in the field. Frisch was thirty-four years old, and second base remained his best position. "We camped out near second base like a couple of conventioneers," Frisch recalled the unsuccessful experiment.[51] After the first weeks of the 1933 season it was clear that the Cardinals had no chance of winning without a competent shortstop. The team was under .500 and seemingly headed for another, unacceptable second-division finish. Rickey decided it was time to make a trade that would have lasting implications in his remarkable story as well as the history of baseball.

10

Prelude to the Gashouse Gang

"Sidney, you must help me!" Branch Rickey was on the telephone, pleading with Sidney Weil, owner of the Cincinnati Reds. It was early in May 1933, and the Cardinals' major-domo was laid up with the flu in a New York hotel room, but no minor ailment was going to stop Branch Rickey from doing his baseball business. The 1933 season was only a few weeks old, and the impatient Cardinals mastermind was convinced that his team had no chance of contending if they did not plug the gaping hole at shortstop caused by Charley Gelbert's injury. It so happened that Sidney Weil was also in New York, traveling with the Reds, and Rickey seized the opportunity to make a trade.

"Sidney, I need a shortstop and you have a young man I can use, Leo Durocher," Rickey implored Weil. "You need pitching and I can help you out there. Don't you think it's time to deal?" Branch Rickey and Sidney Weil were more than just baseball partners and competitors. They had developed a genuine friendship based on their shared roots in Ohio and their mutual devotion to the credo of hard work, community service, and religious commitment. "It made no difference to Branch that Sidney was not a Christian," Weil's son, Irwin, a professor of Russian literature at Northwestern University, wrote in a moving family memoir. "[Rickey] correctly perceived that heaven did not preclude Kosher hot dogs, and the temperaments of truly religious people touched each other."[1]

In addition to their warm personal connection, Rickey was drawn to Sidney Weil's business success story. Like Robert Hedges, Weil had adjusted to modern times, making the successful transition from operating a horse-and-buggy business to running a thriving automobile agency that became lucrative enough for him to fulfill a boyhood dream by buying his hometown Cincinnati baseball team. It was Weil's misfortune, however, to have purchased the Reds on the eve of the great stock market crash in October 1929. Soon he was deeply indebted to local banks, and when some of them failed in the first years of the Great Depression, Weil fell into perilous economic straits. In 1934 he would have to sell the team to radio mogul Powel Crosley.

In May 1933, however, Weil was still trying to make moves to improve the Reds on the field, and he liked doing business with Branch Rickey. In fact, he had tried to entice his St. Louis colleague to join Cincinnati as general manager when Rickey's five-year contract with Sam Breadon had expired in 1932, but the executive did not want to leave St. Louis nor did Breadon want him to go.[2]

Weil had to be content with trading with, instead of hiring, Branch Rickey. He was pleased with the acquisition of former Cardinals Taylor Douthit, Cliff Heathcote, and Wally Roettger, and after two years of trying, on the eve of the 1932 season, Weil had obtained Chick Hafey.[3] Rickey was upfront about the slugger's serious sinus condition, but when he was healthy enough to play Hafey did well in Cincinnati.

Weil was thus more than willing to listen to Rickey's proposal for Leo Durocher, but as one horse trader to another, the Cincinnati owner wanted to make sure that his colleague knew the nonbaseball side of the shortstop's story. "You know about Leo Durocher's off-field baggage, don't you, Branch?" Weil asked. "I have heard the rumors, Sidney, but I know that he has a great will to win," Rickey replied, "and his playing abilities have been endorsed by two men I have the most respect for, Miller Huggins and Ed Barrow." Indeed, when Durocher was signed by the New York Yankees in 1925, Ed Barrow's chief scout, Paul Krichell, raved about Durocher's great hands and overall "moxie." Durocher's future as a hitter was uncertain, but Barrow knew the importance of defense at shortstop, so he authorized Krichell to sign the young man for a bonus reportedly of $7,500.[4]

In 1928 twenty-two-year-old Leo Durocher made his Major League debut as a reserve middle infielder for the Yankees. Branch Rickey saw his skills firsthand during the New Yorkers' sweep of the Cardinals in the 1928 World Series when he served as a defensive replacement for second baseman Tony Lazzeri. The St. Louis executive didn't mind Leo's taunt-ing the Cardinal crowd, always preferring confident, even cocky players to phlegmatic, "anesthetic" ones who put you to sleep with statistics that don't contribute to winning ballgames. Rickey also dismissively called the more passive players "pantywaists."

Lack of confidence was never one of Leo Durocher's problems. When he arrived in Florida in 1928 for spring training, his trunk was larger than Yankees owner Jacob Ruppert's. Known to change his outfits several times a day, his laundry bill would be twice as high as the millionaire beer baron's. Manager Miller Huggins, who saw in the young shortstop the same kind of gritty competitive player he had once been, called Du-rocher aside and reminded him that he was in Florida to train for the season, not to party. As a rookie who had not yet made the team, Leo somewhat toned down his lifestyle in deference to his mentor, who al-ways encouraged him with the exhortation "Little guys like us can win games."[5]

Actually, Durocher, at five foot nine, was not that little, but he was a scrappy street fighter, supremely confident in his abilities (and no doubt masking insecurities about his impoverished upbringing on the wrong side of town). He enjoyed the night life of Prohibition-era New York and quickly made friends with the high-living, big-spending crowd that hung around the sports and entertainment world. Quite possibly, Durocher was the first Major Leaguer to have a day in his honor after being in the Major Leagues for only two months and playing in only ten games. On June 23, 1928, hundreds of his fans from western Massachusetts and many of his high-living New York friends flocked to Yankee Stadium to honor the local boy with gifts and support. It didn't matter that he didn't play in either game of a Yankees' doubleheader loss to the Red Sox. His friends thought Leo deserved a salute for being in the big time. After the game a big party was held, where Prohibition booze flowed and the shortstop's admirers danced to the music of Vincent Lopez. Durocher himself stayed away from alcohol, but he loved the attention of the glam-orous entertainment crowd.[6]

However, in his two years as a part-time player with the Yankees, Duro-cher was never popular with his teammates or the opposition. Babe Ruth labeled him the "All-American Out" and reportedly accused him of pilfering his wristwatch. In one of Durocher's first games against Ty Cobb, who was winding down his career with the Athletics, the brassy shortstop tripped the future Hall of Famer as he was rounding second, heading to third. Cobb threatened grave retaliation if the brash rookie ever tried that maneuver again, and Ruth in this instance protected his teammate from the Georgia Peach's wrath.[7]

When manager Miller Huggins died suddenly before the end of the 1929 season, the handwriting was on the wall for Durocher's career with the Yankees. His fate was sealed when he cursed at general manager Ed Barrow, who refused to raise his salary for 1930. Barrow felt he had more pressing issues to deal with than the insolent salary demands of a light-hitting shortstop. Barrow placed Durocher on irrevocable waivers, and Sidney Weil reportedly outbid Connie Mack's Philadelphia Athletics for his new shortstop.[8]

Durocher was banished to a chronic tail-ender in Cincinnati, a team that would win no more than sixty games in his three full seasons in the Rhineland city from 1930 to 1932. Although he continued to play a fine defensive shortstop, his batting average lagged in the low .200s. Off the field Leo continued to live in the fast lane. He quickly located the gaming tables and pool halls in Cincinnati and across the Ohio River in Kentucky. Before long he piled up a considerable number of debts, for which Sidney Weil was held responsible. In New York Durocher had passed so many bad checks that one angry stationery store owner near Yankee Stadium plastered them on his front window.[9]

After alerting Branch Rickey to Durocher's spendthrift ways, Sidney Weil filled him in on details about Durocher's messy private life. Shortly after arriving in Cincinnati, Durocher had married Ruby Hartley, an aspiring showgirl and waitress who had broken a prior engagement to the son of one of Weil's business associates. When Hartley became pregnant Durocher wasn't prepared for fatherhood, and the marriage soon hit the rocks. Divorce proceedings commenced when Ruby was discovered having an affair with a concessionaire at the Reds ballpark in Cincinnati. One witness in Durocher's behalf was his mother, Clara Durocher, who discovered the adulterous couple in a room in the hotel where she was working as a chambermaid.[10]

At the divorce trial Durocher charged that his wife was an incorrigible drunkard, and Hartley countercharged her husband with desertion and domestic violence. Shortly before the start of the 1933 season, the divorce of Leo Durocher and Ruby Hartley became final, with Leo giving up all rights to the baby girl. It was situations like these in Durocher's past (and future) that led one wit to describe his life as a Horatio Alger story "as if the script had been written by Mickey Spillane."[11]

Branch Rickey cringed when Sidney Weil recounted the story of Durocher losing all rights to his child. Family meant everything to Rickey, and if he could create an ideal scenario, all his players would enjoy the pleasures and responsibilities of marriage and warm domesticity. However, the paternal executive had been around professional ball players long enough to realize that some of them were "matrimonial cowards" and that many lacked what he called "the inner braces" to devote themselves to family life.

Rickey would soon discover that the shortstop had grown up in a poor West Springfield, Massachusetts, neighborhood where French was spoken more than English. His father worked for the Boston and Albany railroad but earned little money. Neither did his mother at menial jobs, so Leo, one of six children, learned early on to live by his wits. The executive certainly was familiar with many great young athletic talents who found the pool hall a far more congenial atmosphere than the study hall. As for Leo's aggressive, almost delinquent behavior off the field, Rickey was used to dealing with such types from his earliest days as a country schoolteacher. It probably wasn't a shock to him when he learned that Durocher had been expelled from high school for punching a mathematics teacher.[12] Rickey was always confident that he could reason, inspire, and straighten out the wayward member of any flock.

Sidney Weil's cautionary tales thus did nothing to dampen Branch Rickey's interest in obtaining the shortstop. If anything, they piqued his interest in undertaking what Branch Rickey Jr. would soon call "Dad's favorite reclamation project." Before they finalized the trade details, Weil offered some final advice to Rickey on the best way to deal with Durocher. He suggested that he try to talk to him fifteen minutes at the beginning of each day and tell him what opportunities for him lay ahead in the day and what pitfalls may be out there too. Weil also warned Rickey with a resigned sigh, "The things he does sometimes, he can't help them."[13]

Rickey trusted Weil's judgment of people and thanked him for the advice. They proceeded to work out the trade, in which Durocher would come to St. Louis along with pitchers Frank "Dutch" Henry and Jack Ogden in exchange for two pitchers, the 1931 rookie sensation Paul Derringer and Allyn Stout, and third baseman Sparky Adams. Rickey considered Adams, the diminutive infielder he had once confused with the batboy, expendable because Pepper Martin could handle third base now that Ernie Orsatti was the regular center fielder and Joe Medwick had taken over in left field.

The key to the deal for Cincinnati was Paul Derringer. Except for his World Series failures, Derringer had been a bellwether and innings eater in the St. Louis rotation. However, Rickey felt he had enough pitching, with newcomers James "Tex" Carleton from Texas Christian University and southpaw Bill Walker, obtained in a trade with the Giants, to join Dizzy Dean, Jess Haines, and Bill Hallahan on the starting staff. You had to give up something to get something was a good horse trading principle, Rickey and Sidney Weil both agreed.

Derringer had also been a constant salary holdout, and his libertine lifestyle off the field, earning him the nicknames "Dude" and "Duke," was not to Rickey's liking. (Bill Turner, a longtime Rickey assistant, says that the executive always took seriously the nicknames players gave each other as an insight into their character.)[14] Shortly before the trade was made, publicity director Gene Karst remembered an angry discussion between Rickey and Derringer that could be heard in other Cardinals offices. Afterward Rickey followed Derringer out of the office, shouting the most profane words Karst had ever heard from his God-fearing boss.[15]

The trade was completed on May 7, 1933. With the Reds and the Cardinals both in New York City for their games against the Giants and the Dodgers, Sidney Weil thought it best to inform Durocher of the trade in person because he knew that the fiery shortstop would take the news hard. "To St. Louis? To Rickey?" Durocher cried when Weil broke the news in Leo's hotel room. "I am not going," Durocher cried. "I won't work on his chain gang, never, never, never!" Weil replied, "Leo, the deal is done, and since Mr. Rickey is here in New York, why don't you go over to his hotel and at least meet him?"

The disgruntled shortstop and his thoughtful ex-owner headed to

Rickey's hotel for what would be a memorable first encounter. As Weil and Durocher entered Rickey's room, the indisposed executive was propped up in his hotel room bed, still suffering with the flu, wearing an old-fashioned Victorian stocking cap and reading a Gideon Bible. Vowing to be on his worst behavior, hoping against hope that he could cause Rickey to rescind the trade, Durocher pulled up a chair to Rickey's bed and put his foot on the bedspread. "I've heard about your chain gangs and your coolie wages, and I don't want any part of it," Durocher snarled. He complained that he had made few friends in baseball, and whenever a supporter came along like Miller Huggins or Sidney Weil, he was taken away from him. The frustrated player said that he'd rather go back home to Springfield than play for a cheapskate.

Except for a few sniffles and coughs from his bed, Rickey silently listened to Durocher's rants. Then it was time for him to speak. "Young man, you have said a lot of things about me, and some of them may be true," Rickey began diplomatically. "But you are a ballplayer and a good one. Why do you think I traded for you if I didn't think you could help us win a pennant?" Durocher listened silently as Rickey began to build up verbal momentum, getting carried away as usual with the sound of his words as he sought to win over a skeptical player. "You say that you won't report and won't play for the Cardinals, is that right?" Rickey asked. Durocher mumbled a barely audible yes. "How would you feel, young man, if because we had to play an inferior shortstop, our team lost the pennant? Don't you realize that with you in our lineup we can win another pennant? Have you been buried in the basement in Cincinnati for so long that you have forgotten why you are playing this game?"[16]

Like so many players before him, Leo Durocher was getting won over by Rickey's mesmerizing salesmanship. His resolve to sabotage the trade quickly faded. From their first meeting, a peculiar yet genuine rapport developed between the erudite and schoolmasterly Rickey and the streetwise and belligerent Durocher, a bond that would deepen through many controversies in the years ahead. Rickey loved Durocher's competitive zeal and his knowledge of inside baseball. They were likeminded in their willingness to try any play and use any player to win a game. Rickey noted early on that Durocher had a keen if unschooled intelligence, which the executive confidently planned to develop and, ideally, domesticate.

Rickey's florid vocabulary awed the new Cardinals shortstop, who, after an early encounter, rushed to the dictionary to find out what his new boss meant by "tranquility." Soon Durocher was gushing, "Why, if you absorb only half of what Mr. Rickey says, you'll come out ahead."[17]

Rickey would also soon learn and take mental note of his new short-stop's color blindness. Durocher never forgot that it was a fellow motor-cycle battery factory worker on the assembly line in Springfield, a black man named David Redd, who had encouraged him to take a chance on the adventure of pro baseball. "You can always come back to the factory," Redd counseled, and a grateful Durocher always left tickets for Redd whenever his friend came to town.[18] Ten years later, when it was time for Branch Rickey to break the color line in baseball, he believed without a doubt that Leo Durocher would be the ideal manager to shepherd whomever was chosen to lead that cause.

As the encounter in Rickey's hotel room drew to a close, Durocher promised he would report to the Cardinals at the Polo Grounds the next day, May 8, 1933. An arrangement was reached that once he arrived in St. Louis, Durocher would be placed on a strict spending allowance. Rickey told Weil to send all of Durocher's extant bills to the Cardinals of-fice, where a payment schedule to creditors would be worked out. Some of Durocher's debts were incurred to gamblers, and Commissioner Lan-dis wanted to know more, but as in the case of Rogers Hornsby, Rickey and Weil convinced Landis that none of these obligations compromised Durocher's standing in the game.[19]

As often happens in the immediate aftermath of a baseball trade, a team's performance improves. The Cardinals went 19-7 in Durocher's first games as the new shortstop. He was having fun playing baseball again for a team whose future looked far more promising than the hapless Reds. His arrival solidified the St. Louis infield defense, with Frank Frisch back at second base, Pepper Martin at third base, and Jim "Rip" Collins, who had first base all to himself with Jim Bottomley traded to the Cubs.

Durocher was on good behavior in his first months as a Cardinal, re-alizing that he was in debt and that Commissioner Landis had an eye on his gambling associations and penchant for writing bad checks. The shortstop didn't want to sabotage what might be his last chance at being with a successful organization. In fact, of the colorful cast of characters he joined in St. Louis, Durocher was usually just an innocent bystander to many of their pranks and bouts of temperament.

For instance, during the shortstop's first appearance in Cincinnati a month after the trade, a big ruckus broke out during batting practice when former teammates Dizzy Dean and Paul Derringer got into a fist-fight in full view of early-arriving fans at the ballpark.[20] Neither player was hurt and Dean laughed it off afterward, but perhaps the colorful Cardinals pitcher felt lingering resentment that Derringer had made the 1931 world championship team while Dean was sent back to the Minors. Or maybe Dean was just feeling his oats as a rising national star and was living up to his reputation as Branch Rickey's most "unpredictable boy."

Unfortunately, the Cardinals' improved play in the first weeks after Durocher's arrival did not sustain itself. With the arrival of summer the team began to sink toward the second division. One of the most disappointing days occurred in New York two days before the Fourth of July, the traditional midpoint of the 154-game baseball season. The Cardinals were swept by the Giants in New York by identical 1–0 scores. The first game went eighteen innings, with Carl Hubbell, the Giants' ace southpaw, edging Tex Carleton. In the nightcap Roy Parmelee beat Dizzy Dean before forty thousand happy fans at the Polo Grounds. Dean would reclaim the headlines on July 30, 1933, when he set a Major League record of seventeen strikeouts in a victory over the Cubs, but despite an occasionally breathtaking individual performance, the Cardinals were once again not a pennant-contending team.

In late July 1933 Sam Breadon exercised his managerial trigger finger by firing his two-time World Series manager Gabby Street. Breadon decided that Street had lost the respect of the veteran players, and couldn't motivate the younger ones. It was a judgment that many sportswriters and some members of the team thought valid. St. Louis at the time was only one game over .500, and Breadon expected much more so Street walked the plank. As always, Branch Rickey couldn't change Breadon's mind when he decided on managerial changes, but the vice president did suggest that Frank Frisch would be the ideal replacement. He was working well with newcomer Durocher in the vital middle of the diamond, had passion for the game, and hated to lose.

When Frisch met with Breadon and Rickey, the second baseman was initially reluctant. He feared that the extra duties as player-manager would hamper his abilities on the field. (Frisch later said in retirement that his only regret in baseball was that his dual duties cost him a chance at 3,000 career hits; he finished with 2,846.)[21] However, when Rickey turned on his salesman's spigot, the ambivalent infielder could not say no, especially since Breadon also wanted him to accept. The owner had been forever grateful to the "Fordham Flash" for making the Hornsby trade look good, and the fiery second baseman thus felt a double sense of duty to accept the job.

Frisch took over the Cardinals in late July and led the team to a 36-26 record. Overall, St. Louis finished at 82-71, good enough only for fifth place, nine games behind the pennant-winning Giants, and also trailing the Cubs, Pirates, and Braves. The Giants, led by player-manager Bill Terry in his first full season as successor to the legendary John McGraw, won the 1933 World Series over the Washington Senators, returning the championship flag to the National League in a hard-fought five-game Series. Yet, in a sign of the economically depressed times, the World Series was not played to capacity, even though the owners waived the traditional rule that every customer must buy strips of tickets for three games. Although tickets were available on a daily basis, not one game sold out.[22]

The decline in World Series attendance was not surprising because during the regular season the world champion Giants had suffered a loss of more than 200,000 fans from their average attendance in the prede-pression 1920s. They drew only 604,471 fans in 1933. In the leanest year of the Great Depression, aggregate Major League attendance was down 4 million from 1930 totals, and total Minor League attendance was off significantly too.[23]

St. Louis attendance mirrored the national decline. The Cardinals drew only 256,171 fans, averaging a paltry 3,327 per game, a loss of al-most 25,000 fans from 1932.[24] A trend that truly alarmed Sam Breadon was that since the record-breaking season of attendance in 1928, the Cardinals had lost more than half a million paying customers. Things were far worse for the St. Louis Browns, who suffered through an embar-rassing 1933 season, in which only 88,113 spectators came to see a last-place team that lost ninety-six games.[25] Around the time that Frank Frisch became Cardinals manager, Rogers Hornsby, with Branch Rickey's help, was named Browns manager, but nothing could change the fortunes of a team stuck indefinitely in the second division.[26] Hiring Hornsby was the last major act of frustrated owner Phil Ball's career; he died soon thereafter on August 22, 1933.

The year 1933 brought disappointment to Branch Rickey not just on the Major League level. As a man who loathed having to fire anybody, he made the reluctant decision in late spring to replace Larry MacPhail as president of the Columbus Redbirds. As he had promised, MacPhail had proven to be a great promoter, and despite the depression the Redbirds set attendance records in the attractive new stadium equipped with lights and featuring the typical MacPhailian promotions. In 1933 Columbus would celebrate its first pennant winner since 1907, but MacPhail wouldn't be around to enjoy the celebration.

One factor in MacPhail's dismissal was an operational extravagance that made cost-conscious Sam Breadon and Branch Rickey blanch. As a devotee of aviation, Rickey did not mind that MacPhail pioneered in flying the Redbirds on road trips, even if some of the players were too airsick to play afterward.[27] However, during a visit to MacPhail's Columbus office, Breadon and Rickey noticed office rugs and walnut wood paneling far more luxurious than the spartan surroundings at the team's main office in St. Louis. MacPhail tried to explain that the rugs were a gift from a contractor, who was pleased that the team president had awarded him a bonus for completing his work ahead of schedule.[28]

Another bone of contention between the home office and Columbus centered on MacPhail's complaint that St. Louis recalled too many players to the Majors who were fan favorites and contributors in Columbus. There was also a concern that MacPhail was paying his Minor League players under the table more than was allowable by regulation, an infraction that resulted in a fine imposed by the American Association.[29]

It is possible that all these problems could have been worked out, but MacPhail's tempestuous personality, especially when influenced by alcohol, ultimately grew too embarrassing. The last straw was when the volatile operator, in one of his inebriated rages, got into a late-night shouting match with the bartender in a road hotel where the Columbus Redbirds were staying. As MacPhail reached higher and higher dudgeon, he insisted that the desk clerk rouse all the players. He was going to find a better kind of hotel, he roared, one that would not employ such a blankety-blank bartender.[30]

The brilliant executive stayed out of baseball for over a season and even pledged not to touch alcohol for a whole year. "Why don't you make it permanent?" Rickey suggested, with the enthusiastic encouragement of Herman MacPhail, Larry's half brother.[31] It was too much to expect permanent sobriety from the impatient, exuberant promoter, but the teetotaling Cardinals vice president always believed that one's good work habits outweighed one's private indiscretions. Rickey highly recommended MacPhail to Powel Crosley when the position of Cincinnati general manager opened up in 1935. MacPhail was on his way to a stormy, successful Major League front office career that would lead him to the Dodgers and, after World War II, to the Yankees and a turbulent collision with his onetime sponsor who had taken his place in Brooklyn.

As Branch Rickey assessed the difficult year of 1933 in his annual postseason meeting with his staff, the feelings of loss and defeat stuck in his competitive craw. It had been nearly a decade since the Cardinals had been out of the pennant running two years in a row. "Never grow accustomed to the emotions of continuous defeat" remained a maxim Rickey lived by, and he vowed that the new season would be better.

As 1934 spring training, the always hopeful time of rebirth, neared, Branch Rickey believed that the Cardinals had a fighting chance to re-emerge at the top of the National League. Rickey analyzed the 1933 season's statistics and saw plenty of hope. In his first full season Joe Medwick justified the trade of Chick Hafey by leading the Cardinals with 18 HR and 98 RBI to go with an impressive .306 BA. As the successor to Jim Bottomley at first base, Rip Collins had brought his batting average up to .308, but his power numbers had dropped to 10 HR and 68 RBI. At least, Collins' nickname was one that pleased Rickey, because it was related to baseball, not off-field behavior. He was "Rip" because of the authoritative sound his bat made on contact with the ball.

Rickey also drew hope from looking at how well the Cardinals as a team had done in key categories in 1933. They led the league in runs scored, doubles, and stolen bases, the first two usually a sign of a con-

tending if not championship team. The pitchers led the league in strikeouts and tied with the Boston Braves for saves, but individually the results
had been mediocre in 1933. Dizzy Dean won twenty games for the first
time, but he also lost eighteen. Newcomer Tex Carleton was a solid 17-
11, and veteran Bill Hallahan turned in a 16-13 record, but venerable
Jess Haines, at 9-6, was the only other pitcher on the staff with a winning
record.

As always, Rickey expected a boost from the farm system in 1934. Dizzy
Dean never ceased to remind the Cardinal brass that his brother Paul,
two years younger, should already have been in St. Louis. In 1933, in
his fourth Minor League season, Paul Dean put it all together, winning
twenty-two games at Columbus as he led the Redbirds to the pennant
and a victory in the Little World Series. He surely was ready for the big
show, Dizzy Dean believed, and Branch Rickey certainly hoped that Dizzy
was right about his brother.

Late in February 1934 the Cardinals began to trickle into their Bradenton, Florida, spring training camp. Publicist Gene Karst drove Branch
Rickey's automobile from St. Louis so the team executive could ride as
a passenger in the Buick convertible of his friend St. Louis industrialist
Walter Weisenburger, the president of the National Association of Manufacturers. After holding his own in an exhibition billiards match with
world champion Frank Taberski, Leo Durocher, now an all-year resident
of St. Louis, headed to Bradenton. A speeding ticket in Chattanooga,
Tennessee, and a driving rainstorm did not prevent Durocher from arriving on time for his first spring training as a Cardinal.[32]

The pundits predicted wide-open pennant races, with Bill Terry's New
York Giants favored to repeat as National League champion, but several
contenders were ready to challenge them, including the Cardinals, with
Frank Frisch primed for a full year as player-manager. St. Louis fans were
hoping that Frisch would duplicate Rogers Hornsby's success of a world
championship in his first full year of managing. *New York Post* sportswriter
John Lardner, the ranking member of the talented literary Lardner family now that Ring Lardner had passed away the previous summer, agreed
that the Cardinals deserved watching, especially Leo Durocher and Pepper Martin. "Between them they have more energy and fire than you'll
find in the entire rosters of many clubs," Lardner wrote.[33]

If one believed in bad omens, the preseason of the New York Giants opened on a sad note. On February 25, 1934, word came from just outside New York City that John J. McGraw had died at age sixty of uremic poisoning at his home in New Rochelle. One of the great eminences in National League history hardly had any time to enjoy his retirement before he passed away. Branch Rickey was saddened by the loss of a respected rival and a trusted baseball friend. "He was an artist and a pioneer," Rickey said upon learning of McGraw's death. "He was the first man to think for the batters after the count on the pitchers had reached two strikes and no balls, or three and two."[34]

The other disconcerting note for the Giants seemed minor at the time, but as the 1934 season unfolded to its dramatic end, the incident foreshadowed disaster for the New Yorkers. At a pre–spring training press conference, Bill Terry wondered aloud why he had heard nothing about the prospects of the Brooklyn Dodgers for the coming year. Their business office did not seem to be open, and Terry asked the reporters matter-of-factly, "Is Brooklyn still in the league?" The Giants manager, never at ease with the aggressive New York sportswriters, did not realize that the New York newspapers would report Terry's plaintive question as an arrogant affront to a whole borough. Casey Stengel, the Dodgers' colorful manager, rejoined that Brooklyn was indeed still in the league. "Tell that to Bill Terry," he said to the sportswriters. "And I don't care what you fellows call my club—the Daffiness Boys, the Screwy Subs, or anything, just as long as they hustle."[35] Stengel was speaking for Brooklyn's proud, rambunctious fans, who kept Terry's ill-worded question in mind and hoped for revenge sometime during the coming season.

As Walter Weisenburger and Branch Rickey pulled into Bradenton in late February 1934, Rickey's churning, always restless mind contemplated a possible bombshell trade. He was concerned about his catching. He wasn't sure if Virgil "Spud" Davis, who he had obtained from the Phillies in an off-season trade for Jimmy Wilson (who became the Philadelphia manager), could handle the team's pitching. There was a prospect named Bill Delancey who might make the grade, Rickey thought, but he could never be certain when a Minor Leaguer was ready. There was a Boston Braves catcher, Al Spohrer, who intrigued him. Boston was interested in Frank Frisch, and Burgess Whitehead had been waiting in the wings for at least two years as the second baseman of the future. "Should I trade Frisch for Spohrer?" Rickey asked himself.[36]

After mulling over the possibility, Rickey decided that trading the popular player was too risky. He realized that Frisch remained a favorite of Sam Breadon, and he thought that the second baseman also deserved the chance to manage the Cardinals for at least a full season. The ferocious gentleman did not yet know what a glorious season lay ahead in 1934, a year when his Cardinals would captivate a national audience and become known to history (if not yet to contemporaries) as "The Gashouse Gang." However, as Frank Frisch prepared to address the troops for the first time in spring training, Branch Rickey was brimming with hope for a return to the top of the National League.

11

The Triumph of the Gashouse Gang

As Frank Frisch took the helm at Bradenton for his first spring training as manager, he gave a short speech, reminiscent of Rogers Hornsby's confident talk at the start of 1926. "We can win it all, if you give you it all," the Fordham Flash said.

"If any of you humpty-dumpties don't think we can win, turn in your jock straps now, and [team secretary] Clarence Lloyd will get your train ticket back to the coal mines or farm, or wherever the else you can starve these days."[1] Frisch added that his philosophy could be summed up in a simple phrase: "Win today's game." The inspirational thought was hung up in the clubhouse by team trainer Harrison "Bucko" Weaver.

Unlike Hornsby's 1926 camp, Frisch worked the Cardinals hard. Resorting to Rickey's regimen when he was manager, the feisty skipper scheduled two practices, one in the morning and one in the afternoon, and emphasized the fundamentals of playing winning baseball. "Sliding is not simply falling down," Frisch declared. "The purpose is to avoid the tag." Frisch covered every aspect of base running, instructing infielders on the proper method of applying the tag and instructing base runners on the proper way of taking leads off bases and eluding the tag. Conversely, he made sure that his pitchers practiced the proper techniques of holding runners on base.[2]

Once the season began Frisch told his charges that they should report to the ballpark by noon for batting practice (most games were still played at three o'clock in the afternoon). He said he would not impose a curfew per se, but he expected his players on the road to be in bed by midnight. If he had doubts about certain players exploring the wonders of the night in National League cities, Frisch was not hesitant about hiring private detectives. However, he would be far surer about his suspicions than Billy Southworth had been during the rookie manager's difficult half season as manager in 1929.

Frisch had one more announcement as the 1934 training season began. He introduced a new team captain, Leo Durocher, who he felt had the right kind of competitive smarts and leadership skills. With Durocher as captain Frisch's own load as player-manager could be reduced. Branch Rickey approved the choice, and probably suggested it, reasoning that in giving Durocher more on-field responsibility, it might limit his penchant for questionable off-field associations. There was a new member of the Durocher admiration society—Jane Rickey, who was captivated by the shortstop's boyish sense of adventure and genuine love of children. With her husband's enthusiastic encouragement, she kept her eyes open for a possible marital match for the team's new captain.

One big story in the Bradenton camp was the arrival of Paul Dean, fresh from his big season at Columbus. It was sportswriter hyperbole that created the nickname "Daffy" for Paul, because the younger Dean was as quiet and noncontroversial as Dizzy was talkative and cocky. Dizzy, though, was more than willing to speak for them both, predicting that "me and Paul" would combine for forty-five wins in 1934 and that ninety-five victories would bring the Cardinals the pennant.

However, as exhibition games started in early March, neither Dean was signed for the upcoming season, and Dizzy was complaining that Paul's contract offer was insultingly low. Roy Stockton of the *Post-Dispatch*, who was Dizzy Dean's regular ghost writer, wrote that Rickey was getting impatient and planned to charge Paul for postage if he didn't sign and mail back his contract immediately. Dizzy shot back that Paul would pitch for no salary until he won fifteen games and would then charge $500 a win. "And the club turned that offer down!" Dean moaned. "You can't tell what a club's going to do nowadays."[3]

By mid-March both Deans did sign—Paul probably for around $3,000, close to standard for a rookie, and Dizzy probably for a few thousand dollars less than the $12,000 he said he was getting. However, the colorful pitcher's fame was growing, and he would more than triple his salary in commercial endorsements. In fact, Dizzy Dean was growing into the role of a national celebrity. There was need for a new larger-than-life hero now that Babe Ruth was nearing the end of his career. (Ruth would leave the Yankees after the 1934 season and would retire from baseball in June 1935, soon after hitting 3 home runs in a game for the Boston Braves.)

Dizzy Dean was ready, willing, and able to play the role of national folk hero, and there was no telling what Branch Rickey's unpredictable boy might do next. In one exhibition game Dean hit seven members of the Giants after the New Yorkers scored seven runs off him. "They ain't going to beat the Master like that," Dizzy declared.[4] When the bell rang for opening day on Tuesday, April 17, 1934, Dizzy was ready for the big occasion, easily beating the Pirates, 7–1.

However, in a sign that the depression was still hurting the pocketbooks of fans, only 7,500 spectators paid their way into Sportsman's Park. Although interest in Major League Baseball was undimmed, that enthusiasm was not necessarily converted into box office receipts. The Cardinals did not help matters locally by deciding not to carry games on the radio in 1934, feeling that the broadcasts were keeping fans away. It was a decision Sam Breadon probably made on his own, because Branch Rickey always believed that good radio broadcasts attracted customers. As matters turned out the lack of daily, pitch-by-pitch news hurt the gate even more, and before the end of the year the Cardinals allowed some limited radio broadcasts to resume and then restored them fully in 1935.[5]

In the first weeks of the 1934 season the Dean brothers did not hit their stride immediately. Paul Dean was actually winless until early May, but when they both started rolling, the wins came in bunches. Their dominance came in handy because of a freak injury to Bill Walker, who broke a leg in a pregame accident when Joe Medwick hit him with a batting practice line drive. Although Walker often walked more people than he struck out, he was a crafty pitcher, and his absence opened a big void on the Cardinal mound. When spitballer Burleigh Grimes, a hero of the 1931 World Series, was released a month into the season, it became evident that the burden of pitching for the 1934 Cardinals would fall mainly on Dizzy and Paul Dean.

The rivalries among the three 1934 contenders—the Giants, Cardinals, and Cubs—were particularly fierce. On Sunday, May 20, Dizzy outdueled the Giants' Carl Hubbell before nearly forty thousand fans in New York.

It was the future Hall of Famer Hubbell's first loss of 1934, and sweet revenge for the Cardinals' 1-0 doubleheader losses to the Giants a year earlier. The Dean-Hubbell duels were taking their place in American lore alongside other American cultural tandems of the 1930s—radio's Fibber McGee and Molly and Amos and Andy, and bank robbers Bonnie and Clyde Barrow, who were shot to death by the authorities three days after Dizzy beat Hubbell.[6]

Then, just ten days after his victory over Hubbell, Dizzy made a startling announcement. He proclaimed that he was going on a sit-down strike in behalf of his poorly paid brother. The national press, especially in New York, liked to say that the Cardinals paid "coolie wages," but Sam Breadon insisted that the team's payroll ranked in the top half of the National League. Always averse to discussing specific salaries in public, Branch Rickey was willing to engage in a general colloquy with Roy Stockton on what constituted a fair Major League salary.

"The average should be $6500 for a star player," Rickey said. "And he should be able to play for eight years." He added that a thrifty player should be able to save $5,000 of his salary. Stockton rejoined, "Mr. Rickey, do you save $5,000 out of each $6,500 you earn? You have help at your house, your children go to the best schools, you eat well, travel, and have automobiles." Rickey replied, "Well, of course, a player could not expect to save $5,000 if he lived like that."[7]

Not surprisingly, Dizzy Dean's sit-down strike did not last long. Even St. Louis writers, not prone to side with Branch Rickey in salary disputes, pointed out that pitcher Hal Schumacher, now in his second full season with the Giants, received the same $3,000 as a rookie that Paul Dean was earning. *New York Post* sportswriter John Lardner observed that the Deans would have a much better case if they weren't just asking for more money for themselves. "'Strike a blow for the Deans!' is Dizzy's motto," Lardner noted. "Strike a blow for oppressed ivory everywhere" would be a better strategy, the writer suggested.[8] (Of course, collective action by the baseball players was still decades in the future.) Dizzy Dean soon ended his work stoppage, reportedly upon the pleas of Jess Haines, the elder statesman on the pitching staff. As was usually the case, quiet Paul Dean was noncommittal, going along with Dizzy's actions only out of a sense of family loyalty.

A crisis with the unpredictable pitcher averted for the moment, St. Louis baseball fans returned to following the pennant race. It was the hottest summer in St. Louis in over sixty years; for thirty days in a row the temperature soared above one hundred degrees, and the heat wave would kill over a hundred people in the Midwest. The sweltering weather was tough on the home team, but it was also a burden on the visitors. One day near the end of June, Dizzy Dean and Pepper Martin decided to mock the visiting Giants. They grabbed some old scorecards and rubbish, lit a big fire in front of the dugout, and, to the great delight of the fans, Dizzy started doing a dance as Martin and other teammates cheered him on.[9]

At the All-Star Game break in early July, the Cardinals were in third place, two games behind the second-place Cubs and four behind the league-leading Giants. At twelve games over .500 they were positioned for a good second half of the season. At the second annual All-Star Game, the Cardinals' representatives did well. Dizzy Dean pitched three effective innings, and Frank Frisch and Joe Medwick each homered. However, for the second year in a row, the American League won, 9–7. (What is most remembered about the 1934 All-Star Game is that, while pitching in his home park of the Polo Grounds, Carl Hubbell made baseball history by striking out five future American League Hall of Famers in a row: Babe Ruth, Lou Gehrig, Jimmy Foxx, Al Simmons, and Joe Cronin.)

When the pennant race resumed, the Cardinals hit many bumps in the road. Aging Frank Frisch had aggravated a charley horse in the All-Star Game and was slumping at the plate. Paul Dean lost three games in a row, and his confidence began to wane. The press was grumbling that Sam Breadon and Branch Rickey didn't seem to want to improve the team because the Cardinals were carrying only twenty-one players on the roster, two short of the twenty-three-man limit, introduced in 1932 as a depression cost-cutting measure.[10]

The Cardinals reached a nadir on Sunday, August 12, 1934, when they were swept by the Cubs in a doubleheader in Chicago. They were still in third place, but seven and a half games behind the Giants and certainly not playing pennant-winning baseball. The next day the team assembled to play an exhibition game at Detroit's Navin Field against the Tigers. It was another one of the many exhibition games scheduled by Branch

Rickey and Sam Breadon to broaden the team's fan base, to provide a payday for management, and not least, as far as Rickey was concerned, to keep players from getting into extracurricular trouble.

However, Dizzy and Paul Dean were missing in action. Disconsolate about the loss of the Sunday doubleheader, the first time they had ever lost two games on the same day in the Major Leagues, the brothers decided to skip the exhibition game. Instead, they accepted an offer to attend a barbecue with some friends south of Chicago. Everyone in the organization was in a snit about the absence. Their teammates were enraged that the pitchers skipped out while the rest of the team had to play a meaningless game. Forty thousand Tiger fans were upset that they were missing a chance to see baseball's largest drawing card, who were supposed to coach first and third base.[11] Perhaps angriest of all was St. Louis player-manager Frisch.

Frisch had usually defended Dizzy Dean from his critics. He might be crazy, the Fordham Flash would say about the unpredictable pitcher, but it helps to be crazy to play the devilish game of baseball. However, running out on the team, and dragging along his kid brother, was the last straw. He announced the indefinite suspension of both Deans, and Rickey and Breadon gave him their full support.

When Dizzy and Paul returned to St. Louis from the barbecue, they took the news of the their suspension defiantly. Dizzy took off his uniform and, in front of sportswriters and photographers, tore it into pieces. When another wave of reporters and cameramen came into the Cardinal clubhouse, Dean obliged by taking another uniform and ripping that up too. "Old Rickey's handy with a needle, ain't he?" Dean said sarcastically.[12] His action, of course, only hardened the position of management.

Meanwhile, the Cardinals started to play winning baseball. They rattled off seven wins in a row as the team started to prove to itself that it was more than just the Dizzy and Paul Dean show. Leo Durocher in particular voiced the sentiment that the Cardinals would show the Deans that they could win without them. Branch Rickey was not surprised at the sudden winning streak. "Football coaches pray for an incident such as this," he confided to publicity director Gene Karst. "They want something, some development, which can change the direction of the team, fire it up to superhuman effort."[13] Rickey, of course, understood that a baseball season was much longer than a football season and that fever-pitch intensity could not be maintained for every game. However, the veteran executive firmly believed that a great team rises to the challenge of being undermanned, especially as the dog days of summer wear on.

After a few days of his suspension Paul Dean wanted to return, was quickly reinstated, and pitched a complete-game victory on Friday, August 17. Dizzy Dean still held out, feeling as the virtual successor to Babe Ruth that he had the stature to pull off a remarkable rebellion. With his having already earned his twentieth victory on August 8, Dean's considerable ego had been slaked by his growing national stature among fans and sportswriters.[14] For instance, the nationally syndicated Grantland Rice, who had immortalized the "Four Horsemen" of the Notre Dame football backfield in the 1920s, had recently penned an elegy, "Dizzy Gunga Dean (If Mr. Kipling Doesn't Mind)."[15]

Dean decided to plead his case in front of baseball commissioner Kenesaw Mountain Landis. He drove seven hours to Chicago and told the czar, "I want to get back to pitching baseball. And I'm willing to do anything necessary to straighten this out." The commissioner called a hearing for all parties in St Louis for Monday, August 20. "You go back to St. Louis and be at the Park Plaza Hotel at ten o'clock on Monday morning," Landis told him. "And when I say 'ten o'clock,' I don't mean 'one minute after ten.'"[16]

To the pitcher's dismay Landis barred sportswriters from the hearing, but the canny, media-savvy commissioner opened a vent in the hearing room window so the horde of reporters could hear the vociferous testimony that dragged on for four and a half hours. Having boycotted an exhibition and publicly insulted the team by tearing up his uniform, Dean did not have much of a case except to rail about the cheapness of the Cardinals and the lowly salary of his brother. He complained that he was worried about a sore arm he got pitching against the Cubs and that his brother was worried about an ankle injury.

In reply, with Branch Rickey playing the role of lead attorney, Frank Frisch spoke ardently on behalf of the team unity that the Deans had disrupted. He was backed up by captain Leo Durocher, team physician Dr. Robert Hyland, and trainer Harrison Weaver. When it was time for Rickey to state his case for the team's fair treatment of the Dean brothers, he felt confident. Although the pitchers' insubordination, and not their salaries, was at issue in the hearing, Rickey stated that he believed his pay scale was fair. Because of depression cutbacks all team salaries had been cut. Frisch, who once earned $28,000 as solely a player was now making $18,500 as player-manager, and veterans Pepper Martin and Bill Halla-han were receiving only $9,000 a year. With less experience Dizzy Dean was earning around $7,500.[17] Exact salary figures would not be known by the players until their union many decades later demanded them, but in a time of economic depression and social unrest, players were largely grateful for having jobs and the stature of being Major Leaguers. Thus, when Rickey asked Dean in front of Landis why he did not think his sal-ary was adequate, the pitcher had no easy rebuttal.[18]

Acting expeditiously, Landis ruled on the same day as the hearing that the Cardinals were in their right to suspend the Deans for boycotting the exhibition. "Ballplayers owe their public a certain obligation, and you two boys owed the City of Detroit, the management of the Tigers, and the management of the Cardinals something important in their lives," Landis declared. "Dizzy, I support them fully."[19] When Dean received the bad news, *St. Louis Globe-Democrat* sportswriter Martin J. Haley wrote, "his facial expression indicated he could not believe what he heard. . . . It seemed as if he felt that his best friend had turned against him."[20] With no other cards to play Dean had no choice but to accept his fate. Yet there was a spirit of compromise in the air as Breadon and Rickey slightly reduced both the fines and the number of days without pay.

The extra rest must have helped their arms because the Deans were dynamos down the stretch. Dizzy was on his way to a 30-7 season, the National League's first thirty-game winner since Grover Cleveland Alex-ander with the 1917 Phillies. He was second in the league in ERA at 2.66, and his 312 innings pitched were third in the league. Paul Dean logged a 19-11 record, pitching 233 innings to an ERA of 3.43. The brothers' total of forty-nine wins was four more than the forty-five Dizzy had promised in spring training. They were especially effective against the Giants, com-bining to win most of the twenty-two games the Cardinals played against Bill Terry's team in 1934.

No two victories were bigger than the doubleheader they won at the Polo Grounds on September 16 in front of more than sixty-two thousand fans, the largest crowd in the history of the National League. The start of the first game was held up for more than half an hour to allow the fans to enter a stadium that had only fifty-five thousand seats. What made the 5–3 and 3–1 victories especially sweet was that the Dean brothers beat the Giants' two aces, Carl Hubbell and "Prince" Hal Schumacher.

Despite the sweep the Cardinals still trailed the Giants by three and a half games, and many sportswriters bemoaned the games lost to the New Yorkers earlier in the season. The players, though, were optimistic, knowing that if they kept on winning they would put great pressure on the Giants. On Friday, September 21, the Deans swept another doubleheader against the Dodgers in Brooklyn. Dizzy pitched a 3-hit shutout in a 13–0 first-game romp, and Paul outdid his brother by throwing a no-hitter in a 3–0 victory in the second game, the first Cardinals no-hitter since Jess Haines threw one in 1924. Afterward puckish Dizzy said that if Paul had told him he was going to pitch a no-hitter, he would have thrown one first.

The doubleheader sweep brightened Branch Rickey's mood. It took away some of the gloom from the news earlier in the day that German immigrant Bruno Hauptmann had been charged with murder in the kidnapping and death of the infant son of Charles Lindbergh. Rickey thought back to the joyous Sunday afternoon in June 1927 when Lindbergh, recently returned from his solo flight across the Atlantic, did the honors of raising the 1926 Cardinals' championship flag at Sportsman's Park. Rickey had grieved when he learned that the Lindbergh baby had been kidnapped, but he thought that the aviation pioneer had made an error in judgment by not going through regular police channels in the attempt to recover his child.[21]

Hauptmann's arraignment brought back to Rickey all the sadness in the Lindbergh story that once seemed like a wonderful American success saga, the story of a "lone eagle" who had conquered the unknown with brilliance and courage. "At least, we have the pennant race to enjoy and be thrilled with," Rickey may well have thought to himself. "It does free our minds for a little while from thinking about the world's troubles." Earlier, in August 1934, Adolf Hitler's Nazi government had taken full control of Germany after the Reichstag fire destroyed the meeting place of the German legislature. Rickey feared that before long there would be even worse news coming from Germany.

When the Cardinals returned to St. Louis for the last week of the regular season, they still trailed the Giants by two games but only one in the lost column. If they won their remaining six games and the Giants lost one, the worst the Cardinals could do was finish in a first-place tie and play the New Yorkers in a three-game playoff. On the last Tuesday of the regular season Dizzy Dean beat the Pirates, 3–2, while the Giants were losing to the Phillies. The two teams were now all even in the lost column, and the Cardinals had the momentum of expecting to win while the Giants were going into a slump at the worst possible time of the season. Looming at the end of the New York schedule were two home games against the hated Dodgers, whose diehard fans were salivating at the thought of exacting revenge on the Giants and manager Bill Terry, who had arrogantly asked in the preseason, "Is Brooklyn still in the league?"

The Cardinals seemed primed to pull off a thrilling, come-from-behind pennant victory when a distraction arose within the team family. On the morning of Wednesday, September 26, an agitated Leo Durocher stormed into Branch Rickey's ballpark office with an urgent nonbaseball matter on his mind. The team captain was hopelessly in love and felt that his mind was wandering on the baseball field. He begged Rickey to put in a good word with his girlfriend, Grace Dozier, whose divorce had recently become official. "I want to marry her today," Durocher said. "She doesn't want to disrupt the team, but I told her that you wouldn't mind." The lovelorn player promised that he would be back in plenty of time for the game later that afternoon. He handed his boss Grace Dozier's phone number and begged him to call her.[22]

Of course, Branch Rickey always loved the caring and security that marriage brought to ballplayers in their precarious profession. The idea of a wedding in the last week of a pennant race, though, was a new one for the ferocious gentleman. Yet he felt that Grace Dozier had been a good influence on Durocher. A single mother raising a teenaged daughter, she was a well-respected member of the St. Louis community, a businesswoman who manufactured her own line of junior-size clothes for young women under the name of Carol King Designs. She sold many of her creations to the Rickey daughters, and it may well have been Jane Rickey who played matchmaker for Leo and Grace. The Texas-born Dozier was a few years older than her beau, who always called her "Mom." Both Jane and

Branch Rickey (who, incidentally, also called his wife "Mother") thought that she had already improved Durocher's manners and wardrobe. Gone were his flashy threads, loud ties, and pointed shoes, replaced by more elegant clothes bathed in softer colors.[23]

Wanting to make his team captain happy and more focused on baseball, Rickey phoned Grace Dozier. "Do you know what you are getting yourself into?" Rickey asked the elegant designer. Dozier replied that she loved Durocher but didn't want to interfere with his baseball at a critical time of the season. Rickey looked at his watch and told her, as his captain beamed opposite him, "Mother and I both think you make a very good couple. You have my blessing." After he hung up, he told his shortstop, "Get going, boy, and make sure you are back in plenty of time for the game!"

An elated Durocher summoned his best man, Cardinals center fielder Ernie Orsatti, and off they went to meet Grace Dozier at a downtown St. Louis courthouse for a civil ceremony. The free-spirited Orsatti made a show out of juggling the wedding ring in front of the justice of the peace but wasn't charged with an error, and the marriage ceremony went off without a hitch. Manager Frisch, not thrilled by the hurried wedding, was pleased when the groom and his best man returned in time to take the field for the Cardinals against the Pirates. No one was happy, however, when Pittsburgh's Waite Hoyt shut out the Cardinals, 4-0. Frisch could be heard muttering afterward that Leo should have waited until after the season to get married.[24]

Fortunately, the Giants also lost on Wednesday, so the teams were still tied in the lost column. Shaking off the loss to Hoyt, the Cardinals moved half a game from first place on Thursday as Bill Walker, recovered from his broken leg, won his twelfth game, 8–5, beating the Reds and ex-Cardinal Paul Derringer. Bridegroom Durocher had two hits and scored two runs.

After the game many of the Cardinals journeyed to a downtown theatre to see the premiere of a new Hollywood melodrama, *Death on the Diamond*, starring Robert Young and Madge Evans. Filmed in part at Sportsman's Park in July, the film featured several Cardinals as extras, with Ernie Orsatti playing a crucial role as a base runner who is shot while running the bases.[25] Orsatti, a Los Angeles native, was no stranger to films, having appeared in 1927 with Wahoo Sam Crawford in the baseball scenes of Buster Keaton's silent film *College*. (Although it has been often written that Orsatti served as a stunt double for the comedian, the outfielder said that Keaton always performed his own physical comedy and that he was used mainly for long shots when Keaton was otherwise occupied. In a delicious irony, Orsatti originally was more interested in film than baseball, but when he starred on Keaton's studio baseball team, the comedian insisted that he give pro baseball a chance. After his retirement Orsatti joined several of his brothers as Hollywood actors' agents.)[26]

On Friday, September 28, while the Giants were idle, Dizzy Dean shut out the Reds, 4–0. There was now a flat-footed tie for first place, and the weekend games would most likely decide the pennant. Both teams had their aces ready—the Dean brothers in St. Louis and Carl Hubbell and Hal Schumacher in New York. On Saturday, September 29, as Paul Dean was pitching the Cardinals to a 6–1 victory, word came from New York that Van Lingle Mungo and the Dodgers had beaten Roy Parmelee and the Giants, 5–1. It was estimated that half of the almost fourteen thousand fans at the Polo Grounds were Brooklyn rooters who brought horns, whistles, and angry passions to the home of the hated enemy.[27] The Cardinals were now in sole possession of first place for the first time since early June.

If Dizzy Dean won on Sunday the pennant would belong to St. Louis. "Give me a few runs and there won't be a playoff," Dean predicted. By a happy coincidence both Deans were going to be honored on Sunday on "Diamond Day," an event their ardent fans had earlier planned to bestow the gifts of diamonds on their heroes, win or lose. Before an excited, overflow crowd of 37,402, Dizzy Dean didn't disappoint his admirers, throwing a 9–0 shutout to earn his thirtieth victory of the 1934 season.[28] During the game the pennant was officially clinched when word came from New York that the Giants had lost again to the Dodgers, 6–1. Afterward a disconsolate Bill Terry said that if the Dodgers had played as hard all year as they did against the Giants, they wouldn't have finished in sixth place. Brooklyn manager Casey Stengel gleefully rejoined, "Well, if the season lasted another month and we kept playing him, he'd finish in last place!"[29]

For the Cardinals it was their fifth National League title in nine years, and they did it by pulling off one of their patented late-season streaks. They won twenty out of their last twenty-five games as the Giants were losing thirteen of their last twenty. In the jubilant victors' clubhouse after the victory, Rip Collins led the team in choruses of the hopeful depression era hit tune, "We're in the Money," and Dizzy Dean, Joe Medwick, and longtime coach Buzzy Wares gave a boisterous rendition of the old song: "I want a girl, just like the girl that married dear old dad."[30]

For the city of St. Louis it was shades of 1926 again. For over four hours crowds spilled into the streets, and police gave up directing traffic. Impromptu veterans' bands serenaded passersby. Automobiles and office windows were festooned with "depression ticker tape" (toilet paper), and chants of "Bring On the Tigers," the American League pennant winners, echoed all over town.

The dramatic come-from-behind pennant victory and the large home crowds on the final weekend buoyed the spirits of Cardinals management. Admitting that he was too stunned by the comeback (and the Giants' collapse) to know what to feel, Branch Rickey said, "The way the club has come through in the last two weeks is enough to make anyone proud of them, and certainly no one could be more proud than I am."[31] In early September, when the Cardinals trailed by seven games, Sam Breadon had virtually given up hope for the pennant, but he was now thrilled by the victory. "We know we've put up a great fight, and if you can't win after such a fight, why the next best thing is to lose gracefully," he said. "But it don't look much like we'd have to be graceful, does it?" he chortled.[32]

However, despite the big September weekend crowds, the Cardinals would draw only 325,056 fans in 1934, more than 400,000 off their record attendance of 1928, and an increase of less than 70,000 from 1933.[33] Disappointed at fan support for the past three years, Breadon was beginning to drop hints about moving the team to Detroit, a city that, though also hit hard by the depression, attracted 919,161 fans to see their 1934 champion Tigers. Although the Michigan city was at the hub of a metropolitan area twice the size of St. Louis, Breadon was feeling unappreciated. On the last Friday of the regular season, when only 5,500 paid to see Dizzy Dean shut out the Reds, Breadon complained about the small crowd. Sympathetic sportswriter Roy Stockton agreed that "several minor league cities" would support baseball better than St. Louis.[34] However, with the thrill of a World Series imminent, Breadon felt that his economic concerns could wait.

The matchup of the Detroit Tigers and the St. Louis Cardinals in the 1934 World Series was a special one for the American heartland because it presented the first all-Midwest battle since the infamous 1919 "Black Sox" Series between the Chicago White Sox and the Cincinnati Reds. The Tigers, in the Series for the first time since 1909, had won the American League pennant relatively easily, building up a comfortable lead by late August. Although they sputtered in September, they still beat the Yankees by seven games on their way to 101 victories.

The Tigers were managed by catcher Mickey Cochrane, one of the cogs on Connie Mack's last great Philadelphia Athletics teams that had opposed the Cardinals in the 1930 and 1931 World Series. Cochrane, who hit .320 with 76 RBI in 1934, was one of four future Hall of Famers on the 1934 Tigers. Second baseman Charlie Gehringer was another; he hit .356 with an astounding 127 RBI for a second baseman, while leading the league in assists. Young first baseman Hank Greenberg came into his own with a .339 BA, 26 HR, and 139 RBI. The fourth future immortal was left fielder Leon "Goose" Goslin, who hit .305 with 13 HR and 100 RBI.

As a team the Tigers led the American League in batting, runs scored, and stolen bases. The Detroit pitching staff had two twenty-game winners with gaudy records, tall right-hander Lynwood "Schoolboy" Rowe (24-8) and left-hander Tommy Bridges (22-11). Elden Auker and Fred "Firpo" Marberry each won fifteen games. On paper the Tigers looked to be the superior team, having won more games and having more balance in pitching and offense than the Cardinals.

Except for the Dean brothers St. Louis seemed to lack pitching depth. Newcomer Tex Carleton did finish at 16-11, but he tired in the late season because of an unusual allergy to the sun, a vexing problem in an age of total day baseball.[35] Bill Walker's 12-4 record and 3.12 ERA looked good on paper, but he was inconsistent and would not perform well in the upcoming competition. Former World Series hero Bill Hallahan was only 8-12 in the regular season but had won his last four decisions and was still considered valuable in clutch situations.

On offense the Cardinals were very balanced. They led the National League in runs scored, doubles, batting average, and slugging average. The defense tied with the Giants for the most double plays, and the pitchers led in complete games and shutouts and were second only to the Giants in team earned run average.

When it came to spirit and will to win the 1934 Cardinals had no peer. There is a compelling photo of the St. Louis starting lineup, taken before the first game of the 1934 World Series. They are posed on the front step of the dugout, their arsenal of bats laid out on the ground before them, and a look of joyous pride and ferocity is etched on their faces.[36] The team was ready to compete and to win by any means necessary.

In an oddity of history the name Gashouse Gang did not become widely used to describe this aggregation of Cardinals until after May 1935, when a cartoon by Willard Mullin in the *New York World-Telegram* popularized the image of a scrappy team of roughnecks, wielding bats like clubs, walking by two huge gas tanks on the wrong side of town. In conjunction with an earlier comment made by Leo Durocher to New York sportswriter Frank Graham that the American League would never allow a "rough gashouse outfit" like the Cardinals into its more sedate sanctum, the compelling nickname of the Gashouse Gang was attached a year after their triumph and become an indelible part of baseball history.[37]

Whatever the origins of the nickname, Pepper Martin exemplified the spirit of the team. Playing without a jockstrap or sanitary hose, he possessed the indomitable will to win that Branch Rickey saw as the essential ingredient of any champion. Martin did not have a notable statistical year at third base in 1934—he hit .289 with 5 HR and 49 RBI and was charged with a league-leading 19 errors—but his hatred of the opposition was so great that in games that were one-sided, he was known to take ground balls at third base and throw the ball at the runner, not to the first baseman.[38] Off the field, however, Martin remained his genuine, gentle, fun-loving self, happily devoted to his hobby of midget car racing and dabbling in managing professional prizefighters, one of whom, Junior Munsell, became a light-heavyweight contender.[39]

On the other side of the infield, the powerful switch-hitting Rip Collins came into his own with a league-leading 35 HR and .615 SA while hitting .333 with 128 RBI. As Frank Frisch and Branch Rickey had hoped,

Collins capably filled the shoes of Jim Bottomley. The Fordham Flash himself had another solid year offensively, with a .305 BA, 75 RBI, and 74 R. He was inevitably slowing down at the advanced baseball age of thirty-five, but he was savvy enough to know how to conserve his energy. His adept double play partner, Leo Durocher, had in 1934 the first of two outstanding offensive years, with 3 HR and 70 RBI to go with a .260 BA, a significant improvement over his low .200 averages in Cincinnati. Hitting .277 in 332 at-bats, Burgess Whitehead provided substantial relief help for Frisch in his first extensive Major League experience after a few years of Minor League seasoning.

Joe Medwick provided the expected outfield offense with a .319 BA, .529 SA, 18 HR, and 106 RBI. Medwick also led National League left fielders with 14 errors because he often had his mind more on hitting than fielding. His indifferent attitude toward defense understandably caused much distress among the Cardinal pitchers. Dizzy Dean and Tex Carleton more than once used their fists to try to beat Medwick into better outfield concentration.[40]

Ernie Orsatti provided adequate defense in center field to go with a .300 BA with 31 RBI in 337 at-bats. Every pennant winner needs unexpected productivity from an unlikely source. The 1934 Cardinals' most pleasant surprise was right fielder Jack Rothrock, a switch hitter who had returned to the Majors after many years in the Minors. Playing in every game, he hit .284 with 72 RBI and contributed steady defense and a solid outfield arm.

The catching was split between Virgil "Spud" Davis, a Cardinal in the late 1920s who had returned in the trade for Jimmy Wilson, and the rookie Bill DeLancey, who emerged out of the farm system to become a valuable player and leader. In only 253 at-bats in 1934 the Greensboro, North Carolina, native compiled a .316 BA, .565 SA, 13 HR, and 40 RBI. DeLancey had a knack for the timely hit, and he called a very intelligent game from behind the plate. Rickey wrote in *The American Diamond* that DeLancey was the best he had ever seen at sensing when a hitter had missed his pitch and helping a pitcher capitalize on the batter's frustration. Rickey would include him on his list of great catchers he had signed (along with Roy Campanella).[41] DeLancey was also one of the great pranksters on a team of cutups. It was rare for a rookie to display leadership qualities off the field, but the young catcher had a knack for relaxing and making friends among his teammates.

The 1934 World Series looked like a very competitive matchup, but with Dizzy Dean as a main attraction anything might and could happen. A crisis loomed shortly before the Cardinals were slated to leave for Detroit and the opening of the Series. Dizzy Dean disappeared. Certainly he couldn't be boycotting a game in Detroit again, could he? No, Dean had been invited to accept an award at a local Masonic lodge, and he was preparing to attend.

When Branch Rickey heard about the latest caper of his unpredictable pitcher, he sighed. Despite Dean's constant wrangling about his and his brother's salaries, Branch Rickey loved his pitcher's colorful and competitive nature and he encouraged many of his antics as crowd-pleasing attractions. Rickey had even brought up from Houston in the middle of the 1934 season Elmer Dean, Dizzy's older brother, a renowned peanut vendor supposedly blessed with a Major League arm, but Elmer quickly tired of life up north and returned home.[42]

When the executive heard about Dizzy's wanting to receive the Masons' award in person before the World Series, he invited the unpredictable pitcher to his country home. He was able to convince him that he needed to be with his teammates in Detroit. Honors and parades could await the successful completion of the World Series, Rickey told Dean. Before he said good-bye to his star hurler, Rickey took leave of his dinner guests to give his ace a tour of his impressive property and is said to have promised him the gift of any horse, any gun, or any dog.[43]

Dean and the rest of the Cardinals entrained together to the 1934 World Series. As the Tigers were taking batting practice during a workout the day before game one, Dizzy stole the show. Clad in street clothes, he barged into the batting line, wisecracking, "Lemme show ya a *real* ballplayer at work."[44]

The next day, Dean, unlike many starting pitchers who prefer time to themselves before a big game, was in the center of all the pregame festivities. With newsreel cameras rolling, Dean and Pepper Martin strode toward the Detroit dugout. "They don't look like tigers to me, Pepper, they look more like pussycats," Dean taunted. He turned to Hank Greenberg, the first great Jewish Major League ballplayer, and in the ethnic vernacular of the day said: "Hello, Mose. What makes you so white? Boy, you're shakin' like a leaf. I get it; you done heard that Old Diz was goin' to pitch. Well, you're right. It'll be all over in a few minutes. Old Diz is goin' to pitch, an' he's goin' to pin your ears back."[45]

They say it's not bragging if you can perform, and Dizzy delivered a complete-game victory in game one, allowing 8 hits in an 8–3 St. Louis romp. The Detroit infield made 5 errors, and Hank Greenberg's solo home run was no match for the thirteen-hit St. Louis attack led by Joe Medwick's 4 hits, including a home run. After the game Dean was hooked up by a radio phone with American explorer Admiral Richard Byrd. "Howdy there Dick Byrd down at the South Pole," the irrepressible Dean said. "I didn't have nary a thing on the ball," the pitcher told the explorer about his 150-pitch effort. "It was a lousy, tick-flea-and-chigger-bit ball game." (For his short conversation, Dean was paid $500.)[46]

On the morning before game two, the Dean brothers and their wives were invited to tour Henry Ford's mansion outside of Detroit. A press entourage was welcomed, and the cameras were clicking and the pens scribbling as the automobile magnate asked Dizzy how the Tigers would do in the Series. "You're in trouble, boss," the self-assured hurler told Ford. A motorcycle escort returned the pitchers to Navin Field in time for the hijinks before the second game of the Series. Movie comedian Joe E. Brown and baseball clown Al Schacht staged a mock fight on the diamond, and referee George Raft, a Hollywood actor who appeared in many gangster movies, counted out Brown.[47]

In game two it was the Cardinals' turn to make the costly errors. Rip Collins and Bill DeLancey let a foul ball fall between them with St. Louis nursing a one-run lead in the bottom of the ninth. Given a second opportunity Tigers outfielder Gee Walker tied up the game with a single, and Detroit won on Goose Goslin's twelfth-inning single after two walks from Bill Walker. Bill Hallahan pitched eight very creditable innings, but through no fault of his own he couldn't repeat his victories of 1931.

With Detroit and St. Louis only a few hundred miles apart, and in an economy still battered by the depression, there was no travel day in the 1934 World Series. In game three Paul Dean showed no rookie jitters as he pitched a complete game, beating Tommy Bridges, 4–1. The Tigers frustrated themselves and their fans by leaving thirteen men on base. Pepper Martin brought back memories of 1931 by hitting a double and a triple and scoring two runs.

The exciting World Series evened up the next afternoon as Elden Auker pitched Detroit to a 10–4 victory. The Tigers scored six unanswered runs in the seventh and eighth innings as they battered the Cardinals' non-Dean pitchers, especially losing pitcher Bill Walker. Disaster almost struck the Cardinals during the fourth inning when Dizzy Dean came in as a pinch runner during a rally that briefly tied the game. Trying to break up a double play at second base on a ball hit by Pepper Martin, Dean was hit in the head by second baseman Charlie Gehringer's attempted relay to first base. The pitcher went down in a heap and was carried off the field. When he regained consciousness in the clubhouse, Dean's first question was, "They didn't get Pepper at first, did they?"[48] He was still "in the game," showing the kind of competitive ferocity that Branch Rickey loved in Dean and all of the Gashouse Gang. Fortunately, Dean was not badly hurt, leading one wit to suggest a mythical headline, "X-Rays of Dizzy Dean's Head Show Nothing."

Dizzy was cleared to play for the rest of the Series, but incredulous sportswriters asked manager Frank Frisch why he had allowed his valuable pitcher to risk injury as a pinch runner. "Dean kept pulling my sleeve and begging me to use him," Frisch explained. "I did not think it even remotely possible that he could be injured in such a role."[49]

In the pivotal game five, the last game in St. Louis for the 1934 season, Dizzy Dean pitched against Tommy Bridges, losing 3-1, with Charlie Gehringer's sixth-inning home run the deciding blow. The Cardinals scored only on Bill DeLancey's home run in the bottom of the seventh. After all the excitement, turmoil, and spectacular finish to the regular season, the Cardinals were faced with the daunting prospect of winning the Series on the road in Detroit.

Yet they were ready for the challenge, just as the first champion Cardinals team of the Rickey era had been in 1926. In game six Paul Dean restored the victorious family name by beating Schoolboy Rowe, 4–3, in a tense contest. In an age when, mercifully, the designated hitter did not yet exist, Paul Dean drove in the ultimate winning run with a single in the seventh inning.

The Series was all tied up, and the game at Detroit's Navin Field on Tuesday, October 9, would decide the baseball championship of the world. It was 1926 and 1931 all over again for the Cardinals, a seventh game with everything on the line. Dizzy Dean begged for the chance to avenge his loss in the fifth game. Worn out by the unpredictable pitcher's antics during the season, however, Manager Frisch was leaning toward pitching his well-rested veteran Bill Hallahan. In the rare role of mediator, Leo Durocher told his volatile teammate to apologize to Frisch for any embarrassment he may have caused him during the year and to tell him that he simply had to have the ball for the seventh game.

Dizzy followed Leo's advice, apologizing to Frisch, and the manager relented and chose him as his starter. Dean was in fine form for the climactic game of the 1934 season, and player-manager Frisch wound up having the key hit in the top of the third inning. After a long ten-pitch at-bat with the bases loaded against Elden Auker, Frisch lined a double down the right-field line and all three runs scored. After the game Frisch was jubilant, but the grouchy perfectionist was not fully satisfied. "I should have had a triple," he said, "but I was skylarking into second base watching all those runs score."[50] In all the Cardinals scored seven runs in the third inning, and Dean went on to pitch a complete-game, six-hit, 11–0 shutout, the most one-sided whitewashing in World Series history.

Game seven is most remembered for the brawl that erupted in the top of the sixth inning when Joe Medwick slid hard into third baseman Marv Owen after belting a triple. Owen took issue with the husky St. Louis outfielder's coming in spikes high and took a swing at him. In a twinkling both players were grappling in the dirt around third base. Both benches emptied, and the frustrated Detroit crowd hooted and started hurling trash, fruit, and vegetables. Tigers second baseman Charlie Gehringer later remarked, "I have no idea where they got all that produce from!"[51]

When Medwick went out to play left field in the bottom of the sixth inning, the pelting resumed. Commissioner Landis assembled the managers of both teams near his first base box. With the score 11–0 and the likelihood of a Detroit comeback doubtful, Landis ordered Medwick removed from the game for his own safety. Frisch and Medwick were enraged. The St. Louis player-manager offered a compromise, suggesting that Medwick could move to right field, where there were no bleacher fans ready to throw objects. They also argued that if Medwick had to leave, so, too, must Marv Owen, who actually started the fight, but Landis insisted that his decision was final.[52]

Medwick was forever miffed at his ejection because he already had collected eleven hits in the Series and thus missed a chance to tie or break Pepper Martin's 1931 record of twelve. Branch Rickey made no public comment on the brouhaha, although he was glad that the game could be resumed without further incident. He was thrilled by the victory, of course, and pleased that newlywed Leo Durocher had an outstanding World Series, playing errorless defense and contributing seven timely hits, including three in the vital game six, which tied the competition.

Thanks to Navin Field's forty-thousand-plus seating (increased to nearly fifty thousand in 1935), the Series brought record shares to both the winners and the losers. A full share for each St. Louis player was $5,941.19, and the losing share was $4,313.90 each.[53] There was no voting for a most valuable player in the World Series until the 1950s, but if there had been, the Dean brothers would certainly have shared the prize. They won all four of the St. Louis victories.

After the Series Dizzy Dean was eager to capitalize on his fame by touring in vaudeville, doing commercials on the radio, and endorsing products in newspaper advertisements. Rickey assigned the job of scrutinizing Dean's endorsement offers to William DeWitt, his longtime assistant who had recently been named treasurer of the Cardinals. DeWitt suggested the proper ones and rejected the less savory ones. It was estimated that Dean's postseason rewards more than tripled his $7,500 salary, and De-Witt earned at least 10 percent commission on Dean's commercial activities. However, after an investigation by Commissioner Landis, some of DeWitt's larger cuts were reduced.[54]

The future looked rosy for the start of another Cardinals powerhouse to rival the four pennant winners between 1926 and 1931. St. Louis was world champion again on the Major League level, and the Cardinals' farm clubs were regularly winning on all levels of the Minor Leagues. Columbus had beaten Toronto to win the Little World Series for the American Association over the International League. What Rickey liked to call his "production and duplication" system was working very economically. The *Sporting News* estimated that the entire 1934 St. Louis championship roster cost only $40,000 to assemble.[55]

Yet scarcely a month after the Cardinals' triumph in the World Series, a momentous shift in team ownership almost occurred. Word began to filter into the newspapers that Sam Breadon was seriously considering selling the team to Oklahoma oilman and philanthropist Lewis Haines Wentz. Breadon had come to realize that it was a pipe dream to think that Tigers owner Frank Navin would allow the Cardinals to move into his Michigan territory, and the St. Louis owner was concerned about his declining profits. He had been stymied at his efforts to bring night baseball to St. Louis, first by the opposition of the other National League owners and second by his inability to make a deal on constructing lights with his stubborn landlord, the Browns' owner Phil Ball, and his successor, financier Donald Barnes.

By the late summer of 1934, Breadon began to seriously consider an outright sale of the team that he had called his own for nearly fifteen years. The plot thickened when, at the end of the regular season and during the World Series, Lew Wentz was often seen in the company of Branch Rickey. The two men traveled together by train to the opening and closing games of the World Series in Detroit, and Rickey also gave Wentz a guided tour of several of the Cardinals' farm team facilities.[56]

It is not clear when Rickey and Wentz first met. Perhaps it was in the 1920s at some religious or philanthropic activity, or maybe it was at a postseason baseball dinner. The two men found out that they had much in common. They were both fervent Methodists, Sunday school teachers, teetotalers, and Rotarians, and each was deeply involved in charitable activities and community service. Wentz funded the Oklahoma Crippled Children's Society, built a public pool and camp in his adopted home of Ponca City, Oklahoma, for use by the Boy Scouts and other youth groups, and provided free movies for local residents. In the early 1930s the staunch Republican served as the Oklahoma State Highway commissioner, suing the Democratic governor to maintain his position.[57]

Lewis Haines Wentz was a member of Rickey's generation, born in Iowa in 1879 and raised in Pittsburgh, Pennsylvania, one of seven children of a blacksmith. Haines was a good semipro baseball player who, while still in high school, competed as a "ringer" for a team connected with the college that became the University of Pittsburgh. Soon he became baseball coach for all the Pittsburgh high schools. In 1911 Wentz had headed to work in the Oklahoma oil fields and after World War One struck it rich in Ponca City. A bachelor, Wentz was proud to be a called "a lone wolf," a man who ran a major company without a corporate structure. In 1927 an Internal Revenue Service report listed him as the sixth richest man in the United States, based on his paying taxes of more than $5 million. In 1934 he was still listed among the very wealthy Americans. "I escaped the stock market crash for the simple reason that I didn't play the market," he told Taylor Spink of the *Sporting News*.[58]

Wentz was a great baseball fan, who once said that he "wouldn't miss a World Series for all the oil in Oklahoma." In the 1920s he had inquired if Barney Dreyfuss were interested in putting the Pirates on the market, but the longtime Pittsburgh owner wasn't interested in selling the favorite team of the oilman's youth. Wentz had also looked into the possibility of buying the Giants or the Dodgers, and in the fall of 1934 it seemed that Lew Wentz seemed to have found a willing seller in Sam Breadon.[59]

As the rumors of the impending sale intensified in early November 1934, Ed Wray penned in the *Post-Dispatch* a possible farewell valedictory entitled "The Strange Case of Sam Breadon." Wray wondered why the Cardinals owner considered himself a "pariah" when the team had been so successful under his stewardship. The chamber of commerce estimated that over $600,000 had been spent by tourists coming to town for the middle three games of the World Series. Wray surmised that Breadon might be tired of fans and players calling him cheap, even though the owner claimed that his 1934 payroll was the fourth highest in baseball. Perhaps, Wray suggested, Breadon was weary of having his good business sense called "mere niggardliness and success repaid with obliquy."[60]

The plot thickened on November 11, 1934, when Wentz flew into St. Louis, checked into a hotel under an assumed name, and went to visit Breadon at his estate in the country. They engaged in serious talks about a sale but could not agree on a price. When the Cardinals did not look like a pennant winner in early September 1934, Breadon had said he would jump at anyone offering him $1.5 million for the team, but now his asking price had reportedly become more than $2 million because of the Major League team's recent success plus the vast farm system holdings that would also be part of any deal.[61]

When asked in mid-November for a comment on a possible sale to Wentz, Branch Rickey said, "My opinion is that there will be no sale." However, because the voluble executive was rarely satisfied with a simple declarative statement, he added, "However, I can be made to change my opinion in a half an hour. Further than that, I don't care to say anything."[62] By Thanksgiving the proposed sale was dead. Sam Breadon had phoned Wentz and told him that he was leaving for Florida in half an hour. If he wanted to buy the team at the owner's price, Breadon said, he should call back within that time. If not, the deal was off. Wentz did not respond to the ultimatum, and Sam Breadon remained the principal owner of the St. Louis Cardinals.[63]

It is interesting to speculate about what the history of St. Louis baseball and Branch Rickey's personal story might have been if Lew Wentz had bought the Cardinals. Certainly Rickey's personal relationship with an owner would have been the best since his early days on the St. Louis Browns under Robert Lee Hedges. When the sale looked imminent Wentz told the *Sporting News*: "I like to go places in my airplane. What would be more fun than taking a jump from St. Louis to Rochester, to Columbus, or to Houston?"[64] A similar devotee of aviation, Rickey would have loved to accompany Wentz on his journeys, for he was a man the passionate executive admired for his sincere philanthropy and staunch Republicanism. Although Wentz was not a spendthrift, the budget for farm system development and Major League salaries probably would have increased. Sam Breadon's iron determination to provide an annual dividend of at least 8 percent per share to the stockholders would likely have eased.

Looking back some time later at the sale that didn't happen, Branch Rickey surmised that Lew Wentz had suffered "a heart attack," that is, he lost his nerve when considering the tremendous expenditure of owning a team.[65] The two men remained good friends and occasional hunting buddies, and ten years later, when Rickey was the president and general manager in Brooklyn and the Dodgers were up for sale, Rickey wrote Wentz: "If there is one remaining live coal of interest in [buying a baseball team], I would like to talk to you about it."[66] Wentz declined; he passed away on June 9, 1949, at age seventy-one.

The ownership and management of the Cardinals thus remained unchanged. Although there is no doubt that Branch Rickey's courting of Lew Wentz as a potential new owner did not sit very well with Sam Breadon, the future still looked rosy for the organization in both the major and the Minor Leagues, and Rickey looked forward to 1935 with more anticipation than usual. He saw in his baseball world a championship team poised to repeat, and hungry young players ready to come up and make their mark. In his family life he eagerly anticipated the June graduations of his two oldest children, Mary and Branch Jr., from Ohio Wesleyan. He had been pleased when both had enrolled at his alma mater in 1931; on campus they would both meet their future life mates. The ferocious gentleman knew that there were no guarantees in baseball or life and that the competition would always be hard, but he expected to prevail. Little did he know that the Gashouse Gang had reached its peak and that the next few years would once again be years of some contention but mainly frustration.

12

Years of Frustration

In May 1935, Branch Rickey received the sad news that his mother had died following a stroke in Crystal Springs, Florida.[1] In their advancing years Rickey's parents had found a place near Tampa to escape from the severity of the Ohio winter. At age seventy-nine Emily Brown Rickey was not in good health overall, and the news of her passing was not totally unexpected. Still, it proved a shock to her devoted son. His deepest regret in baseball remained that many people continued to think that his mother made him promise to stay away from the ballpark on Sunday. He realized it was fruitless to explain the subtlety of a gesture intended to honor her genuinely spiritual nature.

After the funeral and burial in Scioto County, Ohio, Rickey returned to St. Louis and was pleased that the Cardinals were leading the league in the early weeks of the 1935 season. The combination of seasoned veterans and confident newcomers was making the team look formidable. Terry Moore was emerging in the key position of center field as Ernie Orsatti was relegated to reserve duty. Born in Alabama but raised outside St. Louis in Collinsville, Illinois, Moore would become a good hitter, with a career .280 BA and .399 SA, but he took special pride in his fielding, considering it just as important to prevent runs as to score them. Manager Frank Frisch was notoriously hard on rookies but came to value highly Moore's defensive play, especially since the rookie had to cover a lot of the ground with Joe Medwick, whose mind was not always focused on defense, in left field.[2]

Resigning himself to his decline as a player, Frisch shared second base in 1935 with Burgess Whitehead, long his heir apparent. They combined to drive in 88 runs and worked well with shortstop Leo Durocher, who had a career year offensively, batting .265 with 8 HR and 78 RBI. Early in the season, however, Durocher was involved in an unpleasant off-the-field incident. He got into a scrape with a woman union activist who was harassing his wife, Grace Dozier Durocher, as she crossed a picket line to go to work at the factory where she designed her clothes for young women. "You are walking the streets for nothing," Durocher snarled, "and while you are starving, my wife is getting as much in one day as you would in a week."[3]

When the protester was arrested and fined, St. Louis unionists grew enraged at Durocher's role in the incident and called for a boycott of Cardinals games. Sam Breadon and Rickey were hardly sympathetic to union activity, but they were concerned about a possible loss of fan patronage. Rickey was at his diplomatic best in defusing the controversy. The "club cannot exercise control" over the private life of a player, he said, but he added, "I hold no brief for conduct of any player, on and off the field, which may be offensive."[4] Although Durocher would not issue an apology, the love of baseball transcended labor solidarity in the hearts of most fans, and the boycott did not materialize.

If the captain-shortstop stayed out of controversy for the rest of the year, the same could not be said for Dizzy Dean. At the end of May, while pitching against the Pirates in Pittsburgh, Dean became infuriated at home plate umpire George Barr's calls on balls and strikes. Petulantly, Dean started to lob pitches to the plate, and Pittsburgh hitters belted his halfhearted tosses all over Forbes Field. Enraged manager Frisch yanked Dean from the game, and the pitcher was greeted by a chorus of boos as he walked back to the dugout. Within days $50,000 worth of Dizzy Dean clothing for kids and adults was returned to St. Louis by a chain of stores in Pittsburgh.[5]

In June Dizzy caused another ruckus when he refused to acknowledge his fans in St. Paul, Minnesota, with even a tip of his cap during one of the Cardinals' ubiquitous exhibition games. Tickets had been sold to see a hero and a legend in the flesh, but Dean just sat sulking in the dugout. A few days later Dizzy apologized in an open letter to a St. Paul newspaper, and Rickey and Breadon decided not to fine him. Dean responded, "I don't care if they didn't fine me, they're still a chain gang."[6]

Despite the antics of the unpredictable Dean, the Cardinals seemed to have control of the 1935 pennant race. They rattled off fourteen victories in a row in late July and led the Cubs by two games on Labor Day. Then the Chicagoans put together the greatest September stretch run in baseball history, winning twenty-one games in a row. (The Giants had won twenty-six in succession in September 1916, but they were not in a pennant race and wound up in fourth place.) Highlighting the streak was a doubleheader sweep of the Cardinals and the Dean brothers that put the Cubs in first place to stay. The Chicagoans, managed by Charley Grimm, were on their way to their first pennant since 1918.

Making the loss of the pennant particularly painful for Branch Rickey was that three key Cubs pitchers had been developed by the St. Louis farm system. Tex Carleton, a member of the 1934 world champions, had been traded after the season (for cash and two journeymen pitchers who never won a game for the Cardinals). Carleton won eleven games for the 1935 Cubs; two ex–St. Louis farm hands, William Crutcher "Big Bill" Lee and Lon Warneke, each won twenty for the Chicagoans; and Warneke, nick-named the "Arkansas Hummingbird," won the only two games the Cubs managed against the eventual 1935 world champion Detroit Tigers.

After the Series Branch Rickey sat down with Charley Barrett, Bill DeWitt, and the rest of his staff for the annual review of the year. The Cardinals had won ninety-six games, one more than their 1934 world championship team, but still fell four short of the Cubs' one hundred victories. Although disappointed at failing to repeat as champions in 1935, Rickey realized that when an opponent wins twenty-one in a row in September, you had to tip your cap to the victors. Sam Breadon was also disappointed in the lost pennant, but he was buoyed by an increase in attendance to 506,084 paying customers. It was still far short of the 1928 record of over 760,000, but given the ongoing depression, it was a good sign for the health of the franchise that 175,000 more paying customers came to Sportsman's Park in 1935 than in the world championship year of 1934.[7]

Individually, the Dean brothers combined for forty-seven wins, with Paul matching his 1934 total with nineteen, and Dizzy's twenty-eight victories being only two below his 30-7 season of 1934. Once again they combined for nearly half of the team's victories. Offensively, Joe Medwick and Rip Collins had solid years, leading the team with 23 HR each and 126 and 122 RBI, respectively, but both men slumped in September when the pennant was on the line. Right fielder Jack Rothrock, who contributed unexpectedly in 1934, came down to earth in 1935, falling to a .273 BA, 3 HR, and 56 RBI.

The Cardinals received an impressive 101 RBI out of the catching position, but Bill DeLancey, who shared backstop duties with Virgil "Spud" Davis, was limited to 103 games in 1935 because of a nagging cough. After the season he was diagnosed with pleurisy, a serious lung disease, and the dry air of the American Southwest was recommended for his recuperation.

When he learned of DeLancey's illness, Branch Rickey's mind flashed back to the untimely passing of two 1922 Cardinals, Bill Dillhoefer and Austin McHenry, deaths that shocked him and he felt helpless to prevent. With the advances in medical science in the last decade, Rickey vowed that DeLancey would have the best of care, and he personally supervised the catcher's treatment. He paid tuition for the nursing courses that DeLancey's wife took to take care of her husband, whose lungs had to be drained every other day. In 1937 Rickey would create a farm club in Albuquerque, New Mexico, mainly for DeLancey to manage. By spring training 1940, with Rickey's encouragement, the catcher felt strong enough to attempt a comeback.[8] But he lasted for only a few games and soon returned to his chicken and fruit ranch in Arizona, where he would die on his thirty-fifth birthday, November 28, 1946.

Despite the tough loss of the 1935 pennant, nothing could detract from Branch Rickey's feeling of satisfaction about his family's achievements and adventures during the year. In June, Mary and Branch Jr., his eldest children, both graduated from Ohio Wesleyan. Soon thereafter Branch Jr. took off to Albany, Georgia, to begin learning the ropes at the lowest level of the St. Louis Minor League system. Although he had competed in wrestling in college, avoiding baseball and the constant reminders that he was Branch Rickey's son, he loved the beauty and challenges of the diamond sport and was eager to start a front office career.

As a graduation gift for Mary, Rickey presented her with the latest model Ford Phaeton convertible car. Both he and his wife, Jane, gave their blessings to a summer trip in which the three oldest daughters, Mary, Jane, and Alice, would drive the car out to Colorado to pick up the youngest girls, Sue and Betty, who were attending a summer camp. All five girls would then drive back to St. Louis, camping out at national parks each night along the way. The Rickeys imposed only two ground rules on their daughters. There would be no driving at night, and they had to phone their parents every evening.

"They took a lot of criticism from their friends and neighbors," Jane Rickey Jones recalls. "People asked, 'How could you let your girls go so far away from home without a chaperone?' But Mother and Dad loved life, they trusted us, and they wanted us to love and enjoy life, too."[9]

The trip was indeed an adventure and had its share of close calls. One night a bear came sniffing into one of the campsites. "We lay very quietly until he finally went away," Mary Rickey Eckler recalls. "That story we didn't share with Mother and Daddy until many months later," Jane Rickey Jones adds with a laugh.[10] On their way back to Missouri, the girls ran out of money and had to wire home for cash. The money soon arrived, and the trip went on its merry way. It was all part of the experience of living life fully that was the credo of the Rickey family.

One evening, not long after the adventurous summer trip, Branch Rickey's spontaneous enthusiasm led to hilarious embarrassment. He was supposed to be escorting his daughter Mary, who was slated to make her debut in St. Louis society in December 1935, to a meeting of a local book club. On their way to the literary event, the ferocious gentleman suddenly had a better idea. There was a wrestling match downtown that promised to be a real corker. "Let's go there instead, Mary," he exclaimed. Imagine mother Jane Rickey's surprise the next morning at the family breakfast table when she opened the morning newspaper to a picture of a wrestler landing in the lap of two ringside spectators, Branch and Mary Rickey. "Branch, how could you?" a flabbergasted Jane Rickey asked her husband. "Branch, how could you?"[11]

The omens for the 1936 season were not good from the first days of spring training, when Branch Rickey was faced with a public, full-fledged holdout by Dizzy Dean. The pitcher had national fame on his side, a lot of wins to his credit, and an antagonist in the talkative Rickey, and to a lesser degree in the more reticent Sam Breadon, who easily could be painted as miserly. Dean announced that if his salary weren't increased to $25,000 he would sit out the year. As he often did Dizzy made it a point to contrast his meager pay with that of veteran Cardinals pitchers Bill Hallahan and Jess Haines, who had not been nearly as productive as he and his brother Paul had been. Dizzy also derided the catching skills of Spud Davis and let it be known that he preferred not to pitch to him. In the time-honored stance of the holdout, Dean announced that he had other business opportunities to pursue and that he could live without baseball if his contract terms were not satisfied.

Branch Rickey was an old hand at dealing with players wanting more money, and he was serenely confident of being able to use his verbal skills to talk down any player's salary demands to a level more to his liking. The executive also realized that preseason holdouts usually provided harmless newspaper copy for fans until the regular season started. He and Sam Breadon both understood that Dizzy Dean was a valuable commodity, a great pitcher, a great competitor, and a rarity in any sport, a big drawing card. Yet neither management figure liked constantly being called a skinflint in the press.

Accordingly, Rickey wrote a letter to his stubborn pitcher, urging him to report to camp and to act like a loyal teammate in the upcoming season. Taking issue with Dean's criticism of his fellow pitchers and catcher Spud Davis, Rickey implored Dean not to "arrogate to himself the prerogatives of [manager] Frank Frisch."[12] Dean, seeing an opening to receive even more favorable publicity, passed the letter on to Roy Stockton, who offered his services in writing a public reply to Rickey. "The President of Constitute of Tecknological would have had a tough time finding out what it was that Mr. Rickey wanted to say," Dean/Stockton began. The pitcher emphasized his major contributions to the Cardinals in the past two seasons. "I am lopsided on one shoulder from that wheel, an' the grindstone has my nose as flat as a policeman's foot," the colorful pitcher continued. "What the heck does Mr. Rickey want me to do—play the outfield or lead the boys' band?"[13]

By the middle of March, however, Dizzy Dean relented and signed a contract for 1936. Dizzy and his wife, Patricia Nash Dean, decided that there was no point in holding out any longer. As a result of his petulant actions in 1935, the pitcher's commercial endorsements had plummeted and his popularity had taken a beating. Dean claimed he signed for $24,000, a thousand less than he was asking, but St. Louis sources indicated that the figure was closer to $17,500.[14]

No sooner had peace come to the Dizzy Dean front than another disturbing note hit the St. Louis organization. Early in April 1936, while being driven by Bill DeWitt to the Minor League camp in Albany, Georgia, Branch Rickey was seriously injured in an auto accident. During a driving rainstorm, a fully loaded lumber truck had entered the highway without slowing down and collided almost head-on with DeWitt and Rickey's car. The team treasurer suffered minor cuts and bruises, but Rickey, in the passenger seat, was knocked unconscious when his head collided with the rearview mirror and he was rushed to a nearby hospital in serious condition.[15]

Rickey remained hospitalized for over a week, but within a day or two he was having his Major and Minor League baseball work forwarded to him. He was still very much the same impatient man of action who wanted to postpone an appendectomy in 1923 in order to attend a Minor League meeting. When the doctors discharged him in time to make St. Louis for opening day, they assured the baseball executive that he had incurred no permanent injuries and that his broken ribs and collarbone were healing properly. But they were concerned about his persistent double vision. He would have to wear an eye patch for many weeks, and as always, doctors advised that he slow down his work pace. However, with a pennant race about to begin, the idea of taking time off was too ludicrous for Branch Rickey to consider.

He returned to St. Louis in time to see the Cardinals get off to a good start in the 1936 regular season. The 1936 Cardinals were a powerful outfit, led offensively by left fielder Joe Medwick, who hit .351 and led the league in two categories: 64 doubles, still a National League record, and 138 RBI. Another powerful hitter was first baseman John Mize from Demorest, Georgia, who had been signed by Rickey's ace scout of the southern hinterlands, Frank Rickey.

Mize's road to the big leagues had not been smooth because he was not particularly well coordinated. His ability to hit the long ball was his one major baseball tool. Before the 1935 season Rickey traded him to the Cincinnati Reds, but since his physical condition was suspect he was returned to St. Louis as damaged goods. Team physician Dr. Robert Hyland performed a rare operation to remove growths from Mize's pelvic bone, the product of his riding mules and horses bareback in his youth.[16] The first baseman recovered sufficiently to have an outstanding rookie season in 1936, hitting .329 with 30 2B, 19 HR, and 93 RBI in only 414 at-bats. He split first base time with Rip Collins and, after the season, would have the job all to himself when Collins was traded to the Cubs with pitcher Roy Parmelee in a deal that brought back pitcher Lon Warneke to the St. Louis organization.

As powerful as Mize and Medwick were, Branch Rickey always liked teams built around speed, and the 1936 Cardinals could really burn on the base paths. Pepper Martin, now playing right field, led the league with 23 SB and had his best statistical offensive season, with a .309 BA, 11 HR, 76 RBI, and 121 R. Another fine base stealer was second baseman Stuart Martin (no relation), who stole 17 bases and hit .298 with 41 RBI. He played more than eighty games, as Frank Frisch, nearing the end of his career, hit only .274 with 26 RBI. Leo Durocher had the highest batting average of his career, .286, but his RBI fell off to 58. On defense Frisch's range was declining at second base, a point that Durocher noted more and more often, leading to a major problem between the two fiery competitors.

It was on the pitching mound that the 1936 Cardinals seriously tailed off. Dizzy Dean once again led the staff, but his twenty-four victories were four fewer than 1935. He again led the league in innings pitched, 315, and complete games, 28. Unfortunately, 1936 was the beginning of the end of Paul Dean's career. Hampered by a sore arm all season, Paul won only five games and threw just ninety-two innings. After winning nineteen games in both 1934 and 1935, Paul Dean would win only eight more games for the Cardinals (and four more for the Giants, in 1940.) The St. Louis team ERA ballooned to 4.64, the second worst in the National League. Only the Phillies, losers of over one hundred games, had a higher team ERA.

The Giants, presumed out of the race when they fell ten games behind in July, provided the great streak of 1936. It wasn't as late and as long as the Cubs' twenty-one wins in a row in September 1935, but from the end of July to the end of August 1936, they won twenty-six of twenty-eight games, led by their two future Hall of Famers, pitcher Carl Hubbell and right fielder Mel Ott. To Rickey's dismay the Giants were also greatly aided by the play of second baseman Burgess Whitehead, who had been traded after the 1935 season for Roy Parmelee and outfielder Phil Weintraub, neither of whom ever shone in a Cardinals uniform. Whitehead hit .278, with 4 HR, 47 RBI, and he scored 99 R.

In 1936, the Cardinals wound up finishing in a tie for second with the Cubs in 1936. They won only eighty-seven games, seven fewer than the Giants, who were to square off for the first time since 1923 against the Yankees in the World Series. Rickey hoped that the Giants would uphold the honor of the National League, but the Giants fell victim to the slugging American League juggernaut, who won the Series in six games. The Yankees were on their way to a second dynasty, winning the first of four World Series in a row.

The annual after-the-season review by Branch Rickey and his staff of loyalists was not marked by good news. Cardinals attendance fell by more than 50,000, to only 448,078 paying customers, a loss that did not please Sam Breadon.[17] However, far from pulling out of the baseball business, as he had threatened to do just two years earlier, the sixty-year-old Breadon was actually getting more involved. At the end of 1936 Sam Breadon sold his last automobile agency, leaving him comfortable financially and free to spend more time with the Cardinals.

Although an irreparable rift would arise between baseball's odd couple, it was still a year or two in the future. In the summer of 1936, with more than a year left on Rickey's five-year contract, Breadon had offered Rickey another five-year renewal that would run through the end of 1942. Breadon wanted to tie up Rickey's services, lest he be tempted by an offer to run another team, such as the Brooklyn Dodgers, who were reportedly interested in wooing him east.[18] However, Rickey was satisfied with his life and accomplishments in St. Louis, and he signed on again with Sam Breadon for service to stretch until at least the end of the 1942 season.

It was good for Branch Rickey to know that he had the security of a well-paying job in St. Louis. In the nation and the world at large, however, he was growing increasingly pessimistic about the drift toward the "welfare state" at home and the rising dangers of fascism and communism abroad. Speaking often at Republican party functions, he tried to exhort his audiences about the dangers of statism and the need to fight vigorously for traditional American liberty.

His worst fears about what Franklin D. Roosevelt's presidency would mean for his cherished value of free enterprise had come true, and trying to stem the tide of the burgeoning welfare state, he was active in the 1936 Republican campaign in behalf of the G.O.P. presidential candidate, Kansas governor Alf Landon. Rickey saw the election as a clear choice between "government of law" and "government of men by executive order." Speaking to a Republican district convention, Rickey declared: "If the issue is between Communism and the Constitution, I am a Constitutionalist. . . . If between facism [*sic*] and the Constitution, I am a Constitutionalist; if between the New Deal as exemplified by Mr. Roosevelt and the Constitution, I am still a Constitutionalist."[19]

The electoral results in November 1936 did not surprise Rickey, but they dismayed him deeply. Both the Missouri gubernatorial and United States Senate races went to Democrats, and Franklin Roosevelt won reelection to the presidency in a landslide over Alfred Landon. Whatever hopes Rickey had for a Republican resurgence seemed to be on hold indefinitely. As saddened as he remained by Herbert Hoover's serving as a convenient scapegoat for the country's economic woes, Rickey concluded that the severity of the economic depression made the electorate wary of voting for a change back to Republican-led government.

Family life, though, continued to bring Branch Rickey his greatest joy. In December 1936 he walked down the aisle of Grace Methodist Church in St. Louis to give away his oldest daughter, Mary Emily Rickey, to John Eckler, a Phi Beta Kappa graduate of Ohio Wesleyan who was headed to law school at the University of Chicago. The previous June Branch and Jane had traveled to Dayton, Ohio, to attend the wedding of Branch Jr. to Mary Iams at her family church. The paterfamilias was gratified that, like his sister, Branch Jr. had met his spouse at Ohio Wesleyan.

As the Cardinals convened for 1937 spring training in Bradenton, Rickey was looking for better years from Dizzy Dean and other members of the Gashouse Gang. However, the omens as the exhibition season of 1937 began were not good. The Cardinals lost nine of their first twelve pre-season games, prompting Rickey to say publicly that the team might be overrated. He probably was trying to light a fire under his players, but he knew that the Cardinals had to improve the pitching after their subpar performance of 1936. He hoped that the trade for Lon Warneke would make a difference; the right-hander from Arkansas would win eighteen games for the 1937 Cardinals but with a high ERA of 4.54.

Rickey sensed that the fate of the Cardinals would ride once again on the right arm of Dizzy Dean. Dizzy's almost-annual holdout went on until the middle of March, when he signed for a reported $25,500 and agreed reluctantly to a "good conduct" clause. During the off-season Dean had once again complained about the performance of some of his teammates, charging that they had given only "minor league support for a guy who pitched his arm off."[20] Rip Collins and Terry Moore weren't pleased at the criticism and had some choice things to say in the papers about Dean's bellyaching. Both Rickey and Sam Breadon loathed players sniping at one another in the press, and Dizzy pledged to be on good behavior.

Yet, shortly before the end of spring training, the unpredictable boy was involved in another messy incident. After a loss to the Reds in an exhibition game in Tampa, Dizzy and Patricia Dean and Joe Medwick were standing around in a hotel lobby. Mrs. Dean noticed that Jack Miley, a rotund sportswriter for the *New York Daily News* (who bore some resemblance to movie comedian Oliver Hardy), had just come out of a hotel elevator. "Dizzy, there's the writer who is always writing nasty things about you," Pat Dean said. The pitcher confronted Miley, who, during Dean's holdout, had written, "For a guy picking cotton for 50 cents a day a few years ago, Diz has an amusing idea of his own importance." Dean told Miley, "I don't want a $120-a-week man writin' about me." Miley retorted, "I don't write about bush leaguers."[21]

Tempers started to rise, despite an attempt by Irv Kupcinet, a young sportswriter and former University of North Dakota football player, to play peacemaker. Cooler heads did not prevail, and soon fists started flying. Nobody knew who threw the first punch, perhaps it was Joe Medwick, but at the end of the scuffle Kupcinet had a black eye and manager Frank Frisch was lying on the ground under an urn of ashes and a lamp. The newspapers, of course, had a field day with the story. "Attack on

Writers 'Marks' Gas House Gang" headlined the front-page story of the April 8, 1937, *Sporting News*.[22]

Distressed at the news of the altercation, Breadon and Rickey publicly criticized Dean for getting into a scrape with a member of the press. Privately, they told him that they understood his emotional reaction to Miley's nasty words. Rickey especially sympathized with Dean because of his own occasional run-ins with unsympathetic writers. (Brooklyn was still in Branch Rickey's future, so he had seen nothing yet.)

"Anybody can write anything they like about me as a ball player," Dean said. "But I think I'm entitled to certain personal privacy."[23] The top St. Louis brass did not disagree with Dizzy's sentiment, but they made it clear that the only way for him to have the last laugh was to pitch well and lead the team to a championship.

Unfortunately, 1937 would prove a disappointing year for both Dean and the Cardinals. The team never truly contended, finishing fourth, fifteen games behind the pennant-winning Giants. Attendance dropped to 430,811, a loss of almost 20,000 from 1936, despite a national increase in both major and Minor League attendance.[24] The team's decline occurred despite the massive offensive years of the "M" squad, Joe Medwick and John Mize, who finished one-two in the National League in batting and slugging average and RBI. Medwick won the Triple Crown, with a .374 BA, 154 RBI, and 31 HR (he shared the home run title with Giants right fielder Mel Ott).

As Rickey realized, however, great offense alone will not win pennants, and the 1937 Cardinals fell off in pitching and defense. Frank Frisch played very little as his career neared the end, and his replacements, Stu Martin and Jimmy Brown, were not of championship caliber. Leo Durocher slipped all the way to a .203 BA, shades of his first years in the National League with the Reds. His griping about the limited defensive range of his keystone partner intensified. After the season Durocher was traded to Brooklyn, a move encouraged by manager Frisch, who probably feared that Leo was waiting to take his job. Although Pepper Martin enjoyed a good year statistically, with a .304 BA and a .475 SA, his stolen bases dropped from a league-leading 13 in 1936 to 9, and injuries limited his playing to only ninety-eight games.

The biggest factor, though, in the Cardinals' disappointing year of

1937 was the decline of Dizzy Dean. He started the season winning his first five starts, but on May 19, 1937, during a home game against the Giants, Dean again let his emotions get the better of him. An unusually large midweek crowd of over twenty-six thousand gathered at Sportsman's Park to see Dean duel with Carl Hubbell, one of baseball's great head-to-head pitching attractions. In the top of the sixth inning with the Cardinals trailing, 2-1, Dean got into a nasty row with home plate umpire George Barr after the arbiter called a balk. Barr, the same umpire Dizzy had complained about in Pittsburgh two years earlier, called Giants shortstop Dick Bartell back to the batter's box after Dean thought he had retired him on a pop-up.

Dean and manager Frank Frisch vehemently protested Barr's balk call to no avail. Given a second life Bartell lined the next pitch to right field for a single, and when Pepper Martin muffed the ball, a run scored. After another single and an error by Terry Moore, Dean and the Cardinals found themselves trailing, 4–1. The volatile pitcher was fuming, blaming all the unfortunate events on the balk call made by his nemesis George Barr. For the rest of the game Dean threw at the head of every Giants hitter (except his former St. Louis roommate Burgess Whitehead). Still irate a few days later, Dean addressed a youth dinner in the suburban St. Louis town of Belleville, Illinois, and called George Barr and National League president Ford Frick "the two greatest crooks in baseball."[25]

Frick was indignant at the pitcher's remark and threatened an indefinite suspension. Dean denied that he ever made the inflammatory remarks, said that he had been misquoted, and was able to get several sportswriters to vouch for his denial. Branch Rickey and Sam Breadon were again not happy about Dean's outburst, but they did not want their major drawing card suspended.

Ultimately, Frick suspended Dean for only a few days, hardly a punishment for a pitcher who didn't work every day, and never fined him. Dean refused to sign any written apology for his actions. "'I ain't signin' nuthin'!'" was Dizzy's mantra, and it became a popular slogan throughout the country.[26] (As Dean rode to national fame, many schoolteachers had criticized his untutored language as a bad influence on youth, but the pitcher memorably reminded his critics, "A lot of people who don't say 'ain't' ain't eatin'.")

On the eve of the All-Star Game in July, National League manager Bill Terry, skipper of the defending league champion Giants, announced Dean's selection as starting pitcher. Dean, however, still in a snit about his run-ins with Barr and Frick, threatened not to go to the game in Washington DC. Wanting to appease his meal ticket, Sam Breadon offered the pitcher his private plane and escorted Dean to Griffith Stadium personally.[27]

Dizzy Dean probably wished that he had never kept his date in Washington. In front of a crowd that included President Franklin Roosevelt, Postmaster General James Farley (a future candidate for baseball commissioner), and several members of the United States Supreme Court, Dizzy got through the first two innings and the first two batters in the third inning unscored on by the American Leaguers. Then Joe DiMaggio singled, Lou Gehrig hit a home run, and the next batter, Cleveland Indians outfielder Earl Averill, smashed a line drive that broke the big toe on Dizzy's left foot. Dizzy recorded the out, but he limped off the field, trailing 2–0 and ultimately taking the loss in the American League's 8–3 victory, their fourth triumph in the first five All-Star Games.[28]

It was the first serious injury that the hyperactive, supercompetitive player had ever suffered, and he was advised by team physician Robert Hyland and team trainer Harrison Weaver not to rush himself back into action. Ten days later he tried to return to the mound and, almost inevitably, developed arm problems from adjusting his landing position on his injured foot. He did not pitch after mid-August, and he limped to the finish line with a mediocre record of 13-10 in only 197 innings. His 2.69 ERA, though, was still respectable.

Dizzy Dean trade rumors arose, but Branch Rickey said bluntly, "He's not on the market. There is no market for him."[29] Annoyed by the pitcher's public whining, Rickey suggested that Dean should take off all of 1938 and maybe even retire if he were ailing so badly. With Dean out of action for the last six weeks of the season, and with no pennant race drama, attendance faded in St. Louis for a team that finished in fourth place with only 81 wins, fifteen games behind the pennant-winning Giants.

As if the Cardinals' year weren't discouraging enough for Branch Rickey, the National League champion Giants took their lumps in the

World Series. Rematched against the Yankees, they lost in five games as New Yorkers watched the same result in the second subway series in a row. Rickey and the Cardinals organization took another blow when the Columbus (Ohio) Redbirds, the American Association champion, won the first three games of the Little World Series against the Newark Bears, the International League champion and the Yankees' top farm club, only to lose the next four games. Making the loss even more excruciating was that Columbus won all the games played in New Jersey but lost all four played in Ohio.[30]

The state of the world was again turning uncertain and bellicose in the fall of 1937. A so-called "Roosevelt recession" had set in, in large part due to the president's attempt to balance the budget and cut back on public welfare programs. Branch Rickey did not mind the reduction in federal doles that he believed sapped personal initiative, but he was aware that many small businesses were also suffering losses as great as or even greater than those of the initial years of the Great Depression. Overseas, totalitarianism was on the march in Europe, with Adolf Hitler in total control of Germany and annexing nation after nation in Central Europe, using the excuse that the Versailles Treaty after World War I had unduly punished his nation.

In Eastern Europe Josef Stalin was consolidating his power in the Soviet state, using the Moscow Trials to eliminate almost all of his old Bolshevik comrades. American liberals and radicals could not believe the confessions of the former revolutionaries, but an individualist conservative like Branch Rickey understood that whether the old Bolsheviks were telling the truth or were coerced into false confessions, an ideology that glorified the state and not the individual was bound to be self-defeating.

Brutality and devastation seemed on the rise everywhere. Spain was being ripped apart by a civil war, and Rickey was heartsick at the invasion of China by the Japanese in the summer of 1937. Through his close association with international outreach programs of the Methodist church, he knew many Christian missionaries who had traveled to China, and the bloodshed in that ancient nation grieved him terribly.

At a December 14, 1937, sports banquet in St. Louis, where a record number of more than one thousand people turned out to honor Joe

Medwick, the Cardinals' Triple Crown winner and the National League's Most Valuable Player, Rickey poured out his concerns about the world situation and emphasized his abiding belief in the beauty and necessity of baseball. "While all the world is jittery, Nanking is burning tonight, the rivers are red with blood and the Spaniards are flying at each other's throats, there can come a pause in which we, in this country, can stop and pay honor to one in a competitive sport," he orated. "When we can come together at a time like this and recognize the super-excellency of someone not at war, but in competitive playing—a young man who loves to play—Joe Medwick."[31]

Branch Rickey was well aware of the American people's deep reluctance about getting involved again in foreign quarrels. When President Roosevelt gave a speech in Chicago in October 1937, declaring that the United States must "quarantine the aggressors" in Europe and Asia, Rickey applauded. Sooner or later, Rickey sadly agreed with Roosevelt, it was likely that another world war would have to be fought to preserve liberty and freedom. Although most of the American public did not respond positively to Roosevelt's "quarantine" speech, on this one issue Rickey was in total agreement with the Democratic president.

As the new year of 1938 began, Branch Rickey's concern for freedom was not just national and global. He felt that his baseball business's freedom might also be in jeopardy as the result of Commissioner Landis's latest investigation of the Cardinals farm system. Virtually every team in baseball now had a developmental system, even the wealthy big-city teams. The Yankees had started a Minor League affiliation program in 1932, hiring George Weiss to administrate it. The deaths of anti–farm system patriarch John McGraw in 1934 and longtime owner Charles Stoneham in 1936 led the Giants, too, to embark on a player development program. The *Sporting News* editorialized in January 1937 that Commissioner Landis may be "pained, but scarcely surprised to note a baseball world that has been completely 'Rickeyized.'"[32]

As far as Rickey was concerned, he felt that he had saved the Minor Leagues in the worst years of the Great Depression. By 1933 the number of leagues had shrunk to eleven, and the size of class D team rosters had shrunk to fourteen. By 1937 the number of leagues had risen to thirty-seven and would total forty-four by 1940. Rickey took pride in his role in their rebirth. After the Cardinals' World Series triumph in 1934, Rickey received Sam Breadon's go-ahead to expand his amateur tryout camps. As a result, by the end of the 1930s, the St. Louis organization would possess rights to nearly 750 players.[33]

Commissioner Landis, however, still concerned about the vastness of Rickey's system, had assigned his assistant Leslie O'Connor to supervise a thorough investigation of his adversary's empire. There was admittedly a personality conflict between the profane Landis and the religious Rickey, whom the commissioner described to his friends as a "hypocritical Protestant bastard wrapped in those minister's robes," but he was not primarily motivated by a personal vendetta.[34] Landis genuinely believed that individual players should be allowed to rise to the pinnacle of the Major Leagues without impediments created by any organization. Since his first days as commissioner, he had encouraged all players, Major and Minor Leaguers, to come to see him in Chicago or at least put into writing any complaints about maltreatment.

Branch Rickey, on the other hand, believed that his farm system taught the players the correct way to play the game, afforded far better pay than ordinary labor, and provided good moral training for the athletes. Rickey genuinely saw himself as a great paternalist who was providing a priceless opportunity for the eager, hungry, talented young player. He bristled at any claim that he was blocking a boy's path to advancement. He loathed Landis's "edicts," by which the commissioner could both take away a St. Louis Minor Leaguer and force the Cardinals to keep a Major League player on the roster without citing any baseball rules.

In the middle of January 1938, Commissioner Landis summoned Branch Rickey to the former judge's winter home in Bellaire, Florida. Landis had zeroed in on Rickey's control of at least two teams in the Three-I League (named for the three states of Illinois, Indiana, and Iowa). Danville, Illinois, was the Cardinals' team of record in the league, but Landis discovered that Rickey also had a relationship with a team in Springfield, Illinois, that was not registered. Under this arrangement Springfield had to accept players from Danville.

"Have you a right under this agreement to say to Springfield, 'You shall not take that player?'" Landis grilled Rickey, who admitted that he had that right. Landis wanted to know if it was good for Springfield and good for the Three-I League for Rickey to have such power. Rickey replied, "Many a club makes an agreement that is bad for itself. It is entirely a question of can a man make a deal for himself." Not satisfied with the answer, Landis asked Rickey to admit that his control of both Danville and Springfield was as "big as a house, isn't it?" Unyielding, Rickey said, "It is not as big as a house."

Landis countered, "I think it is as big as the universe." The commissioner continued, "This is just as important in the Three-I League as it would be in the National or American Leagues. You two fellows are in a fight for the pennant and Springfield says: 'Here I have a chance of getting a player.' You have the power to say: 'You can't do it.'"[35]

Rickey did not agree with the commissioner's equating the situation in the lower Minor Leagues, where development was more crucial than winning a pennant, with that of the big leagues, where winning a title was paramount. Moreover, he felt that Landis was blind to the point that Minor League executives had thanked Rickey and the Cardinals for saving baseball in their small towns. Obviously, Landis and Rickey had an irreconcilable conflict. The commissioner ended his hearing, telling his adversary that he would rule sometime during spring training.

In 1938, for the first time since Rickey managed the St. Louis Browns in 1914, his spring headquarters would be based in St. Petersburg, Florida. The St. Louis executive was looking forward to a reunion with Al Lang, the Rotary Club leader who had become one of the biggest promoters of baseball's so-called "Grapefruit League" of spring training.

Rickey had many holes to fill in the Cardinals lineup. With Leo Durocher traded to Brooklyn, the team was again looking for a shortstop. Joe Stripp, obtained from the Dodgers in the Durocher trade, was given a long look, but he was not an everyday player. (After he retired Stripp would open a baseball school in Florida.) Always enamored of football athletes, Rickey invited star quarterback Sammy Baugh of Texas Christian University to try out at shortstop. Baugh had played both sports in college and obviously had the arm for the long throw from the shortstop hole, but Frank Frisch wondered whether the football star would ever hit Major League pitching.[36] Although Baugh would play some baseball at the Cardinals' Columbus farm in 1938, he ultimately signed with the pro football Washington Redskins, where he went on to a Hall of Fame football career.

In coming to St. Petersburg the Cardinals were joining the Yankees, who a decade earlier had been lured to Florida by Al Lang. The first game of the exhibition season between the two accomplished franchises drew a record-breaking crowd of nearly seven thousand fans. The start of the game was held up for several minutes, waiting for the arrival of an honored guest, Alf Landon, former governor of Kansas and defeated 1936 Republican presidential candidate. When Landon finally entered the ballpark, he was on the arm of the Mr. Republican of the St. Louis Cardinals, Branch Rickey.[37]

Dizzy Dean was looking fit in the early workouts, a promising sign that his injuries had healed over the winter. Once again it seemed that Dean would be a key to the Cardinals' success, because the team's pitching seemed mediocre. Only left-hander Bob Weiland, drafted from the Minor Leagues, and "Fiddler" Bill McGee (so nicknamed because he played the violin in the "Mississippi Mudcat" band that Pepper Martin had organized) had the makings of consistent winners.

On March 23, 1938, the shoe finally dropped on Kenesaw Mountain Landis's investigation into the practices of the St. Louis farm system. In a nine-page, five thousand–word ruling, the commissioner decreed that the Cardinals organization was guilty of multiple violations in covering up players and not registering controls over Minor League teams. "No club should contract away its right and obligation to get competitive playing strength as needed and whenever obtained," the commissioner ruled in a case that came to be known as the "Cedar Rapids decision," because Cedar Rapids, Iowa, was one of the Minor League teams accepting St. Louis players without registering them with the Minor League's ruling body, the National Association.[38] The owners of the farm clubs in Cedar Rapids, Springfield (Illinois), and Sacramento (California) were fined between $500 and $1,000. Landis also made free agents of at least seventy-four St. Louis farm hands, who had been either illegally signed or illegally transferred. (In another example of the complicated baseball system, the number of freed Minor Leaguers has also been given as ninety-one.)[39] Only one of the players proved truly significant in baseball history, outfielder Pete Reiser, who would wind up in Brooklyn and play a major role in the upcoming Larry MacPhail–Branch Rickey–Leo Durocher–Brooklyn Dodgers melodrama.

Sam Breadon and Branch Rickey received no advance notice of the commissioner's decision. They learned the news along with the sportswriters in St. Petersburg. The Cardinals brass deferred comment until they had time to digest Landis's ruling, although Rickey said he might soon have "a 5,000 word comment" of his own.[40] Although the decision was an embarrassment to the organization and cost the team players worth an estimated $200,000, it could have been worse. Landis could have directly reprimanded and fined Breadon and Rickey, but he did not. He could have fined the Cardinals' Minor League teams more heavily, but William Bramham, president of the National Association, intervened in Rickey's behalf. Even if Landis were unconvinced that Rickey had saved the Minor Leagues, Bramham, based in Durham, North Carolina, had firsthand knowledge of the basic truth in Rickey's statement. Landis also allowed the Cardinals to bid again on the players he liberated as long as they were registered openly and correctly. In an era when most players believed in the reserve system's restrictions, the majority of the freed farm hands returned to the Cardinals' fold.

Shortly after Landis's ruling Sam Breadon left spring training earlier than usual. He was returning to St. Louis, Rickey told the press, "to look at a few records." Branch Rickey, never one to take a negative ruling lying down, was urging some kind of legal recourse against Landis. After some deliberation Breadon decided to take no action. "Landis is the last word," he said soon thereafter. "He has the authority to act 'in the best interests of the game.'"[41]

Rickey was not pleased with Breadon's passive acceptance of the Cedar Rapids decision, an arbitrary "edict," as the ferocious gentleman would call it time and again. However, he understood the reality of the political situation in the front office. Sam Breadon was the boss, whereas Branch Rickey was only an employee, even if an extremely well-paid and well-known one. There was nothing Rickey could do about Landis's ruling but accept it and turn to the immediate job at hand: building another championship team in 1938. On the eve of opening day 1938 Branch Rickey was ready to provide the most graphic evidence of the demise of the Gashouse Gang Cardinals. He was preparing to bid adieu to that "very unpredictable boy" Dizzy Dean.

13

More Years of Loss, and Farewells to Dizzy Dean and Charley Barrett

"Boys, we're going to the movies," Branch Rickey announced to his daughters as he burst into his big house in the St. Louis countryside. "I've just traded Dizzy Dean. The newspapermen are going to be calling, and I don't want to talk to them now."[1] Despite the falloff in the pitcher's productivity in 1937, Rickey's decision to trade the popular Dean had not been an easy one. The colorful pitcher had been on good behavior in spring training 1938. There had been no Dean incidents, no punching of reporters or badmouthing of teammates. St. Louis sportswriters were even beginning to refer to "this year's quiet edition of Dizzy Dean." It had been so peaceful in the Cardinals spring training camp in St. Petersburg that the biggest noise came from the strains of Pepper Martin's Mississippi Mudcat band, entertaining local residents and tourists from the veranda of the Detroit Hotel, the team's headquarters.[2]

Although Dizzy's popularity remained high in St. Louis, the Associated Press had voted him "the biggest disappointment in sports" for the year 1937.[3] Dean was only twenty-seven but had logged a lot of Major League innings since he burst on the scene as an ace pitcher in 1932. As noted earlier, Dizzy's brother Paul had begun to break down in 1936. Before the end of spring training 1938, Branch Rickey told Roy Stockton of the *St. Louis Post-Dispatch*: "He's through. Dead arm. No question about it. You can bet everything you have. No, we can't count on Paul Dean at all."[4]

As opening day of the 1938 season neared, Branch Rickey had to face the question of Dizzy Dean's future as a Cardinal. Was it time to apply one of his famous dictums, "It is better to trade a player a year early than a year late"? Rickey agonized over the decision because despite Dean's constant public criticisms of him as a skinflint, the executive was fond of the pitcher as both a person and a player. "Dean was most always playing a role," Rickey remembered fondly ten years after the trade. "Had a tremendous lot of pretense and showmanship."[5] His desire to be the best in his field made an enduring impression on his boss. If a rival threw a good knuckleball or screwball against the Cardinals, Dean insisted on trying to throw a better one.

No slouch himself as an agitator, Rickey loved to prod Dean to superior performance. One day, when Dean asked out of pitching because he was aching, Rickey begged him to take his turn on the mound because, he told him, a prominent governor and his staff had traveled hundreds of miles to see him. When Dean was persuaded to pitch, Rickey hastily rounded up some friends to pose as the visiting dignitaries. On other occasion, on a sweltering summer afternoon in St. Louis, Dean was hit on the head by a line drive off the bat of Giants second baseman Burgess Whitehead, his former teammate. Rickey rushed down into the clubhouse to see how his ace pitcher was faring. A lump the size of a coconut had formed on Dizzy's head, but the pitcher calmly sat on a training table, smoking a cigarette. Noting his pitcher's quick recovery, Rickey almost coaxed Dean to return to the game until team physician Robert Hyland put a stop to Rickey's reckless idea.[6]

There is no doubt that the executive was going to miss Dean's boyishness and love of pranks. By April 1938, however, he made the professional decision that Dizzy Dean's usefulness to the Cardinals had passed. With Sam Breadon's approval Rickey started secret negotiations with the Cubs, burning up the long-distance telephone wires to Catalina Island in California, where the Chicagoans were in spring training. Rickey threw out different combinations of players to Clarence "Pants" Rowland, the Pacific Coast League president and a former Cubs scout, who was representing Chicago owner Philip Wrigley Jr. in the trade talks.

On April 16, 1938, as the Cardinals were winding up a preseason city series game at Sportsman's Park against the Browns, Branch Rickey and Sam Breadon made the blockbuster announcement. Dizzy Dean had been traded to the Cubs for veteran right-handed pitcher Curt Davis, southpaw pitcher Clyde Shoun, journeyman outfielder George Tucker "Tuck" Stainback, and $185,000 in cash, a huge amount of money for the time. The trade was consummated only after Rickey insisted on language in the transaction that the Cubs had full knowledge that Dean was "unsound in arm."[7]

After the exhibition game with the Browns had ended, Pants Rowland came down to the Cardinals dugout to introduce himself to Chicago's newest player. Dizzy Dean did not know Rowland and thought he was just another autograph seeker. When the scout said, "You're one of us now, Dizzy," the pitcher soon understood. Ex-Cardinal Dizzy Dean walked back into the clubhouse to collect his gear and shake hands with his former teammates, putting an especially warm arm around his brother Paul's shoulder. "Don't worry, guys," Dizzy said. "I'll make sure you all get World Series tickets."[8]

The Cardinals were stunned at the loss of their colorful if volatile teammate. Sportswriters heard a few players mutter that "the pennant just walked outside the door." Suddenly, Branch Rickey and Sam Breadon made a rare dual appearance in the clubhouse, explaining that they still expected the team to do well and become a champion. Although Dizzy took some parting shots at the cheapness of the Cardinals front office, Breadon and Rickey took the high road. They wished him the best in Chicago, noting, though, that since 1934 there had been no pennants in St. Louis. "He has not been everything we expected," was as far as Branch Rickey's public criticism would go.[9]

Breadon and Rickey braced for a public uproar in St. Louis. Although the reaction was not as bitter and angry as the protest over the Rogers Hornsby trade in 1926, Rickey's daughter Jane recalled reading a newspaper headline, "Rickey Sells Dean for Cash and Two Hamburgers."[10] It was surely a potentially risky move to trade a onetime ace pitcher to one of your fiercest National League rivals, but Branch Rickey was never skittish about trading with league contenders. As we have seen, he had dealt pitchers Tex Carleton, Bill Lee, and Lon Warneke to the Cubs, and second baseman Burgess Whitehead to the Giants. You have to have the courage of your convictions in making trades, Rickey believed, knowing that the eventual outcome, especially involving young players, might not be known for years.

Outfielder Tuck Stainback would play only six games with the Cardinals before being dealt away, but Rickey saw promise in the twenty-six-year-old left-hander Clyde Shoun from Mountain City, Tennessee. Some hopeful writers even dubbed Shoun the "next Dizzy Dean." Shoun was nicknamed "Hardrock," perhaps for his toughness (or perhaps for his stubbornness on the mound). His biggest year in St. Louis would be 1940, when he won thirteen games. He also led the National League in appearances in both 1939 and 1940.

The key to the trade for Rickey was Curt "Coonskin" Davis, a late-blooming, thirty-four-year-old pitcher from rural Greenfield, Missouri. Davis did not arrive in the big leagues until 1934, but in his first two seasons, he won thirty-six games for the second-division Phillies. Traded to the Cubs in the middle of 1936, he compiled a 21-14 record for Chicago with a respectable ERA of around 3.75. Statistically, Davis would do fairly well in St. Louis, winning twelve games in 1938 and going 22-16 in 1939 before being traded to Brooklyn in 1940.

Curt Davis, however, was obviously no Dizzy Dean. Not only did he lack the charisma of the departed pitcher, he was a control pitcher who walked few but struck out only thirty-six batters in his first year as a Cardinal. He logged only 173 innings, compared to Dean's usual workload of 300-plus innings a year. Although Dizzy Dean won only seven games for the 1938 Cubs and pitched just seventy-five innings, his ERA was a sparkling 1.81 and he lost only one game. He was also a great drawing card in a year when the Cubs won the pennant and attracted over 950,000 fans.[11]

Meanwhile, the Cardinals in 1938 fell out of the first division to sixth place, nine games under .500. The short explanation for the decline was productive but not timely offense and weak pitching and defense. The Cardinals led the league in runs scored, and Joe Medwick and John Mize had characteristically solid offensive years. Medwick's 122 RBI led the league, and Mize's .337 BA, 27 HR, and 102 RBI looked good on paper. However, Mize also made 15 errors, the most of any National League first baseman, and the team's fielding percentage was last in the league. The new double play combination of second baseman Stu Martin and short-stop Lynn Myers was mediocre defensively and subpar offensively. Injuries limited Pepper Martin to ninety-one games, and though he hit .294, he scored only 34 R, with 38 RBI. The ERA of the pitching staff ranked sixth, identical to the overall final standing of the 1938 team. Southpaw

Bob Weiland was the team's big winner at 16-11, but Lon Warneke, at 13-8, and Curt Davis, at 12-8, were the only other double-digit winners on the staff.

The second noncontending season in a row cost Frank Frisch his manager's job sixteen games before the end of the season. Having managed for over five seasons, Frisch had enjoyed the greatest longevity of the managers hired by Sam Breadon, but the owner was getting impatient for a return to the top of the standings. As usual, the managerial switch was made by Breadon with little input from Rickey. Coach Miguel "Mike" Gonzalez, a longtime member of the organization, ran the team for the rest of the year on an interim basis, finishing with an 8-8 record. As a result of the poor team and the absence of Dizzy Dean as a drawing card, attendance plummeted alarmingly. Only 291,000 fans came to see the Cardinals in 1938, an average of barely 3,500 a game, and a loss of almost 140,000 from 1937.[12]

Reduced to the role of vicarious spectator in the World Series for the fourth straight year, Branch Rickey hoped that the Cubs would represent the National League well against the Yankees. The 1926 Cardinals had been the only team to beat the New York juggernaut in the World Series, but the 1938 Yankees would not be denied, sweeping Chicago in four straight games. In so doing, Joe McCarthy's Bronx Bombers established a record that the 1931 Cardinals had denied Connie Mack's Philadelphia Athletics: for the first time since the World Series began in 1903, a team won three world baseball championships in a row.

Dizzy Dean did enjoy a last hurrah in game two at Wrigley Field. His flaming fastball a thing of the past, Dean kept the Yankees at bay, holding on to a tenuous 3–2 lead until the top of the eighth inning when Yankees shortstop Frank Crosetti timed one of Dean's tantalizing slow pitches and belted a two-run home run, sparking the Yankees to a 6–3 victory. Branch Rickey thought to himself that his former star had pitched heroically and that if it had been four years earlier, the New Yorkers wouldn't have had a chance against him.[13]

Visits to Wrigley Field during the baseball season of 1938 were thus not happy ones for Branch Rickey. First, he saw the archrival Cubs soar over his Cardinals in the regular season, and in the World Series he had to endure the Cubs getting trounced as the National League representative. However, in the two other major realms of Branch Rickey's life, religion and family, Chicago in 1938 provided him some very rewarding experiences.

During the first week of February 1938, Rickey was among the four thousand delegates to a United Methodist council held in conjunction with the two hundredth anniversary of John Wesley's "strange warming of the heart" experienced while he was attending a Moravian meeting on Aldersgate Street in London. The religious movement of Methodism dated its inception from John Wesley's conversion to a very personal kind of religion after he heard a reading from Martin Luther's preface to St. Paul's "Epistle to the Romans." Next to the transformation of Saul of Tarsus to the missionary Paul on the road to Damascus, John Wesley's Aldersgate conversion is perhaps the greatest transformational moment in the history of Christianity.[14]

Assigned the welcome task of spreading the gospel to young delegates, Rickey fired up the audience with a passion that the *Chicago Tribune* called an "'Onward, Christian Soldier' address." Rickey then listened as Bob Feller, the Cleveland Indians' sensational young pitcher, told the audience about the importance of church attendance. Feller, whose fame was so great that his high school graduation had been broadcast live on national radio, was accompanied by his pastor from Van Meter, Iowa, Reverend Charles Fix, who said approvingly, "If all the members of my church were as regular as Bob, I wouldn't have anything to worry about."[15]

The platform passed by the young delegates surely showed the influence of Branch Rickey, who was deeply concerned about the rising threats of totalitarianism and war. Youth must "face threats against freedom with realism," the document stated. "But to do this we must develop spiritual techniques for tapping sources of power. These include Bible reading as a laboratory manual, small groups sharing fellowship, exploration and mutual support, regular practice of personal devotions, and a constant study of changing social conditions and needs."[16]

Also attending the Chicago conference with Rickey was a young minister from Los Angeles, Karl Everette Downs, who was building a considerable following in the black neighborhoods of the Southern California metropolis.[17] One of Downs's parishioners, and soon to be his close friend, was a very talented young athlete from Pasadena who soon would be making his name at the University of California at Los Angeles in football, basketball, track and field, and baseball. The young man's name was Jack Roosevelt Robinson.

The historic linkage of Rickey, Robinson, and Downs was a few years away, but the spirit of the Wesleyan brotherhood and belief in opportunity for all people, regardless of color, certainly infused all the attendees at the two hundredth anniversary celebration in Chicago. After all, it was John Wesley in 1774, on the eve of the first antislavery movements in England and the United States, who wrote with anguish about the slave trade: "Do you never feel another's pain? . . . When you saw the flowing eyes, the heaving breasts, or bleeding sides and tortured limbs of your fellow creatures, was [*sic*] you a stone or a brute? . . . When you squeezed the agonizing creatures down in the ship, or when you threw their poor mangled remains in to the sea, had you no relenting?"[18]

In addition to service to God and baseball, the third realm of Branch Rickey's trinity of passions was his family. Visits to Chicago in the late 1930s brought him close to the mini-family that his three oldest daughters had temporarily established in the second city. Mary Rickey's husband, John Eckler, was attending law school at the University of Chicago; Branch Rickey's daughter Jane was a student at the Chicago Art Institute; and Alice Rickey, in between semesters at Swarthmore College in Philadelphia, was taking drama courses in Chicago. A love of life, art, and adventure infused the daughters' household to the immense satisfaction of the paterfamilias.[19]

When he wasn't visiting family, scouting farm teams and young prospects, speaking to church groups, or drumming up support for Republican candidates for office, Branch Rickey made time for an annual postseason duck hunting expedition with friends in rural Missouri and Illinois. He had put on weight over the last few years and hoped that the fall 1938 hunt could be undertaken with horses. "I can see you snickering about this suggestion," Rickey wrote his physician friend Dr. Cameron Harmon of Carbondale, Illinois, whose brother Clarence, a minister, was another close friend. "But I am considerably heavier, and I don't care to exhaust myself completely when I am not accustomed to walking at all." He concluded his letter with eagerness to find out all about the doctor's venture into black gold futures. "I hear only glorious reports about the Oil Fields near Centralia," Rickey wrote eagerly with unabashed capitalist ardor.[20]

As 1939 spring training commenced in St. Petersburg, Florida, Branch Rickey was hopeful that the dismal performance of the 1938 Cardinals was an aberration. Although Rickey was growing more estranged from Sam Breadon, who Rickey felt had too docilely accepted Commissioner Landis's Cedar Rapids decision, Rickey was glad that Breadon had hired Ray Blades, a longtime Rickey loyalist, as the new Cardinals manager. After a broken leg in 1926 had reduced him to only a part-time player, Blades turned to coaching and managing in the Cardinals' Minor League system with great success.

Blades was truly one of Rickey's ferocious gentlemen. In private life Blades was quiet and well-mannered, traits that certainly pleased his mentor, but when it came to baseball matters the former World War One army sergeant swore like a sailor and hated to lose with a passion. One year, early in his career, when Blades was cut in spring training and sent to the Minor League camp, he had to be restrained from strangling one of then-manager Rickey's coaches.[21] Rickey loved the fire in Blades's belly, the competitive zeal that could justify breaking the legs of one's grandmother if she were blocking second base on a potential double play.

If there was one flaw in Blades's managerial makeup, however, it was his impatience with pitchers. In an age when starting pitchers were expected to go deep into games, and when "finishing what you started" was a baseball precept as well as a moral one, Blades was known to warm up several relievers early in games. It caused the starting pitchers to grow anxious, looking over their shoulders, and the relievers to worry about throwing too many pitches in the bullpen. Yet, in some ways, Blades's theory of getting relievers involved in the action foreshadowed the rise of bullpen dominance decades later. He also was renowned for his ability to invent and relay signs to his players.[22]

Despite Blades's fiery leadership and the big bats of Joe Medwick and John Mize, the Cardinals quickly fell behind in the 1939 pennant race. The Cincinnati Reds, managed by former Cardinals skipper Bill McKechnie, took command early with an outstanding pitching staff led by two veterans, converted third baseman Bucky Walters and former Cardinal Paul Derringer. Yet St. Louis fans, certain there was plenty of time to catch their suddenly emergent Ohio rivals, were ready to provide loyal support. On June 18, 1939, a "Pepper Martin Day" was celebrated at Sportsman's Park. Among the gifts the popular "Wild Horse of the Osage" received was a tractor, which the crowd favorite, as one sportswriter related, "drove out of the arena as if it were a Roman chariot."[23]

Enjoying the festivities was chief scout Charley Barrett, who had signed Martin off a class D, Greenville, Texas, roster fifteen years earlier. Branch Rickey's associate felt a special warmth toward the colorful fan favorite because Martin always gave him public credit for finding him and heading him toward the Major Leagues. It was rare for a player to publicly acknowledge a scout, and Barrett was truly touched.

Sadly, barely two weeks after "Pepper Martin Day," on the Fourth of July 1939, the Cardinals suffered a major blow when Charley Barrett, age sixty-eight, died suddenly of a heart attack after returning home from scouting an amateur game. Branch Rickey was in Rochester, observing the Cardinals' top farm club, when he learned of Barrett's passing. Deeply grieved and not yet wanting to talk publicly about his personal loss, Rickey sent a telegram to the St. Louis newspapers, noting that "one of [Barrett's] leading contributions to baseball was his fine, wholesome advice to and his influence upon young players." He added, "Never a 'yes' man, he was my closest friend in baseball."[24]

The highlights of a thirty-five-year friendship flashed through grieving Branch Rickey's mind as he prepared to make the sad journey back to St. Louis for the funeral. He thought of how they had met as opponents in the Texas League, and of what a fine fielder and base runner Barrett had been, even though he never learned to hit the curve ball or make the big leagues as a player. His keen ability to spot talent and his character and optimistic, obliging spirit had made him a wonderful scout, Rickey reflected. He thought of the enormous list of future Major Leaguers his late friend had signed—the first ones, Art Fletcher, Charley Grimm, Bill Killefer, Muddy Ruel, Hank Severeid; and, later, for the Cardinals, Lester Bell, Jim Bottomley, Pepper Martin, Heinie Mueller, Tom Thevenow, and on and on. He remembered the fun of going on the road with Bar-

rett seeking raw talent, and the pranks they had pulled in St. Louis, haul-
ing Jane's rugs into the barren team office to convince Minor League
owners that the Cardinals were run by people who paid their bills. An
indefatigable idealist, Barrett had wished that more Major League and
high Minor League teams did more to help support the lower Minors, a
sentiment that Rickey wholly endorsed.[25] Waves of grief engulfed the St.
Louis executive as he realized that he would never see Barrett again and
had not had the chance to say good-bye. He allowed himself a good cry.

Rickey and Sam Breadon joined manager Ray Blades, team captain
Pepper Martin, former team officials Clarence Lloyd (now retired in
Georgia), William DeWitt (now general manager of the Browns), Warren Giles (now general manager of the Reds), and team lawyer George
Williams as pallbearers at the Barrett funeral at St. Louis's Blessed Sacra-
ment Catholic Church. A large contingent of baseball people paid their
respects, among them retired scout Dick Kinsella, the most trusted ivory
hunter for the late John McGraw's Giants.[26]

By the end of July 1939, the Cardinals slipped further back in the pennant race. The Reds stretched their lead over the second-place Cardinals
to ten and a half games. It seemed that Branch Rickey's greatest satisfaction would have to come from the fine showings by most of the Cardinals' Minor League farm clubs. Then, all of a sudden, in early August the
Major League team caught fire and won ten games in a row. Fans came
back to Sportsman's Park after the disappointments of the prior two seasons. In mid-August, nearly forty thousand fans jammed the ballpark to
see the Cardinals, behind the solid pitching of young Morton Cooper
and veteran Curt Davis, sweep a Sunday doubleheader from the Reds.
Cincinnati's lead was under double digits, and the Cardinals seemed
headed for another classic late-summer roll.

After four straight years of declining attendance, the Cardinals were
gaining fans again, ultimately drawing more than 400,000 fans in 1939—
again far short of the 1928 record of almost 762,000, but still an increase
of more than 100,000 from 1938.[27] The Reds, though, were going to be
tough to catch, and the September schedule favored them because they
played twenty-three of their final twenty-six games at home, most of them
against second-division opponents.

The Cardinals were still alive, however, and Rickey decided to augment the roster for the final stretch. To infuse some youth in the mound corps, he called up two promising left-handers from the farm system, Max Lanier and Elwyn "Preacher" Roe. Rickey usually didn't like to deprive Minor League teams of good players and drawing cards during their pennant races, but if the parent club had a chance at a pennant, Rickey was not afraid to make the move.

Lanier and Roe were not yet ready to contribute much in 1939, but the rest of the Cardinals were eager to bring St. Louis its first pennant in five years. On Sunday, September 17, the Redbirds pulled out a 6–5, come-from-behind win over the Braves to cut the Reds' lead to three and a half games. It was an emotional day at Sportsman's Park because it marked Sam Breadon's first appearance in a month. In August the owner had sustained serious spinal injuries in a fall from a horse at his country estate, and for a man who prided himself on his good physical condition, his recuperation had been slow and painful.[28]

Yet, instead of building on the momentum of the Sunday victory, the Cardinals treaded water for the next week. When they went into Cincinnati for a doubleheader on the final Tuesday of the regular season, they were still three and a half games behind the league leaders and had to sweep the Reds to keep alive realistic pennant hopes. Both teams were hot, with the Cardinals winning eighteen out of their last twenty-one, but the Reds had kept pace with a 16-4 streak of their own.

Pennant fever was high in Cincinnati as the Reds had a chance for their first World Series appearance in twenty years. The infamy of the Black Sox scandal in the 1919 Series had tainted Cincinnati's victory that year, although many observers thought they would have won even if all of the White Sox had played the games honestly. There were many ex-Cardinals on the 1939 Reds, all eager to clinch the pennant over their former team. Among them were manager Bill McKechnie, outfielders Stanley "Frenchy" Bordaragay and Ival Goodman, infielders Billy Myers and Lew Riggs, pitcher Paul Derringer, and Rickey's protégé in the front office, general manager Warren Giles.

More than thirty-four thousand fans jammed Crosley Field to see the Reds win the crucial first game, 3–1. Mort Cooper kept the Cardinals' slim hopes alive by shutting out Cincinnati in the nightcap, 6–0. The next day, "Fiddler" Bill McGee cut the lead to two and a half games by shutting out Bucky Walters, the eventual league Most Valuable Player, 4–0, before more than twenty-five thousand fans.

On Thursday, September 28, 1939, Paul Derringer pitched the pennant clincher over his former team, winning 4–2 despite giving up fourteen hits. Derringer gave credence to the old baseball adage "If you don't walk people and don't give up too many home runs, it will take many singles to beat you." Even three errors by shortstop Bill Myers did not rattle the veteran pitcher, who gave up hits in every inning except the ninth, when, smelling the pennant, he retired St. Louis in order. The Cardinals had dug themselves a hole in the early innings through wildness by Max Lanier and Curt Davis, and bad base running in the late innings had crippled the Cardinals' comeback. Down by only one run in the seventh inning, Joe Medwick was thrown out trying to stretch a double into a triple, and reserve first baseman/outfielder Johnny Hopp was picked off second base with nobody out in the eighth inning.[29]

Ruefully, Branch Rickey tipped his cap to the veteran Derringer. He had never been enamored by the off-the-field, libertine lifestyle of his former pitcher, who had been nicknamed "Dude" and "Duke" by his fellow players because of a penchant for changing clothes five times a day. A man with a great temper, Derringer had gotten into his share of altercations with fans over the years and had once thrown an inkwell at the equally volatile Larry MacPhail, his former Cincinnati general manager.[30]

Yet Rickey never disputed the importance of veteran experience on the mound. Derringer's twenty-four victories and Bucky Walters's twenty-seven wins accounted for more than half of Cincinnati's total of ninety-seven, all of them vital as Johnny Vander Meer, who in 1938 had pitched back-to-back no-hitters, won only five games in 1939. Both Derringer and Walters profited from the tutelage of manager Bill McKechnie, who said simply and wisely, "I like older pitchers."[31]

Once again Branch Rickey would have to spend early October on the sidelines, rooting for another National League team in the World Series. He hoped that the Reds would be able to end the Yankees' dominance. However, it was not to be, as the Bronx Bombers swept the Reds to add to their remarkable record, now four World Series victories in a row. Paul

Derringer and Bucky Walters did not pitch badly, but they were outshone by Yankee starters Red Ruffing and Monte Pearson and the batting heroics of Joe DiMaggio, Bill Dickey and Charley Keller.

As Branch Rickey gathered his staff early in the fall of 1939 for the annual postseason analysis of the year past and the years ahead, he was not without hope for the team's future. Although another year without a pennant was hard for the competitive executive to endure, he noted many good signs for the future. The Cardinals had won ninety-two games, breaking the ninety-win barrier for the first time since 1935. As a team they led the league in batting and slugging average, runs scored, and doubles, and their team ERA was second only to the champion Reds.

Individually, many Cardinals had enjoyed fine seasons. Despite Ray Blades's overmanagement of the pitching staff, the hurlers performed nobly. Curt Davis won twenty-two and saved seven games, logging 248 innings. Mort Cooper, a star hurler of the future, won twelve games in his rookie season. (North Carolinian Cooper was the older brother of catcher Walker Cooper, who would also soon make his mark with the Cardinals.) Two other farm system products, right-handers Lon Warneke and Bob Bowman, chipped in with thirteen victories apiece. Clyde Shoun led the team in appearances with 53 and went 3-1 with a 3.76 ERA and 9 saves.

The big hitters contributed impressively. John Mize led the league in hitting with a .349 BA, with 28 HR and 108 RBI. Joe Medwick saw his home run numbers fall to 14 but batted a solid .332, slugged .507 with 117 RBI and 98 R. In his first full season, right fielder Enos Slaughter, soon to be nicknamed "Country" Slaughter, emerged from the North Carolina tobacco fields to hit .320 with 12 HR, 86 RBI, and 95 R. He led the league with 52 doubles, showing his speed and power. Slaughter topped the league charts in most outfield assists and put-outs. He also led the league in errors, but, as usual, Branch Rickey discounted overzealousness in the search for victory.

Slaughter's rise through the farm system had been fitful, and some members of the organization thought that right-handed-hitting outfielder John Rizzo was the better prospect at Columbus. However, Rizzo was traded to Pittsburgh, where he had one big year in 1938, with 111 RBI, but then faded from the scene. Slaughter would enjoy a nineteen-year Major League career and ultimately would be elected to the Hall of Fame.

Despite the Cardinals' second-place finish, Rickey felt optimistic about the team's future because Enos Slaughter was just one of fifteen players from the farm system who had at least a taste of Major League action in 1939. To streamline the organization and perhaps to ward off future investigations by Commissioner Landis, Rickey had terminated nine of his Minor League working agreements and had limited those he maintained to class D teams consisting only of "raw rookies."[32]

In sum, Rickey saw the Cardinals as poised to soon regain their rightful perch at the top of the National League. If all went well in 1940, he would be looking forward to the challenge of taking on the Yankees in the World Series and overturning the Yankees dynasty. He understood that the rich big-city teams had built-in advantages, but he relished the challenge of beating them by hard work and astute evaluation.

He had the utmost respect for Edward Barrow's and George Weiss's achievement in creating the New York juggernaut, but he was growing peeved at unfair advantages taken by the reigning baseball champions. Not only were Yankees scouts denigrating the Cardinals to prospective ballplayers as a "cheap outfit," but they were also offering amateurs money for college tuition as an inducement to sign. The domination of the sport by rich owners had been Rickey's bête noire ever since he started working in baseball, and he had recently persuaded the National League owners to pass a rule forbidding the signing of college players until after their classes had graduated. However, the Yankees dominated American League councils so thoroughly that no such provision was passed by the younger league.[33]

Despite his good feelings about the resurgence of the Cardinals as a winning organization, Rickey's disappointment with some of Sam Breadon's business decisions was intensifying. Although Ray Blades was rehired as manager for 1940, during the middle of the 1939 season Breadon had fired Donald Beach as auditor of the Columbus Redbirds farm club. Rickey considered Beach part of his extended family, a fellow Ohio Wesleyan alumnus and Delta Tau Delta fraternity brother. Although Rickey was able, through his wide network of baseball connections, to help Beach find a similar job in 1940 with Buffalo in the International

League, Breadon's peremptory firing was an obvious slap at Rickey and his loyal associates.[34]

Another salvo from Breadon came at the end of 1939 when the owner, despite declaring a dividend for the stockholders, announced a 10 percent cut in salaries of all Cardinals front office personnel.[35] Breadon's decision enraged Rickey, and its callousness must have reminded him of his own peremptory firing as manager in 1925. Accordingly, in 1939, the vice president and general manager gave his blessing for Branch Rickey Jr., who had been steadily working his way up the ladder of the Cardinals Minor League front office system, to go to work in the Brooklyn Dodgers farm system under Larry MacPhail. In *The American Diamond*, Rickey would call his consent for Branch Jr. to work for the tempestuous MacPhail "the most grievous decision I ever faced," but he obviously preferred the temperamental, alcohol-abusing MacPhail to the capricious Breadon as his son's employer.[36]

It has often been said that from Sam Breadon's point of view, his estrangement from Branch Rickey began with his "embarrassment" at Landis's Cedar Rapids decision. In fact, it is likely that the rift started much earlier. Rickey and Breadon were always an odd couple—respected business associates but never close friends. From Breadon's viewpoint, probably the first incident in the inevitable break occurred at the end of the 1934 season when Rickey was involved in oilman Lew Wentz's aborted attempt to buy the team. Breadon claimed to Roy Stockton, his chief confidant among the St. Louis sportswriters, that Rickey would have earned a $100,000 commission if the sale to Wentz had materialized.[37]

When the Cardinals started to lose out on pennants regularly after 1934, Breadon began to wonder whether Rickey was worth his expensive contract, especially after 1936, when the owner, recently retired from the automobile business, got more involved with the daily operation of the team. Probably a final hardening of Breadon's anti-Rickey stance occurred in the aftermath of his horseback riding accident in the summer of 1939. In many ways Breadon never fully recovered physically or psychologically from his mishap. Always a man of few words and one stubbornly set in his ways, these traits hardened in the last years of Rickey's contract. Soon, it was obvious to friends of both men that Rickey's long tenure with the Cardinals was coming to an end. More than once Rickey would say to friends, "I would rather dig ditches for a few cents an hour than to work for Sam any longer than my contract requires."[38]

Early in December 1939 Rickey took a break from his work and his worries to go bear hunting with friends outside Asheville, North Carolina. His trip was curtailed, however, when he received word that back home in Lucasville, Ohio, his father, Jacob Frank Rickey, had died at age eighty-three following a heart attack.[39] Rickey rushed back to Scioto County, where he and his two brothers laid their father to rest next to Emily Brown Rickey in the hillside cemetery.

Returning home to be with his family in St. Louis at Christmas, Branch Rickey was concerned about the state of affairs in the baseball office. Yet, as the new year of 1940 approached, there were three more years left on Rickey's contract, and there was no way that he wasn't going to fulfill its terms and devote himself to the restoration of the Cardinals to the top of the National League. It was also a time of international uncertainty, with a new European war having erupted in September 1939 following Germany's invasion of Poland and England's decision to aid the Polish by declaring war on Germany. In the United States, a fierce nationwide debate raged over whether to get involved in the hostilities. Defying precedent, President Franklin Roosevelt was running for a third term in 1940. Clergyman Norman Vincent Peale, Rickey's good friend and a fellow Ohio Wesleyan graduate, was getting active in anti–third term activities.[40] More than ever, there was "trouble ahead, trouble ahead" in every realm of Branch Rickey's life. Yet, with his faith in God, family, and baseball undimmed, and believing that every crisis brought opportunity, Branch Rickey was ready to face the new decade prepared for anything.

14

Going Out on Top

Although Branch Rickey sensed that his time with the Cardinals was drawing to a close, he betrayed little sense of his dissatisfaction in public and he remained great copy for sports and feature writers. On March 31, 1940, a national Associated Press story entitled "Lawyer, Churchman, Politician—That Is Rickey, Boss of Cardinals" appeared in Sunday newspapers all over the country. The wire service reporter could not help being impressed by the many sides of Rickey, who, in addition to his religious activities, mentioned his collection of books by and about Abraham Lincoln, a founding father of the Republican Party. "The study of Lincoln is the study of government," Rickey declared and summed up the saga of his life thus far when he observed, "I was fortunate in my contacts and making friends."[1] Although the journalist didn't mention that Rickey also engaged in the serious hobby of breeding chickens, the article was accompanied by a photo of Rickey, clad in bowler hat and bow tie, holding a rooster. Rickey got ribbed by his friends for looking like comedian Ed Wynn in the snapshot, but a casual reader had to be drawn to the depth of emotion expressed in the face of Rickey as he gently cradled the bird (although it was probably not the prize-winning cock that once won $3,000 in a competition).[2]

When the 1940 baseball season began, any hopes that the Cardinals would improve on their ninety-two-win 1939 season quickly dissipated. The team staggered out of the gate and fell quickly into the second division. On Tuesday night, June 4, the team hosted the Brooklyn Dodgers in the Cardinals' first night game at Sportsman's Park. More than twenty thousand fans watched in dismay as the Dodgers scored five runs in the first inning and went on to an easy 10–1 victory. It was a night filled with misfortune for the home team. Pepper Martin was ejected from a game for the first time in his career for arguing ball and strike calls with umpire George Barr, Dizzy Dean's longtime antagonist. The fans' booing of the home team throughout the one-sided contest convinced Sam Breadon that it was time to change managers.[3]

Ray Blades was fired, and Billy Southworth was summoned from Rochester to replace him. Although Rickey was resigned to Breadon's making managerial decisions unilaterally, he had in previous seasons at least an inkling of the owner's impatience with an incumbent skipper. The ousting of Blades and the summoning of Southworth caught him totally by surprise, adding further to the growing rift between the two executives. Blades was a longtime Rickey man, and his mentor undoubtedly likened the owner's latest peremptory firing to his own dismissal in 1925. Their records were almost identical, with Rickey at 13-25 and Blades just a game better at 14-24. Mike Gonzalez managed the Cardinals for six games, five of them losses, before Breadon and Southworth agreed on contract terms.

A few days after the arrival of the new manager, the Cardinals made more stunning news when Joe Medwick and pitcher Curt Davis were traded to the Dodgers for $125,000 and four journeymen players: outfielder Ernie Koy, utility player Bert Haas, and pitchers Carl Doyle and Sam Nahem. Medwick, still only age twenty-nine, was one of the team's last links to its gloried Gashouse Gang past. However, since his Triple Crown year of 1937, Medwick's productivity had been gradually declining.

Medwick was still a .300 hitter capable of driving in and scoring one hundred runs a year, but Rickey sensed that he was no longer a dominant figure at the plate. He also had always been a difficult player to fit into a team framework. Medwick liked to say he played baseball for "base hits and buckerinos," and his interest in the defensive side of the game was sporadic. Medwick was thus a prime candidate for a Branch Rickey trade of a player a year too soon rather than a year too late.

The slugger welcomed the change in scenery because he grew up near New York in Carteret, New Jersey, where he had been a great high school football and baseball player. Knute Rockne had tried to recruit him to

Notre Dame, but Rickey's persuasiveness won him over to baseball. When Rockne was killed in a plane crash in 1931, Medwick was convinced he had made the right choice of sports.[4]

Medwick had started his professional career for a class D team in Scott-dale, Pennsylvania, playing for manager Eddie Dyer, a former Cardinals pitcher from Rice University. He rose quickly through the farm system and, in Houston, became a big star with the nickname of "Ducky" Med-wick because a little girl thought he walked like a duck. Branch Rickey loved the name and urged Houston president Fred Ankenman to use it as a promotional tool; thus a candy company was contacted to make "Ducky" bars. Medwick, however, hated the name, much preferring "Muscles" as a sobriquet, or "Mickey" (he had played football under the assumed name of Mickey King). He also didn't like Houston manage-ment capitalizing on the loathed nickname and tried to get a cut of the proceeds from sales of the candy bar.[5]

In leaving St. Louis Medwick was not going to miss money dealings with Branch Rickey. The slugger often used an agent to drum up his value to the team, not a wise way of getting on the good side of the wily executive. The outfielder told the story of how he once tried to negotiate a raise with the Cardinals mastermind as Rickey was shaving without any soap. "I thought I'd seen more blood than Count Dracula," Medwick said.[6]

Leo Durocher, who had become Brooklyn manager in 1939, was ea-ger to reunite with the slugger, his onetime St. Louis roommate. He en-couraged Dodgers general manager Larry MacPhail to make the trade. MacPhail had taken over the struggling Brooklyn franchise in 1938, and just as he had done in Columbus and Cincinnati, the master pro-moter had brought banner crowds and competitive baseball to the most populous and underappreciated borough of New York City. By 1940 the Dodgers were a pennant contender, and MacPhail was convinced that Medwick was the missing piece to add to the Dodgers lineup. Some avid Brooklyn fans even called his acquisition the biggest deal since Babe Ruth was purchased from the Red Sox.[7]

However, just days after Medwick's arrival in Brooklyn, he was hit in the head and knocked unconscious by an errant fastball from Cardinals pitcher Bob Bowman. The incident drove Larry MacPhail berserk be-cause he remembered overhearing Bowman telling Medwick in the team hotel that morning, "You're going to get yours today, Joe." The Dodgers executive thought the beaning was intentional, and according to *Brooklyn Eagle* sportswriter Tommy Holmes, he "raced across the field, screaming, 'Coward!' and trying to hit Bowman with a folded newspaper." The irate executive tried to get ballpark police to arrest the pitcher for premeditated malice and sought an investigation by local authorities, but cooler heads prevailed. National League president Ford Frick checked into the incident and concluded that the beaning was an accident. Medwick had probably been tipped off by a Brooklyn runner at second base that a curveball was coming and had no time to react to the inside fastball. (While in the hospital, Medwick received a call from an outraged Dodgers fan that volunteered to get revenge for the slugger by cutting off Bowman's arm. "That was Brooklyn," Medwick recalled years later to author Robert Hood. "They were rough then.")[8]

Medwick missed only a few games; when he returned he did hit .300 for the Dodgers in 1940, with 14 HR and 66 RBI, but the quick bat of his glory days in St. Louis was gone forever. However, the players Rickey had obtained for the Cardinals did not contribute much in their new surroundings. Medwick's replacement in St. Louis, Ernie Koy, a former University of Texas football star, hit .312 with only 8 HR and 52 RBI. Bert Haas never played for St. Louis, and the pitchers Carl Doyle and Sam Nahem made minor contributions before fading from Major League Baseball. (Rickey had been intrigued by Sam Nahem's potential and his background as a Syrian Jew from Brooklyn, who was planning to study law.[9] Nahem, however, never mastered the art of changing speeds on his pitches, and the lack of decent pay in baseball ultimately led him to a career in union organizing in Northern California; in the 1990s, he produced a film about the Jewish Holocaust.)[10]

The Cardinals still had some moments of glory in the 1940 season. After Billy Southworth took the reins from Ray Blades, he directed the team to a 69-40 record and a third-place finish. John Mize led the league with 43 HR and 137 RBI, as did Terry Moore in center-field put-outs. Lon Warneke and Bill McGee both won sixteen games, and Clyde Shoun, the one holdover from the Dizzy Dean trade, won thirteen and, for the second straight year, appeared in the most games in the National League (fifty-four).

During the 1940 season Marty Marion emerged as the cornerstone of the infield. In the slender six foot two, 170-pound Marion, nicknamed "Slats" and "Mr. Shortstop," the Cardinals had found an enduring replacement for Leo Durocher at one of the most vital positions on the diamond. Born in South Carolina and raised in Atlanta, Georgia, Marion had been scouted by Frank Rickey and signed after high school by Branch Rickey. The youngster managed to obtain a most unusual stipulation from the executive, a four-year contract for both himself and Johnny Echols, his best friend and high school teammate. Marion's father was a devout Baptist who had no use for baseball as a profession, and Rickey undoubtedly saw it as a challenge to convince the elder Marion to allow his son to play ball.[11]

As their baseball lives evolved, Marion rose steadily in the St. Louis chain while Echols, originally considered a better prospect, did not meet expectations. In fact, by Echols's third year, the front office wanted to release him, but he reminded his bosses that the contract gave him four years of protection. "Mr. Rickey was the lord and master in those days," Marion recalls. "He had to keep Echols for four years, and he didn't like it. He threatened to send him to every Cardinals farm club in the country, and he did send him to most. But he played for four years, as he was promised."[12]

Marion's emergence gave the Cardinals a better hitter than Durocher (his career BA was .263 and SA .345, to Durocher's .247 and .320), and he was as great a fielder. His arrival also symbolized the growing ascendancy of Sam Breadon in the Cardinals organization because the owner considered Marion "his favorite player," the shortstop recalls. However, Breadon was an equally hard bargainer on money issues. "We agreed to a bonus for hits one year, but rain washed out some of the games near the end of the season," Marion says. "On the last day, the sun came out, and I was able to play and get the hits. But Mr. Breadon told me that if the rain had come, there would have been no bonus. 'A deal's a deal, he said.'"[13]

In spite of some bright young lights appearing in the Cardinals' firmament, 1940 turned out to be another year for the Cincinnati Reds. There was no real National League pennant race as Cincinnati won one hundred games and their second straight league title, finishing twelve games ahead of the Dodgers and sixteen ahead of the Cardinals. Bucky Walters and Paul Derringer were again twenty-game winners on a staff that had, by far, the best team ERA in the league. Cincinnati also led the league in fielding, a testament to manager Bill McKechnie's belief in the primacy of defense in winning baseball.

The Detroit Tigers broke the Yankees' streak of four straight pennants by nosing out the Yankees by one game and the Cleveland Indians by two. In the World Series Branch Rickey was pleased that the Reds restored National League honor as the one-two pitching punch of Paul Derringer and Bucky Walters won all four games. Former Cardinals farm hand out-fielder Ival Goodman and former St. Louis catcher Jimmy Wilson were other key contributors to the Reds' seven-game Series victory. Derringer won the seventh game, 2–1, besting veteran Louis "Bobo" Newsom in a taut pitcher's duel. Although he did not like Paul Derringer's lifestyle, Branch Rickey again tipped his cap to the veteran's savviness.

After the end of the 1940 season baseball work took a momentary back seat for Branch Rickey as he devoted a large part of his boundless energy to working for the election of his friend Forrest C. Donnell, the Republican candidate for governor of Missouri. It was an office that some of Rickey's Missouri Republican friends, sensing that his rift with Sam Breadon was irreconcilable, had suggested that the baseball executive might be interested in seeking himself. They had also wondered if Rickey might consider a campaign against Harry S. Truman for the United States Senate. (Like Truman, Forrest Donnell's middle initial stood for nothing.)[14] The sportsman was flattered by the suggestions and considered himself a staunch party loyalist, vehemently opposed to Franklin Roosevelt's New Deal intrusions into the private enterprise system. However, because he was nearing age sixty and in the small minority of Missouri Republicans who supported Roosevelt's interventionist foreign policy against international aggressors, it is not likely that Rickey would have thrown his hat in the ring. He was always available, however, to help a friend seeking political office.

After the Cardinals' first World Series championship in 1926, Rickey had campaigned for George Howard Williams, his good friend and attorney, in the lawyer's effort to win a full term for a U.S. Senate seat. After the sudden death of Selden Spencer in May 1925, Williams had been appointed by Governor Samuel Baker to finish the remaining term, but Democrat Harry Hawes beat Williams in the November 1926 election. Hawes had made his name opposing the Ku Klux Klan at the Democratic 1924 national convention and was an ardent anti-Prohibition candidate, whereas Williams's positions on legalized liquor and other issues seemed too unclear to many voters.[15]

Forrest C. Donnell was another good friend, and Rickey leaped at the opportunity of helping him. Donnell and Rickey were both teetotalers, active members of the St. Louis Grace Methodist Episcopal Church, and very involved in community service activities. Donnell served on the board of managers of the Missouri State School for the Blind and was president of the St. Louis City Evangelical Union. What gave special flavor to the 1940 Missouri governor's race was that Donnell's opponent, Democrat Lawrence McDaniel, was also a member of the same Methodist church, and the older Donnell benignly looked upon McDaniel as a protégé, a star Sunday School pupil in his Bible classes. When the church embarked on fund-raising drives, *Time* magazine reported, McDaniel and Donnell would oblige "by holding humorous mock trials in which the legal chums and such pupils as square-jibbed, religious Branch Rickey . . . debated such subjects as 'To bob or not to bob' (when bobbed hair was a grave matter); Resolved. the hen is flightier than the Ford etc."[16]

The good feeling between the fellow parishioners would not survive the 1940 campaign. The Republicans made an issue of McDaniel's Democratic Party connections to imprisoned Kansas City boss Thomas Pendergast, who had been jailed for vote fraud and accepting bribes from insurance companies. The Donnell campaign charged that bossism was alive in St. Louis too. They criticized McDaniel's performance as city excise commissioner, a patronage position in which, the Republicans claimed, he had been delinquent in his supervision of liquor regulations.[17]

Although Donnell had never run for elective office before, the St. Louis lawyer had made a good name for himself by spearheading a movement within the state bar association to make lawyers more professional and community minded. One of his campaign pledges was to support the creation of special state prosecutors if local law enforcement officers were lax in performing their duties.[18]

For Branch Rickey the issues and the choice of candidates could not be more clear-cut: an honest, upright lawyer and good citizen versus a machine politician tied to corrupt liquor interests. Even though he was born in farm country, Donnell had been an urban lawyer for most of his adult life and he needed help in the rural areas, where he was an unknown quantity. Rickey was in his element talking to farmers, hunters, and storekeepers. With characteristic passion, the baseball executive crisscrossed rural Missouri, knocking on doors, attending town and American Legion meetings, tirelessly talking up the candidacy of his friend.

Pundits predicted that 180,000 "inarticulate voters" would decide the governor's race, and when the results came in late on election night, Forrest Donnell had bucked the Democratic tide in Missouri, which reelected Senator Truman and President Roosevelt, and pulled out an upset victory over Lawrence McDaniel.[19] In an election where most statewide Democrats won by 90,000 vote majorities, there was little doubt that Donnell's margin of victory of more than 3,500 votes came from the rural precincts Branch Rickey had won over.[20]

However, the Missouri Democrats refused to concede defeat. They demanded a recount but dawdled in establishing the machinery because they controlled the state legislature. When the standoff continued into December, the Democrats decided not to seat a new governor, an act that infuriated the outgoing state chief executive, Lloyd Crow Stark. Although Stark, a wealthy apple grower, was a Democrat, he had a maverick streak. The Pendergast machine had helped to elect him, but once in office Stark set in motion the machinery to indict the Kansas City boss. He had harbored aspirations for Senator Truman's seat in the 1940 primary, but when he lost Stark gave up any feeling of party loyalty.[21] He refused to give up the governor's office until the recount of the 1940 election was completed. Inauguration Day was scheduled for January 13, 1941, but the results were still not certified. *Life* magazine awarded "an All-American prize for political buffoonery" to the state of Missouri.[22]

As the recount dragged on through the end of January, Branch Rickey flew to Boston to appear as a main speaker at the city's annual baseball writers' dinner. Before a packed audience of eight hundred, Rickey tied together his love of baseball and his concern for the state of the world as only he could. "We must hold on grimly to the things in life which are normal," he declared. "We do not want to yield to the futility which France showed."[23] When France had fallen in three weeks in June 1940 to the invading Nazi armies, Rickey had been especially anguished because his son-in-law, John Eckler, was scheduled to start in the fall of 1940 a postdoctoral law fellowship at the University of Paris.[24]

"We do not want anything to do with dictators," Rickey declared to his Boston audience. "I hate dictators, in government, in politics, yes, in baseball, too." The combative St. Louis executive was making reference to another recent edict by Kenesaw Mountain Landis in which the commissioner decreed that every rookie a team had purchased before August 15 of the previous year could not be optioned to the Minor Leagues until he had a tryout in spring training lasting through at least March 23. Rickey countered by asking why Landis should limit his ruling. Why not disallow any Minor League assignment, he suggested sarcastically, if someone in the Major Leagues wanted the player?[25]

Rickey's dander was bound to rise whenever the rulings of Commissioner Landis were involved. He said often that Landis would be of more service to baseball if he better publicized the merits of the sport among high schools and colleges, many of which were abandoning baseball programs.

Rickey was satisfied, though, that he had won his ongoing argument with the commissioner that there was a need for Minor League teams to be affiliated with big league teams because Major League owners were more likely to provide sufficient capital than were local investors.[26] Indeed, at the recent December 1940 winter meetings, Commissioner Landis had cried uncle in his war on farm systems. He gave up his principled objection to the control of Major League organizations over farm team players as long as all the players were duly registered with the commissioner's office and the National Association.[27]

Branch Rickey, however, had not come to Boston primarily to rail at the commissioner. The majority of the ferocious gentleman's late January 1941 remarks were elegiac, devoted to wistful thoughts of baseball's past. He nearly broke into tears at the sight in the audience of aged Red Sox scout Hugh Duffy, who as a Boston player in 1894 had hit .438. Rickey evoked the memory of the doomed Cardinals outfielder Austin McHenry, who, during his fatal illness in 1922, drew boos from the grandstand crowd because of his failing play. "But when he got back near the Knothole Gang, they cheered him as they always had," Rickey said. "Men abandon their friends in the give and take of ordinary industry, but boys are always loyal to their heroes." Tying together all his themes of sport and sportsmanship in a troubled world at war, Rickey concluded that he "would rather have his children admire [Red Sox shortstop] Joe Cronin than the career of Napoleon Bonaparte."[28]

When the executive returned to St. Louis, he was happy to learn that the recount in the governor's race was finally completed and that Forrest Donnell's margin of victory had actually increased to more than five thousand votes. On February 15, 1941, Donnell was inaugurated as Missouri's governor in the state capital of Jefferson City. In a ceremony filled with pomp and circumstance, Donnell was joined by an ornately dressed honor guard, including his military adviser, honorary colonel Wesley Branch Rickey.[29] (In 1944 Donnell would be elected to the U.S. Senate, winning the seat of Harry Truman, who had been elected vice president of the United States.)

Before heading for spring training in late February 1941, Branch Rickey attended a meeting of the Cardinals' board of directors at which Sam Breadon made official the permanent rift between the two executives. He told the board of his intention not to renew Rickey's contract when it expired at the end of the 1942 season. With war clouds in the air and other economic uncertainties, Breadon said that he did not believe that an expenditure of more than $250,000—Rickey's $50,000-a-year salary for five years (plus his bonus in profitable years on player sales)—made good business sense. He wanted to give the board and Rickey early notice because in the past he had always told his longtime associate at least a year in advance his intentions about the long-term contract.[30]

This was not news to Rickey, of course, but it didn't become news in St. Louis until late June 1941 when the *Post-Dispatch* headlined, "Rickey to Leave Cards? Way Paved for Move after 1942." Neither the team president nor vice president wanted to discuss the meeting. When Roy Stockton asked Rickey if he had asked the board in February to table Breadon's proposal, Stockton quoted the executive, "I never made a request of a board meeting in my life—to the best of my knowledge."[31]

With the certainty that his Cardinals career would be over after the 1942 season, Rickey pondered other career choices. Insurance executive Carroll Otto, his neighbor in St. Louis County, arranged an interview for Rickey with a top official of the Mutual Benefit Life Insurance Company in Newark, New Jersey. A deep believer in the value and virtue of life insurance, Rickey made a trip east to meet with the executive only to learn that the man had canceled the meeting because he had second thoughts about bringing into his organization as formidable a presence as Rickey.[32]

Putting thoughts about alternative plans for the future into the back of his mind, Branch Rickey turned his focus on the 1941 season. He felt confident that the Cardinals were ready to soar again. After Cincinnati's easy waltz to the 1940 pennant, the 1941 baseball season brought back to the National League its tradition of fiercely contested pennant races. It featured one of the tightest two-team races in baseball history. The Brooklyn Dodgers and St. Louis Cardinals were so tightly bunched from June onward that Tommy Holmes of the *Brooklyn Eagle* called the race "quite possibly the longest stretch drive in major league history."[33] The hand of Branch Rickey was intimately involved in the construction of both teams. Virtually all of the Cardinals, led by John Mize and Marty Marion in the infield and by Terry Moore and Enos Slaughter in the outfield, and the two leading pitchers with seventeen wins each, Lon Warneke and left-hander Ernie White, had been signed by Rickey scouts, Rickey's brother Frank foremost among them.

Branch Rickey's influence was almost as great on the Brooklyn side. He had given Dodgers general manager Larry MacPhail his first baseball job in 1931 in Columbus, Ohio. He had brought Brooklyn manager Leo Durocher to St. Louis in the 1933 trade with Cincinnati. Among the key former Cardinals on the 1941 Dodgers were Joe Medwick in left field, who hit .318 with 18 HR and 88 RBI in 1941, and pitcher Curt Davis, the key player in the Dizzy Dean deal, who won thirteen games in 1941.

Most important of all the Brooklyn ex-Cardinals was Harold Patrick "Pete" Reiser, who became the first player in baseball history to win a batting title in his first full year. Elected National League Rookie of the Year in 1941, Reiser hit .343, and his .558 SA, 39 2B, 17 3B, and 117 R all led the league. He also contributed 17 HR and 76 RBI. Signed as a teenager off the St. Louis sandlots by Charley Barrett, Reiser, one of twelve children, was a switch hitter who possessed the serene confidence of an exceptional athlete that no pitcher or situation could ever scare him.[34]

After Commissioner Landis's Cedar Rapids ruling had made the budding star a free agent, Rickey tried to "loan" Reiser to MacPhail and the Dodgers, but once Leo Durocher saw in spring training how good a player Reiser was, there was no way that the Cardinals were going to get him back. He was born "with the gift of speed and the urge to run," Rickey once said with admirable brevity about Reiser's spectacular talent. Baseball observers who saw Mickey Mantle emerge in the 1950s said that Reiser might have become a better all-around player if he hadn't played with such abandon that he often injured himself running into unpadded walls. A ten-year career BA of .295 and SA of .450 do not begin to tell the story of what might have been.[35]

The 1941 Brooklyn–St. Louis pennant race went deep into September. Serious injuries to starting outfielders Terry Moore and Enos Slaughter severely hurt the Cardinals' chances, but they were a plucky bunch that would not fade away. In August, to bolster the pitching staff, Branch Rickey dipped into the farm system to bring up a twenty-year-old left-hander from the Houston farm club, Howard Pollet. In September, after Rochester's season ended, Rickey also recalled a former left-handed pitcher he had converted to the outfield, Stan Musial.

Every great pennant race needs a climactic September confrontation between contenders, and in 1941 one materialized in a three-game series at Sportsman's Park. After the teams split the first two games, the final meeting of the season between the bitter rivals matched two right-handers, the Cardinals youngster Morton Cooper versus the Dodgers veteran Whitlow Wyatt, whom Larry MacPhail had rescued from the Minor Leagues. It was a classic pitcher's duel, a scoreless tie for seven innings. In the top of the eighth inning two Dodgers veterans, outfielder Fred "Dixie" Walker and second baseman Billy Herman, hit back-to-back doubles and produced the only run of the game. The Dodgers went on to win the 1941 pennant with one hundred victories, edging the Cardinals by three games.

That the Cardinals stayed so close to Brooklyn was in some ways a minor miracle because the Dodgers led the league in every offensive category as well as team ERA, and they also had two twenty-two-game winners in Kirby Higbe and Whitlow Wyatt. The Cardinals did have depth in their staff, however. In addition to seventeen-game winners Lon Warneke and Ernie White, St. Louis had six pitchers with ten victories or more, including ten from rookie left-hander Max Lanier.

After the Dodgers clinched the pennant by beating the Braves in Boston, a jubilant Larry MacPhail journeyed to the 125th Street station of the New York Central Railroad to join the triumphant Dodgers on their victory ride to Grand Central Station. In a gesture of sportsmanship, Branch Rickey joined his exultant rival in saluting the conquering heroes. However, Leo Durocher had gotten word that a horde of fans would be waiting at 125th Street. To avoid a mob scene he ordered the conductor to bypass the station. MacPhail and Rickey were lucky to keep their hats from blowing away as the train whizzed by. Rickey chuckled at MacPhail's discomfiture, not yet realizing what a soap opera "life with Leo" would present him in barely more than a year. The fuming MacPhail was ready to fire Durocher for insubordination when he reached his manager later that night, but the two men quickly made up in order to appear together at the tumultuous pennant parade in Brooklyn, which an estimated 1 million people attended.[36]

The World Series of 1941 matched the Dodgers and the Yankees for the first of what would be seven times in the next fifteen years. Although the Cardinals were a nonparticipant for the seventh straight season, a string of failure that gnawed at Rickey (as well as Sam Breadon), Rickey had to admit that it was a most dramatic Series, one that set the stage for the excruciating contests that lay ahead for Brooklyn players and fans.

Game four at Ebbets Field would be remembered for one of the most dramatic and painful endings in World Series history. With the Yankees leading the Series two games to one, the Dodgers were leading 4–3 and were one strike from evening the competition. With two out and no one on base, Yankees outfielder Tommy Henrich swung and missed at a 1-2 pitch from Brooklyn reliever Hugh Casey, but the ball got away from catcher Mickey Owen and Henrich was safe at first base. Taking full advantage of the break, the Yankees scored four runs, and won, 7–4. "The condemned jumped out of the chair and electrocuted the warden," remembered Tommy Holmes.[37]

Branch Rickey felt anguish for Arnold Owen, as he always called the Missouri farm boy he had signed for the Cardinals in the mid-1930s. It moved the executive deeply to learn that five thousand Brooklyn fans gathered outside the clubhouse after the game, waiting for the catcher to tell him that he was still one of their own and not to get down on himself. (Later, Owen received letters of support from the four corners of the country.)[38] However, the next day, the Dodgers lost, 3–1, in a game not as close as the score indicated. The Yankees had won another World Series, their fifth in the last six years.

All plans for the 1942 season took a back seat when on December 7, 1941, the Japanese bombed the American fleet at the Pearl Harbor naval base on Hawaii. Patriotic to a fault, Rickey even considered volunteering himself for the military once again. Turning sixty on December 20, 1941, however, he realized, reluctantly, that active duty was out of the question, but he would be in the forefront of the Missouri war bond drive with Governor Forrest Donnell.

Commissioner Landis conferred with President Roosevelt about what would be the most prudent and patriotic way for baseball to proceed. Landis was as politically opposed to Roosevelt's philosophy and long presidency as Branch Rickey was, but he was putting himself at the service of the leader of the nation. When Roosevelt gave the "green light" for baseball to proceed with the season, Branch Rickey continued to make plans for his final year at the helm of the Cardinals.

He saw no reason why 1942 should not be the year the Cardinals returned to the top of the National League. Their 97 wins in 1941 had been the greatest number of St. Louis victories since the world championship team of 1931 won 101 games, and attendance rose by more than 300,000 fans. After drawing 324,078 in 1940, the 1941 Redbirds had drawn 633,645, one of the few teams in the National League to show an increase.[39] With an influx of maturing talent from the farm system, Rickey felt that the Cardinals were not far away from reaching the top again.

Since he never felt that home run power was a necessary attribute for a winning team, in late 1941 Rickey traded slugging first baseman John Mize to the Giants for journeymen pitchers Bill Lohrman and Johnny McCarthy, backup catcher Ken O'Dea, and $50,000 in cash. Not yet twenty-nine, Mize was seemingly still in his prime and was only two years removed from leading the league in batting and slugging. However, Rickey had begun to notice some slippage in Mize's performance, and he wasn't enamored with the first baseman's constant griping about his contract. After his rookie season in 1936, no doubt influenced by Dizzy Dean's and Joe Medwick's regular salary complaints, Mize tried to get an agent to negotiate his contract. There was thus no love lost between Rickey and the first baseman who was one of the Cardinals, like Enos Slaughter, who erroneously believed that the executive didn't want to win pennants but wanted only to finish close enough to the top to draw fans and turn a profit.

Another factor in Mize's trade might also have been manager Billy Southworth's desire to increase the team's speed. Southworth loved a running team, and Mize was notoriously slow on the bases. Mize's replacements, Ray Sanders and Johnny Hopp, were not long ball threats, but they could run and would contribute to a 1942 Cardinals team that would be memorably nicknamed the "St. Louis Swifties."

The 1942 pennant race again came down to a head-to-head battle between the Cardinals and the Dodgers. Leo Durocher understood full well that for a champion to be truly considered a champion, it had to repeat; a truly great team could not be a one-season wonder. The Dodgers responded to the challenge and by early August had built a seemingly commanding ten-and-a-half-game lead. Yet a healthy St. Louis team had only begun to fight. The dog days of summer slowly caught up with the aging Dodgers, who were severely hurt in early July when Pete Reiser ran into a wall chasing a fly ball in St. Louis. The Cardinals went on to engineer one of the greatest stretch runs in baseball history, winning forty-three out of their last fifty-two games.[40]

As always Rickey relied on his experience and cunning to bolster the team. He outfoxed Toronto's general manager Lee MacPhail (Larry MacPhail's son) in a Minor League trade. Like many young people in baseball, Lee MacPhail had started his baseball career with the help of the paternal Branch Rickey, who also had influenced young MacPhail's choice of Swarthmore College, where he became friendly with Rickey's daughter Alice. When it came to matters of the baseball business, however, Rickey would take advantage of any rival.

During the 1942 season MacPhail was serving as general manager of the Toronto Blue Jays, an International League team without any Major League affiliation. In August Rickey phoned young MacPhail and offered him a Minor League first baseman at Rochester, Jimmy Ripple, who he said could help the Blue Jays make the playoffs. "We'll have to make some kind of deal," Rickey cooed to the unsuspecting MacPhail, suggesting that St. Louis receive a hurler in exchange. "I don't know your staff," Rickey noted innocently. "What pitchers do you have?" When MacPhail mentioned the name Bill Beckmann, Rickey said he would be acceptable. Late in the 1942 season, as MacPhail was attending a game in Brooklyn, he noticed a familiar-looking pitcher warming up in the bullpen. "I checked the scorecard," MacPhail recalls. "Bill Beckmann, and I knew I had been had."[41] Beckmann would win one game for the Cardinals in relief in a year when they would win the pennant by two games.

The climax of the stirring pennant race arrived in mid-September 1942 when the St. Louis Swifties came into Brooklyn's Ebbets Field with the Dodgers' once-huge lead cut to one game. Whitlow Wyatt and Morton Cooper matched up again, but Cooper reversed the tables of 1941, winning, 2–0, as third baseman Whitey Kurowski, one of the Cardinals' most inspirational players, hit the game-winning home run. A native of the coal mining area near Reading, Pennsylvania, Kurowski had a deformed right arm, the result of a childhood battle with polio, but thanks to an operation by Cardinals team physician Dr. Robert Hyland, Kurowski was able to perform brilliantly in the Major Leagues.[42] When the Cardinals won the second game of the series at Ebbets Field, they moved into first place, where they remained for the rest of the season. They would win 106 games to the Dodgers' 104.

Statistically, the Cardinals almost totally turned the tables on the Dodgers in one season, leading the league in every offensive category except home runs (the Giants led in that category, with John Mize the individual league leader with thirty). St. Louis pitchers also compiled the most strikeouts and posted the lowest team ERA. Mort Cooper was the winningest pitcher in the league, with a 22-7 mark, and he also led in ERA with 1.78, earning him the league Most Valuable Player Award. Rookie John Beazley was 21-6, and Max Lanier finished 13-8. In addition to the winner Mort Cooper, the Cardinal Enos Slaughter finished second, and Marty Marion seventh in the MVP balloting.[43]

The Dodgers produced no twenty-game winners but did have six pitchers with at least 10 wins, led by Whitlow Wyatt's 19-7 and Kirby Higbe's 16-11 records. However, the overall age of the team caught up with them down the stretch. Irascible team president Larry MacPhail had foreseen trouble brewing even when the Dodgers were riding high with their big midsummer lead. Knowing that the Cardinals would never quit, MacPhail warned the Dodgers that they would lose if they got complacent. Veteran Brooklyn outfielder Dixie Walker scoffed at the warning and reportedly bet MacPhail $200 that they would still win the pennant by eight games.[44]

Walker lost the bet, and soon after the 1942 season MacPhail lost the team. Dodgers stockholders were growing disgruntled because they had received no significant dividend since MacPhail took over in 1938. He may have turned the Dodgers into a contender, but the brilliant executive followed to excess the business dictum that to make money you must spend money. The last straw for management was probably when MacPhail spent $50,000 to purchase aging right-hander Bobo Newsom from the Washington Senators in a futile attempt to stem the Dodgers' slide.[45] Rather than wait for a possible firing, MacPhail resigned to enter the quartermaster's division of the United States Army in Europe as a lieutenant colonel.

Branch Rickey's last World Series as the organizing genius of the St. Louis Cardinals proved a stirring swan song. It was a rematch of the 1926 battle between the smallest metropolitan area and the biggest city in the nation, St. Louis versus New York. The haughty Yankees had won their sixth pennant in the last seven years, beating the Boston Red Sox by nine games.

Game one was played at Sportsman's Park in front of 34,769 fans. The Cardinals committed four errors, and Red Ruffing held them hitless for seven innings. St. Louis was trailing, 7–0, in the bottom in the ninth, but they rallied for four runs, knocking Ruffing out of the box. Despite a 7–4 loss the Cardinals showed that they could play with the awesome New Yorkers and would not be intimidated.

A Game two crowd of 34,255 was thrilled when the Cardinals evened the Series at one game apiece as rookie John Beazley beat Ernie Bonham, 4–3. Stan Musial and Whitey Kurowski, two more young graduates of the farm system, got the big hits in the St. Louis win.

When the Series shifted to Yankee Stadium, the Cardinals silenced crowds of more than sixty-nine thousand each day. They won Game three behind rookie southpaw Ernie White, who shut out Spurgeon "Spud" Chandler and the Yankees, 2–0. It was the first blanking of the Yankees in World Series play since St. Louis's Jess Haines had turned the trick in 1926. The Cardinals won a game four slugfest, 9–6, as catcher Walker Cooper and shortstop Marty Marion drove in the deciding runs in the late innings.

The St. Louis Swifties completed their remarkable rise to the top on October 5, 1942, when John Beazley outdueled Red Ruffing, 4–2, in game five. Whitey Kurowski broke up a 2–2 tie in the top of the ninth inning with a two-run home run. In the bottom of the ninth inning Yankees second baseman Joe Gordon was on second base with one out, with the tying run at the plate. Shortstop Marty Marion slipped behind the unobservant Yankees runner, Walker Cooper fired a throw down to second, and Gordon was picked off. One out later the St. Louis Cardinals had repeated their 1926 World Series victory over the Yankees, and this time it took only five games. After the Series the Yankees fired their trainer, Earle "Doc" Painter, because they believed that his Cardinals counterpart, Harrison "Bucko" Weaver, had done a better job of preparing his players physically and mentally. Weaver seemed to be putting a hex on them with voodoo signals from the visitors' dugout.[46]

With the country at war and many of the players knowing that they would soon be heading into the military, the jubilation in St. Louis was more restrained than the eruption after the 1926 and 1934 victories. Similar feelings of restrained joy flowed through Branch Rickey. He was elated that the Cardinals, with a team of homegrown players, had bested the big-city boys. He took satisfaction in the opinion of many baseball insiders that an all-star team from his top farm clubs at Rochester, Columbus, and Sacramento might have been the third-best team in baseball in 1942.[47]

Of course, Rickey also felt sad that his nearly quarter century of baseball life in St. Louis was coming to an end. The rumor mill was working overtime about his plans for the future. Knowing that St. Louis was the preferred home for the executive, many pundits thought he might return to the St. Louis Browns. His protégé William DeWitt was now the Browns' general manager, and the team had risen from the depths of the second division to finish a strong third in 1942. Roy Stockton even wrote a story in the *Post-Dispatch* reporting that Rickey's coming to the Browns was a done deal.[48] However, team owner Donald Barnes, a local banker, simply did not have the financial means to pay Rickey the salary he felt he deserved. Another rumor surfaced that the Detroit Tigers might be interested in Rickey's services. General manager Jack Zeller had tried to build a farm system in the late 1930s, but all he got for his trouble was the wrath of Commissioner Landis, who stripped the Tigers of more players than he had taken away from the Cardinals.[49] It was suspected that Zeller might want to call on Rickey's expertise in building a winner, but this rumor, too, was unfounded. Branch Rickey was clearly a National Leaguer at heart.

The hottest rumor of the baseball postseason proved to be the accurate one. Only a few weeks after his last Cardinals team beat the Yankees in the World Series, Branch Rickey would be returning to the big city to replace Larry MacPhail as the president and general manager of the Brooklyn Dodgers. Rickey negotiated a contract similar to the one he enjoyed in St. Louis. He would receive a base salary of a reported $40,000, which would increase to $65,000 after the war ended. He again would earn a percentage of about 10 percent from the sale of every Brooklyn player in the Major and Minor Leagues.

The country boy from Ohio, who had felt at home in the bucolic countryside outside St. Louis, had his misgivings about moving to the big city. However, the determining factor in Branch Rickey's coming to Brooklyn was the chance to build another team alongside his son, Branch Rickey Jr., who had become increasingly frustrated and ignored in the last months of combustible Larry MacPhail's regime. Buffalo sporting goods executive Dick Fischer, a Minor League administrator who had become a good friend of both Rickeys, had written Rickey Sr. about how disappointed Junior had become with the MacPhail regime, even to the point of not even wanting to come to work.[50]

Branch Rickey had a lot of loose ends to tie up in St. Louis. He regretfully sent a letter of resignation to Governor Forrest Donnell, giving up his position on the state war bond drive. The close friends and community-minded Methodists had brought Missouri to the top of the list as the most productive bond sellers per capita in the nation; not long after he arrived at his new position in New York, Rickey would be deeply involved in the Brooklyn war bond committee.

"War overshadows everything," Rickey had said soon before he went to serve in the Army Chemical Corps during World War I. He believed the sentiment even more urgently in World War II. Three of his sons-in-law were in military service, and his daughter Alice was a flier in the Women's Air Service Project; her husband, Edward Jakle, was also a pilot. If Branch Rickey Jr. had not been diagnosed with diabetes at the end of the 1930s, he too would have been in the military service. The younger Rickey was nonetheless deeply involved in the war effort, leading blood drives and organizing greeting committees to welcome home service personnel from the battlefields.[51]

As Branch Rickey late in 1942 cleared out his office in Sportsman's Park for the last time, tears flowed from his secretary of fourteen years, Mary Murphy (whose older sister, Margaret, had been the Browns' office secretary since the first days of Phil Ball).[52] "Sure I'll miss him—won't you?" Murphy asked *Sporting News* correspondent Dick Farrington.[53]

The sportswriters of St. Louis had a more ambivalent relationship with Branch Rickey because they never could understand his many interests and passions or his inevitable circumlocutions of speech. In an aside to one of the writers not long before he left St. Louis, Rickey mentioned that he didn't think he had accomplished that much in his life, although he was pleased that he had finally learned to translate Cicero's speeches from Latin to English.

By the end of Rickey's reign in St. Louis, Roy Stockton of the *St. Louis Post-Dispatch* had become Rickey's severest critic and Sam Breadon's closest ally. In a piece for the *Saturday Evening Post* entitled "A Brain Comes to Brooklyn," Stockton appraised Rickey's tenure in St. Louis with a dry eye. He noted the outgoing executive's money consciousness and how he was always looking for commissions in deals. Stockton hinted at his vanity, noting that if Rickey did not like his picture in the newspaper, he would supply a studio portrait. As far as his ability as a baseball evaluator, however, Stockton had only praise. Nobody could be "as quick to see fine knee action in a runner, rhythm in a throwing arm, and timing at bat," he wrote. As for Rickey's prospects for succeeding with an aging team in the demanding borough of Brooklyn, Stockton concluded with the observation, "Those who know believe he'll find a way, and baseball will experience another revolutionary innovation of some kind."[54] Neither Stockton nor anyone else yet realized how prophetic these words would be.

PART III

The Birth of the Mahatma, 1943–1950

Rickey was one of the slyest men who ever lived,
but in all fundamentals, a man of honor.

—*John Chamberlain,*
Life with the Printed Word

15

A Branch Grows in Brooklyn

"If our aim is to make Brooklyn the baseball capital of America, by Judas Priest, we'll do it," Branch Rickey was expostulating early in February 1943 in Brooklyn before one of his favorite audiences, a Rotary Club. Arthur Daley, sports columnist for the *New York Times*, was in the audience, and he made the noble effort of trying to keep up with the rolling cadences of the Dodgers' new president. "The Yankees made New York the capital of the American League and they didn't do that by any chance or any luck," Rickey exclaimed, warming to a favorite theme of hard work overcoming all obstacles. "They did it by personnel, industry and program. They have been winning not because God has been smiling on them and on no one else. They toiled and they sweated to get something, and they got it."

Rickey professed that in his short time on the job in Brooklyn, he had come to understand and admire the underdog attitude of local fans. "Brooklyn has more industries than New York, but most of the executive offices are in Manhattan. What happens then?" he asked rhetorically. "The Brooklynites resent Manhattan getting all the credit. They have a real pride in their own and refuse to become parasitical," he answered his own question. "When anything comes along distinctly Brooklyn, they rally behind it because it is an expression of themselves, even an entity as lowly as a baseball club," he proclaimed. As often in his life, a note of self-criticism for devoting himself to baseball instead of larger things crept subconsciously into Branch Rickey's utterances.

Yet Rickey chortled with glee when noting the fierce loathing felt by Dodgers fans for the Manhattan-based Giants. "'Poo on the Giants,' they

say, and they are right," he boomed. "It is the pooling of support behind the team, by George, which makes it successful." He concluded his
talk with one of his favorite after-dinner stories about a "superannuated"
minister in the small college town of Mount Lebanon, Illinois (where
Rickey had received his first honorary doctoral degree, in 1928 at McK-
endree College.) "When his wife died, he had her buried in the cemetery near the college," Rickey recalled. "I'll never forget the inscription
on the tombstone. It said, 'She was more to me than I expected.'" After
Rickey paused to let the laughter subside, he observed, "I never was able
to figure out exactly what he did expect, but I can echo his sentiments in
so far as Brooklyn is concerned."[1]

The Rotary Club members filed out, satisfied that the Dodgers were
in good hands. Admittedly, the attendees were at times overwhelmed by
Rickey's long sentences and big words. "He is a man of many faucets, all
running at once," a local fan would mutter memorably, yet most agreed
that Rickey certainly knew what he was talking about concerning their
beloved sport and hometown team.

In his first weeks on the job in Brooklyn, Rickey even impressed many
of the crusty, hard-bitten New York sportswriters. The well-known teetotaler had not, as feared, shut down the pressroom bar his predecessor,
Larry MacPhail, had thoughtfully provided. He did cancel the advertisements for whiskey on the Ebbets Field outfield walls, a sign that he was
not going to encourage the drinking of alcohol. (In Rickey's last years in
St. Louis, Sam Breadon's acceptance of Hyde Beer as a sponsor for Cardinals radio broadcasts had been another indication of the teetotaler's
waning influence in his former organization.)[2]

Rickey scheduled weekly press conferences in Brooklyn and seemed
to like parrying with the aggressive sportswriters. "I never went through
anything like it before," Rickey admitted to Taylor Spink of the *Sporting News* after one of his first sessions with thirty New York–area scribes.
"These New York reporters are keen, they do not miss a trick. I will say
one thing—they hit hard, but they are clean."[3]

Early on Rickey offered a frank assessment of the Dodgers roster that
Larry MacPhail had left him before going into the war. It was "danger-
ously veteranized," Rickey warned, and the team was thus "sitting on a
volcano of complete and sudden disintegration." He added: "Ball clubs

are too conservative about making changes, championship clubs in particular. That's the reason they deteriorate a lot—they change too late."[4] Branch Rickey made it clear that he was not going to make the mistake of allowing a team to grow old on him.

Writing about the Dodgers' new boss in *PM*, a new daily newspaper in New York published by department store mogul Marshall Field, veteran sportswriter Tom Meany offered a shrewd analysis. He downplayed Rickey's verbosity that led some bewildered sportswriters to label Rickey's office "The Cave of the Winds." When it came to talking to the press, Meany said that Rickey's predecessor, Larry MacPhail, hadn't exactly been terse. Concerning Rickey's reputation as a stuffy "blue nose" and adamant teetotaler, the writer observed perceptively, "He is a dry but not a violent one." Meany had been reading travel writer John Gunther's book *Inside Asia* and was struck by Gunther's description of Mohandas K. "Mahatma" Gandhi, the leader of the independence movement in India, as "an incredible combination of Jesus Christ, Tammany Hall, and your father." The sportswriter thought the definition applied to Branch Rickey and thus dubbed him "The Mahatma," a nickname that would stick throughout Rickey's eventful career in Brooklyn.[5]

Often dubbed "The Brain" in St. Louis, Rickey did not particularly mind being branded "The Mahatma" in Brooklyn. What he came to loathe was the nickname "El Cheapo," coined by Jimmy Powers, sports editor and columnist for the *New York Daily News*, a tabloid with the largest circulation of any New York newspaper. Powers would carry his attack on the former St. Louis "chain gang" operator to such a virulent extent that by 1946 Rickey seriously considered suing Powers for libel. But during the executive's first weeks at the helm in Brooklyn, even Powers allowed the executive to enjoy a honeymoon period.

From the moment he began his new job, Branch Rickey set the wheels in motion to establish the Dodgers as a perennial contender in the National League. With the majority of Major Leaguers lost for the duration of the war, most of the big league teams had ordered a cutback in scouting and development. Rickey, however, convinced the Dodgers' board of directors to increase the budget for player recruitment and development. After the war ended, Rickey argued, the team would have a huge supply to choose from, and, just as he had done in St. Louis, he would bring up the best players to Brooklyn and use the others for trades and sales. He planned to follow his tried-and-tested Cardinals model by setting up tryout camps for under–draft age, young players all over the country. Explaining his plans to his close associate Clyde Sukeforth, Rickey conceded that it would be "an expensive experiment, [but] . . . if we win the war, it will be worth it. If we lose the war, what difference does it make?"[6]

Rickey had another idea for making the Dodgers a lasting powerhouse. He wanted to scout and sign black players and break the "gentleman's agreement" that, since the late nineteenth century, had denied American players of color an opportunity to play Major League Baseball. Rickey first broached the subject to an influential behind-the-scenes personage, George V. McLaughlin, president of the Brooklyn Trust Company, the bank that had kept the Dodgers from bankruptcy during the worst years of the Great Depression. McLaughlin was the trustee for the heirs of Charles Ebbets and Edward McKeever, who owned three quarters of the team.[7] Any important baseball decision would have to be approved by a man who, while not a member of the team's board of directors, carried much weight as a well-connected former New York City police commissioner. He was someone, as Rickey might say, who "counted."

"You might turn up something, so go ahead," the banker told the new team president but cautioned, "My God, Rickey, you've got to know you're doing this not to solve any great sociological problem!"[8] As an ardent supporter of capitalism and a foe of left-wing radicalism, Branch Rickey was, of course, in complete agreement with the banker.

In early 1943, at a top secret meeting at the exclusive New York Athletic Club on Central Park South, the board of directors agreed to the plan Rickey brought to McLaughlin. They pledged themselves to secrecy about the search, agreeing that priority should be placed on finding the right kind of player. If the wrong type of black player were signed—that is, a person with an uncontrollable temper or an attitude of racial superiority—the end result would be disastrous. "If that happens," MacLaughlin said, "you're sunk."[9]

Armed with the full support of, and a significant budget from, ownership, something he had noticeably lacked in his last years under Sam

Breadon in St. Louis, Branch Rickey set about his mission of building another great organization. As always, he chose his staff carefully, seeking hard and loyal workers. He was, of course, more than pleased to have Branch Rickey Jr. as his director of Minor League operations.

Rickey was also thrilled to hire George Sisler as scouting supervisor. A chance encounter with his early protégé at a farewell luncheon in St. Louis set the wheels in motion. The Hall of Fame first baseman had been out of baseball since 1933, making a living as an executive in the printing business and also serving as a national softball commissioner. Rickey considered it an injustice that baseball had not found a place for someone of such distinction who had much to offer as a scout and instructor. Sisler eagerly welcomed the opportunity to work with a man he still usually addressed as "Coach" (or "Mr. Rickey"). "I will be of value to you," he promised in his letter of acceptance, though, like his mentor, Sisler had misgivings about moving to the congested New York metropolitan area.[10]

The Rickey and Sisler families had been very close in St. Louis. George and Kathleen Sisler were frequent bridge partners of Branch and Jane Rickey, and Branch took an interest in the lives and careers of the Sislers' three sons, who, like the Rickey children, attended the Burroughs School in St. Louis. They all would have significant baseball careers: George Jr. as a longtime front office executive in Columbus, Ohio; Dick as a Major League first baseman–outfielder and manager; and Dave as a Major League pitcher. "Branch Rickey was always thinking of little things to help people feel more comfortable about themselves," the Sislers' daughter Frances Drochelman recalls. "My brother Dick sometimes stammered. I remember before one meal, Mr. Rickey asked Dick to recite 'The Lord's Prayer,' and he recited it flawlessly."[11]

Rickey also quickly lured two key scouts and instructors from St. Louis: J. Rex Bowen and Wid Curry Matthews. A native of the small town of Shiloh in southern New Jersey, Bowen played baseball at Salem College in Salem, West Virginia, and not long after graduating in 1933 joined the Cardinals as a second baseman in the lower rungs of the farm system, occasionally doubling as a player-manager. After retiring as a player Bowen returned to Bridgeton in southern New Jersey, where he began a high school teaching career. He never lost contact with Branch Rickey, attracted by the charismatic executive's teaching and coaching skills and his religious outlook, a commitment that Bowen, a Seventh-Day Adventist, shared. He ran South Jersey tryout camps for Rickey's Cardinals in the late 1930s and seamlessly switched allegiance when his mentor moved to the Dodgers. Bowen ultimately earned master's degrees in psychology and counseling and was only a few credits shy of a doctorate. However, he told writer Charles Dexter, "I can teach better and more practical psychology by scouting for Mr. Rickey."[12]

Wid Matthews had been a Major League player. A left-handed hitter and thrower, Matthews was a reserve outfielder for the Washington Senators' World Series teams of 1924–25. In 1936 he joined the Cardinals as a Minor League coach and instructor. A native of Raleigh, Illinois, Matthews married a woman from Mississippi and was based in Hattiesburg when he answered the call to join the Brooklyn organization.

The ferocious gentleman did not succeed in luring to Brooklyn everyone he wanted. He put a full-court press on his former trainer in St. Louis, Harrison "Bucko" Weaver. Weaver had played football for Rickey at Ohio Wesleyan, and in the 1920s he expressed a wish to travel on one eastern trip with the Cardinals. Before he knew what happened, Weaver, a licensed osteopath, was seduced to become the Redbirds' full-time trainer.[13]

The baseball executive understood that a good trainer—someone who knew how to repair cuts and bruises and, even more important, to soothe and stoke athletic egos—was an unheralded part of a championship team. Knowing Weaver's misgivings about living in the East, Rickey tried to sell him on his new home. "I like Brooklyn. It is not New York," Rickey wrote his friend with the same passion he used in giving his Rotary addresses. "It is homefolks. I go over to New York [Manhattan] only when I have appointments or some function. Pooh with New York! Two poohs!"

Knowing that Weaver had earned patents on many practical gadgets to aid a ballplayer's life, such as foam comfort shoe insoles, an air-conditioned baseball cap, and sinus clamps for better breathing, Rickey suggested that New York would afford him better commercial opportunities for distributing his clever inventions. "There is more publicity here in one minute than there is in St. Louis in a lifetime," he counseled. "There just isn't any measuring rod long enough to rate the value of [these] things in Brooklyn."

. Rickey tried to sell Weaver on Brooklyn's cooler summer climate, compared to St. Louis's steamy humidity. Knowing the trainer's love of boating, Rickey wrote: "The ocean is here, the rivers are here, the inland lakes are here. . . . All the sports are close at hand, the best there is in the field of art and music start here and end here." He pulled out all the stops in his concluding spiel. "Opportunity with its long hair in front dangling down to his shoe-tops approaches you," Rickey implored his longtime associate. "Sieze [*sic*] him before his slippery bald head behind leaves you nothing to grab except St. Louis."[14]

In the end Weaver was too much a son of the Midwest to migrate to crowded, hectic, and too politically left-wing New York. Rickey retained Harold "Doc" Wendler as the Dodgers team trainer but remained in touch with his old friend. During the presidential election year of 1944, Weaver wrote "my dear Branch" that he was "quite concerned over our country's future and I do not want it to go deeper into National Socialism. . . . I am living only until Nov. 7. If the present philosophy of Government is to be perpetuated and State Rights, private Enterprise and our Constitution junked, then I am going to retire to my Boats for the rest of my life and call it a day."[15] (In 1952 Weaver retired from baseball and enjoyed the election of retired general Dwight Eisenhower, the first Republican in twenty years to win the White House; Weaver died in 1955.)

Although Branch Rickey did not expect Brooklyn to challenge for the pennant until at least a year or two after the end of the war, he hoped that the parent Brooklyn club would at least be respectable in the standings. Rickey conceded the 1943 pennant to his former team because he had left them with enough depth in the roster to overcome their losses to the military. "Why, Sam Breadon could do a Rip Van Winkle in the Catskills for five years and not have anything to worry about," Rickey predicted.[16] In Brooklyn he would have to cope with a less than ideal squad of aging veterans. Yet he had one asset that he looked forward to maximizing: the managerial wizardry and passion of Leo Durocher.

Rickey had never operated a team with Durocher as manager, although when he traded him to Brooklyn after the 1937 season, he told Leo that, if he kept out of trouble, managing would be in his future. "Brooklyn isn't as bad as it is painted," Rickey at that time advised Leo's wife, Grace Dozier Durocher. "Just don't let Leo paint it too often."[17] After he took the managerial reins of the Dodgers in 1939, Durocher quickly fulfilled his promise, finishing third his first year, second in 1940, and winning the pennant in 1941. The 1942 Dodgers won 104 games but were passed by the fast-closing Cardinals.

Many observers felt that Brooklyn had lost the 1942 pennant because, before the games, Durocher and his chief lieutenant, Charley Dressen, had been playing too many rounds of high-stakes card games with the players. The losses in the clubhouse may have affected the play of some of the Dodgers on the field. Rickey himself loved to play cards, and he and Durocher were to engage in memorable wartime spring training bridge games, even drawing crowds of spectators who marveled that the two men seemed to be competing against each other though ostensibly were partners.[18] Card playing for high stakes in a baseball clubhouse, however, was another matter entirely. Before rehiring Durocher as manager, Rickey implored him to stop the in-house gambling. Although the manager argued that he had returned the lost money to the players if they performed well on the field, he promised to limit future card games to small change. Charley Dressen was not so fortunate. Rickey did not at first rehire Dressen for 1943 because he was also a horse player as well as a card player, and for the moment Rickey had decided that two vices were one too many.[19]

Rickey was disappointed to learn that Durocher was separated from his wife, Grace Dozier, the elegant St. Louis dress designer. The divorce would become final in 1944, yet such was the power of Leo's magnetic personality that she admitted that her flame for him still burned. "Possibly I am kidding myself, but I feel like some day I will have my Daddy back—a bigger and better man," she wrote Rickey shortly before the 1943 World Series. "I am truly in hopes that he will continue under your guidance and am sure with such a master he cannot go astray."[20]

Nothing in the Branch Rickey–Leo Durocher relationship was ever uncomplicated, and they probably would not have wanted it any other way. Yet, if not for a reprieve from Uncle Sam, Durocher might never have managed for Rickey in Brooklyn. Before the start of 1943 spring training, Durocher was summoned to a draft board physical in St. Louis. If Durocher were to be lost for the duration, Rickey had other managers in mind. Older loyalists, such as Burt Shotton and Ray Blades, were available. There was even a possibility that Bill Terry, who resigned from the Giants after the 1941 season, might be lured out of retirement, but all speculation ended on March 1, 1943, when the St. Louis draft board of thirty-seven-year-old Leo Ernest Durocher granted him a military exemption because of a perforated eardrum. Wiseacres in the press suggested that Leo's loud arguments with umpires had damaged his hearing, but whatever the cause of his disability, a new and momentous phase in the intriguing, volatile relationship between Branch Rickey and Leo Durocher was about to begin.

Because of wartime restrictions on gasoline, Commissioner Kenesaw Mountain Landis had decreed that all spring training camps must be north of the Potomac and Ohio Rivers and east of the Mississippi. "It sounds like a treaty with the French and Indians," one wit commented.[21] As Rickey's New York City rivals headed to New Jersey—the Yankees to Atlantic City and the Giants to Lakewood—the Dodgers prepared for a trek fifty miles north to Bear Mountain, a resort area just south of the Catskill Mountains. Rickey arranged for the Dodgers to be housed and fed at the Bear Mountain Inn, a well-known hostelry whose proprietor, John Martin, was an avid Dodgers fan. Through his many military contacts, Branch Rickey also obtained access to West Point's indoor facilities on the wintry days when Bear Mountain's outdoor diamonds would be unavailable.

It was a happy, hopeful day as several groups of Dodgers and their families, accompanied by some sportswriters, took a ferry ride across the Hudson River to New Jersey and switched to a bus for the trip to Bear Mountain and the start of the most optimistic time of the baseball year, spring training. Normally, Branch Rickey wasn't eager to have families come to spring training, but during wartime he encouraged the players to bring their wives and children. He had been reading Carl Van Doren's *Secret History of the American Revolution,* with its tales of heroes like George Washington and scoundrels like Benedict Arnold, and its accounts of memorable battles that occurred near the training camp. Rickey urged his players and their families to explore some of the historic places from the early days of American history. The history-loving executive did not expect many of his charges to take up the offer, but at least he had made the suggestion.[22]

As the 1943 season began it became clear that Branch Rickey's prediction of a Cardinals romp to the pennant had been accurate. They would win 105 games and would finish 18 games ahead of the Cincinnati Reds. Unfortunately, his hope for a relatively respectable year for the Dodgers with Leo Durocher at the helm was in jeopardy on the eve of the early July All-Star Game. Although the team was playing above .500 ball, a full-scale mutiny of the players against the manager almost broke out. Rickey had rehired Charlie Dressen, Durocher's third base coach, to act as a buffer between the pugnacious manager and his players, but it took some diplomacy by Rickey himself to avert a crisis.

The trouble came to a boil on Friday night July 9, 1943, after an exciting game in which the Dodgers beat the Pittsburgh Pirates, 7–6, on a squeeze bunt by second baseman Billy Herman in the bottom of the tenth inning. After the game manager Durocher was not celebrating but fuming at pitcher Bobo Newsom for throwing a spitball in the third inning with a runner on third base. Young catcher Bobby Bragan, a former shortstop who had recently arrived in a trade with the Phillies, missed the pitch and the tying run scored. Durocher accused Newsom of deliberately showing up the young receiver, but the pitcher retorted that he had thrown a fastball, not a spitball, and suggested in salty language that Durocher should play people who can catch the ball.[23]

The manager was furious at Newsom's insolence, but it was in character for the cocky South Carolinian, who had won two games for the Tigers in the 1940 World Series and earned him for a time the status of highest-paid pitcher in the Major Leagues.[24] "You're suspended for three days," Durocher bellowed, "and if Mr. Rickey supports me, I hope it is made permanent!"

New York World-Telegram sportswriter Tim Cohane interviewed Durocher in his office after the blowup, and Leo was still so livid about his confrontation with Newsom that he made the tactical error of telling the sportswriter the story of the pitcher's suspension without first telling the team. Regular interviewing of the players in the clubhouse after a game would not be the norm in daily sportswriting until after World War II, so Cohane shared the news of Newsom's suspension with his colleagues in the press box.

The day after the incident Durocher was holding court with the writers in his office when shortstop Harold "Arky" Vaughan walked in, took off his uniform, threw it at the manager, told him what he could do with it, and stalked out. Vaughan, a future Hall of Famer whose best years had been spent with the Pirates, was not known for hotheadedness, and his outburst puzzled everybody. It turned out that Vaughan had read Garry Schumacher's story in the *New York Journal-American* about the Durocher-Newsom argument and the pitcher's suspension. The most soft-spoken of all the Dodgers, Vaughan, an Arkansas native, was perhaps showing his solidarity with South Carolinian Newsom. Outfielder Dixie Walker, who lived in Birmingham, Alabama, also threatened to turn in his uniform. An open foe of Durocher (the feeling was mutual), Walker suggested that Newsom's punishment might justify some kind of strike against the manager.[25]

"Schumacher wasn't even in the clubhouse last night!" Durocher bellowed. The manager demanded a copy of the story, read through it, and said it was filled with lies and distortions. He summoned Schumacher, who said that he stood by the story and that Tim Cohane had been his source. Durocher wanted to see Cohane immediately, but the writer wasn't at the ballpark on Saturday because the *World-Telegram* didn't publish on Sunday. Durocher grabbed a phone, called the sportswriter at home, and ripped into him for his story. He demanded that Cohane come to the ballpark immediately, but on his day off there was no way the writer was coming to subject himself to the manager's abuse.

Branch Rickey, who liked to steer clear of the petty spats that inevitably came up in a long baseball season, almost always avoided the clubhouse, considering it the manager's domain. With a possible mutiny at hand, however, he hurriedly entered the fray. He convinced Arky Vaughan to stay with the team, but since he'd torn off and turned in his uniform, Rickey and Durocher decided that Vaughan couldn't play that day. (They might have had flashbacks to Dizzy Dean's tearing up his uniform in one of his snits in 1934.) The players, who were still smoldering with resentment at their manager, had skipped batting practice, and fifteen thousand fans at Ebbets Field were now wondering what was happening.

The players soon decided that no good would come from boycotting the fans, so they went out to play with a vengeance, scoring ten runs in the first inning en route to a 23–6 walloping of the Pirates.[26]

Rickey hoped that Durocher's desire to suspend Newsom could now be worked out privately. However, there was still the matter of Cohane's feeling enraged that Durocher had impugned his journalistic integrity. Since the writer hadn't been at the ballpark on Saturday to defend himself, he phoned Branch Rickey at home, urgently asking for a chance to address Durocher in front of the team before the Sunday doubleheader. "I want all the ballplayers and all the newspapermen there, and I'll face your Mr. Durocher and everybody will have a chance to find out who is lying," Cohane insisted.[27]

Contrary to what has been written about this controversy, there is no evidence that Branch Rickey broke his vow to avoid baseball on the Sabbath. He did not attend the Sunday meeting, but he felt that he had no choice but to allow the meeting to occur because Cohane's reputation had been challenged by Durocher. Before the Sunday, July 11, 1943, doubleheader at Ebbets Field against the Pirates, a remarkable scene unfolded in the Dodgers clubhouse. Durocher sat on an equipment trunk with his legs dangling nervously, as Cohane paced the floor, presenting his case like a prosecuting attorney. Nothing new was revealed that hadn't already been written in the papers, and not surprisingly none of the players volunteered any new information. The only one who seemed to be enjoying the proceedings was irrepressible, unrepentant Bobo Newsom.[28] After the meeting the Dodgers went out and played the doubleheader, salvaging a split by winning the second game.

The All-Star Game break was at hand, and many players planned to leave town and get away for a few days from the grind of the long season. Probably realizing how unusually stressful the events during the Pittsburgh series had been for most of the Dodgers, Branch Rickey arranged with John Martin to provide a retreat at the Bear Mountain Inn for those players not leaving the New York area during the few days off.[29]

Meanwhile, most of the Brooklyn baseball community awaited Branch Rickey's decision on the fate of Leo Durocher. Most of the sportswriters thought that Durocher would be fired, and a rumor circulated that he offered to resign. However, the New York writers had not been around the executive long enough to realize that he had a real aversion to canning any employee and that he possessed a special feeling for Durocher. Rickey believed in the primacy of the manager's role as leader, and he was impressed that Durocher had stood up for his young catcher Bobby Bragan against the veteran Bobo Newsom's insolence. The pitcher's lack of remorse for his action may have been the last straw factoring into Rickey's decision.

On Tuesday, July 12, the day of the All-Star Game in Philadelphia, Rickey announced that Durocher was remaining as Dodgers manager and that his suspension of Newsom would be upheld. Three days later Rickey traded Newsom to the St. Louis Browns for two journeyman, left-handed pitchers, Fritz Ostermuller and Archie McKain. (In an amusing sidebar to the story, not long after backup catcher Bobby Bragan arrived in Brooklyn, he went in to ask Branch Rickey for a raise in salary, as a recently traded player often did. "Son," Rickey said, with a knowing chuckle, "you are going to be sitting on the bench so much that they will call you 'Judge.'")[30]

No sooner had the threat of player rebellion against Leo Durocher died down than Rickey himself was faced with his first experience of frontal opposition by Brooklyn fandom for his player personnel moves. The grumbling had started when Rickey sold outfielder Joe Medwick to the Giants shortly after the Fourth of July. In his three seasons in Brooklyn Medwick never became the force he had been as a feared member of the St. Louis Gashouse Gang, but he was still a threat to hit the long ball and had his ardent supporters. The rumblings against Rickey's trading away fan favorites when they grew too expensive started to build, and Jimmy Powers, writing in the *Daily News*, began to rev the engines of his "El Cheapo" campaign.

The criticisms intensified at the end of July when Rickey announced the trading of first baseman Dolph Camilli and pitcher Johnny Allen to the hated Giants in exchange for journeymen pitchers Bill Lohrman and Bill Sayles and utility infielder Joe Orengo. Dolph Camilli was a genuine Brooklyn hero, a powerful left-handed-hitting and excellent fielding first baseman, who, after his purchase by Larry MacPhail from the Phillies, had won the 1941 National League Most Valuable Player Award. When news of the trade reached Brooklyn fans during a game at Ebbets Field, Rickey needed a police escort when he left the ballpark to go home.[31]

The Allied invasion of Sicily vied for space on the front pages of New York newspapers with the news of the departure of the popular Camilli. Jimmy Powers accelerated his "El Cheapo" campaign, encouraging fans to protest. "Rickey the Wrecker," "Go Back to St. Louis, You Bum," and a uniquely Brooklynese placard, "Leave Us Have MacPhail," were some of the signs carried by outraged fans parading in Ebbets Field and in front of the Dodgers business office on Montague Street near the Brooklyn Borough Hall.[32]

The negative response stunned Rickey and his family, who started to fear taking taxis in case their identity became known to the cabdrivers. Yet the fans' overreaction to the Camilli trade was a classic example of emotion overcoming reason. Camilli was in the downward arc of his career, no longer able to pull pitches over the 32-foot screen down Ebbets Field's cozy 297-foot right-field line, and no longer demonstrating quick footwork around first base. In fact, it had taken a personal visit by Branch Rickey to the first baseman's California vineyard before the start of the 1943 season to convince the slugger to keep playing. Rickey played on Camilli's patriotism, pleading that in wartime fans needed their heroes to perform for them, and perhaps he also agreed to an increase in the first baseman's salary.[33] However, by 1943, the first baseman's skills had so eroded that at the time of the trade, his numbers in 353 at-bats were a paltry .246 BA, .374 SA, 6 HR, and 43 RBI. In a frank admission to a sportswriter, Camilli said, "If I can't help the Dodgers finish in the first division, how could I help the Giants in last place?"[34] He never reported to Brooklyn's archrival, and except for a few at-bats with the Red Sox in 1945, his career was over at the time Rickey traded him.

Nonetheless, fan discontent, stoked by the newspapers, continued. The passion of the Dodgers fans both enthralled and bewildered Branch Rickey. One of his reasons for a summer 1943 visit to Larry MacPhail at his military headquarters in Washington DC may have been to query his predecessor on the mind of the Dodgers fan.[35] Even the *New York Times*, "the paper of record" and thus more restrained than the emotional tabloids, was printing letters critical of the new regime in Brooklyn. "In less than a year the new leadership has dismembered a magnificent baseball team and has smothered its vitality," wrote Mrs. Ernest Rowan. "With Branch Rickey still in power we may look for further mutilations."[36]

However, the veteran executive was unbowed in his determination to rid the Brooklyn roster of veterans who were no longer productive. In words virtually identical to the ones he had uttered to St. Louis sportswriters at the start of his Cardinals reign nearly a quarter century earlier, Rickey declared: "I could be tempted to join the howling fans, but the fact remains that whatever changes were made were calculated to help the club. I do not propose to deviate from such calculations . . . to help the club."[37]

Although the Dodgers would suffer a ten-game losing streak around the time of the Camilli trade, Leo Durocher was bolstered by the vote of confidence from his boss. He righted the team's ship and brought Brooklyn home in third place, with an 81-72 record. Three holdovers from the MacPhail era—Whitlow Wyatt, Kirby Higbe, and Curt Davis— were the three double-digit winners on the Brooklyn staff, and veteran second baseman Billy Herman had a productive year with a .330 average and 100 RBI, an impressive number since he hit only 2 home runs. The Dodgers finished five and a half games behind the second-place Cincinnati Reds, but a whopping twenty-three and a half games behind the pennant-winning Cardinals. However, in the 1943 World Series, the Yankees reversed the 1942 outcome, easily beating the Cardinals in five games. Although the two teams were clearly the best in their respective leagues in 1943, it was diluted wartime baseball. Branch Rickey was trying to be patient until the real Major Leaguers came back from the war. When they were combined with the youths he was scouting and signing, he remained confident that the Dodgers would be a team to be reckoned with for years to come.

Rickey's first Brooklyn Dodgers tryout camps began in the summer of 1943, and he followed the pattern that had been so successful with the Cardinals. The groundwork for the camps had been laid in letters sent to several thousand high school and college coaches, who were asked for their player recommendations. An advertisement placed in the national young men's magazine *Argosy* widened the net among the youths without school connections. Another advertisement in the *Sporting News* dramatically used capital letters, "BOYS!" to encourage all aspiring players over age sixteen to come to the tryout sessions. "If you expect to enter the armed forces of the United States in the near future, DO NOT let this fact keep you from attending one of these camps," the advertisement proclaimed. "The Dodgers are looking ahead. They are anxious to see you in action now and judge your baseball ability. The Dodger organization will be able to place many players after the war. Who knows? Perhaps you have a baseball career awaiting you!"[38]

Rickey's vast dragnet included an invitation to young Japanese American athletes living in the internment camps established by the U.S. government in the panic after the bombing of Pearl Harbor. In a letter of welcome to the unfairly incarcerated youths of Japanese descent, Dodgers farm director Branch Rickey Jr. wrote simply, "The fact that these boys are American boys is good enough for the Brooklyn club."[39]

In late July 1943 a few thousand hopeful baseball players flocked to locations all over the country to show their skills in front of twelve of Rickey's most astute scouts and developers: George Sisler, Wid Matthews, Ted McGrew, Tom Greenwade, Clyde Sukeforth, Jim Ferrante, Branch Rickey Jr., Lee MacPhail, Harold Roettger, Rex Bowen, Mike Kelly, and Joe Labate. The July camps were so successful that the club continued the program in August. Rickey Sr. impressed on his staff that the expansion of the vast Cardinals farm system had actually come out of these tryout camps. So many potentially good players attended the camps, Rickey explained, that the Cardinals had needed to find farm clubs where they could develop. He emphasized that the camps were the stimulus for the creation of more farm clubs, not vice versa.

Loyal scout Rex Bowen was well versed in the Rickey method and expectations. "We don't want the fellows who demand that [bonus money]," Bowen told local sportswriters as he planned a southern New Jersey tryout camp. However, as Bowen said, "if our scouts think they'll develop in three or four years into average ballplayers we sign them." The scout said that one importance of the program was in making contact with family members who show up to support their boys. "You can make a lot of friends in any tryout camp not only of the camp squad, but among their friends and relatives," he noted.[40]

One teenager paid his own way from Waycross, Georgia, to a Lancaster, Pennsylvania, camp. Because some of the hopefuls had not yet graduated from high school, their names were kept secret so that other

Major League teams did not find out about them and file a complaint with the baseball commissioner's office that the Dodgers were signing under-age players.

Not surprisingly, Branch Rickey's initial Brooklyn tryout camps turned up many diamonds in the rough that would shine for the Dodgers after the war. At an Indianapolis camp two promising teenagers impressed the scouts: Gil Hodges, who immediately signed and even had 2 at-bats for the Dodgers at Ebbets Field in 1943 before going into the Marines, and pitcher Carl Erskine, who signed after the war. Out of a camp in Ohio George Shuba, a Brooklyn reserve outfielder from 1948 to 1955, was signed. Among the 1,500 hopefuls who tried out at a Long Beach, California, camp was a tall, thin outfielder, Edwin Snider, who grew into the sturdy, power-hitting, Hall of Fame Brooklyn Dodgers center fielder Duke Snider. After a tryout at Ebbets Field, pitcher Ralph Branca, a recent high school graduate from nearby Mount Vernon, New York, was signed.[41]

All the teenage signings were assigned to lower Minor League teams until their draft boards came calling. Jake Pitler, manager of the Newport News, Virginia, farm club (and later a fixture as Brooklyn first base coach), noted with amusement that he was running a team in wartime where many players were too young to shave and who read comic books and ate candy bars on the team buses.[42] However, Rickey and his staff correctly reasoned that it would be a good experience for the youngsters to get their feet wet in professional baseball before they had to report for military duty.

By the end of 1943 there was definitely a feeling in the nation that the tide in the war was turning in favor of the Allies. Adolf Hitler's Nazi armies were suffering heavy losses during their attempted invasion of Russia. A second front in Europe, via an invasion of France, was being planned for 1944. After many early setbacks in the Pacific, the American-led troops were beginning to take the initiative in the war against Japan. With many members of his family serving in the military, Branch Rickey intensely followed the developments in the Allied cause. Twice during the war he broke his vow not to come to the ballpark on Sunday. In late April 1943 he appeared at a war bond rally at Ebbets Field held in conjunction with a round-robin exhibition game against the Yankees and Giants. Later, Rickey appeared at the ballpark to support broadcaster Red Barber's blood drive for the American Red Cross.[43]

As for his own living situation, Rickey was trying to adjust to life on the East Coast, but it had not been easy. As much as he said publicly that he liked the spirit and surroundings of Brooklyn, he remained an unreconstructed country boy who craved wide open spaces. Living in the vast, crowded, and complicated New York City area was not his ideal place of residence. "I'm not a plutocrat, but I need room to whoop and holler with my dogs," he told a *Look* magazine reporter.[44]

Branch and Jane Rickey's first lodging in the New York area was in a rental house in Bronxville, in the northern New York suburb of Westchester County. However, Rickey regularly got lost making connections between subways and commuter trains. A few months later he cut down his commuting time by moving to Queens, the New York City borough east of Brooklyn. He found a house in an interesting neighborhood, Forest Hills Gardens, not far from the Forest Hills tennis stadium, the site of the annual United States Tennis Association's championship. Rickey's new home was also only a few minutes' drive from the Richmond Hill, Queens, neighborhood where Branch Rickey Jr., lived with his wife, Mary Iams Rickey, and their two young daughters, Caroline, six, and Nancy, four. (A son, Branch Barrett Rickey, named after Charley Barrett, would be born in 1946.)

Forest Hill Gardens was a planned community, funded by the largesse of Olivia Sage, the philanthropic widow of industrialist Russell Sage. Mrs. Sage also endowed an interdenominational Protestant Church-of-the-Gardens, which opened in 1912. It was crafted with stones from European quarries and featured exquisite stained-glass windows. Before long, Branch Rickey was a member of the Church-of-the-Gardens board of trustees and a featured speaker at father-son banquets and other church functions.[45]

Although Forest Hills was a leafy suburb with a solid community and an ecumenical church, it still lacked the open spaces that Branch Rickey had grown accustomed to in the Midwest. He kept his eyes and ears open for a country retreat. During his first spring in Brooklyn in 1943, Branch and Jane Rickey paid a social visit to S. Raymond "Pinky" Thornburg and his wife, Pherbia Thomas Thornburg, two close friends and Ohio Wesleyan graduates active in alumni affairs. They lived on Quaker Hill in Pawling, New York, about sixty miles north of New York City. Rickey fell in love with the area near the Connecticut border, where visible to the west were the foothills of the Catskill Mountains and to the east loomed the Berkshires. Pinky Thornburg was a trader in Asian commodities, and he and Pherbia were very involved in Christian missionary activities in Asia, activities close to Branch Rickey's heart.

On one of his early visits to the Thornburgs, Rickey met Pherbia's brother, Lowell Thomas, and struck up an immediate friendship with the famous national radio broadcaster. Like Rickey, Thomas had been born in a small town in Ohio, but at the age of eight he moved to Colorado with his parents, who were schoolteachers turned doctors. After graduating from the University of Colorado, Thomas went to Europe and got his big break during World War I when he broadcast reports from the battlefront. In the 1920s Thomas became one of the first regular news voices on radio and was also frequently seen on movie screens, narrating newsreels and movies about his world travels. "Come with me to lands of history, mystery, and romance," Thomas always floridly opened his travelogues.[46] In face-to-face conversation he was equally passionate and inspiring, qualities that quickly made him one of Branch Rickey's new friends.

Lowell Thomas hosted frequent Sunday afternoon salons at the Barn, a Quaker Hill community center, which he had built with stones from the Egyptian pyramid of Cheops, the Greek Parthenon, St. Peter's Basilica in Rome, the Great Wall of China, and George Washington's Mount Vernon estate.[47] Many of Thomas's neighbors, including broadcaster Edward R. Murrow and New York State governor Thomas Dewey, attended these salons as did, on occasion, Branch and Jane Rickey. "I wish I could live just down the hill from you, Lowell," Rickey wrote Thomas after one particularly endearing encounter. "But it is out of the question."[48] Property on Quaker Hill was just too expensive, but Rickey remained close friends with Thomas. When the adventurer was off on one of his world travels, the baseball executive would occasionally substitute for him on the radio. Rickey and Thomas also contributed financial assistance and occasional articles to *Guideposts*, a widely circulated self-help Christian magazine published near Quaker Hill in Pleasantville, New York.[49]

Sometime in 1944 Rickey finally found an affordable East Coast country property to his liking. It was an old farmhouse near Chestertown on the Eastern shore of Maryland. Two hundred miles from New York City, it would become Branch Rickey's rustic escape for the next six years. Many were the weekends he stayed over until early Monday morning to grab extra hours of country living. He hired a tenant to work on the farm while he was away in Brooklyn. The property was never a money-making proposition, but owning and being close to a farm had always been vital to Rickey's inner peace.[50]

Although Branch Rickey did not expect the Brooklyn Dodgers to contend for the pennant in wartime, he was disappointed by the plummeting of the team in 1944 to seventh place. Winners of eighty-one games in 1943 the Dodgers plunged to a 63-91 record in 1944. At one point during the summer the team lost fifteen games in a row, bringing back for many fans unhappy memories of the "Daffy Dodgers." "There can be artistry in ineptitude," Rickey was quoted in the press, but, of course, many Brooklynites didn't find the remark funny.[51] The only thing that Dodgers fans could take pride in was the hitting of Fred "Dixie" Walker, who won the 1944 National League batting title with a .357 average, edging out Stan Musial by 10 points. A onetime member of the New York Yankees, Walker excelled in hitting against the Giants, always a good way to become a Dodger fan favorite. He added to his popularity by appearing regularly at community functions, soon becoming known as the "People's Choice," or, as pronounced in Brooklynese, "The Peepul's Cherce."[52]

The poor showing of the 1944 Dodgers was, of course, explainable because the core of the team of the future was in the military: shortstop Pee Wee Reese, a regular since 1941 who had been obtained by Larry MacPhail in a Minor League deal with the Red Sox; pitchers Ralph Branca and Carl Erskine, first baseman Gil Hodges, and center fielder Duke Snider, all teenagers spotted at the 1943 tryout camps; and the still-unknown players of color being secretly scouted. With the war not yet won, most Major League teams were filled with the very old and the very young, and the Dodgers were no exception. In 1943 and part of 1944 the Dodgers played forty-one-year-old outfielder Paul Waner, who had established his Hall of Fame career with the Pirates and was still a .300 hitter. On the other end of the spectrum was sixteen-year-old short-stop Tommy Brown, a local boy signed out of the playing fields of the Brooklyn Parade Grounds. In 146 at-bats in 1944 Brown hit a woeful .164, but he was a good enough player to make the Dodgers after the war as a useful utility player.

Another youngster who got his feet wet in the 1944 season was pitcher Clyde King, who was signed out of the University of North Carolina and rushed up to Ebbets Field to make his debut within twenty-four hours. King would become a Branch Rickey favorite, a college boy with a strong religious background who loved to play bridge and taught some of his teammates the card game that was a particular favorite of the incessantly game-playing executive.[53]

Although disappointed in the showing of the 1944 Dodgers, Branch Rickey was putting together a solid organization of hard-working, loyal people. In 1944 he added another important component with the hiring of Harold Parrott as traveling secretary. Like a trainer a traveling secretary was a very underappreciated member of a team family, the man who makes the hotel and Pullman car arrangements and assigns roommates on the road.

Parrott was a sportswriter for the *Brooklyn Eagle,* a venerable local newspaper whose history traced back to before the Civil War and whose contributors had included poet Walt Whitman and Henry Chadwick, the inventor of the baseball box score.[54] Parrott was at first not interested in leaving the newspaper to work for the Dodgers, but Rickey had trained his eye on him for some time. He liked articles the journalist had written about him during his years in St. Louis.[55]

Little did Harold Parrott realize he was being scrutinized for a position when Rickey asked him for his opinion of two people who were interested in the team's road secretary job, Emil J. "Buzzie" Bavasi, a holdover Brooklyn front office man from the MacPhail days, and Ed Staples, who had come to Brooklyn from St. Louis. The next morning Parrott dutifully produced a written report for Rickey and began to read it "like a little boy turning in a composition to Teacher," Parrott remembered in his insightful *The Lords of Baseball.* Soon Rickey interrupted and said, "I might as well tell you that you are the one I really have in mind for this position, but I did want to get your ideas on how it should be handled."[56]

As an interesting aside, in 2002 the sons of Harold Parrott issued a new edition of *The Lords of Baseball*, which added their memories of traveling on the road with their father and the Dodgers. They noted that on Sundays Branch Rickey would always find a Catholic church where the boys could worship. "He sat in the last pew throughout the whole service," the oldest sons, Lynn and Tod Parrott, recalled.[57]

The year 1944 also brought sadness for the Rickey family. Late in April Rickey received word that his older brother, Orla, on the road as a shoe salesman, had died suddenly of a heart attack in Rockford, Illinois. Rickey made a sad journey to Lucasville to bury his brother, the first baseball pitcher he had ever caught, in the family plot in the hillside Scioto County cemetery.[58] As he said good-bye to his brother, Branch Rickey thought to himself that all that was left of the immediate family of Emily and Jacob Frank Rickey were himself and his younger brother, Frank, whom he was soon to hire as a Dodger scout.

Branch's ties with the Midwest were seemingly beginning to fray against his wishes. Although no one was injured and a priceless pipe organ was rescued, a fire at his home in St. Louis County in the fall of 1943 had cost him half of his possessions. The blaze was started inadvertently when his daughter Mary Rickey Eckler was discarding some papers into the fireplace, and the flames started to engulf the house. The quick thinking of neighbor Carroll Otto, the insurance executive, prevented the damage from being worse.[59]

Far better news awaited Rickey in the middle of 1944 concerning the economic future of the Dodgers organization. The chaotic ownership structure of the team was beginning to clear up. The heirs of Edward McKeever, the building contractor who had become Charles Ebbets's partner shortly before Ebbets Field was erected in 1913, informed banker George McLaughlin that they were ready to sell their quarter interest in the Dodgers. McLaughlin asked Rickey if he wanted to buy into the team, and he was immediately interested. He would have to borrow on the copious amount of life insurance that he carried, but he obviously felt that the investment would be a good one.

Another person interested in buying into the Dodgers was the team's chief counsel, Walter Francis O'Malley. O'Malley, born in the Bronx in 1903, was the son of Edwin O'Malley, a former New York City commissioner of markets who had suffered serious losses during the Great Depression. By contrast, Walter O'Malley's legal career took off in the 1930s when he became a specialist in foreclosures. He soon became a protégé of George McLaughlin, who had brought the lawyer into the Dodgers' fold when the banker needed someone to examine the Dodgers' finances in the pre–Larry MacPhail era when the team teetered near bankruptcy. McLaughlin asked O'Malley if he were interested in buying into the Dodgers, and the lawyer certainly was, but he, too, like Branch Rickey, couldn't afford a down payment on the team.[60]

Accordingly, McLaughlin structured a tripartite syndicate that brought in a third partner, John L. Smith, chairman of the board of the Pfizer Chemical Company, who became the treasurer and chief stockholder of the Dodgers. Born John Schmitz in Germany in 1891, Smith came to Brooklyn in his teens and rose to become both an able laboratory chemist and a successful business executive. Under his leadership Pfizer became intimately involved in the mass production of both citric acid in the 1930s and penicillin in the 1940s.

Smith participated in sports as a young man in Brooklyn, running the half mile for a local athletic club. He also loved to watch sports, especially boxing and his beloved Brooklyn Dodgers. He lived within a half mile of Ebbets Field and was thrilled to become part of the ownership of his favorite team. He looked forward to the postwar age of Brooklyn baseball as much as any baseball-mad Flatbush denizen. He would thoroughly disarm and win over the players with his unabashed enthusiasm, regularly coming into the clubhouse on Sundays, waving pennants and acting as a cheerleader. As an owner Smith would bring a refreshing attitude. "I don't expect to make money in baseball," said Smith, a very private man, in a rare interview. "I just don't want to lose any."[61]

In the summer of 1945 the Rickey-O'Malley-Smith partnership cemented its position as the dominant force in Brooklyn ownership when the heirs of Charles Ebbets agreed to sell their 50 percent portion of the Dodgers. George McLaughlin arranged the sale to the triumvirate, who now owned three quarters of the ball club. The other 25 percent of the Dodgers was still owned by Marie "Dearie" McKeever Mulvey, daughter of deceased Brooklyn judge Steve McKeever (Ed McKeever's brother), and her husband, James B. Mulvey, an East Coast representative for the Metro-Goldwyn-Mayer movie company. Dearie McKeever Mulvey was a great baseball fan who had missed only a few games since Ebbets Field opened.[62] She and her husband were not interested in selling, but as long as the three triumvirs agreed on policy they had operating control of the team. As Tommy Holmes wrote in his indispensable history *Dodger Daze and Knights,* the creation of the Rickey-Smith-O'Malley group meant that "the ownership of the club passed from the executors of estates into the control of living, breathing people."[63]

Spring training in 1945 was once again at Bear Mountain, and Leo Durocher was at the helm of a team poised to forget the disastrous season of 1944. Durocher was refreshed from a late winter United Services Organization (USO) tour of Europe on which he had talked baseball to the American troops and sung the praises of the "smartest boss" he ever had, Branch Rickey. As part of his program for taming and domesticating Durocher's wild side, Rickey always tried to provide Leo with opportunities to work with the military. While in St. Louis Rickey arranged for his favorite reclamation project to become an assistant baseball coach at the U.S. Naval Academy in Annapolis and was thrilled when they invited him back for a second season.[64] During spring training at Bear Mountain the executive also used his influence with the U. S. Military Academy at West Point for his manager to be hired as an assistant baseball coach.[65]

Durocher seemed intent on keeping his mind on baseball in 1945. The previous spring he had severely tested Rickey's patience by missing an important organizational meeting to appear on a radio comedy show. Rickey instructed road secretary Harold Parrott to inform his manager that he would have to make "an election of professions," baseball or show business. The chastened manager sped back to Bear Mountain and barged into the meeting, proclaiming, "You were running against Milton Berle and I voted for you."[66] Later that summer, though, Durocher almost pushed Rickey's patience to the breaking point when he went to the racetrack instead of attending an exhibition game for the benefit of the armed forces, but as always he charmed himself back into his boss's good graces.[67]

Durocher started the 1945 season on good behavior, and by early June the feisty manager had the Dodgers in first place, where they would remain for a good part of the summer. Then, on Saturday night, June 8, 1945, during a Phillies-Dodgers game at Ebbets Field that Brooklyn would win easily, 10–4, he snapped.

The incessant heckling of a leather-lunged fan sent Durocher over the edge. In the intimate confines of Ebbets Field any loudmouth could be heard, and one particular fan had been on the manager's case since the beginning of the season. Leo instructed a friend, Joe Moore, a burly, longtime ballpark policeman, to "invite" the bellicose fan down beneath the stands near the Dodger dugout for a "conversation." The fan, as innocent as he was loud, complied, thinking it would be a chance to meet the famous Leo Durocher.[68]

During the bottom of the sixth inning, heckler and skipper met face to face. According to a front-page story in the next day's *New York Times*, Durocher snarled, "You've got a mother, how would you like to call her names?" Whereupon patrolman Moore, not waiting for a reply, hit the unsuspecting fellow with a "blunt instrument." Durocher followed suit, and the fan wound up with a broken jaw, a black eye, and two head bruises. The victim staggered home, but when he realized the extent of his injuries, he went to a police station to file charges. Accompanied by a police officer he returned to the ballpark, where the game was still in progress, and Durocher and Moore were arrested and charged with felonious assault. The fan was not only a former star football player at Brooklyn's Thomas Jefferson High School but also a twenty-three-year-old war veteran, wounded in the Pacific, who was now working for the United States Customs House. His name, improbably, was John Christian.[69]

Christian filed a civil suit for damages against Durocher and Moore, and Rickey and the rest of the front office quickly approved payment of $6,500 to the ex-serviceman, hoping that the matter was closed. (Entertainer Danny Kaye, one of Durocher's show business friends, and Sidney Weil, the former Cincinnati owner, reportedly contributed to the settlement.)[70] However, the Brooklyn district attorney's office was enraged by the incident and initiated criminal proceedings against the manager and the policeman. The case would not be tried for a year, but it was another blot on Durocher's dossier.

If Branch Rickey felt any irony in the name of the victim, John Christian, he didn't say so. In fact Rickey defended Durocher to the hilt in the latest controversy. At a Brooklyn Rotary Club luncheon a few days after the incident, Rickey praised Durocher for defending his team and cited one of his favorite pet phrases. We are a "team of ferocious gentlemen," he declared, vowing that the Dodgers would "stand as a unit against indecent and vulgar remarks from those in the stands."[71] Just as Rickey had absolved Durocher in the Bobo Newsom incident because he stood up for rookie catcher Bobby Bragan, he interpreted the latest incident as a leader of men standing up for his players against the vile epithets of a hoodlum.

Rickey's loyalty to Durocher was seemingly absolute, and as Rickey defended his manager the fans, for a change, were almost wholly on Rickey's side. In June 1946 John Christian's case against Durocher and patrolman Moore would be heard in a Brooklyn criminal court, but a jury of Brooklynites, who were obviously Dodgers fans, voted an acquittal after barely a half hour's deliberation. The ex-athlete was evidently not a good witness for himself, and Durocher was represented by a high-powered defense attorney.[72]

In his zeal for rescuing his favorite field leader, Branch Rickey undoubtedly made himself believe that Leo Durocher had been victimized by the unworthy fan. Although the paternal executive would readily admit that the combative Durocher possessed "the most fertile ability to turn a bad situation into something infinitely worse," he was also coming to believe that Durocher had no peers as a baseball manager.

The world war was almost over. Victory in Europe, "V-E" Day, had been celebrated on May 8, 1945, and Branch Rickey felt that the defeat of Japan was imminent. It was nearing time for him to implement his daring new strategy at expanding the player pool in baseball to include players of color. Branch Rickey was convinced that Leo Durocher would be the best manager to lead the new player, whoever he might be, into the uncharted waters ahead. More than in any situation Branch Rickey ever faced in baseball, there would be "trouble ahead, trouble ahead," but he felt prepared for any eventuality and excited about a historic opportunity in the making.

1. (*Left*) Branch Rickey enjoys the pleasures of a fungo bat as manager of the St. Louis Browns, c. 1914. Photo by Charles Conlon. National Baseball Hall of Fame Library, Cooperstown NY.

2. (*Below*) Three prides of St. Louis: Cardinals owner Sam Breadon, future Hall of Fame second baseman Rogers Hornsby, and business and field manager Branch Rickey, c. 1923–1924. National Baseball Hall of Fame Library, Cooperstown NY.

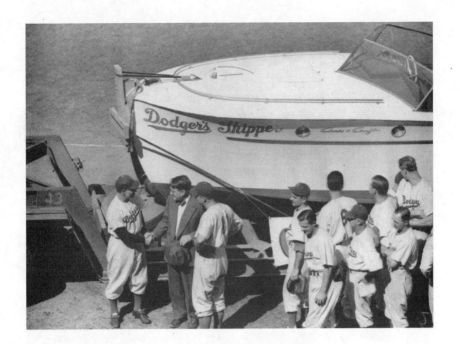

3. (*Opposite top*) Paternal Branch Rickey reads
a story to his granddaughters Nancy (left) and
Caroline Rickey (right), late 1930s. Sporting
News ZUMA Press.

4. (*Opposite bottom*) The gentleman chicken
farmer with one of his prize flock, late 1930s.
AP/Wide World Photos.

5. (*Above*) Dodgers outfielder Dixie Walker
(left) presents Branch Rickey with a gift from
the players, a forty-foot cabin cruiser, before a
game at Brooklyn's Ebbets Field, September
25, 1946. Manager Leo Durocher is on
Rickey's left. Photo by John Lindsay. AP/Wide
World Photos.

6. (*Above*) Rickey and Durocher sign the nose cone of the
Dodgers' team plane in spring training, c. 1947. Behind Rickey
from left to right are Florida state representative Merrill Barber,
Florida governor Millard Caldwell, and Dodgers co-owner
Walter O'Malley. To the left of Durocher, wearing uniform
number 1, is Dodgers shortstop Harold "Pee Wee" Reese.
Courtesy of Walter J. Skiscim.

7. (*Opposite top*) A dark day in Brooklyn, April 9, 1947: Leo
Durocher (second from left) gets word of his yearlong
suspension from baseball as members of the team board of
directors, Walter O'Malley (left), John L. Smith (center), Judge
Henry Ughetta, and Branch Rickey (right), look on. AP/Wide
World Photos.

8. (*Opposite bottom*) Rickey (center) at a Vero Beach airport with
Dodgers executive Fresco Thompson (second from left), and
Bud Holman (second from right), member of the Dodgers
board of directors and local aviation executive, c. 1949.
Courtesy of Walter J. Skiscim.

9. (*Opposite top*) Connie Mack, patriarchal owner of the
Philadelphia Athletics, with Branch Rickey and Vero Beach
mayor Alex MacWilliam, c. 1949. Although Mack was
vigorously opposed to Rickey's program of baseball integration,
the two remained good friends and likeminded baseball
developers. Courtesy of Walter J. Skiscim.

10. (*Opposite bottom*) Dodgers fans, players, and team officials
at the Hotel St. George in Brooklyn for the October 7, 1949,
dinner honoring two pennant winners, the 1916 Dodgers and
the 1949 Dodgers. Rickey is seated third from right, behind the
microphone at back. Unfortunately, two days later, the Dodgers
lost the 1949 World Series to the Yankees in five games.
Courtesy of Walter J. Skiscim.

11. (*Above*) Branch Rickey (left) with his friend Lowell
Thomas, radio broadcaster and world traveler, c. 1949. Rickey
was at times a guest and substitute host on his fellow Christian
activist's radio shows. Historical Society of Quaker Hill and
Pawling NY.

12. (*Opposite top*) Walter O'Malley (standing) takes over from
Branch Rickey (left) as Brooklyn Dodgers president, October
26, 1950. AP/Wide World Photos.

13. (*Opposite bottom*) Branch Rickey and some of his Pittsburgh
Pirates staff, spring training early 1950s. Rickey is at the far
left; the others are (left to right) Rex Bowen, Clyde Sukeforth,
Bill Burwell, Fred Haney, Sam Narron, and Lamar Dorton.
Special Collections and University Archives, Rutgers University
Libraries.

14. (*Above*) Branch Rickey (left) and Rutgers philosophy
professor Houston Peterson (center), Pittsburgh Pirates spring
training, 1954. Rickey was returning a favor after the polymathic
professor had invited the executive to speak at the university
two years earlier. The players (left to right) are Frank Thomas,
Sid Gordon, and Gene Hermanski. Special Collections and
University Archives, Rutgers University Libraries.

15. (*Above*) Branch Rickey (right) and Jackie Robinson, recently retired from baseball and active in civil rights work, at an NAACP dinner, New York City, November 22, 1957. AP/Wide World Photos.

16. (*Opposite top*) The ferocious gentleman in studio portrait repose, 1962, not long before getting back into harness as a St. Louis Cardinals consultant. Yale Divinity School.

17. (*Opposite bottom*) Branch Rickey (left) and fellow Ohio Wesleyan alumnus Reverend Dr. Ralph Sockman discuss plans for a new building at the International Christian University in Japan, December 8, 1964. The two men had promised each other that each would speak at the other's funeral. A year and four days later Sockman eulogized Rickey at St. Louis's Grace Methodist Episcopal Church. Yale Divinity School.

18. Jane Rickey accepts her husband's
posthumous plaque at the Baseball Hall
of Fame in Cooperstown, New York, July
1967. The other honorees are Yankees
pitcher Red Ruffing (left) and Pirates
outfielder Lloyd Waner (right). Courtesy
of Ruth Mann Stoecker.

16

The Secret Path to the "Young Man from the West"

When, shortly after his arrival in Brooklyn, Branch Rickey began scouting players of color, he initially considered the Latin American countries to be the major source of talent. As usual, the persuasive executive was able to enlist a wide variety of people in his important cause, making sure, however, that he kept secret his main motive: breaking the color line in the Major Leagues. He asked his old friend and fraternity brother Robert M. Haig, a Columbia University professor of political economy, to keep an eye on talent in South America. He enlisted a new friend, Jose Seda, a young New York University physical education graduate student, to keep him abreast of talent in Seda's native Puerto Rico. Rickey also sent one of his top professional scouts, Tom Greenwade, to Mexico to evaluate carefully infielder Silvio Garcia, whom Rickey had seen playing for the New York Cubans in the American Negro Leagues and whom Leo Durocher had raved about after seeing him play in the Cuban winter leagues. Brooklyn's manager even compared Garcia to Rogers Hornsby.[1]

Sometime in 1943 Greenwade turned in a negative report on the dark-skinned, Cuban-born Garcia. The right-handed-hitting shortstop couldn't pull the ball and was too much of a cutup, Greenwade cabled Rickey in a secret code that never identified a player by name. "He'd stick his head out over the dugout and the Mexican fans would throw limes at him," Greenwade recalled.[2] Rickey soon realized that the Latin American players might have a language barrier to cope with as well as the color line, so he directed his attention to scouting American players of color.

There was ample opportunity to appraise American black players during the war because many wartime exhibitions were being played between Negro League players and white Major Leaguers in the service. Rickey assigned Greenwade and other key scouts—Wid Matthews, George Sisler, and Clyde Sukeforth—to observe these games and write up reports on every player. The executive had seen many of the great stars of the Negro Leagues perform, including slugging catcher Josh Gibson and the age-less Satchel Paige. In a homage to legendary Pittsburgh Pirates shortstop Honus Wagner in *The American Diamond*, Rickey wrote: "Only one man in my acquaintance was more devoted to baseball or cared less about anything else—Satchel Paige."[3]

However, the executive doubted whether Gibson and Paige, at their advanced baseball age (the catcher was over thirty, and the pitcher might have been closer to forty), could contribute to the Major Leagues when the opportunity arose. Physically, they could probably compete well, Rickey thought, but he questioned whether either could handle the enormous mental pressure of breaking the color line in baseball. Paige's lifestyle was independent and libertine—"I'm not married, but I'm in demand," he once said blithely—and he was notoriously unreli-able about appearing on time for games. Josh Gibson also led the life of the wandering ballplayer, vulnerable to bodily temptations. His off-field life was "not encouraging," Rickey told sportswriter Arthur Mann, who had become his close friend in Brooklyn and who, in October 1946, would join his staff as special assistant.[4] (Gibson would die in January 1947 at age thirty-five.)

Branch Rickey was well aware of the growing movement in the United States for equal rights for people of color. He knew that A. Philip Ran-dolph, president of the Brotherhood of Railway Porters union, had threatened a march on Washington in June 1941 if President Frank-lin Roosevelt didn't sign an executive order banning discrimination in government hiring. Roosevelt complied, creating the Fair Employment Practices Commission (FEPC), and a proposed March on Washington, twenty-two years before the demonstration led by the Reverend Dr. Mar-tin Luther King Jr., was called off. Rickey had noted with concern the wartime race riots in New York, Philadelphia, and Detroit, and was dis-tressed when, on June 22, 1943, the Detroit Tigers even had to postpone a game because of racial disturbances close to Briggs Stadium.[5]

Branch Rickey understood that with a world war being raged against an enemy who believed in the superiority of the white Aryan race, the continued example of race discrimination in the United States was, at best, an embarrassment to the American war effort and, at worst, a policy of indefensible, sustained injustice. Early in 1944 Gunnar Myrdal's pioneering study of race in the United States, *An American Dilemma,* was published, highlighting in definitive detail the failure of white America to apply its great creed of equality and democracy to black Americans. Myrdal's thesis received animated discussion at the Rickey family dinner table and among his friends.[6]

Yet for all his genuine indignation at race discrimination, Rickey remained a very conservative man, fearful of any leftist, collectivist, or—worst of all—Communist agitation of the race issue. It was acceptable for Rickey that the non-Communist, black weekly newspaper, the *Pittsburgh Courier,* had been leading the crusade for integration in baseball since the mid-1930s. Once the United States entered World War II, Rickey had applauded the *Courier's* pithy "Double V" slogan, victory over fascism abroad and racism at home, and by the end of the war he would grow close to sportswriter Wendell Smith, one of the *Courier's* most ardent advocates for integration.

It was the input of the Communist newspaper the *Daily Worker* in the integration crusade that disturbed the extremely anti-Communist Rickey. Since the late 1930s *Worker* sports editor Nat Low and sports reporter Lester Rodney had regularly made a point of asking baseball owners and players what they thought about stars of the Negro Leagues playing in the white Major Leagues. In 1941 Rodney asked Leo Durocher the question, and the outspoken Brooklyn manager replied, "Hell, yes! I'd sign them in a minute if I got permission from the big shots."[7] Not surprisingly, baseball commissioner Kenesaw Mountain Landis was not pleased with Leo's comment and called him on the carpet, telling him that it was not the field manager's purview to make comments on overall baseball policy. Landis disingenuously continued to reiterate that there was no such thing as a color line in baseball and that the owners could sign any qualified players they wished.

(Although Branch Rickey was vehemently opposed to the ideology of Communism, he always maintained a human interest in people, regardless of their political views. "He probably hated the very idea of a communist covering the Dodgers from 'his' press box," Lester Rodney remembers, but Rickey treated the journalist professionally. One day, when the Ebbets Field press box elevator was broken, Rodney recalls that all the writers and team officials had to walk upstairs on an old spiral staircase. "It came to pass that Rickey was climbing those circling steps and I was the next one ascending," Rodney remembers. "About halfway up, he paused, panting a little, looked down at me and said, 'Well, young man, there's more than one way to heaven.'")[8]

As World War II continued, the issue of integrating baseball would not die. Bowing to pressure from Nat Low and Wendell Smith, Pittsburgh Pirates owner William Benswanger in the summer of 1943 invited Baltimore Elite Giants catcher Roy Campanella and New York Cubans pitcher Dave Barnhill to a tryout. However, his offer had so many qualifications—"You would have to start at the bottom . . . the pay would be low"—that Campanella never got his hopes up.[9] His skepticism was well founded because, bowing to pressure from the other owners, Benswanger, son-in-law of the late Pittsburgh owner Barney Dreyfuss, canceled the invitation.

Similarly, a proposed workout in front of Clark Griffith, owner of the Washington Senators, never materialized. Griffith, who had managed Branch Rickey on the Highlanders in 1907, had said that he would not object to looking at two stars of the Homestead Grays of the Negro National League, Josh Gibson and first baseman Walter "Buck" Leonard (the so-called "black Lou Gehrig"). The Grays played some of their home games at Griffith Stadium, as well as at Pittsburgh's Forbes Field, but once again, because of pressure within the ownership fraternity, Griffith backed off and never scheduled a tryout. Not only were almost all baseball owners racially conservative, but it was also in their short-term economic interest to maintain the status quo. Griffith and Benswanger were among several Major League owners earning fees of approximately $100,000 from Negro League teams, who rented their stadiums while the white Major League teams were on the road. Conservative racial attitudes and the bottom line of economics thus posed a formidable obstacle to racial integration.[10]

Baseball's annual meetings were held in New York in December 1943, and Paul Robeson, a world-renowned black singer, actor, and social activist, was invited to address the owners. Currently starring on Broadway in the title role in Shakespeare's *Othello*, Robeson made an eloquent speech to the moguls. "They said that America never would stand for my playing Othello with a white cast, but it is the triumph of my life," the gifted performer said, concluding with a plea that the owners sign black baseball players and fulfill the promise of American democracy.[11]

Before the meeting Landis had instructed the owners to refrain from asking Robeson any questions about integration. The commissioner's strategy was simple: let him speak, and then let him go away in silence. The baseball leaders thought the tactic a wise one, and all complied. Two black sportswriters, Wendell Smith and Sam Lacy, were very disappointed at the lack of discussion at the owners' meeting. Both were integration minded, and Lacy, soon to become a prominent writer on the *Baltimore Afro-American*, thought that Robeson's involvement in left-wing politics and unfamiliarity with the contemporary sports scene would make it easy for the owners to ignore the issue.[12] (A quarter century earlier Robeson had been an all-American football player at Rutgers University.)

It must have been hard for voluble Branch Rickey not to make a comment of some kind to Paul Robeson, but the activist's name was increasingly linked to anticapitalist organizations and he had recently lived in the Soviet Union. Although Rickey accepted the current political reality that the Soviet Union was a necessary ally in World War II against the greater evil of Nazi Germany, he was always profoundly distrustful of supporters of atheistic communism in any guise in any country.

Rickey considered Paul Robeson's story the sad tale of a man whose harsh experience of racism had so corroded him that he lost faith in the American system. "He can say anything he pleases in this country about his government or anybody or anything, and still be asked to play Othello on the New York stage," Rickey noted years later. "In Russia, he could not say a word against totalitarian controls without getting a ticket to Siberia. But Robeson didn't think of this. He was hurting too badly."[13] As Rickey listened to Robeson speak to the owners at the end of 1943, the executive was more than ever convinced that the pioneer in breaking the color line would have to show by stoic example that the American system worked, if only every person were given a fair chance to succeed.

Although Branch Rickey disapproved of lily-white baseball, he shrewdly understood that the stand-pat, reactionary nature of the owners could be used to his advantage as he mapped out the proper strategy for integrating baseball. "You have two years to stay ahead of your competition when you come up with a new idea in baseball," Rickey liked to say. The notion had proven true with the farm system, and he was proud of being the first man to develop his own players inexpensively. He was flattered that most other teams were now copying his idea.

For his second great baseball revolution, Rickey understandably wanted to be the first to mine the vast, untapped market of black talent and to sign the best players for the Dodgers. Given his natural inclination toward convolution and indirection, and his accurate assessment of the explosive social repercussions sure to follow, he felt that he must keep his scouting of black players a secret, except from his family. After he had found the right black player to be the race pioneer and had signed others of great skill, he fully expected the Dodgers would be contenders and champions for years to come. "I will happily bear being called a bleeding heart, and a do-gooder, and all that humanitarian rot," he chortled to Dodgers road secretary Harold Parrott.[14]

Yet there was more than an unashamed economic motive and a baseball businessman's competitive zeal in Branch Rickey's signing black players. There was also a genuine Wesleyan Methodist conscience at work. One of his favorite litanies went, "The Negro has never been really free in this country. Legally free since the Civil War yes, but not politically or socially free, and never morally free."

There were many revealing signs of Branch Rickey's racial conscience during his years in St. Louis. One day in the early 1930s Rickey was in a courthouse with his teenaged daughter Jane, helping her appeal a traffic ticket. He overheard a judge in another courtroom, berating a black defendant on trial for murder. "Dad walked right over and busted right in on the grilling," Jane Rickey Jones told Jackie Robinson biographer David Falkner. "He just didn't want to see the guy mistreated. . . . He wound up giving the guy his card and . . . hired him as a chauffeur!"[15]

When he gave his frequent talks at the John Burroughs prep school in St. Louis, the charismatic baseball leader always made a point of stressing the value of sports to a just and democratic society. Bill Turner, a Burroughs student who first met Rickey at a Boy Scout jamboree in 1929, remembers that during one semester Branch Rickey Jr. spent time in the St. Louis black neighborhoods, writing up his observations and experiences as a school assignment. The project also became a subject for rousing dinner-table discussion in the Rickey household.[16] Alan Henderson, a former mayor of Palo Alto, California, whose father was an Ohio Wesleyan roommate of Branch Rickey, remembers the Cardinals executive visiting his family during the 1930s and often talking about the great black athletes in the United States and how unfair it was that discrimination prevented them from having a chance to compete fully.[17]

When the Jackie Robinson signing was made public in October 1945, Rickey mentioned many times the story of coaching Charles "Tommy" Thomas, the black Ohio Wesleyan catcher who wept at the injustice of the color line, and how the idealistic executive vowed one day to eliminate discrimination. As we have seen, the Thomas story was true, but so are these other examples of Branch Rickey's genuine Christian commitment to racial fairness.

The Rickey family often made individual gestures of racial compassion. Frank Rickey, Branch's brother and a top baseball scout, helped pay the way for Octavius, a black man from North Carolina, to see the Cardinals play and win the 1942 World Series in New York. Helping to foot the bill was fellow North Carolinian Burgess Whitehead, the former Cardinals second baseman.[18] It would be up to Branch Rickey after the war to make an even grander individual gesture for the greater collective good.

As Branch Rickey waited for World War II to end, the question for him was not whether integration should occur in baseball, but when and how? He had applauded the recent achievements of black athletes in individual sports. He had hailed sprinter Jesse Owens's great success at the 1936 Berlin Olympics, when he won four gold medals under the sneering, disbelieving nose of Chancellor Adolf Hitler, showing the world the ludicrous nature of the Nazi Germany master-race theory. In 1937 Joe Louis became the heavyweight boxing champion of the world, dethroning James Braddock in a fight in Chicago, which, incidentally, Rickey attended.[19] In 1938 Louis avenged his only loss with a savage one-round knockout of German Max Schmeling, inflicting another blow to Aryan superiority. While living in St. Louis Rickey witnessed many of the thrilling bouts of "Hammerin'" Henry Armstrong, who would hold an unprecedented three legitimate world boxing titles at the same time in the late 1930s (featherweight, lightweight, and welterweight). Most knowledgeable sports observers thought that, except for a bad decision by boxing judges, Armstrong would have won the middleweight title too.[20]

However, track and field and boxing were individual sports, and Rickey pondered deeply the question of how best to bring a black player into the team sport of baseball, where he must be a teammate as well as an individual star. A start certainly had been made in football, where college teams had been integrated with some success since the late 1920s. By the late 1930s the University of California in Los Angeles (UCLA) featured a backfield that was three-fourths black: Kenny Washington, Woody Strode (who would later become a film actor, appearing in *Spartacus*, among other films), and someone named Jackie Robinson, an all-around athlete who also starred in track and field, basketball, and (probably his weakest sport) baseball.

Although Branch Rickey continued to miss living in the Midwest, he realized that he could never have pioneered signing a black player in St. Louis, the southernmost city in the Major Leagues. Racial segregation was enforced at Sportsman's Park until May 1944, and when Rickey lived in St. Louis the sportswriters would at times refer in print to black people as "darkies." ("1939 holds more promises than a Dixie darkey paying off the dining room furniture on the installment plan" is one of the more jarring examples.)[21] In Brooklyn, a borough of proud ethnicities and genuine sports passions, Rickey thought there was a far better chance of succeeding in what soon became known as, and what he liked to call, "the great experiment."

In February 1944 Rickey addressed a Brooklyn Rotary Club with some general thoughts on the race situation in America and the prospects for bringing black players into the big leagues. He stressed that the strategy for integration must be a cautious one, and, as always, he warned against radical race agitators who wanted to achieve their ends by force. Rickey drew on the analogy of Prohibition, which he had experienced firsthand and which, he concluded with a saddened heart, had done more harm than good for the antialcohol cause. Although he had been serving since 1936 on the Methodist Church's Board of Temperance, Prohibition, and Public Morals, the Brooklyn president was aware that organized crime had been the great beneficiary of Prohibition and that many innocent people had died as a result of the gang wars and the effects of bad bootleg alcohol. (Rickey, of course, had not forgotten that his own brother had been almost killed in the line of duty as a Prohibition marshal in the 1920s and had to stand trial before he was acquitted of murdering a bootlegger.)

If the wrong player or players were picked to racially integrate baseball, Rickey warned the Rotarians, the cause of integration could be set back for generations, just as Prohibition had seriously weakened the temperance movement. As Carl Rowan, one of Jackie Robinson's best biographers, has perceptively noted, Branch Rickey and other baseball people "were afraid a Negro baseball star would find himself besieged by white women eager to give him their affections. The image of Jack Johnson and his three white wives was always before them." Rowan added that Rickey was seeking a "clean-living family man whose character was above reproach."[22] (Jack Johnson, the first black heavyweight champion, flaunted his libertine lifestyle before World War I, resulting in the passage of national legislation, the Mann Act, designed to prosecute him for allegedly traveling with minors across state lines.)

Meanwhile, Branch Rickey's optimism about the ultimate Allied victory was proving true, though neither he nor anyone else really knew how long it would take. In hindsight World War Two reached what would be the beginning of the end on June 6, 1944, with the D-day invasion of France by several hundred American warships, more than ten thousand aircraft, and almost two hundred thousand men. To honor the importance of the day, Major League Baseball postponed all regularly scheduled games on June 6, 1944, and most Minor Leagues did the same. "I have two sons over there," Rickey's friend Frank Shaughnessy, president of the International League, spoke for most people in the sport. "I am not much interested in baseball today."[23]

A few months later, in November 1944, two momentous domestic events affected Branch Rickey's life as a citizen and baseball executive. On Election Day, President Franklin Delano Roosevelt won an unprecedented fourth term, outpolling New York Republican governor Thomas Dewey by fewer than 3 million votes. It was the four-term president's smallest margin of victory, but Branch Rickey was again disappointed by the Republican loss. It was not just that Dewey's running mate was Rickey's friend Ohio governor John Bricker but also because, on the race issue, Rickey believed that the Republican party was more open to change than the Democrats, who had to cater to the outright racist beliefs of their southern wing. By contrast the Republican Party platform endorsed continuing the FEPC and stated in words dear to Branch Rickey's heart: "No problem exists that cannot be solved by American methods. We have no need of either the communistic or fascist technique."[24]

The significant event in Rickey's baseball life occurred on November 25, 1944, when baseball commissioner Kenesaw Mountain Landis died at age seventy-eight. Rickey told reporters that Landis's greatest legacy had been restoring the public's trust after the Black Sox scandal. He added that it would be hard to find someone "as rigid and strong" to replace Landis.[25] Privately, however, Rickey was thinking that one obstacle to his integration plan was now removed. He realized that Landis, a fierce opponent of his farm system, would surely have tried to find a way to oppose his second baseball revolution, breaking the color line and being the first to do it and thus get a head start on the best players.

Yet Rickey was well aware that Landis's enforcement of the color ban was not simply the commissioner's personal prejudice but a reflection of the views of most of the baseball owners, who were not about to rock the boat of traditional American social mores. Rickey was very conservative too in his belief in God, mother, country, and Americanism. However, he also knew that change was the engine of a successful capitalist system, and he was impatiently awaiting the end of the war and the opportunity to open up the baseball business to deserving new black talent. He understood, though, that something more than a new, pro-integration commissioner in baseball would be needed to engineer the change. He believed that some impetus from forces outside baseball would be needed to start the ball rolling.

On the morning of March 13, 1945, Branch Rickey was drinking his coffee and reading the newspaper in his spring training lodging at Bear Mountain. Suddenly, he looked up from his paper with an animated expression on his face. "What's wrong, dear?" Jane Rickey asked her husband, wondering what now was bothering her easily agitated mate. "It says in the paper, Mother, that Governor Dewey has just signed the Ives-Quinn Law!" he exclaimed. "They can't stop me now!"[26] And in a twinkling the ferocious gentleman was out of the door and on his way to the practice fields.

The Ives-Quinn Law was indeed a major breakthrough in legislation against racial discrimination. Slated to take effect in July 1945, the new law was cosponsored by New York State Assembly majority leader (and future U.S. Senator) Irving M. Ives, an upstate Republican, and State Senate minority leader Elmer Quinn, a New York City Democrat. It would impose a fine of $500 or a jail term up to a year on employers who refused to hire anyone for reasons of race.[27] The Ives-Quinn Law established a New York State Commission Against Discrimination, which took its lead from the federal Fair Employment Practices Commission.

Knowing that he now had state law on his side, Rickey turned to another part of the groundwork he was laying for his still-secret project, bringing Dodgers radio broadcaster Red Barber into his confidence. In late March 1945 the Brooklyn team president invited Barber to a quiet lunch at Joe's restaurant, a favorite downtown Brooklyn hangout of Dodgers officials. Since 1939, when Larry MacPhail brought Barber to Brooklyn from Cincinnati to broadcast Dodger games, the "Ol' Redhead" had become an indispensable part of the Brooklyn baseball community. His gentle southern accent and his use of such colorful expressions as "tearing up the pea patch," "the bases are FOB, Full Of Brooklyns," "sitting in the catbird seat," and "Oh, doctor!" had brought him a large following among Brooklyn fans, who knew original language when they heard it. Barber's broadcasts were often so riveting that many people switched from listening to radio soap operas to following Brooklyn Dodgers baseball story lines.

As would-be teachers and professors, Branch Rickey and Red Barber shared much in common. If the Great Depression hadn't made jobs in academia hard to find, Red Barber might well have become an English literature professor. Branch Rickey was always attracted to lively, intellectual, and religious people like Barber, who was involved in church activities and charitable causes. Barber helped out in Rickey's war bond

drives, and Barber enlisted Rickey to speak on behalf of American Red
Cross blood drives in Brooklyn. (Before the war, Barber recalled, it was
"an unwritten law not to say 'blood' on the air.")[28] The Barber-Rickey
friendship grew deeper through their patriotic service in time of war.

As Rickey planned his racial integration program, he understood that
Barber's broadcast voice would be a vital asset in the successful acceptance of a black ballplayer in the Major Leagues. However, he knew that
his broadcaster was a native of the South, a railroad man's son who was
born in Columbus, Mississippi, moved to Sanford, Florida, when he was
ten, and attended the University of Florida in Gainesville. Regardless of
Barber's fine education Rickey sensed that his broadcaster had the same
prejudices as the southern ballplayers, who made up more than a third
of the Major League rosters. Growing up in southern Ohio, near the border states of Kentucky and West Virginia, Rickey had been reared among
people with racial prejudice. Still, the baseball executive believed in reason and fairness, and he had once again hung in his office in Brooklyn
the framed saying of Scottish philosopher William Henry Drummond:
"He who will not reason is a bigot, he who cannot reason is a fool, and
he who dares not to reason is a slave." Rickey was convinced he could use
reason in winning over Walter "Red" Barber to his daring plan.

Rickey almost always addressed his employees by their given Christian
names, and he had plenty to confide to Walter at their private lunch in
late March 1945. "The stage lost an actor of consummate skill and range
when Rickey cast his lot with baseball," Barber wrote, recalling the momentous meeting with Rickey in his book *1947—When All Hell Broke Loose
in Baseball.* "He didn't talk like anybody you'd ever talked with. He was a
formidable man, a strong man, an intelligent man. And he knew it."[29]

Barber listened intently as Rickey filled him in on his top-secret search
for the right kind of black player and his unforgettable experience with
Charley Thomas at Ohio Wesleyan. Rickey's last words to the broadcaster
made the most impact, Barber recalled: "'I don't know who he is, or
where he is, but,' and he said very slowly, very intently, very positively, 'he
is coming.'"[30]

When Red Barber went home that night to discuss Rickey's plans with
his wife, Lylah, he felt certain that he would have to resign. He believed
that he could not broadcast fairly the exploits of a black man on a field

equal with whites. Every thing in his background was geared to believing that the black man should be in a subordinate place. Although he didn't consider himself a racist, Barber had seen the robes of Ku Klux Klansmen in his youth and knew about the harsh penalties inflicted on black people who did not know their place. Like most southerners, and like many people in the North, too, Barber simply did not question the unspoken code against racial equality.

Lylah Barber was another native of the Deep South. In fact, her family had been slaveholders who had been reduced to poverty after the Civil War. However, she knew that her husband liked his job, liked Brooklyn, and liked working for Branch Rickey. "You don't have to quit tonight. You can do that tomorrow," she advised. ". . . Let's have a martini."[31] Lylah Barber, in effect, was following the advice of Branch Rickey's grandfather Ephraim Rickey, who always counseled "belly rest" before making a big decision.

After a good night's sleep Red Barber realized that he could be fair to anyone who performed on the playing field. He would just report what he saw on the field without prejudice. The broadcaster was reminded of the passage in *The Book of Common Prayer*, a late-sixteenth-century work from Elizabethan England that was one of his and Branch Rickey's favorite sources for inspiration: "and hast opened the eyes of the mind to behold things invisible and unseen."[32] Red Barber did not resign but instead prepared himself to broadcast and report, simply report, the momentous games of the years ahead.

Barely a week after Rickey's lunch with Red Barber, the tireless executive was confronted by a commotion at the Dodgers' Bear Mountain spring training camp. Ever the cautious revolutionary, Branch Rickey did not want surprises as he planned his bold program of racial integration. However, on the morning of Friday, April 6, 1945, he was hurriedly summoned from one of the practice fields to discover Joe Bostic, a Harlem sportswriter, camped out in his office. Bostic was demanding a tryout for two players from the Negro Leagues, Newark Eagles pitcher Terris McDuffie and New York Cubans first baseman Dave "Showboat" Thomas.

Neither McDuffie nor Thomas was considered a star player, and both were over age thirty, too old to be considered real prospects. Yet Joe Bostic was an activist, a longtime crusader for integration, who wrote for a newspaper funded by Harlem congressman Adam Clayton Powell, a firebrand in the civil rights cause. Bostic wanted to force the hand of the baseball establishment. He felt that the lordly Yankees wouldn't be interested in black players, nor would the rudderless Giants, so why not try the team of the underdog, the Dodgers? He evidently had earlier tried to see Rickey two times at his Brooklyn office but had been turned away, so he did the next best thing by coming to the spring training camp. If nothing else Bostic was assured of getting a back-page headline like the Sunday *Daily News*'s "Dodgers Try Out Negroes."[33]

Although the black journalist realized that McDuffie and Thomas were probably not of Major League caliber, he was friendly with them because they hailed from his hometown of Mobile, Alabama. They were also the only players, he later admitted, who were "willing to face the wrath of the man." Other Negro League players simply did not want to risk losing lucrative postseason Caribbean baseball opportunities by abandoning the existing Negro Leagues.[34]

For someone committed to a careful, methodical approach to integrating baseball, Branch Rickey was appalled and angered by Bostic's tactics. He also was repelled at the journalist's affiliation with a radical newspaper. Although the periodical was not directly associated with the communist movement, FBI director J. Edgar Hoover branded the *People's Weekly* "a very helpful transmission belt for the Communist Party."[35] Yet, despite Rickey's ferocious feelings against forceful agitation of the race issue, the executive was still a gentleman, and one always interested in new baseball talent. The man who had invited interned Japanese Americans to his tryout camps was not going to give the impression that he would turn away black players from his spring training camp. He invited McDuffie and Thomas to return the next day, and he pledged to evaluate their prospects.

On Saturday, April 7, 1945, in front of the watchful eyes of Branch Rickey and manager Leo Durocher, the pitcher and first baseman worked out for about an hour. Having played winter baseball in Cuba, McDuffie looked sharper than Thomas, even if his change-up was not slow enough, Rickey said. But their age was definitely against them. Afterward Rickey read Bostic the riot act, repeating what he had said before to more admiring audiences. "I am more for your cause than anybody else you know, but you are making a mistake using force," he declared. "You are defeating your own aims."[36]

April 1945 was a month bringing many harbingers of change. On April 12 Franklin D. Roosevelt died at his vacation home in Warm Springs, Georgia, ending the longest presidency in American history. Missourian Harry S. Truman became president at a time when World War II was almost won and racial ferment at home was growing. In another sign that the demands for racial equality were penetrating a baseball business usually impervious to change, on April 16, 1945, three players from the Negro Leagues—Cleveland Buckeyes outfielder Sam Jethroe, Philadelphia Stars infielder Marvin Williams, and Kansas City Monarchs shortstop Jackie Robinson—worked out at Fenway Park in front of Boston Red Sox officials. The tryout had been forced on the Red Sox in large part by the pressure of an activist local Boston assemblyman, Isadore Muchnick (no relation to the St. Louis sportswriter and wrestling promoter Sam Muchnick), and sportswriter Wendell Smith of the *Pittsburgh Courier,* whose newspaper paid the expenses of the three black players.[37]

All of the players performed well, especially Jackie Robinson, who peppered the "Green Monster," Fenway's short left-field wall, with line drives and hit well to all fields. Red Sox officials were polite to the black players and to Wendell Smith, but at the end of the session they basically told them, "Don't call us; we'll call you." The team never contacted them again, and the Boston Braves never even worked them out, as they had promised.

Jackie Robinson was fuming at being led on a wild goose chase. He had left the Kansas City Monarchs of the Negro American League to make the trip at the behest of Wendell Smith, who had become a friend when the *Pittsburgh Courier* did yeoman service in publicizing Robinson's 1944 court-martial at Fort Hood, Texas, for refusing to go to the back of a military bus. "Listen, Smith, this is why I hesitated to come," Robinson vented at his friend. "It burns me up to come 1,500 miles to have them give me the runaround."[38]

Robinson and the other black players headed back to their Negro League teams, who hadn't been thrilled at their departure in the first place. Significantly, however, Wendell Smith did not return immediately to Pittsburgh, detouring instead to Brooklyn for a meeting with Branch Rickey. When Smith had phoned the Dodgers president with the news that Jackie Robinson had excelled at the Boston tryout, Rickey invited him to his office. That the Brooklyn president wanted Smith to report on the Boston tryout in person indicated that the two men had already begun more than a passing acquaintanceship.

In the expanded edition of Jerome Holtzman's classic oral history of sports writing, *No Cheering in the Press Box*, Wendell Smith recalled Branch Rickey's reaction to Smith's report on the star of the Red Sox tryout. "Jackie Robinson! I knew he was an All-American football player and an All-American basketball player," Rickey exclaimed. "But I didn't know he played baseball."[39]

At their Brooklyn meeting Smith tried to size up the nature of Rickey's interest in Robinson. He had heard rumors that Rickey wanted to start a new black league, but perhaps there was something else in the mind of that intense, lively, bushy-browed executive sitting across from him, Smith thought. Certainly Rickey wasn't giving anything away, but the two men hit it off personally. They shared their love of baseball, probably making small talk about the thrilling 1934 World Series, in which Rickey's Gashouse Gang Cardinals had defeated Smith's hometown Tigers.

As Rickey came to know Wendell Smith better, he learned that the writer had been a star high school baseball player in Detroit who was deeply hurt when a white scholastic rival, Mike Tresh, was signed by the Chicago White Sox. Smith, victimized by the "gentleman's agreement," had been ignored by all the Major League teams and had decided to become a sportswriter on a mission to crusade against the injustice of the color line.[40]

The Brooklyn executive was impressed by the earnestness and ambition of the young black sportswriter. Although Rickey didn't exactly take Smith into his confidence at their first Brooklyn meeting, he certainly gave the journalist the impression that Jackie Robinson was a player the Dodgers were going to evaluate thoroughly. Because secrecy was still Rickey's operating procedure, the executive told Smith to use a code name in future discussions of Robinson, "The Young Man from the West."[41]

Soon thereafter, as Branch Rickey continued to plot secretly to find the best player to break the color line, baseball's ruling establishment made another gesture to respond to the rising calls for racial justice. On April 24, 1945, at the same meeting where the owners elected U.S. senator Albert Benjamin (A. B.) "Happy" Chandler (a Democrat from Kentucky) as the second commissioner in baseball history, the owners announced the formation of a four-man commission to investigate the possibilities of racial integration. Named to the committee as management representatives were Branch Rickey and Larry MacPhail, who had returned from the war in January 1945 to become president and co-owner of the Yankees. The other members of the committee were black sportswriter Sam Lacy and black Philadelphia magistrate Joseph Rainey, who had some experience as a Negro League administrator.[42]

Rickey was quite willing to serve on the committee while, of course, keeping secret his advanced private scouting program. Sam Lacy got the sense that the Brooklyn executive might be amenable to granting the existing Negro Leagues some kind of Minor League status, perhaps a special four-A ranking, to ease the transition to the Major Leagues. However, it soon became clear that Larry MacPhail had no real interest in having the committee meet and function successfully. According to Lacy's memoir, *Fighting for Fairness*, after a few unsuccessful attempts at getting the four members together, Rickey telephoned the Baltimore sportswriter. "I'm going to ask Larry if he would meet with us one more time," Rickey said. "If he gives me some excuse or just refuses, . . . we will just give up on him and let nature take its course."[43] In the middle of 1945, Sam Lacy did not know exactly what Branch Rickey meant by "let nature take its course," but the black journalist was becoming aware that the Brooklyn leader was one baseball management person who had a genuine interest in integration.

Then, on May 7, 1945, Rickey seemed to take at least a sideways step, perhaps even a backward one, in the movement toward racial equality. At a press conference in his Brooklyn office, Rickey made the surprise announcement that the Brooklyn Dodgers were sponsoring a team, the Brooklyn Brown Dodgers, that would be part of a new six-team Negro League to be called the United States League (USL). Beginning in June 1945 the Brown Dodgers would play a one hundred–game schedule against the five other cities in the league—Chicago, Detroit, Pittsburgh, Philadelphia, and Toledo. Standing alongside Rickey were the new league's president, Cleveland attorney John Shackleford, who had played in the Negro Leagues in the 1920s; Brown Dodgers manager Oscar Charleston, who in his playing days had been known as "the black Ty Cobb"; and USL vice president Augustus "Gus" Greenlee. Although John Shackleford was the nominal president, vice president Gus Greenlee was the driving force behind the new league, which had been chartered in December 1944, initially with franchises in Atlanta and St. Louis but soon replaced by Toledo and Brooklyn.[44]

In the remarkable, tumultuous history of the Negro Leagues, Gus Greenlee had been a major player. Born in Marion, North Carolina, in 1897, he arrived in Pittsburgh in 1916, part of the "Great Migration" of black Americans away from the tyrannies of the post–Civil War South. After seeing action in France during World War I and receiving a piece of shrapnel in his leg for his efforts, he returned to Pittsburgh. During the exciting ferment of the 1920s and 1930s, Greenlee made his fame and fortune in the "numbers" business, the illegal but very profitable private lottery operation that thrived in the black neighborhoods. The very definition of a high-living sportsman, Greenlee opened the Crawford Grill in the Hill district of Pittsburgh (immortalized in the plays of August Wilson), and it became one of the must-visit places for the national as well as local black sporting and entertainment elites.[45]

Gus Greenlee's baseball credentials were equally impressive. He was the inspiration behind the East-West Negro League All-Star Game, which made its debut in 1933, the same year that the white Major League "Midsummer Classic" had begun. Greenlee owned and operated one of the greatest teams in baseball history, black or white: the Pittsburgh Crawfords, featuring such stars as fleet outfielder and stolen base king James "Cool Papa" Bell, first baseman Buck Leonard, catcher Josh Gibson, and Satchel Paige. The Crawfords rented Forbes Field for their home games, but Greenlee grew indignant at the second-class treatment at the Pittsburgh Pirates' home park. Among other indignities the white management refused to allow the black players to use the showers, so Greenlee in 1932 built his own stadium, Greenlee Field, equipped with lights and seating capacity for nearly ten thousand fans.[46]

Unfortunately, the ballpark did not have a roof, and when Greenlee suffered business losses before World War Two, he had to sell the stadium, which soon was torn down. When business improved during the war, Greenlee tried to reenter the Negro Leagues but was rebuffed by black owners who feared his urge to dominate. A man who liked to be in charge, Greenlee decided to cast his lot with a third league.

It is not clear exactly when Greenlee first encountered another man who liked to be in charge, Branch Rickey. Nor can it be stated definitively whether Rickey knew that Greenlee was a numbers kingpin, but it is very likely that the astute Rickey was well aware of Greenlee's background. Two years before he died, Rickey told Jackie Robinson that he had spent $30,000 of Brooklyn money in "that racket colored league—that's what it was, pure racket."[47]

Yet, with Gus Greenlee at his side at the maiden press conference of the United States League in Brooklyn on May 7, 1945, Branch Rickey betrayed no sense of irony when he denounced the existing Negro American and Negro National Leagues as "organizations in the zone of a racket." He decried their lack of formal contracts with the players and the absence of a reserve clause that bound players to their teams and forced them to honor their obligations to perform. (Branch Rickey was always consistent about the need for a reserve clause in any kind of professional baseball.) The Brooklyn president also used the occasion to rail against the booking agents, who took exorbitant fees of up to 50 percent to schedule the Negro League teams at the established white ballparks.[48]

One of the most singular and outspoken Negro League owners, Effa Manley of the Newark Eagles, a white woman who chose to pass for black, attended the press conference and fired angry questions at Rickey. "Why didn't you try to enter our league instead of forming a new one?" Manley demanded. Rickey deferred the question to President Shackleford, who answered honestly that the existing leagues had spurned any meetings with the new circuit.[49]

Although the established leagues in both white and black baseball greeted the formation of the USL with great skepticism, in May 1945 Branch Rickey and Gus Greenlee had a genuine mutual interest. Greenlee was happy to be back in baseball and talked of creating an enterprise where black players could be trained to soon enter the Major Leagues. In sponsoring the Brown Dodgers, Rickey now had an above-board reason to scout black ballplayers without the need for code words and suspicion from his fellow owners.

After the announcement of the United States League, Branch Rickey sat back and enjoyed the peevish and unsuspecting reactions to the new league. Washington Senators owner Clark Griffith, who earned important rental fees from the Homestead Grays, dismissed Rickey's ploy as a belated grab to gain rental monies for himself. "Mr. Rickey is attempting to destroy two well-organized leagues which have been in existence for some time and in which colored people of this country have faith and confidence," Griffith said.[50] From another viewpoint black activists for integration were furious at Rickey for seemingly becoming another plantation overseer. Ludlow Werner of the *New York Age* exclaimed: "Did you ever hear such double talk from a big pompous ass in your life? I predict that it'll be a cold day in hell when that big windbag puts a Negro in a Brooklyn uniform."[51] The six-team United States League barely lasted a full season, expiring before the end of 1946, but it certainly served its role as a smokescreen for disguising Branch Rickey's ultimate purpose.

With the announcement of the USL, Rickey's scouts could now openly evaluate black players, and by the early summer of 1945 most of Rickey's key scouts had watched Jackie Robinson play with the Kansas City Monarchs. All filed positive reports, with some reservations. George Sisler was impressed with Robinson's speed, passion, and athletic intelligence but doubted that he possessed the arm strength to play shortstop in the Major Leagues. Mississippian Wid Matthews had his reservations about Robinson's demeanor on the field. He was too much of a "hot dog" in his mannerisms, the scout believed, but he thought he was superb at protecting the plate with two strikes on him. Tom Greenwade thought Robinson was the best bunter he had ever seen.[52]

Rickey soon learned that Robinson's overall athletic credentials, beyond his football stardom, were truly remarkable. For a black man in the age of segregation, Robinson was already an athletic legend in Southern California. *Los Angeles Examiner* sportswriter Vincent X. Flaherty had dubbed Robinson "the Jim Thorpe of his race," comparing him to the great Native American athlete of the early twentieth century who won

track and field gold medals at the Olympics and played professional baseball and football. Duke Snider, who would become Robinson's teammate
in Brooklyn, grew up in Southern California, and he and his friends were
awed by Robinson's athletic exploits. At UCLA the talented athlete let-
tered in football, basketball, track and field, and baseball. He was good
enough in track to set a National Collegiate Athletic Association record
in the broad jump, and there were times when he left a baseball game to
compete in a track event and then rushed back to the diamond. Speed
and power ran in the Robinson family; his older brother, Mack, won a silver medal at the 1936 Berlin Olympics, finishing second to Jesse Owens
in the 200-meter sprint.[53]

From reports provided by Wendell Smith and by his own sources in
Southern California, Branch Rickey was also thoroughly investigating
the personal character of Robinson. The executive was aware that some
West Coast sportswriters had been critical of the black athlete's constant assertion of his constitutional rights and having what one called
"a genius for getting into extra-curricular scrapes."[54] Rickey was aware
of Robinson's military court-martial in 1944 but knew that he had been
acquitted. The wily, idealistic executive understood that what sportswriters might call an "uppity" attitude in black players would be praised
as admirable aggressiveness in white players. He considered Robinson's
passion for his race a major plus as he sought the best candidate to
break the color line.

The ferocious gentleman was becoming very eager to meet Jackie Robinson. Robinson's success in team sports bode well for his future, the
executive thought, because he evidently knew how to compete without
fear against and alongside white players. Above all, however, Rickey was
insistent that the pioneer chosen to break the color line would have to
be not only an exceptional athlete but also a disciplined, strong-willed
person, keeping the larger goal of equality of opportunity for an entire
race in mind.

In August 1945 the time was finally ripe for Rickey to move toward
the climax of his secret scouting project. On August 14, 1945, eight days
after American planes dropped the first atomic bomb on Hiroshima
(and five days after the dropping of the second bomb on Nagasaki), the
Japanese formally sued for peace. Rickey sighed with deep relief. The

Second World War was at last over, and for Branch Rickey, who had never doubted the successful outcome of the war, it was now time to accelerate plans for his next contribution to baseball history—and indeed American history. He set about preparing for the most momentous job interview he would ever conduct in his long, event-filled baseball career.

17

An Historic Meeting in Brooklyn

Shortly after V-J Day Branch Rickey called Clyde Sukeforth into his Brooklyn office. Sukeforth, a taciturn native of Maine, was one of the most trusted members of Rickey's inner circle. A former backup Major League catcher, he played for ten seasons in the Major Leagues before his career was curtailed because of a hunting accident. He retired with a .264 BA and .331 SA in 1,237 at-bats, and by the 1940s he had become a valuable jack-of-all-trades for the Dodgers as scout, pitching coach, Minor League instructor, and manager. Earlier in the 1945 season, at age forty-three, Sukeforth had even caught some games for the Dodgers when Leo Durocher's squad was strapped for healthy bodies.

Of all Rickey's evaluators Sukeforth was the only one who had yet to see Jackie Robinson in action. To get another independent viewpoint about the player's abilities and limitations, Rickey told him to go to Chicago, where Robinson would be playing for the Kansas City Monarchs against the Chicago Lincoln Giants. Knowing George Sisler's reservation that Robinson might not have a Major League shortstop's arm, Rickey advised Sukeforth to carefully observe his throwing. "If you like what you see, Clyde, bring him back with you to Brooklyn," Rickey said. "If he can't get away from his team, well, maybe I will come out and see him." The scout made a mental note that if Branch Rickey would be willing to travel to Chicago to see the player in person, his own mission was not merely about looking to sign a prospect for the Brooklyn Brown Dodgers. "This could be the real thing," Sukeforth thought.[1]

On August 24, 1945, Sukeforth arrived at Comiskey Park in Chicago and introduced himself to Robinson as a scout for Mr. Branch Rickey, who was running the Brooklyn Brown Dodgers of the new United States League. Sukeforth said that Mr. Rickey was interested in him and would like to evaluate his throwing arm. Robinson had scarcely heard of Branch Rickey and was understandably suspicious of strangers peddling him baseball stories (as he had discovered at the bogus Boston Red Sox tryout). Anyway, he was injured, having hurt his shoulder stumbling on the ground going into the shortstop hole, and would be unable to play for a few days. "Don't make a regular throw," Sukeforth told Robinson. "Just field a fungo grounder and make an underhand toss to first."[2] The player consented to make a few throws from shortstop to the scout, who, dressed in street clothes, caught the tosses at first base. Since Robinson couldn't play for about a week, Rickey's emissary invited him to come to Brooklyn to meet his boss.

Robinson did not know what to make of Sukeforth's proposition, but he accepted the scout's invitation to get more acquainted at Sukeforth's hotel after the Negro League game. As they entered Chicago's Stevens Hotel late that evening, Sukeforth slipped a little money to the elevator operator to allow Robinson to accompany him in the passenger elevator and not endure the indignity of having to use the freight elevator.[3] As they began to get to know each other, Sukeforth was immediately impressed by Robinson's intelligence, directness, and seriousness. The scout asked him about his army experience, and Robinson mentioned that an old football ankle injury contributed to his discharge but that it posed no problem in playing baseball.

Sukeforth told Robinson that he was heading out on another scouting trip to Toledo, but that if the player were interested, he should meet him in Toledo and they would go to Brooklyn together. Injured, and not thrilled at the chaotic conditions in the Negro Leagues, where he had been playing only since April, Robinson agreed. He told Monarchs manager Frank Duncan that he had to go away on a private business matter. Duncan had not been happy when his shortstop left to try out for the Red Sox in April and was less pleased now, but since he couldn't really stop the player from going, he just urged him to return to the Monarchs as soon as possible.

Robinson met Sukeforth at the Toledo ballpark, and after the game the two men headed for the train station. The scout asked for two seats together in the same Pullman sleeper car. "Yes, together," Sukeforth told the ticket seller. At daybreak Sukeforth asked Robinson if he wanted to have breakfast, but the player said that "he'd eat with the boys," meaning the Pullman porters.[4] When they arrived in New York, Sukeforth went to a hotel in Brooklyn and Robinson went to the Theresa Hotel on 125th Street in Harlem, one of the better-known lodgings in the black community.

At ten o'clock the next morning, Tuesday August 28, 1945, Clyde Sukeforth and Jackie Robinson entered Branch Rickey's fourth-floor office at the Dodgers team headquarters on 215 Montague Street in downtown Brooklyn. Rickey was seated behind a large mahogany desk in a luxurious leather swivel chair, a legacy from former general manager Larry MacPhail. Above him was a giant elk head, a hunting memento given to MacPhail by pitcher Curt Davis.[5] Framed on the walls were photos of Rickey's granddaughters, Caroline and Nancy Rickey (Branch Rickey Jr.'s daughters), Leo Durocher, and the late Charley Barrett, and a portrait of Abraham Lincoln. Off to the side in an illuminated tank were some goldfish, nervously swimming back and forth, exhibiting an uneasiness that Robinson later said matched his own.[6]

In introducing the player to his boss, Clyde Sukeforth said, "Mr. Rickey, this is Jack Roosevelt Robinson of the Kansas City Monarchs. I think he is the Brooklyn kind of player." Branch Rickey rose from his seat, placing his omnipresent cigar in his left hand while offering Robinson a warm handshake. Rickey sat down and "just stared and stared, . . . stared at him as if he was trying to get inside the man," remembered Sukeforth, the only eyewitness to the meeting. "And Jack stared right back at him. Oh, they were a pair, those two! I tell you, the air in that office was electric."[7]

Rickey finally broke the silence. As we have seen, he usually gave a third degree to any potential employee, finding out as quickly as possible about a person's family background, religion, job experience, marital status, ambition, intelligence, and ability to think and express oneself on one's feet. At the Robinson interview, however, Branch Rickey changed the order around, asking immediately, "Do you have a girl?" "I think so," came the reply. "What do you mean, 'I think so'?" Rickey retorted. "Well, a ballplayer's life keeps him away from home so much that I don't know if she is still waiting for me," Robinson said. "Do you love her?" Rickey asked. "Oh, yes, Mr. Rickey, I love her very much. Rachel's a very special girl." "Well, marry her!" Rickey said to a man he had met only moments earlier. "A man needs a wife and a good home, especially when he has a man's work to do."

Rickey went on to ask Robinson about his church affiliations, and he was elated to learn that Robinson was a God-fearing, church-going Protestant. Rickey may have asked Robinson the name of his pastor, and he might have recognized the name of the Reverend Karl Downs, who, seven years earlier in Chicago, had attended with Rickey in Chicago a two hundredth anniversary commemoration of John Wesley's conversion. When Robinson told Rickey that he didn't drink, the executive's eyes lit up approvingly. (Once, while on a double date with a Kansas City Monarch teammate, Robinson threw a glass of whiskey into a lighted fireplace to dramatize the dangers of alcohol.)[8] If the subject of Robinson's birthday came up, Rickey undoubtedly would have been pleased that the ballplayer was born on the same day as Branch Rickey Jr., January 31, but five years later, in 1919. He was not young for a potential Major Leaguer, Rickey thought, but he was young enough.

Rickey next inquired about Robinson's situation in the Negro Leagues. "Are you under contract to the Kansas City Monarchs?" "No, sir, we don't have contracts," Robinson gave the answer that Rickey already knew, but he wanted to make sure. "Do you have any agreements—written or oral—about how long you will play for them?" "No, none at all. Just pay day to pay day," Robinson answered.

After he finished with his barrage of questions, Branch Rickey suddenly looked deep into Jack Robinson's eyes. "Do you know why you were brought here?" he asked. "Something about the Brown Dodgers and a new Negro league?" Robinson replied tentatively. "No, that isn't it," Rickey exclaimed. "I want you to play for the Brooklyn Dodgers organization. Perhaps on Montreal to start with."

"Montreal? Play for Montreal?" Robinson exclaimed. He did not like the life in the Negro Leagues, he was openly critical of it, and once he proved a success in the big leagues in 1947, he wrote scathingly in *Ebony* magazine about the poor working conditions and dissolute behavior in the Negro Leagues.[9] He was eager to escape the second-class conditions of the segregated leagues, but he didn't expect an offer to aim directly for the Major Leagues.

If the opportunity to make the Major Leagues and become a race pioneer in the process overwhelmed and excited Robinson, he wasn't prepared for the next stage in the momentous meeting. "I know you're a good ballplayer," Rickey exclaimed. "What I don't know is whether you have the guts." When physically challenged Robinson always was quick to defend his manhood. He told Rickey that he wasn't afraid of anybody or anything on a playing field. Rickey interrupted. "I'm looking for a ball player with guts enough not to fight back," he roared.

Branch Rickey, the dramatic actor manqué, Lionel Barrymore playing Thaddeus Stevens, began to describe vividly and act out physically the threats Robinson would endure as the first black player in twentieth-century Major League Baseball. Rickey took off his jacket and got down on the floor, imitating a base runner sliding into second, kicking Robinson in the shins, imitating the actions of a racist opponent barreling into Robinson with spikes vengefully high. He probably shouted the "n" word and voiced other epithets that opponents would yell at Robinson. He asked the stunned athlete how he would react when white waiters wouldn't serve him on the road, railroad conductors turned their backs on him, and other situations of discrimination in America arose that Rickey deplored but felt that he could change through the actions of a great black baseball player. The key to the success, Rickey stressed, was that Robinson could not fight back against the indignities.

Suddenly, the passionate executive pulled out of his desk drawer a heavily marked passage from one of his favorite books, Giovanni Papini's *The Life of Christ*. Papini (1881–1956) had been a Harvard student of William James, the philosopher-psychologist who wrote "The Moral Equivalent of War," one of Rickey's favorite essays. Papini had been an atheist, but in researching his history of the life of Jesus Christ, he had became an enthusiastic convert to Christianity. Papini's book had moved Rickey to order copies for all his children one Christmas.[10]

Branch Rickey read Jackie Robinson the words from Jesus that Papini had underscored: "Ye have heard that it hath been said, An eye for an eye, and a tooth for a tooth: But I say unto you, That ye resist not evil: But whosoever shall smite thee on thy cheek, turn to him the other also." After listening to Branch Rickey's amazing mixture of oratory and psychodrama, Jack Roosevelt Robinson said simply, "I have two cheeks, Mr. Rickey. Is that it?" Rickey nodded with deep satisfaction.

The executive did not yet know the extent of Jackie Robinson's competitiveness and will to win, which Rickey would later compare to Ty Cobb's. Yet, after their initial Brooklyn meeting of almost three hours, Rickey's intuition told him he had found his man. Branch Rickey sensed in Jackie Robinson everything that he wanted in a race pioneer—great talent, fierce competitiveness, good personal and family values, and a commitment to uplift his race. Clyde Sukeforth remembered that when Robinson promised Rickey at the end of the interview that he would provoke no racial incident, "Well, I thought the old man was going to kiss him."[11]

"Nobody will ever know the hell Robinson went through in those [first] seasons," Rickey told *Newsweek* sports columnist John Lardner ten years later. "He has never opened his face about it, about the details. He never will. Proud man. When *he* made it, it was made."[12] For his part Robinson was immediately won over by Rickey's compelling combination of competitiveness and spirituality. He recalled that at their first meeting, his "piercing eyes looked at me with such meticulous care, I felt almost naked," but once he got to know him, he felt that "he was like a piece of mobile armor, and he would throw himself and his advice in the way of anything likely to hurt me."[13]

Robinson was captivated by Rickey's recounting of a favorite "trouble ahead, trouble ahead" story about an old Ohio couple taking their first railroad trip. They were afraid that their train would not make it through the mountains and would plunge over a precipice. Yet they reached their destination safely, and Rickey told Robinson, "That's the way it is with most trouble ahead in this world, Jackie—if we use the common sense and courage God gave us. But you've got to study the hazards and build wisely."[14]

As their initial meeting drew to a close, Rickey reached into his drawer and offered Robinson a standard Minor League contract for a player assigned to the Dodgers' highest-classification team, the Montreal Royals in the International League. He would receive $600 a month, and also a $3,500 signing bonus, a relatively high figure from Branch Rickey, a man who loathed the concept of bonuses for unproven talent. Yet he rightly saw Robinson as a special case and expected that he was getting a bargain as a baseball businessman.

At the end of their historic first meeting, Branch Rickey's last words were to admonish Jackie Robinson to follow strict secrecy about their meeting. Robinson could tell his family and his fiancée, Rachel Isum, but no one else. Rickey had not yet decided on when to announce "The Young Man from the West" as his race pioneer.

Ideally, Rickey wanted to wait until the end of the regular college football season in late November or even until after the bowl games on New Year's Day. Local New York City politics, however, forced him to move up his timetable. During the summer of 1945 an End Jim Crow in Baseball Committee, supported by Communist New York City councilman Benjamin B. Davis, was picketing the three Major League ballparks with photographs of dead and wounded black soldiers. Underneath the graphic pictures was the caption "Good enough to die for their country but not good enough to play for organized baseball."[15]

New York City mayor Fiorello LaGuardia also wanted positive action on racial equality. Unlike the late President Franklin Roosevelt, LaGuardia had decided not to run for a fourth term as mayor, but the onetime Italian immigrant wanted to add a farewell laurel of improved race relations to his progressive legacy. LaGuardia urged all three local Major League teams to join his Committee for Unity, which had been established in the wake of the Harlem race riots in 1943, and to make a pledge to conform to the Ives-Quinn antidiscrimination law and sign black players as soon as possible.

Branch Rickey for the Dodgers and Larry MacPhail for the Yankees had pledged their teams' willingness to join the Committee for Unity, but the Giants' Horace Stoneham, who had inherited the team from his father Charles Stoneham in 1936, rejected the mayor's appeal in no uncertain terms. He denounced the "professional do-gooders" on LaGuardia's committee for interfering with the private enterprise of the baseball business. Although Larry MacPhail did agree to give the Yankees' tacit support to a call for integration, he privately supported Stoneham. MacPhail wanted no part of a committee made up of what he also branded as "social and political drum-beaters."[16]

The executive director of the Committee for Unity, New York University sociology professor Daniel K. Dodson, hoped that Branch Rickey would view things differently and was delighted when he hit it off immediately with the paternal Brooklyn executive. Once again Rickey struck up a friendship with a man of similar background and convictions. The sociologist Dodson, the son of poor white sharecroppers, was raised in the small Texas town of Mt. Vernon and had attended McMurry College, a small Texas school named after a Methodist bishop. After earning a master's degree from Southern Methodist University in Dallas, he obtained his doctorate at New York University. Dodson belonged to the Christ Methodist Church in New York and was active in the Boy Scouts, the Girl Scouts, and the YMCA. His views on education were similar to Rickey's in that he believed that true learning occurred less from "erudition" than through "community involvement."[17]

Branch Rickey found in Daniel Dodson such a kindred spirit that, after the baseball executive's investigators performed a background check on the sociologist to make sure he had no left-wing tinge in his background, he brought him into his confidence. He told Dodson about the Dodgers' already advanced scouting of black players and confided that at least one and possibly several black players would be signed before the start of the 1946 season. The two men discussed in detail the least painful way to reveal the breaking of the color line in baseball to players, fans, owners, and the society at large. Dodson thought that the sooner Rickey made his decision public, the better prepared everyone would be for the dramatic change in the 1946 season. To allow sufficient time for the white players to adjust to the new working conditions, the sociologist suggested that the end of the 1945 baseball season might be the ideal time for the announcement. Dodson also forewarned Rickey that Mayor LaGuardia wanted quick action on ending discrimination, preferably before the November election.[18]

Rickey preferred waiting until after the election for he too, like his fellow baseball owners, had an aversion to being labeled a "do-gooder." However, circumstances hastened Rickey's announcement. Early in October 1945 the LaGuardia Committee on Unity issued what it called a "tentative proposal submitted purely on the basis of discussion." The report listed the pros and cons of prospective racial integration in baseball. Problems of acceptance in the South during spring training and among southern players year-round were noted. Difficulties in hotel arrangements in border cities were also mentioned, but the working draft concluded forcefully that there was "little doubt that New York City's baseball public would certainly support the integration of Negroes on the basis of their abilities. There was never a more propitious moment than the present, when we are just concluding a terrible World War to suppress the theory of racial superiority, to put our house in order."[19]

When Rickey learned from Dodson that Mayor LaGuardia planned to make baseball integration the subject of his regular Sunday afternoon radio address on October 18, 1945, the baseball executive decided that he must act quickly. He implored Dodson to use his influence on the mayor to postpone his talk on racial justice because, shortly, there would be favorable news on integration in baseball. Dan Dodson had not known Branch Rickey for very long, but he put his reputation on the line when he convinced LaGuardia to change the subject for his weekly radio remarks. The mayor chose to devote his Sunday radio talk to a general plea for patriotism and community service instead of a call for specific actions on behalf of racial equality.[20]

Branch Rickey hurriedly got in touch with Jackie Robinson, who, fortunately, was in New York, preparing to leave soon for ten weeks of winter baseball in Venezuela. Rickey instructed Robinson to go to Montreal for a press conference on Tuesday, October 23, 1945. He would be accompanied by Branch Rickey Jr., director of the Dodgers' Minor League operations.

Shortly before the blockbuster announcement, Branch and Jane Rickey dropped in for a social visit with their friends broadcaster Lowell Thomas and his wife on Quaker Hill, north of New York City. When Rickey confided to Thomas the news of the forthcoming signing, the broadcaster was aghast. According to Rickey's oldest daughter, Mary Rickey Eckler, who was also visiting that day, Lowell Thomas predicted, "Branch, all hell will break loose!" The Dodgers president disagreed. "No, Lowell," he said. "All heaven will rejoice."[21]

On the afternoon of Tuesday, October 23, 1945, the press corps in Montreal gathered for a "major announcement." They had no idea what the news would be, although many writers hoped that it would involve the hiring of Babe Ruth as the new manager of the local team. The scribes nodded hello to team co-owner Hector Racine and greeted Branch Rickey Jr., who had been to Montreal many times in his role as farm director. They were stunned when in strode athletic, black Jack Roosevelt Robinson, who was introduced as the newest member of the Brooklyn Dodgers organization. The writers were told that Robinson would have every chance to make the Montreal Royals in the upcoming 1946 season.

Scheduling Robinson's first professional season in Montreal was a wise strategy because there was no deep tradition of white racism in Canada, which had relatively few people of color. Even so, the reporters in attendance were astounded by the announcement. Al Parsley of the *Montreal Herald* wrote the next day: "This Robinson is definitely dark. His color is the hue of ebony. By no means can he be called a brown bomber or a chocolate soldier."[22] ("The Brown Bomber" was the nickname of heavyweight champion Joe Louis, who was deliberately being promoted as a mild-mannered, unthreatening figure in contrast to the defiantly black, white-womanizing Jack Johnson.)

Genuinely gifted in his public speaking, Jack Robinson was poised and modest in his comments. "Of course, I can't begin to tell you how happy I am that I am the first member of my race in organized baseball," he said. "I can only say I'll do my very best to come through in every manner."[23] For his part Branch Rickey Jr. made it a point to mention how thorough the Dodgers' scouting had been in discovering Robinson, even noting the figure of $25,000 spent on the project. (Harold Parrott later suggested that mentioning the money was a way for Rickey Sr. to refute the ongoing allegations in the tabloids that he was "El Cheapo.")[24] Branch Jr. noted: "Undoubtedly [we] will be criticized in some sections of the United States where racial prejudice is rampant." He said that the Dodgers were "not inviting trouble, but they won't avoid it if it comes." Branch Jr. admitted that "some players now with us may even quit," but he also predicted that "they'll be back in baseball after they work a year or two in a cotton mill."[25]

The reaction of Rickey's colleagues in the baseball business ranged from skeptical to positively vitriolic. For Judge William Bramham, president of the National Association, the governing body of the Minor

Leagues, breaking the color line was a serious breach of American social mores. Speaking from his office in Durham, North Carolina, the Minor League chief denounced Rickey as one of "those of the carpetbagger stripe of the white race" who "under the guise of helping" are really using black people "for their own selfish interests that retard the race." Bramham added sarcastically: "Father Divine will have to look to his laurels, for we can expect Rickey Temple to be in the course of construction in Harlem soon."[26] Clark Griffith and Larry MacPhail added their critical voices, denouncing Rickey's move as a selfish act by a notoriously manipulative colleague.

Most players were noncommittal, although, as the younger Rickey predicted, many southern-born players did not take the news easily and resented the reference to returning to the cotton mills if they didn't like the new development. Privately, many of Robinson's future teammates on the Dodgers were worried about the competition of a black man for their jobs as well as about bad reactions from racially conservative people back home. The aptly named Dixie Walker said, "As long as he isn't with the Dodgers, I'm not worried."[27] Bob Feller, ace pitcher for the Cleveland Indians, opined that on the basis of playing some exhibition games against Robinson, he "couldn't foresee any future" for him. He is "so tied up in the shoulders and couldn't hit an inside pitch to save his neck," Feller said. "If he were a white man I doubt they would even consider him as big league material."[28]

The pitcher's critique was shared by *Daily News* columnist Jimmy Powers, coiner of the "El Cheapo" epithet against Rickey, which he was beginning to use with ever-greater frequency. Powers dismissed Robinson's chances as "1,000 to 1." If Robinson weren't black, he wrote, he would have been assigned to class C. As the Robinson saga evolved into a major story, Powers impugned any possible humanitarian motive of Rickey's, even using the loaded metaphor that readers not be misled by a man who claims to "have a heart as big as a watermelon."[29]

Rickey didn't think that most of the writers would be as vitriolic as Powers, but he was acutely aware that the press coverage of the Robinson breakthrough would be crucial to its success. He hired the respected New York sportswriter Frank Graham to survey his colleagues' reaction to the signing.[30] Most scribes viewed Robinson's signing with an open mind, although they also expressed some skepticism and fear of the uncharted waters Rickey and Robinson were entering.

Two reactions, one white and one black, definitely encouraged the executive. In a column titled "Rickey Explodes a Bomb," the *New York Herald-Tribune's* Al Laney wrote about Jimmie Odoms, a retired Pullman porter, and big baseball fan, who swept the floors of the newspaper's office. A close follower of the Negro Leagues, Odom praised Rickey for his strategy of integration. "Pick out just one good boy. Put him in the minors and let him come up," Odoms said, predicting, "He gonna make it and when he do, . . . the stars ain't gonna fall. . . . They'll be plenty kids ready to try it after Robinson makes good."[31] With words that warmed Branch Rickey's staunch Republican heart, Sam Lacy of the *Baltimore Afro-American* wrote: "Alone, Robinson represents a weapon far more potent than the combined forces of all our liberal legislation."[32]

Rickey was also heartened by the thoughts of Hearst newspaper columnist Bill Corum, who urged in the *New York Journal-American* that Robinson's signing not become "a cause celebre" but should be welcomed by "common sense." Corum and Rickey shared the bonds of a small-town Midwest upbringing (the writer hailed from Boonville, Missouri) and their participation in the Chemical Warfare Service of World War I, when Corum was the youngest and Rickey was the oldest major in the same cause. "Good luck to Rickey! Good luck to Robinson!" Corum concluded his column. "Good luck to baseball, which may be a little slow on the uptake, but which usually gets around to doing the sensible thing in the long run."[33]

Reaction within the Negro League community was generally favorable. Although it has been said that he was embittered by not being selected as the pioneer, Satchel Paige was gracious at the news of Robinson's selection. "They didn't make a mistake by signing Robinson," Paige said. "They couldn't have picked a better man."[34] Negro American League president J. B. Martin also praised Rickey. "I feel that I speak the sentiment of 15 million Negroes in America who are with you one hundred per cent," Martin said. "[We] will always remember the day and date of this great event."[35]

Other Negro league officials were more critical, especially the co-owners of the Kansas City Monarchs, J. L. Wilkinson and Thomas Baird, who were understandably upset that Rickey had signed Robinson without compensating the Monarchs in any way. Baird said sharply, "Rickey reminds me of the man who walked into the room with a rope and at the end of the rope was a horse."[36] The Monarchs owners even contemplated suing Rickey for stolen property, but they were quickly dissuaded by other Negro League officials, who didn't want it to appear that they were standing in the way of Robinson's and other black players' advancement.

The combative Rickey insisted that he did nothing wrong in his signing of Robinson. "There is no Negro league as such, as far as I am concerned," he repeated defiantly, maintaining the same stance he had taken since he had condemned the Negro Leagues in May 1945 as "zones in the form of a racket."[37] However, in the future, as he made plans to soon sign more Negro League players (two of them destined to be great Brooklyn stars, catcher Roy Campanella of the Baltimore Elite Giants and nineteen-year-old pitcher Don Newcombe of the Newark Eagles), the executive made certain that the black players put into writing the lack of contractual agreements with their Negro League teams.[38]

As Thanksgiving 1945 neared, Rickey looked back at the momentous year with a sense of relief and anticipation. The war at last was over and, as he had predicted and felt in every fiber of his heart and mind, the Allies had won over the forces of totalitarianism and darkness. The human cost of war always pained the idealist in Branch Rickey, but he accepted the sad reality that in war as in sports, "You have to pay the price."

He did worry about the shape of the peace to come. As a fervent, idealistic, anti-Communist Christian, Rickey foresaw threats from expanding Communism in Europe and Asia, and it is likely that he foresaw by the end of 1945 how fearful and paralyzing the "Cold War" would become. Yet, on the level he was most acquainted with, youth and sports, Rickey was guardedly optimistic. "I am sometimes quite anxious about the period of transition these young folks will need to go through," he wrote to Franklin P. Cole, his minister at the Church-of-the-Gardens in Forest Hills, who was still on active duty as an army chaplain, "but they have a way of coming out on top."[39]

Most of all Branch Rickey was happy that his sons-in-law had all returned unharmed from the war. One of them, Robert Terry Jones, a Burroughs School graduate from St. Louis who married Rickey's second-oldest daughter, Jane, would be going, so to speak, into the family business as business manager and radio announcer for the Dodgers' Fort Worth franchise in the double-A Texas League. Bob Jones liked to refer to himself, kiddingly, as "Mr. Jane Rickey Jones," because, though he may have married a Rickey daughter, the enormous vital presence of Branch and Jane Rickey was always there. Mary Rickey's husband, John Eckler, also liked to call himself, at times, Mr. Mary Rickey Eckler.[40]

Bob Jones earned the rank of colonel in the military, but he was not a career soldier and was eagerly looking forward to resuming his life as a civilian and a family man. Before he left for Texas, however, Jones was told by one member of the Brooklyn Dodgers organization that he should capitalize on his military status. "I think you should keep the title Colonel," Rickey's partner Walter O'Malley told Jones before he headed south. "No, that's not really my style," Jones replied.[41]

It was not the first or the last time that a Branch Rickey supporter and Walter O'Malley would disagree. There would be friction between the two strong-willed partners starting in the first postwar season of 1946. However, as the energetic baseball executive prepared at long last for the first full year of peacetime baseball, he could not help but feel elated. The time had finally come to see whether his intense scouting and development of white and black players would succeed. Inevitably, there would be "trouble ahead, trouble ahead," but the ferocious gentleman felt that he was on the verge of a truly major accomplishment in both baseball and the larger American society.

18

Prelude to a Pennant

"William, please help me, the room is spinning," Branch Rickey pleaded to Bill DeWitt. It was early in December 1945, and the Dodgers executive and the St. Louis Browns president were in Chicago, attending the Major Leagues' joint session at baseball's annual December meetings. "If I get up, I'll make a fool of myself," an obviously distressed Rickey said to his longtime friend.

DeWitt felt helpless and deeply concerned about his mentor's condition. In the six weeks since Rickey had dropped the bombshell that Jackie Robinson was going to get his chance in the Dodgers organization, he had kept up his usual hectic pace. On this trip Rickey had flown to Columbus, Ohio; motored to Delaware, Ohio, for a meeting of the Ohio Wesleyan board of trustees; returned to Columbus for the annual Minor League meetings; and traveled to Chicago for the Major League conclave.

There was no way Branch Rickey was going to miss this gathering, baseball's first peacetime conference since 1940, and the first convention since A. B. "Happy" Chandler had been elected commissioner in April 1945. Many important issues were on the table, such as the limits of the new commissioner's power, bonus regulations for amateur free agents, and restrictions on signing high school players before graduation. The trade market wasn't in full gear yet because no team really knew what condition their stars would be in when they returned from the military. Some speculated that no big deals would happen until the wartime excess profits tax was lifted early in the new year.[1]

Branch Rickey was in no hurry to wheel and deal because he had faith in his Brooklyn youngsters coming back from the war. Yet he was always a presence at the winter meetings, and there was no way he would miss them. Beneath the surface of collegial greetings and small talk, however, he was subjected to murmurs and long looks from his partners and rivals in the baseball business as they pondered what his latest bold stroke of signing Jackie Robinson would mean for the future of their industry.

Now, at his moment of physical distress, the bracing competition of the baseball business was far from Branch Rickey's mind. His balance was off, he could not stand up straight, and the pain in his ear was overwhelming. "Don't make a scene, William, and draw attention to me," Rickey whispered to Bill DeWitt. "Just try to help me to the door." The concerned younger executive complied and managed to get Rickey back to his hotel room. Branch Rickey Jr. was summoned, and father and son took the next available train back to Brooklyn.

On the trip home Rickey suffered a more severe attack of dizziness, and mordant thoughts that he had a brain tumor raced through his anxious brain. Upon arriving in Brooklyn he was immediately checked into a hospital under the alias "John Doe" to keep the newspapers uninformed about his mysterious condition. The next day he was transferred to a medical facility with more advanced equipment. After several days of tests a diagnosis was finally provided. Branch Rickey did not have a brain tumor, he learned with relief, but was suffering from a very painful and relatively rare condition, Ménière's disease. It was caused by an imbalance in the inner ear, which left a victim subject to vertigo, nausea, and general lack of balance.

Doctors informed him that the ailment might be hereditary because Rickey's late mother, Emily, and late older brother, Orla, had suffered similar symptoms. Sudden movements of the head and body could cause severe attacks, the physicians warned the ailing executive, and there was no cure for the disease except rest and a slower pace of life. Of course, the doctors' prescription of rest did not sit well with Branch Rickey, who said yet again, "I expect my funeral cortege to move at a stately pace." On the eve of building the Dodgers into a dominant baseball organization, he was not going to allow a mere imbalance disorder to disrupt his great plans. He had a list of a few dozen things that had to be done prior to the opening of the Dodgers' first postwar spring training camp in February

1946. If he had to do his work in the hospital, well, reluctantly, he would allow that concession.

Rickey's hospital stay lasted beyond Christmas into early 1946. It was a blow to the paterfamilias, who always looked forward to celebrating the holiday at home, surrounded by the love of his family and the excitement of sharing presents with his children and grandchildren. His spirits were uplifted when his wife Jane, Branch Jr. and his family, and other visiting family members and friends came to celebrate with him in the hospital. The press was still largely unaware of the serious nature of Rickey's hospitalization, but leave it to garrulous Leo Durocher to blurt, "He's in the hospital now," when asked by a reporter on New Year's Eve if his contract with the Dodgers was assured for 1946, which, of course, it was.[2]

From his hospital bed Branch Rickey started making plans for what promised to be a busy and eventful spring training. With the war over the Dodgers had abandoned the icy terrain of Bear Mountain for the broiling sun and warm breezes of Florida. With important decisions to be made about the assignment of more than six hundred players to the twenty-seven Brooklyn farm clubs, the team established several beachheads in the Sunshine State. Major League headquarters would be in Daytona Beach, while most of the Minor Leaguers would train forty miles inland in Sanford. The team also leased some fields at a naval base at Pensacola while Rickey sought a permanent training home for all the players.

One of the first projects on Rickey's agenda was to make sure that Jackie Robinson's first spring training was as stress free as possible. To keep the race pioneer from feeling totally isolated, Rickey signed black pitcher John Wright. On paper the twenty-seven-year-old Wright seemed like a genuine prospect, having starred for the Homestead Grays in the Negro Leagues and compiling in 1945 the lowest earned run average in armed forces baseball.[3] However, Wright, a native of Alabama, never felt comfortable competing against white players, and after one season in the Dodgers' Minor League organization, he returned to the Negro Leagues in 1947.

Next, Rickey brought Wendell Smith, the *Pittsburgh Courier's* crusading, pro-integration sportswriter, directly onto the Robinson support team. Smith had written Rickey before Christmas, informing him that he would be covering Robinson's spring training for the *Courier* and that if he could help in any way, to please ask. Rickey took Smith up on his offer, filling him in about Wright's signing and asking the journalist to keep an eye on both players "because much harm could come if either of these boys were to do or say something or other out of turn."[4] Smith replied that he would glad to oblige, shrewdly adding that he would be available to serve as the chauffeur for the black players in Florida. Rickey, who hated to drive and liked to have a ready supply of drivers handy, promptly hired him, matching his *Courier* salary of $50 a week.[5]

Shortly before Rickey left the hospital in mid-January 1946, Jackie Robinson stopped by for a visit. He was returning from his winter baseball experience in Venezuela and had come to New York to meet his fiancée, Rachel Isum, an honors graduate of the UCLA nursing school, who had been working in the city. Robinson brought Rickey the news that he was planning to get married in California before heading to spring training. As a great proponent of marriage and family, Rickey, of course, was delighted about his player's forthcoming nuptials.

Robinson's visit to his recuperating boss was brief, but both men could sense a bond growing. Despite the formidable gulf between age and youth, owner and player, and white and black, both Rickey and Robinson knew that they were about to embark on a perilous but very worthwhile adventure. Each was profoundly committed to turning Robinson's opportunity into a triumph for all.

The veteran executive was aware that the road to the big leagues was a tough one for any white player. The game was a "fail" sport by definition—a good hitter made out seven times out of ten, and a good pitcher always gave up hits and runs. How a player handled and overcame adversity on the field was a big part of his ultimate success. The aspiring player of color would have to face the same hurdles of the game itself plus all the challenges of racism on and off the field. As an especially paternal team executive, Branch Rickey was dedicated to ensuring that Robinson was treated to a fair playing field on and off the diamond.

One of Rickey's top priorities was finding housing for the Robinson newlyweds in segregated Florida. Normally, Rickey did not encourage players to bring wives to spring training, but in the special case of Robinson, who the executive knew would need the solace of a helpmate, he made an exception. Wendell Smith contacted a college classmate who lived in a big house in the black community of Sanford, and she and her husband agreed to house the Robinsons when they arrived in camp on the reporting date of March 1.[6]

Shortly after Robinson's hospital visit, Rickey happily returned home to Forest Hills, though not to follow his doctors' prescription of rest and relaxation. He was around for as long as it took to prepare for his travel to spring training. In a twinkling he flew off to Florida and soon resumed his usual regimen of sixteen-hour workdays. An early camp was slated for one hundred inexperienced recruits on February 1, and Rickey and his thirty-one coaches were raring to get to work. Rickey had no doubt that the Dodgers organization would shortly surpass what he had built for the Cardinals, and that the "St. Louis Swifties" would pale in comparison to his speedy new team of the future.

March 1, 1946 arrived, and Jackie Robinson was not yet in Sanford, Florida. Nor did he appear the next day, and Branch Rickey, treasuring promptness, was growing impatient. Soon a phone call from Robinson provided an agonizing explanation for the lateness. Neither Rickey nor Robinson had been truly prepared for the ordeal that the newlyweds would face coming from California to Florida. As recounted meticulously in Arnold Rampersad's biography of Jackie Robinson, the indignities that the newlyweds suffered on their trip to Florida were legion. When their overnight plane from Los Angeles landed in New Orleans at 7:00 a.m. for refueling, they were told without explanation that they couldn't reboard. When they were not booked on later flights to Pensacola, the couple decided to get some rest in a hotel in New Orleans that Robinson knew from his barnstorming baseball days. Twelve hours after they arrived in New Orleans, they finally got on a flight to Pensacola, but they were bumped from their connection to Daytona Beach, ostensibly on the grounds that the plane was overloaded. When they saw a white couple walk on board to take their place, they decided to forget about plane connections.

After spending the night in a roach-infested segregated hotel in Pensacola, they hopped on a bus to Jacksonville. En route Jackie Robinson was forced to do what he had refused to do in the Army and had been court-martialed for: move to the back of the bus. After a long wait in the crowded, malodorous, segregated bus station in Jacksonville, Jackie and Rachel made a connection on a bus to Daytona Beach, finally arriving thirty-six hours after leaving Los Angeles.[7]

They were greeted by Wendell Smith, *Pittsburgh Courier* photographer Billy Rowe, and pitcher John Wright. Robinson was glad to see friendly faces after the ordeal of his trip, but he declared, "I never want another trip like that one."[8] His supporters sat up all night with him, hearing his pain and reassuring him that conditions would be far better in the training camp.

Branch Rickey said little to the press during the delay in Robinson's arrival except the euphemism that "bad flying weather in the vicinity of New Orleans" had kept him from reporting on time.[9] Fortuitously, because he did not want too much attention centered on the race pioneer, Branch Rickey was not in camp when Robinson did arrive. The president had flown in the Dodgers' new team plane to Westminster College in Fulton, Missouri, to hear a major foreign policy speech by Winston Churchill.[10] On March 5, 1946, Rickey, a member of Westminster's board of trustees, listened rapt as England's inspiring World War Two leader used for one of the first times the term "the Iron Curtain" to describe the threat that the Soviet Union posed to Eastern Europe and the entire non-Communist world. Although Churchill had recently been defeated in a bid for reelection, his words still carried a lot of weight in the United States, not least in the heart and mind of Branch Rickey, who nodded in agreement with Churchill's Manichean definition of what would define the coming anxious years of the Cold War.

When Rickey flew back to Florida, he tried to treat Robinson's presence in camp nonchalantly, saying that he was just another nice fellow trying to make the team. Of course, he was closely following every aspect of the player's progress. Rickey was cheered when he learned that, on March 4, Robinson's debut at the practice field had gone smoothly, with no untoward reactions by his teammates. The executive was distressed, however, when two days later a band of local bigots in Sanford threatened to march on the house where the Robinsons were staying unless they cleared out of town immediately.[11]

Rickey always feared that ignorant whites in the South and militant blacks in the North could sabotage his plan for integration, because he felt that they were the two groups least susceptible to reasoned argument. He hated to yield to bigots' threats, but he hastily made plans to house the Robinsons with another black family in Daytona Beach. The accommodations were far less appealing than the near mansion where they had stayed in Sanford, but it could not be helped. "When you made Branch Rickey make a move like that," Red Barber, a native of Sanford, later recalled, "it was serious. It had to be!"[12]

Conditions in Daytona Beach were less tense. By the standards of the South, the central Atlantic Coastal city was relatively enlightened. There were black bus drivers, a small black middle class, and a well-regarded black college, Bethune-Cookman; blacks could also try on shoes (but not clothes) in stores.[13] Although they were segregated in the bleachers, many black fans came to see and cheer Robinson's first Daytona Beach workouts.

Spring training was a new athletic experience for Jackie Robinson. The Kansas City Monarchs and most Negro League teams didn't engage in spring training; they simply reported to a southern training camp and started playing exhibition games immediately. In his eagerness to show his worth, Robinson overdid his throwing in the first days of camp. Before the end of his second week he could hardly lift his arm over his head, and he asked out of fielding practice. When he heard the news of Robinson's temporary disability, Branch Rickey hurried over to the Minor League camp. The man who always preached "You have to pay the price" encouraged Robinson to hang tough and keep playing. "Under ordinary circumstances, it would be all right, but these are not ordinary circumstances," Rickey counseled the ailing player. "You can't afford to miss a single day. They'll say you're dogging it, that you are pretending your arm is sore."[14]

Robinson understood and soon was giving every evidence that, despite his limited experience in playing baseball, he was a definite Major League prospect. Although he had played shortstop for the Monarchs, the consensus of Rickey's coaches (and of Negro League personnel) was that Robinson did not have the arm of a Major League shortstop. Since the Montreal Royals had a popular, able player (Stan Breard) at the position, Robinson was told to work out at second base. He was a quick learner, picking up intricacies of the position from one of the career

Minor Leaguers in the Dodgers organization, Alexander Sebastian "Al" Campanis. Born in Greece, Campanis had twenty at-bats for Brooklyn in the war year of 1943, but he knew his future was as a coach and an instructor. He genuinely helped Robinson become a better defensive player as he prepared for his rookie Minor League season. "He had the greatest aptitude of any player I've ever seen," Campanis later said.[15]

One day in mid-March, as spring training progressed, Branch Rickey was watching a Montreal Royals intrasquad game with the team's new manager, Clay Hopper. All of a sudden Robinson made an incredible play on a grounder into the first base hole. "Have you ever seen a human being make a play like that?" Rickey exclaimed, poking Hopper in the ribs for emphasis. The discomfited manager turned away from his boss for a moment and then asked quietly, "Mr. Rickey, do you really think a nigra is a human being?"

Rickey was stunned by Hopper's question. He swallowed hard and said nothing. There was nothing in Rickey's formidable arsenal of intellect and vocabulary that could undo in a few words what generations of prejudice had created within the heart and mind of the southern-bred baseball man. Hopper was a native of Mississippi who had been reluctant to manage Robinson because he was afraid of what his neighbors would say back home. Rickey, though, had bluntly informed Hopper that he had no choice. The baseball lifer, who had been working for the executive since he had joined the Cardinals organization in the 1920s, had pledged to treat Robinson like any other player, so Rickey let Hopper's racist remark pass without comment.

One good example of how the Royals manager fulfilled his promise to his boss was illustrated later in spring training. Hopper enlisted Paul Derringer, the former Cardinals and Reds pitcher who was winding up his career in the Minor Leagues at Indianapolis, to test Robinson's mettle by throwing a bevy of knockdown pitches at him in an exhibition game. When the race pioneer didn't back down and dug in at the plate after every brushback pitch, Derringer told Hopper, "Clay, he will do."[16]

(Considering the good baseball training Robinson received from coaches who had been bred in prejudice, it is hard not to think that if Branch Rickey were still alive and running the Dodgers in 1987, Al Campanis would not have been fired for his insensitive remarks on the

ABC News network television show *Nightline,* when he said that black people lacked the "necessities" to hold front office positions. Rickey would not have liked the remark, of course, but he always believed that reason would ultimately win out over bigotry and that one unfortunate remark should not be allowed to undo all the good works of a person's career.)

Meanwhile, the first post–World War II baseball spring training camps were abuzz with other major developments. Robert Murphy, a Harvard-educated former examiner with the National Labor Relations Board, was trying to organize Major League players into a union. After hearing tales in Boston from members of the Red Sox and Braves about underpaid players and the one-sided baseball contract, Murphy paid his own way to Florida, trying to see if the ballplayers wanted to join his fledgling American Baseball Guild. Not surprisingly Murphy had minimal impact in the Dodgers camp, where Branch Rickey and Leo Durocher made it clear that no union organizer was welcome. Murphy would receive the greatest support from the Pirates, in the strong union city of Pittsburgh; a majority of players actually voted to strike an early June 1946 game before they were talked out of it by management and antiunion players.[17]

In spring training 1946 a more direct threat was posed to the Dodgers by the Mexican League, a baseball organization trying to lure American Major Leaguers south of the border with promises of far greater salaries. Mexican League raids were the brainstorm of Jorge Pasquel, a wealthy Mexico City businessman, and his three brothers. Pasquel, a flamboyant figure who carried a gun and had food served to him in his ballpark box on a silver tray, bragged, "With money I can buy anything. Every man or woman has a price."[18]

Pasquel directed his Florida emissaries to bring suitcases filled with money to the hotel rooms of star Cardinals outfielder Stan Musial, Yankees shortstop Phil Rizzuto, and many other players. Pasquel's agents were also in Daytona Beach trying to lure several Dodgers to Mexico. "Assassin of careers! Assassin of careers!" Branch Rickey shouted at one of Pasquel's employees, adding more profane verbiage that surprised sportswriters used to hearing no expletive stronger than "Judas Priest!" from the God-fearing executive.[19] However, there was no way that the Brooklyn president was going to allow any interloper to invade his spring training camp, which, after the long years of diluted wartime baseball, was at last brimming with the kind of prospects Rickey had dreamed of since he first took over the Dodgers.

The Mexican League recruiters were persistent. They visited Jackie Robinson, trying to tempt him with lucre, but he quickly dismissed them.[20] They made a run at Pete Reiser, the Dodgers' oft-injured but immensely talented switch-hitting outfielder, but Rickey convinced the player to stay in Brooklyn. "I don't believe he wanted to be a man without a country," Rickey said in one of his heartfelt, if chilling, defenses of the established baseball order.[21]

The Dodgers did lose two players they were counting on for 1946: catcher Mickey Owen and Puerto Rican outfielder Luis Olmo. Olmo never reported to Daytona Beach in 1946, going straight from Puerto Rico to Mexico, but Owen did come to camp. Rickey thought he could sign the Missouri farm boy, who had made his Cardinals roster as a twenty-one-year-old in 1937, but the catcher was not satisfied with Rickey's contract offer. When it became clear that Owen was tempted by the Mexican offer, Rickey had no trouble convincing team counsel Walter O'Malley and other members of the Brooklyn board of directors to take legal action.

Once again an offending sportswriter—Ray Gillespie of the *St. Louis Star-Times*—had drawn Rickey's ire. The Dodgers president claimed that Gillespie was serving as an agent for the Pasquels by trying to deliver Owen (Brooklyn property) to Mexico. Owen denied that Gillespie was doing anything improper except translating messages from the Pasquels. A Missouri lower court granted the Dodgers a temporary injunction, but at the end of May 1946 a St. Louis circuit court judge ruled in favor of the sportswriter. "Inspired by a zeal for 'scoops,' Gillespie aggressively pressed his opportunities," Judge Rubey Hulen wrote, but he decreed that there was nothing illegal about a reporter's seeking an exclusive story.[22]

"I beat the great Mr. Rickey in court," Gillespie reminisced years later to sportswriter and oral historian Jerome Holtzman. The St. Louis writer had known the executive since the 1920s and had once considered taking a Minor League front office job with the Cardinals' Danville, Illinois, farm club until Rickey intimate Charley Barrett advised him that the boss thought his career path should focus on sports writing, not management.[23] However, pleasant relations in the past were insignificant to Branch Rickey if he thought Gillespie was actively helping the Mexican League woo American players. The Brooklyn president was ready to take any steps needed to protect management's strict control of the player market. Another twist to the Gillespie story was that Cardinals owner Sam Breadon offered to foot $2,500 of the sportswriter's legal bills.[24] It is a measure of the feeling of mutual bitterness lingering between the former St. Louis associates that the tight-fisted Breadon was willing to shell out a goodly sum to help Gillespie in his court battle against the Brooklyn president.

Late in May 1946 Breadon himself was stung by the Mexican League when his ace southpaw pitcher, Max Lanier, headed south after starting the season with a 6-0 record. Lanier was joined by his teammate second baseman Lou Klein. A somewhat panicked St. Louis owner soon flew to Mexico to visit Pasquel, pleasing the Mexican mogul no end but outraging Breadon's American partners. In June Commissioner Happy Chandler fined Breadon $5,000 for breaking ranks in the establishment's complete opposition to recognizing the Mexican League as anything but a loathed "outlaw" league. (The fine, though, was never collected.)[25]

As events played out, the Mexican League experience of Mickey Owen and other American players proved short lived and unhappy. Owen's team, the Veracruz Oilers, languished in the league cellar despite having eight American players, including Lanier and Klein. The exiles were uncomfortable with the unfamiliar surroundings of a foreign country, and most came back quickly, Mickey Owen among them. Yet Commissioner Chandler issued an edict in June 1946 declaring that all those who went to Mexico would be banned for five years. The ruling was to provoke several legal suits against baseball, but Chicago Cubs general manager Jim Gallagher expressed the imperial hauteur of baseball's establishment when he said, "The spectacle of Mickey Owen languishing on a Missouri farm will do more to keep players from jumping this winter than anything Mr. Rickey or the rest of us could do."[26]

In June 1946, as Rickey was receiving an honorary degree from the University of Rochester for his efforts in fostering sportsmanship and interracial goodwill with the signing of Jackie Robinson, he was asked for his view of the Mexican League challenge. As always, in public he was the picture of confidence. He said that he was all in favor of expanding baseball opportunities, but he criticized the Mexican League for going through the back door and raiding players instead of knocking on the front door and asking for recognition.[27]

Still, the threat of the "outlaw" league and Robert Murphy's American Baseball Guild led to an extraordinary late August 1946 meeting of the owners, who usually met as a group only in December. The beginning of the baseball players pension dates from this meeting because a few owners, including the Yankees' Larry MacPhail and the Cubs' Philip Wrigley, shrewdly reasoned that offering players postbaseball security in the form of a pension would likely nip in the bud any union activity.

Another subject discussed at the special midsummer meeting was Branch Rickey's signing of Jackie Robinson and other black players. Larry MacPhail presented a report of a three-man committee, consisting of himself, Sam Breadon, and Phil Wrigley, that was very critical of Rickey's program of racial integration. The study noted that already in 1946 at some of Montreal's games in Newark and Baltimore, black spectators accounted for more than 50 percent of the attendance. If integration occurred in the Major Leagues, the report warned, "a situation might be presented . . . [that] could conceivably threaten the value of the Major League franchises."[28] MacPhail's thinly veiled meaning was that the presence of black players on the field might attract too many black fans to all-white ballparks and thus threaten the property values of the teams.

When the report was presented for discussion, Branch Rickey was stunned by its content. However, it was not voted on but instead was quickly gathered up and locked away, with most of the copies destroyed. As we shall soon see, in February 1948, in the glow of Robinson's successful rookie Major League season in 1947, Rickey went public with the existence of the report. In late August 1946, however, Rickey simply sat quietly at the owners meeting, confident that the tide of integration could not be turned back and that the success of his program would be determined, as it should be, by excellence in performance on the field.

On April 18, 1946, Jackie Robinson's Montreal Royals debut could not have gone better. Before a packed house of more than twenty-five thousand fans at Jersey City's Roosevelt Stadium, Robinson homered twice for the visiting Royals and went five for six, powering a 14–1 Montreal rout over the New York Giants' top farm club. In addition to a horde of white and black New York City writers covering the event, one interested and pleased spectator was catcher Roy Campanella, who would soon leave for Nashua, New Hampshire, where he and nineteen-year-old black pitcher Don Newcombe had been signed to the Dodgers' class B farm team in the New England League. (They would play for manager Walter Alston, who had been signed by Rickey's Cardinals in the 1930s and had one Major League at-bat as a pinch hitter for Johnny Mize in 1936.) Campanella and Newcombe would lead Nashua to a pennant in 1946 and would play out the year without any untoward racial incidents.[29]

With only a few exceptions Robinson's year in the International League was also played out without racial tension. At first, however, league president Frank "Shag" Shaughnessy was nervous about Robinson traveling to the border state city of Baltimore, Maryland. He pleaded with Rickey, an old friend he had known since he managed the Cardinals' Syracuse farm club in the early 1920s, not to bring the black player. However, the Brooklyn president insisted that there would be no backing down on the principle that Robinson was a member in full standing of the Royals, and where the team went, he went. Period. Shaughnessy relented and soon became a great advocate of integration, realizing that the race pioneer was a catalyst for a record-breaking season of attendance in the International League.[30]

When Robinson and the Royals came to play in Jersey City and Newark during the 1946 season, Rickey and many staff members came to see Robinson play and to offer encouragement. Occasionally, a New York sportswriter stopped by to observe a historic story in the making. Walter Wellesley "Red" Smith, a future Pulitzer Prize winner who had joined the staff of the *New York Herald Tribune* in the fall of 1945, was impressed by both Robinson's skills as an athlete and his aplomb in dealing with the writers. When asked if he had been subjected to extensive razzing from crowds and fellow players, Robinson said, "It hasn't been worse than anything I heard in college football."[31]

W. C. Heinz of the *New York Sun* encountered Robinson while visiting the New Jersey training camp of heavyweight champion Joe Louis, who was preparing for his second fight with Billy Conn. Montreal's prize rookie was on the injured list, but Heinz was impressed that Robinson, although he would be out of action for a few more days, wanted to be back with the Royals well before game time, as players on the active list were required to do. Robinson implored the writer to drive him to the ballpark on time, and Heinz obliged.[32]

Branch Rickey was pleased but not surprised at the great success Jackie Robinson was having in Montreal. However, he did not expect that the Brooklyn Dodgers would truly contend with the Cardinals until 1947. Yet Leo Durocher had the team in first place for a good portion of the 1946 season. The team was getting inspired play from its double play combination of shortstop Pee Wee Reese, back from the Navy, and second baseman Eddie Stanky, a wartime pickup from the Phillies Minor League system. A former high school soccer star from Philadelphia, Stanky was the son-in-law of Dodgers coach Milt Stock, who had played third base for the Cardinals in the early 1920s.[33] Nicknamed "The Brat" for his pugnacious style of play, Stanky would earn one of Branch Rickey's highest accolades: "He can't run, he can't hit, and he can't throw, all he can do is beat you."

In the outfield the Dodgers were led by right fielder Dixie Walker, who batted .319, with 9 HR and 116 RBI. Although his numbers—.284, with 3 HR and 35 RBI—didn't reflect his coming stardom, center fielder Carl Furillo, one of the youthful World War Two signings, was beginning to establish himself as a Major Leaguer. He was an excellent outfielder whose shift to right field later in the 1940s would cement his starter status and maximize a fearsome throwing arm, nicknamed the "Reading Rifle." When he wasn't injured Pete Reiser patrolled left field and would hit .277, with 11 HR and 73 RBI.

The Brooklyn pitching wasn't outstanding, but veteran Kirby Higbe, back from the war in Europe, led the staff with seventeen wins. Young southpaws Joe Hatten and Vic Lombardi contributed fourteen and thirteen victories, respectively. Hank Behrman, a local boy from Maspeth, Queens, won eleven games, as did reliever Hugh Casey, back from the Navy, who compiled an excellent 1.99 ERA. At catcher, Bruce Edwards came up from the Mobile farm club in the Southern Association to fill the void left by the departure of Mickey Owen for Mexico. His statistics were not impressive—.267 BA, 1 HR, and 25 RBI—but he called a good game behind the plate.

Durocher's hunger for a 1946 pennant was growing so intense that he tried to convince Rickey to call up Jackie Robinson for the stretch run.[34] Eddie Stanky was entrenched at second base, but the Dodgers had weaknesses at first and third base and left field (all positions, incidentally, that Robinson would play later in his Brooklyn career). However, Rickey did not seriously consider promoting Robinson. He wanted the race pioneer to complete a successful full season in the Minor Leagues. There was no way that Branch Rickey wanted to risk arousing the extraneous factors of racial and social unrest that bringing up Robinson in the middle of a pennant race might entail.

Meanwhile, 1946 was a great year for sports spectatorship all over the country as the nation was at last freed from the sacrifices of the world war. Attendance was particularly booming in Brooklyn, delighting players, fans, and owners alike. By August the Dodgers shattered their single-season record on their way to a league-leading total of 1,796,824 fans.[35] To accommodate the demand the Dodgers occasionally scheduled morning-afternoon doubleheaders with separate admissions for each game. Many spectators grumbled about money grubbing by the management, but the interest was so high that the fans, of course, continued to come. One morning Branch Rickey came out of his office to calm and chat with the crowd on line waiting for tickets.

Rickey was used to the excitement of pennant races in St. Louis, but the Missouri fans tended not to come in droves until the last few games of September. In Brooklyn Rickey was often overwhelmed by the fan frenzy and by the fever pitch stirred up all season long by the more than a dozen daily New York area newspapers covering the Dodgers and the effective radio broadcasts of Red Barber. Paradoxically, as the pennant race heated up, Jimmy Powers's "El Cheapo" attacks on Rickey in the *New York Daily News* reached new lows. Never one to take press criticism easily, Rickey grew so enraged that he instructed Arthur Mann and other associates to prepare a dossier of Powers's unfounded charges for possible legal action.[36]

Although the Mexican League raids had died down and the league itself would shortly disband, Powers continued to charge that the Dodgers paid "coolie wages" compared to other teams in the National League. He even started a campaign to run Rickey out of Brooklyn, presumably because Rickey's manner was so pompous and irritating that he didn't belong there with the common people. "Shall we send him over Niagara Falls in a barrel?" Powers asked his readers. "Shall we maroon him on Bikini atoll?" The scribe asked his readers for their ideas. Powers quoted one reader who suggested "that all fans get together and each donate a $20 bill upon entrance to the park." The virulent journalist endorsed the idea. "If the fans will help fill these barrels with $20 bills," Powers wrote, "perhaps Rickey's desire for milking money out of the franchise will be satisfied and he will pack his carpet bags and go away to another town and run his coolie payroll there."[37]

Although Rickey was talked out of suing Powers for libel by Walter O'Malley, John L. Smith, and other members of the Dodgers' board of directors, he also took great umbrage at a comment by Joe Williams, columnist for the *New York World-Telegram*. The writer charged that Rickey's midseason trade of second baseman Billy Herman to the Boston Braves was another sign that he didn't really want to win a pennant. Williams was repeating the argument that John Mize and Enos Slaughter used to make on the Cardinals: that Rickey's goal was always to draw enough fans to come in a close second, masking that his real goal was in making money in sales. "It is a lie," Rickey told his staff with great emotion.

It seems that he wouldn't be Branch Rickey if he weren't harboring a grudge against some sportswriter. It was his least attractive character quirk, perhaps a product of both his deep respect and his fear of what he called the "mighty fourth estate." If he liked a writer and the feeling was mutual, he thought nothing about inviting the scribe to his country house and welcoming him to sleep over. Journalists who weren't regular baseball beat writers, such as Charles Dexter and John Chamberlain, received wonderful stories as a result, but in his almost childlike innocence, so peculiar in a man of such intelligence, Rickey couldn't understand that other writers with less access might get jealous.[38]

Rickey's saving grace was that rarely, if ever, did he let his petulance interfere with the operation of a ball club. Nor did he lose the general respect and admiration of most of the players. During the last week of the 1946 season, with the Cardinals and Dodgers locked in another neck-and-neck race for the pennant, two remarkable events at Ebbets Field revealed the unusual bond between Rickey and most of his athletes during the first season following World War II.

Before the game on Wednesday night, September 25, the players invited Rickey down to the field and presented him with the gift of a forty-two-foot cruiser, for which each member of the team had contributed $125. "This is to say that we think you are tops in our book," team spokesman (and later National League player representative) Dixie Walker told Rickey in front of the Ebbets Field fans, some of whom nonetheless booed the executive.[39] The players' unusually generous gesture was a response to Rickey's recent announcement that every member of the team would receive a Studebaker automobile. The gifts were courtesy of Paul G. Hoffman, president of the auto company and Rickey's friend and fellow Delta Tau Delta fraternity brother. (In the 1950s, Hoffman would become president of the Ford Foundation and, later, managing director of the United Nations Special Fund.) Walter O'Malley was not in favor of the automobile gifts, grousing about the tax liability that might incur on the team treasury, but for Branch Rickey there was no way that these cars would not be bestowed. "I'm going to give you those autos whether you finish first or second," he said. "And I want to say you've done a wonderful job."[40]

On the last day of the 1946 season the Dodgers found themselves tied for first place with the Cardinals, each with ninety-six wins. In one of the heart-wrenching turns that make pennant races an experience not for the fainthearted, St. Louis and Brooklyn both lost on Sunday, September 29. Mort Cooper, the ex-Cardinals pitcher who was now with the Braves, beat the Dodgers, 4–2, but St. Louis lost to Johnny Schmitz and the Cubs. As befitting the spirited, first post–World War Two season, St. Louis and Brooklyn would now meet in the first pennant playoff in Major League history.

The Dodgers won the coin toss, and Durocher elected to open the best-of-three series in St. Louis, with the last games to be played at Ebbets Field. The strategy backfired when Howard Pollet, the mild-mannered southpaw from New Orleans whom Rickey had signed as a teenager, beat Ralph Branca, 4–2. At Ebbets Field two days later, Dodgers left-hander Joe Hatten didn't get out of the second inning as the Cardinals won,

8–4, sweeping the playoff and earning their way into the World Series. The Dodgers didn't go down quietly. They rallied for two runs in the bottom of the ninth inning and loaded the bases with two out. Looking for a long ball with the potential tying run at the plate, Durocher sent up six foot seven first baseman Howard Schultz to pinch-hit for lighter-hitting Eddie Stanky. But Harry Brecheen, another outstanding St. Louis left-hander, struck out Schultz to end the Dodger season and bring the Cardinals their fourth pennant in the last five seasons.

The clubhouse scenes after the game reflected the remarkable influence Branch Rickey continued to have on both teams. In front of the sportswriters St. Louis manager Eddie Dyer gave an emotional tribute to his former boss: "There is something I want you all to know. It was Branch Rickey who assembled this team. It was Branch Rickey who signed me as a pitcher back in 1922 and, when my arm went dead, persuaded me to continue as an executive and taught me every bit of baseball I know. If this is a good team, and it was today, then most of the credit is his. He got these ballplayers while he was still in St. Louis. If I am a successful manager, it's because he made me one."[41]

Over in the Dodgers clubhouse Rickey made a rare appearance. He, too, was very emotional, but he wanted the team to know that he had never thrown in the towel on the season. With tears in his eyes he called sportswriter Joe Williams's charge, repeated in that morning's newspaper, that he didn't really want to win "a lie. I want none of you young men to leave here and go home with the idea that I don't want to win every day, every year. Because I do, with all my heart."[42] He added that the Dodgers might have lost to a better team in 1946, but he predicted that Brooklyn was the team of the future. The reign of the Cardinals was over, Rickey said, and the Dodgers were on their way. Success in the Minor Leagues buoyed Rickey's optimism as Montreal won the International League title, Fort Worth took the Texas League crown, and St. Paul contended for the American Association pennant. The Cardinals' top farms at Rochester, Houston, and Columbus all languished in the second division.[43]

Branch Rickey's prophecy would prove entirely accurate. After the Cardinals conquered the Boston Red Sox in seven thrilling games in the 1946 World Series, St. Louis would not win another pennant until 1964.

Starting in 1947 the Dodgers would win six out of the next ten National League pennants and come agonizingly close to two others.

After saying good-bye to his scrappy 1946 team, Rickey went upstairs to the press box to say a few words for a national radio hookup. His gracious concession speech was widely applauded inside and outside the game. An ardent Brooklyn fan who lived near Ebbets Field was moved to write the executive with his words of condolence. "The team fought gamely against tremendous handicaps, . . . outclassed player to player, but never man to man," wrote fan Harvey Weinstein. "You are no longer 'Mr. Rickey,' a name in the newspaper but a warm human being. You are no longer the penny-pinching ogre of the 'Chain Gang,' no longer 'the non-alcoholic Rickey' (John Kieran) but very much one of the boys, one of Brooklyn." Weinstein concluded his letter with the sincere hope that "you will remain at the Brooklyn helm for many years, that there will be peace on earth and good will toward men, and that somehow, somewhere, you will find a left-handed pull hitter."[44]

As Branch Rickey sat down with his staff for the annual postseason review of the year, he thought that there was far more good news than bad. The parent Dodgers had almost won a pennant in 1946 that Rickey never thought was possible so soon after the war. The fine showing confirmed his belief that Leo Durocher was the best manager in the game.

In the Minor Leagues Jackie Robinson had completed a highly successful first year in the Dodgers organization, leading the Montreal Royals to a Little World Series title over the Louisville Colonels of the American Association. It was the sweetest kind of victory for Robinson and his teammates. After losing three games in a row at Louisville, where some Kentuckians taunted him with the worst race baiting he heard all season, the Royals won four in a row before the home crowd. After the victory the fans were so delirious that they wouldn't leave the ballpark. When Robinson came out of the clubhouse in street clothes, his admirers began grabbing at him and the player's friends had to spirit him away. "It was probably the only day in history," Sam Maltin wrote in the *Pittsburgh Courier*, "that a black man ran from a white mob with love instead of lynching on its mind."[45]

After hitting .349, stealing 48 bases, and playing often-spectacular defense at his new position of second base, Robinson was the unanimous choice as Most Valuable Player in the International League. Roy Campanella and Don Newcombe also excelled at Nashua, and there was promise aplenty among the white players at Brooklyn's farm club affiliates.

Never one to mull too long about the past, Branch Rickey soon was thinking about the 1947 season and the opportunity for Jackie Robinson to make the Brooklyn club. By arranging to move spring training headquarters from Daytona Beach to Havana, Cuba, Rickey hoped that the preseason in 1947 would prove less stressful for Robinson and the other black players, who would not have to endure the strict Florida segregation statutes. He was planning an adventuresome travel schedule, with games in Panama and Venezuela as well as Cuba. It was the idealistic executive's hope that playing games in front of people of color would make his white players more comfortable playing alongside Robinson and other black players. Rickey harbored the genuine, if naive, hope that once his white players saw how good a player Jackie Robinson was, they would virtually demand that he become a teammate in 1947.

However, as he looked forward to the adventure of the 1947 season, Branch Rickey couldn't help but feel a growing concern about the internal politics in the Brooklyn front office. The ambition of his partner Walter O'Malley was obviously growing. It wasn't just that O'Malley spoke out against the tax implications of Rickey's gifts of the Studebaker automobiles to the players as a reward for their fine 1946 effort. O'Malley was also upset that his partner had refused to accept extra money for the radio broadcasts of the playoff games against the Cardinals. Rickey told the sponsors that they had paid for a full season of games and that as far as he was concerned the playoff was part of a full season. (The interpreters of baseball's official record book certainly agreed with Rickey's position.) The team lawyer was not pleased when Rickey said that playoff proceeds would go to the team's fifty front office employees.[46]

O'Malley was not yet in a position of power to make the major business decisions, but Rickey sensed that the young attorney was eager to one day take control of the team. Road secretary Harold Parrott was telling his boss stories of O'Malley and his cronies at their Brooklyn hangout making fun of Rickey's piety and mannerisms and virtually playing "pin the tail on the donkey" games with Rickey's picture as the target on the wall.[47]

However, as long as John L. Smith, the third partner in the controlling triumvirate of the Dodgers, was in Rickey's corner, the ferocious gentleman's position was secure. Smith had undergone a cancer operation in 1946, but he seemed to have recovered quickly. Although Smith would come to consider some of Rickey's baseball expenditures "extravagant," he deferred completely to the veteran executive on matters of baseball judgment. "I know him to be the best man in the business," Smith told Taylor Spink in June 1946. "He is a fine operator, a moral man, a man with faith and principles, . . . and genuinely interested in youth." He added, "I know that the baseball writers kid him a lot about his double talk, so-called. But he is a very coherent man, believe me."[48]

Rickey had another cause for concern as he looked ahead to 1947. A rivalry with Yankees general manager Larry MacPhail was intensifying. Although in 1946 the brilliant promoter had nearly tripled Yankees home attendance to an all-time Major League record of 2,265,512, the Bronx Bombers had missed out on two pennants in a row since MacPhail had come to the Bronx.[49] Already extremely vocal in his criticism of Rickey's cornering the market on black players, MacPhail was jealous that his one-time mentor had usurped his place as the mastermind in Brooklyn. He was beginning to target Rickey's coaches, hiring Red Corriden and Charlie Dressen for 1947, and was rumored to be making a pitch for Leo Durocher too. He also was trying to woo Red Barber to the Bronx.

As Rickey made his final plans for the 1947 season, he was concerned about Durocher in more ways than MacPhail's possible designs on him. He was worried that the off-field behavior of his irrepressible manager might become a major distraction. Brooklyn's Roman Catholic Church hierarchy was expressing its dissatisfaction with the manager's incorrigibly belligerent behavior and messy private life. It was sending signals to Walter O'Malley, a leading local Catholic layman, that the Catholic Youth Organization (CYO) would end its support of the Knothole Gang, the program Rickey had pioneered in St. Louis and brought to Brooklyn, if Durocher weren't removed.[50] Although the manager had been quickly acquitted in May 1946 of the assault charges brought by fan John Christian for the previous year's altercation at Ebbets Field, many leading Brooklyn Catholics thought Durocher was a time bomb waiting to go off.

There was no doubt that Leo was a great fan favorite for bringing Brooklyn the 1941 pennant, for coming close in 1946, and perhaps most of all for being his vital, take-no-prisoners self, a personality that appealed to the underdog mentality of the much-maligned borough. Rickey shared the fan sentiment that nobody matched Leo Durocher as a field leader. With Jackie Robinson due to get his shot at the big ball club in spring training, Rickey felt strongly that he needed his dandy manager to shepherd and protect the black pioneer. The Dodgers were truly on the cusp of something magnificent, Rickey believed, and before it was too late he decided to try to preempt the danger to Durocher and, indirectly, to himself, as the manager's greatest patron. As it turned out Rickey's strategy would backfire and set in motion one of the most turbulent off-seasons in his adventurous saga.

19

When All Hell Almost Broke Loose

If Branch Rickey needed another reminder that Leo Durocher was not a choir boy off the field, he received a vivid one the afternoon that the Dodgers lost the 1946 playoff to the Cardinals at Ebbets Field. Going down to the clubhouse to commiserate with Durocher and the players after their valiant 1946 run at the National League pennant, Rickey was blocked at the entrance by a big, burly fellow. "Just a minute, Pop," the stunned executive was told. "Stand back!" A bodyguard for movie actor George Raft was blocking the door while Raft was in the clubhouse, extending his sympathies to his good friend Leo Durocher.[1]

Raft's friendship with Durocher dated back to the late 1920s when Durocher was a young Yankees shortstop and Raft was an occasional Broadway actor, gifted ballroom dancer, and baseball-loving man about town, a habitué of all the hot spots in Prohibition-era New York. Ten years older than Durocher, Raft, born George Ranft, was raised in the tough New York City neighborhood known as Hell's Kitchen. Like his friend Leo, Raft quit school early on to live by his wits, hanging out in pool halls and doing odd jobs for local mobsters. When he was eleven years old Raft said that he had a dream job, serving as a mascot and go-fer for the New York Highlanders (before they became known as the Yankees).[2]

In the 1930s Raft headed to Hollywood, where he appeared as a gangster in many movies. His on-screen persona was very convincing because he was friendly in real life with many big-time mobsters, including Owen Madden, Al Capone, and Benny "Bugsy" Siegel. The actor also cultivated relationships with many baseball people. Leon "Goose" Goslin gave him the bat with which the Tigers star won game seven of the 1935 World

Series.[3] Raft and Durocher grew so close that they stayed in each other's apartments when visiting the opposite coast. They wore similar wide-brimmed hats with low crowns and employed the same tailor for their custom-made clothes. The actor once said of their friendship, "We used each other's suits, ties, shirts, cars, girls."[4]

In baseball circles a red flag had hovered over George Raft for some time. In 1941, when then-commissioner Landis learned that Raft had won $100,000 betting on baseball, he ordered Durocher to rescind his offer of four World Series tickets to the actor.[5] The Raft-Durocher connection raised eyebrows again in 1944 when a wealthy man was duped out of $12,000 during a crap game with loaded dice at the manager's New York apartment. Durocher was at spring training in Bear Mountain the night of the incident, but Raft was the host of the evening. He, too, wasn't involved in the dice game but was playing gin rummy at another gaming table in a night of typical revelry chez Durocher.

The victim in the dice game didn't bring the matter to the authorities until months afterward and no criminal charges were ever filed, but the police fed the newspapers with the details because the activities of high-living celebrities always made for good copy. By 1946 rumors were circulating about Durocher's ties to New York mobster Joe Adonis and about Raft's close friendship with Bugsy Siegel (who would be murdered in 1947). Durocher denied to Branch Rickey any connection with Adonis, saying that his only link to the gangster was that he once provided baseball equipment for one of the gambler's favorite charities.[6]

Scandal-mongering newspaper reporters, however, would not let the Durocher-Raft connection die. On October 26, 1946, Westbrook Pegler, a syndicated columnist for the *New York Journal-American*, the largest of the national chain of Hearst newspapers, wrote the first of a series of three scathing articles about the actor and the manager and their unsavory lifestyle and associates. There were no new disclosures of fact in Pegler's series. He basically rehashed the story of the loaded dice game in Durocher's apartment and the manager's penchant for surrounding himself with people Pegler called "Hollywood characters—jerks, one sport writer called them recently." The columnist added that Brooklyn's manager attracted so many hangers-on "that a baseball writer can't get into his dressing room during the season."[7]

Pegler was a one-time sportswriter himself who at times had supported the underdog in a variety of causes, but in recent years he had wielded his pen as one of the more vitriolic yellow journalists. He concluded his series of articles with the warning, "Durocher's choice of companions has been a matter of deep concern to Branch Rickey, the business manager of the Dodgers. The old practice of 'whispering out' players and even managers for 'the good of the game' could be revived."[8]

Always fearful of the power of the press to besmirch a reputation, Branch Rickey was indeed concerned that his prodigal son was heading for thin ice, running toward trouble and not away from it. On the eve of what Rickey hoped would be a historic 1947 season for the Dodgers, he did not want his manager's off-the-field indiscretions to jeopardize the team's future. In preparing his stories Pegler had telephoned the executive at home, urging him to dismiss his manager and warning that he planned more exposés if he did not. The writer said that Durocher should be fired because he was "a moral delinquent" who "would drag Rickey and baseball down to his own level of shame and shameful companions."[9]

Branch Rickey, of course, was not going to be intimidated by anyone, and he tried to reason with Pegler. Rickey may have been slightly acquainted with the journalist because both of them had occasionally attended Lowell Thomas's Quaker Hill Sunday afternoon salons.[10] In their long phone conversation the Dodgers president defended his manager as an able strategist and leader of men on the playing field. He also did good works off the field, Rickey argued. He had entertained troops during World War Two, and, in fact, as they spoke he was on his way to give baseball clinics to American troops stationed in Italy. The executive tried to sway Pegler's thinking by using a historical analogy. He mentioned that in his long baseball career, he had seen Babe Ruth suspended for insubordination and Ty Cobb accused of gambling and fixing games, but both these heroes were ultimately cleared and restored to baseball's pantheon.[11]

Branch Rickey probably did not expect that he could persuade Pegler to drop his venomous crusade, and indeed, in December 1946, the columnist came out with more anti-Durocher diatribes. But at least the executive had tried to dissuade the acidulous writer to control his pen. (Bill

Veeck Jr., the maverick baseball owner, once said that the last words on his deathbed of his father, Chicago Cubs president William Veeck Sr., were, "Push inter-league play, and beware of Westbrook Pegler.")[12]

Regardless of Pegler's vitriol, Rickey knew that Leo Durocher always lived close to the edge of trouble. He was aware that his manager was continuing to live in George Raft's Hollywood apartment, even though he told Leo that he must move out.[13] The Dodgers president pondered an important decision. He had recently re-signed Durocher to a contract that, at $50,000 a year, would make him the highest-paid manager in baseball. He was mulling the right time to publicly announce the renewal. However, the possibility that Durocher's underworld connections were more serious than he imagined frightened him. When Commissioner Landis was alive he could read the riot act to the manager in ways that the benignly paternal Rickey could not bring himself to do.

Branch Rickey could rarely be direct and threatening with anyone, especially with Leo Durocher. He operated by indirection, a family trait akin to his mother's disciplining little Branch not with harsh words but, rather, by praying on her knees to God that she must do a better job of teaching her son the right way to behave. Branch Rickey could not effectively say to Leo Durocher, "You *must* cut all ties to George Raft." Somebody else would have to do it.

Rickey wondered if baseball commissioner Happy Chandler should be informed of Durocher's dangerous connections and whether he should be the one to order him to end his associations with disreputable people. In considering what turned out to be a momentous (and disastrous) decision, Rickey huddled primarily with Arthur Mann, who had joined Rickey's staff in October 1946 as a special assistant.

Mann was a person of many talents, all of which drew him to Branch Rickey. He had been an artist, an actor, and a beat sportswriter for the *New York World* who left daily writing after the newspaper was bought in the 1930s by the Scripps-Howard syndicate and became the *World-Telegram.*[14] He had been published widely in national magazines and made his home on a farm in Cherry Plain, New York, many miles north of the city. Rickey was impressed by Mann's erudition; he knew Latin and quoted it to his friend's delight. They shared a love of Protestant hymns, and in their spare time they would belt them out with Mann at the piano.[15] They both believed in the rightness of the racial integration cause and were strong anti-Communists. Rickey had given Mann exclusive information about the scouting and signing of Jackie Robinson that the writer utilized in some of the first articles about the race pioneer.[16] The journalist's impression of Rickey at the annual New York baseball writers' dinner was so hilarious that the joke among the sportswriters was that Mann had been hired by Rickey to prevent him from doing his impersonation.[17]

However, Mann's new position as special assistant to the president perplexed other people in the Brooklyn organization. E. J. "Buzzie" Bavasi, who worked under Branch Rickey Jr. in the Minor League department, never really knew what Mann's duties were nor did office secretary Jane Ann Jones (no relation to Rickey's daughter Jane Rickey Jones).[18] Rickey had no explanation, except that everyone in the office knew that Arthur Mann had Rickey's ear, and when you were a friend of Branch Rickey it was a unbreakable bond.

Rickey and Mann decided that Commissioner Chandler should be told about Durocher's troublesome associations and that Chandler should be the one to order him to cut his ties with unsavory people. In mid-November 1946 Rickey dispatched Mann to meet with Chandler at the commissioner's office in Cincinnati. The main purpose of the meeting was to inform Chandler about Durocher's indiscretions, but Rickey also wanted Mann to express his displeasure with Larry MacPhail's recent signing of coach Charley Dressen. The Brooklyn president believed that Dressen had verbally agreed to a two-year contract to remain as coach that would be invalid only if Dressen got an offer to be a Major League manager. MacPhail, though, had gone ahead and hired Dressen.[19]

Chandler knew little about Durocher's off-the-field lifestyle, but when Mann told him the stories about the manager's unsavory connections, the commissioner was immediately concerned. Mann gave Chandler Durocher's phone number in Hollywood, which happened to be located at George Raft's apartment. When Chandler called he was told that Durocher was not home but was rehearsing for the Jack Benny program at the NBC radio studios. When he called the studio Chandler was informed that Leo could not be disturbed because he was in rehearsal. "Tell him that Commissioner Chandler is on the phone," Chandler roared. "That will disturb him."[20] Durocher hurried out to take the phone call and agreed to meet the commissioner shortly before Thanksgiving on a golf course in Berkeley, California.

In bringing Chandler into the Durocher case, however, there was a big risk involved. The late Judge Landis was familiar with Durocher's antics, and though he often rebuked him he basically liked Leo's spirited pugnacity. Chandler, though, had no personal connection with the incorrigible manager. He had met him only casually at ceremonial baseball functions when he was still a Kentucky politician gazing in awe at his baseball heroes.

Commissioner of baseball since April 1945, Chandler had been placed in the unenviable position of following the legendary Kenesaw Mountain Landis. He was being increasingly subjected to wide criticism as a do-nothing, and even inept, successor. In one of his first acts as commissioner in 1945, Chandler had given his verbal approval to American League umpire Ernie Stewart's attempt to organize a union. However, American League president William J. Harridge summarily fired Stewart and pointedly told Chandler that the issue was "a league matter."[21] The commissioner's five-year ban on the defectors to the Mexican League had spawned many lawsuits, and many observers felt his action was too severe. There were also several incidents of fixes during the Minor League season in 1946, soon to result in lifetime expulsions by the National Association, the Minor Leagues' ruling body.[22] Chandler had been largely silent about these disturbing episodes, drawing more criticism for his passive leadership. As he flew to California to meet Leo Durocher for the first time in his role as putatively baseball's most powerful individual, he likely was looking for an issue to prove that he was every bit as big a man as Judge Landis had been.

At their November 22, 1946, meeting Chandler immediately asked Durocher to provide him with the names of his friends and acquaintances of dubious reputations. The manager mentioned George Raft, Joe Adonis, Bugsy Siegel, and two New York bookies, Max "Memphis" Engelberg (who actually once put "bookmaker" in the "occupation" column in a tax return) and Conrad "Connie" Immerman, who had been running the Harlem nightspot Connie's Inn since the murder of gambler Owen "Owney" Madden. Chandler ordered Durocher to move out of Raft's apartment and to cut off his connections with the other men. Durocher protested that he and George Raft spent little time with each other and even used separate telephones when they visited, but the manager reluctantly agreed. "They'll call me a louse, but I'll do it," Durocher said.[23]

Then, probably because Rickey had told Leo to unburden himself of every possible problem, Durocher informed Chandler of his latest love affair with movie actress Laraine Day, best known for her role as the nurse in the popular *Dr. Kildare* movies. Given the manager's inevitable penchant for entanglements, there was a complication. Laraine Day was still married to Jack Hendricks, currently employed at a Southern California airport. As the commissioner sat in stunned silence, Durocher provided the details of the affair. It happened that Jack Hendricks was a drinker and that Laraine Day was a Mormon who neither drank nor smoked. The marriage had been on the rocks for a long time, according to Durocher, when he entered to push it over a cliff. He told Chandler that as soon as her divorce was final, he and Day would be married in January. He added that he and Laraine were so enamored with each other that he was staying in her apartment, much to the chagrin of her husband.[24]

Happy Chandler, the strait-laced, God-fearing former governor and senator of the conservative state of Kentucky, had heard enough from the streetwise city slicker Leo Durocher. He had never encountered anyone like him, with his escapades right out of pulp fiction. "You are going to conduct yourself properly, or I'm going to have to discipline you," Chandler said to Branch Rickey's prodigal son, parting words that Rickey himself could never utter directly.[25]

In the short run, alerting Chandler to Durocher's problems allowed Branch Rickey to feel that he had done due diligence on an issue concerning the good of the game. He called a late November press conference in Brooklyn announcing Leo's return as manager, and it went off swimmingly. With great flair Rickey announced that Durocher's $50,000 a salary made him the highest-paid manager in baseball "not by a little, but by a great deal, a very great deal."[26] The feisty, rehired manager expressed confidence about the 1947 season and uttered a desire to remain as Brooklyn manager "until the day I die." As for the rumored attempt by Larry MacPhail to woo Durocher to manage the Yankees, Rickey treated the subject lightly. He said that he was glad that his manager was in demand by other teams because it showed that the rival executives had good taste.[27]

However, the long run danger was that Happy Chandler was now watching every move of the Brooklyn manager, and as always Durocher could not help turning a sticky situation into a terrible tangle. Early in January 1947 the triangle of Durocher, Day, and Hendricks made headlines when Hendricks sued the Dodgers skipper for alienation of his wife's affections. The *Los Angeles Examiner*, a Hearst syndicate newspaper, ran the headline "Durocher Branded Love Thief."[28] A California court did grant Laraine Day her divorce on January 20, 1947, but state law required a wait of one year for remarriage. The defiant lovebirds ignored that requirement and hopped to Mexico, where they obtained a Mexican divorce and then returned across the border to El Paso, Texas, where they were married in late January 1947.

California Superior Court judge George Dockweiler was outraged at the newlyweds' action and threatened to overturn Day's divorce decree. He made the transcripts of the court proceedings public, with all the details of Durocher's role in the end of Laraine Day's marriage to Hendricks. Once again the press had a field day of headlines and charges and countercharges. The unrepentant Brooklyn manager accused Judge Dockweiler of being "unethical and publicity-conscious," and another judge agreed with Durocher. Day's divorce decree was sustained.[29]

Meanwhile, back in Brooklyn, Branch Rickey was kept informed of all these twists and turns in the soap opera "As the World of Leo Turns," and he sighed wearily. He tried to believe what Durocher promised to him once he had become again a happily married man: he would be on very good behavior after spring training began in Havana because, as Durocher reflected years later in his autobiography, *Nice Guys Finish Last*, "I had the commissioner, the judiciary, the clergy and the crusading press watching every move I made."[30]

Branch Rickey did not know what to expect when spring training commenced in Cuba in February 1947. For the time being Jackie Robinson was still on the Montreal Royals roster, but Rickey wanted Robinson to have every chance to make the Dodgers. As he had done the prior spring in Daytona Beach, Rickey took special steps to facilitate Jackie Robinson's spring. While Rachel Robinson was back in California with Jackie Robinson Jr., born in November 1946, Rickey hired Wendell Smith to be Jackie Robinson's roommate. Rickey understood that the pressures on the black player were bound to intensify, and he thought that the presence of the *Pittsburgh Courier* sportswriter would be a calming influence. "You should not worry about the plans they have for you," Smith wrote to Robinson in California before the start of spring training. "[Mr. Rickey] is a very methodical man and will see to it that you are treated right. All you have to do is take care of Jackie Robinson on the playing field and he will do the rest."[31]

As the "great experiment" in racial integration neared a major test in 1947 spring training, Rickey was taking heart from reading a recently published little book, *Slave and Citizen*, by Columbia University Latin American history professor Frank Tannenbaum. In his book Tannenbaum argued that slavery in the Latin American nations had not been as pernicious as in the United States because, south of the American border, the slave had always been considered a "moral being" with a soul bestowed by God. Such was not the case under the harsher American Protestant form of slavery, Tannenbaum argued. Despite the death of the "peculiar institution" after the Civil War, too many white people held on to their feeling of superiority because of a feared loss in status. As a Christian moralist and committed idealist, Rickey was captivated by Tannenbaum's analysis that with the passage of time, increased education, the rise of a black middle class, and greater proximity between the races, the American racial dilemma would be ameliorated, if not totally solved.[32]

Rickey was so enthralled by Tannenbaum's thesis in *Slave and Citizen* that he began to carry around a battered copy of it with his own notes on racial progress stuffed into its pages. It became for the ferocious gentleman as valuable a source book in the area of race relations as his black loose-leaf notebook stuffed with player information had been during his days running the Cardinals.

Rickey soon developed a friendship with Tannenbaum, who had led the kind of adventurous as well as intellectual life that the ferocious gentleman always admired. Born in Austria in 1893 Tannenbaum moved with his family to a New England farm in 1905. In 1914 he took part in a demonstration of unemployed workers in New York City that turned violent, and he was jailed for a year. A sympathetic warden helped him to attend Columbia, where he made Phi Beta Kappa. In the early 1920s he served in the United States Army in the South, where he witnessed racism firsthand, and he drew on those experiences for his first book, *Darker Phases of the South*, published in 1924.[33]

In 1956 Rickey implored his knowledgeable and concerned friend to issue an updated edition of *Slave and Citizen*. "There is no problem facing us nationally or internationally comparable to the Negro problem," Rickey wrote Tannenbaum. Ever the cautious conservative progressive, Rickey hoped that a revival of Tannenbaum's work would dissuade radical black militants from acting with "quick ardor in whetting its knife for forceful surgery."[34]

Before Rickey flew to Cuba for the start of 1947 spring training, he decided that he had one more major step to take to lay the best possible foundation for the emergence of Jackie Robinson on the 1947 Dodgers. He was concerned that serious trouble might arise if there was too much celebration by Robinson's black fans. As fearful as Rickey was of southern white bigots, he remained firm in his belief that northern black militants could also disrupt the integration program if they provoked a defensive reaction in the white community.

On Tuesday night, February 5, 1947, Rickey spoke to a select gathering of thirty local black leaders at the Carlton YMCA in Brooklyn. The Dodgers president, his special assistant Arthur Mann, NYU sociology professor Daniel Dodson, and Judge Edward Lazansky (the latter two members of the now-defunct former mayor LaGuardia's Committee for Unity) were the only white people in the room. Before he began speaking Rickey asked that everything he said be kept in confidence. His topic was how best to plan for Robinson's acceptance in the New York black community.

Branch Rickey always felt most at home at a YMCA, where he had worked as a young man and often spoke and mesmerized his audiences. As was his custom in important lectures he discarded his written remarks and talked extemporaneously. He began by stressing the moral rightness of the cause of racial integration, and the bravery of Robinson, who had already been through a crucible of fire. He has held up nobly, Rickey said, and should be applauded for his courage and restraint.

Rickey, the dramatic orator, paused for effect. He said that he did not know yet if Robinson would make the Major League roster in the upcoming spring training. "But I do know this," he said bluntly. "If he is brought up to the Dodgers, one big risk to his success is that the Negro people themselves will ruin it."[35] There were gasps in the room from the black middle-class group of educators, clergymen, realtors, morticians, and government employees, but he won them over by painting a dire picture of black people strutting, having parades, getting drunk and into fights, all because one of their own had made the Major Leagues.

"You must remember that white ballplayers are human beings too," Rickey explained. "That old green-eyed monster, jealousy, also moves among them, and it is only natural that they will resent the heaping of praise and awards upon a Negro who has not been in the major leagues long enough to prove himself." He continued, "We don't want Jackie Robinson wined and dined until he is fat and futile. We don't want what can be another great milestone in the progress of American race relations turned into a national comedy and an ultimate tragedy."[36] The conservative revolutionary concluded sharply: "If any individual, group, or segment of Negro society uses the advancement of Jackie Robinson in baseball as a triumph of race over race, I will regret the day I ever signed him to a contract, and I will personally see that baseball is never so abused and misrepresented again!"[37]

As the audience of black professionals left the Carlton YMCA meeting, they thought deeply about Rickey's talk. After being horrified and somewhat insulted at Rickey's first barrage, they got the message about the dangers of in-group aggression. They realized that the black community, like the white community, had its deep divisions, distrusts, and snooty attitudes toward the poorer and less refined of their own. As a result of the YMCA gathering the black leaders agreed to follow Rickey's cautionary program. They printed up signs reading "Don't Spoil Jackie's Chances" and posted them prominently in black churches, community centers, schools, stores, taverns, and wherever black people congregated.[38]

Shortly after addressing the black leaders in Brooklyn, Rickey flew to Cuba for the start of spring training. It was the first time that Rickey had led a team to train outside the United States (although Larry MacPhail had brought the team to Havana in 1941 and 1942). The Dodgers were headquartered at the opulent Hotel Nacional overlooking the Caribbean, and the Royals were based at a new boarding school for the Cuban military elite fifteen miles outside of Havana. However, the four black players on the Montreal roster—Robinson, Campanella, Don Newcombe, who won sixteen games in Nashua in 1946, and thirty-six-year-old left-handed pitcher Roy Partlow—were consigned to a shabby Havana hotel. It was an inconvenience that disturbed Jackie and Rachel Robinson, but cautious to a fault, Rickey explained that he had made the arrangements because "he didn't want a possible racial incident to jeopardize the situation."[39]

On March 10, 1947, the Royals and Dodgers hopped a plane from Cuba to Panama to meet in a series of exhibition games that Branch Rickey thought would showcase Robinson's unquestionable Major League abilities. However, far from the veteran Dodgers clamoring for Robinson's promotion, just the opposite was happening. Rickey received word that some of the players were contemplating preemptive action against the presence of the race pioneer. Although an actual petition was probably never drawn up, several southern-born players were intent on creating pressure to prevent the Dodgers from promoting Robinson to the Major League roster.

Veteran outfielder Fred "Dixie" Walker was one of the ringleaders. Walker was a native of the Deep South, born in the small town of Villa Rica, Georgia, now living in Birmingham, Alabama, where he operated a sporting goods store. When he was originally signed by the Yankees, it is said that Walker waited a long time before he told his unreconstructed Confederate grandmother what team he was playing for, and, as noted earlier, when Walker heard the news of Robinson's signing in October 1945, he said pointedly, "As long as he isn't with the Dodgers, I'm not worried."

Others in the anti-integration group were two more southerners, pitcher Hugh Casey and reserve catcher Bobby Bragan, and one player from the North, Pennsylvanian Carl Furillo. However, another southerner, pitcher Kirby Higbe, did not think the protest was a good idea, and he informed road secretary Harold Parrott about what the players had in mind. Parrott quickly told Rickey and Durocher, who wasted no time confronting the problem.[40]

The manager summoned the entire team to a midnight meeting in the kitchen of an old army barracks in Panama City, where the team was staying. Clad in bathrobe and pajamas, Durocher read the players the riot act. The fiery skipper told them what they could do with, and where they could stick, their alleged petition. "I'm the manager of this ball club, and I'm interested in one thing. Winning," Durocher told the team, in the undoubtedly sanitized though assuredly accurate version in *Nice Guys Finish Last.* "I'll play an elephant if he can do the job, and to make room for him I'll send my own brother home," he added. "From everything I hear, [Robinson's] only the first. Only the first, boys," he roared. "They're going to come, boys, and . . . unless you fellows look out and wake up, they're going to run you right out of the ball park." Yet, like a true leader of men in baseball battle, Durocher offered a carrot as well as a stick to his charges. "He's going to win pennants for us," he said. "He's going to put money in your pockets and money in mine."[41]

The next day it was Branch Rickey's turn to lay down the law in individual conferences with recalcitrant players. If Rickey was disappointed that the players hadn't come asking him to bring up Robinson, he didn't let on. He just firmly told them that if any member of the team didn't want to play with Robinson, he would surely oblige the player with a trade. Soon thereafter Dixie Walker wrote him a letter asking to be dealt, and reserve catcher Bobby Bragan told Rickey frankly, "Ah don't intend to make myself a goat for a mess Ah didn't create."[42]

The rebellion had been nipped, and, fortunately, as far as Rickey and the organization were concerned, little if any news of the uprising made the press. Robinson went on to hit .625 with 7 SB and 6 RBI in the Panama exhibition series against Brooklyn. With Eddie Stanky entrenched as the Brooklyn second baseman, Robinson was handed a first baseman's glove, a position he never had played. With the help of George Sisler and others in the organization, he gradually began to feel adequate at the new position. Cautious to a fault, however, Rickey still made no announcement of Robinson's call-up to the Dodgers; he remained on the Royals' roster.

There was a significant postscript to the opposition of both Dixie Walker and Bobby Bragan to Robinson's presence, changes in attitude that bore out Branch Rickey's belief that reason and proximity would overcome bigotry. Both players eventually became great admirers of the race pioneer. Walker said that the Dodgers would not have won the 1947 pennant without him, and he called him a "gentleman." Although Rickey did almost trade Walker to the Pirates early in the 1947 season, he held on to the veteran outfielder after another injury to Pete Reiser. Walker would make a valuable contribution to the 1947 Dodgers, with a .308 BA, 31 2B, 9 HR, and 94 RBI, and an outstanding 97:26 walk-strikeout ratio.

If Walker had been willing to serve as a player-manager, Rickey would have had him manage the Dodgers farm club in St. Paul in 1948. However, the outfielder still wanted to play, so Rickey packaged him to Pittsburgh in a big trade before the 1948 season, with Brooklyn receiving two future stalwarts in return, pitcher Preacher Roe and third baseman Billy Cox. Often accused of being cheap, Rickey actually received just $1 for Walker's contract so Walker himself could pocket the $10,000 waiver price. The gesture was another example of Rickey's genuine paternalism within the strict limits of the reserve system. As with Clay Hopper, Rickey realized that Dixie Walker's racial attitudes were deeply entrenched and might be impossible to temper, but he wasn't going to ignore Walker's other abilities as a player, a coach, and a community-oriented leader.[43]

As for Bobby Bragan, the catcher played in only twenty-five games for the Dodgers in 1947, but he was ready to start a Minor League coaching and managing career in the Brooklyn organization and later under Rickey in Pittsburgh. "He showed me a lot when he stood up for his beliefs in Panama," Rickey reflected years later. "It made me believe in his future as a leader."[44] It warmed Rickey's heart that Bragan quickly became a big advocate of integration, agreeing with him that only runs and hits are important in baseball, not color of skin. In a phone interview in May 2005 Bobby Bragan declared, "The three greatest men I ever met in my life were Jackie Robinson, Branch Rickey, and Billy Graham."[45]

The player rebellion against Jackie Robinson was nipped in the bud in spring training, but controversy involving Leo Durocher could not be averted, even though he arrived in Havana trying to be inconspicuous.

With his marriage to Laraine Day not yet official in the United States, Durocher decided at first not to bring his new wife to Cuba, fearing too much of a crush from the press. He also was keeping his vow to stay away from his gambler friends. When given an opportunity to meet Charles "Lucky" Luciano, a well-known gangland kingpin, the manager refused to shake his hand and fled to the security of his hotel room.[46]

Yet the life of a taciturn hermit was not made for Leo Durocher, nor was it for talkative Branch Rickey. The climactic brouhaha in Durocher's off-season of travails started innocently enough. In his March 3, 1947, "Durocher Says" column for the *Brooklyn Eagle*, a regular feature for the newspaper ghosted by Harold Parrott, the Brooklyn manager said that he was treating seriously the upcoming exhibition series against the Yankees in Caracas, Venezuela. He said that he wanted to get even with Larry MacPhail for pilfering his coaches Charley Dressen and Red Corriden and for trying to lure him to the Bronx. "I want to beat the Yankees because MacPhail knows in his heart that I love Brooklyn," Durocher/Parrott wrote, "always want to manage there and regard Branch Rickey as my father." The manager added that when MacPhail couldn't woo him away, he "resolved to knock me, and to make life as hard as possible for me."[47]

Out of context the column seemed like harmless early spring training banter. Like many people who use ghost writers, Durocher hadn't read what Parrott wrote, but if he had he likely would not have raised an objection. Both Harold Parrott and special assistant Arthur Mann evidently thought that it was a good idea to enliven spring training with stories of the two warring executives, Rickey and MacPhail, and to use Durocher as the critic of the ex-Dodgers executive, not Rickey.[48] The strategy turned out to be another disastrous tactical error because the column offended MacPhail, who was in increasingly high dudgeon about Rickey's usurping his place in Brooklyn and beating all his partners to the market for black players. MacPhail was probably also thinking, "I trained in Havana before Rickey, and I bought the Montreal franchise before Robinson played there. Who does Rickey think he is, claiming all the credit for the Brooklyn organization?"

MacPhail's irritation escalated into something far more serious a few days later when, during another game against the Yankees back in Havana, Rickey noticed with dismay that gamblers Memphis Engelberg and Connie Immerman were seated in MacPhail's private box. After the game the Dodgers president, never bashful about making a point publicly, asked the writers what would have happened if the betting moguls had been in the Brooklyn box. When Engelberg and Immerman returned the next day, Dick Young, a youthful, enterprising sportswriter for the *New York Daily News*, asked Durocher for a comment. The manager obliged, saying, "Where does MacPhail come off, flaunting his company with known gamblers right in their faces?" He declared: "If I even said 'Hello' to one of those guys, I'd be called up before Commissioner Chandler and probably barred."[49]

MacPhail was enraged at Durocher's claim that the gamblers sitting in his box were his guests and was even angrier that Rickey had made the criticism a day earlier. He demanded an investigation by Commissioner Chandler that he hoped would lead to penalties on the two Brooklyn leaders for libeling him.

When he received MacPhail's complaint the commissioner thought wearily, "Durocher making headlines again?" Since Durocher was the accuser and not the accused, Chandler at first tried to talk MacPhail out of pursuing any action. However, the Yankees' passionate leader was driven to continue his vendetta against Rickey. He started working on a fifty thousand–word brief and enlisted American League president William Harridge to join the complaint.[50]

Chandler owed his job largely to MacPhail's support in 1945, and the commissioner was becoming increasingly aware of the growing dangers of gambling in all sports. In December 1946 two members of the New York Giants football team, Frank Filchock and Merle Hapes, had been permanently disqualified for refusing to report a bribe attempt before the Giants' National Football League championship game against the Chicago Bears. Middleweight boxing champion Ray Robinson and contender Rocky Graziano had also recently admitted to being offered bribes, and a few more Minor Leaguers had been banned for life by National Association czar William Bramham for betting on baseball.[51] Acceding to MacPhail's wishes, the commissioner called a meeting of all the parties for Sarasota, Florida, on March 24, 1947.

Unfortunately, one of the main defendants, Branch Rickey, could not attend. As Rickey was preparing to fly from Havana to Sarasota, he learned that Jane Rickey's brother, Frank Moulton, had died and that the funeral was scheduled for Lucasville, Ohio, on the same day as the hearing. Family always came first with Branch Rickey, who asked for a postponement, but Chandler refused. Rickey asked his old friend from St. Louis, attorney George Williams, who had retired to Sarasota, to represent him at the hearing. Representing the Dodgers as an organization were the team's chief counsel Walter O'Malley, Arthur Mann, and farm director Branch Rickey Jr. Leo Durocher appeared without representation by counsel.

Commissioner Chandler and his assistant Walter Mulbry were the judge and jury at the March 24 hearing, which convened on the top floor of a Sarasota hotel that during World War Two had been used as a night club.[52] In the wonderland of baseball jurisprudence, there was no official record kept, but Arthur Mann made copious notes, which he used a few years later for his book *Baseball Confidential: Secret History of the War among Chandler, Durocher, MacPhail and Rickey*. Harold Parrott testified that though he worked for the Dodgers, he had indeed written the "Durocher Says" column in question. Chandler told him that he must choose between being a baseball man or a writer, and he chose the former, never ghosting again for Durocher.[53]

Larry MacPhail was the major witness. Reading from a prepared statement, he attacked the March 3 "Durocher Says" column for impugning his integrity by "implication or innuendo." However, during questioning by Chandler, MacPhail denied he was conducting a feud with the Dodgers, and he had no word of criticism for Durocher himself. When it was the manager's turn to speak, he made light of Parrott's ghosted story, calling it "just another rhubarb" with MacPhail, a man he had fought with many times in Brooklyn and always made up with quickly. He apologized for any hurt he might have caused the Yankees executive. MacPhail quickly embraced Durocher, and to prove that there were no hard feelings, he took the clipping of March 3 and ripped it into pieces.[54]

Commissioner Chandler, however, was not through with the investigation. He seemed determined to throw the book at Durocher, indicating as much when he told a reporter before the hearing, "Somebody may wind up getting kicked out of baseball." Although he later denied making the statement, he also said that as governor of Kentucky he had sent men to the electric chair, "so I am not going to be timid when I get ready to take action."[55]

Chandler called another hearing for March 30 in St. Petersburg, which Branch Rickey was able to attend along with the other principals. It was clear that the commissioner was worried about the gambling scandals in sports and about Durocher's past associations with betting, both inside and outside the clubhouse. He brought up the subject of the manager's high-stakes card games with players in the pre-Rickey years. Baseball's leader directed more pointed questions to Yankee officials about the gamblers in MacPhail's box in Caracas, and who might have provided their tickets. Although he admitted to a friendship with Memphis Engelberg, MacPhail vehemently denied that he had provided the tickets to the gamblers. However, his road secretary, Arthur Patterson, indicated that he might have "conceivably" supplied them; he just did not remember.[56]

Before the hearing ended, Chandler called in the Brooklyn delegation for a private conference. "How much would it hurt you folks to have your fellow out of baseball?" the commissioner asked. A shocked and tearful Branch Rickey replied, "Happy, what on earth is the matter with you?"[57] He argued that his manager had more character than the owner who brought the charges. Chandler did not make an immediate ruling, irritating MacPhail, who expected an exoneration, and worrying Branch Rickey, who was wondering whether Leo Durocher's worst fears were correct and the commissioner was primed to throw the book at his controversial skipper.

Outside events were conspiring against Branch Rickey's prodigal son. The combination of fears of fixed games and Durocher's marital complications were creating a perfect storm against him. Rickey's eloquent appeal to a crusading Brooklyn priest—"Can we ignore a tremendous force like [Durocher], and surrender it to Satan?"—had fallen on deaf ears.[58] On March 1, 1947, the Catholic Youth Organization of Brooklyn had announced that it was withdrawing its support of the Brooklyn Dodgers Knothole Gang because of the presence of a manager who is "a powerful force for undermining the moral and spiritual training of our young boys."[59] Around the same time, Commissioner Chandler also received a letter from United States Supreme Court Justice Frank P. Murphy that echoed the Brooklyn Catholic hierarchy's position that Durocher was a menace to the moral fiber of American youth.[60]

When the Dodgers returned to Brooklyn a week before the April 15 opening day of the 1947 season, Chandler still had rendered no decision in the case. On Wednesday, April 9, the Dodgers were playing an exhibition game at Ebbets Field against the Montreal Royals. Branch Rickey was sitting in his office with farm director Branch Rickey Jr., Arthur Mann, Emil J. "Buzzie" Bavasi (the younger Rickey's assistant), and other staff members. They were discussing the news release that they would issue later in the day announcing Jackie Robinson's promotion to the Dodgers.

The telephone rang; it was Commissioner Chandler calling. Rickey picked up the phone, mumbled a greeting, and sat silently for several moments as he listened. Then, all of a sudden, Buzzie Bavasi heard Branch Rickey swear for the first time in Bavasi's presence. "You son of a bitch!" Rickey yelled. "You son of a bitch!"[61] The ferocious gentleman slammed down the phone and broke the bad news to his staff. Commissioner Chandler had fined Harold Parrott $500 for ghostwriting the "Durocher Says" column that started the latest controversy. The Dodgers and Yankees as organizations had both been fined $2,000 for continuing their feud in the press. Coach Charley Dressen was suspended thirty days for signing a coaching contract with the Yankees while still in the employ of the Dodgers.

Worst of all, Rickey informed his colleagues, Chandler had imposed a season-long suspension of Leo Durocher for "an accumulation of unpleasant incidents" and "publicity-producing affairs."[62] According to Bavasi, after the staff absorbed the shocking news, Branch Rickey Jr. asked his father if he had told the commissioner about the decision to call up Jackie Robinson. "No!" Rickey Sr. thundered. "It's a league matter."[63]

During the sixth inning of the April 9, 1947, exhibition game against the Montreal Royals, Arthur Mann brought out to the Ebbets Field press box copies of a short press release that stated, "The contract of Jackie Robinson has been purchased from Montreal. He is to report immediately." Not surprisingly, however, the Durocher suspension story made the biggest headlines the next day. Most of the sportswriters outside New York weren't disappointed that Durocher had been banished. However, the reaction among Brooklyn fans was outrage, and the majority of New York sportswriters thought the punishment too severe. Even Larry MacPhail was stunned by the decision. Although privately he had to enjoy Rickey being robbed of his most competitive field general, MacPhail said, "There was nothing to justify even a five-minute suspension of Durocher."[64]

The baseball season was due to start in less than a week, and the Dodgers, with the first black Major League player in the twentieth century in their lineup, had no manager. In the interim loyal coach Clyde Sukeforth agreed to fill in until a permanent successor was named. As Rickey often did when faced with a crisis, he dramatically asked his associates for their help. "I am going over a cliff, and I am falling, falling, and only one man can help me. Who can he be?" Rickey asked. He considered hiring Joe McCarthy, who had resigned from Larry MacPhail's Yankees early in the 1946 season, feeling that his great record of thirteen pennants and nine World Series titles had not earned him the irascible MacPhail's respect. McCarthy, though, needed more time away from the game. (He would lead the Boston Red Sox to a playoff for the pennant in 1948.) Rickey thought about Bill "Is Brooklyn Still in the League?" Terry, but the former Giants first baseman and player-manager was permanently retired from the game.

Branch Rickey finally decided on someone who might have been his first choice all along: Burt Shotton. Retired in Bartow, Florida, Shotton was virtually unknown to New York fans and even some sportswriters, but Rickey considered him an astute baseball man and an absolutely loyal, teetotaling friend. Rickey wired Shotton that he was needed immediately in Brooklyn. "See nobody, say nothing," he instructed. Once again, the executive was facing more than his usual share of "trouble ahead, trouble ahead," but in a crisis Branch Rickey knew that he could always rely on the help of his friends.

20

When Most of Heaven Rejoiced

While Branch Rickey was awaiting the arrival of Burt Shotton from Florida, interim manager Clyde Sukeforth led the Dodgers to two victories in two tries over the Boston Braves at Ebbets Field. Jackie Robinson's Major League debut on Tuesday, April 15, 1947, was nowhere near as spectacular as his International League debut a year earlier in Jersey City. Batting second and facing Boston's formidable Johnny Sain, Robinson was hitless in four plate appearances, but he laid down a beautiful bunt in the seventh inning that caused a wild throw and triggered a rally leading to a 5–3 win. Still learning his new position of first base, he was removed for defensive purposes in the ninth inning. The paid attendance was 26,283, about 7,000 short of capacity. It was estimated that half of the crowd consisted of people of color, who came to cheer on the race pioneer. Sportswriter Tom Meany noted a certain subdued quality to the throng, perhaps due to the absence in the Brooklyn dugout of loud, belligerent Leo Durocher.[1]

When Burt Shotton arrived in Brooklyn three days later, he was without an overcoat, wearing two-toned shoes, and carrying only an overnight bag. He had come to chilly, almost wintry, New York on a mission to help an old friend and didn't expect to stay long. Shotton had little inkling about what was on Rickey's mind but was prepared to do anything that could help out his old friend Rick. Rickey knew his friend well, describing him as a "Colonel House kind of a fellow, [who] would go anywhere and do anything I had to have done."[2] (Colonel Edward House had been President Woodrow Wilson's right-hand man.)

Shotton thought he had retired after serving as a wartime coach for

Cleveland Indians player-manager Lou Boudreau, but once he learned the meaning of Rickey's sos call, he quickly accepted the challenge. Retirement was overrated, Shotton said later. "It's a hell of a thing when a man has good health and enough money, and absolutely nothing to do," he said. "I was all wrong when I said I was through with baseball. This is the only life for an old pepper pot like me."[3]

On a handshake deal with Rickey, Shotton agreed to manage the Dodgers for the 1947 season. Salary wasn't even discussed, though it was later reported that Shotton would earn $25,000 a year, or half of Leo Durocher's salary. When asked by a team staff member for measurements for his uniform, Shotton said that it wasn't necessary. When he left the Indians, Shotton had decided his days in uniform were over, and he wasn't going to change his mind. He would manage in street clothes like Connie Mack (and Rickey in his last years as field manager with the Cardinals). Unlike Mack, however, Shotton did not wear a suit with a starched collar; instead, he donned a Brooklyn baseball cap, a Dodgers warmup jacket, and a pair of slacks.

Just three hours after Branch Rickey dropped Burt Shotton's formidable assignment into his lap, Shotton prepared to manage the Dodgers as they were beginning a series with the hated Giants in the Polo Grounds. However, the new manager almost missed his first game when a taxicab driver, unfamiliar with New York's labyrinthine traffic patterns, got lost. He was driving over the Triborough Bridge away from Manhattan when a policeman spotted them and escorted Shotton to his proper destination.[4]

Shotton lost his first game as the Giants hit six home runs in a 10–4 rout. But Jackie Robinson hit his first Major League home run in the loss, and the signs were good that he wasn't going to be intimidated by Major League pitching. After the game Shotton, the polar opposite of Leo Durocher in terms of brassy persona, admitted, "Aside from having seen some of the players in spring training, I know practically nothing about the club."[5] He said that for the first few days, he would just sit and watch and would rely on input from his coaches, especially Clyde Sukeforth.

It soon became clear that Robinson was growing accustomed to the unfamiliar position of first base and no longer would need late-inning defensive replacements. The Robinson story as a racial and social drama was another matter. The race pioneer was keeping to his pledge not to fight back at provocations, but during the Philadelphia Phillies' first visit to Ebbets Field on April 22, his patience was tested to the fullest. Phillies manager Ben Chapman orchestrated a torrent of racial insults at Robinson from the visitors' dugout. "Hey, nigger, why don't you go back to the cotton field where you belong?" went one vicious cry. "Hey, snowflake, which one of those white boys' wives are you dating tonight?" came another virulent insult.[6]

Chapman, a native of Tennessee now living in Alabama, was a former Major League outfielder who, during World War II, had tried to hang on in the Major Leagues as a Brooklyn pitcher. Playing for the Yankees in the 1930s, Chapman got involved in a controversy after directing anti-Semitic remarks at some fans, but he insisted that his vicious attacks on Robinson were no different from the typically rough, ethnic insulting ballplayers commonly inflicted on one another.[7]

Robinson's teammates knew better, and slowly but surely team unity behind Robinson, which Rickey had craved from day one of the great athlete's arrival, began to form. Second baseman Eddie Stanky shouted at Chapman, "Why don't you pick on someone who can defend himself?" When Branch Rickey heard about the Dodgers rallying to the beleaguered Robinson's side, he was overjoyed. He cited to his associates one of his favorite passages from Alexander Pope's "Essay on Man":

> Vice is a monster of so frightful mien
> As to be hated, needs but to be seen
> Yet seen too oft, familiar with her face
> We first endure, then pity, then embrace.[8]

As Rickey interpreted the development, the players had endured Robinson's trial of fire, pitied the perpetrators of hate, and, last and most important, embraced their comrade.

Another racial crisis loomed during the first visit of the archrival Cardinals to Brooklyn in early May. The weather in the Northeast turned rainy, and the Dodgers were rained out two days in a row before St. Louis came to town. The delays meant reporters seeking rainy day stories; one of the big stories uncovered was the possibility of an anti-Robinson strike by the Cardinals before the first game in Brooklyn on Tuesday, May 6. Although undoubtedly most players, especially the journeymen, were fearful of losing jobs to black players, it seems highly unlikely that the Cardinals or any other team in Major League Baseball would have walked out of their contractual obligations, however dissatisfied they were at the racial integration of their sport. The ironclad reserve system was still very much in force, especially with the defeat of both Robert Murphy's American Baseball Guild and the waning of the Mexican League. As Rickey said confidently to Arthur Mann, "You couldn't get enough ballplayers to agree on any one thing to pull a strike. It's bogey-man stuff."[9]

Obviously, though, there had been talk among the most anti-black Cardinals about some kind of rebellious action. Cardinals owner Sam Breadon had been concerned enough to fly into New York to meet with manager Eddie Dyer and National League president Ford Frick, but the three-game series was played without incident on the field. The Cardinals won the series by taking the last two games behind strong pitching by southpaws Howard Pollet and Harry Brecheen. On Friday, May 9, the day after the end of the series, Stanley Woodward, sports editor of the prestigious *New York Herald Tribune*, broke the story of the alleged plan to strike in the first of two consecutive stories copyrighted by the newspaper.

Woodward wrote that the players' goal was "to gain the right to have a say on who shall be eligible to play in the major leagues," but he lauded Ford Frick's firm preventive action. The National League president had written a letter to Breadon in which the league official declared unequivocally that Robinson was a player in good standing and that any action against him by opposing players would result in permanent suspension. "You will find that the friends you think you have in the press box will not support you, that you will be outcasts," Frick warned the anti-Robinson faction. As for the rumors that some Cardinals might delay taking action against Robinson until Brooklyn soon made its first road trip to St. Louis, Woodward wrote prophetically: "Publicity probably will render the move abortive." He added that "it can now be honestly doubted that the boys from the Hookworm Belt will have the nerve to foist their quaint sectional folklore on the rest of the country."[10]

Another crisis seemed in the making when, immediately after the St. Louis series, the Dodgers embarked on their first trip of the season to Philadelphia. Phillies general manager Herb Pennock phoned Rickey and pleaded with him not to bring Robinson. There had been threats on the player's life, Pennock warned, and he could not guarantee his safety. "Very well, Herbert," Rickey replied, "And if we must claim the game nine to nothing, we will do just that, I assure you."[11] (The official score of a forfeit was 9–0.) The games were played, and there were no visible threats on Robinson. Before the beginning of the series, at the suggestion of Rickey and National League officials, Robinson was persuaded to share a public peace offering with Ben Chapman. Reluctantly, Robinson posed for photographers with the Phillies manager as they held a baseball bat. Their hands were not touching, there seemed to be no eye contact, and their smiles were forced.[12] Another indignity of the trip occurred when the Dodgers had to scramble for a new road hotel after the Benjamin Franklin Hotel refused to accept Robinson as a guest. Fortunately, road secretary Harold Parrott found an acceptable if more expensive alternative in the Warwick, which became the team's permanent Philadelphia stopping place.[13]

Despite continuing pockets of hostility toward Robinson among the players, most of the fans warmed to the sight of the electric ballplayer. For liberal-minded rooters Robinson embodied the worthy cause of integration, and he "bore the whole burden of the black athlete with Christlike patience," writer and Brooklyn fan Wilfrid Sheed remembered. "For two years and more he suffered that a hundred Hank Aarons might bloom; indeed, for those years he *was* the civil rights movement to most of us."[14]

From his conservative viewpoint Branch Rickey was thrilled by Robinson's sparkling performance, but he was concerned about too many idolizers surrounding him. Rickey pleaded with the press not to suffocate Robinson and to allow him to become the great player and fine teammate that he was sure he would become. "He's a sideshow attraction!" Rickey complained. "If I had my own way, I'd place a cordon of police around him—give him protection so that he might be a ballplayer!"[15] Shortstop Pee Wee Reese echoed his boss's sentiment. "Why don't they leave that kid alone?" Reese said about the hordes of black and white reporters and photographers always swarming around his teammate.[16]

Despite the circuslike atmosphere surrounding the Dodgers, they were holding their own in the pennant race and were on their way to leading the National League in both home and road attendance. Under the quiet but firm hand of new manager Burt Shotton, they survived a four-game sweep in mid-June inflicted by the defending world champions in St. Louis, and in July they began a thirteen-game winning streak of their own, which featured a turnabout sweep of St. Louis at Ebbets Field.[17] By the end of the month they led the league by ten games and were in command for the rest of the year. Shotton established a set rotation of starting pitchers—Ralph Branca, Joe Hatten, Vic Lombardi, and Harry Taylor—and promised them that they would work in sequence with no favoritism.[18]

The inspired play of Jackie Robinson was a big part of the Dodgers' surge. With his teammates more definitely on his side now, Robinson started hitting with more authority, stealing more bases, and running the bases with such abandon that sometimes a whole rival infield got into the desperate act of trying to stop him. At the end of June Robinson reached a milestone when he stole home for the first time in a game against Pirates left-hander Fritz Ostermuller (the same pitcher Rickey had traded for when he banished Bobo Newsom to the St. Louis Browns in 1943).

Robinson's ability to terrorize and demoralize an opponent's defense any time he got on base was just one asset of Brooklyn's emerging National League juggernaut. Pee Wee Reese was an anchor at shortstop and turned many double plays with his partner Eddie Stanky; the team would finish second to the Cardinals in total twin killings. Stanky was a clutch hitter at the plate, with many of his 53 RBI big ones, as was true of Pee Wee Reese's 73 RBI. In the outfield Carl Furillo was putting together a solid year, with a .295 BA, 8 HR, and 88 RBI. Bruce Edwards continued to be a reliable catcher while picking up his offense to the tune of .295 BA, 9 HR, and 80 RBI.

Only the pitching seemed to be a little short, and an injury to rookie starter Harry Taylor caused Rickey to worry. "I don't have a World Series pitching staff," he moaned to his wife. Jane Rickey, ever quick with a gentle needle, replied, "Are you sure you have a pennant-winning staff?"[19] In mid-August Rickey made a move he hoped would bring the mound corps added strength. He and scout George Sisler traveled to Memphis, Tennessee, to observe Dan Bankhead, who was hurling for the Memphis Blue Sox in the Negro American League. After the game Bankhead and his wife, Charlotte, fed the visitors dinner, and soon thereafter Rickey announced that the pitcher had been purchased from Blue Sox owner J. B. Martin for $15,000.[20]

When the Dodgers' newest pitcher entered a game in relief against the Phillies on August 26, 1947, it marked the first appearance by a black pitcher in a Major League game. Like many of the Negro League hurlers, Dan Bankhead was also a good hitter. He belted a home run in his first at-bat in the Major Leagues, but he pitched in only four games in 1947, without any won-lost record. Bankhead would spend 1948 and 1949 in the Minor Leagues and would win the only nine games of his Major League career for the 1950 Dodgers before returning to what was left of the Negro Leagues. Like John Wright, Bankhead evidently always felt more comfortable playing against black opponents.[21] (Incidentally, one of Dan's four baseball-playing brothers, Sam Bankhead, was said to have been the model for the Troy Maxson character in August Wilson's play "Fences.")

Rickey was happy that Dan Bankhead's color did not attract overwhelming press attention when the pitcher arrived in Brooklyn. The executive always hoped for the day when merit, and not color of skin, determined a person's chance for success. He was thus pleased when two teams in the American League also added black players to their rosters. On the Fourth of July 1947 the Cleveland Indians signed twenty-two-year-old Larry Doby, an infielder-outfielder for the Newark Eagles of the Negro National League. Rickey was well aware of Doby's abilities, but the Dodgers had a full complement of outfield candidates and the last thing Rickey wanted was to corner the market on black players.

Accordingly, the Brooklyn team president was pleased the next season when Cleveland Indians managing partner Bill Veeck, with the approval of owner Alva Bradley, signed ageless Satchel Paige. Paige made the most of his long-delayed opportunity by winning six regular-season games and one in the 1948 World Series. The presence of Paige and a championship team enabled the Indians to draw 2,620,627 fans, shattering the all-time single season attendance of the 1946 Yankees by almost half a million customers.[22]

In July 1947 Rickey's longtime protégé William DeWitt, general manager of the St. Louis Browns, became the third big league official to join the integration program when, with the approval of his new owner, ice and bottling millionaire Richard Muckerman, he signed black outfielders Willard Brown and Hank Thompson for his struggling team. Like his mentor Rickey, DeWitt was motivated by the same combination of fairness and economics. He had noticed that the Cardinals had drawn 100,000 fans when they swept the Dodgers in June, but unfortunately his new players did not boost either the on-field fortunes or home attendance for a Browns team that was destined to lose 95 games, finish in last place, and draw only 320,474 fans.[23] Brown and Thompson were released before the end of the 1947 season. (Thompson resurfaced with the New York Giants in 1949 and would play on two pennant winners in 1951 and 1954.)

Although the Dodgers were never passed after they rode their thirteen-game winning streak in July into first place, the Cardinals were not rolling over in their quest to defend their league title. In a baseball era when teams played each other twenty-two times, the head-to-high rivalries grew intense, especially among the contenders. Despite the St. Louis players' realization that Jackie Robinson was here to stay, the last meetings of the Dodgers and Cardinals in 1947 revealed that racial tensions were still high. In Brooklyn in mid-August, pitcher Harry Brecheen deliberately placed a hard tag on Robinson instead of throwing his easy grounder to first base. Robinson glared at the opposing pitcher and muttered a warning.[24] In another, more famous incident, Enos Slaughter ran down the first base line and missed by inches stepping on Robinson's Achilles tendon as the first baseman was stretching for a throw.[25]

On another occasion, in St. Louis, Cardinals catcher Joe Garagiola tried a similar maneuver as he was running down the line attempting to beat out a double play grounder. An injured Pete Reiser was sitting in the stands next to writer John Chamberlain, who was traveling as Rickey's guest on the team's Beechcraft plane while preparing a magazine profile of the executive. "If he could have come down out of the stands to help his offended teammate, he would have," Chamberlain wrote of Reiser's angry reaction to attempts to seriously injure Robinson.[26]

Robinson escaped serious injury, and like all great players he rose to the occasion when challenged. On his next at-bat after the alleged Garagiola spiking attempt, he hit a home run in a game that the Dodgers won, 4-3. Robinson started on a hot streak in St. Louis, going 11 for 24 as the Dodgers went on to clinch the pennant on September 22, 1947.[27] They would win ninety-four games, finishing five games ahead of the Cardinals.

The honors started to pour in for Jackie Robinson. The *Sporting News* voted him its Rookie of the Year Award. Editor-publisher Taylor Spink wrote austerely that the prize "sifted only stark baseball values. . . . The sociological experiment that Robinson represented, the trail blazing that he did, the barriers he broke down, did not enter into the decision."[28] The September 22, 1947, issue of *Time* featured the Brooklyn rookie on the cover and offered polling evidence that Jackie Robinson was the second most popular entertainer in the country after singer Bing Crosby.[29]

On September 23, 1947, Jackie Robinson Day was celebrated at Ebbets Field. Although Branch Rickey had warned in his February speech at the Brooklyn YMCA about overexultation by black fans, he evidently saw no harm in a festival honoring Robinson. "Days" for white players had been very common for years in baseball, so why shouldn't Robinson's friends and admirers celebrate his achievement? In pregame ceremonies Jack and Rachel Robinson were showered with gifts, including an automobile, a television set (not yet in mass production), and furs. Tap dancer and movie star Bill "Bojangles" Robinson, who once owned an interest in the New York Black Yankees, performed on the Dodgers dugout and declared, "I never thought I'd live to see Ty Cobb in Technicolor."[30] In his brief remarks Robinson spoke with his usual sincere modesty. "I want to thank all my teammates for making me a better player," he said.[31]

Although numbers could never tell the full story of Jackie Robinson's contribution to winning on a baseball field, his 1947 Rookie of the Year season was filled with outstanding statistics—.297 BA, .427 SA, 12 HR, 48 RBI, 31 2B, and 125 R. He led the National League with 31 SB, and his walk-strikeout ratio was an excellent 74:36. He played in 151 of 154 games. Before the last game of the regular season, Burt Shotton offered him the chance to rest and preserve his .300 batting average, but Robinson insisted on playing. He didn't want records for records' sake, and he went 0 for 3, thus finishing at .297 for the season.

For the first time since 1941, the World Series matched the Dodgers and the Yankees, and for the first time ever it was Branch Rickey versus

Larry MacPhail for the baseball championship of the world. In his long experience in the game Rickey had never viewed a World Series in personal terms, as one general manager and front office against another. However, MacPhail had put Rickey through such a wringer in the last year, with his poaching of Brooklyn coaches, his opposition to integration, and his precipitation, however unintended, of Leo Durocher's suspension, that Rickey really wanted to win the World Series, not just for the players and the borough of Brooklyn but also to defeat MacPhail.

Interest was enormous in New York City, and speculation arose that all the games would be played at Yankee Stadium, which had more than double the seating capacity of Ebbets Field. Rickey squelched that idea immediately, however. The World Series had to be a reward for the loyal fans who supported a team all season, he said emphatically.[32]

The World Series opened at Yankee Stadium with Ralph Branca—coming off a season in which he won twenty-one games at age twenty-one—earning the right to open game one. Branca began by pitching four perfect innings but was knocked out in the fifth as the Yankees scored five runs and won, 5–1, behind a strong effort from rookie Frank "Specs" Shea. Game two was a rout by the Yankees as Allie Reynolds pitched a complete-game, 10–3 victory, aided by a home run by Tommy "Old Reliable" Henrich. Vic Lombardi, Brooklyn's diminutive left-hander, lasted only four innings, and two errors didn't help his cause. Most of each Yankee Stadium crowd—73,365 for game one and 69,865 for game two—went home thinking that the 1947 Series was going to be another romp, even a sweep, for the Yankees.

However, when the Series shifted to Ebbets Field, Brooklyn's fortunes turned around. In game three the Dodgers teed off on former teammate Bobo Newsom and reliever Vic Raschi for six runs in the bottom of the second, and the Dodgers held on to win, 9-8, despite home runs by Joe DiMaggio and Yogi Berra.

The fourth game, on October 3, 1947, would go down in baseball history as one of the most dramatic World Series and baseball games ever (only to be surpassed on the same day four years later when Bobby Thomson hit his famous home run against the Dodgers to win the pennant playoff for the Giants). Going into the bottom of the ninth inning, Yankees starting pitcher Floyd "Bill" Bevens clung to a 2-1 lead and was

pitching a no-hitter. The Dodgers had scored one run without a hit because Bevens had been wild, walking nine batters.

With two out Brooklyn had the tying run on second base, carried by
reserve outfielder Al Gionfriddo, who was pinch-running for Carl Furillo. Pete Reiser came up to pinch-hit for pitcher Hugh Casey. The in-
jury-prone Reiser could not run on his damaged ankle (which was found
out later to be broken), but he commanded such respect from the opposition that even though he represented the potential winning run,
Yankees manager Bucky Harris ordered an intentional walk.

Infielder Eddie Miksis ran for Reiser, and Harry "Cookie" Lavagetto
pinch-hit for Eddie Stanky. The veteran utility player swung and missed
at Bevens's first pitch, but on the next one he slashed a double high off
the right-field wall to give the Dodgers an improbable 3–2 victory. Their
winning line score was 3–1–3–3 runs, 1 hit, and 3 errors. An overjoyed
Burt Shotton gave Lavagetto a phone to call his family in California. The
frugal Shotton, working for the frugal Rickey, told the game four hero
"to talk all I want to," Lavagetto told his wife. "He said the phone bill
would be on the club."[33]

As the Dodgers prepared for the crucial game five with the Series all
tied up at two games apiece, Branch Rickey thought back to similar situations in his prime years with the Cardinals. They had won some and
they had lost some when faced with what was, in effect, the first game of
a climactic three-game series. Rickey knew that it was always up to the
pitcher to keep his team in the game.

Rex Barney was slated to start for Brooklyn, and Rickey had great faith
in the natural ability of the twenty-two-year-old Omaha, Nebraska, native,
who was another of his World War Two tryout camp signings. However,
inconsistent control was Barney's major shortcoming. It would soon be
said in Brooklyn, "If the strike zone were high and outside, Rex Barney
would be in the Hall of Fame."

Unfortunately, Barney was wild in game five, walking 10 men in six and
two-thirds innings. He allowed only four hits and two runs, one of them
on a Joe DiMaggio home run, but Frank Shea again pitched a strong
complete game, and the Yankees won, 2–1. Most of the 34,379 fans, the
largest crowd of the Series in Brooklyn, left the last game of the year at
Ebbets Field feeling disappointed once again.

Yet, the next day at Yankee Stadium, the Dodgers evened the Series, winning 8–6. Game six is most remembered for Al Gionfriddo's great catch on Joe DiMaggio's long drive to left field, which prompted radio broadcaster Red Barber to exclaim, "Oh, doctor!" and caused DiMaggio to exhibit a rare piece of emotion on the field, kicking the dirt angrily after the outfielder hauled in his smash. A record number of thirty-eight players were used, and Ralph Branca won in relief, with veteran Hugh Casey getting a save for pitching a shaky but successful ninth inning.

Alas, for Brooklyn fans starved for a world championship, game seven was anticlimactic. The Dodgers lost, 5–2, in a game that wasn't as close as the final score might indicate. Yankees reliever Joe Page pitched the last five innings, allowing only one hit, while Dodgers starter Hal Gregg didn't get out of the fourth inning.

After the game Branch Rickey trudged down to the clubhouse to commiserate with the players for another gallant season that again came up just short. A year ago he had made the same trip to console a team that had just lost a pennant playoff. "You did a great job, boys, and I'm proud of you," he said, adding hopefully, "I'll tell you this, in the next 10 years, you'll beat the Yankees more times in the World Series than they'll beat you."[34] Certainly the Dodgers had nothing to be ashamed of, and Jackie Robinson had performed respectably, going 7 for 27 in the Series with two stolen bases.

When Rickey left the clubhouse he encountered Larry MacPhail, who started to embrace his defeated rival. Rickey was usually gracious in defeat. Back in 1941 he had even waited with MacPhail at the railway station to welcome home Brooklyn's heroes after they had clinched the pennant over Rickey's Cardinals. Six seasons later, however, Rickey felt too bitter about MacPhail's actions and behavior in the past year to be cordial. The last straw may have been a recent comment by the combustible Yankees president that Leo Durocher would never have been suspended if Branch Rickey didn't really want it to happen.[35] In front of a swarm of photographers MacPhail offered a handshake to his defeated rival, but Rickey whispered, "I am taking your hand only because people are watching us, but never speak to me again, never."[36]

MacPhail departed and was on his way to a bravura farewell performance in baseball. At the Yankees clubhouse victory celebration, MacPhail began by congratulating George Weiss for building the Yankee team and himself for building the Dodger team. Before long, however, after imbibing more than his share of alcohol, he abruptly told Weiss that he was fired. Then he interrupted the party to break down in tears and announce his retirement from baseball. After MacPhail exited Weiss was quickly reinstated by the Yankees' other owners, Dan Topping and Del Webb.[37]

When the pain of the World Series loss of 1947 subsided, Branch Rickey could look back at the year with definite satisfaction. The Dodgers had won the pennant convincingly, and Jackie Robinson had proven resoundingly that he belonged in the Major Leagues, obviously breaking the ground for future black players. Brooklyn road attendance doubled as people of color in other cities flocked to see the man Bojangles Robinson had called "Ty Cobb in Technicolor." (In 2004 baseball commissioner Allan "Bud" Selig reminisced about coming from Milwaukee to Chicago as a young man to see Robinson's debut at Wrigley Field, noting that he and his friend were the only white people they saw in the upper deck.)[38] In other National League cities, including Cincinnati and St. Louis, large groups of black fans came to see Robinson from hundreds of miles away. Sportswriters traveling with the Dodgers recalled hearing announcements in the late innings of games, "Will the group from Paducah, Kentucky, please report to your bus outside of Gate 4 for the return home."[39]

After the season the awards and accolades from interfaith and interracial groups started to pile up for Branch Rickey and Jackie Robinson. Rickey was flattered, but he turned down many speaking engagements. He continued to insist that the credit belonged only to Robinson and that it was a sad commentary that a chance for employment for someone so qualified was greeted as such a special thing in what, after all, was an American nation founded on the tenets of liberty and equality of opportunity for all.

In November 1947 Rickey provided another example of his genuine concern about racial fairness when he tried to mediate a dispute between his alma mater, Ohio Wesleyan University, and Rollins College in Orlando, Florida. One of the stars of Ohio Wesleyan's football team was Kenneth Woodward, a versatile black player who excelled at both running back and end. The Battlin' Bishops were scheduled to play Rollins in Orlando the day after Thanksgiving, but because of the segregation laws in Florida, Rollins would play owu only if Woodward didn't accompany the team. Rickey wired C. E. Ficken, the acting president of his alma mater. "I think Ohio Wesleyan might make a major mistake," he warned, if it were to allow the team to play without Woodward. He argued that the school would compromise its integrity if it took such a timorous stand.[40] Rickey discouraged Kenneth Woodward's parents from offering a compromise that would absolve the university of any liability if their son got injured in the game. He wrote them at their home in Columbus, Ohio: "The university got itself into this mess, and it will have to get itself out of it."[41]

On the campus in Delaware, Ohio, for a board of trustees meeting, Rickey phoned the Rollins authorities and tried to get them to rescind their segregationist decision. However, the Orlando college would not bend. Rollins issued a statement that summed up a majority southern attitude in the years before the historic 1954 *Brown v. Topeka Board of Education* Supreme Court decision (and before the success of Jackie Robinson and other black players was fully absorbed and appreciated). "Rollins College has no objection whatsoever to playing in a game in which a Negro participates," the college administrators wrote. "However, a football game is a community affair." After talking the matter over with members of both black and white communities, the small Florida college announced the game was canceled. In "the best interests of racial relations," the school said that it was "unwilling to take action which might interfere with the good progress now being made in Florida, and especially in the local community."[42]

Branch Rickey sighed sadly at the outcome. He had tried to bring reason and his sense of fair play to the college controversy, but he realized that only in professional baseball did he have the ability to influence racial change in a progressive manner. He retreated to his hideaway on the Eastern Shore of Maryland, where he prepared to deal with the first major issue of the postseason, the reinstatement of Leo Durocher.

Commissioner Happy Chandler had been silent about when Durocher's suspension would end. Was it at the end of the World Series? Or at the end of the calendar year of 1947? For his part Durocher had been keeping out of the headlines during the season of his unwanted sabbatical. He was spending most of his time near Hollywood with his new wife, Laraine Day, and their adopted children in the modern house she had tastefully decorated. However, he expected to be reinstated for the 1948 season because he knew that Rickey felt his punishment had been totally unwarranted.

Rickey met with Chandler, and the commissioner reluctantly agreed not to oppose Durocher's return, though he wouldn't endorse it either. "The Commissioner neither approves nor disapproves of the reappointment," Chandler said in a written statement. "It's solely a matter between Mr. Durocher and the Brooklyn Club." He concluded his short release by expressing his hope that "the fans of the country will accept Leo's return in true American style."[43]

Around Thanksgiving Durocher journeyed to Rickey's Chestertown farmhouse for what Rickey hoped would be a secret rendezvous and re-signing. Not surprisingly, enterprising reporters managed to get on the trail. When one sportswriter noted that the local general store shelves were filled with an inordinate number of Oreo cookies, there was good reason to believe that the manager was nearby because informed people knew that Jane Rickey always liked to have plenty of the chocolate cookies, Durocher's favorite snack, on hand.

Just as he had done after the 1942 season when he decided to retain Leo as Brooklyn manager, Rickey took Durocher for a walk in the woods. "We spent the first day traipsing over his . . . farm so that he could introduce me to his cows," Durocher remembered in *Nice Guys Finish Last*. "I had to wear his old clothes, which were five sizes too large for me. . . . I looked like a five-year-old kid whose mother had taken him out for an airing."[44] At the end of the suspended manager's visit to Rickey's rustic hideaway, it was announced that he was rehired for 1948 at the same $50,000 salary as 1947. However, an addendum to the top of the agreement gave both parties "the right to terminate the contract at any time."[45] The clause was added probably because of the continuing pressure from the Brooklyn Catholic Youth Organization, which had reluctantly agreed to continue its participation in the Knothole Gang program, even with the alleged bad influence returning to manage the Dodgers.

As tumultuous as the 1947 season had been in his baseball business life, at Christmastime in 1947 Rickey looked back at another rewarding year as a paterfamilias. In February another milestone had been reached when Betty Rickey, his youngest daughter, married a young engineer, Lindsay Wolfe, she had met at Swarthmore College outside Philadelphia. As a sophomore in 1939, Wolfe, a 140-pound halfback, had played on the school's first undefeated football team, a squad captained by Edward Jakle, who would marry his schoolmate Alice Rickey. So the small Pennsylvania college had a representation in the Rickey family that almost rivaled Ohio Wesleyan's.[46]

With Betty's wedding all six Rickey children were married now, and Rickey beamed with pride at his good fortune. One of his favorite after-dinner speech topics was "The Qualities That a Good Husband Must Have," and Rickey said that "infinite kindness" was the most important attribute of all. When he was asked how it felt to be the father of five daughters and only one son, Branch Rickey always had a ready answer. "For Christmas, the men usually go to their wives' home," he said. "So I enjoy an extended visit with my family every year." He always added that he felt his greatest accomplishment in life had been to earn the love and respect of all the women in his household.[47]

Decades later Lindsay Wolfe shared vivid memories of his first encounters with his in-laws, Jane and Branch Rickey. He first met Jane after his discharge from the Navy at the end of World War II. He was enrolled in a graduate program in mechanical engineering at Stanford University in Palo Alto, California, and one day, as he prepared to drive to the campus laboratory, Jane Rickey asked demurely, "Can I come?" Of course, she was welcome. After Wolfe completed his work in the campus lab, he came outside to see Jane Rickey bent over, dutifully and contentedly picking the weeds out of the university gardens.

Wolfe and his new father-in-law, Branch Rickey, also hit it off swimmingly. When the young engineer told Rickey that he was going into business for himself, his father-in-law exclaimed, "Hallelujah!" Rickey, of course, was a most enthusiastic supporter of the capitalist system and the value of individual initiative. In the 1950s Wolfe would become an officer with Rickey in the American Baseball Cap Company, which the executive established in Pittsburgh to manufacture protective batting helmets for baseball players.[48]

Lindsay Wolfe shared another revealing story about Branch Rickey's undying belief in the enterprising spirit. It happened on a brutally hot Saturday afternoon in the seclusion of Rickey's house on Maryland's Eastern Shore. All of a sudden the doorbell rang. "A door-to-door vacuum salesman appeared, who somehow had found his way to the house in the middle of nowhere," Wolfe remembers. "Branch Rickey became so impressed with the young man that he wound up buying seven vacuum cleaners from the man, one for Jane and himself, and one for each of his children."[49]

The year 1947 had also brought a change in primary residence for the energetic executive, who left the relative roominess of Forest Hills Gardens for an apartment in a big complex on Clinton Avenue in Brooklyn. Arthur Mann already lived there, and George Sisler would, too, when he moved east the next year. Rickey's new home was closer to the team offices and cut down on his commuting time, an important consideration because his chronic condition of Ménière's disease left him vulnerable to sudden attacks. The less he was outside in strange places, the safer he would be.

Although his primary residence was in Brooklyn, Branch Rickey was all the more intent on keeping his Chestertown retreat in Maryland for refuge on weekends, or whenever he could break away from the office. He never would learn to accept the traffic jams of the big city. One day he got caught in a terrible snarl on the highway. Tuga Clements Adams, widow of Bob Clements, one of Rickey's devoted farm system administrators, remembers that Rickey got out of the back seat of his car and starting shouting at the drivers, trying to whip them into shape and get them moving again.[50]

As the 1948 season drew near, Branch Rickey realized that the Dodgers were on the verge of becoming an even better and more successful organization than his Cardinals had been. The Brooklyn team, which he and his staff had carefully selected and developed, had taken the proud Yankees to a seventh game in the World Series. Most of the twenty-seven farm clubs in the Dodgers organization had made the first division, with eight pennant winners among them. All that was missing was a World Series title for Brooklyn, and Rickey fervently believed it was around the corner.

However, he knew that the Dodgers must continue to stay at the top of the National League because he felt the growing pressure from Walter O'Malley, whose concern about the economic bottom line was becoming obvious. Jackie Robinson's presence on the Dodgers had been an artistic success, but the attendance for the 1947 Dodgers, though a team record of 1,807,526, was barely 10,000 higher than that for the 1946 Dodgers.[51] New left and left-center seats had been added in 1947 to increase Ebbets Field's capacity to almost 34,000 and to provide right-handed power hitters with a very cozy target, from only 348 feet down the left-field line to 389 feet in dead center.[52] However, Walter O'Malley was already talking about the need for a larger stadium and soon would commission architect Norman Bel Geddes to draw up a blueprint for a new stadium.[53]

The team counsel was also taking a hard look at every aspect of the balance sheet of the ball club. He was questioning Minor League expenditures, the expense of the team's owning a Beechcraft plane, and especially the cost of Dodgertown, the new spring training facility at Vero Beach, Florida, which would open for the Minor Leaguers in 1948 and by 1949 would fulfill Branch Rickey's dream of housing all the Dodgers Minor and Major Leaguers in one place.[54]

Rickey considered both the airplane and the training complex necessities, not luxuries. He was thrilled that treasurer and chief stockholder John L. Smith had approved both expenditures. As a young man Rickey had been afraid of heights and once had nearly fainted when he looked down from the top of the Empire State Building.[55] However, practicing what he preached about confronting and conquering obstacles, he overcame his fear of heights by flying as much as he could and grew to love the adventure and time-saving attributes of aviation. The opening of Dodgertown at Vero Beach was going to be the fulfillment of a longtime dream, the establishment of a campus for his talented and ambitious athletes.

Whether Branch Rickey would truly be able to enjoy his creations, however, was becoming doubtful. Like Sam Breadon in St. Louis less than a decade earlier, Walter O'Malley was casting a disapproving eye at Rickey's expensive contract, which was due to expire after the 1950 season. The team president's requests for an extension had been ignored.

The Dodgers would have to improve both financially and artistically in the next three years, or else Branch Rickey, who turned sixty-six on December 20, 1947, might have to again start looking for work. Unfortunately, 1948 would be an unsatisfying year on both levels and would not be helped by some poor decisions made by Rickey himself.

21

A Year of Disappointment, Odd Choices, and an Adieu to Leo

Before the start of spring training in 1948, Branch Rickey uttered a frank and accurate appraisal of his approach to baseball and life. Accepting in New York the Graham McNamee award for sportsmanship, named in honor of baseball's first national radio broadcaster, Rickey declared, "I am not afraid of boldness about the things I say I believe, even to the point of rashness." He cited a favorite saying by French writer Anatole France stating that he "preferred a turbulent freedom to a peaceful slavery."[1] As events in 1948 unfolded, however, there was probably more controversy and turbulence than even Branch Rickey wanted, and when the dust finally cleared, Rickey's long baseball marriage to Leo Durocher would be over, his uneasy relationship with the sportswriters would have deteriorated, and his ill-advised venture into professional football would have dealt his reputation a major hit within the Dodgers' board of directors.

Branch Rickey was well aware that every baseball season had its own rhythm, its own story line, and its inevitable peaks and valleys. But he never expected that the Brooklyn Dodgers by Memorial Day 1948 would have plunged into the abyss of last place in the National League. The late May holiday had its share of bad memories for Branch Rickey, who twenty-three years earlier had been fired as manager of a struggling Cardinals team by Sam Breadon. The situation would definitely improve in Brooklyn, Rickey assured himself, because the Dodgers were too talented to stay in the second division for long, but it was not a happy time. How strange life and baseball can be, Branch Rickey must have thought. "In 1948, at last I have Leo Durocher managing Jackie Robinson, and a young, hungry team ready to go all the way, and we are in the basement," he mused sorrowfully.

The local and national press were writing about how the mighty had fallen, and the grumbling of Brooklyn fans was growing loud and nasty, especially during the late May eight-game losing streak at Ebbets Field. Fans were open in their anger at Rickey for trading before the start of the season two popular players, Eddie Stanky and Dixie Walker. They were even booing Durocher, whose frustration was symbolized by using a record number of twenty-four players in one game against the hated Giants on April 21 and still the Dodgers lost the game.[2] Attendance was falling, always a concern for any baseball ownership group, and especially in Brooklyn, where Walter O'Malley was counting the beans and chief stockholder John L. Smith was not eager to lose money.

The poor standing of the Dodgers did not augur well for Branch Rickey's future. But he faced the music as best as he could, continuing to hold his weekly press conferences, where he displayed the kind of frank honesty that sometimes startled writers used to his professorial circumlocutions. He said he was not "infallible," he admitted he might not want to see the lackluster Dodgers play if he didn't have to, and he conceded that he may have made a mistake in trading the pepperpot Stanky.[3]

In another surprising development, Branch Rickey did not deny that Jackie Robinson, the returning National League Rookie of the Year, had been put on waivers, through which interest in his services from other teams was gauged.[4] Rickey did not confirm that waivers were asked on Robinson (and they were surely only revocable ones) because he didn't think the sportswriters had the right to know the confidential dealings within the baseball business. (Twenty years earlier Branch Rickey nearly had a fistfight with St. Louis sportswriter Ed Wray when the writer charged that the executive had once placed pitcher Bill Doak on waivers.) However, there was no doubt that, so far in 1948, Robinson's performance had been disappointing. His batting average might be close to .300, but he had stolen no bases and he looked lethargic on the base paths.

Obviously, though, Rickey had traded Stanky to the Boston Braves in a move made to open second base for Robinson. However, Robinson reported to spring training in the Dominican Republic as much as 30 pounds over his ideal playing weight of 185 to 190 pounds. Durocher was shocked and angry when he saw Robinson's condition. "You look like an old woman," he bellowed. "Look at all that fat around your midsection." Durocher had been looking forward to managing Robinson since he first laid eyes on the talented athlete in spring training 1946. He had pleaded with Rickey to bring up Robinson from Montreal for the pennant drive in 1946 and had urged Rickey not to hesitate to add him to the roster before the start of the 1947 season. "He doesn't just want to beat you," Durocher would later express his admiration of Robinson the competitor. "He wants to shove the bat up your ass."[5]

The player Durocher saw early in March 1948, however, looked nothing like the lithe, whirling dervish he lusted to manage. The reinstated skipper drove Robinson very hard to get into shape under the broiling Dominican sun. He ordered painful "up and down" drills, in which Robinson, dressed in a rubber suit, had a bucketful of baseballs thrown to him, one high and one low, and had to keep going after them until the drill was over or he collapsed from exhaustion.[6] "Robinson will shag flies till his tongue hangs out," Durocher told the sportswriters. "[Coach] Jake Pitler will see to it that Jackie chases every fungo up a palm tree."[7] Often during spring training Durocher could be heard muttering, "He was thin for Shotton, but he's fat for me."

Branch Rickey was not pleased at Robinson's reporting to camp out of shape, but he understood that he was not the first Major Leaguer, nor would he be the last, to lose condition in the off-season. It was a time when ballplayers were not earning millions of dollars in salaries, to say the least, and they had to work to make ends meet. Rickey did not begrudge Robinson's using some of the time after the 1947 season to capitalize on his fame as long as he did not let his celebrity go to his head.

Rickey also understood the extenuating circumstances in Robinson's lack of early condition. Robinson had undergone an off-season operation to remove bone spurs from his ankle, the result of an old football injury. He also was grieving the recent death of his close friend the Reverend Karl Everette Downs, who had died at age thirty-six after a heart operation. Downs was the Pasadena pastor who had channeled Robinson's aggressiveness into sports and, after Robinson's discharge from the Army, had hired him as the basketball coach at Samuel Huston College in Austin, Texas, where the minister had become the president. Downs had officiated at Jack and Rachel's wedding. His loss was made more terrible when the Robinsons learned that he had been denied the facilities of the white hospital in segregated Austin, Texas, which might have saved his life.[8] The tragic indignity was not lost on the fiercely proud race man, Jackie Robinson, and his wife, Rachel. Without saying anything Rickey also understood.

The only truly disturbing note in Robinson's off-season for the Dodgers president was the race pioneer's failure to appear at an early January 1948 speaking engagement in Virginia to support the erection of a war memorial stadium between the towns of Hampton and Newport News. It was a benefit for one of Rickey's beloved bond drives, and he was left to explain to sixty thousand people why Robinson had not appeared. It turned out that the Rookie of the Year was in Los Angeles, waiting for filming to begin on his life story, *Courage*, a movie that was never made. (Two years later, *The Jackie Robinson Story*, produced by a different and more professional crew, would be filmed.) Robinson's explanation for his absence was that he thought that Leo Durocher, living in Beverly Hills with his actress-wife, Laraine Day, had told Rickey that he wouldn't be coming. Later in January 1948 Robinson made amends by traveling to Virginia, where he addressed the chamber of commerce, gave radio interviews, and also spoke at a rally for the new stadium.[9]

Hindsight tells us that the off-season miscommunication between Durocher and Robinson might have given Branch Rickey a signal that the events of the upcoming season were going to be troubling. Robinson had basically established himself as a player and didn't need Durocher's protection, and the manager had gone through such turmoil with his suspension that he might lose his focus as a leader of a band of ferocious gentlemen. Yet, in the off-season of 1947–1948, Branch Rickey thought that all the inevitable "trouble ahead, trouble ahead" would ultimately resolve itself satisfactorily.

Rickey himself was in almost as much demand as Jackie Robinson for speaking engagements. He turned down more requests than he accepted, but one opportunity was too good to turn down, an invitation to address more than 250 people at the annual football banquet at Wilberforce College in his home state of Ohio. Rickey's February 17, 1948, speech to the historically black college made national headlines when he talked with his trademark reckless passion about how fierce the opposition had been to Jackie Robinson's signing. He made public for the first time the owners' meeting in August 1946 that tried to block his effort at bringing up Robinson and other black players to the Majors. He cited Larry MacPhail's secret report, in which the Yankees' co-owner warned about the dangers of black attendance to the economic future of the Major League franchises.

Having the Wilberforce audience in the palm of his hand, Rickey went on to say that MacPhail's findings were approved by a vote of fifteen to one, his own vote being the dissenting one. Although Rickey said that the report was never formally approved, and that the copies were soon gathered up and destroyed, he declared, "Let them deny that they adopted such a report if they dare. I'd like to see the color of the man's eyes who would deny it."[10]

There was nothing like a college audience or a gathering of young people to fire up Branch Rickey. Released from his self-imposed silence on the subject of Robinson's entry into baseball, he went on at length about his philosophy of brotherhood in society. "I believe that racial extractions and color hues and forms of worship become secondary to what men can do," he said. "The denial of equality of opportunity to qualify for work to any one, anywhere, any time, is ununderstandable to me," he added. (The Associated Press reporter covering the story was obviously battling with the daunting task of communicating Rickey's wandering syntax.) "It is not strange that Robinson should be given a chance in America to feed and shelter and clothe his wife and child and mother in a job he can do well, better than most individuals," Rickey continued. "It is not strange that a drop of water seeks to find the ocean."

Rickey was giving another rendition of what would become his standard and highly coveted speech about sportsmanship and racial progress, and he was just getting warmed up. He explained all the details that went into Robinson's signing. He mentioned the $25,000 of ownership money spent secretly on scouting black players. He praised Robinson as "a great credit to his race," adding, "He has great homage coming to him, and his race owes it to him." However, the conservative racial progressive repeated his warning that "we've had to stop parades and excursions in his honor. He must be treated just the same, no better or worse, than a white boy in our game."

Before he left his rapt audience well after midnight, Rickey voiced another major theme that he never ceased to expound upon, the danger of Communist inroads in the integration movement. "Now there is a Communistic effort to get credit for 'forcing' us to sign Robinson, but I warn you to be on your guard against that thing," he cautioned. Rickey concluded with an eloquent prediction. "The American public is not as concerned with a first baseman's pigmentation as it is with the power of his swing, the dexterity of his slide, the gracefulness of his fielding or the speed of his legs," he said.[11]

Rickey's baseball brethren were, of course, not happy with his Wilberforce remarks, and denials came immediately. Bob Carpenter, the DuPont Chemical heir who had bought the Phillies in 1944, called Rickey's charges "ridiculous," and Clark Griffith voiced the old canard, "The door has always been open to those boys if they were good enough to make it into the big leagues." Cubs owner Philip K. Wrigley, who had been on the committee that produced the secret report, had no comment. Neither did committee member Sam Breadon, who, after the 1947 season, had sold the Cardinals to Robert Hannegan, a former St. Louis college football star and postmaster general of the United States. "I am retired, and I think I will stay retired," Breadon said. Cleveland Indians owner Alva Bradley remarked, "Rickey is liable to say anything. This is not surprising."[12]

The Brooklyn president's nemesis, the recently retired Larry MacPhail, was more vituperative in responding to Rickey's speech. He accused his one-time sponsor and colleague in the baseball business of having "double-crossed his associates for his own personal advantage, raided the Negro leagues, and took players without adequately compensating them." MacPhail added, "Churchill must have had Rickey in mind when he said, 'There but for the grace of God goes God.'" Citing one of Rickey's heroes, Winston Churchill, against him was bound to draw a response, although Rickey limited his rejoinder to a terse statement that derided "typically MacPhailian distortions, untruths, and inventions."[13]

Rickey was not interested in getting into another war of words and accusations with Larry MacPhail, especially now that Jackie Robinson was an accepted Major Leaguer and a virtual national hero and Rickey's one-time protégé was out of the baseball business. Moreover, Rickey was immediately reminded by baseball insiders that the August 1946 meeting involved more than a discussion of racial integration. There had also been top-secret discussions about player pensions, the Mexican League threat, changes in the baseball contract to eliminate the ten-day clause, and confidential criticisms of Commissioner Chandler.

Shortly after the Wilberforce speech, Rickey issued a statement in which he said that his remarks, while quoted accurately, had led to "interpretations not intended and certainly not foreseen." As far as the denials from owners that a vote on race was ever taken at the 1946 meeting, Rickey said, "Anyone who makes that statement is fully to be believed." He stressed that he raised the subject at the black college primarily to point out how far baseball had come in less than two years on the issue of equality of opportunity. "I wish very much to say that no club owner in the American or National Leagues, with one exception, has ever protested to me personally the signing of Jackie Robinson by the Brooklyn club and several have expressed approval," he said.[14]

Of course, the press was curious about who was the "one exception" Rickey mentioned as an opponent of Robinson. However, appearing at a Brooklyn luncheon to announce the Dodgers' continuation of a joint program with *Argosy* men's magazine to honor Brooklyn's best Minor Leaguers, Rickey refused to divulge the name. It might have been more prudent to write in his statement that "virtually all" or "most of" the owners supported Robinson's right to play, or somehow phrase it without teasing the writers. But Rickey's style of address could not help being a unique mixture of the conditional and the combative.

There is little doubt, however, that the executive who opposed Robinson was Rickey's old friend Connie Mack, who said publicly during Robinson's first spring training in 1946, "I used to have respect for Rickey. I don't have any more." Mack added that his Athletics would not play the Dodgers in Florida if Robinson came with them.[15]

Although he was saddened by Mack's stance, Rickey was not going to get into a public war of words with his longtime colleague and friend. Rickey always empathized with Mack's problems with ballplayers asking for too much money and was distressed when the Philadelphia owner had to break up his championship teams of 1914 and 1931. For his part, except for his opposition to Robinson and integration, Mack always spoke highly of Rickey in public, and he had the most glowing things to say about him in his autobiography, *My 66 Years in the Big Leagues: The Great Story of America's National Game*, published in 1950. Mack called the Brooklyn executive "a man of great administrative ability, unimpeachable character, and an honor not only to our national game but to the nation."[16] (Mack also mentioned in his book that because of Rickey's great national esteem, when he lived in Missouri it was possible that Franklin Roosevelt might have selected him as a national unity vice presidential pick in 1940, and the entire world, not just the baseball world, may have now be referring to him as U.S. president Branch Rickey.)

It is not surprising that Branch Rickey spoke so eloquently at Wilberforce about the signing of Robinson and his deep concerns for racial justice. Nor is it remarkable that he backtracked from his criticisms of the owners' opposition to integration, because Rickey was very much a vital part of the conservative inner sanctum of baseball's managerial elite. Yet it is hard to fathom what was going on in his hyperactive mind when, shortly before the Wilberforce speech, he got into a war of words with *New York Daily News* sportswriter Dick Young in front of the entire New York press corps.

Young was fast developing a reputation as one of the most persevering and aggressive of the band of hard-edged New York scribes that Branch Rickey liked to parry with but never learned how to neutralize. What particularly riled Rickey was Young's story on February 10, 1948, in which the sportswriter wrote that Ralph Branca had signed his contract for the upcoming season but that the team president "lied when queried later that day whether he and Branca had come to terms."[17] Young was undoubtedly miffed when a story came out in a suburban paper near Branca's Mount Vernon home indicating that the pitcher had signed. However, to call Rickey a liar in print or to his face certainly was guaranteed to draw the executive's ire.

At a crowded press conference at the Dodgers' offices on the day Young's story appeared, Rickey sarcastically read aloud the writer's account of Branca's signing. "The auditory torture in Rickey's gas chamber lasted four solid hours," Rickey quoted Young, "by which time, Branca, after wiping the blood off his ears, was more than willing to take two thousand less and escape with his life."[18] According to Arthur Mann's account in his biography of Rickey, the executive said in an aside, "That's supposed to be clever writing, I guess."[19]

The Brooklyn president next stunned the writers by summoning Branca on the intercom to come into the press conference. The confused young pitcher entered, not knowing why he was needed, but he found out that his boss wanted him to testify, in effect, that when Dick Young called Rickey's office, Branca had not yet signed his contract. They were discussing marriage at the time, and Rickey was asking why his young, handsome pitcher was still a "matrimonial coward." The angry executive and the nervous pitcher both agreed that the actual signing of the contract didn't occur until an hour or two later.

Rickey remained furious at Young, who, not coincidentally, wrote for the *Daily News*, whose chief columnist, Jimmy Powers, had started the scurrilous "El Cheapo" campaign. "I want an apology now, and I want one with a retraction in your newspaper tomorrow," Rickey thundered at the sportswriter. Young did comply, writing a few days later that "Rickey has received a sincere, unqualified apology." However, possessing the press's power to have the last word, he added, "The reporter's big mistake was in failing to technically analyze Rickey's evasive phraseology—an innocent error which could happen to anyone, and usually does."[20] The executive should have known better than to get into a war of words with a reporter, but as we have seen many times in his story, when he felt his integrity was threatened, especially by a sportswriter, he acted passionately and recklessly.

Branch Rickey took another bold and reckless step in December 1947 when he convinced his baseball partners, John L. Smith and Walter O'Malley, that the team should buy the Brooklyn football Dodgers of the fledgling All-America Football Conference (AAFC). The gridiron Dodgers had been playing in the National Football League (NFL) at Ebbets Field since 1930, but except for a few years of contention on the eve of World War Two, they were not a very good team. During the war their owner, Daniel Reid Topping, an Anaconda Copper mining heir who had bought a share of the baseball New York Yankees with Larry MacPhail and construction magnate Del Webb, had taken the best Brooklyn players to form a New York Yankees football franchise. In 1946 Topping had abruptly moved the football Yankees from the older NFL into the AAFC. The new league promised more wide-open football and a truly national presence, with teams in San Francisco and Los Angeles. In 1946 the premier AAFC team, the Cleveland Browns, added two black players—fullback Marion Motley and lineman Bill Willis—and won the league title by beating Topping's Yankees, 14–9, in a hotly contested championship game before more than forty-one thousand fans at Yankee Stadium.[21]

With the postwar spectator sports boom in full bloom, many baseball executives, including Branch Rickey, thought that dual baseball and football ownership made economic sense. In fact, while still in St. Louis, Rickey had expressed an interest in bringing a pro football franchise to St. Louis, but Sam Breadon thought the idea unrealistic and expensive.[22] After the war ended Rickey stated publicly his ardent interest in "putting a football team on the field as soon as practicable."[23]

By the end of 1947 Rickey told O'Malley and Smith that operating a pro football team at Ebbets Field in Brooklyn would be both a good community gesture and, ultimately, a money-making proposition. Rickey argued that since the baseball Dodgers had been the football landlord since the end of 1945, taking over the team would ensure continued rent payments. He tried to assure O'Malley and Smith that the baseball team would not be responsible for prior football debts. The football Dodgers were owned by paper mill executive William D. Cox, whom Rickey had met when Cox briefly owned the baseball Phillies in the early 1940s. In one of his last acts as commissioner, Kenesaw Mountain Landis had expelled Cox from baseball for betting on his own team, and the young executive drifted into a co-ownership of the football Dodgers with Gerald W. Smith, from the family that published Street and Smith sports publications. When Smith bailed out of the operation, Cox was left holding the bag with over $200,000 in losses.[24]

Always wanting to offer a job to someone down on his luck, Rickey proposed William Cox for football team president. "He seeks a job understandably because of his pride," Rickey wrote his partners, "also a desire for vindication or rehabilitation or whatever we may care to call it relating to the Landis decision as well as his economic failure in the operation of the football team."[25] As for reports that the football owner was difficult to work with, Rickey surmised that, like owners in any sport, Cox just wanted to win. The enthusiastic baseball Dodgers president believed that the football Dodgers had a good nucleus of players, and he urged his partners to take over the gridiron squad.

John L. Smith, who deferred totally to Branch Rickey on baseball matters, was solidly opposed to taking on the responsibility for the football team. He correctly thought that the expenditures would far outweigh the profits. Walter O'Malley was skeptical about the football project, but he was willing to be persuaded because Dan Topping had told him that there was money to be made in football, as evidenced by the good Yankee Stadium crowds his football team had drawn.

Early in January 1948 the baseball Dodgers formally announced its takeover of the football team. Joe Trimble, one of the *Daily News* writers more sympathetic to the Dodgers president, wrote, "No longer can anyone point a honest finger at Branch Rickey and accuse him of being a money grubber to the exclusion of all else in life."[26]

One of Rickey's first acts was to name the ubiquitous Arthur Mann as his salaried football administrator. Then he tried to grab some headlines for his new football regime by trying to lure Columbia University football coach Lou Little to the pro ranks. On October 25, 1947, Little's Columbia Lions had shocked the sporting world by upsetting Army, 21–20, thereby breaking the Cadets' thirty-two-game winning streak. Any coach capable of beating one of the military academies was worth hiring, Branch Rickey thought. Rickey invited Little to dinner, where he reportedly offered Little a blank check to coach the football Dodgers, but the Columbia coach was not interested in leaving the secure Ivy League life.

On the recommendation of University of Illinois football coach Bob Zuppke, Rickey next offered the football Dodgers coaching job to Auburn University's Carl Voyles, who had once been Zuppke's assistant. During the same week that Rickey tilted with Dick Young and prepared to orate at Wilberforce, he introduced Voyles to the press as the team's new coach and waxed eloquent about Brooklyn's football prospects. When his new coach expressed a desire for the Dodgers to sign "a great passer," Rickey let it be known that he had recently offered a four-year, $110,000 contract to University of Mississippi quarterback Charlie Conerly. Conerly, though, spurned the bid, which included a $40,000 signing bonus, and announced his intention to complete his spring baseball season as an Ole Miss shortstop and then sign with the New York Giants of the more established National Football League.[27]

In response to Conerly's snub Rickey declared, "It will not be a morale-inducing factor for him to remember as he always will, that he had to pass up such an offer because of a commitment to the Giants." He added, "What's more, I would pay more than $110,000 for a great passer."[28] The irony of Rickey's throwing around six-digit figures for football players while keeping baseball salaries on the low end was not lost on football Giants owner Jack Mara, who had just read about Ralph Branca's signing for $14,000 and Pee Wee Reese fighting for $15,000 a year. "I do not know where this guy gets off talking about morale problems and stuff, considering the business he's in," said Mara, the older brother of long-time Giants patriarch Wellington Mara. "There's no difference between football and baseball contracts, except that a football player has a choice of two leagues."[29]

Yet when Branch Rickey got involved in a project, he could not hold back his enthusiasm. He actually thought he could scout football players as successfully as baseball players, and he instructed many of his scouts and officials to do double duty, evaluating, in particular, small college football games where he thought many overlooked prospects could be found. He must have been thinking back to twenty years earlier when Pop Kelchner found Charley Gelbert for him on the Lafayette college playing fields. To coach the field goal kickers, and to occasionally suit up for a game, Rickey put in a call to the Oklahoma Baptist church where his all-time favorite baseball player, forty-four-year-old Pepper Martin, was very active. He was told that despite the wintry day, the ex–Gashouse Gang leader was outside playing football. Once he was located the fiery ex-Cardinal quickly agreed to join the gridiron Dodgers.

It took until late June, however, for Rickey to find Coach Voyles his "great passer." The Dodgers offered a long-term, nearly-six-figure contract to Bob Chappuis (pronounced "happy-us"), the hero of the University of Michigan's 49–0 trouncing of the University of Southern California in the 1947 Rose Bowl. Chappuis was everything Branch Rickey looked for in an athlete, a mature, married man from Ohio and a war hero. (Near the end of World War II, Chappuis's B-25 had been shot down in Italy, and he survived in enemy territory for over a month with the help of an antifascist family.)[30] Chappuis would perform capably for the 1948 Brooklyn Dodgers, but despite Rickey's predictions, the team was a weak one, losing twelve of fourteen games, its only wins coming against a Chicago Rockets team that finished 1-13.

At the end of 1948 the balance sheet for the football Dodgers was grisly, with the team losing around $300,000. "It cost us all what little Christmas bonus we were getting," Dodgers executive Buzzie Bavasi remembers.[31] In January 1949 the football Dodgers merged with the football Yankees, and at the end of the 1949 season the AAFC disbanded, with its best teams—the Cleveland Browns, the Los Angeles Rams, and the San Francisco 49ers—being incorporated into the NFL. Branch Rickey was saddened that the football venture had not worked out and called the losses "regrettable."[32] Although Walter O'Malley had voted to buy into football, Rickey had been the enthusiastic backer, and the team lawyer thus had another major arguing point to make with the team board of directors that the extravagance of the president made his replacement imperative when his contract expired at the end of the 1950 season.

At the end of June 1948 Branch Rickey reached the painful conclusion that it was time to cut ties with Leo Durocher. Something had seemed to be missing in Durocher's leadership skills since his return from his suspension. His longtime sponsor couldn't quite put his finger on it, but his prodigal son seemed to have lost the fierce intensity that had always been his trademark. Rickey didn't like to think the heretical thought, but it could well be that his manager's marriage to Laraine Day had made the fiery Durocher too domesticated and indecisive. "The management of a baseball club is a jealous mistress," Rickey later reflected. "In earthly terms, he can have no other God."[33] The distracted Durocher shifted the lineup daily but not with great results. Jackie Robinson was removed from second base and put back at first base, while Eddie Miksis and Gene Mauch got temporary tryouts at second, trying to fill the void left by the departed Eddie Stanky.

The reinstated skipper did get one wish fulfilled in June 1948 when Roy Campanella came up to stay from the Dodgers' American Association farm club in St. Paul, Minnesota. If it had been Leo's decision, Campanella would not have sent to St. Paul in May, but Rickey still saw some hope in Bruce Edwards, who was a big cog on the 1947 team but would never be the same after an injury. The team president also hadn't given up on Gil Hodges as a catcher, although Durocher presciently saw first base in Hodges's future, where he became an All-Star (and, arguably, the most deserving player not yet in the Baseball Hall of Fame). Rickey also had an ulterior motive in sending Campanella to the farm in St. Paul; he wanted the catcher to integrate the American Association.[34]

In seasons past Durocher and Rickey could vehemently argue with each other about player personnel and still come to a meeting of the minds. However, when the Dodgers stumbled into a six-game losing streak near the end of June 1948, Rickey decided that Durocher must resign. Since Rickey could rarely bring himself to fire an employee, especially someone as dear to him as his prodigal son Durocher, he was mulling the best way to replace his manager. Maybe he would come up with an idea during a long-planned late June Canadian fishing trip.

Rickey's vacation had to be canceled, though, when he was hospitalized with a bladder infection. Many people close to him feared he had suffered another Ménière's attack, but Jane Rickey, in a rare public comment, downplayed the illness. So did Walter O'Malley, making a rare comment in the sports pages, who said that Rickey was suffering from only a "minor" ailment.[35]

While in the hospital Rickey dispatched road secretary Harold Parrott to Ebbets Field to ask for the manager's resignation. The Dodgers were playing a doubleheader with the Giants, and Brooklyn was far behind in the first game. Parrott found Durocher in the clubhouse after another of his many ejections by the men in blue. When told that Rickey wanted him to resign, Durocher refused. "The Old Man will have to fire me himself, face-to-face, and he hasn't got the guts," Leo roared.[36]

Suddenly, coach Clyde Sukeforth stuck his head in the door to announce that Roy Campanella had hit a two-run homer, and the Dodgers were coming closer in the first game. Parrott and Durocher talked some more to no avail about the resignation. Soon, Sukeforth returned excitedly to announce that Campy had hit a 3-run homer and that the Dodgers had taken the lead. They wound up sweeping the doubleheader and started on a winning streak.

With his manager still employed, Rickey checked out of the hospital to recuperate on his Maryland farm, where he would continue to ponder his manager's fate. The media-savvy Durocher told columnist Bill Corum of the *New York Journal-American* about Rickey's plans, and Burris Jenkins, the newspaper's cartoonist, lampooned the executive as hiding behind a haystack on his farm.[37] Of course, Rickey's decision would not be determined by press satire or criticism, but his swirling, hyperactive mind considered the alternatives. There was certainly every likelihood that Durocher would rebound as a winning manager, and he thought that the surge upward might have even started with the latest winning streak. Yet the internal politics of Rickey's situation in Brooklyn also had to be considered. Even though Durocher had returned to manage, and the Catholic Youth Organization (CYO) had resumed its support of the Knothole Gang program, many priests and CYO leaders made no secret of their distaste for him as a bad influence on youth.

Rickey decided that he still wanted Durocher to resign, but the solicitous paterfamilias wanted his prodigal son to land on his feet. As only Branch Rickey could, he masterminded an unprecedented midseason swap of New York managers. Fortuitously, Horace Stoneham was planning to fire Mel Ott as the Giants' manager at the upcoming All-Star Game break. Stoneham phoned Rickey asking whether Burt Shotton was available as Ott's replacement. The Giants owner was stunned when Rickey informed him that he could choose either Durocher or Shotton. It didn't take long for Stoneham to decide. At forty-one, Durocher was more than fifteen years younger than Shotton and had far more fan and sex appeal. Once the Giant fans got over the shock of their hated Brooklyn rival now managing their side, Stoneham and Rickey were sure that they would adopt Leo as one of their own.

On July 16, 1948, the shocking shift of managerial chairs was announced to a stunned New York sports world. Mel Ott, the man about whom Leo Durocher had said, "He's a nice guy, and see where he is? In last place," was gone from the Giants' home in the Polo Grounds, and Leo Durocher was in.[38] Burt Shotton, the quiet man who dressed in street clothes and who had led the Dodgers to the 1947 pennant, was back at Ebbets Field. Branch Rickey's old friend, who graciously had let Leo Durocher manage the National League team in the 1948 All-Star Game, had been back in retirement in Florida, but when his friend Rick asked for help, Shotton was always ready to oblige.

The Dodgers responded well to Shotton's return. Away for less than a year, he knew most of the personnel, and the players knew that he always had Branch Rickey's ear. Under the leadership of the quiet, noncontroversial manager (dubbed KOBS, "Kindly Old Burt Shotton," by Dick Young in the *Daily News*), the Dodgers actually moved into first place briefly in late August 1948, but it was a mirage. They fell back to third at the end of 1948, seven games behind the pennant-winning Braves and one game behind the Cardinals. The fans never believed in the 1948 team, and the Dodgers lost more than 400,000 from their record attendance of 1947, drawing only 1,398,967 in 1948.[39]

Still, they were close to becoming the dominant team that Branch Rickey was confident he would build when he took over before the 1943 season. The 1948 Dodgers would lead the National League in stolen bases, with 114, 46 more than any other team. Pee Wee Reese and Jackie Robinson were becoming a sublime double play combination and productive offensive players. Reese hit .274, with 9 HR and 75 RBI, and after his slow start Robinson came in with respectable numbers, .296 BA, .412 SA, 12 HR, 85 RBI, 38 2B, 22 SB, and 108 R. Gil Hodges, a 1943 wartime signing, was settling in at first base. Although he hit only .249, he produced 11 HR and 70 RBI. Roy Campanella played in eighty-three games, and his .258 BA, 9 HR, and 45 RBI gave only a hint of his productivity ahead. Billy Cox, the shortstop Rickey plucked away from the Pirates in the Dixie Walker trade, was beginning to feel comfortable at third base. Duke Snider, another 1943 signing, was showing signs that he had finally mastered knowledge of the strike zone and was ready to claim center field, with Carl Furillo moving to right field.

It was on the pitching mound where the Dodgers in 1948 once again fell short. The staff led the league in both walks and strikeouts and almost walked as many as they fanned. Young Rex Barney was one of the big culprits. Although he led the team with fifteen wins and 247 innings pitched, he walked 122 men and struck out only 138, far from the ideal ratio of at least twice as many strikeouts to walks. Rickey still retained great hopes for the right-hander, who did toss a no-hitter against the Giants at the Polo Grounds on September 9, 1948. However, Barney would never master control. He would be out of Major League Baseball after 1950, winning only thirty-five games in his career.

Ralph Branca fell off from his twenty-one-win season of 1947 but still turned in a respectable 14-9 record in 1948 and seemed young enough to rebound. Another bright spot for the future was Elwyn "Preacher" Roe, a thirty-three-year-old left-hander from Arkansas so nicknamed because he once attended ministerial school. He won twelve games after coming to Brooklyn with Billy Cox in the Dixie Walker trade and was beginning to justify the promise Rickey saw in him when he was signed by the Cardinals in the late 1930s.

Going into the off-season, Branch Rickey took consolation in knowing that he had built a promising team soon likely to jell. He was saddened, though, when the National League lost the World Series. Despite Billy Southworth's managing and Eddie Stanky's scrappy play, the Boston Braves fell to the Cleveland Indians, four games to two. The Dodgers executive was glad, though, that Cleveland's Satchel Paige became the first black pitcher to win a World Series game. Rickey was also pleased to learn that Horace Stoneham was getting into the black player market too. Stoneham had signed for the Giants outfielder-infielder Monte Irvin, and, as noted earlier, he was to give Hank Thompson, the former St. Louis Browns infielder, a second chance. In the wings was center fielder Willie Mays, who would burst on the Major League scene early in the 1951 season.

As always for Branch Rickey, where there was life there was hope in spite of all the "trouble ahead, trouble ahead" in any mortal's existence. However, in addition to the disappointing 1948 baseball year, he suffered two more blows, one in politics and one in the family. In November the Republican Party failed to regain the White House for the fourth straight election. New York Republican governor Thomas Dewey, whom Rickey had met at Lowell Thomas's salons, was favored to beat incumbent president Harry S. Truman and was pronounced the winner in a classic, embarrassing *Chicago Tribune* headline, "Dewey Beats Truman." However, Truman had whistle-stopped the country by train and, taking advantage of the still-functional if tattered Franklin D. Roosevelt coalition, he retained the White House for the Democratic Party.

The other hard blow for Branch Rickey and his family at the end of 1948 was the passing in late December of his mother-in-law, Mary Moulton, who had been a part of his household for nearly thirty years (since the death of her husband, Chandler Moulton). She lived to be almost one hundred years old. In her last years, as her eyesight failed, Branch Rickey would read aloud to her from Shakespeare and the English Romantic poets. Rickey often called her "a benediction on my life."

Branch and Jane Rickey made the sad journey to Scioto County to lay Mary Moulton to her eternal rest in the hills of southern Ohio. Rickey wept alongside his wife, gathered himself and his thoughts, and prepared for the return trip to Brooklyn. The Dodgers leader felt certain that a strong, competitive season lay ahead in 1949, even if he could not be sanguine about his ultimate future in the organization. However, if Rickey privately sensed the disturbing parallel to his last years in St. Louis under Sam Breadon, he remained publicly the picture of confident leadership.

22

A Branch Bends in Brooklyn

Branch Rickey looked forward to the 1949 season with great optimism. Although most of the pundits predicted a second-place finish at best for the Dodgers, Rickey felt otherwise. The nucleus of the team was coming back and was young and hungry. Early in January he described the upcoming squad as his "most promising team" since he had arrived in Brooklyn, perhaps his "best ever." "I had opportunities to make deals, but I didn't make them." he said. "I like what I have too much to make fairly even 'horse' deals," added Rickey, who, of course, came from a long lineage of horse traders.[1]

Rickey was pleased that Burt Shotton was going to manage the team from the very first day of spring training. No longer would he have to arrive as Leo Durocher's replacement after the season started. From day one of the opening on March 1 of Dodgertown—the Dodgers' new permanent training headquarters in Vero Beach, Florida—Shotton would be in command. The facility had opened for Minor Leaguers in 1948 and had attracted a *Life* magazine cover story, replete with photos of young players hard at work under the guidance of the man the publication called the "parsimonious panjandrum."[2] The year 1949, though, would be the first time when all of the Dodgers, from the Majors to class D, would be training in one place.

Everyone in the organization was thrilled with the new facility, with the exception of Walter O'Malley, who continued to complain that it was too expensive.[3] Rickey insisted that the creation of Dodgertown at Vero Beach was well worth the expense. The Dodgers could now put behind them the tensions and inconveniences of the past three springs in Florida and Central America, and Rickey would realize his dream of establishing a permanent baseball college campus where all the players could be trained by a faculty of superlative teachers under the direction of the ferocious gentleman himself. That the land was once home to a United States naval base added to the satisfaction of ultrapatriotic Branch Rickey.

Rickey meticulously organized each day, from morning reveille and breakfast to the postdinner lectures, delivered by either the executive or a member of his staff. All meals were communal in a big cafeteria, where posted on the wall was a sign borrowed from the military, "Take all you want, and eat all you take."[4] Free orange juice from the copious groves nearby was available all the time.

A typical day began with the running up of the American flag at dawn and the reciting of the "Pledge of Allegiance" by Herman Levy, the camp mailman and night watchman.[5] After the communal breakfast there were calisthenics for everyone, followed by separation into groups. Some pitchers worked on throwing techniques, while hurlers with control problems were sent to work in the pitching strings. All pitchers took regular breaks from throwing activities to go to the sliding pits, where they worked on proper technique. Meanwhile, the hitters were working at batting tees or against pitching machines. Before lunch they all assembled in center field to work on defensive drills with Wid Matthews, one of the most highly respected of Rickey's loyal and hard-working staff of scouts and instructors. (This year, 1949, would be Matthews's last spring training with the Dodgers. After the season, the man who reportedly once called Branch Rickey "the greatest man since Jesus Christ," accepted the position of general manager of the Chicago Cubs.)[6]

The afternoon was devoted to infield and outfield practice followed by intrasquad games. After communal dinner Rickey held a nightly meeting with the staff, where he discussed the day's activities and planned the rosters for the twenty-seven farm teams in the Dodgers system. The day ended with a lecture in the dining hall on some subject concerning inside baseball. Attendance was voluntary, but since there was little night life in the isolated town of Vero Beach, most players attended.

Rickey's lectures often went over the heads of the athletes, but some of the players just enjoyed hearing the sound of Branch Rickey's mesmerizing voice. A typical Rickey speech would combine his love of aviation and baseball with a lesson in color blindness:

> I am 40,000 feet above the ground. I have high-powered glasses, but as I look down all I can see is specks, specks that seem to be moving. "Yes," you say to me, "those are human beings. They have two legs and they do move." Now I don't know whether these specks are Chinese or whether they are black or green or blue. But I know that some can run better than others, and hit better, and throw better, and I simply want to find the nine who can do these things best, without caring what color they turn out to be.[7]

Rickey was pleased when Jackie Robinson reported to Vero Beach with all the Major League players on March 1. He looked considerably lighter than he had a year earlier. Rickey's effective if not-too-subtle Christmas gift of a scale, the athlete's fierce pride in his abilities, and his knowledge of his importance as a pioneer all primed him for what would turn out to be the best year of his career.[8] In 1949 Robinson would be joined for the entire season by two black teammates, Roy Campanella and Don Newcombe, the latter emerging as the first black pitcher in a regular rotation in Major League history. (In 1948 Satchel Paige had mainly pitched in relief for the Cleveland Indians.)

One standard interpretation of Jackie Robinson's career is that, beginning in 1949, after three years of being restrained by Branch Rickey, the race pioneer was "unleashed" by Rickey to play and speak with abandon. Robinson did send a message to his taunting opponents upon arriving in spring training. "They better be rough on me because I am going to be rough on them," he warned.[9] However, in uttering these remarks, Robinson was basically expressing his confident, aggressive self. That Branch Rickey had some kind of omnipotent control over Jackie Robinson does not do justice either to their memory or to the movement for equality, which they tried to trigger by example, not rhetoric. "Jackie was not on a leash. It was Jackie Robinson who kept Jackie Robinson from exploding," Pacific Coast League president Branch Barrett Rickey, Rickey's grandson and son of Branch Rickey Jr., told Robinson biographer Arnold Rampersad. "He had a given a pledge he believed in and he stuck by it—that's all."[10]

At Vero Beach, Robinson took full advantage of the instruction provided by two of Rickey's most respected instructors, George Sisler and Pepper Martin. Martin, who slid headfirst during his career, helped Robinson refine his feet-first sliding technique. Sisler worked on Robinson's balance at the plate, reminding him to always prepare for the fastball while adjusting to the curve ball.[11] Unlike the tortuous time the overweight Robinson experienced in 1948 spring training, he rounded quickly into shape in 1949 and hit over .500 in exhibition games. He was poised for a great season.

So was center fielder Duke Snider, who was ready to become an everyday player and a major contributor on offense and defense. In an earlier spring training Rickey had commanded the young Californian not to swing a bat, but to stand behind a batting cage and identify the pitches as either balls or strikes. After the Brooklyn staff was satisfied that Snider knew the strike zone, he was free to resume his batting practice and polish his stroke. The center fielder did not stick on the varsity roster in 1947 and 1948, but by 1949 he looked confident at the plate, prompting Burt Shotton to say prophetically, "If he hits, we win the pennant. It's as simple as that."[12]

On the way north from spring training the Dodgers stopped off in Atlanta for a three-game series against the Minor League Atlanta Crackers. The Ku Klux Klan had threatened demonstrations in front of the ballpark if the Dodgers brought their black players with them. However, this was the spring of 1949, not 1946 or 1947. Robinson was a nationally renowned figure, and Campanella and Newcombe were on the verge of National League stardom. Rickey did not foresee a problem in Georgia, and he accurately predicted that "the only danger from mob violence would come from people with pens in the hands, [seeking autographs]."[13] The Klan's disruptive efforts fizzled, and record-breaking crowds cheered the integrated Dodgers as they played and won the exhibition games in Atlanta.

Pleased with the progress of his integration program, Branch Rickey continued to speak his mind publicly on other issues he perceived of patriotic concern. Just before the opening of the baseball season, he addressed a luncheon meeting of the Baltimore Chamber of Commerce and made headlines by denouncing the continuing antitrust lawsuits brought against organized baseball by former New York Giants outfielder Danny Gardella and two former Cardinals pitchers, Max Lanier and Fred Martin. All three had jumped to the Mexican League in 1946, and when they had asked for reinstatement to the Majors, Commissioner Happy Chandler had slapped the five-year ban on them. The players' cases against the baseball system were winding their way through the federal judicial system, but Rickey could not resist the opportunity to link the rebels against the baseball establishment with dangerous political enemies of the republic. "Those people who oppose the reserve system have avowed Communist tendencies," he declared.[14]

There was immediate fallout from Rickey's connecting an antimonopoly lawsuit with the international Communist conspiracy. John L. Flynn, one of the lawyers for plaintiffs Max Lanier and Fred Martin, wrote Rickey an angry letter, threatening a defamation suit for being called a Communist in a public forum. A somewhat chastened Rickey turned the matter over to the Dodgers' team counsel, who was, of course, his increasingly ambitious rival Walter O'Malley. Publicly O'Malley replied that "Mr. Rickey neither stated nor inferred" that Flynn had connection with Communists, and that Rickey's remarks meant "absolutely nothing" except that it was an another example of his partner's penchant for wordy speech. Not immediately appeased, Flynn continued to threaten to sue "to recover substantial punitive damages" for the "vicious slander as maliciously intended" of Rickey's remarks.[15]

O'Malley soon met Flynn face to face and persuaded the attorney for the ex–Mexican League players to drop any legal action. But O'Malley also mentioned to his fellow lawyer that Rickey was a "fool" for risking a slander suit, and among the Dodgers' board of directors, O'Malley was winning more points as an effective leader qualified to replace Rickey as team president at the end of the 1950 season.[16]

If Branch Rickey felt discomfort at his increasingly precarious situation inside the Dodger hierarchy, his well-honed actor persona disguised it. The fast start of the Dodgers in the 1949 pennant race buoyed his spirits, though it was clear that the National League was poised for another of its traditional dogfights. The defending league champions, the Boston Braves, had a shot at repeating, and the St. Louis Cardinals were also clear contenders. The Philadelphia Phillies, who hadn't been in a World Series since 1915, were also showing signs of life. Leo Durocher, however, had not yet started using his influence on owner Horace Stoneham to bring the Giants the kind of players who would make his new team a scrappy contender. The new manager's frustration spilled over into another altercation with a fan after a game in late May, which led to headlines and threatened lawsuits. However, when it became clear that the spectator had initiated the problem by trying to steal Durocher's cap, the issue quickly faded away.[17]

In mid-June, with fewer than five games separating the first four teams in the National League, Branch Rickey headed to Cooperstown, New York, to be the main speaker at the eleventh annual National Baseball Hall of Fame inductions. Rickey never believed the story that Abner Doubleday had invented the game of baseball in the lovely small town on Otsego Lake. ("The only thing that Doubleday started was the Civil War," he liked to say about the soldier who returned Confederate fire at Fort Sumter, South Carolina, and ultimately rose to general.) Yet he considered the Hall of Fame an excellent idea and was glad to honor the newest inductees, among them recently deceased Yankees pitcher Herb Pennock, and seventy-nine-year-old Charles "Kid" Nichols. As a left-handed pitcher for the Boston Nationals in the late nineteenth century, Nichols had won 361 games, including a never-yet-matched seven straight seasons with 30 or more victories.

Before the ground was broken for a new wing at the Hall of Fame, Rickey reached deep into his oratorical playbook for his heartfelt view of what baseball meant to him and the country. "Why [is] baseball so special?" he asked his audience. "First the beauty of it; second, the comparative freedom from danger of injury to participants; third, the marvelous exactitudes and precision of measurements relating to human skills." Rickey expressed his hope for a time in history when sportsmen, philosophers, and artists were honored as much as military men.

"I am confident that sports in America can furnish the virtues of war—if there are any. We can hold it up to the world as the national pastime of America. We are not astray when we honor the people who have given of their lives to a great sport. They are men who have contributed largely to the sum happiness of the people. They each bore the banner, 'Not honors, but honor.'"[18]

When Rickey returned to Brooklyn the contenders began to separate themselves from the pretenders in the 1949 National League pennant race. The Phillies and Braves faded, and once again the race would come down to a battle between the Dodgers and the Cardinals. Jackie Robinson was leading the Brooklyn charge. On July 1 he was hitting .361, running the bases with his customary élan, and participating in a great double play combination with Pee Wee Reese. Rickey told sportswriter John Lardner: "Watching the play of Reese and Robinson is one of the true joys of my life."[19]

Robinson would go to win the league batting title at .342 and the stolen base crown with 37. Robinson was convinced by manager Burt Shotton that he could fill the bill as the fourth-place, cleanup hitter in the batting order, and his final 1949 power numbers justified his skipper's confidence: .528 SA, 16 HR, 122 RBI, and 124 R. He played in every one of the Dodgers' games and would be voted the Most Valuable Player of the league.

Rookie Don Newcombe was on his way to a 17-9 season and selection as the National League's first Rookie of the Year. Roy Campanella was establishing himself as a feared hitter; in the 1950s he would twice win the league's Most Valuable Player Award. His 1949 numbers were excellent for a catcher in his first full year: .287 BA, .498 SA, 22 HR, and 82 RBI. All three black Brooklyn stars were selected to play in the All-Star Game at Ebbets Field on July 12, 1949, and so was the American League's race pioneer, Cleveland's Larry Doby. Robinson led all National League vote-getters, and only the Boston Red Sox's Ted Williams drew more votes. Pee Wee Reese and Preacher Roe also made the team from the Dodgers. In a slugfest before a sold-out Ebbets Field, the American League won, 11–7, aided by 5 National League errors. Robinson doubled in the first inning and scored 3 runs but had no other hits. Neither Campanella nor Doby got a hit.

For Branch Rickey and Jackie Robinson, July 1949 did not bring only an All-Star Game and the daily challenge of staying atop the torrid National League pennant race. On Monday, July 18, 1949, in the middle of the finest season of his career, Robinson also traveled to Washington DC to read a statement and testify before the House Un-American Activities Committee (HUAC). The anti-Communist political climate of the United States had heated up in the summer of 1949. China had fallen to the Communists in the spring of 1949, and tensions between the United States and the Soviet Union were intensifying. The United States' World War II ally had exploded an atomic bomb and was working on a hydrogen bomb.

The domestic "Red Scare" was also increasing. Alger Hiss, a high-ranking U.S. State Department official, who had been with Roosevelt, Stalin, and Churchill at the February 1945 Yalta summit meeting and at the April 1945 San Francisco conference that established the United Nations, was on trial for perjury about his prewar relationship with Whittaker Chambers. Chambers, a former Communist who was now a staff writer for *Time* magazine, accused Hiss of belonging to a Communist cell in the 1930s that transported secret information to the Soviets. Hiss's first trial had been deadlocked, but the former official was on trial again for perjuring himself about his relationship with Chambers. Hiss would be convicted and sent to prison in 1950.

Branch Rickey, ever on the alert about what he perceived as Communist dangers to the United States, railed against Hiss's rise in the government and "the disgraceful presence of a traitor sitting with our president at Yalta."[20] What drew Jackie Robinson into the vortex of raging domestic American politics was the tempest created by Paul Robeson's mid-April 1949 speech in Paris, France, in which the singer, who had lived in the Soviet Union, told a left-wing audience, "It is unthinkable that American Negroes would go to war on behalf of those who have oppressed us for generations against a country which in one generation has raised our people to the full dignity of mankind."[21]

The House Un-American Activities Committee reacted swiftly to Robeson's charges. It sought statements and testimony from influential and patriotic black Americans. Mary McLeod Bethune, the president of Bethune-Cookman College in Daytona Beach, the campus that had been friendly to Jackie Robinson in his first spring training in 1946, criticized Robeson's statement. "I think he has missed his cue and has entered the stage during the wrong scene," Bethune said.[22] The *Pittsburgh Courier* called Robeson's comment "a pathetic statement."[23]

471

Long antagonistic to Robeson's radicalism, Branch Rickey believed that Robinson's example as a great player and an exemplary person would provide a stirring antidote to naysayers about America. He encouraged him to add his patriotic voice to the committee's list of supporters. On July 8, 1949, Robinson received a telegram from the chairman of the HUAC, John S. Wood (a Democrat from Georgia), inviting him to testify at a hearing in ten days. It was not exactly a subpoena, but there was little doubt that Robinson's reputation in an increasingly fearful American society would suffer if he ignored the request. In fact, the HUAC had been interested in Robinson's appearance for well over a year, but there had been a delay when the previous HUAC chairman, Parnell Thomas (a Democrat from Texas), fell ill and was then charged, convicted, and imprisoned for embezzlement.[24]

Initially, baseball's race pioneer was lukewarm about testifying. Although he did not know Robeson personally, the ballplayer always felt positively disposed to anyone outspoken about racism in America. When Robeson talked about growing up in Princeton, New Jersey, and being pushed off the street by white racists, Robinson empathized with his outrage.

The Brooklyn Dodgers' hierarchy also had mixed feelings about the wisdom of Robinson going to Washington. "We took a straw vote, and it came out 10–2 against, because most of us were afraid of what Robinson would say," Buzzie Bavasi remembers.[25] However, the two dissenting votes in the Brooklyn front office—by Branch Rickey and Arthur Mann—were the most influential at the time, and thus Robinson prepared to make his unprecedented in-season congressional appearance.

"I knew Mr. Rickey wanted me to go to Washington," Robinson told Carl Rowan years later. "He figured that an appearance before that committee, in which I would speak boldly but wisely, would be the final stroke necessary to establish forever the Negro's place in baseball—and possibly in America."[26] Rickey and Mann prepared drafts of a statement for Robinson to read to the committee, but none were satisfying. It was mutually decided that the player would work better with a black collaborator, who could best express Robinson's feelings for democracy and against communism.

Lester Blackwell Granger, the executive director of the National Urban League, a leading civil rights organization, was selected to work on Robinson's speech. Born in Newport News, Virginia, in 1896 Granger graduated from Dartmouth College in Hanover, New Hampshire, and worked as a social worker in the Midwest until he was hired by the antidiscrimination organization in 1940. During World War II Granger was actively involved as an advocate for blacks in the United States Navy, pushing for the rights of equal citizenship in a still-segregated military, and was honored for his efforts after the war.[27] In a prior issue of *Common Ground* magazine in which Rickey's invitation to Japanese ballplayers in the internment camps to the Dodgers' tryout camp was lauded, Granger wrote an article that argued voluntary associations were a better vehicle than bureaucratic government commissions for achieving lasting racial integration. "Minorities cannot accept the status of wards of the Federal government, and at the same time demand equal partnership rights," Granger wrote.[28] His views won Branch Rickey's seal of approval.

Granger himself testified before HUAC on July 14, 1949, and minimized the extent of Communist influence among black Americans. He returned four days later to sit in the overflow audience in the congressional hearing room as Jackie Robinson testified, with his customary clarity and sincerity, about his people's belief in American ideals despite a history of prejudice and discrimination. Robinson said he felt a "responsibility" to speak as a "colored American, with thirty years experience at it." He strove to separate himself from Communist propaganda while enlisting himself in the cause of racial justice. He said that black people in America had been "stirred up long before" the Communists came on the scene, he said, and they would be "stirred up long after the party has disappeared—unless Jim Crow has disappeared by then as well."

As far as Robeson's speech was concerned, Robinson said, "I haven't any comment to make, except that the statement, if Mr. Robeson actually made it, sounds very silly to me." The ballplayer said that black Americans would act in future wars as they had acted in the recent ones. "They'd do their best to help their country stay out of war," he said. "If unsuccessful, they'd do their best to help their country win the war—against Russia or any other enemy that threatened us." Dismissing Robeson's argument, Robinson said that blacks would not be swayed "by a siren song sung in bass," a metaphor that caught the ear and eye of the press and would be widely quoted. "The Negro people can achieve freedom and equality without the help of the Communists, and we do not want it," Robinson concluded.[29] Branch Rickey especially loved the last sentence, in which Granger and Robinson tied together the fight for freedom and the fight against communism.

Given Robinson's great celebrity, the committee waived its rule against photography. Jack and Rachel Robinson were deluged by cameras before and after the hearing but could not stay long because Jack had a game to play in Brooklyn that night against the Chicago Cubs. Without missing a beat Robinson played a key role in the game, drawing a walk in the sixth inning, stealing second, and going to third on a wild throw from the catcher. A pitch or two later he stole home. In the eighth inning he tripled and rattled Cubs pitcher Russ Meyer so badly that the pitcher balked and Robinson scored an insurance run in the Dodgers' 3–0 victory. "Public speaking must agree with me," he quipped after the game.[30]

Rickey's success in building a second great organization, and starting a racial revolution along with it, was attracting increasing press coverage. He graced the cover of the August 8, 1949, issue of *Newsweek*, photographed intently trying to balance three baseballs in one hand with a globe of the world in the background. The story, "Man of Empire," was a glowing tribute to his achievements in baseball, his tireless working pace, and his ability to work without much sleep. "What's [sleep] good for outside of 'knitting up the ravell'd sleave of care'?" the erudite executive asked. Not being a fan of Napoleon Bonaparte, Rickey probably did not like the title of the story, but otherwise he was pleased by the recognition.[31] (An unapologetic Victorian, Rickey in 1948 had successfully convinced the publisher of Leo Durocher's book about his Brooklyn baseball life to change the title from what the executive thought was the demeaning *Bums* to *The Dodgers and Me*.)[32]

The Dodgers' 1949 pennant, their second in three years, did not come easily, but as Rickey often said, "The hard way may be the best way." The Cardinals held a slight lead on the Dodgers with two weeks left in the season, but Brooklyn won two out of three games in St. Louis, with Preacher Roe pitching a shutout in the rubber game. When they returned east to finish the season, the Dodgers were only half a game out of first place.

Big crowds flocked to Ebbets Field for the final home games on the next to last weekend of the season. On "Don Newcombe Day," the big pitcher's fans presented him with an automobile and other gifts in pre-game ceremonies. The impressive rookie showed his thanks by winning his sixteenth game easily, an 8–1 victory over the Phillies. The next day, however, on "Pee Wee Reese" Day, the Dodgers lost, 6–4. They would have to win the pennant on the road, and they left from Brooklyn trailing the Cardinals by one and a half games. In the American League the Yankees trailed the Red Sox by the same margin, but they would be playing at home for the rest of the season.

On paper the Dodgers had the tougher schedule because they would meet the first-division Braves and Phillies while the Cardinals battled the Pirates and Cubs, also on the road. But St. Louis stumbled, and Brooklyn pulled ahead by sweeping a doubleheader in the rain in Boston. Preacher Roe and Don Newcombe outpitched the formidable Braves duo of Warren Spahn and Johnny Sain, the aces of the defending National League champion. The pennant was clinched in Philadelphia on the last day of the 1949 season when Jack Banta came out of the bullpen after Newcombe and Rex Barney failed to hold sizable leads. Pitching despite a painful blister on his finger, Banta kept the Braves at bay until the Dodgers won in ten innings, 9–7, as Duke Snider drove in the go-ahead run.

Attendance rebounded in Brooklyn as an exciting 1949 Dodgers team combined with a close pennant race attracted 1,633,747 fans to Ebbets Field, almost 175,000 fewer than the record-setting year of 1947 but still an increase in attendance of almost 235,000 from 1948.[33] Now it was time, Branch Rickey believed fervently, for the Dodgers to avenge their losses of 1941 and 1947 and finally beat the Yankees in the World Series. He understood the fierce desire of the underdog Brooklyn borough to arrive at last in the promised land of victory. Maybe the third time would be the charm.

The Yankees, however, under their first-year manager Casey Stengel, were on a roll. They won the American League pennant in dramatic fashion, beating the Boston Red Sox at Yankee Stadium in the last two games of the season to win the flag by one game. They also had their legendary mystique of near invincibility, having won seven of the previous thirteen World Series.

Although not close friends, Casey Stengel and Branch Rickey had shared several decades of baseball history. Stengel played outfield for the Dodgers before World War I, and for the Giants when they faced the Yankees in three straight World Series from 1921 to 1923. He had managed bad Brooklyn teams in the 1930s and, later, bad Boston Braves squads too. Stengel advised that the best way to cope with Branch Rickey when the sly and tireless executive was in a trading mood was to let him talk for two hours and when he finished and asked, "Is it a deal?" say, "No!" and walk out.

Now that Stengel was leading a good team, he was eager to end all the jokes about his incompetence as a manager. He also had the aura of Yankee Stadium on his side. When the Dodgers came to the Bronx to play game one of the 1949 Series at the Stadium, they were directed to the third base clubhouse because the home team had recently moved to the first base clubhouse. The Yankees, though, hadn't taken all their possessions. "When we entered the visitor's locker room, we were not only confronted with the atmosphere of being in a national shrine," Brooklyn pitcher Carl Erskine remembered, "but we also noticed that still in place, and not yet moved to the Yankees' side, were the lockers and uniforms . . . of Babe Ruth and Lou Gehrig."[34]

Although the first three games of the 1949 World Series were close and well played, the perhaps-intimidated Dodgers did not provide the drama of the 1941 and 1947 Series. The teams swapped 1–0 shutout victories in the first two games. In game one Tommy Henrich broke up the scoreless game with a home run in the bottom of the ninth off Don Newcombe, who later said, even though he lost, that it was the best game he ever pitched.[35] Preacher Roe evened the Series the next day, beating Vic Raschi, as the Dodgers' left-hander made the second-inning run scored by Jackie Robinson on a single by Gil Hodges hold up for the victory. Roe thus fulfilled the promise that Branch Rickey had seen in him when he was signed by the Cardinals. "One day, son, you will win a game in the World Series," Rickey had said to Roe and numerous other hurlers as he sought to fix in their minds a cherished goal of their profession. Wanting to win the World Series more than at any time in his career, Rickey burst into the Dodgers clubhouse to congratulate Roe. With cigar butt clenched firmly in his mouth, he followed Roe into the shower to make sure his embrace was completed. What difference did a little water on his clothes mean at a time of great jubilation?[36]

However, when the Yankees came to Ebbets Field, they took charge of the Series, never trailing in sweeping the three games in Brooklyn. Game three, though, was as tense and exciting as the first two games. Ralph Branca pitched well, and it was a 1–1 tie going into the top of the ninth inning. But pinch hitter Johnny Mize knocked in two runs with a single to give the Yankees the lead, and they held on for a 4–3 victory. Solo home runs in the bottom of the ninth inning by Roy Campanella and Luis Olmo (reinstated from the Mexican League) only made the final score tantalizingly close.

Oh, the vagaries and vicissitudes of baseball, Branch Rickey thought after the game. Mize had been one of his own, discovered by his brother Frank Rickey on the playing fields of Georgia. Traded to the Giants after the 1941 season, Mize had come to the Yankees late in 1949, just in time to crush Brooklyn's hopes. It was sweet revenge for the big first baseman who had always felt underpaid and underappreciated by Branch Rickey and the Cardinals.

After game three the Dodgers hosted a banquet honoring the members of the 1916 National League champion Brooklyn team. Although the 1916 team had lost the World Series to the Boston Red Sox, Rickey toasted their competitiveness and legacy of achievement. He also happily announced that the last federal antitrust law suit against baseball's reserve system had been settled out of court. Outfielder Danny Gardella had accepted a cash settlement plus an invitation to spring training in 1950 with the St. Louis Cardinals, an offer made by the Cardinals' new owner Fred Saigh. (Gardella did not make the team in spring training, and never played again in the Major Leagues.)[37]

Rickey was, of course, thrilled that the last legal challenge to the reserve system had been beaten. He had recently distributed to his fellow baseball brethren a law journal article written by his son-in-law John Eckler that affirmed the wisdom of the antitrust exemption granted to baseball in 1922 in a unanimous opinion written by Oliver Wendell Holmes, chief justice of the United States Supreme Court. Rickey heartily enjoyed a colorful metaphor his son-in-law used in defending baseball's status quo. "The rationale of the Federal case is that baseball is not trade or commerce," Eckler wrote, "and it is submitted that the court's decision would have been quite the same had the facts shown that every ball park was located on a state line and the players had to pass from one state to another as they ran from first to second base."[38]

The glow of good feeling at the dinner honoring the old Dodgers quickly faded to disappointment as the current Dodgers were not up to the task of beating the Yankees. Games four and five were over early, as the Yankees knocked Don Newcombe out of the box in the fourth inning of game four, and the next day Rex Barney didn't make it out of the third inning. "Wait 'til next year" was again the plaintive wail heard across Brooklyn. A disturbing pattern was obvious to all: three World Series against the Yankees in the 1940s, and three losses in a row. Brooklyn players would have to be satisfied with the losers' share of $4,165, compared to the Yankees' cut of $5,884 a man.[39]

The defeat was another great disappointment to Brooklyn fans and a tough loss to take for Branch Rickey, who had been so optimistic at the start of the year. He was particularly peeved at Preacher Roe's inability to make a second start in the World Series because a line drive off the bat of Yankees outfielder Johnny Lindell in game two had injured a finger on his gloved hand.

Rickey tried to motivate Roe "to pay the price" by telling him the story of Bill Hallahan's courage during the 1930 pennant race for the Cardinals when, with his nonpitching fingers bruised, he took the ball and won a key game. To Rickey's chagrin he couldn't convince Roe to do likewise, calling it "his biggest disappointment of 1949."[40]

After the World Series ended, Rickey engaged in a public dispute with Yankees general manager George Weiss about which team had the better farm system. Weiss had started the contretemps when he said, "Where would Brooklyn be if it had not raided the Negro leagues for Jackie Robinson, Roy Campanella, and Don Newcombe?" Weiss also claimed that his organization had a better record in the Minor Leagues, but Rickey, of course, did not let the criticism go unanswered. First, he took issue with Weiss's now-familiar charge that Rickey had "raided" the Negro Leagues, saying that the word had "an unpleasant connotation" and was not true in any legal sense. Then he cited numbers proving that in the thirteen leagues where the Dodgers and Yankees both had farm teams, Brooklyn's affiliates had nine teams in the first division to only four for the New Yorkers. Ever the clever logician, Rickey rested his case by saying that the issue was not where would the Dodgers have been without black players but "where would the Yankees be without their white players?"[41]

Before the annual baseball winter meetings in December, Rickey recharged his batteries by going on a fishing trip with Burt Shotton near his manager's home in central Florida. The camaraderie with his former player and virtually oldest friend in baseball was special for Rickey. "Rick could replay a whole season during one hour of fishing," Shotton marveled.[42] They agreed that the Dodgers had not lost the World Series but that the Yankees had won it with better pitchers and more timely hitters.

Although Rickey liked to tease the writers about possibilities for change, there was no doubt that Shotton was returning in 1950 because Rickey placed him in the upper echelon of managers, along with John McGraw and Connie Mack. All were great leaders of men, he felt, blessed with the rare ability to alternately soothe and stoke fragile athletic egos. What Rickey said admiringly about Pepper Martin could also be said about Burt Shotton. "He is as was"—there was no pretense in the man. He was a baseball lifer who did not drink or lead a colorful life off the field. While managing the Dodgers he lived with his wife in the St. George Hotel in downtown Brooklyn. One night he ordered from room service two Manhattans, expecting delivery of two bowls of his favorite fish chowder. When the waiter brought up two glasses of alcoholic Manhattans, Shotton simply sent them back.[43]

However, the manager's inability to provide lively quotes created many detractors in the press. He was not forthcoming with colorful stories to tell the writers. After Don Newcombe got knocked out in the fourth inning of game four in the 1949 World Series, Shotton kept the press waiting for ten minutes and then snapped, "Just what the hell would you like me to say?"[44] Contentious Dick Young of the *Daily News* continued to refer to him in print as "KOBS," Kindly Old Burt Shotton. The nickname was not as virulent as "El Cheapo" was for Rickey, but Young and Jimmy Powers both worked for the same newspaper and Shotton was not going to go out of his way to be quotable for the writers, especially for newspapers that had trashed his friend Rick.

By the late 1940s Jimmy Powers had added radio and television assignments to his newspaper work. According to Dodgers front office executive Buzzie Bavasi, who was an eyewitness to the encounter, Shotton was invited to appear on Powers's program on WPIX, the newspaper's television station. "The show started with both men seated at a table," Bavasi recalls. "Before Jimmy could say a word, Burt stood up and said, 'Jim, you and I have played golf together, fished together and hunted together, and now I am finally glad to meet you.' With that, Burt walked off the set. Funny thing, Jimmy never mentioned Burt in his column again."[45]

By the end of the 1940s Jimmy Powers had also terminated his "El Cheapo" campaign against Rickey. The reason was not primarily because the Dodgers had proven consistently successful on the field under Rickey's management, but because a member of the Brooklyn front office, probably Minor League administrator Harold Roettger, had received anonymously a copy of a letter Powers had written during World War Two to Colonel Robert McCormick, publisher of the *Daily News*. The sports columnist expressed many racist and anti-Semitic opinions in the letter. "If [gossip columnist Walter] Winchell and the rest of the Jews had their way," Powers had written, "America would be a vast concentration camp from Maine to California. There wouldn't be enough barbed wire to hold back all the decent Christians maligned by the Jews and all who run with them." Roettger, the gentlest of Rickey's compassionate staff, wanted to go public with the letter, but Rickey insisted on letting the matter drop. "We never should have taken Powers seriously," the ferocious but idealistic gentleman concluded.[46]

If one of his worst press antagonists was now muted, Branch Rickey had no illusions about what the coming year of 1950 would bring. Two pennants in three years meant nothing. "What have you done for me lately?" was the operative view in the organization, Rickey understood. Leo Durocher might be gone and the Catholic Youth Organization placated, and the economic losses of the football Dodgers may have been fading into history (although there were still the last checks to be paid to quarterback Robert Chappuis).[47] However, Rickey and his hand-picked loyal manager Burt Shotton were still the ruling faces of the Brooklyn management, and Walter O'Malley was eager to ascend to the team presidency. It was more than ever clear to Rickey that he could be out of a job by the end of the 1950 season.

The thought of idleness repelled Rickey, but his brain and his spirit could never slow for long. As Branch Rickey celebrated Christmas with his family, he looked forward to the new year with the same passion he always felt. If what lay ahead in the new year was indeed going to be his swan song in Brooklyn, he wanted 1950 to be a banner year.

23

A Branch Is Chopped in Brooklyn

At the start of spring training in Vero Beach in 1950, Branch Rickey made a bold statement. He not only predicted a pennant for the Dodgers but forecast a Yankees-Dodgers World Series. The remark prompted his former favorite prodigal son, manager Leo Durocher of the New York Giants, to comment sarcastically that maybe the rest of the teams in Major League Baseball shouldn't even bother to play the season.[1]

After the end of the 1949 World Series, Burt Shotton had said that if the Dodgers obtained another starting pitcher, they would win in 1950. However, his friend Rick did not make any major deals in the off-season, figuring that the young staff, headed by Don Newcombe, Ralph Branca, and Carl Erskine, was maturing and would only get better. He was losing faith in Rex Barney but was confident that Preacher Roe still had plenty of wins to contribute from his left arm. He may have been peeved at Roe for not pitching with discomfort when the Dodgers desperately needed a victory in the 1949 World Series, but he considered the southpaw a veteran presence that every pennant-winning pitching staff needed.

As far as the rest of the team was concerned, Rickey beamed with confidence. Roy Campanella was becoming a rock of steadiness and production behind the plate. The infield of Gil Hodges, Jackie Robinson, Pee Wee Reese, and Billy Cox was still in its prime (although, every now and then, Rickey lamented that because of the color line Robinson did not arrive in Brooklyn until he was a baseball-old rookie at twenty-eight). Billy Cox's bat at third base was perhaps questionable, but Bobby Morgan, a twenty-three-year-old farm system product who was the 1949 International League MVP and hit .337 with 112 RBI, was going to have a chance to take away Cox's starting job.[2] (Morgan, however, would never make it as a regular, with an aversion to flying not helping his cause.)

Rickey assessed two thirds of the prospective 1950 Dodgers outfield with satisfaction. Carl Furillo was making right field his own with an exemplary combination of offense and defense. Duke Snider had taken over in center field and was becoming the kind of power hitter Rickey had envisioned when he was signed during the World War II tryout camps. Although he led the National League in strikeouts with 92 in 1949, Snider had shown that he was in the big leagues to stay in 1949 when he hit .292 with 23 HR and 100 RBI.

Left field remained a revolving door for the Dodgers. One reason the position was undermanned in 1950 was that, before the start of the season, Rickey sold black center fielder Sam Jethroe to the Boston Braves for over $100,000. "It was the first time in my life I have a sold a man who may be better than what I have," Rickey admitted to sportswriter Stanley Woodward. "I may have impoverished myself." However, he frankly admitted that he wasn't sure if Brooklyn ownership and the players were ready for another black regular on the team. He said that Brooklyn's scouting in the South had been hurt by the signing of the black players, but at least by selling Jethroe to the Braves, another Major League club had broken the color line. "When more clubs have Negro players," Rickey told Woodward hopefully, "it may be that we shall be able to overcome prejudice in those areas and reestablish our scouting fields [in the South]."[3]

In 1950 Gene Hermanski had the most at-bats in left field, with 289; he was subbed for on occasion by Tommy Brown, George Shuba, and Cal Abrams. Abrams's base running was not a strong part of his game. During one spring intrasquad game in 1950, Branch Rickey was sitting in the dugout next to Joe Oliffe, a seventeen-year-old Minor League pitcher who was the son of Rickey's neighbor on the Eastern shore of Maryland and had been signed in the kitchen of Rickey's country hideaway. "Joe, Jr., if you want to learn how not to run the bases," Rickey said, pointing to Abrams, who was uneasily taking his lead, "watch that guy at second base. That young boy needs some help."[4] On the last day of the 1950 regular season, when the Dodgers needed to beat the Phillies to force a playoff for the pennant, Abrams took a hesitant lead off second base as the potential winning run in the bottom of the ninth inning at Ebbets Field but was thrown out at home plate, trying to score on Duke Snider's single. The Dodgers went on to lose the game in the tenth inning.

Nightmares of lost pennants, however, were far from Rickey's mind as the Dodgers assembled in Vero Beach in 1950. The team was brimming with confidence as the first workouts started. Dodgertown at Vero Beach was now in its second year of full use, and it was taking on the air of a bustling baseball college campus, complete with extracurricular hijinks.

It was the first spring training for young future Hall of Fame broadcaster Vin Scully. "I walked into the lobby of the old barracks one night after dinner," Scully remembers. "There was a huge throng of players cheering and whooping it up, and at first I thought they were playing a crap game because they were gathered in a semi-circle looking down." Scully worked his way through the crowd to get a closer look. "There was Branch Rickey Jr. on the ground arm wrestling Chuck Connors," he recalls. "That's the way it was in those days."[5] (Connors was soon traded to the Cubs, and his brief Major League career would soon be eclipsed by his television work as star of the long-running series *The Rifleman.*)

Scully had been hired on Red Barber's recommendation and was told to introduce himself to Branch Rickey after one of his Vero Beach lectures. "I thought he was going to ask me about baseball," Scully remembers. "But he only wanted to talk about me. He asked, 'Are you married?' 'Oh, no,' I said. 'Are you engaged? Are you going steady?'" Rickey continued his standard barrage of questions at the young broadcaster, a recent graduate of New York's Fordham University. "All of a sudden, he sat bolt upright and said, 'Get a girl! Go steady, get engaged, get married,' and slammed the table." Rickey gave Scully the parting words he always gave to ballplayers. "A lot of people are going to know you, and you will have a lot of time on your hands, and that's dangerous. Be careful!"[6]

There was one major absentee as spring training began, but it was an excused absence. Jackie Robinson was in Hollywood, playing himself in *The Jackie Robinson Story.* Unlike *Courage,* the film that was never made after Robinson's rookie season in 1947, Eagle-Lion Films had some able professional people working on the production. Director Alfred Green had recently scored a hit with *The Jolson Story,* a movie about entertainer Al Jolson; producer Mort Briskin and screenwriter Ross Hunter were also well known in their fields; and rising actress Ruby Dee was cast as Rachel Robinson.[7]

Arthur Mann, no longer a special assistant on the payroll in Brooklyn, was a special adviser on the film and a script cowriter. For a time Mann also toyed with the idea of putting himself forward to play the role of Branch Rickey in the movie, but in this instance, the executive put his foot down, if in his uniquely indirect way. He sent a memo to office secretary Jane Ann Jones instructing her to tell Branch Jr. to inform the producers of the film that although Arthur Mann was his personal representative to the production, they "must not be influenced by the authoritative position which Arthur occupies."[8] Just because Mann had impersonated him for years at baseball writers' dinners and had been an actor, Rickey argued in the memo, did not mean that he was qualified to play him in the movie. Mann took the news well and kept Rickey informed as the project evolved because he knew that his boss did not want anyone in the baseball business portrayed negatively in the film. Just as he had never criticized Connie Mack's antiblack stance in public, Rickey took pains to make sure baseball's initial foes of integration wouldn't be caricatured in the movie.

The Jackie Robinson Story premiered in May 1950. Robinson performed well, bringing great authenticity to the baseball action scenes and ably delivering his lines. Playing Branch Rickey, veteran character actor Minor Watson presented a plausible likeness of the Brooklyn executive. The actor was undoubtedly aided by once taking in a game with Rickey after the Dodgers leader had been impressed with the actor's performance in the Broadway play, *State of the Union*. *New York Herald Tribune* columnist Bob Cooke visited the set during the shooting and was impressed by Watson's mastery of a favorite Rickey litany: "I want to win pennants. And we need ball players."[9]

The movie was not a big box office success, but Rickey was certainly pleased that the strains of "America the Beautiful" were often heard on the soundtrack, most noticeably in the final scene as Jackie and Rachel Robinson, with the United States Capitol building in the background, strode hand in hand to testify for Americanism and against Communism at the House Un-American Activities Committee hearings in Washington.[10]

Jackie Robinson reported to Vero Beach without missing too many early practices, and, when the season opened in mid-April he got off to a solid start. Once again the 1950 National League pennant race promised to be another competitive battle between the Dodgers and the Cardinals, with perhaps a dark horse lurking in the weeds, the Philadelphia Phillies, who in 1949 had finished in third place, 8 games over .500 with an 81-73 record. They soon became known as the "Whiz Kids" because of the veritable youth of a lot of their key players: starting pitchers Robin Roberts and Curt Simmons and reliever Jim Konstanty, catcher Andy Seminick, right fielder Del Ennis, third baseman Willie "Puddn'head" Jones, and shortstop Granville "Granny" Hamner. In left field for Philadelphia was Dick Sisler, the second of three sons of George Sisler, Rickey's trusted scout and close friend. Although the Dodgers were in first place for the first two months of the season, the Phillies swept a series at Ebbets Field at the end of June to send a message that the young upstarts were here to stay at the top of the league.

Meanwhile, Branch Rickey was more than ever in demand for interviews. Although he was well aware that his situation in the front office was precarious, he betrayed no sense of his job insecurity. Tex McCrary and Jinx Falkenburg, *New York Herald Tribune* society and entertainment writers, caught up with Rickey at his Brooklyn office, where he regaled "Tex and Jinx" with tales of his early days in baseball. He recalled the thrill of making the Major Leagues in Cincinnati and backing up his boyhood hero, catcher Heinie Peitz. He told the story of his first meeting with Cincinnati owner Garry Herrmann, who supported his refusal to play on Sunday (even if manager Joe Kelley did not). After he became an integral part of baseball management, he forged a friendship with Herrmann. At league meetings, he told Tex and Jinx, "I always sat next to Mr. Herman [*sic*], we never argued then, either."[11]

Rickey confided to Jinx that he was trying to quit smoking cigars after one of his daughters criticized him for rebuking her for smoking cigarettes. They made a bet on who could stop first. Each wrote a check, the paterfamilias for $500 and his daughter, probably Betty, the youngest, for $100, and both were put in safekeeping with "Mother" (Jane Rickey). "That was four long months ago," Rickey told Jinx as he chewed on a drooping, unsmoked cigar. "I hate to admit how tough it is. But the first four months are the hardest—I'll hold out!" Although they were likely unaware of the backstage battle going on behind the scenes in Brooklyn,

Tex and Jinx observed presciently about the polymathic Branch Rickey that he "would rather read Plutarch's 'Lives' than the bank account of the Dodgers."[12]

In late May and early June 1950, the *New Yorker* published a two-part series by writer Robert Rice, who, like John Chamberlain and Charles Dexter in seasons past, had with Rickey's blessing been allowed to travel with him and observe firsthand his frenetic pace. Rice captured a key part of the ferocious gentleman's personality when he wrote that "although he is privately a cheerful man, [he] is professionally as dead serious as if he were the president of the Metropolitan Life Insurance Company or a Justice of the Supreme Court—jobs his admirers are sure he could have qualified for if he had put his mind to them."[13] Rice watched Branch Rickey Jr. as he tried to keep up with his indefatigable father's endless travels. There were always professional games to see, amateur prospects to scout, long drives to make, and planes and trains to catch. "You know how Dad walks—like a man killing snakes," the younger Rickey confided to the journalist. "I've never in my life walked alongside him."[14] Branch Jr. added with a sigh that there was always something going wrong and that it was always his fault.

Rice concluded his series with a portrait of the executive in his box seat on a day when the Dodgers rallied to win a game in the bottom of the ninth inning on a Gil Hodges home run. The journalist was impressed that Rickey was both happy about the victory and dissatisfied with the poor defense and pitching by the opposition. "Look at that third baseman," Rickey complained. "He should be playing six feet farther from the base." After the pitcher threw an 0-2 pitch to Hodges down the middle of the plate for the game-winning home run, Rice heard Rickey explode: "A man should go to the penitentiary for a pitch like that." The Dodgers' major domo added that he knew the losing pitcher. "He's a conscientious boy . . . has a fine mother," he said, but he won't learn from his mistake, Rickey predicted. He'll say that God was against him and that the home run was only a pop fly. However, Branch Rickey, the embodiment of the Protestant ethic of individual responsibility, disagreed vehemently. "Why, when that boy pitches like that to Hodges," he said, "he isn't giving God a chance."[15]

Robert Rice's profile contained only a passing comment that Rickey owned and operated the Dodgers with "two silent associates," Walter O'Malley and John L. Smith. In July 1950, however, the silent associates became widely known as the fates conspired to accelerate Branch Rickey's departure from Brooklyn. As Rickey and Walter O'Malley were meeting in Chicago with other Major League Baseball owners the day before the All-Star Game at Comiskey Park, word came from Brooklyn that John L. Smith had died of cancer at age fifty-eight. The pharmaceutical mogul had survived an operation in 1946 to continue leading a vigorous life and in his last months had even assumed new duties as chairman of the board of Pfizer. It was a sad irony that his company, which pioneered in mass producing penicillin and saved the lives of thousands of wounded World War Two soldiers, had just put into production another antibiotic, terramycin, that might have prolonged Smith's life if he had lived.[16]

Passing up the All-Star Game, Rickey and O'Malley flew immediately back to New York on the team plane to attend the funeral. Only pleasantries, if that, were exchanged on the flight to Brooklyn. With Smith having passed away, Rickey knew the odds were stacked against continuing his tenure in Brooklyn and, ideally, one day handing the reins over to Branch Rickey Jr., who since 1947 had been elevated to the position of assistant general manager.

Not only had Walter O'Malley led the opposition to Rickey's receiving an extension of his lucrative contract, but the lawyer had been openly courting the support of Smith's wife (and now widow), Mary Louise "Mae" Smith. "You don't want to entrust the business to that 'farmer,' do you?" *New York Herald Tribune* sportswriter Harold Rosenthal more than once overheard O'Malley denigrating Rickey to Mrs. Smith.[17] O'Malley was obviously referring to his partner's ungainly way of walking, his occasionally slovenly dress, and the regular afternoon naps he took in his office, work breaks Rickey likened to the ones the farmers took in his father's alfalfa fields. The small-town Ohioan at times would even nap on the floor of the Dodgers team plane, causing alarm among associates who did not know where he had wandered.

As long as John L. Smith was alive, Rickey's tenure in Brooklyn had been secure. The baseball executive might not get the contract extension he wanted as long as O'Malley was on the board of directors, but Smith came from a chemical industry where executives did not receive contracts. If their work was good, they stayed on; if not, they were gone. Smith did believe that some of Rickey's expenditures were "extravagant," especially in the disastrous Brooklyn football Dodgers adventure. Yet the chemist had respected Rickey's judgment in all baseball matters and had never doubted his competence. Despite what some sportswriters called "great pressure in high places," meaning, no doubt, the hierarchy of the Catholic church in Brooklyn, Smith had sided with Rickey on the return of Leo Durocher after his suspension.[18] If Smith had lived, an accommodation to keep Rickey at the Dodgers' helm might have somehow been arranged.

With the chemist departed, however, all bets were off. O'Malley quickly won from Mrs. Smith the voting rights to her family's quarter ownership of the team. The ambitious partner now controlled 50 percent of the team, Rickey held 25 percent, and Jim and Ann Mulvey continued to hold on to their quarter of the team. O'Malley could garner a clear majority control if the Mulveys were interested in selling, but they were not. (The couple with deep roots in Brooklyn would keep their share of the team for many years, even after the team's move to Los Angeles, before they did finally sell to O'Malley in the 1960s.)[19]

With the Mulveys' stake unavailable, Walter O'Malley attempted to buy out Rickey. Because he felt he was in the driver's seat, O'Malley's first offer was for exactly the amount each member of the triumvirate had paid in 1945, less than $350,000. This was a "tactical error," O'Malley biographer Andy McCue has written, and Rickey turned the offer down immediately.[20] When George McLaughlin had put together the O'Malley-Rickey-Smith triumvirate during World War Two, the Dodgers were not particularly profitable. By 1950 the team was veritably the first "America's Team" with a growing national as well as loyal local following. The organization was showing a profit despite the overhead from the far-flung operations of the farm system and Rickey's lucrative contract.

In one of his last appeals to the board of directors, Rickey argued that he had taken over a team that had a capital deficit of $200,000 in 1943 and now had a surplus of more than $2.5 million. An organization that in the war year 1943 had five farm teams and 250 players, almost 100 of which were inactive, now had twenty-five farm clubs and 637 players. Ebbets Field was no longer mortgaged but owned free and clear, and the team also owned ballparks in Fort Worth, Montreal, and Cambridge, Maryland. Rickey estimated that the book value of the entire holdings of the ball club exceeded $4 million.[21]

Branch Rickey did not want to sell and abandon his second great creation in baseball, one which, with the success of the racial integration movement, had attained a social significance far beyond anything he had achieved in St. Louis. Yet Rickey was strapped for cash because he had borrowed heavily on his life insurance to buy into the team and his stock portfolio had not performed well.[22] Rickey's options in Brooklyn were limited and not pleasant. He did not want to leave, but if he didn't sell he might find himself working for O'Malley after his contract expired in October. Branch Rickey could never work under anybody after all he had achieved in baseball, especially for someone who had been maneuvering against him for years and who would certainly demand economies in his operation.

The only card Rickey had to play was a clause in the original 1945 agreement that stated that if any of the three partners wanted to sell, the other partners would have to match the offer. Rickey needed a financial angel who could get him a better price for his Dodgers stock than O'Malley's lowball offer.

Enter John Wilmer Galbreath, chairman of the board of the Pittsburgh Pirates. Galbreath had entered baseball in 1946 as part of an ownership syndicate that bought the Pittsburgh Pirates from William Benswanger, son-in-law of the team's late patriarch Barney Dreyfuss. Pittsburgh hadn't won a World Series since 1925 or appeared in one since 1927. In 1948 young slugger Ralph Kiner had helped the Pirates to a fourth-place finish and home attendance figures that led the National League, but by 1950 Pittsburgh was back in the second division and World Series contention seemed a long way off.

A prominent realtor and former president of the National Association of Real Estate Boards, John Galbreath thought that only one man could reverse the Pirates' fortunes and bring them a championship: Branch Rickey. Seventeen years younger than the outgoing Brooklyn president, Galbreath had first met Rickey in the 1930s at a Columbus Redbirds game when Rickey was still running the St. Louis Cardinals. They shared a similar small-town Ohio upbringing and vigorous work ethic. They were sons of hard-working farmers from the south-central part of the state; Galbreath's grandfather had also been a Methodist minister. As a freshman in high school the future mogul played shortstop on a team whose senior catcher was John Bricker, the future governor and senator of Ohio and a friend of Branch Rickey.[23]

Galbreath worked his way through Ohio University, waiting on tables and operating a photography business that sold pictures of students to their doting parents. He rose to lieutenant in an artillery division in World War One and after the war entered the real estate business in Columbus. He made his first million by combining land plots that had no liens and defaults into major tracts. Soon thereafter he added to his fortune by building prefabricated houses for workers with modest incomes. By the 1940s Galbreath's company had offices in Chicago, Cleveland, New York, and Columbus. With Rickey-like energy, Galbreath in one day would often fly to all the cities where he had subsidiaries and be back for work in his home office the next day. "I hope I die in Ohio," Galbreath once said. "I can't think of a more glorious crown than one of the sod of Ohio." In addition to his real estate activities and his baseball ownership, Galbreath was an avid horseman, whose Darby Dan farm outside Columbus was beginning to challenge the fabled Kentucky bluegrass stables for horse racing supremacy.[24]

Ohioan Galbreath wanted in the worst way for Ohioan Rickey to take over the Pirates. He contacted William Zeckendorf, a fraternity brother and millionaire New York City realtor who had recently put together the package to sell land for the construction of the United Nations headquarters along New York's East River. The forty-five-year-old Zeckendorf was a New York native with only a passing interest in baseball, but he devised a plan with Galbreath to increase the price for Rickey's share of the Dodgers.

Zeckendorf would offer O'Malley $1 million for Rickey's slice, nearly three times his partner's initial bid. Although the Brooklyn lawyer would likely be suspicious of someone wanting to buy only one quarter of the team, he would have to match the bid if he wanted to be rid of his rival. Rickey would receive the $1 million, leave Brooklyn, and be welcomed with open arms into Galbreath's Pittsburgh Pirates organization. A final twist to the plot was that if O'Malley met Zeckendorf's price, he would also have to pay the realtor an additional $50,000, the cost of having "tied up" Zeckendorf's capital during his unsuccessful bid for the team.[25] The real reason for the extra $50,000 was Galbreath's idea of giving a gift of an extra $50,000 to Branch Rickey.

As all these machinations of high finance were going on outside the view of the players and fans, the Phillies had taken command of the pennant race. On September 19, 1950, they led the second-place Braves by seven and a half games and the Dodgers by nine games. Never in their checkered history had the Brooklyn Dodgers won two pennants in a row, and it looked as if the Dodgers would once again not repeat as league champions. During an August dinner honoring local sandlot players, Rickey lashed out at the "complete satiety" and "complacency" of his players.[26] Perhaps he was speaking out of frustration about the likely end of his tenure in Brooklyn, but it certainly looked like a September without baseball excitement in Brooklyn.

The team's biggest problem had once again been inconsistent pitching. By the end of the season the Dodgers would outscore the Phillies by 125 runs and lead the league in home runs, batting average, and slugging average. On defense they made the fewest errors, and thanks in large part to Pee Wee Reese and Jackie Robinson, they turned the most double plays. But the team gave up 100 more runs than the Phillies.[27] Its ERA was 4.28, compared to the Phillies' league-leading 3.50. Jack Banta, Rex Barney, and Ralph Branca all slumped. The team was also carrying two bonus players—Billy Loes, a local pitcher from Queens who Rickey thought could develop into a productive fan favorite, and first baseman Wayne Belardi, but both weren't ready for the big leagues. However, according to the baseball rules at the time, since Loes and Belardi had received over $4,000 to sign, they had to remain on the Major League roster for at least two years.

Brooklyn attendance was plummeting. The gains of 1949 were obliterated as the team would draw only 1,185,896 in 1950, a loss of over 450,000 fans.[28] The decline could be attributed to many factors: the rise of an automobile culture in the suburbs, parking space limited to seven hundred cars at Ebbets Field, free televising of all home games, and a disappointing team for most of the summer. Weekday attendance at Ebbets Field was embarrassingly small. Crowds of five thousand or less were common, bringing back wan memories for Branch Rickey of lean days in St. Louis.

Then, on the edge of autumn, when all had been given up for lost, the Dodgers suddenly caught fire and the Phillies, perhaps not used to the rarefied atmosphere of first place, began to lose. The Dodgers swept a late September series in Philadelphia, and looming on the final weekend of the season were two games with Philadelphia at Ebbets Field. When the slumping Phillies arrived in Brooklyn, their lead had shrunk to two games. The Dodgers could tie the Phillies for the pennant with a sweep of the series.

Pennant fever returned to Flatbush. On Saturday, September 30, before more than twenty-three thousand fans, the Dodgers won, 8–3, and pulled within one game of first place. Home runs by Duke Snider and Roy Campanella helped Erv Palica earn the victory (a week earlier in Philadelphia, Palica had pitched a two-hit shutout and belted a grand slam in an 11–0 rout). For the second time in five National League seasons, a tie and a playoff for the pennant were a distinct possibility if the Dodgers won the Sunday matchup of team aces Don Newcombe and Robin Roberts.

Sunday, October 1, 1950, turned out to be a day of drama and irony. More than thirty-five thousand rabid fans were shoehorned into Ebbets Field, while another twenty-five thousand were turned away. Because it was a Sunday, Branch Rickey was at home, listening to the game on the radio and watching it on television. (Years before the term became fashionable, the ferocious gentleman was indeed a multitasker.) George Sisler was sitting with his wife, Kathleen, in Rickey's Ebbets Field box, rooting for the Dodgers but certainly hoping that their son, Phillies left fielder Dick Sisler, also did well—just not too well.

The game was scoreless until the top of the sixth inning when Del Ennis, Philadelphia's right fielder, who would lead the league in 1950 with 126 RBI, singled to left field, driving in the first run of the game. The Dodgers immediately answered with a Pee Wee Reese home run down the right-field line that hit the thirty-eight-foot screen and landed in a little ledge alongside it, a very rare occurrence at Ebbets Field.[29]

The Dodgers had a great chance to win the game and tie for the pennant in the bottom of the ninth inning. Utility outfielder Cal Abrams was on second base, and Pee Wee Reese was on first with none out. Duke Snider singled to center, and the speedy Abrams rounded third and was sent home by third base coach Milt Stock, who took a chance on center fielder Richie Ashburn's weak throwing arm. But Stock hadn't noticed that Ashburn was breaking in on the pitch because Phillies shortstop Granny Hamner had moved toward second base, hoping for a pick-off attempt on Abrams. Robin Roberts pitched anyway and Snider singled, but Abrams was out at home by at least ten feet.

The Dodgers were a good base running team (they had to be if managed by Burt Shotton and developed by Branch Rickey), so Reese alertly took third base and Snider took second on the throw home. With runners on second and third and one out, a championship team should have been able to win the game. But Robin Roberts pitched out of the jam. After walking Jackie Robinson intentionally with first base open, Roberts got Carl Furillo to pop up to the infield. Then, in one of those excruciating "what if" moments that mark the life of a baseball fan, Gil Hodges hit a fly ball to center field deep enough to score a run from third base, if there had been fewer than two outs. But Hodges's fly was the third out, and the Dodgers missed their golden opportunity to tie for the pennant.

In the top of the tenth inning, with Don Newcombe still pitching, the Phillies got the first two runners on. Richie Ashburn hit into a force play at third base on an attempted sacrifice bunt. The situation was still runners on first and second, now with one out. Up stepped left-handed-hitting Dick Sisler, who had already hit three singles to right field. Newcombe tried to keep the ball away from Sisler's power, but his pitch caught too much of the plate and the left-handed hitter sliced the ball over the left-field stands for a 3-run home run and a 4–1 lead. Roberts retired the Dodgers in order in the bottom of the tenth, and the Phillies claimed their first pennant in thirty-five years.

Although the elder Sisler did murmur afterward that he felt happy and terrible at the same time, he and Branch Rickey never discussed publicly their feelings about Dick Sisler's pennant-winning home run, A few months later *American* magazine writer J. B. Griswold tried to get Rickey to talk about the crushing blow, but the executive claimed that he did not remember that Sisler hit it. "Oh, yes, I'd forgotten it was Dick. It was a mighty nice hit," was all that Rickey would say.[30] It was just part of a hard-fought game, Rickey and the senior Sisler maintained. Don Newcombe hadn't thrown a bad pitch; Dick Sisler had just hit it well.

Philadelphia's jubilation was short-lived because the Yankees swept them in the World Series in four well-pitched, close games. Just as in 1949 against the Dodgers, the Yankees were just a little better in every category, not the least in mystique.

After Branch Rickey and the Dodgers missed out on the pennant on the last day of the season and the first day of October, the executive watched helplessly for the rest of the month as the inevitable end game of his tenure in Brooklyn played out. In late September Rickey had announced publicly that he was selling his share of the Dodgers to William Zeckendorf. It was headline news in New York City at a time when the business side of the sport was rarely reported in the newspapers. The New York realtor enjoyed the attention of the pack of sportswriters who hung on his every word, because his business activities had, of course, never received such intense coverage. The millionaire builder said that he was thinking about asking Jim Mulvey if he were interested in selling, which would then give him 50 percent of the team. He added that he would definitely consider asking Branch Rickey to stay on as general manager. Close observers of the baseball industry were skeptical of Zeckendorf's intention, however, when the realtor admitted that the "entire package [was] arranged by [John] Galbreath."[31]

Walter O'Malley always doubted that William Zeckendorf's offer was legitimate because he didn't think that any savvy investor would want to buy only one quarter of a thriving enterprise. The Dodgers chief counsel believed the rumors that Galbreath wanted Rickey to come to Pittsburgh and was just doing his fellow Ohioan a favor by finding someone like Zeckendorf to raise the price for Rickey's shares of Brooklyn stock. However, O'Malley could not be 100 percent certain that Zeckendorf's offer was not for real. He postponed a meeting of the Dodgers' board of directors to ponder his next step.

As in his last days with Sam Breadon's Cardinals, Rickey publicly hedged on his future plans. It was clear he preferred to stay put. "Would a man of my age, 69 on December 20, after having remained here for eight years, and enjoying his job, want to pull out?" he asked rhetorically.[32]

A rumor of Rickey's return to St. Louis resurfaced, prompted in part by a casual remark by Jane Rickey that she would like to live in St. Louis again.[33] A visit to Rickey's longtime friend in St. Louis, Browns president William DeWitt, led reporters to ask whether Rickey was going to buy into the Browns. Opera singer Helen Traubel had recently bought a modest amount of shares in the team, and there was no doubt that DeWitt was looking for more investors. Rickey deflected all questions, having, in fact, asked John Galbreath if he wanted to buy the Browns to allow Rickey to return to St. Louis, but the Pirates owner had no desire to leave Pittsburgh.[34]

Before he left St. Louis Rickey parried some more with the sportswriters. As always, he expressed himself freely about the state of the world. Since June 1950 the United States had been at war again, mobilizing troops and materiel to protect South Korea from an invasion by North Korea. Rickey did not think that the hostility would evolve into World War III, but he was fully behind any battle against Communist incursion. He continued to express his ongoing concerns about juvenile delinquency and his belief in the importance of sports in combating deviant behavior by the young. He publicly congratulated his ten-year-old grandson, Rickey Eckler, for winning a $5 prize from his grandfather for providing "a suitable definition" for each of the three types of boys that Rickey insisted were universal: "juvenile delinquents, morons, and gentlemen."[35]

When it was time to fly back to Brooklyn, Branch Rickey realized that his time with the Dodgers was coming to an end. He expected Walter O'Malley to meet William Zeckendorf's price, and though Rickey would get a handsome return for his share of the Dodgers, he realized that his era of rewarding accomplishment in Brooklyn would be over. Vivid memories flashed through his mind not just of victories on the field but of special moments of unbridled joy he had experienced running the Dodgers. He smiled, thinking of the day when he was being interviewed in his office by Taylor Spink of the *Sporting News* and a world champion checkers team from China stopped by for a visit. In front of Spink's astonished eyes, Rickey, a checker shark from way back, rolled up his sleeves and got down on the floor to play a game against the youngsters. As Spink left to catch a plane to the West Coast, Rickey instructed assistant

Buzzie Bavasi to put a sign on the office door, "Board Meeting In Progress. Do Not Disturb." After Spink arrived in San Francisco, he phoned the Dodgers office with an important question on his mind. "Who won the game?" he asked.[36]

Rickey chuckled at the memory of one of his chauffeurs in Brooklyn. "Dave was a corking good fellow," Rickey recalled. "He sure knew his way around all over town, even if he was a socialist, left-wing mollycoddle." He thought of the time he asked Dave to drive him to a game in Philadelphia, but the chauffeur hemmed and hawed and finally said he couldn't because he was wanted by the authorities in Pennsylvania.[37] Rickey ended his daydreaming and returned to his apartment in Brooklyn, ready to face whatever happened.

The last days of October 1950 provided their share of momentous events in American history. On Monday, October 23, in San Francisco, Al Jolson, who had just returned from performing for the troops in Korea, died while playing cards with friends at the St. Francis Hotel. On the war front, American troops moved slowly into Manchuria and were only fifty miles from the Chinese border. And on Tuesday, October 24, in Brooklyn, Walter O'Malley held a press conference, announcing that he had accepted William Zeckendorf's bid of $1 million-plus for Branch Rickey's share of the Dodgers. He was measured in his words with the press. "There has never been any pressure on Rickey to cut down on his operations," O'Malley said. "He has done well for us. The record speaks for itself." Regarding the issue of limited profits and dividends for the team shareholders because of Rickey's expenditures, O'Malley said that no investor has "realized as much as six per cent on invested capital. I am sure that some stockholders would like to collect more on their investment. I'd rather win the world series."[38]

When Walter O'Malley found out, however, that the extra $50,000 check he had to make out to Zeckendorf wound up almost immediately endorsed to Branch Rickey, he realized that he had been taken. Soon after he took the helm as president of the Dodgers, he made it a sin, payable by a $1 fine, to mention Rickey's name in the team office.[39] He also saw to it that the Dodgers would not schedule any Florida exhibition games with the Pirates, Rickey's likely new destination.

On Thursday afternoon, October 27, the final scene of Branch Rickey's eight dramatic years in Brooklyn was played out in Brooklyn's Bossert Hotel, near the Dodgers business office on Montague Street. As Rickey entered room 40 of the hotel, he surveyed the legion of sportswriters with whom he had tilted with so often and who had rarely understood his verbiage or his thinking processes. For old times' sake Rickey decided to engage in a little verbal jousting with the writers.

"Comest thou to see the reed blowing in the wind?" he asked, inquiring whether they knew the source of his quotation. The writers played along for one last time. "*Gone With The Wind?*" a muffled voice suggested. Rickey gave a mock wince at the blatantly wrong answer. When Milton Gross of the *New York Post* correctly identified the Book of Matthew as the correct answer, Rickey went through his familiar pantomime of putting a gold star in the reporter's notebook.[40]

Then it was time for the formal transfer of power from Branch Rickey to Walter O'Malley. Rickey introduced the new team president as "a man of youth, courage, enterprise, and desire." His successor responded, "I have developed the warmest possible feelings of affection for Mr. Rickey as a man," adding, "I am terribly sorry and hurt personally that we now have to face this resignation." Finally, Rickey couldn't take any more of the fake bonhomie. "I have just received a telegram," he said, pausing dramatically for effect, "from a man who is shipping me a prize bull to my farm in Chestertown. I contemplate studying a new tangent in handling the bull."[41]

In the give-and-take with reporters following the announcement of his departure, Rickey talked about his future plans. He was mum on the likelihood of his going to Pittsburgh, in large part because O'Malley couldn't afford to buy all of Rickey's stock and the problem of an individual owning stock in two teams still had to be ironed out (as it also had to be in 1927 after Rogers Hornsby's trade to the Giants). "I don't want to be idle," Rickey said. "I don't see how you can get any fun out of doing nothing." He talked wistfully about a long-postponed trip to France, where he wanted to show Jane Rickey the battlefields on which he had fought and she wanted to tour the lovely gardens of the old country. "I'd like to write a newspaper column but I am afraid I don't have the stuff," Rickey said, frankly admitting his aversion to the discipline of writing.[42]

Yet, when Rickey set his mind to it, he wrote well, if inevitably with convolutions. An October 1950 issue of *Collier's* featured Rickey's attempt at prophecy, "World Series 2000 AD" His optimistic bent was never more on display than when he predicted a World Series played in triple-decked stadiums with seating capacity for two hundred thousand and televised to the "four corners of the globe." He foresaw "superbly conditioned, scientifically trained and selected athletes, drawing salaries exceeding those paid the stars of today." He scoffed at the idea that televised games would turn baseball into a studio show. "The man who saw the contest on television still has to take a back seat to the man who can say, 'I was there.'"[43]

Rickey added many entertaining tidbits to his article. He recalled that an obscure utility infielder of the 1920s, Walter Lutzke, pioneered in bringing a three-fingered fielder's glove into the game. "Contemptuously labeled a 'coward's glove' by old-timers, it soon gained universal adoption," Rickey wrote with glee. He made a provocative point about intentional bases on balls. He understood that they were first brought into baseball to limit Babe Ruth's "magnificent home run records" and to set up a double play. But Rickey believed that "some penalty should accrue" the pitcher who walked someone on purpose. He suggested that a count of 1-0 or 2-0 on the next batter might be a rules change worth considering.[44]

Clearly, Branch Rickey, nearing age seventy, had a future as a spokesman for baseball, an elder statesman like retired financier Bernard Baruch. Many of his friends urged him to slow down, to pull the governor up on the throttle a little bit. Rickey's friends Arthur Mann and Red Barber investigated broadcasting possibilities for him, but they turned up very few prospects that would truly occupy him and could afford him the kind of "emolument" he expected. The challenge of turning a third baseball organization, the Pittsburgh Pirates, into a champion was the one on the table for the ferocious gentleman, and as a man of action who needed to feel that he counted in the world, he decided to take it.

There is a fascinating question of "if-history" posed by Rickey's decision to go to Pittsburgh. If he had known how few prospects were in the Pirates organization, would he have accepted the arduous task of rebuilding another organization at his advanced age? He left the Dodgers with a consistently contending Major League team and more than six hundred farm hands, but the Pirates' cupboard consisted of fewer than two dozen genuine prospects, many of whom would soon be headed for the Korean War draft.

In one of the larger ironies in the saga of Branch Rickey, part of the reason for the Pirates' downtrodden status was a series of poor trades John Galbreath had made with Rickey in the late 1940s. One major coup for Brooklyn had been the 1948 deal in which Rickey obtained Preacher Roe and Billy Cox for the aging veteran Dixie Walker and a bunch of Dodger farm hands, who were more suspects than prospects. Galbreath soon tired of being ridiculed in Pittsburgh for his deals and swore he would never trade with his fellow Ohioan again. However, his chortling rival bet him one of the realtor's fancy new suits that, within a year, Galbreath would buy another Brooklyn player worth more than $50,000. "You're on, Branch," Galbreath had said. Rickey won the bet, as the Pirates owner, in dire need of infield help, purchased farm hand Monte Basgall from Rickey for $50,001. "Branch Rickey boasted more about that suit he had won from Galbreath than about the dozens of one-sided deals he put over," Harold Parrott recalled in *The Lords of Baseball*.[45] (A final kicker to the story was that Basgall soon returned to the Dodgers organization, where he became a coach for many years.)

By early November 1950, however, the legacy of Rickey's one-sided trades with Galbreath was conveniently forgotten by both men as the Pittsburgh owner introduced Branch Rickey to the local press and community as the new vice president, general manager, and limited partner of the Pirates. Once again he would be blessed with a five-year contract at approximately $100,000 a year, with assurance of a consultant's salary of $50,000 a year for five years after 1955.

Galbreath provided other perks for Rickey that made his offer an impossible one to refuse. He introduced Rickey to real estate brokers in Pittsburgh, who found him a residence in the exclusive Fox Chapel section. The new home brought back for Jane and Branch Rickey pleasant memories of their happy years at their big St. Louis county estate. The new property similarly had a big house, a cottage that Rickey turned into an office, and plenty of horses and farm animals for his growing breed of grandchildren to enjoy on their regular visits.

Galbreath also provided Rickey the opportunity to buy land and a house on the huge, remote freshwater Northern Ontario island of Manitoulin on Georgian Bay. Of all the extra benefits Galbreath offered the passionate executive, owning a country place on the water was undoubtedly the most tempting. The retreat on Maryland's Eastern shore was simply not large enough for the paterfamilias to entertain all the grandchildren, who, before Rickey died, would number nineteen plus a great-grandson. Branch Rickey was to cherish his place on the distant Canadian island, which would help to keep alive the Rickey family tradition of shared fun and togetherness.

As for the cause and the calling of his new job, Branch Rickey said he was ready at age sixty-nine to accept a new challenge in a new city in the National League, and one much closer to his beloved Ohio. He would bring many loyal staff with him, including scouts Rex Bowen, Edward McCarrick, and Clyde Sukeforth; administrator Harold Roettger; and farm director Branch Rickey Jr. In 1952 Sam Narron, a catcher Rickey had originally signed for the Cardinals, would also join him. In Brooklyn Rickey had hired Narron, the cousin of current Cincinnati Reds manager Jerry Narron, as baseball's first bullpen coach.[46]

Branch Rickey Jr.'s departure from Brooklyn was more bittersweet. He had worked in the organization since 1939, more than three years before his father's arrival, and had been intimately involved in every aspect of scouting and development as Brooklyn became the most successful organization in the National League. He had a special feel for pitchers, and he was probably more understanding about the perils and pitfalls of their difficult craft than his father. He would be less likely to proclaim, as his father had said recently, "It's not the rabbit in the ball, but the quail in the pitcher."[47]

However, staying in Brooklyn was not an option for the younger Rickey. Walter O'Malley told him that he appreciated his work over the years but that he could not, after building a case for the board of directors against his father's extravagance, employ another Rickey in his organization.[48] As Harold Rosenthal put it in the *New York Herald Tribune*, the days of Rickey "flying 2,000 miles to Texas to observe a blister on the finger of a Double-A pitcher at Fort Worth" were over.[49]

Rickey Sr. offered positions in Pittsburgh to Buzzie Bavasi and another top assistant, Fresco Thompson, but since both had been hired by Larry MacPhail in the pre-Rickey era, they were not tainted as "Rickeymen." O'Malley made offers to keep them as vice presidents with significant duties, and the young executives stayed on with the perennially contending Dodgers. The joke among New York sportswriters was that Buzzie Bavasi's title should have read "Vice-President in charge of Dick Young," because O'Malley knew the harm that a discontented journalist could cause among a team's fans. Young, though, would no longer have a target to write about in "KOBS," Kindly Old Burt Shotton, because O'Malley did not retain the manager, the ultimate Rickey man. He replaced him with Charlie Dressen.

As Rickey started work on the Pirates, he warned his new Pittsburgh constituency that it might take five years to bring a pennant to the victory-starved city but said he was ready to lead the charge. It was a good thing that Branch Rickey still remembered his old injunction "Never grow accustomed to the emotions of continuous defeat," because he surely was going to taste more of it in the years ahead than he ever wanted to experience again.

PART IV

"My Greatest Thrill in Baseball Hasn't Happened Yet,"
1951–1965

I don't care who picks the fruit. I intend to live each day
as if I am going to live forever.

—*Branch Rickey in the late 1950s, remembering the words of his
octogenarian father, Jacob Frank Rickey, as he planted
peach trees not long before he died*

24

A Branch Doesn't Grow Fast Enough in Pittsburgh

Branch Rickey knew that the Pittsburgh Pirates organization he was assuming responsibility for was thin in talent, but how bereft of real prospects the Pirates actually were proved a shock. When Rickey assembled the team in San Bernardino, California, for 1951 spring training, he looked over an assemblage of Pittsburgh talent that was almost as lacking in championship personnel as the 1919 Cardinals he had gathered at the Washington University of St. Louis gymnasium.

To complicate matters Rickey had hardly been given a clean bill of health by his doctors, who as always urged him to slow down. Of course, the passive life and the life of a semiretired man were simply not for Branch Rickey, regardless of his age or physical condition. "I can't seem to keep from working at high speed," Rickey admitted to journalist J. B. Griswold, who was writing an aptly entitled profile for *American* magazine, "Rickey Starts in the Cellar Again."[1] He added that it was a good thing that he took the Sabbath off or he would not have lasted as long as he had.

Branch Rickey was unable to face the prospect of idleness. He truly believed what he lectured the players about endlessly, that "idleness was the devil's workshop." Television and radio commentary and writing might be fulfilling for other people, Rickey decided, but he was a baseball lifer, and he had come to Pittsburgh to bring the pennant-hungry city its first world title since 1925. It wouldn't happen overnight and he had warned John Galbreath that his services and his program would be expensive, but Rickey had supreme confidence in his ability to lead another organization out of the wilderness. As he had done in Brooklyn, one of

Rickey's first decisions was to increase significantly the budget for Pittsburgh scouting and development. He tripled the number of scouts and instructed them to beat the bushes for speedy, youthful, hungry players.[2]

With a long-range rebuilding project in mind, Rickey retained Bill Meyer as manager in Pittsburgh. After many successful years leading the Yankees' Kansas City Blues farm club in the American Association, Meyer had taken the Pirates' reins in 1948 and brought the team home in fourth place, with an 83-71 record, while Pittsburgh led the National League in attendance, drawing more than 1.5 million fans.[3] However, the team's record was reversed in 1949, to 71-83, and they fell into the cellar in 1950. Rickey decided that the decline in performance wasn't Meyer's fault, and since building an organization from the ground up was more important than any cosmetic changes at the Major League level, he had no problem with Meyer's returning as manager.

Rickey talked optimistically about a five-year plan for bringing the pennant to Pittsburgh, and he vowed that the team would show definite progress toward contention sooner. Except for home run hitter Ralph Kiner, however, the Pirates team he inherited had no other outstanding player or special strength. When asked by J. B. Griswold for a prediction on the eve of his first season at the Pittsburgh helm, Rickey said frankly, "In the manner of an old fellow I knew out in Ohio,—first division me hope, second division me spec, but I may end up at the bottom."[4]

With a weak Major League team and a barren farm system, Rickey decided that the Pirates had no choice but to enter the bonus market for young talent. In principle Rickey was vehemently opposed to offering large bonuses to unproven amateurs. The level of competition was not always easy to gauge among the amateurs, and since pitchers were usually the best athletes on the youth level, it was difficult to forecast how they would fare when they faced more proficient professional hitters.

However, the bonus market was growing as the sixteen Major League teams were increasingly competing for young talent. In his last year in Brooklyn Rickey had authorized bonuses for 20 percent of the 125 players he signed, even though most of them, with the exception of pitcher Billy Loes, didn't make a mark in the Major Leagues. In Pittsburgh Rickey felt that he had no choice but to gamble on bonus players, and in 1951 he spent nearly half a million dollars on untested athletes, almost none of whom made the grade.[5]

A bonus problem fell into Rickey's lap as the result of a signing early in 1950 by the previous Pirates administration. Paul Pettit was a teenaged, left-handed pitcher from Los Angeles who received $100,000 to sign plus the additional perks of an all-expenses-paid honeymoon in Hawaii and a contractual commitment to nine years of employment. Fourteen of the sixteen Major League teams had bid for the left-hander, including Rickey when he was still in Brooklyn. "He's the [Bob] Feller type," the supersalesman said at the time. "Maybe at this time next year a lot of people will be sorry that they didn't offer $200,000."[6]

However, when he saw the nineteen-year-old Pettit in 1951 spring training, Rickey realized that the ballyhooed youngster was not ready for the big leagues. "Could be an embryonic neurotic," Rickey observed in a memo to John Galbreath. "Complains a great deal. . . . fearful lest his elbow . . . will get sore again."[7] Pettit, one of the many Pirates called up for military duty in 1951, would win only one game for Pittsburgh in 1953 before disappearing from the Major Leagues. (He did try a comeback as an outfielder in the Minor Leagues before retiring.)

That Pittsburgh was forced to go with unproven pitchers like Pettit demonstrated one great weakness of the Pirates: their lack of Major League pitching depth. Although Rickey liked the future of some young pitchers he inherited, especially Bob Friend and Vern Law, the young hurlers would not be ready to contribute until much later in the 1950s. Law had been signed on a tip from United States Senator Herman Welker (Republican from Idaho) to his Gonzaga College classmate Bing Crosby, who owned a small interest in the Pirates.[8]

Rickey was thus forced to build his 1951 Major League staff around Murry Dickson, whom he had signed for the Cardinals in the late 1930s. The thirty-four-year-old Dickson had adopted a knuckleball as his "out" pitch in the late stages of his career. In a characteristically blunt if humorous memo to John Galbreath in the spring of 1951, Rickey described the veteran pitcher as "a scatterbrain, which may explain a scatter arm." Dickson has great stuff, Rickey said, but he couldn't make up his mind on what pitches to throw. "He reminds me of the fellow in the army who complained of every job given to him and was unsatisfactory in all of them, and finally was given the job of sorting potatoes," Rickey wrote Galbreath. Even that job was no good because it worried him to death. When asked why, the soldier said, "It was the damned decisions."[9]

The 1951 Pirates were doomed to a seventh-place finish with a 64-90 record, thirty-two and a half games behind the first-place Dodgers and Giants (who would engage in a dramatic postseason playoff won by the famous home run by the Giants' Bobby Thomson off the Dodgers' Ralph Branca). Murry Dickson did win twenty games, but he also lost sixteen, with a high 4.02 ERA. No other Pittsburgh pitcher won in double digits. The team ERA was the league's worst, and even more disturbing, the pitchers registered more walks than strikeouts.

On offense Pittsburgh's run production was in the bottom half of the league, and they were last in stolen bases. The only star the Pirates could offer their fans was left fielder Ralph McPherran Kiner, who was in the middle of an unprecedented streak of leading the National League in home runs seven years in a row. As the Pirates sank to competitive oblivion, Kiner's home run bat became the team's one drawing card. It was common for fans to stay at games only until Kiner's final at-bat and then head for the exits. In 1951 Kiner led the league in four categories: 42 HR, .627 SA, 124 R, and 137 BB (with only 57 SO), while hitting .309 with 109 RBI. As Branch Rickey knew well, however, fans came to see a winning team, not just one player's productivity. Attendance in Pittsburgh fell to under 1 million for the first time since 1948 as only 980,590 came to Forbes Field, a loss of almost 200,000 from 1950.[10]

Realizing that pennant contention in Pittsburgh was a long way off, Branch Rickey was happy in his first year at the Pittsburgh helm to encourage ceremonial celebrations of baseball. He heartily approved using Pittsburgh's home park for the filming of some scenes in the Hollywood movie *Angels in the Outfield*. Directed by Clarence Brown, the film starred Paul Douglas (in real life, once a baseball broadcaster) as a crusty manager who is mellowed through the influence of a newspaper society reporter, played by Jan Sterling. The cinematic Pirates' improbable march to the pennant is aided by a group of angels, a "Heavenly Choir Nine," led by a cherubic little girl played by Donna Corcoran (who was being ballyhooed as "the next Shirley Temple").[11]

Angels in the Outfield had its world premiere in Pittsburgh in midsummer 1951. Around the same time, the club hosted another sentimental event, a reunion of the 1925 Pirates, Pittsburgh's last World Series winners. More than a dozen members of the championship team returned to their scene of triumph and were feted by grateful local fans. Future Hall of Fame outfielder Max Carey, a one-time base-stealing champion, was moved to send Rickey a letter of thanks that opened with a Victorian couplet: "Genius, that power which dazzles mortal eyes, is oft but perseverance in disguise." Writing from Fort Wayne, Indiana, where he was managing the Fort Wayne Daisies in the All-American Professional Girls Baseball League, Carey declared, "I can assure you that *everyone* was and will continue to be sincerely grateful to you and should pay handsome dividends in the public relation's [*sic*] department, if not also from a baseball standpoint." (Before he chose baseball for a living, Carey, born Maximilian Carnarius, had trained in a seminary.)[12]

As the losses mounted in his first season in Pittsburgh, Branch Rickey maintained his optimism that his dedicated and astute scouts would find new talent to turn the Pirates' fortunes around. In August 1951 Edward McCarrick signed a young center fielder he had been following since his days in Brooklyn under Rickey. McCarrick first witnessed the youngster when he was playing in a summer league all-star game under the assumed name of "Connie Cutts" (to avoid losing college eligibility for accepting pay for play). He impressed the scout with his speed, range in the outfield, and strong throwing arm. His hitting was problematic, but there was very little offense in a game dominated by a left-handed pitcher, who was also playing under an assumed name. The southpaw's real name was Ed "Whitey" Ford, a future New York Yankees Hall of Famer who would break into the big leagues in the middle of 1950 with a bang, winning his first nine decisions and the clinching game in the Yankees' World Series sweep of the Phillies.[13]

After he came to Pittsburgh, McCarrick kept following the progress of "Connie Cutts." He sought out the young center fielder after one game and asked about his background and his real name. "Mario Cuomo from Queens, New York, sir," was the reply. The future governor of New York was now a freshman enrolled at St. John's University, not far from his home. "I think Mr. Rickey would like you," McCarrick told Cuomo. "We are prepared to pay you a $2,000 bonus to join the Pittsburgh organization." Cuomo was stunned at the offer, having read that Mickey Mantle, who had made the Yankees as a rookie in 1951, received only an $1,100 bonus to sign.[14]

Standing in the way of Cuomo's pro baseball career was his skeptical father, Andrea Cuomo, who ran a small grocery store and opposed anything that might keep his son from getting a college education and improving his status in life. When McCarrick relayed to Rickey the senior Cuomo's objection, the paternal executive swung into action, being a master at convincing parents that the baseball life was a worthy one. He wrote a letter to Andrea Cuomo praising him for the stance he had taken but emphasizing that a boy could both go to college and play professional baseball. Rickey promised that the Pirates would let Mario finish his school term before sending him to a Minor League team to begin his development.

The senior Cuomo relented, and early one morning in August 1951, McCarrick journeyed to Andrea Cuomo's Queens grocery store and went into the back room where, surrounded by slabs of salami and provolone, he signed Mario Cuomo to a Pittsburgh Pirates Minor League contract.[15] As part of the agreement, Mario would work out with the Pittsburgh Minor Leaguers over his spring semester break in 1952 and then start his career in class D at the end of the school term.

Cuomo promised the St. John's student newspaper he would try to interview the famous Branch Rickey while he was training in Florida, and the gregarious executive was more than willing to oblige. "You could see right away that he was extremely didactic, extremely intelligent, extremely analytical, and was very interested in religion," Cuomo says. He remembers that Rickey provided every member of the Pittsburgh organization with a subscription to *Guideposts*, the Christian self-help magazine on whose board the executive served.

"When I told him that I had been an altar boy, and a 'shabbos goy,' he wanted to know all about it," Cuomo recalls. The youngster explained to Rickey that a "shabbos goy" was a non-Jew who did physical chores at orthodox Jewish synagogues on the Jewish Sabbath, when no physical work was allowed. Cuomo and Rickey talked some more about religion and philanthropy, but suddenly the passionate executive turned his penetrating gaze on the young player. "I'm not certain you want to play this game," he said, obviously testing Cuomo's competitive desire, as he did in all his interviews with prospective players. Cuomo responded well enough to convince Rickey that he was serious about trying to master the game of baseball.

When Cuomo put on his hat as a college reporter and asked Rickey how he evaluated a player, the avuncular Rickey replied, "Let's do it together!" He explained that in scouting, he gave hitting one point, and throwing and fielding another point, adding that he was very impressed by the throwing arms of the Latin American ballplayers who were coming into baseball. (As we shall soon see, one of the best, belonging to Roberto Clemente, would be plucked away from the Dodgers in less than three years.) The third attribute that Rickey told Cuomo he looked for was speed, and he awarded it two points because speed wins you games on both offense and defense.

Before the interview ended Rickey imparted some general wisdom to the raw rookie. "You've got to be wary of not thinking too much in this game," he counseled. "Before a game and after a game, that is fine and good. But not when you are in the batter's box. You must have certain instincts that you hone so they are second nature. You can't be thinking about your stance, your hand position, and guessing what the pitcher is going to throw when you are getting ready to hit."[16]

The year 1952 would be Mario Cuomo's only season as a professional. He was beaned late in the year and suffered a hematoma, a swelling on the brain. "We only had one helmet in the dugout and it was considered a sissy thing to wear one," Cuomo recalls. "I never saw the ball and it hit me on the back of the head, and I was knocked unconscious."[17] (By 1953 batting helmets would be required throughout the Pittsburgh organization.) Doctors wanted to perform an exploratory operation, but Cuomo declined. He was doubtful about his baseball future, even though, after hitting .254 with ten doubles and triples, he was offered a Minor League contract for 1953.[18] He returned home to Queens and started on the path toward graduation, law school, and politics.

(A postscript to Cuomo's brief baseball career was an encounter with Mickey Mantle in 1985 when Buffalo dedicated a new baseball stadium, which had been built with the help of $25 million from Cuomo's New

York State government. The Pirates were running the Buffalo franchise at the time, and they unveiled a plaque containing Cuomo's Minor League contract. At a press conference afterward, Mantle was asked, "Do you know that the Governor got more money than you did to sign?" Mantle replied, "I know all about this Coomo. The two dumbest scouts in the history of baseball are the one who gave me $1,100, and the one who gave this bum who never got out of Class D $2,000."[19] Incidentally, it was Tom Greenwade, Rickey's former Brooklyn scout, who signed Mantle for the Yankees.)

Although Cuomo and many other youngsters signed by Rickey's Pittsburgh scouts did not pan out, the accent remained on youth for the Pirates. Rickey was very excited about a program he was starting in the early fall in 1951, an instructional league for promising young players. Instead of attending the World Series, another subway series between the Yankees and Giants, Rickey journeyed to Deland, Florida, where nearly sixty Minor Leaguers and four young members of the Pittsburgh Major League roster were engaging in an intensive program under the keen eyes of Pittsburgh scouts and instructors. Rickey hoped that at least a year of development in the Minor Leagues could be eliminated by this hothouse method.

However, including the Major Leaguers in the Deland invitation rubbed Ralph Kiner the wrong way. The slugger, who was the team player representative (and soon to be the National League player representative), complained that the players from the Major League roster were risking injury by giving up their off-season time to perform without salary. Rickey countered that the Pirates were assuming all expenses and that if players had other pressing duties of work or school in the off-season, they would be excused.[20]

Rickey was peeved at Kiner for injecting himself into what the executive felt was management's prerogative, but the slugger enjoyed a special status as Pittsburgh's lone drawing card, a home run hitter billed by some writers as a "second Babe Ruth," who was being paid accordingly. After his first big home run seasons in 1947 and 1948, his salary reportedly climbed to $65,000 a year, and as he continued his long ball heroics it reached $100,000 in the early 1950s. "Home run hitters drive Cadillacs, singles hitters drive Fords," Kiner is supposed to have said, though he later credited a teammate, pitcher Fritz Ostermuller, for the memorable saying.[21]

Given Branch Rickey's historic opposition to players rights activists and excessive salaries, it was inevitable that Rickey would soon start contemplating a trade of Ralph Kiner. Union activity alone, though, would not be a sufficient reason for a trade, since Rickey was very aware of Kiner's "gate power" in Pittsburgh. However, in a memo he wrote to John Galbreath before the start of 1952 spring training, Rickey warned the owner about the coming decline of the slugger, who would turn thirty in October 1952. "He is slowing up. His running speed is not as good as it was, and his arm is by no means the arm he once had," Rickey wrote. To counter the oft-cited statistic that Kiner's home run percentage per at-bat was second only to Babe Ruth's, Rickey presented unfavorable comparisons between Babe Ruth and Kiner:

> Babe Ruth could run. Our man cannot.
> Ruth could throw. Our man cannot.
> Ruth could steal a base. Our man cannot.
> Ruth was a good fielder. Our man is not.
> Ruth could hit with power to all fields. Our man cannot.
> Ruth never requested a diminutive field to fit him. Our man does.[22]

Rickey was referring to "Greenberg Gardens," the special left-field "short porch" that the previous management installed in 1947 for Kiner and Hank Greenberg, who had come to Pittsburgh in what would be the last season of the former Detroit Tigers and future Hall of Fame slugger's career. (The smaller dimensions reduced the distance down the left-field foul line by 30 feet, to 335 feet, and also cut down some of the left-center-field alley, which had been 407 feet.)[23] Another problem with "Greenberg Gardens" was that Pittsburgh pitchers felt victimized by the closer fence, and some of the Pirates' left-handed pull hitters wanted a similar inviting target in right field for themselves.[24]

Rickey was obviously preparing Galbreath for an eventual trade of Kiner, but the team builder was not satisfied with the few offers he had received for the slugger. As the one player who could draw fans, Kiner was to remain in Pittsburgh for another full season. However, rarely in Branch Rickey's baseball life had a situation looked so dire. Financially, the Pirates were in far worse shape than Rickey had thought when he made the decision to lead the organization. Early in 1952 he invested $200,000 of his own money in the team to show his commitment. Pittsburgh attorney Thomas Johnson, Rickey's increasingly critical and far more financially well endowed rival on the Pirates' board of directors, added a similar amount to the treasury, but as Rickey well knew from his long experience in the sport, money without talent was of little help in building a contender.[25]

The 1952 Pirates suffered through one of the worst seasons in Major League history. By Memorial Day Pittsburgh was 8-32, and twenty and a half games behind the eventual pennant-winning Dodgers. They limped home with a 42-112 record, fifty-four and a half games behind the Dodgers, who won 20 of the 22 games played against their former boss's rag-tag team. With little protection in the batting order, Ralph Kiner produced his lowest numbers since his rookie year—.244 BA, .500 SA, 37 HR, and 87 RBI. Home attendance continued its downward path, falling to 687,000 in 1952, a loss in one season of almost 300,000 fans.[26]

Despite the suffering in his immediate baseball world, Branch Rickey was still very much in demand as a speaker in the outside world. He turned down more awards than he accepted, but when he did speak he was forthright in his espousal of racial justice and denunciation of Communism. In the summer of 1952 he accepted an award from a Negro Elks organization in Atlantic City, New Jersey, and predicted that the success of the racial integration of the Dodgers showed the country that "a rapid solution to our domestic racial problems" was in sight if too much government interference did not occur.[27] Accepting a fair play and sportsmanship award from Brith Sholom, a Jewish community group in Philadelphia, Rickey said that the United States needed a "rebirth of old-time patriotism" and a firm declaration against those "men who tear down our national ideals and national freedom."[28]

Visits to college campuses were always delightful occasions for the professor manqué, and Rickey was pleased to travel to Rutgers University in New Brunswick, New Jersey, to take part in festivities honoring the new school president, Lewis Webster Jones. On May 7, 1952, Rickey joined a symposium, "Knowledge and the Zest of Life," chaired by Houston Peterson, a polymath Rutgers philosophy professor. The baseball executive shared the stage with modern dancer Martha Graham, Franklin Roosevelt's former secretary of labor Frances Perkins, *Publishers Weekly* editor Frederick Melcher, Smithsonian Institution zoology curator Waldo L. Schmitt, and New Jersey's poet-physician William Carlos Williams.

Rickey nodded in agreement when editor Melcher urged the actual reading of great books, not just synopses of and background about them. As Rickey smiled his approval Martha Graham told the assemblage "that the only freedom in life was that of a discipline that we have chosen." When it was his turn to speak, Rickey praised the sportsmanship of true fans, who were more concerned about a player's "graceful swing" and his "marvelous slide than in the pigmentation of the skin or the last syllable in a name."[29]

It is unclear when Rickey first met symposium organizer Houston Peterson, but it could have been in the 1940s when Peterson hosted many forums on public issues at New York's Cooper Union, with such prominent guests as Eleanor Roosevelt, writer Thomas Mann, and anthropologist Margaret Mead. It might have been through a Lowell Thomas connection, because Peterson was a frequent guest and host on radio programs. A "public intellectual" before the term became common, Peterson authored many books on a wide variety of subjects, ranging from a study of Shakespearean sonnets to an analysis of the work of the poet Conrad Aiken (intriguingly titled *The Melody of Chaos*) to biographies of sex education advocate Havelock Ellis and his award-winning *Thomas Huxley, Prophet of Science*. Later, Peterson would write a book on his romance with aviation in the early days of the twentieth century. All these topics intrigued Branch Rickey and drew him close to a man who was descended on his mother's side from Sam Houston, the governor of Texas who stood with the Union in the Civil War and was extremely outspoken about the need for American ideals to be granted to every citizen regardless of race or color.[30]

Refreshed as always by an experience on a college campus, Rickey returned to Pittsburgh with renewed optimism. Despite the ongoing disastrous year on the Major League level, Rickey took solace in knowing that his scouts were continuing to look for the young talent that would ultimately turn the Pirates into a contender. Barely a month after Rickey regaled the students at Rutgers, he brought up to Pittsburgh one of the first cornerstone players of a future champion. That the newest Pirate was a local boy only made the news more exciting. His name was Richard Morrow Groat, and he hailed from the Pittsburgh township of Swissvale. He had just completed a remarkable athletic career at Duke University in Durham, North Carolina, earning All-American honors twice in both baseball and basketball.

"Mr. Rickey had his eye on me for a long time," Dick Groat remembers. While the executive was still with the Dodgers, Rickey's scout Rex Bowen had paid a visit to Groat's parents to see if they were amenable to their son's playing pro baseball. They were receptive, but they wanted their son to first complete college. During Groat's junior and senior years, Bowen, now working for Rickey in Pittsburgh, invited the promising youngster to work out with the Pirates during the summer. Raised as a Pirates fan, Groat leaped at the chance to put on a Pittsburgh uniform in practice and then watch a game in the company of Branch Rickey.

During one night game Rickey turned to Groat and cooed, "If you sign a contract tonight, Richard, I can guarantee you that you'll be starting for us against Cincinnati tomorrow." Groat replied, "I can't do that, Mr. Rickey. I owe my senior year to Duke." But the young athlete added, "If the offer is still there when I am finished at Duke, I will accept." "I understand and appreciate your loyalty, Richard," Rickey replied. "And I guarantee you that the offer will be there next spring."[31]

Groat had a spectacular senior year in 1952, leading the Blue Devils to both the NCAA basketball tournament and the College World Series. Meanwhile Rickey's bond with the Groat family was growing. He was the featured speaker at the athletic award banquets of both Duke and the township of Swissvale. Upon Groat's graduation in June 1952, Rickey offered the shortstop a Major League contract with a signing bonus reportedly between $35,000 and $40,000. Because the bonus was over $4,000, Groat was required to remain on the Major League roster for at least two years. However, Rickey was convinced that Groat was worth the money and that he had the goods, like George Sisler, to be that most rare of Major Leaguers, one who never needed any seasoning in the Minor Leagues.

Rex Bowen and Rickey agreed that despite his below-average running speed for a middle infielder, Groat had extraordinary agility, flexibility, and far-above-average mental aptitude and toughness. "He was so limber that he could place his palms on the ground without bending his knees," Rex Bowen remembers.[32] Harold "Pie" Traynor, Pittsburgh's immortal third baseman who was also working in the Pirates' front office, concurred. "He's fast on his feet, has a good arm and splendid coordination gained from his playing basketball," Traynor said.[33]

On the eve of summer in 1952, twenty-one-year-old Dick Groat joined the Pirates in New York for a series against the Giants. After sitting on the bench for the first game, he made his debut the next day, pinch-hitting successfully, and on his third day in the big leagues Dick Groat became the Pirates shortstop for the rest of the calamitous 1952 season. He would have the highest batting average of any regular, .284, with 1 HR and 29 RBI. He committed 25 errors in the ninety-five games he played, but usually they were the errors of enthusiasm that Branch Rickey forgave. Groat clearly showed that he was a building block of the future.

Unfortunately, Groat was inducted into the Army after the 1952 season, and he would spend the entire 1953 and 1954 seasons in the military. He was stationed at Fort Belvoir, Virginia, and was able to stay in shape by playing on the camp's baseball and basketball teams, both of which won All-Army titles. He even tried out for football and made the Belvoir team as a punter and place-kicker, but when his coach tried to persuade him to play defensive back, Groat drew the line. "I could imagine Mr. Rickey's reaction to me playing football and breaking a leg," Groat laughs.[34]

In November 1952 Rickey enjoyed a moment he had been waiting for since 1932: the election of a Republican presidential candidate, Dwight Eisenhower, the former general in command of Allied forces in Europe in World War Two. When Eisenhower's World War II memoir, *Crusade in Europe*, was published, Rickey urged his friends and family to make it required reading.[35] He deeply admired Eisenhower as a soldier. He did not know how good a political leader the new president would prove to be, but he was gladdened by the return of solid business values and a real patriot to the White House.

As someone who believed in a two-party, democratic system, Rickey may have shied away from the virulence of the anti-Democratic party Republican slogan of the 1952 campaign, "Twenty Years of Treason," but there was no doubt that both Branch and Jane Rickey deeply feared the continuing threat of Soviet Communism. In a rare interview Jane gave to a reporter for the *Pittsburgh Press* Sunday newspaper supplement, she talked about a Latvian couple that the Rickeys had recently "adopted" and helped to adjust to their new life after they fled from their Communist country. "Their greatest concern is that the Americans aren't taking the Russians as seriously as they should," Jane Rickey warned.[36] Her husband did come to believe—like most Americans, including many Republicans—that Wisconsin senator Joseph McCarthy's anti-Communist crusade against subversives in government was excessive. He had "a good fastball, but no control," was the way Rickey phrased it, but both Branch and Jane Rickey remained steadfast anti-Communists.[37]

Rickey's viewpoint was reinforced after paying a call to the Westminster farm in western Maryland of ex-Communist Whittaker Chambers, a visit probably arranged by mutual conservative Republican friends. Chambers, whose accusations against Alger Hiss in many ways had defined the Cold War in the United States, had recently written *Witness*, his memoir of his journey away from Communism and toward democracy and religion. Rickey chatted with Chambers citizen to citizen and farmer to farmer. They shared their mutual belief in the rightness of the anti-Communist cause and their preference for the rural life. Before the baseball executive went back to Pittsburgh, he gave Chambers's teenage son John an autographed baseball. "It was the first baseball I ever owned," John Chambers recalls.[38]

As spring training convened for the Pirates in 1953, Ralph Kiner was still a member of the team, but the handwriting on the wall about his departure was clearer than ever. In the past John Galbreath had negotiated directly with the slugger on his contract, but the owner decided to let Rickey represent the team in the next contract talks. It promised to be a hard bargaining session. After Branch Rickey Jr. failed to reach terms with Kiner in a personal visit to the slugger's southern California home, the elder Rickey tried his hand in direct contact. "Ordinarily a player who hits .244 is given a decrease in salary," Rickey told reporters.[39] (He added one of his most memorable quips about Kiner's value to the team. "We finished last with you and we can finish last without you," he said.)

However, Kiner remained the one last hero in Pittsburgh, and Rickey understood that the fans were almost uniformly on the slugger's side. On the other hand, with the nation still at war in Korea, many players in the armed forces, and Kiner receiving one of the highest salaries in baseball, the slugger didn't have universal support. Even attorney Thomas Johnson, Rickey's greatest antagonist on the Pirates' board of directors, took issue with Kiner's "nonchalance" about arriving at games late and leaving early.[40] Ultimately, he accepted a pay cut, though probably not the full 25 percent allowable at the time, and reported (late) to spring training.

The Pirates were trying something new in the spring of 1953—training in Havana, Cuba, where Rickey's 1947 Dodgers had begun their pennant-winning season with pioneering Jackie Robinson heading for his spectacular rookie season. However, it was obvious to Cuban baseball fans that Rickey's Pirates were a far cry from the contending Dodgers. The sad sack reputation of the Pittsburgh team had reached the Cuban capital, and with gate attraction Ralph Kiner holding out, no game drew more than four thousand; paid attendance reached a low of three hundred at one game.[41] Work would be cut out for the new Pittsburgh manager, Fred Haney, who had managed the St. Louis Browns in the late 1930s and more recently had been the skipper of the Hollywood Stars, the Pirates' thriving affiliate in the Pacific Coast League. Haney replaced Bill Meyer, who left voluntarily, growing tired of all the losing.

Because of military obligations the Pirates were still missing two key pieces to their future success: pitcher Vernon Law and shortstop Dick Groat. The pitching would remain lackluster, with the biggest winner, Murry Dickson, logging a 10-19 record in 1953. The other hurlers were either too old (Ted Wilks and Howard Pollet, both of whom Rickey originally signed for the Cardinals) or still too inexperienced (Bob Friend).

Rickey always loved having brother tandems on his teams, with Paul and Dizzy Dean on the Gashouse Gang Cardinals being the most successful. In 1953 he brought up a double play combination, the O'Brien twins, Eddie and Johnny, signed out of Seattle University, where they had been basketball All-Americans. Putting on his best salesman's spiel Rickey predicted, "They can't miss, I'll wager that."[42] They did miss, however, as they were overmatched offensively. Unlike Dick Groat, the O'Briens' high-water marks as athletes would only be in basketball.

In the first weeks of the 1953 season, the Pirates gave their fans a little glimmer of hope, rattling off five victories in a row in early May. Rickey, in his best Rotarian enthusiasm, praised Pirates fans for their vigorous support and denied that he planned to trade Kiner. After the streak ended, the Pirates resorted to their losing ways. On June 4, 1953, with the team already in seventh place, fifteen games behind the Dodgers (who began the season by winning the first nine games and were never passed afterward), the shoe finally dropped on the long-rumored Ralph Kiner trade.

Kiner, infielder-outfielder George Metkovich, catcher Joe Garagiola, and left-handed pitcher Howard Pollet were traded to the Cubs for out-fielders Bob Addis and Gene Hermanski, and first baseman–outfielder Preston Ward, catcher Toby Atwell, infielder Gene Freese, left-handed pitcher Bob Schultz, and more than $100,000. Atwell, Hermanski, and Ward were all originally signed by Rickey in Brooklyn, and Garagiola was signed by the executive in St. Louis.

(Yogi Berra, Garagiola's boyhood friend from the Italian neighbor-hood in St. Louis known as "The Hill," was not signed by Rickey, who had told Berra that he would never go higher than Triple A. However, when Rickey came to the Dodgers, he told the future Hall of Famer that he was indeed a prospect but, knowing that his time was almost over with the Cardinals, he didn't want to sign him for St. Louis. He tried to sign Berra for Brooklyn, but the catcher was already committed to the Yankees.)[43]

The Kiner trade was announced before a regularly scheduled game in Pittsburgh against the Cubs, and all players involved hastily changed uni-forms and played for their new teams. The Pirates won their first game without Kiner, 6–1, but the loss of their main drawing card accelerated the downward trend of attendance. From a team record of 1,517,000 in 1948, attendance fell to 572,757 in 1953.[44] The Pirates won only fifty games in 1953, an improvement on the meager forty wins of 1952 but hardly an augury of future success. Mired again in the basement of the National League, the Pirates would trail the seventh-place Cubs by fif-teen games.

If it is true that the best trades in baseball help both teams, it turned out that the mammoth Kiner trade hurt both teams. No player in the deal emerged as a Major League regular. Rickey had expected big things from Preston Ward, but the left-handed hitter finished his nine-year career with a .253 BA in 2,067 at-bats. Rickey confided to Arthur Mann for a June 1954 piece in *Sport* magazine titled "Has Rickey Failed in Pittsburgh?" that he thought Ward was more focused mentally on going into business with his father-in-law after the season than on his baseball career.[45]

On the other hand, as Rickey had predicted a year earlier, Kiner was in decline. Bothered by a chronic bad back, he played only one full year with the Cubs and one more with the Cleveland Indians in 1955 before his premature retirement at age thirty-three. None of the other veterans the Cubs obtained in the Kiner trade added significantly to their Major League laurels.

Although Rickey's scouts were busily trying to replenish the once-barren Pirates, the organization still lacked depth of talent. It was obviously not like his prime years with the St. Louis Cardinals, when he could always replace a Chick Hafey with a Joe Medwick and a Jim Bottomley with a Rip Collins. To replace Kiner the Pirates called on Frank Joseph Thomas, who was the closest thing the Pirates had to a power slugger. Raised in Pittsburgh only a short walk from Forbes Field, Thomas had the advantage of being a hometown boy, and he had the mental toughness to deal with the added pressure of playing before friends and family.

Thomas put up respectable numbers in nearly six full seasons in Pittsburgh (he would retire from a sixteen-year career with a .266 BA and .454 SA), but he struck out almost twice as many times as he walked and never had the charisma of the departed Kiner. As a young player, though, he commanded a far lower salary, and like most of the younger players, he had to fight hard to get raises. When asked nearly fifty years later about life under the Rickey regime in Pittsburgh, he said, "Next question."[46]

Ralph Kiner might have been traded from Pittsburgh, but he was not forgotten. An expected fallout from the trade was the rising tide of anti-Rickey commentary on the air and in print. Broadcaster Bob Prince, a close friend of the slugger, said that all Rickey received in exchange for Kiner was six jockstraps.[47] The beleaguered general manager was irritated by Prince's frequent disparaging comments about the team in his broadcasts, but he wasn't about to censor on-air comments.

However, when *Pittsburgh Press* sportswriter Les Biederman wrote soon after the trade that the team the Pirates fielded one night in June 1953 "probably presented the lowest paid nine men on a big league team in recent years," Rickey took great offense. The outraged executive wrote John Galbreath that although he had received his share of press criticism over the years, he never went "past the writer himself with any kind of protest." However, he felt Biederman had crossed the line "with malice and distrust and . . . personal accusations." Rickey told the *Pittsburgh Press* publisher that he would not talk to Biederman again, and Taylor Spink, editor and publisher of the weekly *Sporting News*, replaced Biederman as its Pittsburgh correspondent. Spink gave as his reason Biederman's "sour attitude towards the Pirates for some time and particularly Rickey."[48]

If Pittsburgh was becoming a crown of thorns professionally for Branch Rickey, he was still widely regarded in other parts of the nation. October 1953 promised to be a time of relaxation and further recognition. Early in the month Branch and Jane Rickey traveled to Billings, Montana, to stay at a mountain resort and rekindle ties with the spectacular region where forty years earlier they had thought he would be embarking on a career as an Idaho lawyer.

The nature-loving executive was looking forward to a hunting trip with friends. He was also going to receive an honor from the Billings Mustangs Minor League team as "one of the wisest men in the game of baseball." One of the men behind the award was Robert Cobb, a Billings native who lived in Hollywood, where he owned and operated the Brown Derby restaurants and had invented the "Cobb salad" (known for its mixture of meat, cheese, and greens). Cobb also owned the Hollywood Stars' Pacific Coast League franchise, which had been a Brooklyn Dodgers affiliate in the 1940s. As Cobb was going to his first meeting with Branch Rickey in Brooklyn, he was warned by a cab driver to be wary of "El Cheapo," but once he met the avuncular executive in person, he was mesmerized. When Rickey left for Pittsburgh, Cobb immediately shifted his Hollywood team's affiliation to the Pirates.[49]

After his Montana trip Rickey paid a visit to his favorite area in the world, southern Ohio, where on October 16, 1953, his hometown of

Stockdale and Jane Moulton Rickey's hometown of Lucasville celebrated "Branch Rickey Day" and he gave an inspirational talk to the high school students. Three days later he attended a ceremony in Cleveland, where he was honored as one of the fifty greatest native sons of Ohio. The next night he was a guest on the television show of Bob Hope, a Cleveland native and longtime screen partner of Bing Crosby, a part owner of the Pirates. Rickey took in stride Hope's kidding about the misfortunes of the Pittsburgh team.[50]

Within days of returning to Pittsburgh, however, Rickey had to return to Ohio on a sad mission. While working on his farm in Lucasville, Branch's younger brother, Frank Wanzer Rickey, had died suddenly of a heart attack at age sixty-five. Dismissed from his scouting job in Brooklyn when Walter O'Malley took over, Frank Rickey had returned to his occupations as a horse trader and fruit farmer. Frank left his wife and seven children well taken care of, but Branch Rickey ached at the loss of his spirited younger brother. He himself was all that was left on the earth from the immediate family of Jacob Frank and Emily Brown Rickey. With a heavy heart Branch Rickey buried his brother in the hills of Scioto County, thinking to himself about how swift were the changes in fortune God brought to human lives. Only a few days earlier he had been honored in Lucasville and Stockdale as the town's most noteworthy citizen. Now he was returning to bury his brother.

One blessing of working in baseball is the feeling of rebirth every new spring training brings. When Rickey traveled in 1954 to Fort Pierce, Florida, the third different Pittsburgh spring training camp in the past three years, Rickey believed that the bottom had been reached and that the Pirates would show progress in the coming season. He was buoyed by a visit from Houston Peterson, the philosophy professor who had invited Rickey to speak at Rutgers in the spring of 1952. Peterson observed many of the team's daily practices, and in the evenings the two voracious readers enjoyed conversations on a wide variety of subjects ranging from the importance of games and sports in a nation's cultural life to the chances for lasting world peace, with the Korean War having ended with an uneasy truce in June 1953.

Peterson shared the good news that his latest book, *A Treasury of the*

World's Greatest Speeches, would be out later in 1954. The mammoth collection would begin with Moses's proclamation of the Ten Commandments and end with President Eisenhower's first inaugural speech of January 1953. Rickey was pleased to learn that included in Peterson's volume was John Wesley's "free grace" sermon, in which the founder of Methodism denounced the doctrine of predestination because it "destroys the comfort of religion, the happiness of Christianity, [and] also destroys our zeal for good works."[51]

Rickey refused to believe that another miserable season was foreordained in Pittsburgh, but 1954 showed scant improvement in the Pirates' fortunes. Frank Thomas became the new Ralph Kiner in that he had very little offensive help in the batting order. His 94 RBI would be nearly double the amount produced by any other Pittsburgh hitter. The pitchers again had the worst team ERA in the National League, 4.92. Not surprisingly with such numbers, the team finished last again, with a 53-101 record, forty-four games behind Leo Durocher's pennant- and World Series–winning Giants and eleven games behind the seventh-place Cubs.

The economic strains within the Pittsburgh organization were becoming obvious. Before the start of spring training, Murry Dickson had been traded to the Phillies with cash being the main consideration in return. Andy Hansen and Jack "Lucky" Lohrke, the utility infielders obtained in the deal, proved of little help. Infielder Danny O'Connell, taken from Brooklyn in the Minor League draft, was back from the Army; ostensibly in his prime at age twenty-six, he was Rickey's most marketable player. Faced with the necessity for cash to keep the organization afloat, Rickey received more than $100,000 for the middle infielder from the Milwaukee Braves in exchange for veteran pitcher Max Surkont; veteran third baseman Sid Gordon; young pitchers Curt Raydon, Fred Walters, and Larry Lasalle; and outfielder Sam Jethroe, the fleet black center fielder Rickey had originally signed for the Dodgers. Although O'Connell was hardly a Rogers Hornsby (he would hit .260 in a ten-year career), it was the kind of trade—youth for limited and fading veterans—that Rickey had always resisted making earlier in his career.

Surkont would lead the staff with only nine wins, and he also led in losses, with eighteen. Although Bob Friend and Vern Law, back from the military, showed improvement, they were not yet consistent pitchers. Nor was twenty-five-year-old right-handed rookie Bob Purkey, a local Pittsburgh boy. Purkey would go only 3-8, with far more walks than strikeouts in 1954. As happened so often with second-division teams, the Pirates could not be patient with an unrefined talent. Purkey didn't emerge as a regular starter until 1957 when he was traded to Cincinnati, where he had his best years. Sadly, the Pirates in the latter stages of Branch Rickey's regime were not being patient with prospects.

When he took over the Pirates in late 1950, Branch Rickey made a strong commitment to scouting black players, an area that prior Pittsburgh administrations had never explored. Twenty-two of fifty-five commissioned Pirates scouts were hired from black colleges and high schools, among them Eddie Robinson, Grambling University's noted football coach.[52] Rickey was encouraged when Joe L. Brown, one of the Pirates' leading Minor League administrators, reported about his warm reception on scouting trips to the Deep South. Brown (who was film comedian Joe E. Brown's son) had first met the executive in the 1930s when the youngster came to St. Louis for the summer and wound up living with Dizzy and Patricia Dean. ("Now I have two teenagers in the house," Patricia had said.) Brown told his boss that throughout the segregated South, black athletic and academic officials had all been eager to assist the Pirates when they found out that he was working for Branch Rickey, the man who had signed Jackie Robinson and opened up baseball to talented black players.[53]

In 1954 the mantle of the first black member of the Pittsburgh Pirates would be draped upon second baseman Curt Roberts, who came from the baseball-rich area of Oakland, California. At McClymonds High School Roberts had played for coach George Powles, who tutored future Hall of Fame outfielder Frank Robinson; two more outstanding Major League outfielders, Curt Flood and Vada Pinson; and basketball immortal Bill Russell. After high school Curt Roberts went immediately into pro ball, playing for the Kansas City Monarchs under manager Buck O'Neil. He picked up valuable baseball tips from teammates Satchel Paige and Hilton Smith and from two big league stars of the future, catcher Elston Howard, who in 1955 would become the first black member of the Yankees, and shortstop Ernie Banks, a future Chicago Cubs Hall of Famer.[54]

Before the 1954 season started, Rickey sat down Curt Roberts and his wife, Christine, down in his Forbes Field office and, in essence, gave him the same kind of talk he had first given Jackie Robinson. "I want to know every bill you've got," Rickey told the couple. "I want to know how you and your wife get along. I want to know every worry you've got, because it's going to be rough."[55] During the season Jackie Robinson sent Roberts a letter of support. "I hope you understand why I am writing and will accept this letter in the manner that I write it," the race pioneer wrote the rookie. "Your job in Pittsburgh is a ticklish one, you have to be careful, just as I had to be for a while. . . . Just don't defeat yourself by giving up."[56]

Jackie Robinson's breakthrough was seven years in the past, but there had not been a groundswell for integration in the Major Leagues. Although the National League had welcomed black players more than the American League had, baseball was still very cautious and conservative about race equality; half of the sixteen Major League teams were still all white.

Roberts received a full shot at being the Pirates' regular second baseman in 1954, but he hit a mere .232, with 36 RBI and only 47 R. His walkstrikeout relationship was positive, 55–49, but he didn't utilize his speed effectively. "He is the worst fly ball hitter on the club," Rickey moaned.[57] Although Roberts was adequate defensively, his overall play did not warrant maintaining his status as a regular. Roberts received only a handful of at-bats in 1955 and 1956 before leaving the Majors permanently. (He died at age fifty in Oakland in 1969.)

It was a sign of the times during Rickey's troubled reign in Pittsburgh that he was falling just short on some key signings. He expressed interest in two members of the Kansas City Monarchs—shortstop Ernie Banks and second baseman Gene Baker—and in Oakland, California, high school outfielder Frank Robinson, but the purse strings of the Galbreath ownership were tightening.[58] The Cubs signed future Hall of Famer Banks and Baker, later a Pittsburgh scout, and the Reds inked future Hall of Famer Robinson. All possessed the kind of talent that Rickey, in a better economic situation, would not have let get away.

In 1954 the Pirates also lost out to the Dodgers in the bonus bidding for Sandy Koufax, the Brooklyn-bred left-handed pitcher who would become a Hall of Famer. Scouts Edward McCarrick and Clyde Sukeforth were very enthusiastic about Koufax as a prospect. Sukeforth raved about "the boy's habits and disposition" and his physical qualities. "I mean the good Lord was good to him," Rickey's veteran scout said about Koufax's limber body and huge hands.[59] (They were the hands of a basketball player, which at the time was Koufax's best sport.) However, John Galbreath felt that he had been burned too many times before by bonus babies who didn't pan out, and he refused to increase his offer of a $15,000 bonus. Brooklyn signed the left-hander, who took years to develop; once he did, however, the wait was well worth it.[60]

It was not much consolation for a man who prided himself on being a consistent winner on the baseball playing field, but in the summer of 1954 Branch Rickey did add to his literary output by contributing a thoughtful, analytical piece to *Life* magazine, "Goodby [*sic*] to Some Old Baseball Ideas." Aided considerably by the calculations of statistician Allan Roth, who had remained in Brooklyn when Rickey went to Pittsburgh, Rickey presented a highly mathematical formula for deciding what factors were most valuable in determining a team's success. Claiming that his method was "96.2 per cent successful," and based on over twenty years of numbers that were crunched for him, Rickey argued that you can determine a championship team by deducting the runs it allowed from the runs it scored.

In analyzing pitching the intense executive asserted that he must take issue with Connie Mack, who thought it was at least 70 percent of the game. Yankees major domo George Weiss, on the other hand, thought it was only 35 percent, but Rickey—on the basis of the statistics that Roth analyzed for him—now thought pitching accounted for only 30 percent of the game. He made it clear that he was not ignoring the psychological and other intangible qualities that produce winning baseball. "Could you measure the arrogance of a Rogers Hornsby as he got ready to take his cut, Walter Johnson's utter indifference to the identity of any batsman who ever faced him?" he asked. Of course not, Rickey said, but anything modern and scientific that might provide a winning edge for a baseball team was something that always interested him.[61]

Just before Thanksgiving 1954 Rickey's and the Pirates' luck began to change for the better. Having the first selection in the Minor League draft because the Pirates had the worst record in baseball, Pittsburgh selected twenty-year-old outfielder Roberto Clemente off the roster of Brooklyn's Montreal farm club. The youngster from Carolina, Puerto Rico, was destined to be the Pirates' first great black player and a future Hall of Famer. During the 1954 season the Dodgers had tried to "hide" Clemente—that is, not play him very much—because they had paid him a bonus of more than $4,000, making him eligible for the draft. The Dodgers realized that the Puerto Rican's tools were too obvious to overlook—the great throwing arm, the speed, the quick wrists, and, most of all, the desire to succeed.

Branch Rickey had watched Clemente play for the first time during the Puerto Rican winter league season in 1953–54. Playing left field for the Santurce Crabbers, alongside the already established New York Giants star Willie Mays, Clemente made a great catch and fired a mighty throw to home plate. After the game Rickey called the young Puerto Rican over and, of course, wanted to find out all about his life and ambitions. When Clemente told Rickey that he loved baseball "more than eating," the Pittsburgh general manager was delighted. When he discovered that Clemente was not yet married, he urged him to tie the knot soon. "Find a nice girl and marry her," Rickey advised. "Get *that* out of the way and you can really settle down to the business of baseball," Rickey said, predicting a great career for the young man.[62]

There were weeks during the 1954 season when Clemente, on orders from Brooklyn, did not play, but there was no way that Rickey and his Pittsburgh staff would overlook the outfielder's promise. Another top scout, Howie Haak, joined the chorus of Pittsburgh personnel writing glowing reports about Clemente. On Clyde Sukeforth's last visit in the summer, Sukeforth told Montreal manager Max Macon, "Take good care of our boy," knowing full well that the Pirates would claim the talented Puerto Rican after the season.[63]

Being drafted from Brooklyn hastened Clemente's entrance to the big leagues. He became Pittsburgh's regular right fielder in 1955, but like virtually all rookies, he suffered through growing pains. His numbers were not outstanding in his rookie year: .255 BA in 474 at-bats, 5 HR, 47 RBI, and 48 R. Looking closer at his statistics, however, he had 23 2B, 11 3B, and 18 assists in the outfield. He was showing flashes of what was going to be a Hall of Fame career that ended with a total of exactly 3,000 hits, and a stirring performance in the Pirates' 1971 World Series triumph over the Baltimore Orioles. Although Rickey was disappointed that Clemente never became an adventurous base runner and base stealer, there is no doubt that his drafting was another important step on the road to better times in Pittsburgh.[64] (Tragically, on New Year's Eve 1972, Clemente perished at age thirty-eight in a plane crash while traveling to Nicaragua to help earthquake victims.)

Another sign of hope for the future on the 1955 Pirates came with the return of Dick Groat from the military. It took some time for the shortstop to regain his batting stroke, and he had to survive a "semiscare" tactic in spring training from Branch Rickey, a veiled threat to send him down to the Minors. Groat remembers seeing Rickey one day shaking his head disapprovingly as he watched the player muttering at himself in the batting cage. In a voice just loud enough for the shortstop to hear, Rickey was saying, "There is no way that the boy can improve. He never was an All-American in baseball and basketball."[65]

Groat soon regained his stroke, and at the start of the season he was again the starting shortstop. However, there was still the issue of Groat's wanting to play pro basketball as well as pro baseball. "Basketball was fun to me, and baseball was work," Groat explains. "Baseball does things to your coconut. Like making an error and watching that guy score on a home run. In basketball, you commit a turnover and you can make it back in a hurry on defense with a good play."

The Fort Wayne Pistons of the National Basketball Association owned basketball rights to Groat, and coach Charlie Eckman told him that owner Fred Zollner was prepared to offer the All-American more money than the Pirates and still allow him to leave for spring training every year. "Mr. Rickey had doubled my salary when I returned from the military," Groat remembers, but the versatile athlete was tempted to try both sports. However, the well-prepared Rickey was ready if the shortstop wanted to cite the example of six foot eight Gene Conley, who was a pitcher for the Milwaukee Braves and a backup center for the Boston Celtics. "Don't bring up Conley with me, Richard," Groat recalls the conversation with Rickey. "As a starting pitcher he only works every fourth or fifth day, and he's only a backup center in basketball. You are a regular player in both baseball and basketball. I think you should realize that eventually you won't justify your salary in either sport."[66] Convinced by Rickey's formidable powers of persuasion, Groat reluctantly gave up plans to play both sports and started on the path to become an all-star shortstop and linchpin of two world champion teams, the 1960 Pirates and the 1964 Cardinals.

Summing up his experience with Branch Rickey, Groat states, "I never had a problem with Mr. Rickey about money. He was always fair with me."[67] Groat likened Rickey's manner to the shortstop's sister Elsie, a high school teacher who, Groat says, always knew "my mind and the direction it was going."[68] The shortstop hasn't forgotten the lessons in life Rickey imparted in his weekly talks to the young and impressionable Pirates. There was Rickey's admonition to "never play checkers with a man who brings his own checkerboard." He also remembered another piece of advice from the paternal executive. "There are good debts like mortgages, and bad debts like gambling debts," Groat recalls Rickey saying, adding wistfully that few teams today offer Rickey's wise advice to young players, who make so much more money than in his day but also have more opportunity to lose it.[69]

Even with Roberto Clemente and Dick Groat in the lineup, the 1955 Pirates were still not a winning team. After a few good weeks early in the season, they fell back into their customary position at the bottom of the second division. Pittsburgh finished in the cellar again with a 60-94 record, thirty-eight and a half games behind the pennant-winning Dodgers, who finally won a World Series, beating the Yankees in seven games.

In the 1955 World Series, Johnny Podres pitched a 2–0 shutout in game seven. Perhaps fittingly, the young left-hander was one of Rickey's last signings for the Dodgers. Late in the 1950 season, as Rickey's struggle with Walter O'Malley for control of the franchise was nearing its climax, Podres worked out at Ebbets Field. As he was demonstrating his wares, he heard Rickey's booming voice bellowing, "Don't let that kid get away."[70]

Despite the 1955 Pirates' poor won-loss record, there were signs of hope. First baseman Dale Long led the team with 79 RBI, Rickey's spring training experiment with him as a left-handed catcher a distant memory.[71] Bob Friend, at last harnessing his considerable talents, led the league in ERA with 2.83, to go with a 14-9 record. Vern Law was beginning to establish himself, showing a 10-10 mark. Although the team was still last in stolen bases, they led the league in triples. Still, the bottom line for any team in baseball remains wins and losses, and Branch Rickey accepted that basic fact. Attendance had dropped nearly a half million fans since Rickey's arrival with his ballyhooed five-year plan. In 1954 it fell to 475,494, almost a 100,000 loss from 1953, and it fell again in 1955, to 469,397.[72]

The 1955 season was the last one on Rickey's five-year contract, and though owner John Galbreath publicly stated his continuing support for his fellow Ohioan, it was no secret that a change was being contemplated when the contract ended. As the builder of the United States Steel skyscraper in Pittsburgh and the Socony tower in New York, the realtor was flush with business success. Summer Tan, his Darby Dan stable horse, had finished third in the 1955 Kentucky Derby, and Galbreath was impatient for similar improvement in baseball on the way to an eventual championship.[73] Without the successes in St. Louis and Brooklyn to cushion his disappointment, Branch Rickey faced another unwanted exit from a treasured baseball position.

On October 19, 1955, the changing of the guard was officially announced. Joe L. Brown was brought in as the new general manager. Branch Rickey was retained as a "senior consultant," the $50,000-a-year job for the next five years that John Galbreath had included as an additional incentive to lure Rickey from Brooklyn. Unlike the previous bitter partings with Sam Breadon and Walter O'Malley, which had forced the executive to change residences, Rickey would remain in Pittsburgh, and he announced that he intended to see more games in 1956 than he had in previous years. He was confident that the team was on the upswing, and he wanted to support their efforts. "I want to be an ambassador without portfolio," he said. "I am not going to desert the ship."[74]

Branch Rickey Jr. would stay on as director of the farm system. "By all rights, young Branch should have been promoted to the top post," Joe L. Brown recalls. "He knew everything about everybody in the organization, and I told him that. He was very gracious, and said that he would do anything to help me."[75] Unfortunately, from a public relations stand-point, by the end of the 1955 season in Pittsburgh it was not feasible for a Rickey to have any role in the forefront of Pirates baseball. Sadly, the name had come to be associated in the Steel City with failure.

Branch Rickey, now nearly seventy-five years old and unpredictably af-flicted with attacks of Ménière's disease, was widely expected to officially retire. Many summaries of his career and profiles of his life appeared in newspapers. Bill Corum, who was fond of his fellow Midwestern farm boy, featured him in the first of his Hearst newspaper series on "The Most Unforgettable Men I Have Ever Known." Calling Rickey "The Man Nobody Knows," he praised his baseball evaluative abilities and marveled at Rickey's inability to let down any person having bad luck. Corum, who had once dubbed Rickey "The Great Rotarian," coined another evoca-tive term, describing Rickey as a "warm iceberg," a man who seemed ominous and foreboding at first glance but on closer contact was a truly caring and compassionate person.[76]

As the year 1956 dawned Branch Rickey looked forward to celebrat-ing his fiftieth wedding anniversary to Jane Moulton Rickey. All of his six children and nearly twenty grandchildren would gather at the big house in Fox Chapel. However, for the first time in over forty years, he would not be running a Major League Baseball organization. He made it clear, however, in a letter he sent to his daughters, that he was planning to bounce back.

"I am not down and out,—not at all. In fact, I think am on the spring board of happier days," he insisted. He said he was writing because "doubtless you have been perplexed by no inside news on my so called 'retirement.'" He hoped that he could work out a good relationship with Joe Brown as the new Pirates' boss. If not, Rickey pledged that he would do "exactly what Judge Landis told the old reprobate whom he sent to Leavenworth Penitentiary for two years. Under repeated falsetto protests that he 'couldn't stand it,' the Judge told him, 'Well, sir, you do the very best you can.'"[77]

Anybody who knew Branch Rickey knew that he could not and would not remain idle for long. There would always be some new challenge to undertake and some new cause to espouse, ideally involving his life's calling of baseball.

25

Mr. Rickey Prepares to Do the Continental

Branch Rickey's life as a senior consultant with the Pirates was predictably unfulfilling. His replacement, Joe L. Brown, understandably wanted to make his own mark on an organization that was beginning to show signs of promise. In a trade early in the 1956 season, whose groundwork had been laid before Rickey left for his forced semiretirement, center fielder Bill Virdon was obtained from the Cardinals for outfielder Bobby Del Greco and left-handed pitcher Dick Littlefield. The bespectacled Virdon, who had come to St. Louis as a Yankees Minor Leaguer in a trade for Enos Slaughter, would become an important member of the Pirates, a career .267 hitter with outstanding defensive skills, as they headed into contention.

Another building block fit into the Pirates' edifice during the 1956 season was second baseman Bill Mazeroski. Rickey's scouts had signed the Wheeling, West Virginia, native, and before he left the general manager's chair, the aging executive gave him the thumbs-up as a budding prospect. In a seventeen-year career that led to election to the Baseball Hall of Fame, Mazeroski became renowned for his lightning-quick pivot on the double play. He is most remembered for his home run in the bottom of the ninth inning of game seven of the 1960 World Series against the Yankees that brought Pittsburgh its first world championship in thirty-five years.

With Virdon, Dick Groat, and Mazeroski, the Pirates were getting strong up the middle, an absolute requirement for any pennant winner. Bob Friend continued his improvement in 1956 with seventeen victories and a league-leading 314 innings pitched. Despite the good signs, however, the Pirates still finished 1956 with a poor record, 66-88, twenty-seven games behind the pennant-winning Dodgers. Pittsburgh finished seventh only because the Cubs were six games worse. When the Pirates continued to languish for more than one hundred games in 1957, Joe L. Brown replaced Bobby Bragan as manager with Danny Murtaugh, who had been a journeyman Pirates second baseman.

Brown felt a greater rapport with Murtaugh than with Bragan, who had been hired by Branch Rickey after Fred Haney was replaced in 1955. Ironically, it was Bragan's criticisms of Dick Groat as a shortstop that contributed to his ouster. Rickey's signing of Groat in 1952 was, of course, one of his greatest contributions to Pittsburgh's success, but Bragan didn't think that the Duke graduate was a championship-caliber shortstop. To Bragan's credit, the deposed manager soon admitted that he had evaluated Groat incorrectly, not appreciating sufficiently his baseball smarts and winning attitude.[1]

Branch Rickey followed the fitful progress of the Pirates from afar. Although he had talked about seeing many games in 1956, there was no need to go to the office when there wasn't much real work for him to do and where his presence was a reminder of the embarrassing defeats of the past five years. He did remain in demand on the lecture circuit, where "The Perils of Complacency" and "Idleness as the Devil's Workshop" were two of his favorite topics, and where, as always, he could work himself into high dudgeon on the dangers of worldwide communism. He reserved special scorn for leftist professors who embraced the writings of Karl Marx without having read the work of Thomas Jefferson and James Madison. In his speeches to college students, he frequently invoked the spirit of George Washington at Valley Forge. "I don't like silent men when personal liberty is at stake," he would say, "and I grow suspicious of them. This is not a time for silent men."[2]

He gladly lent his support to Donald Chanen, a young, small college football coach from Oklahoma, who in the mid-1950s was starting a new organization, the Fellowship of Christian Athletes (FCA).[3] Rickey contributed his name and money to FCA and convinced several of his friends to do likewise. One of the athletes active in the group was future Hall of Famer Robin Roberts, the Philadelphia Phillies pitcher who had beaten the Dodgers on the last day of the 1950 regular season (the game that turned out to be the last one in Branch Rickey's Brooklyn career). Roberts remembers how Rickey, the well-known teetotaler, made his audience feel at ease by telling a story on himself: "He said that his doctor had ordered him to have a bottle of beer before dinner to relax." Roberts recalls Rickey adding, "I've got to quit this because I like it too much."[4]

Another player active in the Fellowship of Christian Athletes was Brooklyn Dodgers pitcher Carl Erskine, whom Rickey had a great influence on as both a player and a person. Erskine credits the executive with making him appreciate the connections between the good techniques of a successful ballplayer and the regular church attendance of a good Christian. "Faith is like a red thread that runs through every part of people's lives," Erskine remembered Rickey's saying. "It makes no difference . . . if [you] are a ballplayer, a truck driver, a housewife." Rickey also suggested that pitchers should meditate before big games, and Erskine followed that advice on the day in October 1953 when he pitched a shutout against the Yankees and set a World Series record of fifteen strikeouts. In many pressure situations on the mound, Erskine drew on the spiritual executive's insight. "I would get renewed confidence when I looked at a baseball and saw those red stitches," Erskine wrote in *Carl Erskine's Tales from the Dodger Dugout*.[5]

Branch Rickey was also in great demand as a speaker on civil rights and race relations. His speeches were characteristically passionate and eloquent. "Of course the Emancipation Proclamation by Lincoln made the southern Negro slave free," he told an Atlanta audience in January 1956, "but it never did make the white man morally free. He remained a slave to his inheritances. And some are even today."[6] He wondered aloud about that "something in human nature that gets contaminated with fear," but he said the problem must be faced honestly if it is to be cured. There could be no finessing the basic issue of racial justice, Rickey declared, or else you were the "moral pickpocket" he always decried, a person who was too scared to bludgeon you but who would sneak away with something from your pocket when you weren't looking.[7]

"The American public not only in the south, but all over the place has a secret feeling that the Negro is really inferior by nature," Rickey wrote to nationally prominent black journalist Carl Rowan in 1958. "The long years of unequal opportunity and menial service caused this sort of unconscious belief. I think the stark fact of it ought to be brought to the public's attention in every way we know how."[8] Rickey's 450-word article, "How It Looks from Where I Sit," for *Look* magazine's May 27, 1958, issue also made the point crisply about the need for full equality of opportunity.

As his semiretirement began Branch Rickey was still living in the big house in the Pittsburgh suburb of Fox Chapel. In addition to the eighteen-room house and the cottage Rickey turned into an office, he owned over one hundred acres of adjoining land, where he could indulge his love of the farm life. There was a huge barn, where he housed farm animals and many ponies that his grandchildren could delight in and ride when they came to visit.

Branch Rickey Jr. and Mary Iams Rickey and their children did not have far to come because they lived just across a clearing from their parents' home. Caroline Rickey, Branch Rickey Jr.'s oldest daughter, was already attending Ohio Wesleyan; her younger sister Nancy would also shortly enroll at her grandfather's beloved alma mater; and the youngest child, Branch Barrett Rickey, born in 1946, would attend OWU in the 1960s.

The other Rickey children and grandchildren were scattered across the country—in Columbus, Ohio; St. Louis; Los Gatos, California; Philadelphia; and Elmira, New York—and couldn't come often enough to satisfy the boundless devotion of Branch and Jane Rickey. The rambunctious paterfamilias would greet every Rickey offspring with a bear hug and an earnest exclamation, "You're Grandpa's favorite grandchild." Many mornings the young Rickeys were aroused by a wakeup kiss from their impish grandfather, his face filled with shaving cream.

In their love of life, games, and each other, Branch and Jane Rickey provided an abundance of stories that have become part of Rickey family lore. Some grandchildren remember saying good night to Branch and Jane as they were seated at a chessboard, and the next morning, when they came down for breakfast the game was still in progress. Others have a memory of their grandparents' falling asleep on their bed with each one's head nestling in the other's feet.

Perhaps the best example of the playful restlessness of Branch Rickey is revealed in a story that took place at the family retreat on huge Manitoulin Island on Georgian Bay in Northern Ontario. It was a serene summer afternoon, and the Rickey clan of all ages was gathered at the edge of the bay. There was hardly a cloud in the sky, and the only sound that could be heard was made by the ripples in the water. Suddenly, the blissful silence was broken by a loud "Ow!" from one of the grandchildren, who had been hit in the face by a watermelon seed. Accusations and denials ruptured the calm of the summer day, but, finally, by a process of elimination, the culprit was discovered. It was Grandpa Branch Rickey, who, after finishing a slice of his favorite fruit, spit out the seed at an unsuspecting youngster. "He just couldn't stand too much quiet," Molly Eckler Emery, Mary and John Eckler's daughter, says. "He had to shake things up."[9]

Having family nearby was a necessity for Branch and Jane Rickey. When Branch found out that Jane Rickey's grandnephew Richard Moulton, a 1954 graduate of the United States Military Academy at West Point, had come to work in Pittsburgh for an engineering firm, Rickey implored him to buy a house near Fox Chapel. It would have been too long a commute for the young man, but he and his wife did come regularly to visit for Sunday night dinner. "He, John Eckler and Senator John Bricker were instrumental in getting me my appointment to West Point," Dick Moulton says. "I think my uncle always was sorry that he hadn't gone to West Point or Annapolis. He was a big booster of the academies, and he seemed to know everybody." Moulton, who played tackle for West Point's football team, remembers one day during a freshman practice, Army's head coach Earl "Red" Blaik strode past the young plebe and inquired, "How's your uncle?"[10]

"I have never met anyone as generous as Uncle Branch," Dick Moulton declares. "If somebody needed money for college tuition, he always provided for them." Moulton remembers that whenever there was a new baby born in the Rickey or Moulton families, Branch sent flowers, chocolates, and a bedside lamp.[11]

In August 1957 Branch Rickey took on a new assignment when he was named by President Dwight Eisenhower as a public member of the Commission on Government Employment Policy. The civil rights movement was gathering steam, inspired by both the 1954 Supreme Court decision

Brown v. Topeka Board of Education, which outlawed public school segregation, and the seminal, earlier example set by Branch Rickey's signing of
Jackie Robinson and other black players.

The new chairman of the commission was forty-nine-year-old Reverend Archibald James Carey Jr., a clergyman and alderman from Chicago
and the son of an African Methodist Episcopalian bishop. After running
an unsuccessful campaign for Congress in 1950, Carey gave a stirring
speech on civil rights to the 1952 Republican national convention that
has been called a precursor to Martin Luther King's "I Have a Dream"
speech in 1963. Carey declared that black people in America wanted
"nothing special. Just what everybody else wants, nothing more and
nothing less."[12] As always Branch Rickey found himself invigorated by a
younger person who shared his passion and idealism. A close friendship
was forged from their work together on the equal opportunity commission, and before long the two men were fishing buddies.

Shortly before Thanksgiving 1957 Rickey traveled to New York to accept a scroll of achievement at a dinner of the National Association for
the Advancement of Colored People (NAACP). Jackie Robinson, who had
retired from the Dodgers after the 1956 season, was the chairman of the
NAACP fund-raising drive. New York Democratic governor Averell Harriman, Robinson, and noted jazz musician Duke Ellington were all slated to
speak to the gathering of more than a thousand people at the Roosevelt
Hotel. Rickey promised not to talk too long, sharing Archibald Carey's
story about a longwinded speaker at a similar function who prattled on
at such length that there was only one person left in the auditorium. The
orator thanked the solitary fellow for staying, but the man confessed, "I
am the next speaker." Rickey did orate for over a half hour, moving the
audience with the story of his successful shepherding of Robinson into
the Major Leagues and urging them as civil rights advocates not to run
away from the term *prejudice* but, rather, to face it and conquer it.[13]

During Robinson's speech Rickey felt a glow of paternal warmth when
the race pioneer praised him "not only for daring to break the color
line in major league baseball" but for having given him sage advice and
guidance in every aspect of life. Rickey listened in sadness as Robinson
told the audience about Willie Mays's difficulty at finding housing in
San Francisco because of the color of his skin. (The month before, as we

will soon see, the Giants and Dodgers had moved from New York to the West Coast.) Robinson also criticized the recent cancellation of singer Nat King Cole's national television program, a rejection that had led the embittered entertainer to comment, "America is afraid of the dark." The outspoken ex-ballplayer called both incidents the product of "poisonous race hate."[14]

Although Rickey felt that Robinson at times could overreact to anything that he perceived as a racial slight, he empathized with his struggle and was fully supportive of Robinson's ferocity in the fundamental cause of equality of opportunity. He always felt delight to be in his company and wished only that they could have more time together.

During Branch Rickey's brief pre-Thanksgiving visit to New York City, he sensed an unaccustomed gloom in the air of the normally bustling big city. Scarcely a month earlier, on an off day in the 1957 World Series between the Milwaukee Braves and the New York Yankees, Walter O'Malley had made official what had been rumored for months: the Brooklyn Dodgers were moving to Los Angeles while the New York Giants were heading to San Francisco. New York would be without National League baseball for the first time since the league was founded in 1876. Although the news was not unexpected, the announcement caused a deep wound in the heart of New York baseball fans. Adding insult to injury, National League president Warren Giles, who started in baseball in the 1920s as an administrator of one of Branch Rickey's St. Louis farm clubs, indicated that he was in no hurry to bring a club back to New York.[15] In "One-Horse Town," New York newspaper cartoonist Willard Mullin, whose 1935 drawing of the St. Louis Cardinals Gashouse Gang had indelibly etched Rickey's feisty team into the minds of baseball fans, sketched a far more quiescent figure, sleepy Father Knickerbocker pulling a broken-down old steed named the Yankees.[16]

Branch Rickey reacted to the abandonment of New York with sadness and anger. He believed that change was necessary and good for any institution, and since the end of World War Two, he had often spoken in favor of bringing Major League Baseball to new cities, preferably through the mechanism of a third Major League. His friend Hollywood Stars owner Bob Cobb often talked about Los Angeles as a Major League city, and an idea was even floated in the early 1950s about making the entire Pacific Coast League a third big league.[17] Yet Rickey never dreamed that Southern California's gain would come at the expense of New York, the nation's largest city and an undeniable baseball hotbed. If he had remained in Brooklyn in an influential position of ownership, Rickey told a Pittsburgh sportswriter, "I could never have become involved in a conversation about moving the team."[18] Writing in *The American Diamond,* not long before his death, Rickey added, "It was a crime against a community of 3,000,000 people to move the Dodgers. . . . A baseball club in any city in America is a quasi-public institution, and in Brooklyn the Dodgers were public without the quasi. Not even a succeeding generation will forget or forgive the removal of its Dodger team."[19]

Walter O'Malley's uprooting of the Brooklyn Dodgers was seismic in the baseball industry because the prior franchise shifts in the 1950s had been of second division or poorly attended teams. In 1953 the logjam of sixteen Major League franchises in eleven cities, unchanged since the National Agreement of 1903 established the American League as equal to the National League, had been broken when the Boston Braves moved to Milwaukee. After winning the pennant in 1948 and drawing nearly 1.5 million fans, the Braves had fallen on hard times in Boston, drawing only 281,278 in 1952.[20] The Red Sox had become the dominant team in Boston, and the Braves were looking for greener pastures in Milwaukee, where their triple A team was located. Although Branch Rickey, still in authority in Pittsburgh at the time, was loath to abandon historic Boston, he approved the decision to move to the Wisconsin city when he learned of the Braves' big losses in recent years.[21] The Milwaukee Braves proved an immediate success as over 1.8 million fans flocked to the new County Stadium in the team's initial year of 1953. The team would average more than 2 million a year in attendance for the next four years as the Braves won back-to-back pennants in 1957 and 1958 and a World Series in 1957.[22]

The next two franchise shifts of American League tail end teams were not nearly so successful. In 1954 the St. Louis Browns became the Baltimore Orioles, and in 1955 the Philadelphia Athletics were transplanted to Kansas City. Civic pride spurred promising crowds in the first year of the Baltimore and Kansas City franchises, but once the fans realized that the Orioles and Athletics were still second-division teams, attendance dropped off.

What the first three shifts of Major League franchises had in common was that all involved teams who were second-division in quality and played in cities that, quite probably, could no longer support two teams: Boston, St. Louis, and Philadelphia. Few people thought that the Browns could compete with beer baron August Busch Jr., who bought the Cardinals in 1953, nor could Connie Mack, Rickey's old friend, compete against Robert Carpenter, the DuPont chemical company heir who bought the Phillies in 1944.

When Walter O'Malley announced the abandonment of Brooklyn for Los Angeles, it was the first time a successful franchise left its historic home. As an ardent believer in the capitalist system and the rights of private property, Branch Rickey did not deny the Brooklyn owner the right to move his property, but he felt saddened for the loyal fans of Brooklyn. However, Rickey knew from painful experience all about the great ambitions of Walter O'Malley and his ability to build a plausible case to attain his ends.

O'Malley had long complained that Ebbets Field was antiquated, lacked parking, and was located in a neighborhood changing for the worse. People did not want to come to games at night anymore, O'Malley warned, showing sportswriters letters of complaints he was receiving from one-time season ticket holders.[23] Envious of Milwaukee, with a new stadium drawing larger crowds than Brooklyn, O'Malley presented the City of New York with a proposal for a new stadium in downtown Brooklyn near a confluence of many railroads and subways. The imperious and powerful New York City Parks commissioner Robert Moses dismissed O'Malley's stadium idea out of hand, saying the city did not condemn property for the interests of private enterprisers. Moses suggested an alternative plot of land in the adjoining borough of Queens, near the 1939 World's Fair site in Flushing (where oilman Harry Sinclair had threatened to move a Federal League team in 1916). O'Malley countered that Brooklynites would not go all the way to Queens to see a game.[24]

In 1956 O'Malley had scheduled seven games in Jersey City, one with each National League rival, and announced that he planned to leave Ebbets Field permanently by 1960. John Lardner quipped that the Dodgers were "1/600 of the way to Los Angeles" and wondered aloud if it would still be Brooklyn without the Dodgers.[25] Before the start of the

1957 season, the die was truly cast when O'Malley worked out a swap of Minor League cities with Cubs owner Philip Wrigley, who owned the Los Angeles franchise in the Pacific Coast League. Chicago received the Fort Worth franchise of the Texas League, a team that Rickey in the 1940s had built into one of the jewels of the Brooklyn Minor League system. Like Braves owner Lou Perini when he was preparing to move to Milwaukee, O'Malley now controlled Los Angeles, the territory where he wanted to move.

The last piece of the puzzle for O'Malley was finding a partner for his West Coast adventure. In the spring of 1957 the National League approved Horace Stoneham's request to vacate New York, and it was widely thought that the Giants were headed to Minneapolis, home of the organization's top triple-A franchise. However, concerned about travel costs to the West Coast, the senior league took the position that it would approve a move to California only if two teams made the switch. Although Stoneham had already made monetary commitments to Minneapolis, the persuasive O'Malley convinced him that a San Francisco–Los Angeles rivalry would rekindle the New York–Brooklyn competition.[26]

There was some sympathy in New York for Stoneham's plight because the Giants had fallen out of contention since their last world championship year of 1954. Leo Durocher, who led the team to the 1951 and 1954 pennants, resigned late in the 1955 season, and by 1957 the Giants drew barely 650,000 fans, one-third of the attendance coming from the eleven games with their hated Brooklyn rivals.[27]

There were few mixed feelings, however, when the Dodgers decided to leave—only rage at the betrayal. The team had drawn over a million fans for twelve seasons in a row and in that period had won six pennants and one World Series and had finished within a game of a pennant three other times. To be sure, the arc of attendance was shifting downward in the 1950s, but the interest and ardor of Brooklyn Dodgers fans were undiminished.

But for Walter O'Malley, the temptation to tap into the Southern California market was irresistible. There was a huge population, available land for a new stadium, vast parking opportunities, and quite possibly a pay-television bonanza. Probably somewhere deep in O'Malley's unconscious, he also felt that he had to show the baseball world that he, too, was as great a baseball revolutionary as Branch Rickey had been.

Branch Rickey continued to believe that every crisis brought with it opportunity. As he surveyed the changing baseball map from his forced retirement in Pittsburgh, he was concerned about the decline of popularity in his beloved sport. In 1958 National League baseball did receive a big boost in attendance from its new West Coast franchises, especially in Los Angeles, where the Dodgers would be playing in the cavernous ninety-three-thousand-seat Coliseum, built for the 1932 Olympics and used primarily for football. (It was said that the Coliseum had room for ninety-three thousand fans and only two outfielders because its left-field fence was a ridiculously close 251 feet from home plate.) Other cities in the league were not gaining fans, however, and Major League Baseball as a whole was in definite decline. Since the record-breaking seasons of 1948 and 1949, when total attendance vaulted for the first time over the 20 million mark, the graph had been declining; by 1957 about 3 million paying customers had been lost.[28]

The American League was especially suffering. In New York in 1958 the Yankees had the baseball market all to themselves, and yet they lost more than 65,000 fans from their 1957 total, even though they were on their way to a fourth straight American League pennant.[29] National League fans in New York would not go to see games in the "other" league, and even American League fans were reacting negatively to the snub of the city by National League moguls. The decline of attendance in two other American League cities was even more dramatic. In 1957 the Cleveland Indians, who had drawn more than 2.6 million fans in their championship year of 1948, attracted fewer than 664,000 fans, and the Washington Senators in the same year drew fewer than 390,000 spectators.[30]

The Minor Leagues were in greater disarray, a situation that especially troubled Branch Rickey because the development of young players was the cause closest to his heart. There were now fewer than half the fans, leagues, and teams than had existed in the peak year of 1949, when 41 million fans came out to see 446 teams in fifty-nine Minor Leagues.[31] The problems were acute at both the top and the bottom of the Minors. Many class D leagues had folded, and top triple-A cities were suffering declining attendance because of three main factors: indiscriminate televising of Major League Baseball into Minor League areas; the loss of top cities such as Milwaukee, Baltimore, and Kansas City to the Major Leagues; and the rise of professional football. Some pundits were even claiming that football had surpassed baseball as the nation's most popular sport.

For Branch Rickey, who liked and had coached football, there would never be a substitute for baseball. Not only was it the best sport, but it reflected for him the perfect expression of the American national character. He was still aching to get involved with the sport more directly than in his distant consultant's role with the Pirates. He wanted to play a role in bringing back baseball to its prior prominence. The idea of expansion through the vehicle of a third Major League was bubbling through his mind and was on the verge of exploding into a great cause.

Rickey was only temporarily set back by a heart attack on the night of February 20, 1958, which occurred shortly after he returned to Pittsburgh from a meeting in Washington DC of the Commission on Government Employment Policy. He remained in the hospital for almost three weeks but was released with "very much improvement," the hospital reported.[32] He was instructed to lose weight, take his heart medicine (what he called "his TNT pills"), and reduce stress in his life.

Of course, he would not be Branch Rickey if he weren't working hard on an important mission of some kind, stressful or not. Without a vocation, especially in baseball, Branch Rickey felt like a fish out of water. He yearned to be involved in the Major League action, and if at his advancing age no existing Major League team was going to come calling, then it was time to beat the drums for the cause of a third league.

Taylor Spink, editor and publisher of the *Sporting News*, was always willing to give Rickey a forum, and Rickey made a strong case for the adventurous new idea in a front-page story in the May 21, 1958, issue of the sports weekly. He stressed that there were 75 million more people in the United States than at the turn of the century, when the American League earned parity as the second Major League. "The time is ripe for the majors to expand," Rickey declared. "It should be the creation of the present two leagues, . . . formed with their cooperation, if possible, and if not, then without their co-operation." The latter situation "would result in a war, which should be avoided," he said. "But a third major is something we must have soon."[33]

Rickey argued that the problem with expansion into two ten-team leagues was that it only added two more tail end teams. In the long run fans would not come to see a team that had no real chance of contention, Rickey said. However, if a league was started from scratch, there would be equal competition among eight teams. "A man with half the capacity of the late Ban Johnson, who organized the American League, could form a third Major League today," the restless executive emphasized, citing the name of a fellow son of Ohio and one of his favorite people in baseball history.[34]

Stung by the loss of their two historic baseball franchises, politicians and power brokers in New York City were beginning to swing into action. Mayor Robert F. Wagner Jr. established a commission empowered to bring another baseball team to Gotham and was looking for a point man to spearhead the effort. He sought the advice of banker George V. McLaughlin, who had brokered Walter O'Malley's stake in the Brooklyn Dodgers in the early 1940s, only to feel bitterly betrayed by his protégé's abandonment of the city. McLaughlin suggested the name of a corporate lawyer, William Alfred Shea, whose first New York job had been with McLaughlin's Brooklyn Trust Bank, to head the baseball commission.[35]

Shea was a fifty-two-year-old native of New York whose baseball interest had first been aroused when his Spanish teacher at George Washington High School introduced him to Yankees pitcher Herb Pennock, the educator's nephew. Shea won a basketball scholarship to New York University but transferred to Georgetown University in Washington DC, where he earned a law degree in 1931. Returning to New York, Shea rose quickly in the world of corporate law. With his talent, congeniality, and connections with George McLaughlin and another prominent personage, William Casey (who ultimately became head of the Securities and Exchange Commission and the Central Intelligence Agency), Shea became known as "the unofficial chairman of the state's unofficial permanent goverernment."[36] He was thus perfectly situated to shape a coalition to build a new stadium to attract another Major League team to New York. Time was of the essence because Ebbets Field was slated to be demolished in February 1960 and the Polo Grounds soon thereafter.

Shea's first strategy had been to lure an existing National League franchise to New York. He investigated the possibilities in Cincinnati, Philadelphia, and Pittsburgh, but the Reds, Phillies, and Pirates played in one-team towns and local ownership was reluctant to sell to an outsider. Pressuring the National League to expand was Shea's next strategy, but league president Warren Giles, wittily dubbed by John Lardner as a "well-known immobilist," remained uninterested in helping New York.[37]

Shea solicited the advice of baseball commissioner Ford C. Frick, the former National League president who had replaced Happy Chandler in the commissioner's office in 1951. Frick ostensibly possessed the same powers that the first commissioner, Kenesaw Mountain Landis, insisted upon—to act in the "best interests" of baseball. Frick was somewhat more encouraging than Giles had been. He told Shea that he was in favor of expansion, maybe even of a third league, and said that "deep in my heart I expect it to come within five years."[38]

However, the commissioner was vague about the mechanism for opening up the baseball business. It became clear to Bill Shea that Ford Frick was not going to take a lead in helping new franchises emerge but was only going to respond to what the most powerful owners in the established leagues wanted him to do. Somebody would have to shake up the status quo, Shea realized, and on the suggestion of George McLaughlin, who had witnessed Branch Rickey's successful handiwork firsthand in Brooklyn, the lawyer made a call to the semiretired baseball executive.

Bill Shea quickly fell under the Branch Rickey spell. The Irish American big-city lawyer was taken by the energy and idealism of the aging executive, twenty-five years his senior. For his part Rickey again had found a younger man to be inspired and motivated to do great deeds. "New York deserves another corking good baseball team, and baseball deserves you," Rickey flattered Shea. "But, you know, baseball moves very slowly. They are afraid of change and of thinking outside of the box." Rickey convinced Shea that his initial attempt to entice an existing National League franchise to move to New York had been the wrong strategy. He encouraged the well-connected lawyer to be outspoken in public against baseball's resistance to change, while the veteran executive hoped to persuade the owners behind the scenes to welcome a third league.

The physical condition of the ferocious gentleman was still precarious, and more than once Shea murmured to sportswriters, "God willing, he is with us next season."[39] Mentally, though, Rickey's mind was still sharp, and he relished the intellectual challenge of solving the paradox that there were not enough Major League players for two potential ten-team leagues but that two hundred Minor Leaguers on eight brand-new teams would ultimately excel. Rickey noted that if you took the stars in the current Major Leagues and eliminated them from the overall player talent pool, there remained mainly journeymen in the big leagues. He observed: "Not every ballplayer on the Giants is a Willie Mays. But that does not mean that Willie Mays is the only big league ballplayer on the Giants."[40] He believed that the new league could draw on some of the current journeymen in both the Major and the Minor Leagues while devoting itself to developing its own players.

Branch Rickey was aware that the problem of player procurement was huge, and he had conflicted emotions on how best to proceed. After all, he was the man who had built his career on signing and developing thousands of players, keeping the best of them for his parent teams in his successful careers in St. Louis and Brooklyn and trading or selling the rest to interested and often outwitted buyers. All of Rickey's prior baseball operations had been enabled by the overwhelming power of the perpetual reserve system, which granted the player only the right to retire or to hold out temporarily for better terms.

For the third league to succeed Rickey knew that some of the total control of the reserve system would have to be removed. He had made individual exceptions in the past in the case of such star players as George Sisler and Rogers Hornsby, but he had been very uncompromising in defense of the strict restrictions on virtually every other player. He also needed the goodwill of the very owners whom, until his unsuccessful experience in Pittsburgh, he had regularly outmaneuvered. Those owners had enjoyed Rickey's down years with the Pirates, and they were in no hurry, to say the least, to help him start a new league.

It was a tough position for Rickey, but publicly he did not betray any sense of contradiction, because by 1959 the time seemed right for the third league cause. For one thing, political pressure was building on the established baseball owners. For the third straight year Congress was planning to hold hearings on monopolistic controls in professional sports. The motive behind the investigation was not simply the rage of jilted New York City legislators, such as Brooklyn Democratic representative Emanuel Celler, who chaired a House antimonopoly subcommittee and had called a hearing in 1957 when it was becoming clear that the Dodgers and Giants were leaving town. Others in Congress from all over the country were in a serious mood because the United States Supreme Court had denied antitrust exemption to professional boxing in 1955 and to professional football in 1957. The high court had also called baseball's unique exemption from normal trade and commerce laws an "anomaly" that Congress had the power to, and should perhaps, rectify.[41]

Aware of a possibly changing political climate, the established baseball owners held a rare spring meeting on May 21, 1959, at John Galbreath's Darby Dan racehorse farm outside Columbus, Ohio. The moguls were, of course, aware of rumbles about a third league and sensed that Branch Rickey was in the middle of it, but they professed to be unconcerned. They gave lip service to the idea that expansion was probably a good idea, but they dictated a series of requirements that any new team must meet. Among the conditions, which Yankees co-owner Dan Topping modestly called the "Ten Commandments," were that new teams represent cities no smaller than the smallest in the existing Major Leagues (Kansas City, with less than a half million residents); that they provide a new stadium with at least thirty-five thousand seats; and that they also be prepared to indemnify the Minor League cities and leagues they cause to relocate.[42]

All of these issues were going to loom as huge obstacles, but Branch Rickey advised the third league backers to first get their ownership groups together. By the summer of 1959 Bill Shea was on the verge of announcing a prestigious group of investors for the proposed new franchise in New York. The group included Dwight "Pete" Davis Jr., wealthy son of the sportsman who had donated the Davis Cup for the international amateur tennis competition; financier Herbert Walker, whose uncle had donated the Walker Cup, amateur golf's most coveted prize (and who himself was the uncle and great-uncle, respectively, of future U.S. presidents George Herbert Walker Bush and George Walker Bush); and Mrs. Dorothy Killam, wife of a Canadian lumber magnate who had been an investor in the *Brooklyn Eagle,* the newspaper that, until its demise in 1955, covered the Brooklyn Dodgers enthusiastically.[43]

When Mrs. Killam bowed out of the baseball project, her place was quickly taken by Mrs. Charles (Joan) Payson, sister of John Payne "Jock" Whitney, publisher of the *New York Herald Tribune* and U.S. ambassador to Great Britain. Joan Payson had served on the New York Giants' board of directors, where she had pleaded with Horace Stoneham to sell her the team rather than move it to San Francisco. Eager to bring baseball back to New York, she enthusiastically joined the prospective ownership group. (A particularly caring woman, Joan Payson ultimately became the owner of the New York Mets; whenever a player on her team had a baby, she presented a sterling silver gift from Tiffany to the family.)[44]

Branch Rickey never doubted the likelihood of involving prominent and wealthy lovers of sport in a New York City baseball franchise. What especially pleased him were the syndicates developing in other cities. Entrepreneur Jack Kent Cooke was the driving force in Toronto. Describing himself as an "indomitable optimist," Cooke was one of those self-made men who naturally gravitated toward Branch Rickey and were in turn mesmerized by him.

Born in Hamilton, Ontario, in 1912, Cooke was a man of many musical, athletic, and entrepreneurial talents. He played saxophone in the touring Canadian bands of American bandleader Percy Faith and was offered a hockey scholarship to the University of Michigan. The Great Depression of the 1930s curtailed Cooke's college plans, but he soon struck it rich by buying a Toronto radio station and the Canadian version of *Liberty* magazine, *New Liberty*. After World War Two Cooke became a part owner of the hockey Maple Leafs and in 1951 purchased the Minor League Baseball Maple Leafs.[45]

Cooke enlivened the atmosphere of the Toronto baseball park, installing an exploding scoreboard and electric organ and staging prizefights on the pitching mound before and after games. The fans flocked to the ballpark for the entertainment and soon were treated to a good team on the field. In 1952 Cooke was voted the *Sporting News* Minor League executive of the year, and the Maple Leafs won International League pennants in 1954, 1956, 1957, and 1960. In 1954 the Leafs' Elston Howard, destined to break the color line with the Yankees the next season, was International League MVP. Cooke clamored for more black players because he considered them a good gate attraction.[46]

The Toronto mogul was eager to join the new league because he had been spurned several times when he tried to lure existing franchises to Canada. "The city is too cold," went one complaint. "No colder than Cleveland, Detroit or Milwaukee," Cooke retorted. "Your stadium is too small," was another criticism. In a city with a population of over 1.3 million, Cooke vowed that he could get the existing ballpark expanded beyond the current capacity of eighteen thousand seats.[47]

Denver represented a third ownership group Rickey found very promising. The group was headed by Robert Lee Howsam, age forty-one, another enterprising young capitalist, who admired Rickey's record in baseball. "I sat at his feet and tried to absorb everything he said," Howsam recalls. The Colorado executive never forgot Rickey's axiom that once you come up with a new idea in baseball, "you have two years to make it work before other people copy you."[48] Howsam had been a successful small businessman in southern Colorado, growing alfalfa and raising bees. After service in the navy in World War II, Howsam relocated to Washington DC, where he became the administrative assistant of U.S. senator Edwin Carl "Big Ed" Johnson, a three-term senator and twice-elected Colorado governor. From 1945 to 1958 Johnson also served as volunteer president of the Western League, a class A Minor League.

After marrying Senator Johnson's daughter, Howsam moved back to Colorado, where he operated the Western League's Denver franchise, but the circuit fell victim to the decline of the Minor Leagues in the 1950s. Ed Johnson was a big baseball fan, sometimes called the "Abe Lincoln of Colorado" for his six foot four size and his residence in the state dating back to 1909, when he came west from Kansas after contracting tuberculosis (the same year Branch Rickey was afflicted). Never reticent about blasting the excesses of Major League control of players and markets, Johnson looked forward to tangling with the baseball establishment. The third league backers were counting on Johnson's knowledge of Washington, his political pull having strongly influenced the extension of the interstate highway system through western Colorado and the establishment of the Air Force Academy in Colorado Springs.[49]

Houston was the fourth city in the prospective third Major League. Its ownership group was led by the feisty duo of George Kirksey, a one-time nationally prominent sportswriter, and Craig Cullinan Jr., grandson of the founder of the Texaco Oil company. Kirksey grew up in north Texas in Hillsboro, and he liked to wax poetic about the virtues of his small-town upbringing, a trait that endeared him to Branch Rickey. As a United Press sportswriter in Chicago and New York from the mid-1920s through the early 1940s, Kirksey covered twelve World Series, as well as six Sugar Bowls and six Rose Bowls in football, and occasionally wrote features for the national magazines *Collier's*, *Look*, and the *Saturday Evening Post*. Married before World War Two to big band singer Ethel Shutta, it was said of the Kirksey-Shutta liaison that they were "beautiful people before there were beautiful people."[50]

After serving in the European war as the United States Air Force's public relations officer, Kirksey settled in Houston and met Craig Cullinan Jr., who had returned to Texas after graduating from Phillips Andover Academy and Yale. Cullinan and Kirksey watched with great interest in 1952 as oilman R. E. "Bob" Smith pledged $250,000 for the purchase of the Philadelphia Athletics if nine other wealthy Houstonians matched his commitment to the enterprise.[51] However, Kansas City businessmen, led by Canteen Corporation executive Arnold Johnson, who had the key support of the New York Yankees ownership, were better organized, and the Athletics went to the Missouri city.[52]

Undeterred, Cullinan became president of the Houston Sports Association and, with Kirksey, worked to pass a November 1957 referendum that would authorize expenditures for a new baseball stadium. The vote passed by a large margin, and in the summer of 1958 Houston informed officials of both Major Leagues that with a new domed stadium on the drawing board, the city was ready for the big leagues. However, the stalling by the baseball establishment began to grate on the Texans. There were many Houston groups vying to bring Major League Baseball to Houston, including ones fronted by former Cardinals shortstop Marty Marion and former St. Louis manager Eddie Dyer, but Cullinan and Kirksey were ready to throw in their lot with the proposed third league.[53]

The fifth charter member of the new league was Minneapolis–St. Paul. The Twin Cities of the Upper Midwest had actually come the closest to joining one of the existing Major Leagues. After the death in October 1955 of Clark Griffith, the Washington Senators' patriarch-owner, his adopted son Calvin Griffith was tempted by the untapped market of the Twin Cities. Since its last World Series appearance in 1933, the Senators had become a chronic noncontender. If the now-defunct St. Louis Browns had been branded with the saying "First in booze, first in shoes, and last in the American League," the Senators had to endure the equally cruel jibe "First in war, first in peace, and last in the American League."

Spurned by Horace Stoneham in 1957, Minneapolis sporting interests started seriously wooing Calvin Griffith. Abandoning the nation's capital, however, was something that made even the haughty, baronial baseball owners take pause. Calvin Griffith's desire to relocate had shocked all Washington politicians, and even President Eisenhower, during an August 1958 press conference, declared that the baseball team should stay in Washington, while also saying, "I think they should have a little better club." As the pressure mounted on the Washington owner, Calvin Griffith testified in public at the antitrust hearings early in July 1958 that he planned to stay in Washington as long "as is humanly possible."[54]

Minneapolis was understandably feeling jilted again. In January 1959 a bond proposal to expand a new stadium, recently built in Bloomington between Minneapolis and St. Paul, died because construction had been approved only if a Major League team were definitely coming. Tired of being strung along by the old guard in baseball, a bunch of eager young Minnesota capitalists hopped onto the bandwagon of the new league. The group was organized by Wheelock Whitney, a thirty-three-year-old investment banker from St. Cloud, north of the Twin Cities, who, like his friend Craig Cullinan Jr., had attended Phillips Andover Academy and Yale. The young Minnesotan assembled a group of investors from prominent local corporations, including the Dayton department stores, Hamm Brewing, Pillsbury Mills, and the *Star-Tribune* newspaper.[55]

By July 1959 the new league was almost ready to announce itself to the world. Of course, they still faced many problems. They lacked three franchises for an eight-team league, but they were confident that groups in other cities would join once the new circuit was officially established. Preliminary talks had already been held with investors in Buffalo, Atlanta, Seattle, Montreal, and Dallas–Fort Worth. (After all, how could Houston enter a new vigorous enterprise and not its big Texas rival, Dallas?) There were also feelers from business interests in San Juan, Puerto Rico, and Honolulu, Hawaii. None of the teams had any players, of course, but Bill Shea and Branch Rickey assured the new league members that establishing the structure of the organization was the first priority.

Before they were ready to go public, there was the question of a name for the new league. "How about the Third League?" someone suggested. No, too bland came the response. "How about the United States League?" No, if Toronto, Montreal, and other non-American cities came into the league, that name wouldn't do. Finally, Edwin Johnson suggested, "Why not the Continental League?" The name immediately resounded, and the Continental League was born, in name anyway.[56]

On July 27, 1959, a press conference was called for New York City, announcing the birth of the new Major League. It was front-page news in a town still smarting from the loss of the Dodgers and the Giants. As the head of the founders committee, Bill Shea informed the public that a meeting with the two existing Major Leagues was planned for August 18, 1959, at which time a president and a constitution for the Continental League would also be announced. Information on additional cities would also follow soon, Shea said.

Finding a vigorous, knowledgeable president to lead the Continental League was the next urgent matter of business. Bill Shea was asked by his new league brethren to consider taking the post. However, the New York lawyer quickly rejected the idea, saying that the league presidency required a baseball man to deal with the complicated details. All eyes turned to seventy-seven-year old Branch Rickey, who had been interested in a third league for at least several years before the departure of the Giants and Dodgers.

There was no other possibility, and despite his age and physical infirmities, Rickey accepted what he knew would be a major challenge. During his successful years in baseball, he loved the thrill of building a winning team and experiencing the ups and downs of daily competition. Running a league would be a new experience, but one that promised to reward both his unremitting Protestant ethic and his genuine desire to give baseball a needed boost of new teams and new energy.

However, before he could assume the presidency of the Continental League, Rickey first had to dispose of his remaining stock in the Pittsburgh Pirates. On the same day that the new league was announced,

Rickey phoned his former boss John Galbreath to inform him of his plans. The Pittsburgh owner "did not wish me to sell the stock," Rickey wrote in a memorandum to his Continental League colleagues. Galbreath had told him "that if I needed money, he would advance it to me on a loan from the Club." The powerful realtor-owner tried to work on Rickey's sense of loyalty to his longtime baseball colleagues. "He mentioned that he had stood by me from the time he first met me and that he felt that now there was a reciprocal relationship which should be maintained," Rickey wrote. "I said to him these very words: 'You fired me from my present job and you know it,' to which there was no reply."[57]

The break with John Galbreath may not have been as bitter as Rickey's earlier severances from Sam Breadon in St. Louis and Walter O'Malley in Brooklyn, but, clearly, the wound from his defeat remained deep. An arrangement of sale was shortly executed so the proud executive would be able to join the other Continental League pioneers at their first joint meeting with the established leagues on August 18, 1959.

However, before the third league would formally introduce Rickey as its new president, there were hearings to attend in Washington. Tennessee Democratic senator Estes Kefauver had convened another inquiry from his perch as chairman of the Judiciary Committee's Subcommittee on Anti-trust and Monopoly. Kefauver was a lawyer from eastern Tennessee with populist leanings, who had risen to power by beating the entrenched machine of Democratic boss Edmund Crump. In 1951 the Tennessean emerged as a prominent political figure when he chaired nationally televised hearings into organized crime. His earnest, pointed questioning of unsavory mobsters vaulted him into the ranks of 1952 Democratic presidential hopefuls, and he made a good showing in the preference primaries until he lost out to Illinois governor Adlai Stevenson. In 1956, after briefly considering another run for president, Kefauver accepted the vice presidential position on the Democratic ticket as Stevenson lost for the second time to Dwight Eisenhower in the race for president.

Kefauver represented a state that did not have a yearning for Major League Baseball, and although he had played football at the University of Tennessee, he was hardly an ardent fan of spectator sports. However, he was a genuine fighter against monopolistic tendencies in all industries, and he believed deeply in the principle of using the power of the federal government to force monopolistic industries to comply with fair rules of competition. Kefauver had told William Shea in the earliest days of third league planning that he didn't expect the baseball establishment to help the newcomers in any way and that a tough law would probably have to be passed to force compliance. Kefauver's chief counsel, Paul Rand Dixon, was even more blunt, telling Continental League leaders that the baseball owners were an intractable monopoly that would have to be challenged frontally.[58]

Branch Rickey, on the other hand, remained a staunch Republican believer in free enterprise, a man wary of federal interference in the marketplace. Just eight years earlier, during his first year as Pittsburgh general manager, Rickey had told Congressman Emanuel Celler's House judiciary subcommittee hearings that the controls of the reserve system were for the good of everyone involved with baseball—owners, players, and fans. Rickey was not ready in the summer of 1959 to drastically modify his thinking, but he realized that some relaxation of the reserve rules had to be approved for the third league to have access to players.

Introduced to the Kefauver committee as a member of the Pittsburgh Pirates' board of directors, which technically he still was, Rickey did not bring a prepared statement with him but, of course, had many opinions to offer. He responded to the many attacks on baseball owners that had been delivered by Congress members and other critics, including the Continental League's own Edwin Johnson, who had seen his Western League disband after the 1958 season. In his most diplomatic tones, Rickey said: "Do you think that Gus Busch, Powell [*sic*] Crosley, John Galbreath, my good friend Wrigley, or Mr. Yawkey, or Del Webb, oh, it is unkind not to include them all, that they are that definition of sportsmen who would make for 40 years phony deals in the transaction of players' contracts and continue to do it? And maintain their self-respect in their own communities, which they do enjoy?" He answered his own question: "That is unthinkable. It isn't true." Rickey went on to twit Ed Johnson for being angry with all of baseball when he had experience only as president of one Minor League. "You can be a fish in a puddle and think the world is made out of water," Rickey jibed.[59]

Of course, Rickey was not belittling the problems of former Minor

League executives like Ed Johnson and a host of others who had abandoned ownership in the sport. He was genuinely concerned about the plight of the Minors and the decline of Major League Baseball's popularity, but Rickey thought he had a good, voluntary plan to propose—the unrestricted draft of first-year professional players. Teams in the existing leagues and the new third league could select from this pool. Rickey saw the proposal as also cutting down on "this silly thing of paying bonuses to boys that wreck half of them to begin with morally, and create great disturbance in the morale of a club where the bonus player goes."[60] As always the idealist believer in voluntary action, Rickey hoped that the owners would see the wisdom of the draft without the need for legislation.

In response to a question from Kenneth Keating, a Republican senator from Rochester, New York, who was one of the baseball establishment's leading advocates in Congress, Rickey said that he opposed a set limit of any number of players any team could control. "The source of players has hardly been scratched," he declared. "Even in the white fellows it has not been scratched. . . . Japan has not been scratched and two Major League clubs this year I understand are scouting it. Central America, South America, Puerto Rico, Cuba, South Africa even." He added that he also opposed player limitations "because I think the third major must contemplate some small Minor Leagues to develop their own production of [amateur] free agents for the sake of baseball and the country and the good health of it."[61]

The Kefauver hearings ended in late July 1959 without any recommendation on a bill. The legislators were aware that the third league had just been announced and welcomed its upcoming negotiations with the existing leagues for recognition. Kefauver gladly held his legislative recommendation in abeyance but closed with an ominous comment for the establishment. "You might say baseball is under surveillance, even under a shotgun," he warned.[62] Kefauver's rhetoric did not appeal to the idealistic if ferocious gentleman, but in any event Branch Rickey, heart attack survivor and Ménière's disease sufferer, at a few months' shy of his seventy-eighth birthday, was getting ready to lead one final charge to shake up the baseball establishment.

26

The Continental Dance Card Goes Blank

On August 18, 1959, at the Warwick Hotel in New York City, the Continental League introduced Branch Rickey as its first president. The prospective ownership groups from the five cities already in the new league were in attendance, but the focus of attention was, of course, on the aging executive, who had flown down for the occasion from a fishing camp near his northern Ontario retreat. Rickey hadn't encountered such a barrage of inquisitive New York newspapermen since his farewell Brooklyn Dodgers press conference with Walter O'Malley nearly nine years earlier.

The New York press corps and sportswriters throughout the nation were skeptical about the Continental League's chances at success, but the scribes readied their note pads to write down the thoughts of the ever-quotable executive. "So many cities on the Triple-A level have lost baseball because of the encroachments of television," Rickey declared, "that the need for baseball in these growing cities is evident. It is a community responsibility to bring back baseball to these cities that deserve and have long supported baseball."[1]

"Where are you going to get the players?" Rickey was asked.

"Players won't be a problem," he replied. "There are thousands who don't have a chance to play who will jump at a chance that the new league will give them." William Shea interjected that one reason people thought there was a shortage of players was that, with only sixteen Major League teams, many potential athletes thought the odds were too great to make it. Expand the Major Leagues to twenty-four, or even thirty-two, teams, he said, and you would find that the chance for jobs would bring out the new talent. Shea confidently predicted that the Continental League would begin operation in 1961.[2]

"How long will it take to reach parity with the existing Major Leagues?" Rickey was asked. "That's a tough question. I cannot answer it now," the executive said frankly. "Let me tell you this. I am sure that by the fall of 1963, the Continental League will be a position to take part in the World Series."[3] He added that the round-robin tournament among the three leagues would bring more excitement and revenue to baseball than had ever been imagined. The time was ripe for baseball to reassert itself as the national pastime, Rickey declared. "I am alarmed at the subtle invasion of professional football, which is gaining pre-eminence over baseball," he said. "It's unthinkable."[4]

Rickey insisted that the Continental League would not become an "outlaw" league. It did not intend to raid the existing Major Leagues for players, as the Federal and Mexican Leagues had done. Rickey was eyewitness to those unsuccessful leagues, and he maintained that the rebellions ultimately brought only grief and lost money to owners and players. The big question remained, though, what would move the entrenched baseball moguls to act favorably toward the new league? At the league's first press conference, Rickey did not attempt to answer the question but instead put forth his best idealistic gloss on the situation. "It will not be too difficult if the boys in the majors turn a kindly glance in our direction," he said hopefully.[5]

Despite the writers' skepticism, they were impressed by the vigor and passion of Branch Rickey. Although nearly seventy-eight years old and walking with a cane, he exuded the energy of someone half his age. Turning his infirmity into an asset, Rickey waved or banged the cane for dramatic effect, just as for years he had been using a fiercely chewed cigar as a batonlike prop. With his typical sense of drama, he warned that baseball was heading for a funeral if it didn't accept the new blood of the league. He added that neither he nor his colleagues intended to be pallbearers. The writers did not doubt that he was going to roll up his sleeves to set the groundwork for a working organization, but he insisted that he was not going to be a permanent presence. "All I want is a couple of years to get this third league on its feet," Rickey said, "and then I'll let some young fellow take over."[6]

Veteran New York writer Jimmy Cannon tipped his cap to the work ethic and stately bearing of the aging executive. He quoted one of Rickey's favorite family stories about his father planting peach trees not long before he died. "Why are you planting the trees knowing that you won't be around to pick the fruit?" Jacob Frank Rickey was asked. "I don't care who picks the fruit," Branch Rickey's father replied. "I intend to live each day as if I am going to live forever."[7]

No sooner did the press conference at the Warwick break up than did Branch Rickey, Bill Shea, and Jack Kent Cooke represent the Continental League at a get-acquainted meeting with delegations from the American and National Leagues at Commissioner Frick's Rockefeller Center office just a few blocks away. Seven hours later the three league presidents and the commissioner emerged, telling the press that the session had been amicable.

Frick said that he had always been in favor of expansion and that the members of the committee from the established leagues "will support a third league movement and will attempt to avoid interference." He stressed, however, that the conditions that he had laid down earlier must be met, especially new stadiums with more than thirty-five thousand seats and fair indemnities to the Minor League teams the new league would displace. There was no word about a mechanism of making any players available to the new league. Regarding this crucial issue, Branch Rickey implored the established leagues: "We want your co-operation, we need your co-operation, and I can prove to you that a third league will benefit baseball tremendously."[8]

As the Continental League began operations, Rickey admitted to the sportswriters that its office was in his pocket, although soon a small office space was leased in a building on Manhattan's Fifth Avenue. Rickey rented an apartment on New York's fashionable Sutton Place to stay in town some nights, although his home remained in Fox Chapel in Pittsburgh. A skeletal staff of employees was assembled: Ken Blackburn, a World War Two Army officer who had been Rickey's secretary since his Pirates days; Arthur Mann, public relations director for the league; and two secretaries, Margaret Regetz and Judy Wilpon, wife of Fred Wilpon, the future owner of the New York Mets. Houston's George Kirksey, a former sportswriter, agreed to stay on in New York for a few weeks to serve as another of Rickey's assistants and hopefully to garner enough information to write a national magazine story about the new league (a piece that evidently was never published).[9]

Noticeably absent from Rickey's Continental League staff was Branch Rickey Jr., who remained as Pirates farm director. The younger Rickey expressed "surprise" to a wire service reporter about his father's active role in the new league.[10] He had advised Pittsburgh scout Rex Bowen and others to think twice before they abandoned the existing Major Leagues, and most remained in their jobs.[11] (Later in the 1960s, Bowen moved on to scout for the Cincinnati Reds under general manager Robert Howsam and played a significant role in the development of Cincinnati's Big Red Machine teams of the 1970s.) Branch Jr. was beginning to learn Spanish to be able to communicate better with the growing number of Hispanic farm hands in the Pittsburgh system.[12] Junior's breaking ranks with his father led to a temporary strain in father-son relations, but Branch Jr. understood his father's unremitting desire to have a great cause in his life, and Branch Sr., of course, remained a loving father with a deep empathy for his talented and compassionate son, whose diabetic condition was steadily getting worse.

Not surprisingly, Branch Rickey threw himself into his new job with vigor. He spread the word of the Continental League with Wesleyan Methodist vigor to all the people and in all the places that he could. On Sunday night, September 13, 1959, he was a mystery guest on the popular Sunday night television quiz show *What's My Line?* One of the guest panelists was Chuck Connors, Rickey's former Brooklyn Minor League first baseman, enjoying his fame as the star of the TV western series *The Rifleman.* However, it was actress Arlene Francis who correctly guessed that the man behind the screen was Rickey, who could not easily disguise his booming dramatic baritone.[13]

Although the Continental League was still three franchises short of a complete eight-team league and to date had signed no players, Rickey tried to drum up interest everywhere. Not long after his *What's My Line?* appearance, Rickey was riding in a taxicab when he noticed recently retired pitcher Carl Erskine walking down a New York street. Rickey ordered the cab to the curb. "Son, do you want to coach in the Continental

League?" he shouted at the former Dodgers pitcher. "Please come over here, and we'll talk it over." Erskine listened to Rickey's proposal, but he was not interested in staying in baseball. He was heading back to his hometown of Anderson, Indiana, where he would become a prominent banker and community leader.[14]

Despite Rickey's frequent pronouncements that the new league was "as inevitable as tomorrow," there was no gainsaying the major problems ahead for the Continental League. The establishment owners might have said at their meeting at John Galbreath's horse farm in May 1959 that they would welcome new teams to Major League baseball, but, in fact, they were in no hurry to welcome new brethren. They knew they held a very strong hand of cards. They controlled access to all the professional players, they could always lure cities eager for baseball with an invitation to come into the established two-league structure, and, with the federal antitrust exemption, they could act basically as they pleased.

Most sportswriters were, as usual, on the side of the establishment. After the 1959 World Series, won by the Los Angeles Dodgers over the Chicago White Sox in a competition that drew the largest crowds in Series history to ninety-three-thousand-seat Memorial Coliseum, the *Sporting News* took a poll of the scribes on the future of baseball. Sixty-three favored expansion of the existing leagues, thirteen favored no expansion, and six favored the Continental League.[15]

Branch Rickey was aware that he faced enormous "trouble ahead, trouble ahead" in his cause of the third league. Although he cringed at the poor players expansion teams would be offered by the establishment, he understood that most of the charter franchises in the Continental League would be tempted by the prospect. His pipeline to the National League indicated that most owners in the senior circuit were opposed to adding new teams but that the American League was more interested in expansion.

In early November 1959 Rickey decided to meet with American League president Joe Cronin to get a better sense of the junior circuit's intentions. "I have never heard so much solicitude in my life," Rickey wrote in a memorandum to his fellow Continental Leaguers. "About my knee, my heart, my wife, my children, my present, my past, my future."[16] Cronin was interested in everything about Rickey except working collegially with the third Major League. Soon thereafter, Rickey wrote Cronin, asking him to designate the two cities his league was considering to add in the hope that stadium projects in those municipalities could go ahead while the Continental League could begin to find new members. Not surprisingly, Cronin did not tip the hand of his league's intention to a rival president who, though fired by his zeal for the cause of the third league, had no real leverage except his formidable work ethic and reputation.

Rickey was also hearing disturbing rumors that both established leagues were considering expanding to nine-team leagues in 1960. They had already approved interleague trading for the first time, effective after the 1960 season.[17] Although the scheduling difficulties of nine-team leagues would be enormous, some American League owners, jealous of Walter O'Malley's bonanza in Los Angeles, wanted to put a team in Southern California and some National League owners wanted to re-enter New York. The latter move, of course, would effectively kill the chances of the Continental League.

Shortly before the start of baseball's annual December meetings, Walter O'Malley, the most influential owner in the game now that he had successfully pulled off the Dodgers' move to the West Coast, wrote his former partner, ostensibly to allay his fears about nine-team leagues. "Prior to the announcement of the formation of the Continental League I had been advocating privately and within baseball circles, two nine-club leagues to play in three, six-club divisions with a limited interlocking schedule," O'Malley admitted. He said, however, that the idea received little support and was dropped when the Continental League was formed. O'Malley concluded his letter with the likely real reason for his writing it. He inquired whether stories circulating in Los Angeles and San Francisco newspapers were true that the Continental League was considering putting franchises in those West Coast cities. "On that subject I would like to know directly from you if your proposed league has such ambitions," O'Malley asked point-blank.[18]

Rickey replied a few days later, saying that the Continental League had no plans to invade California. However, he remained concerned about the proposed nine-team leagues. "Where would you get the players to compete in a 154-game schedule with the teams in your league?" he asked. "The only reason I can possibly think of for the National League to expand to a ninth club would be to defeat the Continental League by placing a National League franchise in New York City."[19]

As the winter meetings opened in Miami in early December 1959, Branch Rickey was the center of attention. "I have been so covered with olive branches that no one could even see me," Rickey quipped. However, he said that he was "terribly chagrined" that the nine-team league charade was still being discussed in Florida by both leagues. He was upset that Commissioner Frick not only had refused to criticize the idea but had called it "a confirmation of the Columbus commitment" of May 1959 to welcome expansion. "179 million people in our country cannot forever be limited to a well-guarded Major League monopoly in the guise of a 'national game,'" Rickey declared. "The fictitious addition of one or two clubs, in any event, does not meet the need nor the solve the problem." However, as the result of the foot-dragging by the established leagues in Miami, Rickey modified his timetable about the starting date for the third league. "The Continental League is as inevitable as tomorrow, but not as imminent," he said.[20]

The league presidents, Warren Giles of the National and Joe Cronin of the American, were taking turns belittling the Continental as a league without any players or even a full roster of teams. Responding to the naysayers, the Continental League in December 1959 announced the addition of two more franchises. One was in Atlanta, headed by F. Eaton Chalkley, a shopping mall developer and the husband of movie actress Susan Hayward, and the other was located in Dallas–Fort Worth, led by Amon Carter, publisher of the *Dallas–Fort Worth Telegram,* and construction magnate J. R. Bateson. Houston's Continental League owner, Craig Cullinan Jr., kidded Eaton Chalkley about why he wanted to enter the sweaty baseball business when he had a beautiful wife at home, but the lure of joining a new Major League was, of course, irresistible.[21]

The full roster of eight Continental teams was completed in January 1960 with the admission of a Buffalo franchise, led by businessman John Stiglmeier. A longtime bulwark of the International League, Buffalo in 1959 led all the Minor Leagues in attendance, drawing more than 405,000 fans. Rickey was delighted that the Continental League had reached its full complement of eight teams. When asked about the ongoing problems with indemnities to existing leagues and revenue sharing within the league, Rickey spoke in his most avuncular and religious tones. "It is quite a task getting a whole family of children all dressed up and ready to go to church," he said. "You know you will have trouble going to church together, but you also know you will surmount the difficulties."[22]

The year 1960 promised to be one of ferment and possibility throughout the world of professional sports. The American Football League was preparing to challenge the established National Football League, and its deep-pocketed owners were ready to plunge into bidding wars for top college talent. H. Lamar Hunt, the twenty-seven-year-old son of Dallas billionaire oilman Lamar Hunt, was an owner in the new football league, but he also sat in on Continental League meetings in Dallas. He was very impressed when Branch Rickey voiced a cooperative vision for pooling television revenue for the new league. "The American Football League adapted it from the start (1960) and the NFL copied it two years later after efforts had been made by their Commissioner Pete Rozelle," Hunt remembers. "I am often asked where the idea came from, and I would like to give, and have given the credit to Mr. Rickey."[23]

Despite his advancing age and weakened physical state, Rickey's engaging personality and work ethic left a lasting impression on all of the Continental League pioneers. "I can still hear him saying, 'Never grow accustomed to the emotions of continuous defeat,'" Minneapolis's Wheelock Whitney recalls. "When he came to speak at a Minneapolis luncheon, there were 200 people there, listening in total silence, including the waiters and the bus boys."[24]

Rickey told Whitney that when he was a young student, many people ignored him because of his rural accent and background. The Minnesota businessman remembers that Rickey would implore him, "Wheelock, you don't know how risky it is to make a suggestion to someone. Always in your lifetime make sure you give a new idea the attention and credibility that it deserves. In business or politics, it will help you live your life better."[25]

If you worked with Branch Rickey, you would inevitably come under a searching moral microscope. Craig Cullinan Jr., the wealthy and handsome Houston oil heir, had his share of entanglements with women and once expressed his frustration to his new friend and business associate.

Cullinan recalls that Rickey introduced him to Jane Rickey with a withering remark, "Mother, this young man just said something remarkable to me: He said, 'Women were placed on earth for the same reason that dogs were given fleas.'"[26] On another occasion, Rickey offered the stern advice, undoubtedly drawn from a biblical parable, "Men who sin in haste often repent in leisure."

Just as Rickey's strict moral code remained in force during his first venture as a league president, so did his legendary work ethic. Long meetings, lasting well past the dinner hour, were common as Rickey's ingrained desire to succeed knew no bounds, even at his advanced age. He knew the importance of breaks and naps, though, as he had learned from his father's workers on the farm. Most of the younger Continental League executives were not ready for Rickey's endless pace. During one long meeting, Bob Howsam remembers that Rickey pleaded, "Just give me fifteen minutes to go lie down, please." With a chuckle Howsam recalls, "We knew that if he got his rest, we'd be there all night. We refused to let him leave. So he just dropped his pants and laid down on the floor in front of us."[27]

Throughout the first weeks of the new year of 1960, Branch Rickey and Bill Shea continued to beat the drums for the cause of the new league. Yet they faced evident problems without players or stadiums. There was also the thorny question of indemnity rights to the Minor Leagues whose territories were invaded. International League president Frank "Shag" Shaughnessy, an old friend of Rickey's dating back to the 1920s, was playing hardball for the entrenched baseball monopoly. He wanted payment of $1 million each for losing franchises in Toronto and Buffalo to the Continental League. American Association president Edward Doherty was asking $850,000 for the loss of Minneapolis–St. Paul.[28]

The Continental League leaders cried foul, noting that when Horace Stoneham and Walter O'Malley moved their teams to San Francisco and Los Angeles, their entire indemnity to the Pacific Coast League totaled only $850,000. Branch Rickey added that when Walter O'Malley had put out a feeler in early 1960 about whether the new league was interested in buying the Dodgers' Montreal franchise, he mentioned a figure of only $150,000, including twelve players.[29] The Continental

League president said that he turned down the offer because the league preferred Toronto as a franchise and didn't think that Montreal's available players were worth the price. Toronto's Jack Kent Cooke chimed in that the existing Minor Leagues were wildly overstating the value of their territories. Cooke argued that a proper indemnity fee should be more like the $48,000 that the Baltimore Orioles ownership gave the International League in 1954 as a price for taking over that city's main baseball franchise when the St. Louis Browns moved east. Certainly, it should be no more than the $76,000 offered to Buffalo on the Baltimore formula (7 cents per paying customer during the last three years of paid attendance).[30]

In February 1960 the battle lines were drawn in New York City between the Yankees and the new Continental League franchise. The city's Board of Estimate approved the issuing of bonds to build a stadium for the new team in town. It would be on the site in Flushing Meadows, Queens, offered by Robert Moses to Walter O'Malley and rejected by the Dodgers owner before he moved his team to Los Angeles. Bill Shea was overjoyed at the news, and Branch Rickey twitted the old order by saying that he had no desire to play temporarily in Yankee Stadium, "an antiquated ballpark." Yankees general manager George Weiss retorted that a new stadium for "a minor league team" was a waste of money and opined that the city would spend its money more wisely by improving the parking for the established team in town.[31]

In March 1960 another major obstacle was placed in the Continental League path. Commissioner Ford Frick refused to accept a co-operative arrangement for the pooling of players in a proposed new Minor League, the Western Carolina League. Headed by Al Todd, an old friend of Rickey's who had been a backup Major League catcher in the 1930s and early 1940s, the Western Carolina circuit would be operated on the premise that all players were owned by the league and could ultimately be bought by any Major League franchise, including those in the Continental League.

"Absolutely not," decreed Frick. "We can't have one set of rules for one minor league and a different set for everyone else." Frick argued that the pooling might have been acceptable if the Western Carolina League had worked out agreements with existing high Minor League teams, but he would not allow it for teams and leagues that still existed only on paper. Rickey did not take Frick's spurning of the Western Carolina League lying down. "Show me the rule," he railed at Frick, in the outraged manner of his more influential days when he tilted with Commissioner Landis. "There is no such rule."[32]

Rickey put pressure on the commissioner by arranging a meeting with Senators Estes Kefauver and Everett Jordan (Democrat, North Carolina.) The politicians reminded Frick that baseball's monopolistic practices were being scrutinized in Congress. Rickey knew that the veteran baseball man was frightened by the possibility of congressional action against baseball's reserve system controls. Rickey told his third league brethren that the commissioner referred to political intervention in baseball's business as "the haywire thing." Frick reluctantly agreed to allow the formation of the co-operative Minor League, but he insisted that each team charter itself as an independent franchise, not as a member of a league. The establishment's delay tactics did succeed in pushing back the Western Carolina League's opening day to the end of May 1960. Once the season started, Rickey brought in loyal, able Burt Shotton to evaluate players and managers in the new league.[33]

On April 15, 1960, Charles F. Hurth, former president of the Southern Association, was introduced as the general manager of the New York Continental League franchise. A nephew-in-law of Branch Rickey, Hurth hailed from Portsmouth, Ohio, and had begun his baseball career in the 1930s working for the Cardinals' farm teams in Columbus, Ohio, and Columbus, Georgia. Since 1939 Hurth had been based in New Orleans, first operating the Southern Association franchise and then, in the mid-1940s, becoming president of the Southern Association, making him at the time the youngest league president in professional baseball.[34]

Hurth was not Branch Rickey's first choice for the New York job, and the executive mentioned it publicly, perhaps fearing a charge of nepotism. William DeWitt, an enthusiastic backer of both Rickey and a third league, had been the man Rickey sought, but at the end of 1959 DeWitt was named president of the Detroit Tigers. Longtime Atlanta baseball operator Earl Mann was Rickey's second choice, but Mann was not interested in uprooting himself to a new city and dealing with the difficulties of a new league.

Charles Hurth displayed admirable frankness in an early interview with the press. "It is strange to be sitting here as the general manager of a team with no players yet and no new stadium," he admitted.[35] However, he was confident that these vital matters would soon be resolved. It was becoming clear, though, that only Congress could help the Continental League get started.

Once again Branch Rickey was faced with more than his usual internal turmoil. His deep Republican belief in the competitive free enterprise system made him very uncomfortable with the thought of congressional intervention in the baseball system. Legislation limiting the number of players any organization could control certainly went against the grain of a man who had built two vast, successful farm systems in St. Louis and Brooklyn. As a longtime baseball man, he agreed with Commissioner Frick's argument that the Minor Leagues must be preserved. Even if only a tiny fraction of Minor Leaguers ever made the Major Leagues (Frick suggested a ratio of thirty to one), it was the competition provided by career Minor Leaguers that enabled the prize prospects to develop into Major Leaguers.[36]

Yet for the Continental League to have a chance of success, Rickey realized that congressional action would be needed to loosen up some of the Major League monopoly on player production and control. Privately, most baseball people conceded that the absolute reserve clause would not likely survive another major court test, but because there were no cases currently on the docket, the baseball establishment was stonewalling any attempt at change.

For the Continental League to have a chance at succeeding, the latest bill proposed by Senator Estes Kefauver would have to pass. Under the bill that Kefauver introduced in the judiciary committee in May 1960, Title One exempted football, basketball, and hockey from strict antitrust regulation, but Title Two was specifically devoted to baseball. It called for a restriction of any team's reserve limit to one hundred players, with sixty of those players open to an unrestricted draft at the end of every season. Although in the late 1950s no Major League organization controlled as many players as Branch Rickey did in his heyday, the average American League team still claimed rights to 289 players and the average National League team to 391 athletes.[37] Another provision of Kefauver's bill placed a strict thirty-five-mile territorial limit on any Major League team's area of control to allow new cities to get into the baseball business. In addition, Title Two contained criminal penalties for any baseball team or official that violated its provisions.[38]

At the committee hearings on May 19 and 20, 1960, baseball's old guard reacted with predictable outrage to the bill. Commissioner Ford Frick called it "preposterous and vicious," and National League president Warren Giles warned that "it will ultimately do great harm to a great game." Yankees general manager George Weiss did not testify, but in a *Saturday Evening Post* article by Stanley Frank that appeared around the time of the hearing, Weiss pooh-poohed the bill and said, "I cannot believe Congress will take it seriously."[39]

Among the Continental League witnesses, Bill Shea was most enthusiastic, giving it his 100 percent endorsement. Branch Rickey also supported the Kefauver bill, especially after the provisions for criminal penalties were dropped from the final version. Although in prior testimony the creator of the farm system had always opposed restrictions on the number of players a team could develop, he realized that the new league had to have a chance to sign professional talent. Rickey now agreed with the bill's sponsors that, in one season, teams could evaluate professional promise well enough to allow sixty unwanted players to go into a draft. He reiterated his 1959 testimony that another great benefit of the unrestricted draft of first-year professionals would be to cut down on the bonuses paid to untried amateurs.

In what would be his swan song to congressional investigators, the ferocious gentleman was eloquent and pertinent. Rickey peppered his opening statement with heartfelt paeans to baseball's unique glory. In praising the drama of the contest between pitcher and batter, he rhapsodized, "No flurry of fists in the boxing ring rivets the spectators' attention more closely." He testified to the strength of a sport that emerged intact after one of its darkest hours, the fixing of the 1919 World Series. "Even 41 years ago, one little left-handed pitcher [Dickie Kerr] could upset, and did upset, the calculations of the gamblers."[40]

In offering his support of the Kefauver bill, Rickey declared, "Any rule or regulation that removes or tends to remove the power of money to make the difference in playing strength is a good rule," words that echoed the farewell to baseball nearly a half century earlier of Robert Hedges, the St. Louis Browns owner under whom Rickey most enjoyed working. To the opponents of change, who feared the Minor Leagues would collapse if there were an unrestricted draft of first-year players, Rickey argued that the Minors were already on life support. They were being propped up by an insufficient fund of $1 million a year from the Majors. In the past seven years, Rickey noted, the number of Minor Leagues had dropped from 47 to 21, and the number of independent teams, without Major League affiliation, had dropped from 128 to 25.[41]

The eloquent executive argued that the Continental League would give baseball a needed shot in the arm, providing jobs for both Major and Minor Leaguers. He noted that two thirds of the new league's proposed television income would be pooled among all the teams and that the new league would be able to contribute to both a good pension program for its players and the "encouragement of youth, school and college baseball programs."

Rickey stressed that he was trying to save baseball from itself. Even though there currently were no legal cases brought by discontented players, there was reason to be concerned about baseball's decline, and he was frustrated by baseball's inaction. "Trouble ahead, trouble ahead. You will hear it from Mr. Trautman [Minor League, National Association president] and Mr. Frick. This will happen, that will happen, the other thing will happen, upon assumptions that are wrong."[42]

Despite Rickey's eloquence and passion the omens were not good for passage of the bill by the full Congress. Senator Kefauver did not even attend the hearings, having started to campaign for reelection in Tennessee. Although Rickey did testify, he was away from the Continental League office for most of May, in Pittsburgh tending to Jane Rickey, who had just undergone a cataract operation, and battling a bronchial infection of his own.

A major sign of trouble for the Kefauver bill was that the hearings adjourned without the subcommittee reporting favorably on any bill. One of the biggest supporters for the status quo was New York republican senator Kenneth Keating. Even though Keating was from a state that recently had lost two Major League teams, he represented Rochester, an upstate city whose International League franchise would be threatened by the Continental League's moving into nearby Buffalo and Toronto. Keating gave lip service to Major League expansion, but he usually sided with the old order. He called the Kefauver bill "an attack on baseball, and I am against such a strategy."[43]

The bill was due for a vote on the floor of the U.S. Senate sometime in June 1960. It was a portentous and anxious time in the nation's capital. Jockeying for the nominations for president in both parties was going on in earnest with President Dwight Eisenhower retiring after his two terms in office. The recent shooting down of American pilot Gary Powers in his U-2 spy plane over Soviet air space had created an embarrassment for Eisenhower's administration at a time when a thaw with the Soviet regime seemed possible.

Even with the alarm caused by the feared shift of the Washington Senators, changes in the legal status of the baseball industry were not a high priority among the legislating senators. Organized baseball's chief lobbyist, Paul Aldermandt Porter, made it his job to see that the full antitrust exemption remained. Kentucky-bred Paul Porter was on his way to becoming a partner in the high-powered Washington law firm of Thurman Arnold and Abe Fortas. A former chairman of the Federal Communications Commission and administrator of the Office of Price Administration during World War II, Porter had emerged as a renowned lobbyist and behind-the-scenes deal maker in Cold War Washington. Antitrust crusader Congressman Emanuel Celler branded Porter the "generalissimo" of lobbyists.[44]

At first Porter assured the baseball moguls that the Kefauver bill had no chance of passing the full Senate. He assured them that the Continental League would get no more than a dozen votes. Then, behind the scenes, Democratic Senate majority leader Lyndon B. Johnson, of Texas, stepped into the fray. Although Massachusetts Democratic senator John F. Kennedy had built up a clear lead in the presidential primaries, Johnson was still a contender for the presidential nomination. Although not a passionate sports fan, Johnson was in favor of any bill that might accelerate Major League status for Texas. Encouraged to speak out by Craig Cullinan and George Kirksey, leaders of Houston's Continental League franchise, Lyndon Johnson began twisting arms for support for the Kefauver bill.[45] Before long the vote to keep baseball's sanctified antitrust protection was not seen as a sure thing.

Paul Porter heightened his lobbying pressure with a skill that Bill Shea, like Emanuel Celler, ruefully acknowledged, giving one professional lobbyist's tip of the cap to another pro. Porter forged an alliance with a rising liberal star in the Senate, Michigan Democrat Philip Hart, who was chairing the Kefauver subcommittee in the Tennessee Democrat's absence. Hart had ties to the baseball establishment as a small stockholder in his brother-in-law Walter "Spike" Briggs's Detroit Tigers. During the 1959 hearings Hart had downplayed the value of being a baseball investor when asked about its worth by fellow Senate committee member, Colorado Republican John Carroll. "It is hardly the proper investment with which to build up a trust fund," Hart had quipped. Yet the Michigan Democrat still had his inside baseball connections, and he worked diligently with his colleagues to turn them against the Kefauver modifications of the baseball reserve system.[46]

When the vote on the Kefauver bill finally came to the Senate floor on June 28, 1960, timing was conspiring against the Continental League. The legislators were in a hurry to adjourn to prepare for the presidential conventions. Senator Kefauver again wasn't even in Washington, campaigning back home in Tennessee. Senator Joseph O'Mahoney (Democrat, Wyoming) was instructed to vote for the Tennessean's bill and to represent his interests in bringing the reserve system under reasonable restrictions so that the new league could have a fair chance to sign players.

However, through legislative maneuvering, the first vote that came to the floor of the Senate was on a bill introduced by Wisconsin Republican senator Alexander Wiley. It would apply the same antitrust exemptions that baseball already enjoyed to the other sports. When Wiley's bill passed, 45–41, the Kefauver bill supporters knew that they would lose if it came to a vote. They joined the large majority that voted, 73–12, to return the bill to committee. The Continental League backers approved this strategy because they did not want to face a total rejection on the Senate floor.[47]

Rickey tried to rally the Continental League owners. Congress was not going to help them, something that deep down he didn't expect or truly want. "We have to fight now or disband," Rickey exhorted his young colleagues.[48] He urged them to hold together because the idea of a new third league was too good for baseball and for the cities in the Continental League to abandon.

By the summer of 1960 the establishment owners began to realize that some change in the baseball structure was inevitable. There was too much pressure coming from politicians in both parties to stonewall indefinitely. Forty-one votes against the status quo in the late June Senate vote was surely a sign that they couldn't maintain the existing Major League structure much longer. Vice president Richard Nixon, soon to be nominated as the 1960 Republican presidential candidate, was even talking about an international baseball league that would include Havana and Mexico City.[49]

The monopoly of Major League Baseball clearly needed a breath of fresh air and new blood. Even the players were slowly getting rambunctious. They feared that their pension program, established in 1946 to ward off the threats of a union and the Mexican League, was underfunded, and two All-Star Games had been scheduled starting in 1959 to provide more money for their post-playing careers. (The unwieldy second game was dropped after 1962.)

Accepting that the time was ripe to broaden their ranks, the owners of the established leagues decided to invite the Continental League owners to a meeting in Chicago to discuss the mechanics of expansion. On August 2, 1960, a group of expectant, nervous Continental Leaguers arrived in the Windy City, hoping for membership in the exclusive club of baseball ownership.

The most senior member at the meeting—Branch Rickey—was the calmest, and Minnesota's Wheelock Whitney remembers in awe the respect shown to him by the powerful baseball moguls. At one heated point in the discussions, Walter O'Malley raised his voice, shouting, "Goddammit!" Whitney remembers. "He then quieted down, and said, 'Excuse me, Mr. Rickey.'"[50]

After the meeting broke for lunch, the owners and officials of the two established leagues met privately as the Continental League's eight owners, founding chairman Bill Shea, and president Branch Rickey waited in an anteroom as the big boys on the block made their decisions. "We were very nervous," Whitney recalls. "We weren't used to losing, but we knew that we didn't have any cards to play." Craig Cullinan remembers, "We had bluffed because none of our stadiums were ready."[51]

However, after fifty-seven years of an unchanged Major League structure with two eight-team leagues, the owners had faced up to the need for change. The Yankees' Del Webb and the Dodgers' Walter O'Malley, baseball's most powerful owners, called the Continental committee back into the room and announced that the Major Leagues had voted to add four new franchises "and four more at a later time." In a formal statement Walter O'Malley said, "The American and National Leagues recognize the efforts of Mr. Shea and Mr. Rickey."[52] The cheering among the new league members was deafening, but Rickey told them to listen to the terms carefully.

As it turned out, an initial notice to the press was misleading. An erroneous report made the newswires that the American League would add Toronto and Houston and that Minneapolis and New York were to join the National League. In fact, Houston was placed in the National League along with New York, and Minneapolis–St. Paul and Los Angeles would join the American League. Moreover, the Minnesota team was not going to be an expansion team. After several years of trying, Calvin Griffith was granted permission to move the Senators to Minnesota. Realizing the uproar from Congress that would occur, the American League hastily announced the creation of an expansion franchise for the nation's capital. Los Angeles, not a member of the Continental League, was voted into the American League because its market was so vast that Commissioner Ford Frick ruled that it was "an open city," where any team could move without paying indemnity to the existing Dodgers.[53] (Walter O'Malley, however, would find ways to make sure that the new Los Angeles Angels franchise was definitely subordinate in his adopted city.)

Commissioner Ford Frick chortled: "Peace, it's wonderful. I have always favored expansion and this is the best way." Bill Shea was delighted, too, proclaiming that this day was "the greatest baseball event in 50 years."[54] Minneapolis–St. Paul, predictably, was also ecstatic, having achieved Major League status in both football and baseball within a few months in 1960. The birth of the National Football League Minnesota Vikings and now the American League Minnesota Twins eased some of the pain caused by losing the National Basketball Association Minneapolis Lakers to Los Angeles earlier in the year. Houston was happy, too, to become the first Major League city in Texas. However, the rest of the Continental League contingent was shut out.

The sporting press for the most part welcomed the denouement, but with a healthy dose of cynicism. Harold Rosenthal, in the *New York Herald Tribune*, summed up the feeling when he wrote: "There is little doubt that whatever Congressional pressure which has been brought to bear will be eased, and baseball will again be left with its questionable reserve clause dangling in Damoclean fashion over its well-tonsured head."[55]

As Branch Rickey flew home from Chicago, his feelings were decidedly mixed. He was happy for Bill Shea and Wheelock Whitney, whose cities had been awarded Major League franchises, but he felt sad for those cities that had lost out, especially Toronto and Jack Kent Cooke, who had been most optimistic about his city's chances. (Cooke soon turned to professional football, where ultimately he became the majority owner of the Washington Redskins and also chief executive of the Los Angeles Kings hockey team.) Rickey feared for the quality of the play in the expanded Major Leagues because he felt that the inherent problem of ten-team leagues was that all that was done was to add two more bad teams to each league. Phillies owner Bob Carpenter admitted as much at the Chicago meeting. His team would suffer through a twenty-three-game losing streak in 1961, and he was not going to help expansion franchises with good players. "We have a tough enough time getting ourselves out of last place," the DuPont heir said.[56]

Yet, even at age seventy-nine, Branch Rickey was not going to allow himself to grow accustomed to the emotions of defeat. He would never be ready to break from an active involvement with the business and passion of baseball. On a bumpy plane ride back home to Pittsburgh, Branch Rickey wrote his new young friend in Minnesota, thirty-four-year-old Wheelock Whitney, about what the future would hold in store for him as he entered the baseball business.

In a handwriting made nearly illegible by the turbulent plane ride, Rickey said that he was writing because he was impressed by Whitney's "very great strong points of character . . . loyalty sincerity and good sense—candor under pressure—I can not name them all." He warned him that "your people must not trust to the 'help' that may be promised or indeed provided, as coming from the majors. That will be the 'crumbs from the table,'" he counseled. "You will be confronted with a vicious competition, surely unlike anything you have ever imagined. I shudder, really, when I think of what surely is in front of the ninth and tenth clubs in either major league, because and chiefly because of player weakness on the field."

As always, Rickey tempered his well-founded pessimism with fighting optimism. "You must now have a working faith that you will soon be a major league operation," he said, stressing that step number one was choosing a general manager, someone with "*executive ability in the field of baseball experience.* Personal connections or business influence must have nothing to do with your election. . . . Get the best. If you are fortunate enough to get the right man, don't debate the price. Get him."

Step two was to hire a farm director, a chief of the player production department, and preferably an assistant who knew the Major League players as well as the Minor League ones. Rickey warned, though, that during the first year of play, the team would be lucky to win 40 out of 154 games. "The newness of attractions will sustain you for a time, probably so!" he predicted. "But the fantasy wears out rapidly with a discreditable club."

Before ending his letter, Rickey thanked his new friend for his support. "You were very thoughtful in your personal remarks to me. I am a bit uncomfortable to feel that anyone anywhere feels that I am the object for some sort of sympathy or consolation (although it may be and really is an understandable feeling)," he wrote. "About me? I mean to have another fling. St Louis was good to me. So was Brooklyn, and Pittsburgh is coming through!" (Indeed, in two months the Pirates would beat the Yankees in the World Series.) Rickey concluded his letter to Whitney on a note of indomitable optimism. "I have plans—I will keep busy," he promised. "I intend to bring another club to World Series status."[57]

Branch Rickey endured another disappointment in 1960. In November, in a very close election, the Republicans lost the White House, as Massachusetts senator John F. Kennedy defeated vice president Richard Nixon. Although Rickey's powers of persuasion certainly played their part in Jackie Robinson's supporting Nixon in the election, Kennedy carried most of the black vote, which played a big role in securing the Democratic victory.

Branch Rickey, though, was not prepared for retirement in any way. He kept a close watch on developments with the new National League franchise in New York. Of course, he had the ear of his nephew-in-law Charles Hurth, the general manager of the Continental League team that soon would be named the Mets (restoring the name of a late-nine-teenth-century New York franchise, the Metropolitans). Rickey offered Hurth lengthy and basically profound advice on the three issues of major importance for a new team: spring training, Major League scouting, and mass production of free agents.

He urged Hurth to bid for St. Petersburg, which had become in Rick-ey's estimation for "climate, playing field, clubhouse, hotel accommoda-tions, and exhibition game schedule, . . . the most desired training point in the United States." After sharing the facility with the Cardinals since 1938, the Yankees were planning a move to Fort Lauderdale. Rickey urged Hurth to act swiftly, and the Mets did make St. Petersburg their spring training site.

Rickey also urged the fledging New York franchise to adopt a mass pro-duction program with recently signed pro players. "It was the big reason for the success of the Western Carolina League last year," Rickey wrote. "The four sponsoring clubs could form quickly as many leagues as the production of players would require." Rickey offered opinions on a wide variety of other subjects, from Major League scouting to television and radio contracts to area and individual scouting. "Integrity is a precious attribute of every baseball scout," Rickey's memo counseled. "There is more room for the twilight zone double cross in scouting than in any other phase of the baseball business."

As for the new stadium to be built at the World's Fair site in Flushing Meadows, Rickey recommended the name of an architect who had built several Minor League ballparks for him, Gustavus Thompson of Troy, New York. He noted the importance of the field cover and that "the location of the trench is exceedingly important involving the protection against slush or overflow water." As a concession to the glitz and glamour required by New York, Rickey suggested that the scoreboard at the new Flushing Meadows ballpark "should be somewhat pretentious. This matter should have early study." He also put in a good word for Dr. J. B. Martin, president of the Negro American League, the only remaining Negro League. "I believe a deal could be made very soon whereby a sponsoring club or clubs could get the entire production of this Negro League," Rickey suggested. "This would be a very valuable asset to New York."[58] Unfortunately, the Negro American League disbanded in 1961.

The baseball-loving mind and churning work ethic of Branch Rickey were obviously undimmed. On April 10, 1961, however, Rickey received a terrible blow when Branch Rickey Jr. died in Pittsburgh from complications of the diabetes he had been battling since the late 1930s. Because he had stayed in Pittsburgh as farm director during his father's Continental League effort, the younger Rickey had been able to savor the World Series triumph of the Pirates, which he had contributed to greatly behind the scenes. He was only forty-seven when he died.

As a measure of what the family and the family name meant to Branch Rickey, the grieving father asked Mary Iams Rickey, Branch Jr.'s widow, if Rickey's teenaged grandson Branch Barrett Rickey, who went by the name of Barry, could now be called Branch. It was a decision the younger Rickey's family thought touching and apt. Another "Branch that beareth fruit" would live on.[59]

Two months later, still grieving his loss at his Northern Ontario retreat, Branch Rickey suffered his second heart attack in three years. It was serious enough to keep him in a Sudbury, Ontario, hospital for over six weeks. As he recovered he made new friends in the hospital and wondered aloud why Sudbury did not have a Minor League baseball team. When Jane came on her regular visits, he told everyone that she remained for him "the only pebble on the beach," and she appropriately blushed.[60]

Meanwhile, it was clear that Rickey's influence in the operations of the new team in New York was waning. When the franchise had been granted in the summer of 1960, Bill Shea wanted Rickey to consider being general manager, but a combination of factors kept Rickey from accepting. His age and his frail health were among them, and he told Charles Hurth that he didn't want it thought that his primary motive in accepting the Continental League presidency had been to operate another franchise in the established leagues.[61]

M. Donald Grant, the stockbroker who had chief owner Joan Payson's voting proxy, was becoming the power on the board of the directors of the Mets. When Rickey turned down any active involvement, Grant brought in George Weiss, the Yankees general manager who had been summarily fired (along with manager Casey Stengel) after the Yankees lost the 1960 World Series to the Pirates.[62] Charles Hurth was still the nominal general manager, but it was oil and water between Weiss and Hurth. The Mets seized on the opportunity to win disgruntled Yankees fans over to the National League side by hiring Stengel to manage the new team. Hurth was not privy to these moves or to Weiss's decision to win over Brooklyn Dodgers fans by signing aging first baseman Gil Hodges. Hurth believed in building a team with younger players and younger leaders. He resigned and moved to Colorado.[63]

As 1962 began Branch Rickey was still living in Pittsburgh. He had weathered a second heart attack, the tragic early loss of his only son, and the defeat of his dream of a third major league. He hadn't been visible at many baseball functions and ceremonies since his string of defeats had begun in Pittsburgh and the Continental League, but he knew he would be in Cooperstown in July 1962. Jackie Robinson, in his first year of eligibility, had been elected into baseball's shrine of the immortals. "Mr. Rickey" had been the first person Robinson called after he and Rachel learned the news from the Baseball Writers' Association of America. It was an occasion that neither Branch nor Jane Rickey would want to miss.

27

Meet Me in St. Louis, Final Chorus

July 23, 1962, was a cold and rainy day in Cooperstown, New York, but Branch Rickey never let the weather interfere with his plans. Jackie Robinson was being enshrined in the National Baseball Hall of Fame, and Branch and Jane Rickey happily made the trip up from Pittsburgh, driven by their chauffeur, Archie. When it was Robinson's time to speak, he thanked three people who had meant the most to him: his mother, Mallie Robinson; his wife, Rachel Isum Robinson; and "a man who has been like a father to me," Branch Rickey.[1] Jack was thrilled that all three could join him on his special day. Although Rickey felt that the day and the triumph fully belonged to Robinson, he beamed with paternal pride. As he never tired of saying, he had just opened the door of opportunity that should have been opened years before, and Robinson took full advantage of the chance.

After the ceremony ended, John Branch Jakle, one of Branch Rickey's grandsons, took a picture of Rickey and Robinson. Robinson later autographed it and inscribed a message: "I think this photo says it all. Your being with us at Cooperstown was just wonderful. My entire family loved seeing you. May God continue to bless you." Jakle, who pitched for the small Southern California college of Pomona and was scouted by his grandfather, is now a lawyer and keeps the photo proudly on his desk.[2]

Unfortunately, Rickey and Robinson did not have much time to socialize together at Cooperstown. Since their first meeting in Brooklyn, however, they had felt the bonds of a genuine friendship that extended far beyond their public personas as symbols of integration. The executive surely influenced the black pioneer's belief in black capitalism and encouraged his leanings to the Republican Party, which were evident in Robinson's vote for Richard Nixon for president in 1960 and his later employment by New York State governor Nelson Rockefeller.

The two pioneers always quickly responded to each other's business ventures. When Rickey was organizing the Continental League, the baseball executive asked Robinson whether his new employer, William Black, president of the Chock Full o' Nuts coffee company, was interested in investing in the new league. Robinson quickly replied that his boss was not.[3] In the last year of his life Rickey expressed his interest in assisting Robinson's black-owned Freedom National Bank, and he was delighted when Robinson in turn agreed to lend his name for fund-raising for one of Rickey's charitable ventures, the Japanese International Christian University in Tokyo.[4]

Mingling with the baseball brotherhood in Cooperstown was a great tonic for Branch Rickey, who had largely been out of the baseball loop since the Continental League disbanded. He was escorted into the Hall of Fame ceremony on the arm of Frank Frisch, who had just come out with a book that said many flattering things about his one-time Cardinals boss. "Everybody I've ever known who was associated closely with Branch, as scout, manager, player, or clerk, has become forever a Rickey man," Frisch wrote.[5]

The other inductees with Jackie Robinson in the Hall of Fame Class of 1962 were Cincinnati Reds outfielder Edd Roush, Cleveland Indians pitcher Bob Feller, and manager Bill McKechnie. Bob Feller's presence on the same stage as Robinson was ironic given the pitcher's public doubts in 1945 that Robinson lacked the talent to make the Major Leagues. However, the race pioneer held no grudges against the fireballing pitcher, who for years held both the single-game and season strikeout records (until Sandy Koufax broke them). Robinson told Feller that he was glad to be inducted with him.[6]

Rickey was pleased that Bill McKechnie was also being honored. There was no doubt about the veteran manager's credentials for enshrinement. He had won four National League pennants, with the 1925 Pirates, Rickey's 1928 Cardinals, and the 1939 and 1940 Cincinnati Reds; his first and last league champions had also won the World Series. Both McKechnie and Rickey, in their day, had been nicknamed "Deacon" for their religious beliefs and regular church attendance. The executive was moved by the elegiac tone of the manager's acceptance speech, in which he said, "Anything I may have ever contributed to baseball, I am repaid seven times seven today."[7]

Rickey and McKechnie enjoyed talking about old times, but they lamented the current state of baseball, with its two ten-team leagues, which meant more teams in the second division. If only there were a third league, McKechnie sighed, with a real first and second division, instead of at least six teams buried far from a pennant.[8] Rickey grimaced at the reference to the third league, a gallant cause that he had not been able to lead to fruition.

When Branch and Jane Rickey returned to Pittsburgh, they took stock of their lives. Although each was over eighty years old, living life fully was still their goal. It was becoming clear, though, that their eighteen-room house was too big for them alone. Across the clearing they were reminded every moment of the loss of Branch Rickey Jr. It certainly made sense for them to find a smaller house in Pittsburgh or maybe to relocate, perhaps near one of their other children. Then, out of the blue—"almost by accident," Branch Rickey would later say—a phone call came from St. Louis. It was from August "Gussie" Busch Jr., the disgruntled owner of the St. Louis Cardinals. The team had not won a pennant since 1946, and like all owners Busch was getting impatient to win again. "Would you be interested in coming to the Cardinals to work as a senior consultant, Mr. Rickey?" Busch asked.

The bee in Busch's bonnet had been put there by Brown Derby restaurateur Bob Cobb, whom the St. Louis mogul had just visited on a brewery business trip. Cobb was still one of Branch Rickey's biggest admirers, and the feeling was so mutual that the California businessman was one of the few people who felt comfortable enough to drink alcohol in the teetotaler's presence. When Busch vented his frustration at the Cardinals' lack of progress, Cobb said, "The best brain in baseball is sitting in Pittsburgh doing nothing."[9] He suggested that Busch call the one-time St. Louis legend, and the owner leaped into action.

Busch's offer immediately tempted the executive, who was still itching, as he had written to Wheelock Whitney when the Continental League disbanded, to "have another fling . . . and bring another team to World

Series status." However, the issue of what real authority a "senior consultant" would have should have raised a red flag in Branch Rickey's mind. Some members of his family tried to gently make the point to him. Why, at his age and in his shaky physical condition, would he want the stress of direct involvement with a baseball team? After all his years of principled opposition to beer sponsorship of baseball games, did he really want to go to work, in effect, for a brewer who, when he bought the Cardinals, wanted to rename Sportsman's Park Budweiser Stadium?[10] Wasn't he involved enough with the game by working on his highly awaited and long overdue book on baseball for a major New York publisher, Simon and Schuster?

There was also the inevitability of a sticky situation in St. Louis, where there were already in place a general manager, Vaughan "Bing" Devine, and a team president, Dick Meyer, whom Busch had brought over from the brewery. These good questions were brushed aside by the proud octogenarian because meaningful work in baseball trumped all. He saw an opportunity to return to the Cardinals, the team he had put on the baseball map, and to St. Louis, a city he had never wanted to leave, where he had raised his six children and had become a pillar of church and community.

Rickey told Busch that he expected certain privileges. "Like what, Mr. Rickey?" Busch asked. "Well, to bring my secretary, Ken Blackburn, and to be provided with a car and a driver," Rickey replied. "Is that all?" Gussie Busch said with a laugh. Busch could afford almost anything and was used to getting his way, hiring and firing people at will. The multimillionaire lived the life of a baron, residing at Grant's Farm, a 281-acre estate outside St. Louis that had been Ulysses S. Grant's hideaway in the years before Abraham Lincoln called on him to lead the Union Army in the Civil War. Busch had erected on the property a thirty-four-room Renaissance manor and a park that he populated with exotic animals from all over the world. He liked to travel around the estate in carriages pulled by his Clydesdale horses, and in the wintertime he was transported by sleighs.[11]

In late September 1962 Rickey flew to St. Louis at Busch's invitation to sit in on some team organizational meetings. The Cardinals were completing a disappointing season, headed for a sixth-place finish, although they would have a respectable record of 84-78 (due to the vagaries of the ten-team league). They still had a chance to play spoiler in the hot pennant race between the San Francisco Giants and the Los Angeles Dodgers. The Dodgers were coming in to St. Louis for a weekend series, and Cardinals manager Johnny Keane, whom Rickey had signed as an infielder for the Cardinals Minor League system in 1930, asked the renowned executive to speak to the team before the opening game. "He told the boys to watch out for the little things as well as the big ones," Keane said afterward.[12]

Rickey's speech might not have had the power and pertinence of his pep talk before the 1931 World Series, which had fired Pepper Martin to superhuman heights, and by now many of the younger players tended to tune out Rickey's inspirational rhetoric. Yet the Cardinals did win two out of three against the Dodgers, continuing Los Angeles on a downward slide that ultimately forced them into a one-game playoff, which they lost to the Giants. (In an interesting sideline, Leo Durocher was back with the Dodgers as a third base coach for manager Walter Alston. He was the same brassy Leo, speaking what was on his mind, second-guessing Alston's field decisions, and calling corpulent owner Walter O'Malley "Whalebelly" to his face.)[13]

On October 29, 1962, virtually twenty years to the day when Branch Rickey took over the Brooklyn Dodgers, he was officially introduced at a 9:00 a.m. press conference as the newest member of the Cardinals front office. He was surrounded by Bing Devine, Dick Meyer, Johnny Keane, and Gussie Busch, but Branch Rickey could not be in a room without being the center of attention. He held forth in grand style, saying that the Cardinals might "possibly" contend in 1964 but that 1965 seemed to him "a rational objective for a pennant."

When Rickey was asked whether he intended to watch the team's prospects in the upcoming instructional league in St. Petersburg, Gussie Busch interrupted, "I'll bet all the peanuts, doughnuts and chocolate, he'll be there."[14] After the owner finished Rickey announced, "I will go to St. Petersburg for a personal inspection of our young players." Bob Broeg of the *Post-Dispatch*, who had taken over from retired Roy Stockton as the dean of St. Louis sportswriters, observed that "Branch Rickey must have felt like General Douglas MacArthur wading ashore in the Philippines in 1945."[15]

Not surprisingly, within days of the formal announcement of Rickey's return to St. Louis, the front office was in turmoil. Bing Devine, who walked out of the room in the middle of Rickey's press conference, was giving serious thought to resigning. He knew that Busch wanted Rickey and had installed him in the first floor office previously occupied by former Cardinals owner Fred Saigh. Devine understood that the owner paid the bills and could hire anyone he wanted. Yet Bing Devine didn't want or need a "senior consultant." He had worked for the Cardinals for nearly a quarter century, starting out as an office assistant after graduating from Washington University of St. Louis (where he played varsity basketball). He had worked his way up the Minor League front office ladder and in 1958 had been named general manager of the parent club.[16]

Devine believed the Cardinals were on the cusp of contention. In fact, he was finalizing a trade that would bring shortstop Dick Groat from the Pirates in exchange for the younger shortstop Julio Gotay and pitcher Don Cardwell. Devine thought the deal would cement an infield that already had Bill White at first base, Julian Javier at second, and Ken Boyer at third.

Branch Rickey was opposed to the trade and let Devine and others in the front office know it. It was ironic that Groat was the center of the controversy, because Rickey had signed him for Pittsburgh in 1952 and liked him very much as a person. However, as always in Rickey's long baseball career, personal feeling did not get in the way of professional evaluation. Rickey preferred younger players to older players, and that view led him to voice an opinion against obtaining Groat.[17]

The youth-conscious Rickey offered another blunt, very controversial judgment: Stan Musial should retire. The St. Louis legend was coming off a 1962 season in which he hit .330, with a .508 SA, 19 HR, and 82 RBI. However, he was forty-two years old and certainly near the end of his career. Of course, nobody else in the front office, fearing fan backlash, wanted to ease the local legend into retirement, but Branch Rickey had not been hired to be a yes-man. He was going to offer honest evaluations and judgments, and he wasn't going to—and, by disposition, could not—pussyfoot.

Bing Devine and Branch Rickey ultimately worked out an uneasy truce. According to Devine, one day early in Rickey's return to the Cardinals, the older executive called him down to his office and asked him for a ride home because Rickey's usual chauffeur, Ken Blackburn, was unavailable. Rickey and Devine lived only a mile apart in suburban Ladue, and the aging executive thought they might use the time in the car for a get-acquainted session. During the ride it became clear to Devine that Rickey thought he was running the show and the younger man was only going to have a functionary's role. Rickey sensed Devine's discomfort. "Are you and I going to have trouble?" he asked. Devine replied, "Mr. Rickey, you and I already have trouble."[18]

The young general manager was not going to yield his prerogatives, and a clear sign of his continuing authority came a week before Thanksgiving 1962, when he completed the Groat deal with Pittsburgh, obtaining the shortstop and left-handed pitcher Diomedes Olivo in exchange for Gotay and Cardwell. It turned out to be a good deal for St. Louis because, despite his advancing years, Groat was a winner, a genuine first-division ballplayer who knew how to use his abilities to the utmost.

Meanwhile, as best as he could, Branch Rickey settled into his role as a not particularly wanted consultant. He certainly was happy to be back in harness in the game he loved deeply. The press didn't clamor for his opinions as much as earlier, but he was always available when an inquiring reporter came calling. "It is difficult for an eighty-one-year-old man to serve in the capacity of consultant and not be suggestive," he told Frank Graham Jr., who was writing a piece, "Branch Rickey Rides Again," for the *Saturday Evening Post*. He added: "I think I can best render service to the Cardinals by forgetting my age and past titles and getting down to hard work as a scout."[19]

Rickey remembered Graham, the son of noted New York sportswriter Frank Graham, from his last year in Brooklyn when the young man had worked in the Dodgers' community relations department. He regaled the journalist with strong and prescient opinions on the decline of baseball and the surge in pro football. "We must beat football into the new areas in order to control the stadiums," he warned. He talked strongly about meeting the challenges of the civil rights movement. He had recently reiterated his point to six hundred ministers in Ohio that "to advise moderation" is like being "a moral pickpocket." Yet he criticized activist-writer James Baldwin's "venomous writing." Rickey charged: "He has a mind as sharp as steel, but for him *now* was ten years ago."[20]

Despite his uncomfortable situation in the workplace, Branch Rickey was delighted to be back in St. Louis, and so was Jane Rickey. Some of their friends from twenty years earlier were still in town, and social evenings and bridge games resumed almost as if they had never been interrupted. Socializing and playing bridge with Kathleen and George Sisler, in particular, brought special joy to the Rickeys.[21] Always needing family nearby, Branch and Jane found a house in suburban Ladue, across a meadow from the home of their second-youngest daughter, Sue Rickey Adams; her husband, Stephen Adams; and their two young children, Stephen Jr. and Elizabeth.

Having her grandparents live a short walk away felt like a blessing to Beth Adams Louis, who was not yet nine when they returned to St. Louis. "They loved life so much, and their family meant so much to them," she declares. Although both were octogenarians, Branch and Jane Rickey acted half their age, readily communicating their vitality and sense of fun. Grandpa Branch would poke his grandchildren with his cane and occasionally pull off his favorite early-morning prank, awakening them with shaving cream on his face and asking, "Who's my favorite grandchild of them all?" Grandma Jane always had cookies for the kids when they returned from school. For all her genuine belief in education, a hallmark of the Rickey household, Jane exuded an irresistible desire to enjoy life in the moment. "You could come home in the afternoon and say, 'Grandma, I got kicked out of school today,' and she would act as if nothing had happened," Beth Louis recalls. "She would just smile and say, '"Well, dear, what do you want to do today?"'"[22]

At some point in the summer, all the Rickey children and grandchildren would gather at the family house on Manitoulin Island off Northern Ontario. Beth Louis remembers one morning when her grandfather went into town and came back with identical tartan outfits for all his granddaughters. "He presented them to us and we had to try them on and model them for him right away, all standing in a row," she recalls about her paterfamilias.[23]

Spring training in 1963 provided for Branch Rickey a warm reunion in St. Petersburg with Al Lang, the local promoter and former town mayor who had lured Rickey's St. Louis Browns to the city on Tampa Bay in

1914 and started a lifelong friendship with the baseball man. Rickey spent many convivial evenings visiting with Lang and other old friends in the St. Petersburg business, academic, and religious communities.

Many baseball pundits—including Branch Rickey—did not view the Cardinals as real contenders for the 1963 pennant, but with the addition of Dick Groat, the infield of White-Javier-Groat-Boyer was solid defensively. In the outfield Rickey liked what he saw in two of the Cardinals' black players, center fielder Curt Flood, whom he called "perfection," and left fielder George Altman.[24] St. Louis had not initially been in the forefront of signing black players, but by the 1960s they had made up for lost time with such stars as first baseman Bill White, pitcher Bob Gibson, and Curt Flood.

Rickey also saw promise in catcher Tim McCarver. However, he wouldn't be Branch Rickey if he didn't find room for improvement in a player. "McCarver needs to improve his footwork on his throwing," Rickey wrote in a memo to Gussie Busch. "He doesn't need to take two steps before he throws to second base."[25]

For his part, Tim McCarver, today a nationally recognized baseball broadcaster and author, recalls how "intimidating" and "tough" Branch Rickey could be in his role as senior consultant. In the spring of 1963 McCarver had recently been discharged from the military, and as he took his first swings at an old batting cage in St. Petersburg, his batting mechanics were still rusty. McCarver could see that Rickey, who arrived at practice sessions in a chauffeur-driven car, was observing everything on the field from a perch high above the batting cage.

The senior consultant didn't like what he saw of McCarver's swing, and two days later he addressed the whole team. "There is a player I watched at batting practice—and I don't want to mention his name—and he's a young fellow who should know better," McCarver remembers Rickey's critique. "He didn't take the bat back far enough. He'll never hit a fastball like that." According to McCarver, everyone on the team knew that Rickey was criticizing him. At the end of the year, when the Cardinals with a great closing winning streak almost won the pennant, McCarver relates that "Rickey had the nerve to say, 'If we had 25 McCarvers on this team, we would win many pennants.' I despised the guy."[26]

McCarver's opinion is another example of Branch Rickey never leaving anyone neutral about him. Yet Rickey could not be quiet about his evaluations. To a fault he remained the man who wanted to know everything about you and then make you better. When the 1963 regular season began, Rickey continued his internal criticism of Stan Musial. After the Cardinals started the season with a 5-3 record, Rickey drafted a memo to Gussie Busch that bluntly attributed two of the team's three losses to the aging veteran's slow running. Once, a foul fly ball was hit that "could have been easily reached by an outfielder of average running speed," Rickey wrote Busch. The ball fell untouched, and the batter got a second chance at a hit. In another example Musial hit a grounder with the bases loaded that the shortstop fumbled but was still able to turn the double play because Musial lacked the speed to beat the throw to first base. "He is still a grand hitter but not at all the hitter of former days," Rickey concluded.[27] The forty-three-year-old Musial would retire at the end of 1963 after a season with mediocre numbers: .255 BA, .404 SA, 12 HR, and 58 RBI in 337 at-bats. However, Rickey's criticism of the great legend would be leaked to the sportswriters, making the strong-minded executive appear meddlesome.

In 1963 the Cardinals had their best year since 1949 (when they finished only one game behind Rickey's Brooklyn Dodgers). The nucleus of a future championship team was in place, with first baseman Bill White leading the team with a .304 BA, 27 HR, and 109 RBI, and Ken Boyer not far behind at the other infield corner with a .285 BA average, 24 HR, and 111 RBI. The team would lead the league in runs scored, and the pitching surprised a lot of people, with future Hall of Famer Bob Gibson, the Cardinals' first dominant black pitcher, winning eighteen games, as did Ernie Broglio. In the bullpen Ron Perranoski won sixteen games as a reliever and saved twenty-one. The Cardinals won ninety-three games, but the Dodgers won ninety-nine, led by their future Hall of Fame pitching duo of Sandy Koufax and Don Drysdale. Los Angeles went on to sweep the Yankees in the World Series.

Hardly a month after the World Series ended, the American body politic received a terrible blow. The assassination of President John F. Kennedy on November 22, 1963, shocked the Rickey family in St. Louis, as it did the entire nation. The beginning of deeper American involvement in the war in Vietnam began to stir young people in the country, especially those eligible for the military draft, to protest. Branch Rickey wasn't ambivalent about the rise of long-haired, antiwar protesters on college campuses. Speaking to students at Ohio Wesleyan, he called these radicals "treasonous."[28]

Yet visits with his children always tempered Rickey's angrier edges. In the fall of 1963 he spent time with his daughter Jane and her husband, Robert Jones, and their children in Elmira, New York, where they had settled after leaving Fort Worth when Walter O'Malley took over the Dodgers. Rickey enjoyed a visit with philosophy professor Houston Peterson, who had just retired from Rutgers. The two Renaissance men taped two hour-long discussions for New York City–area public television, titled "The Mahatma and the Professor," which were aired on Christmas and New Year's Day in the winter of 1963–64.[29]

As always Rickey took solace and drew hope from his Christian faith. He was delighted when early in the new year of 1964, the Reverend Norman Vincent Peale came to St. Louis for a visit. Peale was a good friend and fellow Ohio Wesleyan graduate whose book *The Power of Positive Thinking* and frequent radio and television appearances had reached millions of believers and would-be believers. "A visit with you is a great inspiration to me," Rickey wrote Peale on Valentine's Day 1964. "I get younger and I want to do more and better." Of course, Rickey sought to connect his belief in God with baseball. "Our Christianity needs more hitting in the pinches. We need to know what we believe and why, and then we will have more confidence in our swing," Rickey observed. "Home runs don't count unless the bases are touched in order. I don't know of anyone who gets more players on first base than you do."[30]

When the Cardinals gathered in St. Petersburg for spring training in 1964, they were hopeful that this would be their year, after the strong finish in 1963. Gussie Busch certainly expected a pennant after eleven years of waiting. Yet the uneasy situation in the front office continued, with Rickey "consulting" and Bing Devine and his staff largely ignoring his advice. Branch Rickey had to accept the conditions, perhaps finally understanding that he was physically unable to take on the burden of fully running a team.

He was, of course, ready to express his opinions on a variety of subjects.

He took the time to write a letter to the *Sporting News* that took issue with a recent column suggesting the Federal League of 1914 and 1915 had been a Major League. As someone who had watched the third league severely hurt both the Browns and the Cardinals, and drive Browns owner Robert Hedges out of baseball, Rickey declared: "In our top minors of the time, there were numerous clubs with better balance and more talent than any Federal League club possessed." He continued authoritatively: "There's an end or purpose to proper statistics, and it is this—major league or not major league. The Federal League was not major league in any respect. It had a few very fine players, but for balanced clubs, our majors were far superior."[31]

Meanwhile, the 1964 season did not start off smoothly for the Cardinals. They were lagging under .500 when Bing Devine pulled off a major trade at the June 15 deadline. He dealt pitchers Ernie Broglio and Bobby Shantz and spare outfielder Doug Clemens to the Chicago Cubs for outfielder Lou Brock and journeymen pitchers Jack Spring and Paul Toth. Rickey had little input into the trade, which turned out to be a great one for St. Louis as Lou Brock, who would become a Hall of Famer, broke Ty Cobb's single-season and career stolen base records.

However, Brock's acquisition did not immediately transform the Cardinals. As the summer wore on, they still trailed the Dodgers, Giants, Reds, Phillies, and Braves, all contenders in what was to make 1964 one of the most competitive of all National League pennant races. Rumors were growing that Gussie Busch was dissatisfied with both Bing Devine and Johnny Keane and wanted to fire one or the other or both. With Branch Rickey behind the scenes, many sportswriters thought they divined his manipulative hand at work. Nothing could have been farther than the truth. Rickey, who didn't like to fire anybody, certainly did not believe in firing managers during the season; it was Sam Breadon who had exercised the itchy trigger finger in years past. Firing a general manager in midstream was even more unthinkable to Rickey, who understood that the general manager had to have a vision for a whole program of development, not just for one Major League season.

Another problem arose over Dick Groat's dissatisfaction with Johnny Keane. Keane, who had a reputation for being a player's manager, still had strict rules he wanted obeyed. In 1963 he had taken the unusual step of releasing left-handed pitcher Maurice "Mickey" McDermott in front of the entire team because he feared the bad influence of McDermott's carousing lifestyle.[32] One baseball rule that Keane wanted enforced was that only he could call hit-and-run plays, when the runner broke for second and the batter had to hit the ball. Dick Groat, however, wanted to signal his own plays.

"I had to call hit-and-run plays on odd counts because I was not a fast runner and hit into a lot of double plays," Groat explains. "I needed the surprise 0-2 and 1-2 count to make it work, and Johnny Keane didn't like the approach."[33] Rickey tried to mediate the dispute, and Groat, an intense but team-oriented player, ultimately apologized to the team. The rift, however, did not help team unity.

In mid-August 1964, with the Cardinals seemingly adrift in the pennant race while mired in fifth place, eight games out of first, impulsive Gussie Busch fired Bing Devine. He replaced Devine with Bob Howsam, who had worked with Branch Rickey in the Continental League as the representative of the prospective Denver team. Of course, the rumors started to swirl that Rickey was at work behind the scenes of this move, though again it was not true. It seemed that Rickey could be blamed for everything, although in his powerless position as consultant, he could actually influence very little. He did highly recommend Howsam, but nobody could tell an imperious owner like Gussie Busch who to hire or to fire.

The front office drama soon took a back seat as the Cardinals rallied in the pennant race. They started winning late-season games, though not as regularly as past Cardinals teams under Rickey; more importantly, the Philadelphia Phillies started losing. With a six-game lead and twelve games left to play, the Phillies lost ten in a row. With Bob Gibson pitching heroically, the Cardinals squeaked into the pennant by one game and won the World Series in seven games over the Yankees, replicating St. Louis's 1926 triumph. After the game Branch Rickey was in the clubhouse, singing the praises of Johnny Keane, looking like Banquo's ghost, *New York Times* sportswriter George Vecsey remembers.[34]

Soon after the World Series triumph, however, the front office soap opera reached its almost inevitable conclusion. Johnny Keane resigned suddenly, taking the Yankees managerial job when Yogi Berra was fired. (Never before in baseball history had both World Series managers been immediately replaced.) Bob Howsam had the unpleasant task of telling Branch Rickey that Gussie Busch had decided his services were no longer needed. With the championship trophy at last in his possession, Busch evidently had decided that he could live without the constant management turmoil.

Howsam approached his assignment with the same unhappiness that Joe L. Brown had felt nine years earlier when he told Rickey that John Galbreath was replacing him in Pittsburgh.[35] The executive never took the emotions of defeat easily, but he sensed that a major shakeup was coming. At least the Cardinals had won another pennant and World Series while he was in harness.

When he went home after the bad news at the office, Branch Rickey found Jane Rickey working at her easel on another painting. From an early age she had shown a talent for art, and in her advancing years she had started to paint regularly. As always, Jane was a sympathetic helpmate to her loving, if often turbulent, husband. "You can finish your book now without any interruptions," she said. He nodded, realizing that his manuscript was long overdue.

Rickey had procrastinated on writing his book for a variety of reasons, not least that he hated to write. It is not surprising that a great talker, storyteller, and man of action would find crafting a written page a confining and frustrating experience. He would complain that one day he was feeling very good about something that he had written, only to read it the next day and tear it up because he felt it was so bad. (Most professional writers could empathize with Rickey's feeling of dissatisfaction.)

Another problem in getting his book rolling was the conceptual issue of its form. In the 1950s Rickey gave freely of his time to answer questions from Arthur Mann, whose book *Branch Rickey: American in Action*, came out in 1957. Rickey had helped Mann promote the book by appearing on the NBC television network's morning show *Today*, but Rickey told friends and acquaintances that he had never read the book, probably wouldn't, and did not think that his good friend was truly a biographer.

Rickey, however, resolutely resisted writing a memoir. He explained his reluctance by saying that as a self-reproving religious man, he refused to believe that he was worthy of such egotistical attention.[36] Without doubt, the biggest factor in his delay in completing his book was a profound feeling that his life story was not over. He said many times that he wanted to contribute to the success of another baseball organization before his days on earth were complete.

Yet Rickey was contracted to do the book, and after the sudden death of Arthur Mann at age sixty-one in January 1963, Robert Riger was found as a replacement. Rickey had been impressed by Riger's book on professional football, *The Pros*, which, in addition to his text, featured Riger's action photographs and drawings of star players of the gridiron. Rickey hoped to make his baseball book a similar venture. Highlighted would be Rickey's short essays on baseball people he called "Immortals," surrounded by Riger's drawings of the Hall of Fame players and his photographs of contemporary baseball players in action.

Like almost everybody who crossed the path of Branch and Jane Rickey, Robert Riger was quickly captivated by the elderly couple, who acted much younger than their age. He was welcomed into their home, was moved to hear Branch Rickey say grace before meals, and was stimulated by the lively conversation at the dinner table. Riger and Rickey would often stay up past midnight, discussing and arguing points to be made in the book. "When we started this thing you were 81, Mr. Rickey, and I was 35," Riger wrote in his introduction. "Now we're finished, and you act like you're 38 and I feel like I'm 84."[37]

Rickey wrote the entire working draft of the book by himself without assistance. Overcoming his writer's block, he rewrote some of his essays on the "Immortals" nine times, giving homage to the baseball people whose life and work he had shared. When he completed his draft, he reviewed his work with Riger, who, as Rickey watched in awe, fit his elegant drawings and photographs into the text.

Much of Rickey's writing is memorable and bears many rereadings. Long out of print and worthy of republication, the handsome, oversized book was entitled *The American Diamond: A Documentary of the Game of Baseball.* Rickey's vivid descriptions of the immortal Hall of Famers are among the book's highlights. Rickey wrote of Pittsburgh Pirates shortstop Honus Wagner: "If immortality means at all continuity of excellence, Honus Wagner is still playing the game." About Ty Cobb, Rickey observed: "His genius was a form of insanity, a do-or-die personal effort to beat someone or something."[38]

Rickey devoted his longest essay to American League founder Ban Johnson. He wrote about Johnson's authoritative style of leadership: "He ruled the roost but he never stopped to crow about it." Still irritated that he had been unable to lead the Continental League to success, Rickey surmised that Ban Johnson would have brought the third league into existence. "He never would have accepted the promises of the American and National Leagues," the exasperated leader of the league that never happened opined.[39]

The American Diamond was completed late in 1964, but Simon and Schuster decided to delay publication until the fall of 1965. Branch Rickey did not mind the delay because, despite his growing physical infirmities, he still considered himself a man of action. He wasn't pleased that the Republicans had lost the White House again in the November election, but he understood that President Lyndon Johnson had been able to use civil rights as an issue in his behalf in ways that Republican candidate Senator Barry Goldwater had not.

When Rickey's good friend the Reverend Archibald Carey Jr., from the Commission on Government Employment Policy, wrote him that he was breaking ranks with the Republican Party on the race issue, Rickey replied that, although he understood Carey's position, he disagreed. "If I believed that the election of Goldwater would mean the slowing down of progress in the field of Civil Rights, I would not vote for him," Rickey explained. The moral and idealistic baseball executive argued that because of President Johnson's involvement in the Bobby Baker and Billy Sol Estes scandals in Washington, he feared a vote for the Democrats would be "a step toward national degradation."[40]

Accepting reluctantly that the baseball world was finally closed to him, Rickey's undimmed work ethic sought other primary outlets. When his alma mater Ohio Wesleyan called, wanting to know if he was interested in spearheading a major capital investment fund-raising drive for physical education and other school projects, he immediately accepted. "Ohio Wesleyan has been very largely responsible for whatever good is in me," Rickey said many times with deep conviction, "and is to be credited with whatever good I may have done."[41]

He toured the Midwest with Robert Holm, a recent Ohio Wesleyan graduate also working on the campaign. Holm was struck by the energy and life force that eighty-three-year-old Branch Rickey still possessed. Rickey enjoyed talking with the students on campus, holding forth on his belief in service, God, family, and country. Occasionally, Rickey would have a reunion with old classmates and teammates. One day Holm watched with delight as Rickey and Harvey Yoder, a former Battlin' Bishop player who was now an attorney in Ohio, went down to the football field and ran through the "billy goat" play that scored a touchdown against Ohio State sixty years earlier. On a more testy occasion Holm watched as the feisty octogenarian tried to coax funds from a wealthy farmer. "I had to step outside because I didn't want to be in the line of fire as those opinionated 80-year-olds starting calling each other names," Bob Holm recalls with a laugh.[42]

Early in February 1965 Rickey journeyed to Tulsa, Oklahoma, to attend the annual Oklahoma Diamond Dinner. Cardinals third baseman Ken Boyer was receiving the first annual Pepper Martin Award for his outstanding season for the world champions. Rickey was always delighted to see Martin, an all-time favorite player of his, whom he called one of "nature's noblemen." Martin owned a cattle ranch in nearby McAlester, Oklahoma, and on the property there was a big lake where he fished and swam and invited the area kids to join him.[43] He had managed Sacramento for Rickey's Cardinals in 1942, and Miami for Rickey's Dodgers in 1949, although he didn't finish the Florida State League season. He had been suspended for the last games of the year after trying to choke an umpire who had made a bad call.

Rickey had laughed when he heard about the incident and Martin's explanation: "I looked at my two hands and darned if I didn't have an umpire's throat between them." Rickey wrote off Martin's indiscretion, saying, "Pepper does get overzealous at times." Martin played Minor League baseball until he was fifty-four and even tried his hand at pitching, compiling a 6-5 record at the tail end of his career. It was a grievous blow to Rickey to learn a month after the dinner that Martin had died of a heart attack at age sixty-one.[44]

When the 1965 baseball season began, Rickey followed the Cardinals on the radio and television, but since his services were no longer needed at the ballpark he didn't attend many games. Under new manager Red

Schoendienst, the 1965 Redbirds fell all the way to seventh, one game under .500, as the Dodgers nipped the Giants in another close pennant race. The Minnesota Twins (the transplanted former Washington Senators) won the American League pennant, and Rickey gladly accepted the offer of Wheelock Whitney to be his guest at the World Series against the Los Angeles Dodgers, a thrilling competition that was won at Minnesota by a two-hit shutout in game seven by Sandy Koufax. "He was, as always, great company," Whitney remembers, "but it would be the last time I saw him."[45]

Shortly after returning home from Minnesota, Rickey fell ill and went to the hospital for tests. The cause of his high fever and latest ailment perplexed his doctors, but when Rickey started to grumble about hospital food and express a desire to get home soon, his family thought he was getting better. When the invitation came to attend his induction into the Missouri Sports Hall of Fame, he insisted that he must go.

After the fateful evening and the speech he never completed, Rickey never regained consciousness. As Jane Rickey and other members of the family kept a constant vigil at his bedside, many people phoned the hospital, hoping for news of improvement. Rickey's loyal friend Red Barber called, and so did Larry MacPhail, whose destructive antics in New York in the 1940s had antagonized Rickey to the point that it ultimately ruined their friendship.

When the end came on December 9, 1965, the news quickly went out across the nation. When told about Branch Rickey's death by sportswriter Phil Pepe of the *New York Daily News*, Jackie Robinson was first at a loss for words. Then he summed up what so many people felt who had known Branch Rickey. "He was always doing something for someone else," Robinson said.[46]

After Branch Rickey was laid to rest next to his parents in the hillside Scioto County cemetery in Ohio, Jane Rickey came back to live her last years in St. Louis, near her daughter's family and her friends. She continued to work at her paintings and remained an ardent and involved grandmother. Along with Kathleen Sisler and many other woman friends, Jane was active with her daughter Sue and granddaughter Beth in "Mother-Daughter" clubs.[47]

When Jane Moulton Rickey passed away in 1971, the Reverend Norman Vincent Peale wrote Mary Iams Rickey, Branch Rickey Jr.'s widow, a condolence note. "Branch's mother and father were two of the greatest, most lovable human beings I ever knew in this life, and I shall never forget them," the clergyman said. "Thank God He makes such people."[48] In 1976 Ohio Wesleyan University honored Branch Rickey by naming its field house after him, and in 2004 the school began a large-scale fundraising drive for its athletic and recreational facilities, naming the program, "Remembering Mr. Rickey." The town of Portsmouth, Ohio, has memorialized Branch Rickey on their flood wall murals with a portrait of him reading bedtime stories to two granddaughters. His brother Frank Wanzer Rickey, the baseball scout and irrepressible life force, is also featured on one of the murals.[49]

There is no simple last word on Branch Rickey, nor should there be. To the players at contract time, he was a formidable adversary. To the bewildered Brooklyn fan, "he was the man of many faucets, all running at once." To his family, however, he was a bulwark of protection and a bottomless source of mirth and affirmation of life. In summing up his experience in working on *The American Diamond* with Branch Rickey, Robert Riger wrote: "I tried to give a name to Mr. Rickey to describe his unique contribution as a man. But after seeing him in the long private hours of discussion, and meeting his friends and working with him and knowing him, battling him, loving him, respecting him, I call him *citizen*. After all—that's what he called Jackie Robinson."[50]

There was a Methodist hymn that was one of Branch Rickey's favorites, and it may stand as the best valedictory to the ferocious gentleman's ardent feelings about life on earth in service to the almighty God above.

> There's a wideness in God's mercy,
> Like the wideness of the sea;
> There's a kindness in His justice,
> Which is more than liberty.[51]

Notes

Prologue

1. "Rickey's Last Speech," *Sporting News*, December 25, 1965, 18; *New York Times*, August 19, 1959, 21.

2. "Rickey's Last Speech."

3. "The Old Brain," *Time*, April 13, 1942, 65.

4. "Rickey's Last Speech."

5. "Rickey's Last Speech."

6. Monteleone, *Branch Rickey's Little Blue Book*, 126.

7. Mann, *Branch Rickey: American in Action*, 8.

8. "Rickey's Last Speech."

9. A June 2005 e-mail to the author from Donald Hughes, Branch Rickey's grandson-in-law, provided an especially penetrating analysis of Zaccheus's appeal for Branch Rickey.

10. (Columbia) *Missourian*, November 14, 1965, 6. Clipping found in the Branch Rickey file, Ohio Wesleyan University Beeghly Library, Delaware OH.

11. *St. Louis Post-Dispatch*, December 14, 1965, 4B.

12. Quoted from an e-mail to the author of June 2005 by Robert Holm, retired assistant to the president of Ohio Wesleyan University and eyewitness to the arrival and departure of the Globetrotters.

13. Tygiel, *Past Time*, 94–95.

14. Cited in Graham Jr., *A Farewell to Heroes*, 234

15. Monteleone, *Branch Rickey's Little Blue Book*, xvi.

16. Graham Jr., *A Farewell to Heroes*, 225.

17. Thompson with Rice, *Every Diamond Doesn't Sparkle*, 58.

18. Launius, *Seasons in the Sun*, 20.

19. Interviews with Mary Rickey Eckler, Sebastopol CA, August 2000, and Jane Rickey Jones, Elmira NY, August 1999.

1. Diamond in the Rough

1. The standard sources for Branch Rickey's first school teaching job are Mann, *Branch Rickey: American in Action*, 7–18, and Polner, *Branch Rickey: A Biography*, 16–18. See also the second part of a penetrating article by Robert Rice, "Thoughts on Baseball—II." The Rickey files at the Beeghly Library at Ohio Wesleyan University in Delaware, Ohio, are also helpful.

2. Polner, *Branch Rickey: A Biography*, 16–17.

3. "Recollections and Reminiscences of Herman M. Shipps," unpublished speech, Rickey file, Ohio Wesleyan University Beeghly Library, Delaware OH. See also "Introducing Branch Rickey."

4. Mann, "The Life of Branch Rickey—I," 76.

5. Lipman, *Mr. Baseball*, 21.

6. Writer Brand Whitlock, quoted in Davies, *Defender of the Old Guard*, 5.

7. Polner, *Branch Rickey: A Biography*, 7.

8. E-mail to the author from Nancy Rickey Keltner, Branch Rickey's granddaughter (Branch Rickey Jr.'s daughter), May 2005.

9. Interview with Mary Rickey Eckler, Sebastopol CA, August 2000.

10. Rice, "Thoughts on Baseball—II," 33; Polner, *Branch Rickey: A Biography*, 13.

11. W. J. O'Connor, *St. Louis Post-Dispatch*, August 19, 1915, D1.

12. Rickey with Riger, *The American Diamond*, 20.

13. Urwin and Wollen, *John Wesley, Christian Citizen*, 29.

14. Polner, *Branch Rickey: A Biography*, 15.

15. Mann, "The Life of Branch Rickey—I," 74.

16. Associated Press, "Lawyer, Churchman, Politician—That Is Rickey, Boss of Cardinals," *Milwaukee Journal*, March 31, 1940, 3.

17. Richard D. Miller, "Branch Rickey at Ohio Wesleyan College—Prelude to Greatness," unpublished paper presented at the 25th convention of the Society for American Baseball Research, 1995.

18. "This Day 50 Years Ago," *Delaware (Ohio) Gazette*, June 15, 1953. Clipping in Rickey file, Ohio Wesleyan University Beeghly Library, Delaware OH.

19. "This Day 50 Years Ago." See also "Introducing Branch Rickey."

20. Polner, *Branch Rickey: A Biography*, 35.

21. Polner, *Branch Rickey: A Biography*, 29.

22. Sports Information, Ohio Wesleyan University, http://bishops.owu.edu/. Thanks to sports information director Mark Beckenbach for providing updated information.

23. Harris, "Branch Rickey Keeps His 40 Year Promise," 6.

24. Polner, *Branch Rickey: A Biography*, 32.

25. Harris, "Branch Rickey Keeps His 40 Year Promise," 4–5.

26. Mann, "The Life of Branch Rickey—I," 79.

27. Harris, "Branch Rickey Keeps His 40 Year Promise," 7.

28. Roberts, "Historically Speaking: Charles Follis," 57.

29. Harris, "Branch Rickey Keeps His 40 Year Promise." See also letters of Branch Rickey and Charles Thomas, especially October 26 and November 1, 1921, in the Branch Rickey Papers, Library of Congress, Washington DC.

30. Rowan with Robinson, *Wait Till Next Year*, 105–6.

31. Mann, *Branch Rickey: American in Action*, 33.

32. Newspaper Enterprise Association sportswriter Harry Grayson, March 20, 1935, part 3 of a series on the career of Branch Rickey, located in the archives of the *Sporting News*, St. Louis.

33. Mann, *Branch Rickey: American in Action*, 34.

34. Lieb, *The St. Louis Cardinals: The Story of a Great Baseball Club*, 64.

35. Mann, *Branch Rickey: American in Action*, 35; *Sporting News*, September 3, 1904, 6.

36. Mann, *Branch Rickey: American in Action,* 35. For more on Garry Herrmann, see John Succoman's chapter in Simon, ed., *Deadball Stars of the National League.*

37. Mann, *Branch Rickey: American in Action,* 37.

38. Branch Rickey to his parents, September 1, 1904, Branch Rickey Papers, Library of Congress, Washington DC.

39. Polner, *Branch Rickey: A Biography,* 38–39.

40. Rice, "Thoughts on Baseball—II," 33.

41. Hanners, "Branch Rickey, College Football Coach," 292.

42. (Allegheny) *Campus,* October 5, 1904, 1 (accessed at Allegheny College library, Meadville PA).

43. (Allegheny) *Campus,* October 6, 1904, 1.

44. (Allegheny) *Campus,* October 12, 1904, 1.

45. (Allegheny) *Campus,* December 7, 1904, 1.

46. (Meadville) *Daily Republican Tribune,* November 7, 1904, 1.

47. Updated records courtesy of Bill Salyer, sports information director, Allegheny College, e-mail to the author, July 2006.

48. Rickey with Riger, *The American Diamond,* 20.

49. Steinberg, *Baseball in St. Louis,* 14.

50. "St. Louis Browns under Hedges . . .," *Sporting News,* December 30, 1915, 2.

51. Steinberg, *Baseball in St. Louis,* 13.

52. Mann, *Branch Rickey: American in Action,* 40.

53. Mann, *Branch Rickey: American in Action,* 41.

54. Mann, *Branch Rickey: American in Action,* 41.

55. Lucas and Smith, *Saga of American Sport,* 242–43; see also Hanners, "Branch Rickey, College Football Coach," 297 n26.

56. Lucas and Smith, *Saga of American Sport,* 287.

57. Branch Rickey to Ray F. Turner, January 12, 1956, Branch Rickey Papers, Library of Congress, Washington DC.

58. (Allegheny) *Campus,* October 10, 1905, 3. "Sam Hill" is a eupheuism for hell.

59. Hanners, "Branch Rickey, College Football Coach," 296–97.

60. Branch Rickey to Alan Rinzler, Simon and Schuster editor, June 21, 1963, Branch Rickey Papers, Library of Congress, Washington DC.

61. (Allegheny) *Campus,* May 1, 1906, 1.

62. Branch Rickey to his parents, March 4, 1906, Branch Rickey Papers, Library of Congress, Washington DC.

63. E-mail to the author from Nancy Rickey Keltner, May 2005.

64. Full text is in (Allegheny) *Campus,* May 22, 1906, 3; partial text is in Polner, *Branch Rickey: A Biography,* 42.

65. Polner, *Branch Rickey: A Biography,* 43.

66. "Baseball Babble," *St. Louis Post-Dispatch,* June 2, 1906, 6.

2. From Catcher to Coach

1. Mann, *Branch Rickey: American in Action,* 48.

2. Richard D. Miller, "Branch Rickey at Ohio Wesleyan College—Prelude to Greatness," (unpublished paper, Society for American Baseball Research, national conference no. 25, Pittsburgh, 1995).

3. John Lardner, "Speaking of Rickey," *Newsweek*, December 9, 1957, 93; see also Mann, *Branch Rickey: American in Action*, 48.

4. Polner, *Branch Rickey: A Biography*, 45.

5. *Washington Post*, June 29, 1907, 10.

6. Raymond Spahr to Branch Rickey, October 30, 1942, Branch Rickey Papers, Library of Congress, Washington DC. "Muckers" in early-twentieth-century usage meant idlers, or people who would not work.

7. Mann, *Branch Rickey: American in Action*, 53.

8. Mann, *Branch Rickey: American in Action*, 7.

9. Polner, *Branch Rickey: A Biography*, 4–5.

10. "Recollections and Reminiscences of Herman M. Shipps," unpublished speech, Branch Rickey file, Ohio Wesleyan University Beeghly Library, Delaware OH; see also *Delaware (Ohio) Gazette*, December 14, 1965, 6, and a March 1966 reminiscence by C. E. Persons, also at the Beeghly Library.

11. Mann, *Branch Rickey: American in Action*, 53.

12. Gertrude Hopping to Robert Haig, September 28, 1908, and October 5, 1908, Branch Rickey Papers, Library of Congress, Washington DC.

13. Ellison, *Healing Tuberculosis in the Woods*, 1, 11, 25.

14. Polner, *Branch Rickey: A Biography*, 49; Hubbart, *Ohio Wesleyan's First Hundred Years*, 111.

15. Hallock and Turner, *Health Heroes*, 31

16. Ellison, *Healing Tuberculosis in the Woods*, 48.

17. R. Taylor, *Saranac*, 131.

18. Gertrude Hopping to Robert Haig, March 15, April 6, and April 14, 1909, Branch Rickey Papers, Library of Congress, Washington DC.

19. Gertrude Hopping to Robert Haig, May 18, 1909, Branch Rickey Papers.

20. *New York Times*, May 19, 1909, 10.

21. Gertrude Hopping to Robert Haig, June 15, 1909, Branch Rickey Papers, Branch Rickey Papers, Library of Congress, Washington DC.

22. Mooney, *In the Shadow of the White Plague*, 140.

23. Mooney, *In the Shadow of the White Plague*, 68.

24. Mooney, *In the Shadow of the White Plague*, 33, 28, 39.

25. Mooney, *In the Shadow of the White Plague*, 41–42.

26. Mann, *Branch Rickey: American in Action*, 55.

27. Mooney, *In the Shadow of the White Plague*, 171.

28. Michael Rosenberg, "Yost Built Michigan to Reflect His Image," *Detroit Free Press*, October 21, 1999.

29. Branch Rickey to Jane Rickey, October 17, 1909, Branch Rickey Papers, Library of Congress, Washington DC.

30. Sports information department, Ohio Wesleyan University, http://bishops.owu.edu.

31. Lucas and Smith, *Saga of American Sport*, 294.

32. Mann, *Branch Rickey: American in Action*, 57.

33. Branch Rickey to "folks" (his parents), January 13, 1910, Branch Rickey Papers, Library of Congress, Washington DC, emphasis in original.

34. Lipman, *Mr. Baseball,* 49.

35. Mann, "The Life of Branch Rickey—I," 80.

36. Rice, "Thoughts on Baseball—II," 38.

37. Noguchi, "The Residue of Design," 17.

38. Stevens, "As the Branch Is Bent," 281.

39. Stevens, "As the Branch Is Bent," 281.

40. Rosenberg, "Yost Built Michigan to Reflect His Image."

41. Mann, "The Life of Branch Rickey—I," 80.

42. Lipman, *Mr. Baseball,* 51.

43. Rickey with Riger, *The American Diamond,* 14.

44. Rickey with Riger, *The American Diamond,* 14.

45. Huhn, *The Sizzler,* 4–11.

46. Huhn, *The Sizzler,* 21–24.

47. Polner, *Branch Rickey: A Biography,* 57.

48. Mann, *Branch Rickey: American in Action,* 64–65.

49. Huhn, *The Sizzler,* 24.

50. Huhn, *The Sizzler,* 24–25.

51. Adler, *Baseball at the University of Michigan,* 35; see also 47 and 49.

3. Branch Rickey and the St. Louis Browns

1. Mann, *Branch Rickey: American in Action,* 65.

2. Lieb, *The St. Louis Cardinals: The Story of a Great Baseball Club,* 158.

3. Edgar Brands, "Barrett Tops All Major Scouts in Service," *Sporting News,* January 24, 1935, 5, 6. There are conflicting reports on the occupation of Charley Barrett's father. Brands mentions that his father was a fireman, but some other sources indicate that he was a streetcar conductor. The elder Barrett might have served in both capacities. See also "King of the Weeds," *Sporting News,* January 6, 1927.

4. Steinberg, *Baseball in St. Louis,* 13.

5. Mann, *Branch Rickey: American in Action,* 70; Fetter, *Taking On the Yankees,* 125–26; Andersen, "Branch Rickey and the St. Louis Cardinal Farm System," 7–12.

6. Mann, *Branch Rickey: American in Action,* 71; *Sporting News,* November 20, 1913.

7. Golenbock, *The Spirit of St. Louis,* 63–64; Steinberg, *Baseball in St. Louis,* 53.

8. *Sporting Life,* September 20, 1913.

9. *St. Louis Times,* September 8, 1913. Thanks to Steve Steinberg for the clippings in this and the previous note.

10. *Sporting Life,* September 20, 1913; Lipman, *Mr. Baseball,* 57.

11. See chapter 6 on Jimmy Austin in Lawrence S. Ritter's classic oral history, *The Glory of Their Times,* 78–90.

12. Butterfield, "Brooklyn's Gentleman Bum," 86.

13. Gough, *Burt Shotton, Dodgers Manager,* 25.

14. Steinberg, *Baseball in St. Louis,* 67, 29; *Sporting News,* October 23, 1913.

15. *Sporting News,* October 16, 1913, 4.

16. Seymour, *Baseball,* 202.

17. Okkonen, *The Federal League of 1914–1915,* 4, 12, 63.

18. Karst and Jones, *Who's Who in Professional Baseball,* 44.

19. *Sporting News,* January 15, 1914.

20. Hunt Stromberg, "Manager Plans Many Innovations," *Sporting News,* January 1, 1914, 5.

21. Stromberg, "Manager Plans Many Innovations."

22. Stromberg, "Manager Plans Many Innovations."

23. W. J. O'Connor, "Rickey Disagrees with Huggins' Method of Managing Major League Baseball Clubs," *St. Louis Post-Dispatch,* December 12, 1913, pt. 4, 1S; see also Mann, *Branch Rickey: American in Action,* 74.

24. O'Connor, "Rickey Disagrees with Huggins' Method"; see also Mann, *Branch Rickey: American in Action,* 75–76.

25. Biemiller, "Florida's Baseball Riviera," 67. Thanks to Donald Hughes for calling my attention to this article.

26. Mann, *Baseball Confidential,* 79; see also Andersen, "Branch Rickey and the St. Louis Cardinal Farm System," 50–51, and Barney, *Thank Youuuu,* 49–50.

27. Steinberg, *Baseball in St. Louis,* 63.

28. Billy Evans, "The Somewhat Different Manager," *Harpers Weekly,* August 27, 1914, 187. Evans may have also played baseball at Ohio Wesleyan under Branch Rickey. See "Introducing Branch Rickey," (Ohio Wesleyan) *Bulletin,* special edition, March 1938.

29. Evans, "The Somewhat Different Manager," 187.

30. "Branch Rickey Discovers the Quality That Makes a Ballplayer Great," in Safire, ed., *Lend Me Your Ears: Great Speeches in History,* 485–87.

31. Hoke, "The Base in Baseball." Thanks to Evelyn Begley for sharing this article.

32. Schwarz, *The Numbers Game,* 56.

33. *Total Baseball,* 106.

34. *Total Baseball,* 106.

35. *Sporting News,* January 28, 1915, 5.

36. Pietrusza, *Judge and Jury,* 155–56.

37. Lowenfish and Lupien, *The Imperfect Diamond,* 90.

38. Pietrusza, *Judge and Jury,* 156.

39. Seymour, *Baseball,* 216.

40. *Sporting News,* August 14, 1915, 6.

41. *Sporting News,* August 14, 1915, 6.

42. Huhn, *The Sizzler,* 40.

43. Huhn, *The Sizzler,* 45–46.

44. Murdock, *Ban Johnson,* 163. See also *Sporting News,* June 16, 1916, 6, and Bernstein, "George Sisler and the End of the National Commission," 95.

45. Rickey with Riger, *The American Diamond,* 20.

46. *St. Louis Post-Dispatch,* July 4, 1915.

47. Huhn, *The Sizzler,* 5.

48. *Total Baseball,* 106.

49. *Total Baseball,* 106.

50. *Sporting News,* December 30, 1915, 3; Steinberg, *Baseball in St. Louis,* 12.

51. Mann, *Branch Rickey: American in Action,* 84.

52. Mann, *Branch Rickey: American in Action,* 86; Peter Kihss, obituary for Roscoe Hillenkoetter, *New York Times,* June 21, 1982, D9.

53. Branch Rickey to George Williams, December 27, 1916, in George Williams Papers, Missouri Historical Society, St. Louis.

54. Huhn, *The Sizzler*, 58.

55. Branch Rickey to George Williams, December 27, 1916.

56. Steinberg, *Baseball in St. Louis*, 73. For more on Mrs. Britton, see the chapter on her in Boxerman and Boxerman, *Ebbets to Veeck to Busch*.

57. John Sheridan, "The Gentle Art of Getting Along," *Fort Wayne Sentinel*, August 15, 1917.

58. Mann, *Branch Rickey: American in Action*, 90.

59. Willis Johnson, *Sporting News*, unpublished article, November 1951. Thanks to Steve Gietschier, *Sporting News* archivist and baseball historian, for sharing this clipping.

4. "War Overshadows Everything"

1. Honig, *The St. Louis Cardinals: An Illustrated History*, 28; Rains, *The St. Louis Cardinals: The 100th Anniversary History*, 19.

2. *St. Louis Post-Dispatch*, March 15, 1917, 8; Steinberg, *Baseball in St. Louis*, 85.

3. *St. Louis Post-Dispatch*, April 4, 1917.

4. Golenbock, *The Spirit of St. Louis*, 83.

5. W. J. O'Connor, *St. Louis Post-Dispatch*, June 26, 1917, 11.

6. John E. Wray, "Sleuths in Plain Clothes to Save Umps from Pop Bottles," *St. Louis Post-Dispatch*, August 1, 1917, 11.

7. Wray, "Sleuths in Plain Clothes to Save Umps," 11.

8. *Total Baseball*, 106.

9. Karst and Jones, *Who's Who in Professional Baseball*, 660; see also Meadows, "How Lee Meadows Rose Above All Handicaps to Become a Star," 310.

10. *St. Louis Post-Dispatch*, August 12, 1917.

11. Lieb, *The St. Louis Cardinals: The Story of a Great Baseball Club*, 69; Rains, *The St. Louis Cardinals: The 100th Anniversary History*, 20.

12. *St. Louis Post-Dispatch*, December 15, 1917; John E. Wray, "Rickey Will Not Buy Release of Jack Hendricks," *St. Louis Post-Dispatch*, December 6, 1917, 12.

13. Photo in *St. Louis Post-Dispatch*, December 30, 1917, 12.

14. "Weeghman Verbally Pounded by Rickey for Offers to Hornsby," *New York Times*, February 14, 1918, 13.

15. *St. Louis Post-Dispatch*, April 1, 1918, 18 (capitals in original).

16. John E. Wray, *St. Louis Post-Dispatch*, February 18, 1918, 14.

17. Edgar Brands, "Barrett Tops All Major Scouts in Service," *Sporting News*, January 24, 1935, 6.

18. *St. Louis Post-Dispatch*, February 3, 1918, 11.

19. John E. Wray, *St. Louis Post-Dispatch*, March 1, 1918, 18.

20. C. Alexander, *Rogers Hornsby: A Biography*, 3.

21. *St. Louis Post-Dispatch*, March 14, 1918, 20.

22. *St. Louis Post-Dispatch*, April 28, 1918, 10.

23. C. Alexander, *Rogers Hornsby: A Biography*, 47.

24. *St. Louis Post-Dispatch*, May 26, 1918.

25. *Total Baseball*, 106.

26. Austin McHenry file, National Baseball Hall of Fame Library, Cooperstown NY.

27. C. Alexander, *Rogers Hornsby: A Biography*, 45.

28. Seymour, *Baseball*, 262–63; see also Bernstein, "George Sisler and the End of the National Commission," 96.

29. *St. Louis Post-Dispatch*, August 2, 1918, 14.

30. Seymour, *Baseball*, 252.

31. Mann, *Branch Rickey: American in Action*, 96.

32. C. Alexander, *Rogers Hornsby: A Biography*, 46.

33. Interview with Christine Jones (Branch Rickey's granddaughter), New York City, November 2000; Polner, *Branch Rickey: A Biography*, 77.

34. Mann, *Branch Rickey: American in Action*, 95.

35. U.S. War Department to Branch Rickey, August 27, 1918, Branch Rickey Papers, Library of Congress, Washington DC.

36. Sisler, "Why I Enlisted in the Army." Thanks to Sisler biographer Rick Huhn for sharing this article.

37. Mann, *Branch Rickey: American in Action*, 97.

38. Lipman, *Mr. Baseball*, 75.

39. Mann, *Branch Rickey: American in Action*, 97. See also Langer, *Gas and Flame in World War I*, 83–93.

40. Rickey with Riger, *The American Diamond*, 18–19.

41. Mann, *Branch Rickey: American in Action*, 97–98.

42. Mann, *Branch Rickey: American in Action*, 90.

5. Necessity Is the Mother of Invention

1. Harold Parrott, *This Week*, Sunday newspaper supplement, *New York Herald Tribune*, August 31, 1941, 6

2. Andersen, "Branch Rickey and the St. Louis Cardinal Farm System," 70.

3. *St. Louis Globe-Democrat*, February 27, 1919, 2.

4. Burk, *Never Just a Game*, 230; see also Steinberg, *Baseball in St. Louis*, 66.

5. Steinberg, *Baseball in St. Louis*, 62.

6. Allen, *The National League Story*, 140.

7. D'Amore, *Rogers Hornsby*, 53.

8. Interview with the late J. Rex Bowen, New Smyrna Beach FL, March 2000.

9. Golenbock, *The Spirit of St. Louis*, 92–93.

10. Honig, *Baseball When the Grass Was Real*, 179.

11. *Total Baseball*, 106.

12. Burk, *Never Just a Game*, 225.

13. McGee, *The Greatest Ballpark Ever*, 90; Dewey and Acocella, *Biographical Dictionary of Baseball*, 450.

14. Lieb, *The St. Louis Cardinals: The Story of a Great Baseball Club*, 94.

15. Golenbock, *The Spirit of St. Louis*, 85.

16. Stockton, *The Gashouse Gang and a Couple of Other Guys*, 14.

17. Andersen, "Branch Rickey and the St. Louis Cardinal Farm System," 62.

18. Mann, *Branch Rickey: American in Action*, 105–6.

19. Broeg, *The Pilot Light and the Gashouse Gang*, 71.

20. Golenbock, *The Spirit of St. Louis*, 93.

21. Broeg, *Redbirds!*, 33.

22. Mann, *Branch Rickey: American in Action*, 143. See also Ward, "Here's an Outfielder Who Always Hustles," 340.

23. Broeg, *Redbirds!*, 85.

24. *St. Louis Post-Dispatch,* January 12, 1920, B1.

25. Lieb, *The St. Louis Cardinals: The Story of a Great Baseball Club,* 73.

26. Rains, *The St. Louis Cardinals: The 100th Anniversary History,* 28.

27. Stockton, "Singing Sam, the Cut-rate Man," 134.

28. Stockton, "Singing Sam, the Cut-rate Man," 132.

29. Lieb, *The St. Louis Cardinals: The Story of a Great Baseball Club,* 75–76.

30. Lieb, *The St. Louis Cardinals: The Story of a Great Baseball Club,* 78–79.

31. Lieb, *The St. Louis Cardinals: The Story of a Great Baseball Club,* 78.

32. Andersen, "Branch Rickey and the St. Louis Cardinal Farm System," 83.

33. Mann, *Branch Rickey: American in Action,* 110.

34. Andersen, "Branch Rickey and the St. Louis Cardinal Farm System," 98.

35. Lieb, *The St. Louis Cardinals: The Story of a Great Baseball Club,* 76–77.

36. Lieb, *The St. Louis Cardinals: The Story of a Great Baseball Club,* 77.

37. Golenbock, *The Spirit of St. Louis,* 90.

38. Mann, *Branch Rickey: American in Action,* 108.

39. Mann, *Branch Rickey: American in Action,* 111.

40. Allen, *The National League Story,* 183.

41. Ward, "A Big League Pitcher Who Came Back," 428.

42. *Total Baseball,* 106.

43. *Total Baseball,* 106.

44. Holway, *The Complete Book of Baseball's Negro Leagues,* 467. See also Dixon with Hannigan, *The Negro Baseball Leagues,* 16–17, and C. Alexander, *Rogers Hornsby: A Biography,* 62.

45. C. Alexander, *Rogers Hornsby: A Biography,* 64.

46. Polner, *Branch Rickey: A Biography,* 79–80.

6. Years of Contention and Frustration

1. Pietrusza, *Judge and Jury,* 345.

2. Pietrusza, *Judge and Jury,* 347.

3. Seymour, *Baseball,* 406–7.

4. Andersen, "Branch Rickey and the St. Louis Cardinal Farm System," 139. See also Graham Jr., "Branch Rickey Rides Again," 66.

5. *Total Baseball,* 106–7.

6. *St. Louis Post-Dispatch,* February 25, 1922; "Pickles Dillhoefer," http://www .baseballlibrary.com/baseballlibrary/ballplayers/D/Dillhoefer_Pickles.stm.

7. *St. Louis Post-Dispatch,* February 28, 1922.

8. Hood, *The Gashouse Gang,* 29.

9. Picture in Broeg, *The Pilot Light and the Gashouse Gang,* 69.

10. J. Roy Stockton, *St. Louis Post-Dispatch,* March 16, 1922.

11. *Lima (Ohio) News,* December 1, 1922, 29.

12. *St. Louis Post-Dispatch,* November 30, 1922.

13. Austin McHenry file, National Baseball Hall of Fame Library, Cooperstown NY.

14. *St. Louis Post-Dispatch,* November 30, 1922.

15. Phone interview with sportswriter Bob Broeg, August 2002.

16. Eisenbath, *The St. Louis Cardinals Encyclopedia,* 36.

17. *St. Louis Post-Dispatch,* July 27, 1922.

18. Lieb, *The St. Louis Cardinals: The Story of a Great Baseball Club,* 96.

19. John Lardner, "That Was Baseball," 148; see also Clark, *One Last Round for the Shuffler,* 76.

20. *St. Louis Post-Dispatch,* August 19, 1922.

21. Lardner, "That Was Baseball," 148.

22. Lardner, "That Was Baseball," 149.

23. *New York Times,* August 17, 1922.

24. Huhn, *The Sizzler,* 140–42.

25. *Total Baseball,* 106–7.

26. *St. Louis Globe-Democrat,* November 23, 1922.

27. Lieb, *The St. Louis Cardinals: The Story of a Great Baseball Club,* 79.

28. Mann, *Branch Rickey: American in Action,* 121.

29. Parrott, *The Lords of Baseball,* 188.

30. Andersen, "Branch Rickey and the St. Louis Cardinal Farm System," 38.

31. Lieb, *The St. Louis Cardinals: The Story of a Great Baseball Club,* 99.

32. L. H. Addington, "The Man Who Lives for Work," *Sporting News,* January 31, 1929.

33. Rains, *The St. Louis Cardinals: The 100th Anniversary History,* 49; James, *The New Bill James Historical Abstract,* 691.

34. "The 'Goat' of the Series," 604.

35. James Isaminger, *Sporting News,* April 5, 1923, 5.

36. Frank Graham, *New York Journal-American,* April 25, 1952, clipping in Fred Toney file, National Baseball Hall of Fame Library, Cooperstown NY. In an interesting sidelight, when he was a member of the Giants, Toney lived for a while in the same Manhattan apartment building as former Cardinals catcher Frank "Pancho" Snyder and the ill-fated Phil Douglas. Clark, *One Last Round for the Shuffler,* 53.

37. *St. Louis Post-Dispatch,* April 11, 1918, 26; *New York World,* December 24, 1917, 17, clipping in Fred Toney file, National Baseball Hall of Fame Library, Cooperstown NY.

38. John B. Sheridan, *Sporting News,* February 22, 1923, 4.

39. Mann, *Branch Rickey: American in Action,* 122.

40. C. Alexander, *Rogers Hornsby: A Biography,* 70; Eisenbath, *The St. Louis Cardinals Encyclopedia,* 9.

41. Karst and Jones, *Who's Who in Professional Baseball,* 867.

42. *Baseball,* April 1925, 499.

43. D'Amore, *Rogers Hornsby,* 46.

44. Phone interview, Bob Broeg, August 2002.

45. C. Alexander, *Rogers Hornsby: A Biography,* 81.

46. "Open Dates Have to Be Filled Some Way," *Sporting News,* September 20, 1923, 1.

47. C. Alexander, *Rogers Hornsby: A Biography,* 81.

48. *St. Louis Post-Dispatch,* September 15, 1923.

49. Joseph Holland, *St. Louis Post-Dispatch,* September 28, 1923, 19.

50. John E. Wray, *St. Louis Post-Dispatch,* September 30, 1923, 2B.

51. *Total Baseball,* 106.

52. Butterfield, "Brooklyn's Gentleman Bum," 83; see also Shotton, "The Batting Order," 297–98.

53. *Total Baseball,* 106.

54. Stockton, "Singing Sam, the Cut-rate Man," 137.

55. Andersen, "Branch Rickey and the St. Louis Cardinal Farm System," 89.

56. Lieb, *The St. Louis Cardinals: The Story of a Great Baseball Club*, 107.

57. Frank Ruppenthal to Branch Rickey, n.d., Branch Rickey Papers, Library of Congress, Washington DC.

58. Interviews with Jane Rickey Jones, Elmira NY, August 1999, and Mary Rickey Eckler, Sebastapol CA, August 2000.

59. Interview with Julia Rickey Peebles, Ohio Wesleyan University, Delaware OH, October 1999.

60. *New York Times*, July 25, 1923, 15; see also Einstein, *Prohibition Agent Number One*.

61. *New York Times*, April 25, 1925, 5.

62. Interviews with Jamie and Julia Rickey Peebles, Ohio Wesleyan University, Delaware OH, October 1999.

63. Interview, Julia Rickey Peebles, October 1999.

64. Frank Wanzer Rickey's new position was acknowledged in a letter that an Ohio district prohibition officer wrote the main office in Washington DC in March 1926. "Mr. Rickey has resigned to accept a much better position than that he now holds," the local official explained. The agent went on to praise Frank Wanzer Rickey as "one of the most loyal, devoted and painstaking officers with whom I have come in contact," adding ruefully, "It is impossible to retain such men in the service these days at the salaries they are getting for their work." I am indebted to Julia Rickey Peebles for sharing this document and her story.

65. J. G. Taylor Spink, *Sporting News*, March 11, 1943, 8; Sid Mercer, *New York Journal-American*, February 25, 1943.

66. Broeg and Miller, *Baseball from a Different Angle*, 185.

7. That Championship Season

1. Lieb, *The St. Louis Cardinals: The Story of a Great Baseball Club*, 110; Devaney, *The Greatest Cardinals of Them All*, 37; C. Alexander, *Rogers Hornsby: A Biography*, 108–9.

2. C. Alexander, *Rogers Hornsby: A Biography*, 109–10.

3. "Where Did Rickey Dig Them All Up?" *Sporting News*, March 31, 1927, 6.

4. Polner, *Branch Rickey: A Biography*, 105. See also Ward, "Lee Douthit," 3. A collision with Chick Hafey in the 1926 World Series caused Douthit to miss the last three games.

5. Charles Chapman to Branch Rickey, March 10, 1921, Branch Rickey Papers, Library of Congress, Washington DC.

6. Bill Bryson, "There's Nobody like 'Em," 549; Edgar Brands, *Sporting News*, January 17, 1935, 6.

7. Lieb, *The St. Louis Cardinals: The Story of a Great Baseball Club*, 100; obituary for Howard Freigau, *New York Times*, July 19, 1932.

8. Broeg, *Redbirds!*, 36; Skipper, *Wicked Curve*, 2.

9. C. Alexander, *Rogers Hornsby: A Biography*, 112.

10. Lieb, *The St. Louis Cardinals: The Story of a Great Baseball Club*, 113.

11. Lieb, *The St. Louis Cardinals: The Story of a Great Baseball Club*, 126.

12. C. Alexander, *Rogers Hornsby: A Biography*, 114; phone interview with Bob Broeg, August 2002.

13. C. Alexander, *Rogers Hornsby: A Biography*, 114.

14. Lieb, *The St. Louis Cardinals: The Story of a Great Baseball Club*, 116.

15. *St. Louis Post-Dispatch*, September 25, 1926.

16. *St. Louis Post-Dispatch*, September 30, 1926.

17. C. Alexander, *Rogers Hornsby: A Biography*, 116.

18. *Sporting News*, October 4, 1926.

19. *New York Times*, October 3, 1926, 1.

20. Rains, *The St. Louis Cardinals: The 100th Anniversary History*, 39.

21. C. Alexander, *Rogers Hornsby: A Biography*, 117.

22. "Train Record Beat by Nearly Three Hours," *New York Times*, October 9, 1926, 11.

23. J. Roy Stockton, *St. Louis Post-Dispatch*, October 17, 1926, 5B.

24. Lieb, *The St. Louis Cardinals: The Story of a Great Baseball Club*, 125.

25. *New York Times*, October 11, 1926, 1.

26. Quoted in Noguchi, "The Residue of Design," 130.

27. "How Old Is Alexander?" *St. Louis Post-Dispatch*, October 11, 1926, 18.

28. J. Roy Stockton, "Winning the Series in Advance," *Sporting News*, November 25, 1926, 5.

29. Reisler, ed., *Guys, Dolls, and Curveballs*, 408.

30. Karst, *Who's Who in Professional Baseball*, 52.

31. *St. Louis Globe-Democrat*, October 19, 1926.

32. C. Alexander, *Rogers Hornsby: A Biography*, 123–24.

33. Golenbock, *The Spirit of St. Louis*, 122–23.

34. Heywood Broun, *Literary Digest*, February 25, 1928, 58.

35. C. Alexander, *Rogers Hornsby: A Biography*, 125.

36. C. Alexander, *Rogers Hornsby: A Biography*, 127.

37. Seymour, *Baseball*, 385.

38. Frisch as told to Stockton, *Frank Frisch*, 57.

8. The Near-dynastic Years and a Place in *Who's Who*

1. Eisenbath, *The St. Louis Cardinals Encyclopedia*, 209.

2. *New York Times*, December 28, 1926, 14.

3. Graham, *The New York Giants*, 171.

4. Graham, *The New York Giants*, 171.

5. D'Amore, *Rogers Hornsby*, 82–83.

6. *Total Baseball*, 106.

7. Broeg, *The 100 Greatest Moments in St. Louis Sports*, 36.

8. Lieb, *The St. Louis Cardinals: The Story of a Great Baseball Club*, 131.

9. Broeg, *The 100 Greatest Moments in St. Louis Sports*, 36.

10. *St. Louis Post-Dispatch*, June 19, 1927, 1.

11. Maranville, *Run, Rabbit, Run*, 65–67; see also Gould, "Considering the Cardinals," 541.

12. *St. Louis Post-Dispatch*, September 30, 1927, 1; Broeg, *The Pilot Light and the Gashouse Gang*, 69.

13. Lieb, *The St. Louis Cardinals: The Story of a Great Baseball Club*, 131.

14. *Total Baseball*, 107.

15. Reverend Franklin Cole, radio speech, "Eliminating the Circle of Worry," December 1947, in which Rickey is cited for the study of history as a way to keep present losses in perspective. Branch Rickey Papers, Library of Congress, Washington DC.

16. Conversation with Rickey biographer Murray Polner, New York City, September 2004.

17. Andersen, "Branch Rickey and the St. Louis Cardinal Farm System," 113.

18. Broeg and Miller, *Baseball from a Different Angle*, 71.

19. Maury White, *Des Moines Register*, April 12, 1987, quotes Forrest Twogood.

20. Lieb, *The St. Louis Cardinals: The Story of a Great Baseball Club*, 83.

21. Mann, *Branch Rickey: American in Action*, 127–28; e-mail to the author from Donald Hughes (Donald Beach's grandson and Branch Rickey's grandson-in-law), May 2005.

22. Polner, *Branch Rickey: A Biography*, 112; *Sporting News*, March 22, 1923, 5.

23. Polner, *Branch Rickey: A Biography*, 95; phone interview with Bob Broeg, August 2002.

24. *Total Baseball*, 107.

25. Lieb, *The St. Louis Cardinals: The Story of a Great Baseball Club*, 133.

26. Eisenbath, *The St. Louis Cardinals Encyclopedia*, 176; obituary for Taylor Douthit, *New York Times*, June 1, 1986.

27. Broeg and Miller, *Baseball from a Different Angle*, 33.

28. *St. Louis Post-Dispatch*, September 21, 25, and 27, 1928.

29. Lieb, *The St. Louis Cardinals: The Story of a Great Baseball Club*, 138.

30. *Optimist Magazine*, c. 1963, 2.

31. See http://www.mckendree.edu.

32. Herbert Hoover, "The American System," October 1928 campaign speech, reprinted in Horwitz, ed., *The American Studies Anthology*, 193–98.

33. Barry, *Rising Tide*, 262–75.

34. Charnley, *The Boy's Life of Herbert Hoover*, 114.

35. Hoover, *On Growing Up*, 91, 29.

36. Mann, *Branch Rickey: American in Action*, 136–37.

37. Polner, *Branch Rickey: A Biography*, 95–96.

38. Interview with Jane Rickey Jones, Elmira NY, August 1999.

39. Interview with Richard Moulton (Branch Rickey's grandnephew), Pittsburgh, July 2004.

40. Dexter, "The Mahatma and the Lip," 63.

41. Dexter, "The Mahatma and the Lip," 63.

42. Interview, Jane Rickey Jones, August 1999.

43. Lieb, *The St. Louis Cardinals: The Story of a Great Baseball Club*, 139.

44. Rickey with Riger, *The American Diamond*, 55.

45. Lieb, *The St. Louis Cardinals: The Story of a Great Baseball Club*, 140.

46. Golenbock, *The Spirit of St. Louis*, 127.

47. Seymour, *Baseball*, 138.

48. *Total Baseball*, 107.

49. Lieb, *The St. Louis Cardinals: The Story of a Great Baseball Club*, 141.

50. Mann, *Branch Rickey: American in Action*, 157.

51. Mead, *Two Spectacular Seasons*, 77.

52. Mead, *Two Spectacular Seasons*, 74.

53. Mead, *Two Spectacular Seasons*, 98; Lieb, *The St. Louis Cardinals: The Story of a Great Baseball Club*, 145.

54. Lieb, *The St. Louis Cardinals: The Story of a Great Baseball Club*, 144–45.

55. Allen, *The Hot Stove League*, 38.

56. Lieb, *The St. Louis Cardinals: The Story of a Great Baseball Club*, 142.

57. Bryson, "There's Nobody like 'Em," 549.

58. Eisenbath, *The St. Louis Cardinals Encyclopedia*, 217.

59. *Total Baseball*, 106; Rabinowitz, "Thriving in Hard Times," 18.

60. Broeg, *The Pilot Light and the Gashouse Gang*, 92.

61. Lieb, *The St. Louis Cardinals: The Story of a Great Baseball Club*, 147.

62. Keith Kernan, "Interesting St. Louisans," *St. Louis Post-Dispatch*, Sunday magazine section, November 9, 1930.

63. L. H. Addington, "The Man Who Lives for Work," *Sporting News*, January 31, 1929.

64. Kieran, "Big League Baseball."

65. *Current Biography Yearbook*, 1943, 653.

66. *Who's Who in America*, 1865.

9. Another Championship Season and Then Decline

1. Kirkendall, *A History of Missouri*, 137.

2. *Total Baseball*, 107.

3. Mann, *Branch Rickey: American in Action*, 166.

4. Pietrusza, *Judge and Jury*, 348–49.

5. Warfield, *The Roaring Redhead*, 26–27.

6. McKelvey, *The MacPhails*, 8–9. See also a family memoir by Irwin Weil, son of Sidney Weil. I am grateful to Professor Weil of the Northwestern University Slavic Languages Department for sharing this document with me.

7. Warfield, *The Roaring Redhead*, 27.

8. Taylor, "Borough Defender—II," 20.

9. Karst, *Who's Who in Professional Baseball*, 612.

10. Karst, *Who's Who in Professional Baseball*, 612. See also Tygiel, *Past Time*, 95–96.

11. *Current Biography Yearbook*, 1945, 375–76.

12. Warfield, *The Roaring Redhead*, 27.

13. Tygiel, *Past Time*, 97; Warfield, *The Roaring Redhead*, 30.

14. Gene Karst to Branch Rickey, November 25, 1930, copy shared with the author by the late Gene Karst.

15. Gene Karst, e-mail to the author, October 14, 1998.

16. Joe Holleman, "A Man of Stature," *St. Louis Post-Dispatch*, May 6, 2001.

17. Gene Karst, e-mails to the author, August 17 and September 13, 1998. After leaving the Cardinals, Karst went to work for Larry MacPhail in Cincinnati in 1935. In the early 1940s he was publicity director for the Brooklyn Dodgers farm club in Montreal in the International League. After World War Two until his retirement, he was employed by the Voice of America. Karst died in St. Louis at age ninety-seven in June 2004.

18. Lieb, *The St. Louis Cardinals: The Story of a Great Baseball Club*, 158.

19. Mann, *Branch Rickey: American in Action*, 162.

20. Mann, *Branch Rickey: American in Action*, 163.

21. Mann, *Branch Rickey: American in Action*, 163.

22. Broeg, *The Pilot Light and the Gashouse Gang*, 119.

23. Broeg, *The Pilot Light and the Gashouse Gang*, 94.

24. Karst and Jones, *Who's Who in Professional Baseball*, 257.

25. Karst and Jones, *Who's Who in Professional Baseball*, 257.

26. Interview with Gene Karst, St. Louis, August 2000; see also Karst, "The Cardinals' First Publicity Man."

27. Pietrusza, *Judge and Jury*, 347; James, *The New Bill James Historical Abstract*, 813–14.

28. Mann, *Branch Rickey: American in Action*, 170.

29. *St. Louis Post-Dispatch*, October 2, 1931; Barthel, *Pepper Martin*, 48.

30. Hood, *The Gashouse Gang*, 170.

31. Karst, e-mail to the author, August 17, 1998.

32. For the Ossian Sweet case, see Boyle, *Arc of Justice*.

33. Polner, *Branch Rickey: A Biography*, unnumbered page before preface; interview with Betty Rickey Wolfe, New York City, November 2000.

34. Polner, *Branch Rickey: A Biography*, 81; Donald Hughes, e-mail to the author, June 2005.

35. Mead, *Two Spectacular Seasons*, 70.

36. "Hoover to Attend World Series Game," *New York Times*, September 30, 1931, 29; *New York Times*, October 4, 1932.

37. *St. Louis Post-Dispatch*, October 11, 1931.

38. *Guideposts*, February 1955, 16.

39. Barthel, *Pepper Martin*, 97.

40. *Sporting News*, December 31, 1931, 1.

41. *Total Baseball*, 107.

42. Rabinowitz, "Thriving in Hard Times," 18.

43. Lester Rice, *New York Journal-American*, February 16, 1948.

44. *St. Louis Post-Dispatch*, February 5, 1932; Broeg, *The Pilot Light and the Gashouse Gang*, 125.

45. Barthel, *Pepper Martin*, 106.

46. *Total Baseball*, 107.

47. Mead, *Two Spectacular Seasons*, 33; Rabinowitz, "Thriving in Hard Times," 19.

48. J. G. Taylor Spink, "'Three and One': Looking Them Over," *Sporting News*, November 22, 1934, 176.

49. Lieb, *The St. Louis Cardinals: The Story of a Great Baseball Club*, 161.

50. Pietrusza, *Judge and Jury*, 319.

51. Frisch as told to Stockton, *Frank Frisch*, 107.

10. Prelude to the Gashouse Gang

1. Family memoir by Irwin Weil, son of Sidney Weil.

2. Mann, *Branch Rickey: American in Action*, 175.

3. *Sporting News*, April 14, 1932, 1.

4. Shaplen, "The Nine Lives of Leo Durocher—I," 68.

5. Durocher with Linn, *Nice Guys Finish Last*, 46.

6. *New York Herald Tribune*, June 24, 1928; Mann, *Baseball Confidential*, 23

7. Shaplen, "The Nine Lives of Leo Durocher—I," 68.

8. Mann, *Baseball Confidential*, 23.

9. Eskenazi, *The Lip*, 46.

10. Eskenazi, *The Lip*, 69–70.

11. Shaplen, "The Nine Lives of Leo Durocher—I," 65.

12. Shaplen, "The Nine Lives of Leo Durocher—I," 66.

13. Shaplen, "The Nine Lives of Leo Durocher—I," 75.

14. Interview with the late Bill Turner, August 2001, Pittsburgh.

15. Karst, *Who's Who in Professional Baseball*, 240.

16. Details of the first encounter between Branch Rickey and Leo Durocher are drawn from Durocher with Linn, *Nice Guys Finish Last*, 76–79; Weil family memoir; and Mann, *Branch Rickey: American in Action*, 177–78.

17. Shaplen, "The Nine Lives of Leo Durocher—II," May 30, 1955, 67.

18. Eskenazi, *The Lip*, 38; Durocher with Linn, *Nice Guys Finish Last*, 40.

19. Broeg, *The Pilot Light and the Gashouse Gang*, 105.

20. *St. Louis Post-Dispatch*, June 7, 1933, B1; C. Smith, *America's Dizzy Dean*, 44.

21. Frisch as told to Stockton, *Frank Frisch*, 46.

22. C. Alexander, *Breaking the Slump*, 72–73.

23. *Total Baseball*, 107.

24. *Total Baseball*, 107; C. Alexander, *Breaking the Slump*, 77.

25. *Total Baseball*, 107.

26. C. Alexander, *Rogers Hornsby: A Biography*, 187–88.

27. Taylor, "Borough Defender—II," 22.

28. Broeg, *The Pilot Light and the Gashouse Gang*, 114.

29. Karst, *Who's Who in Professional Baseball*, 613.

30. Warfield, *The Roaring Redhead*, 32.

31. Mann, *Baseball Confidential*, 244.

32. Hood, *The Gashouse Gang*, 39; Fleming, *The Dizziest Season*, 53.

33. Fleming, *The Dizziest Season*, 53.

34. Martin J. Haley, *St. Louis Globe-Democrat*, February 27, 1934, 8A.

35. Fleming, *The Dizziest Season*, 40–41.

36. Broeg, *The Pilot Light and the Gashouse Gang*, 125.

11. The Triumph of the Gashouse Gang

1. Broeg, *The Pilot Light and the Gashouse Gang*, 120.

2. Fleming, *The Dizziest Season*, 54–55. See also Lane, "The Speed of 'The Fordham Flash,'" 312; and Frisch, "Why Player Oddities Have Their Place in Baseball," 552.

3. Fleming, *The Dizziest Season*, 43.

4. C. Smith, *America's Dizzy Dean*, 51.

5. White, *Creating the National Pastime*, 219.

6. Gregory, *Diz!*, 150.

7. Fleming, *The Dizziest Season*, 57–58.

8. Fleming, *The Dizziest Season*, 107.

9. Gregory, *Diz!*, 155; Hood, *The Gashouse Gang*, 89.

10. Fleming, *The Dizziest Season*, 200.

11. Fleming, *The Dizziest Season*, 206.

12. Frisch as told to Stockton, *The Fordham Flash*, 83. Broeg, *The Pilot Light and the Gashouse Gang*, 133, suggests that Dean called Frisch a tailor too.

13. Hood, *The Gashouse Gang*, 108.

14. Rains, *The St. Louis Cardinals: The 100th Anniversary History*, 73.

15. Golenbock, *The Spirit of St. Louis*, 174.

16. Pietrusza, *Judge and Jury*, 379.

17. Broeg, *Redbirds!*, 76.

18. Gregory, *Diz!*, 174.

19. Pietrusza, *Judge and Jury*, 379–80.

20. Martin Haley, *St. Louis Globe-Democrat*, August 14, 1934.

21. Interview with Jane Rickey Jones, New York City, August 2002.

22. The story of Branch Rickey as intermediary in Durocher's marriage is drawn primarily from Hood, *The Gashouse Gang*, 119, and Shaplen, "The Nine Lives of Leo Durocher—II," May 30, 1955, 64.

23. Eskenazi, *The Lip*, 75–76; Shaplen, "The Nine Lives of Leo Durocher—II," May 30, 1955, 64. See also "Grace Dozier Durocher Honored as a Woman of Achievement by Group Action Council," May 27, 1947, article courtesy of the University of Missouri–St. Louis Archive and Manuscript Division.

24. Hood, *The Gashouse Gang*, 119; Lieb, *The St. Louis Cardinals: The Story of a Great Baseball Club*, 170.

25. *St. Louis Post-Dispatch*, September 28, 1934; Broeg, *Redbirds!*, 127.

26. Harry T. Brundidge, *Sporting News*, February 4, 1932, 5; Jerry Ross, *Sporting News*, February 5, 1947, 7.

27. Feldmann, *Dizzy and the Gashouse Gang*, 131.

28. Rains, *The St. Louis Cardinals: The 100th Anniversary History*, 62, and Fleming, *The Dizziest Season*, 279, raise intriguing questions as to whether Dean actually won 30 in 1934 because of two disputed scorers' decisions that gave him victories.

29. Fleming, *The Dizziest Season*, 281.

30. Fleming, *The Dizziest Season*, 280.

31. *St. Louis Post-Dispatch*, September 30, 1934.

32. *St. Louis Post-Dispatch*, September 30, 1934.

33. *Total Baseball*, 107.

34. J. Roy Stockton, *St. Louis Post-Dispatch*, September 28, 1934.

35. Hood, *The Gashouse Gang*, 11.

36. Hood, *The Gashouse Gang*, sixth page of photos after 123.

37. Cartoon accompanying Tom Meany story, *New York World Telegram*, May 14, 1935; Durocher with Linn, *Nice Guys Finish Last*, 81–82; Eisenbath, *The St. Louis Cardinals Encyclopedia*, 47.

38. Broeg, *Redbirds!*, 116.

39. Hood, *The Gashouse Gang*, 68; Barthel, *Pepper Martin*, 145.

40. Feldmann, *Dizzy and the Gas House Gang*, 39; J. Roy Stockton, "Lord Medwick, of Carteret," *Saturday Evening Post*, March 5, 1938, 28.

41. Rickey with Riger, *The American Diamond*, 157.

42. Gregory, *Diz!*, 166–67; Fleming, *The Dizziest Season*, 200.

43. *Sporting News*, October 11, 1934, 1.

44. Feldmann, *Dizzy and the Gas House Gang*, 141, emphasis in original.

45. Golenbock, *The Spirit of St. Louis*, 189. Dean's words are captured on the soundtrack of the documentary *The Life and Times of Hank Greenberg*, directed by Aviva Kempner, 20th Century Fox, 1999.

46. Fleming, *The Dizziest Season*, 288; Stockton, *The Gashouse Gang and a Couple of Other Guys*, 59.

47. Hood, *The Gashouse Gang*, 129.

48. Staten, *Ol' Diz*, 145.

49. Fleming, *The Dizziest Season*, 300.

50. Broeg, *The 100 Greatest Moments in St. Louis Sports*, 73.

51. Interview with Charlie Gehringer, New York City, October 1986.

52. Umpire Harry Geisel may have been the man who suggested the removal of Medwick to Landis. *Sporting News*, October 25, 1934, 6.

53. Fleming, *The Dizziest Season*, 311.

54. Stockton, *The Gashouse Gang and a Couple of Other Guys*, 63–64; Pietrusza, *Judge and Jury*, 380.

55. Rabinowitz, "Thriving in Hard Times," 24.

56. *Sporting News*, September 27, 1934, 3.

57. J. Alexander, "Lew Wentz," 21, 78; obituary for Lew Wintz, *New York Times*, June 10, 1949, 27.

58. J. Alexander, "Lew Wentz," 81; J. G. Taylor Spink, "'Three and One': Looking Them Over," *Sporting News*, November 22, 1934.

59. "Lew Wentz Bids for Breadon's Championship Cardinals," *New York Times*, November 14, 1934, 26.

60. John E. Wray, *St. Louis Post-Dispatch*, November 16, 1934, 2E.

61. Gregory, *Diz!*, 180.

62. Dent McSkimming, *St. Louis Post-Dispatch*, November 16, 1934, 2E.

63. Lieb, *The St. Louis Cardinals: The Story of a Great Baseball Club*, 175.

64. Dick Farrington, *Sporting News*, November 22, 1934, 5.

65. Interview with Jane Rickey Jones, New York City, October 2001.

66. Branch Rickey to Lew Wentz, March 25, 1944, in Branch Rickey Papers, Library of Congress, Washington DC.

12. Years of Frustration

1. *Lima (Ohio) News*, June 8, 1935; phone interview with Julia Rickey Peebles (Branch Rickey's niece), July 2005.

2. Wilber, *For the Love of the Game*, 220.

3. Feldmann, *September Streak*, 55.

4. *New York Times*, April 29, 1935, 1.

5. Stockton, *The Gashouse Gang and a Couple of Other Guys*, 60–61.

6. C. Smith, *America's Dizzy Dean*, 93.

7. *Total Baseball*, 107.

8. Crichton, "Comeback," 16.

9. Interview with Jane Rickey Jones, New York City, December 2001.

10. Interviews with Jane Rickey Jones, New York City, December 2001, and Mary Rickey Eckler, Sebastopol CA, July 2000.

11. Interview with Mary Rickey Eckler, July 2000.

12. Stockton, *The Gashouse Gang and a Couple of Other Guys*, 66.

13. Stockton, *The Gashouse Gang and a Couple of Other Guys*, 66–67.

14. Staten, *Ol' Diz*, 312. Stockton, *The Gashouse Gang and a Couple of Other Guys*, 68, says that Dizzy's salary was $24,000 in 1936.

15. *New York Times*, April 2, 1936, 32.

16. Mead, "Robert Hyland," 96.

17. *Total Baseball*, 107.

18. Holmes, *Dodger Daze and Knights*, 177.

19. Branch Rickey, speech to Warrenton MO Republican district convention, December 1935, in Branch Rickey Papers, Library of Congress, Washington DC.

20. C. Alexander, *Breaking the Slump*, 131.

21. *Sporting News*, April 8, 1937, 1; see also C. Smith, *America's Dizzy Dean*, 22.

22. *Sporting News*, April 8, 1937, 1.

23. *Sporting News*, April 8, 1937, 1.

24. *Total Baseball*, 107.

25. C. Alexander, *Breaking the Slump*, 136–37.

26. Lieb, *The St. Louis Cardinals: The Story of a Great Baseball Club*, 182.

27. Broeg, *Redbirds!*, 83.

28. F. Lieb, *Sporting News*, July 15, 1937, 2.

29. *New York Times*, September 9, 1937, 28.

30. James, *The New Bill James Historical Abstract*, 159.

31. Edgar C. Brands, *Sporting News*, December 23, 1937, 5.

32. *Sporting News*, January 14, 1937, 3.

33. Burk, *Much More than a Game*, 50, gives the number of farm hands under Rickey's control in St. Louis as 743. Andersen, "Branch Rickey and the St. Louis Cardinal Farm System," 164, gives the number as 732.

34. Pietrusza, *Judge and Jury*, 361; James, *The New Bill James Historical Abstract*, 160.

35. Pietrusza, *Judge and Jury*, 362–64.

36. *New York Times*, March 23, 1938; Frisch with Stockton, *Frank Frisch*, 76.

37. *New York Herald Tribune*, March 13, 1938, III, 1.

38. Pietrusza, *Judge and Jury*, 365.

39. Spink, *Judge Landis and 25 Years of Baseball*, 202, gives the number freed by Landis as ninety-one. Pietrusza, *Judge and Jury*, 364, lists the number as seventy-four.

40. *St. Louis Post-Dispatch*, March 25, 1938.

41. Pietrusza, *Judge and Jury*, 366.

13. More Years of Loss

1. Interview with Jane Rickey Jones, Elmira NY, August 1999.

2. *Sporting News*, March 30, 1938. Martin's band had developed a big following in Minor League cities with Cardinal franchises. It featured "Fiddler" Bill McGee on violin and guitar (reportedly the best musician), Stanley "Frenchy" Bordagaray on washboard, Pepper Martin on harmonica and accordion, Lon Warneke on guitar, Bob Weiland on jug, and occasionally trainer Harrison "Bucko" Weaver on mandolin. Barthel, *Pepper Martin*, 137.

3. *New York Times*, December 21, 1937.

4. J. Roy Stockton, "Paul Dean Through, Branch Rickey Says," *St. Louis Post-Dispatch*, March 23, 1938.

5. Lester Rice, "Branch Debunks Legend of Piety," *New York Journal-American*, February 16, 1948 (part of a series).

6. Lipman, *Mr. Baseball*, 74.

7. Lieb, *The St. Louis Cardinals: The Story of a Great Baseball Club*, 184.

8. *St. Louis Post-Dispatch*, April 17, 1938.

9. *St. Louis Post-Dispatch*, April 17, 1938.

10. Polner, *Branch Rickey: A Biography*, 109.

11. *Total Baseball*, 107.

12. *Total Baseball*, 107.

13. Interview with Gene Karst, St. Louis, August 2000.

14. "Methodism Warmed"; *Christian Century*, May 25, 1938; *Time*, May 30, 1938, 58.

15. "Feller Receives School Diploma," *New York Times*, May 15, 1937, 12. In Feller's second start in the Major Leagues for Cleveland, in 1936, he tied Dizzy Dean's single-game strikeout record of 17. J. Roy Stockton, *Saturday Evening Post*, February 20, 1937, 12.

16. Rev. John Evans, "Methodism to Shift Gears to Face New Age," *Chicago Tribune*, February 5, 1938, 13.

17. List of attendees for Methodist meeting commemorating "the two-hundredth anniversary of the Aldergate heartwarming of John Wesley," Chicago, February 3 and 4, 1938, in Branch Rickey Papers, Library of Congress, Washington DC.

18. Wesley, "Thoughts on Slavery."

19. Interview with Mary Rickey Eckler, Sebastapol CA, July 2000; e-mails to the author from Rickey granddaughters Molly Eckler Emery, Jenne Eckler Pugh, and Nancy Rickey Keltner, May 2005.

20. Branch Rickey to Dr. Cameron Harmon, October 20, 1938, Branch Rickey Papers, Library of Congress, Washington DC.

21. Lieb, *The St. Louis Cardinals: The Story of a Great Baseball Club*, 186.

22. Broeg and Miller, *Baseball from a Different Angle*, 203.

23. Barthel, *Pepper Martin*, 154.

24. *St. Louis Post-Dispatch*, July 6, 1939.

25. Edgar C. Brands, *Sporting News*, January 24, 1935, 6.

26. *St. Louis Post-Dispatch*, July 8, 1939.

27. *Total Baseball*, 107.

28. *St. Louis Post-Dispatch*, September 18, 1939; August 21, 1939, 1.

29. *St. Louis Post-Dispatch*, September 27, 1939.

30. "The Amazing Larry MacPhail," 43.

31. Williams, "Deacon Bill."

32. *Sporting News*, January 4, 1940, 1. See also Noguchi, "The Residue of Design," 62.

33. John Lardner, *Lincoln (Nebraska) Evening Journal*, January 1, 1938.

34. Polner, *Branch Rickey: A Biography*, 115–16; e-mail to the author from Donald Hughes, May 2005.

35. Polner, *Branch Rickey: A Biography*, 116.

36. Rickey with Riger, *The American Diamond*, 166.

37. Stockton, "A Brain Comes to Brooklyn."

38. Polner, *Branch Rickey: A Biography*, 116.

39. *New York Times*, December 12, 1939, 27.

40. *New York Times*, July 22, 1940, 15.

14. Going Out on Top

1. Associated Press story in *Milwaukee Journal*, Sunday, March 31, 1940.

2. J. G. Taylor Spink, interview with Branch Rickey, *Sporting News*, May 30, 1941, 2.

3. J. Roy Stockton, *St. Louis Post-Dispatch*, June 4, 1940, 1B.

4. Barthel, *The Fierce Fun of Ducky Medwick*, 22.

5. Barthel, *The Fierce Fun of Ducky Medwick*, 12–13.

6. Broeg, *The Pilot Light and the Gashouse Gang*, 122–23.

7. "The Amazing MacPhail," 43.

8. Holmes, *Dodger Daze and Knights*, 153; Hood, *The Gashouse Gang*, 230.

9. Harold Parrott, *Sporting News*, May 22, 1941, 3.

10. Phone interview with Sam Nahem, May 2004.

11. Wilber, *For the Love of the Game*, 150–51.

12. Phone interview with Marty Marion, May 2002.

13. Interview, Marty Marion, May 2002.

14. "Just Chums," 16–17; see also *Time*, January 20, 1941, 20.

15. "Hawes Defeats Williams by 35,000 in Senate Race," *St. Louis Post-Dispatch*, November 3, 1926, 3.

16. "Just Chums," 16–17; see also *Time*, January 20, 1941, 20.

17. *St. Louis Post-Dispatch*, September 15, 1940, 7A; Dilliard, "Missouri Has No Governor," 183–84.

18. *St. Louis Post-Dispatch*, October 16, 1940, 6B.

19. Curtis Betts, *St. Louis Post-Dispatch*, November 3, 1941, pt. 6, 1.

20. Holland, "Mr. Rickey and the Game," 48. Campbell Titchener alludes to Rickey's role in Republican Missouri politics at this time without specifically mentioning his role in the Donnell gubernatorial campaign. Titchener, *The George Kirksey Story*, 239. Specific reference to the Donnell campaign can be found in a letter to Rickey's first biographer from a longtime Rickey baseball assistant. Mel Jones to Arthur Mann, July 27, 1955, Arthur Mann Papers, Library of Congress, Washington DC.

21. Dilliard, "Missouri Has No Governor," 183–84; Alexander, "Missouri Dark Mule," 38.

22. "Democrats Try to 'Steal' Missouri Governorship," 32.

23. Jack Malaney, *Sporting News*, February 6, 1941, 6.

24. Interview with Mary Rickey Eckler, Sebastopol CA, July 2000.

25. Jack Malaney, *Sporting News*, February 6, 1941, 6.

26. *New York Times*, February 4, 1944, 21.

27. Burk, *Much More than a Game*, 67.

28. Jack Malaney, *Sporting News*, February 6, 1941, 6.

29. *St. Louis Post-Dispatch*, February 16, 1941.

30. J. Roy Stockton, *St. Louis Post-Dispatch*, June 20, 1941, 1B.

31. J. Roy Stockton, *St. Louis Post-Dispatch*, June 20, 1941, 1B.

32. Carroll Otto to Branch Rickey, February 26, 1941, Branch Rickey Papers, Library of Congress, Washington DC; Dick Kaegel, *Sporting News*, March 5, 1966; Polner, *Branch Rickey: A Biography*, 115–16.

33. Holmes, *Dodger Daze and Knights*, 163.

34. Honig, *Baseball When the Grass Was Real*, 286–89.

35. Along with Honig's oral history interview with Reiser, noted above, Heinz, "The Rocky Road of Pistol Pete," is an indispensable essay about the star-crossed Reiser.

36. Holmes, *Dodger Daze and Knights*, 168.

37. Holmes, *Dodger Daze and Knights*, 168.

38. Owen, "Mystery of the Missed Third Strike," 19.

39. *Total Baseball*, 107.

40. Golenbock, *The Spirit of St. Louis*, 240–42.

41. Lee MacPhail to Lee Lowenfish, March 21, 1998, author's personal collection; McKelvey, *The MacPhails*, 106.

42. Lieb, *The St. Louis Cardinals: The Story of a Great Baseball Club*, 195–96.

43. *Sporting News*, October 10, 1942.

44. Holmes, *Dodger Daze and Knights*, 173.

45. Holmes, *Dodger Daze and Knights*, 174.

46. Lieb, *The St. Louis Cardinals: The Story of a Great Baseball Club*, 201–2.

47. Broeg and Miller, *Baseball from a Different Angle*, 232.

48. J. Roy Stockton, *St. Louis Post-Dispatch*, October 15, 1942, B2.

49. Pietrusza, *Judge and Jury*, 367.

50. Dick Fischer to Branch Rickey, February 14, 1942, Branch Rickey Papers, Library of Congress, Washington DC. For more on Branch Rickey Jr., see J. G. Taylor Spink, "Another Rickey in a Rush—Branch Jr. of Dodgers," *Sporting News*, June 12, 1941, 4.

51. E-mail to the author from Nancy Keltner (Branch Rickey Jr.'s daughter), May 2005.

52. Dick Farrington, *Sporting News*, May 6, 1937, 5.

53. Dick Farrington, *Sporting News*, November 5, 1942, 1.

54. Stockton, "A Brain Comes to Brooklyn," 24, 60.

15. A Branch Grows in Brooklyn

1. Arthur Daley, *New York Times*, February 12, 1943, 32.

2. Harold Parrott, *Sporting News*, March 4, 1943, 5; Polner, *Branch Rickey: A Biography*, 116.

3. J. G. Taylor Spink, *Sporting News*, November 26, 1942, 1.

4. Jerry Mitchell, *New York Post*, November 25, 1942, 37.

5. "Meany's Baseball," PM, October 30, 1942; Gunther, *Inside Asia*, 384.

6. Mike Shatzkin, "Interview with Clyde Sukeforth," BaseballLibrary.com, http://www.baseballlibrary.com/baseballlibrary/features/sabr/sukeforth_interview.stm.

7. Lowenfish, "The Two Titans and the Mystery Man," 170.

8. Mann, *The Jackie Robinson Story*, 11.

9. Mann, *Branch Rickey: American in Action*, 213.

10. Huhn, *The Sizzler*, 254; interview with Dave Sisler (George Sisler's son), St. Louis, August 2000.

11. Phone interview with Frances Drochelman (George Sisler's daughter), St. Louis, June 2005.

12. Interview with the late J. Rex Bowen, New Smyrna Beach FL, March 2001; Dexter, "The Mahatma and the Lip," 63.

13. Stockton, "Double-whammy Doc."

14. Branch Rickey to Harrison Weaver, December 6, 1942, Branch Rickey Papers, Library of Congress, Washington DC.

15. Harrison Weaver to Branch Rickey, August 6, 1944, Branch Rickey Papers, Library of Congress, Washington DC.

16. *Sporting News*, December 24, 1942.

17. Eskenazi, *The Lip*, 94.

18. Holmes, *Dodger Daze and Knights*, 189; see also Parrott, *The Lords of Baseball*, 156–57.

19. Holmes, *Dodger Daze and Knights*, 192.

20. Grace Dozier Durocher to Branch Rickey, September 28, 1943, Branch Rickey Papers, Library of Congress, Washington DC.

21. Holmes, *Dodger Daze and Knights*, 182.

22. Harold Parrott, *Sporting News*, March 4, 1943.

23. Garry Schumacher, *New York Journal-American*, July 10, 1943.

24. Frank, "Big Bobo," 61.

25. Cohane, *Bypaths to Glory*, 40.

26. *New York Herald Tribune*, July 11, 1943.

27. Graham, *The Brooklyn Dodgers*, 241.

28. Graham, *The Brooklyn Dodgers*, 241–42.

29. *New York Herald Tribune*, July 12, 1943.

30. Phone interview with Bobby Bragan, June 2004.

31. Interview with Jane Rickey Jones, Elmira NY, August 1999.

32. *New York Daily News*, August 2, 1943.

33. *New York Times*, March 4, 1943.

34. Allen, *The Giants and the Dodgers*, 185.

35. Marshall, *Baseball's Pivotal Era*, 109.

36. *New York Times*, August 7, 1943, 9.

37. Louis Effrat, *New York Times*, August 10, 1943, 24.

38. *Sporting News*, July 22, 1943 16.

39. Quoted in *Common Ground* (Spring 1944): 86. I am grateful to Professor Robert Shaffer of Shippensburg State University in Pennsylvania for sharing this source with me.

40. *Bridgeton Herald*, July 22, 1943, clippings in the Rex Bowen collection, courtesy of Rex's son, Jack Bowen, Pittsburgh.

41. Golenbock, *Bums*, 91.

42. Mann, *Branch Rickey: American in Action*, 226.

43. R. Barber, *1947—When All Hell Broke Loose in Baseball*, 49.

44. *Look*, June 15, 1943, 73.

45. Pamphlet courtesy of Church-of-the-Gardens, Forest Hills Gardens, Queens NY, and their historian Connie Corson. See also *New York Times*, August 15, 2003, C1.

46. R. N. Smith, *Thomas E. Dewey and His Times*, 318; Polner, *Branch Rickey: A Biography*, 126–27.

47. R. N. Smith, *Thomas E. Dewey and His Times*, 319.

48. Branch Rickey to Lowell Thomas, April 25, 1943, Branch Rickey Papers, Library of Congress, Washington DC.

49. See http://www.guideposts.com.

50. Rice, "Thoughts on Baseball—II"; Chamberlain, "Baseball, Brains, and Branch Rickey"; interview with Branch Barrett Rickey, Ohio Wesleyan campus, Delaware OH, October 1999.

51. Cohane, "A Branch Grows in Brooklyn," 76; Mann, "The Life of Branch Rickey—I," 72.

52. Holmes, *Dodger Daze and Knights*, 185.

53. King with Rocks, *A King's Legacy*, 20.

54. Parrott, *The Lords of Baseball*, 72.

55. Parrott, *This Week*, August 31, 1941, 6, was a particular favorite of Rickey's.

56. Parrott, *The Lords of Baseball*, 150.

57. Parrott, *The Lords of Baseball*, 2001 edition, 324.

58. *New York Times*, April 29, 1944, 15.

59. *New York Times*, November 2, 1943; interview with Mary Rickey Eckler, Sebastopol CA, July 2000.

60. McCue, "Walter O'Malley"; *Current Biography Yearbook*, 1954, 494–95.

61. Lowenfish, "The Two Titans and the Mystery Man," 169–73.

62. Taylor, "Borough Defender—II," 28.

63. Holmes, *Dodger Daze and Knights*, 187.

64. Eskenazi, *The Lip*, 170.

65. Graham, *Brooklyn Dodgers*, 239; Eskenazi, *The Lip*, 169.

66. Parrott, *The Lords of Baseball*, 153–54.

67. Parrott, *The Lords of Baseball*, 153–54; Cohane, "A Branch Grows in Brooklyn," 76.

68. Eskenazi, *The Lip*, 183–84.

69. *New York Times*, June 9, 1945, 1.

70. Eskenazi, *The Lip*, 185.

71. *New York Herald Tribune*, June 15, 1945.

72. Holmes, *Dodger Daze and Knights*, 196. See also Gene De Poris, "Woeful-looking Durocher May Learn His Fate Today," *PM*, April 25, 1946, 10.

16. The Secret Path to the "Young Man from the West"

1. Polner, *Branch Rickey: A Biography*, 146–47; Hal Middlesworth, *Oklahoma City Oklahoman*, June 3, 1947, J2, clipping in the Branch Rickey file, Ohio Wesleyan University Beeghly Library, Delaware OH; Parrott, *The Lords of Baseball*, 202.

2. Middlesworth, *Oklahoma City Oklahoman*, June 3, 1947, J2.

3. Rickey with Riger, *The American Diamond*, 9.

4. Mann, *The Jackie Robinson Story*, 24.

5. *New York Times*, June 23, 1943, 1.

6. Phone interviews with sportswriter Heywood Hale Broun, who covered Rickey's Dodgers for *PM* newspaper, June 2000, and Rickey family friend Alan Henderson, May 2003.

7. Rodney, *Press Box Red*, 70.

8. Lester Rodney to Lee Lowenfish, November 14, 1998, author's personal collection.

9. Tygiel, *Baseball's Great Experiment*, 40.

10. One of the most penetrating analyses of the quandary of the Negro Leagues is Burley, "Negroes in the Major Leagues?" Burley was a sportswriter and entertainment writer who also played a modified kind of boogie-woogie piano known as "skiffle."

11. *New York Times*, December 4, 1943, 10.

12. Sam Lacy, *Fighting for Fairness*, 45.

13. Rickey, "How It Looks from Where I Sit," 101.

14. Parrott, *The Lords of Baseball*, 188.

15. Falkner, *Great Time Coming*, 105.

16. Interview with Bill Turner, Pittsburgh, August 2001.

17. Alan Henderson to Lee Lowenfish, May 2003, author's personal collection; see also Henderson's article "The Man Who Brought Up Jackie," May 14, 1997, http://www.paloaltoonline.com/weekly/morgue/spectrum/1997_May_14.GUESTOP.html.

18. Phone interview with Charles Hurth Jr. (Frank Rickey's son-in-law), March 2003.

19. Margolick, *Beyond Glory*, 225.

20. *Time* cover, June 6, 1938; Broeg, *The 100 Greatest Moments in St. Louis Sports*, 61.

21. L. H. Addington, *Baseball*, February 1939, 421. When Pepper Martin arrived one year in a St. Louis spring training hotel and took a hunting rifle out of his pickup truck, a St. Louis sportswriter wrote, "The sleepy darky on duty at the hotel became suddenly wide awake at this picture and fled to the back thinking it was a holdup." Clifford Bloodgood, *Baseball*, May 1938, 537.

22. Rowan with Robinson, *Wait till Next Year*, 107.

23. *New York Herald Tribune*, June 7, 1944, 18.

24. R. N. Smith, *Thomas E. Dewey and His Times*, 401.

25. *New York Times*, November 26, 1944, 56.

26. Sam Roberts, "Faster than Jackie Robinson: Branch Rickey's Sermons on the Mound," *New York Times*, April 13, 1997, sec. 4, 7; interview with Mary Rickey Eckler, Sebastopol CA, July 2000.

27. R. N. Smith, *Thomas E. Dewey and His Times*, 446; *New York Times*, March 13, 1945, 38.

28. R. Barber, *1947—When All Hell Broke Loose in Baseball*, 48.

29. R. Barber, *1947—When All Hell Broke Loose in Baseball*, 57.

30. R. Barber, *1947—When All Hell Broke Loose in Baseball*, 52.

31. R. Barber, *1947—When All Hell Broke Loose in Baseball*, 63. For the story of the family of Red Barber's wife, see L. Barber, *Lylah*.

32. R. Barber, *1947—When All Hell Broke Loose in Baseball*, 64.

33. *New York Daily News*, April 8, 1945.

34. Lanctot, *Negro League Baseball*, 254.

35. Lanctot, *Negro League Baseball*, 254.

36. Tygiel, *Baseball's Great Experiment*, 46.

37. Lamb, *Blackout*, 36.

38. Rowan with Robinson, *Wait till Next Year*, 99.

39. Holtzman, *No Cheering in the Press Box*, 320.

40. Reisler, *Black Writers/Black Baseball*, 110; Rampersad, *Jackie Robinson: A Biography*, 120.

41. Falkner, *Great Time Coming*, 109.

42. Lanctot, *Negro League Baseball*, 260.

43. Lacy with Newson, *Fighting for Fairness*, 48.

44. Lanctot, *Negro League Baseball*, 263–64.

45. Ruck, *Sandlot Seasons*, 37–40. The entire chapter 5 of this book is a superb treatment of Gus Greenlee.

46. Ruck, *Sandlot Seasons*, 155–57, 163–64.

47. J. Robinson with Dexter, *Baseball Has Done It*, 42.

48. Polner, *Branch Rickey: A Biography*, 158–59.

49. Lanctot, *Negro League Baseball*, 266.

50. Snyder, *Beyond the Shadow of the Senators*, 219.

51. Polner, *Branch Rickey: A Biography*, 159.

52. Mann, *Branch Rickey: American in Action*, 219.

53. Tygiel, *Baseball's Great Experiment*, 61.

54. Tygiel, ed., *The Jackie Robinson Reader*, 5.

17. An Historic Meeting in Brooklyn

1. Clyde Sukeforth as told to Donald Honig, "Oh! They Were a Pair," reprinted in Tygiel, ed., *The Jackie Robinson Reader*, 67 (originally published in Honig, *Baseball: When the Grass Was Real*).

2. Mann, *The Jackie Robinson Story*, 28.

3. Rampersad, *Jackie Robinson: A Biography*, 125.

4. Sukeforth as told to Honig, "Oh! They Were a Pair," 69.

5. Taylor, "Borough Defender—I," 21.

6. Mann, *Branch Rickey: American in Action*, 220.

7. Sukeforth as told to Honig, "Oh! They Were a Pair," 69. See also an interview with Clyde Sukeforth by Gene Karst, Branson MO radio station KSOZ, 1978. I am indebted to the late Gene Karst for sharing this tape with me.

8. Rampersad, *Jackie Robinson: A Biography*, 118.

9. Robinson, "What's Wrong with the Negro Leagues," 16–18. In September 1947 Robinson and his wife and infant son appeared on the cover of *Ebony* with the caption "Family Man."

10. Interview with Jane Rickey Jones, Elmira NY, August 1999.

11. Sukeforth as told to Honig, "Oh! They Were a Pair," 70. See also Lincoln, "A Conversation with Clyde Sukeforth," 72–73.

12. Lardner, "The Old Emancipator," pt. 1, 88 (emphasis in original).

13. Robinson as told to Smith, *Jackie Robinson: My Own Story*, 21; United Press International obituary for Branch Rickey, *Columbus (Ohio) Dispatch*, December 10, 1965, 2A.

14. J. Robinson, "Trouble Ahead Needn't Bother You," 239.

15. Tygiel, *Baseball's Great Experiment*, 69.

16. Dan W. Dodson, "The Integration of Negroes in Baseball," *Journal of Educational Sociology* (October 1954), reprinted in Tygiel, ed. *The Jackie Robinson Reader*, 158; Mann, *The Jackie Robinson Story*, 23.

17. *New York World-Telegram and Sun*, February 21, 1964, clipping in the Dodson Papers, New York University Bobst Library.

18. Dodson, "The Integration of Negroes in Baseball," 162–63.

19. Polner, *Branch Rickey: A Biography*, 171.

20. Polner, *Branch Rickey: A Biography*, 172.

21. Sam Roberts, "Faster than Jackie Robinson: Branch Rickey's Sermons on the Mound," *New York Times*, April 13, 1997, sec. 4, 7; interview with Mary Rickey Eckler, Sebastopol CA, July 2000.

22. Tygiel, *Baseball's Great Experiment*, 72.

23. Rampersad, *Jackie Robinson: A Biography*, 129.

24. Parrott, *The Lords of Baseball*, 98.

25. Tygiel, *Baseball's Great Experiment*, 72.

26. Tygiel, *Baseball's Great Experiment*, 79.

27. Mann, *The Jackie Robinson Story*, 150.

28. Rampersad, *Jackie Robinson: A Biography*, 130.

29. Tygiel, *Baseball's Great Experiment*, 74.

30. Polner, *Branch Rickey: A Biography*, 173.

31. Al Laney, *New York Herald Tribune*, October 25, 1945, 26.

32. Tygiel, *Baseball's Great Experiment*, 75.

33. Corum, *Off and Running*, 232.

34. Rowan with Robinson, *Wait till Next Year*, 123.

35. Rampersad, *Jackie Robinson: A Biography*, 131.

36. Quoted in Lowenfish, "Sport, Race and the Baseball Business," 10.

37. Lanctot, *Negro League Baseball*, 281.

38. Roy Campanella to Branch Rickey, August 6, 1946, Branch Rickey Papers, Library of Congress, Washington DC. There are similar letters from Negro League pitchers John Wright and Roy Partlow in the same folder—July 20 and August 12, 1946, respectively.

39. Branch Rickey to Franklin Cole, November 16, 1945, Branch Rickey Papers, Library of Congress, Washington DC.

40. Interview with Robert Jones, Elmira NY, August 1999.

41. Interview, Robert Jones, August 1999.

18. Prelude to a Pennant

1. *New York Herald Tribune*, December 25, 1945.

2. *New York World-Telegram*, December 31, 1945, 21.

3. Lamb, *Blackout*, 69.

4. Lamb, *Blackout*, 68.

5. Lamb, *Blackout*, 69.

6. Lamb, *Blackout*, 74–75.

7. Rampersad, *Jackie Robinson: A Biography*, 137–38.

8. Rampersad, *Jackie Robinson: A Biography*, 139.

9. Rampersad, *Jackie Robinson: A Biography*, 139–40.

10. Lamb, *Blackout*, 78.

11. Lamb, *Blackout*, 88–89.

12. Marshall, *Baseball's Pivotal Era*, 133.

13. Lamb, *Blackout*, 91–92; Rampersad, *Jackie Robinson: A Biography*, 140.

14. Lamb, *Blackout*, 95.

15. Rampersad, *Jackie Robinson: A Biography*, 145.

16. Roeder, *Jackie Robinson*, 92.

17. Lowenfish and Lupien, *The Imperfect Diamond*, 140–47.

18. Holtzman, *No Cheering in the Press Box*, 339.

19. Holmes, *Dodger Daze and Knights*, 202.

20. Lamb, *Blackout*, 124.

21. Harold Burr, "Mexican War On as Branch Rickey Fires Injunction," *Brooklyn Eagle*, May 7, 1946, 13.

22. Holtzman, *No Cheering in the Press Box*, 343; Lowenfish and Lupien, *The Imperfect Diamond*, 143.

23. Holtzman, *No Cheering in the Press Box*, 341.

24. Holtzman, *No Cheering in the Press Box*, 342.

25. Marshall, *Baseball's Pivotal Era*, 59.

26. Lowenfish and Lupien, *The Imperfect Diamond*, 158.

27. *Brooklyn Eagle*, June 6, 1946.

28. "The Major League Steering Committee Report of August 27, 1946," in Tygiel, ed., *The Jackie Robinson Reader*, 131.

29. Roper and Roper, "We're Going to Give It All We Have for This Grand Little Town."

30. Mann, *Branch Rickey: American in Action*, 235–36.

31. Red Smith, "Model Ball Player," column, August 4, 1946, reprinted in Red Smith, *Red Smith on Baseball*, 15.

32. W. C. Heinz, "Second Base, Brooklyn," *Sporting News*, July 27, 1949.

33. Pete Hamill on Eddie Stanky, in Peary, ed., *Cult Baseball Players*, 42.

34. Golenbock, "Men of Conscience," 18.

35. Fetter, "Robinson in 1947," 185.

36. Mann, *Branch Rickey*, 239.

37. Polner, *Branch Rickey: A Biography*, 128.

38. For two examples of such insightful freelance articles, see Chamberlain, "Brains, Baseball, and Branch Rickey," and Dexter, "The Mahatma and the Lip."

39. *New York Herald Tribune*, September 26, 1946, 38; *Brooklyn Eagle*, September 26, 1945, 15.

40. *New York Herald Tribune*, September 26, 1946, 38. There is some dispute about how many Dodgers players actually received the cars, but pitcher Rex Barney certainly says he did. Barney, *Thank Youuuu*, 53.

41. Mann, *Branch Rickey: American in Action*, 238.

42. Mann, *Branch Rickey: American in Action*, 238.

43. Tommy Holmes, "Rickey's Proteges Face Flock Today," *Brooklyn Eagle*, October 1, 1946, 15.

44. Harvey Weinstein to Branch Rickey, October 3, 1946, Branch Rickey Papers, Library of Congress, Washington DC.

45. Rampersad, *Jackie Robinson: A Biography*, 157.

46. *Brooklyn Eagle*, October 3, 1946, 16.

47. Parrott, *The Lords of Baseball*, 202.

48. J. G. Taylor Spink, "Looping the Loops," *Sporting News*, June 26, 1946, 2. See also Lowenfish, "The Two Titans and the Mystery Man," 165–67.

49. *Total Baseball*, 107.

50. Parrott, *The Lords of Baseball*, 20.

19. When All Hell Almost Broke Loose

1. Marshall, *Baseball's Pivotal Era*, 105.

2. Yablonsky, *George Raft*, 9.

3. Yablonsky, *George Raft*, 98–99.

4. Yablonsky, *George Raft*, 178.

5. Pietrusza, *Judge and Jury*, 346.

6. Mann, *Baseball Confidential*, 41.

7. Westbrook Pegler, "As Pegler Sees It," *New York Journal-American*, October 26, 1946, 3.

8. Westbrook Pegler, "As Pegler Sees It," *New York Journal-American*, October 30, 1946, 3.

9. Mann, *Baseball Confidential*, 37–38.

10. R. N. Smith, *Thomas E. Dewey and His Times*, 320.

11. Mann, *Baseball Confidential*, 65–66.

12. Conversation with Bill Veeck, Baltimore MD, April 1975, after he addressed the author's "Sports and American Culture" class at the University of Maryland Baltimore County.

13. Yablonsky, *George Raft*, 178.

14. Roscoe McGowen, *New York Times*, November 5, 1946, 37.

15. Polner, *Branch Rickey: A Biography*, 186.

16. For example, Mann, "See Jack Robinson."

17. McGowen, *New York Times*, November 5, 1946, 37; Tygiel, *Baseball's Great Experiment*, 92.

18. Buzzie Bavasi, letter to the author, September 29, 1998; Jane Ann Jones, memorandum, November 6, 1946, Branch Rickey Papers, Library of Congress, Washington DC.

19. Mann, *Baseball Confidential*, 46

20. Mann, *Baseball Confidential*, 46.

21. Marshall, *Baseball's Pivotal Era*, 40.

22. Marshall, *Baseball's Pivotal Era*, 106.

23. Marshall, *Baseball's Pivotal Era*, 105.

24. Marshall, *Baseball's Pivotal Era*, 105.

25. Marshall, *Baseball's Pivotal Era*, 105.

26. McGowen, *New York Times*, November 26, 1946, 40.

27. *New York Herald Tribune*, November 26, 1946.

28. Polner, *Branch Rickey: A Biography*, 141.

29. Marshall, *Baseball's Pivotal Era*, 107–8.

30. Durocher with Linn, *Nice Guys Finish Last*, 244.

31. Wendell Smith to Jackie Robinson, February 4, 1947, Wendell Smith collection, National Baseball Hall of Fame Library, Cooperstown NY.

32. Tannenbaum, *Slave and Citizen*, xv–xvii.

33. Cary D. Wintz, entry in *Encyclopedia of the Harlem Renaissance*, vol. 2, ed. Cary D. Wintz and Paul Finkelman, 1158–59 (New York: Routledge, 2004). See also Maier and Weatherhead, *Frank Tannenbaum: A Biographical Essay* (found in Columbia University Rare Book Library).

34. Branch Rickey to Frank Tannenbaum, May 22, 1956, Branch Rickey Papers, Library of Congress, Washington DC.

35. Rowan with Robinson, *Wait till Next Year*, 169.

36. Rowan with Robinson, *Wait till Next Year*, 170.

37. Mann, *Branch Rickey: American in Action*, 255.

38. Marshall, *Baseball's Pivotal Era*, 136; Tygiel, *Baseball's Great Experiment*, 162.

39. Rampersad, *Jackie Robinson: A Biography*, 161.

40. Tygiel, *Baseball's Great Experiment*, 170; Mann, *The Jackie Robinson Story*, 167.

41. Durocher with Linn, *Nice Guys Finish Last*, 205.

42. Mann, "The Truth about the Jackie Robinson Case—II," 152.

43. Mann, *Branch Rickey: American in Action*, 258; phone interview with sportswriter Herman Masin, June 2005; Robinson with Dexter, *Baseball Has Done It*, 45.

44. Lardner, "The Old Emancipator," pt. 2.

45. Phone interview with Bobby Bragan, May 2005.

46. Durocher with Linn, *Nice Guys Finish Last*, 245.

47. "Durocher Says," *Brooklyn Eagle*, March 3, 1947, 11.

48. Marshall, *Baseball's Pivotal Era*, 110.

49. Marshall, *Baseball's Pivotal Era*, 108.

50. Dan Daniel, *Sporting News*, April 2, 1947, 2.

51. Marshall, *Baseball's Pivotal Era*, 106.

52. Gayle Talbot, *Nashua (New Hampshire) Telegraph*, March 24, 1947.

53. *Brooklyn Eagle*, April 10, 1947, 2.

54. Durocher with Linn, *Nice Guys Finish Last*, 254.

55. Marshall, *Baseball's Pivotal Era*, 111.

56. Mann, *Branch Rickey: American in Action*, 252.

57. Marshall, *Baseball's Pivotal Era*, 113.

58. Parrott, *The Lords of Baseball*, 202.

59. Marshall, *Baseball's Pivotal Era*, 108.

60. Marshall, *Baseball's Pivotal Era*, 114.

61. Phone interview with Buzzie Bavasi, October 2, 1998.

62. Marshall, *Baseball's Pivotal Era*, 113.

63. Interview, Buzzie Bavasi, October 2, 1998.

64. Mann, *Baseball Confidential*, 134.

20. When Most of Heaven Rejoiced

1. Tom Meany, *PM*, April 16, 1947.

2. Butterfield, "Brooklyn's Gentleman Bum," 83.

3. Butterfield, "Brooklyn's Gentleman Bum," 88.

4. Mann, *Branch Rickey: American in Action*, 260–61.

5. *New York Herald Tribune*, April 19, 1947.

6. Rampersad, *Jackie Robinson: A Biography*, 172.

7. Mann, "Bad Boy Bounces Back," 27–28.

8. Polner, *Branch Rickey: A Biography*, 196.

9. Mann, "The Truth about the Jackie Robinson Case—II," May 20, 1950, 154; see also Mann, *The Jackie Robinson Story*, 183.

10. Stanley Woodward, *New York Herald Tribune*, May 9 and 10, 1947, reprinted in Halberstam, ed., *Best American Sports Writing of the Century*, 165–69. It is interesting to note that National League president Ford Frick did not inform Commissioner Chandler of the possible strike, and in his story, Woodward derided Chandler's viability as a leader by referring in his article to A. B. (Albert Benjamin) Chandler as "Abie," surely a touch of ethnic stereotyping characteristic of the time.

11. Parrott, *The Lords of Baseball*, 199.

12. Rampersad, *Jackie Robinson: A Biography*, 176.

13. Parrott, *The Lords of Baseball*, 202.

14. Sheed, "And Now Playing Second Base for Brooklyn . . . Jackie Robinson," 82, emphasis in original.

15. Rampersad, *Jackie Robinson: A Biography*, 171.

16. Daley, "Baseball's Showmen—The Dodgers," 18.

17. Moss, "Burt Shotton: The Crucible of 1947," 127.

18. Red Barber, *New York Times Magazine*, September 28, 1947, 22.

19. Mann, *Branch Rickey: American in Action*, 262.

20. *New York Herald Tribune*, August 25, 1947.

21. Rampersad, *Jackie Robinson: A Biography*, 184; obituary for Bankhead, *New York Times*, May 7, 1976, D18.

22. *Total Baseball*, 107.

23. Tygiel, *Baseball's Great Experiment*, 219–20; Mann, *The Jackie Robinson Story*, 184; *Total Baseball*, 107; obituary for Richard Muckerman, *New York Times*, March 17, 1959, 30.

24. Rampersad, *Jackie Robinson: A Biography*, 184.

25. Rampersad, *Jackie Robinson: A Biography*, 184.

26. Chamberlain, *Life with the Printed Word*, 124.

27. Rampersad, *Jackie Robinson: A Biography*, 185.

28. Tygiel, *Baseball's Great Experiment*, 205.

29. "Rookie of the Year," *Time*, September 22, 1947; reprinted in Tygiel, ed., *The Jackie Robinson Reader*, 145–53.

30. *New York Herald Tribune*, September 24, 1947.

31. *New York Herald Tribune*, September 24, 1947.

32. *New York Times*, September 4, 1947, 33.

33. Marshall, *Baseball's Pivotal Era*, 163.

34. Heywood Hale Broun, "I'm Telling You . . .," *PM*, October 7, 1947, 27.

35. Shaplen, "The Nine Lives of Leo Durocher—II," May 30, 1955.

36. Eskenazi, *The Lip*, 219; Holmes, *Dodger Daze and Knights*, 234.

37. Parrott, *The Lords of Baseball*, 117–18.

38. Bud Selig, interview with mlb.com, May 2004, http://www.mlb.com.

39. Interview with Jack Lang (*Long Island Press* sportswriter at the time), New York City, May 1998.

40. Branch Rickey to C. E. Ficken, November 14, 1947, Rickey file, Ohio Wesleyan University Beeghly Library, Delaware OH.

41. Branch Rickey to the Woodwards, November 15, 1947, Rickey file, Ohio Wesleyan University Beeghly Library, Delaware OH.

42. "Rickey's Appeal for Negro Is Lost," *New York Times*, November 25, 1947, 41.

43. "Durocher Returns as Dodger Pilot," *New York Times*, December 7, 1947, 5.

44. Durocher with Linn, *Nice Guys Finish Last*, 271.

45. Durocher with Linn, *Nice Guys Finish Last*, 273.

46. Interview with Lindsay Wolfe (Branch Rickey's ex-son-in-law), New York City, November 1999; Swarthmore College Web site, http://www.swarthmore.edu.

47. Interview with Branch Barrett Rickey, Ohio Wesleyan campus, Delaware OH, October 1999; Dexter, "The Mahatma and the Lip"; Barber, *Walk in the Spirit*, 27.

48. Interview with Lindsay Wolfe, New York City, November 1999. See also "American Baseball Cap Company" file, Branch Rickey Papers, Library of Congress, Washington DC.

49. Interview, Lindsay Wolfe, November 1999.

50. Phone interview with Tuga Clements Adams, May 2004.

51. *Total Baseball*, 107.

52. Ritter, *Lost Ballparks*, 53.

53. Sullivan, *The Dodgers Move West*, 37; Shapiro, *The Last Great Season, 1956*, 35.

54. McCue, "Two out of Three Ain't Bad." See also Buzzie Bavasi to Lee Lowenfish, October 29, 1998, author's personal collection.

55. Harold Burr, "Dodger Boss Overcame Air Fright," *Brooklyn Eagle*, n.d. (probably 1949 or 1950).

21. A Year of Disappointment

1. *PM*, February 25, 1948, 26.

2. *New York Times*, April 22, 1948, 36.

3. *New York Herald Tribune*, May 30, 1948; "Boycott in Brooklyn," 51; *Sporting News*, June 2, 1948, 3–4.

4. Arnold Rampersad, *Jackie Robinson: A Biography*, 201; *PM*, May 26, 1948, 22.

5. Rampersad, *Jackie Robinson: A Biography*, 194; Tygiel, *Baseball's Great Experiment*, 190.

6. Falkner, *Great Time Coming*, 186.

7. Falkner, *Great Time Coming*, 188.

8. Rampersad, *Jackie Robinson: A Biography*, 193.

9. Rampersad, *Jackie Robinson: A Biography*, 191–92.

10. *New York Times*, February 18, 1948, 37. The MacPhail August 1946 report is reproduced in Tygiel, ed., *The Jackie Robinson Reader*, 129–33.

11. *New York Times*, February 18, 1948, 37.

12. *Sporting News*, February 25, 1948; *New York Times*, February 19, 1948.

13. Tygiel, *Baseball's Great Experiment*, 81.

14. *New York Times*, February 24, 1948.

15. Lamb, *Blackout*, 100.

16. Mack, *My 66 Years in Baseball*, 202.

17. Dick Young, *New York Daily News*, February 10, 1948, 47.

18. Mann, *Branch Rickey: American in Action*, 130.

19. Mann, *Branch Rickey: American in Action*, 130–31.

20. Dick Young, *New York Daily News*, February 13, 1948, 65. Incidentally, three years later, when Ralph Branca did get married, it was to Ann Mulvey, the daughter of James and Marie "Dearie" Mulvey, who owned one quarter of the team.

21. *New York Times*, December 21, 1946.

22. Connellsville (Pennsylvania) *Daily Courier*, June 9, 1939.

23. Branch Rickey entry, *Current Biography Yearbook*, 1945, 500.

24. Tommy Holmes, "How Rickey Went into Grid Business," *Brooklyn Eagle*, January 7, 1948, 19.

25. Branch Rickey memo on Football Dodgers, December 20, 1947, in Branch Rickey Papers, Library of Congress, Washington DC.

26. Joe Trimble, *New York Daily News*, January 7, 1948.

27. *New York Times*, February 11, 1948.

28. *New York Times*, February 11, 1948.

29. *New York Herald Tribune*, February 11, 1948; Red Smith, "So Branch Took the $110,000," *New York Herald Tribune*, February 11, 1948.

30. "The Specialist," 72–76.

31. Buzzie Bavasi to Lee Lowenfish, September 29, 1998, author's personal collection; see also Bavasi with Strege, *Off the Record*, 28–29.

32. Polner, *Branch Rickey: A Biography*, 219; Lowenfish, "The Two Titans and the Mystery Man," 172–73; McCue, "Two out of Three Ain't Bad."

33. Shaplen, "The Nine Lives of Leo Durocher," June 6, 1955, 72.

34. Tygiel, *Baseball's Great Experiment*, 241; interview with Bill Turner (Rickey staff member), Pittsburgh, August 2001.

35. *New York Times,* June 27 and June 25, 1948.

36. Parrott, *The Lords of Baseball*, 33.

37. Parrott, *The Lords of Baseball*, 35.

38. Graham Jr., *A Farewell to Heroes*, 208.

39. *Total Baseball*, 107.

22. A Branch Bends in Brooklyn

1. *New York Herald Tribune,* January 8, 1949.

2. "Life Goes to Dodgertown," 116.

3. Marshall, *Baseball's Pivotal Era*, 207.

4. Marshall, *Baseball's Pivotal Era*, 206.

5. Jimmy Powers, undated *New York Daily News* article (probably late March 1948), available at http://www.walteromalley.com.

6. 1949 spring training memo, box 35, folder 2, Branch Rickey Papers, Library of Congress, Washington DC; interview with Rex Bowen, New Smyrna Beach FL, March 2000; Graham Jr., *A Farewell to Heroes*, 217.

7. Roeder, *Jackie Robinson*, 170.

8. Mann, *The Jackie Robinson Story*, 208.

9. Rampersad, *Jackie Robinson: A Biography*, 206.

10. Rampersad, *Jackie Robinson: A Biography*, 207.

11. Rampersad, *Jackie Robinson: A Biography*, 208.

12. Butterfield, "Brooklyn's Gentleman Bum," 88.

13. Rampersad, *Jackie Robinson: A Biography*, 208.

14. *New York Times*, April 14, 1949.

15. John L. Flynn to Walter O'Malley, April 19, 1949, in Branch Rickey Papers, Library of Congress, Washington DC.

16. Polner, *Branch Rickey: A Biography*, 217.

17. *New York Times,* June 1, 1949; Shaplen, "The Nine Lives of Leo Durocher—III," June 7, 1955, 73.

18. *New York Times,* June 14, 1949.

19. Lardner, "Reese and Robinson," 18.

20. Polner, *Branch Rickey: A Biography*, 249.

21. Rampersad, *Jackie Robinson: A Biography*, 212.

22. Ron Smith, "Robeson and Robinson," 180.

23. R. Smith, "Robeson and Robinson," 181.

24. Falkner, *Great Time Coming*, 184.

25. Phone interview with Buzzie Bavasi, October 15, 1998.

26. Rowan with Robinson, *Wait till Next Year*, 206.

27. *New York Times*, February 11, 1946.

28. Granger, "No Short-cut to Democracy," 17.

29. *New York Times,* July 19, 1949; Ron Smith, "Robeson and Robinson," 183.

30. Rampersad, *Jackie Robinson: A Biography*, 215.

31. "Man of Empire," *Newsweek*, August 8, 1949.

32. Mann, *Baseball Confidential*, 164.

33. *Total Baseball*, 107; Fetter, "Robinson in 1947," 191.

34. Erskine, *Carl Erskine's Tales from the Dodger Dugout*, 3–4.

35. Golenbock, *Bums*, 246.

36. Harold Rosenthal, *New York Herald Tribune*, October 7, 1949.

37. Lowenfish and Lupien, *The Imperfect Diamond*, 167.

38. Eckler, "Baseball—Sport or Commerce?," 66.

39. *New York Herald Tribune*, October 10, 1949.

40. J. G. Taylor Spink, *Sporting News*, October 19, 1949, 2.

41. Dan Daniel, "Rickey Blasts Weiss for Claims for Yank Clubs," *Sporting News*, November 2, 1949, 4.

42. Lipman, *Mr. Baseball*, 179.

43. Butterfield, "Brooklyn's Gentleman Bum," 88.

44. *New York Herald-Tribune*, October 9, 1949.

45. Buzzie Bavasi to Lee Lowenfish, September 29, 1998, author's personal collection.

46. Polner, *Branch Rickey: A Biography*, 130.

47. Buzzie Bavasi to Lee Lowenfish, September 29, 1998; see also Football Memo of Arthur Mann in Branch Rickey Papers, Library of Congress, Washington DC.

23. A Branch Is Chopped in Brooklyn

1. *New York Herald Tribune*, March 7, 1950.

2. Shatzkin, *The Ballplayers*, 141.

3. Woodward, "How to Build a Ball Club."

4. Phone interview with Joe Oliffe, November 2000. Oliffe's one year in class D ball was the subject of a *Saturday Evening Post* story, "It's a Long Way to the Majors," August 26, 1950.

5. Interview with Vin Scully, New York City, August 1999.

6. Interview, Vin Scully, August 1999.

7. Rampersad, *Jackie Robinson: A Biography*, 224.

8. Jane Ann Jones to Branch Rickey Jr., "VERY CONFIDENTIAL," February 11, 1950, Branch Rickey Papers, Library of Congress, Washington DC.

9. Bob Cooke, "Enter Minor Watson," *New York Herald Tribune*, March 5, 1950. Edward Herrmann caught more nuances in his portrait of Rickey in the otherwise far-fetched 1995 Home Box Office film *The Soul of the Game*. In the HBO movie, Blair Underwood as Jackie Robinson is incredulous that he, rather than Satchel Paige or Josh Gibson, is getting the chance in Major League Baseball.

10. Rampersad, *Jackie Robinson: A Biography*, 225–26.

11. "New York Close-up," *New York Herald Tribune*, March 8, 1950.

12. "New York Close-up."

13. Rice, "Thoughts on Baseball—II," 30.

14. Rice, "Thoughts on Rickey—I," 38.

15. Rice, "Thoughts on Rickey—II," 44.

16. Rodengen, *The Legend of Pfizer*, 77.

17. Lowenfish, "The Two Titans and the Mystery Man," 175.

18. McCue, "Walter O'Malley"; Rodengen, *The Legend of Pfizer*, 33; phone interview with Buzzie Bavasi, November 2000; Mike Gaven, *Sporting News*, September 27, 1950, 2.

19. Obituary for James Mulvey, *New York Times*, December 4, 1973.

20. McCue, "Walter O'Malley."

21. Branch Rickey to board of directors of Brooklyn Dodgers in minutes of meeting of October 26, 1950, Branch Rickey Papers, Library of Congress, Washington DC; see also Mann, *Branch Rickey: American in Action*, 284.

22. Parrott, *The Lords of Baseball*, 28–29.

23. Sheean, "John Galbreath," 114.

24. Sheean, "John Galbreath," 114. See also http://horatioalger.com and http://columbusoh.about.com. In 1963 Galbreath's Darby Dan farm won the Kentucky Derby with Chateaugay and again with Proud Clarion in 1967. Obituary for John W. Galbreath, *New York Times*, July 21, 1988, D22.

25. Graham Jr., *A Farewell to Heroes*, 234.

26. Graham Jr., *A Farewell to Heroes*, 224; Joe King, "A Goat Grows in Brooklyn," *Sporting News*, August 23, 1950, 1.

27. Gough, *Burt Shotton, Dodgers Manager*, 115.

28. *Total Baseball*, 107.

29. *New York Herald Tribune*, October 2, 1950.

30. Griswold, "Rickey Starts in the Cellar Again."

31. Harold Rosenthal, *New York Herald Tribune*, September 24, 1950, sec. 3, 1.

32. [Dan] Daniel, *New York World Telegram*, October 24, 1950, 39.

33. Ray Gillespie, *Sporting News*, October 18, 1950, 15. This was the same Ray Gillespie whom Rickey had sued four years earlier during the Mexican League uproar.

34. O'Toole, *Branch Rickey in Pittsburgh*, 13.

35. Ray Gillespie, *Sporting News*, November 8, 1950, 1.

36. Buzzie Bavasi to Lee Lowenfish, September 14, 1998, author's personal collection.

37. Interviews with Al Fried, a Brooklyn resident in the 1940s, and Emily Rickey Wolfe, Branch Rickey's granddaughter, who both knew Chauffeur Dave. New York City, November 1999.

38. [Dan] Daniel, *New York World Telegram*, October 25, 1950, 45.

39. Golenbock, *Bums*, 268.

40. Lowenfish, "The Two Titans and the Mystery Man," 175.

41. Lowenfish, "The Two Titans and the Mystery Man," 175.

42. Harold Rosenthal, *New York Herald Tribune*, October 27, 1950, 23.

43. Rickey, "World Series 2000 A.D."; Lowenfish, "World Series 2000 A.D."

44. Rickey, "World Series 2000 A.D."

45. Parrott, *The Lords of Baseball*, 36.

46. Interview with Jerry Narron (Sam Narron's second cousin and, since 2005, manager of the Cincinnati Reds), New York City, August 2002. At one time the Narron family, from Goldsboro, North Carolina, had eight players in professional baseball, all of them catchers.

47. *Sporting News*, July 19, 1950, 5.

48. Interview with Branch Barrett Rickey, Ohio Wesleyan campus, Delaware OH, October 1999.

49. Harold Rosenthal, *New York Herald Tribune*, October 27, 1950; Lowenfish, "The Two Titans and the Mystery Man," 172.

24. A Branch Doesn't Grow Fast Enough in Pittsburgh

1. Griswold, "Rickey Starts in the Cellar Again," 110.

2. O'Toole, *Branch Rickey in Pittsburgh*, 19.

3. *Total Baseball*, 108.

4. Griswold, "Rickey Starts in the Cellar Again," 108.

5. Mann, *Branch Rickey: American in Action*, 289.

6. O'Toole, *Branch Rickey in Pittsburgh*, 125; *New York Times*, February 1, 1950.

7. O'Toole, *Branch Rickey in Pittsburgh*, 36.

8. McCollister, *The Bucs*, 138–39.

9. O'Toole, *Branch Rickey in Pittsburgh*, 36.

10. *Total Baseball*, 107.

11. Review of *Angels in the Outfield*, *Variety*, August 27, 1951, clipping in Branch Rickey Papers, Library of Congress, Washington DC.

12. Max Carey to Branch Rickey, August 6, 1951, Branch Rickey Papers, Library of Congress, Washington DC (emphasis in original); Parrott, *The Lords of Baseball*, 90.

13. Phone interview with Mario Cuomo, March 13, 2003.

14. Interview, Mario Cuomo, March 13, 2003.

15. McElvaine, *Mario Cuomo*, 107.

16. Interview, Mario Cuomo, March 13, 2003.

17. Interview, Mario Cuomo, March 13, 2003.

18. McElvaine, *Mario Cuomo*, 108, 112.

19. Interview, Mario Cuomo, March 13, 2003.

20. O'Toole, *Branch Rickey in Pittsburgh*, 94–95.

21. Kiner with Gergen, *Kiner's Korner*, 13.

22. Polner, *Branch Rickey: A Biography*, 233.

23. Ritter, *Lost Ballparks*, 66–67.

24. O'Toole, *Branch Rickey in Pittsburgh*, 93.

25. O'Toole, *Branch Rickey in Pittsburgh*, 54.

26. *Total Baseball*, 107.

27. *New York Times*, August 26, 1952, 28.

28. *New York Times*, January 22, 1952, 36.

29. *New York Times*, May 8, 1952, 29.

30. Obituary for Houston Peterson, *New York Times*, May 20, 1981, A26.

31. Interview with Dick Groat, Bolivar PA, July 2001.

32. Interview with Rex Bowen, New Smyrna Beach FL, March 2001.

33. Groat with Dascenzo, *Groat: I Hit and Ran*, 32.

34. Interview, Dick Groat, July 2001.

35. Polner, *Branch Rickey: A Biography*, 133.

36. Adele Moyer Allison, "Mr. Rickey's Silent Partner," *Pittsburgh Press Sunday Magazine*, 1952, clipping in Branch Rickey Papers, Library of Congress, Washington DC.

37. Holland, "Mr. Rickey and the Game," 223.

38. Phone interview with John Chambers, May 2005.

39. O'Toole, *Branch Rickey in Pittsburgh*, 96.

40. O'Toole, *Branch Rickey in Pittsburgh*, 97–98.

41. O'Toole, *Branch Rickey in Pittsburgh*, 101.

42. O'Toole, *Branch Rickey in Pittsburgh*, 102.

43. Conversation with Yogi Berra, Montclair NJ, April 2002.

44. *Total Baseball*, 107.

45. Mann, "Has Rickey Failed in Pittsburgh?"

46. Interview with Frank Thomas, New York City, August 2000.

47. O'Toole, *Branch Rickey in Pittsburgh*, 155.

48. O'Toole, *Branch Rickey in Pittsburgh*, 110

49. Mann, *Branch Rickey: American in Action*, 275–76.

50. O'Toole, *Branch Rickey in Pittsburgh*, 114.

51. Peterson, ed., *A Treasury of the World's Greatest Speeches*, 109–14.

52. O'Toole, *Branch Rickey in Pittsburgh*, 160–61.

53. Phone interview with Joe L. Brown, December 1999.

54. O'Toole, *Branch Rickey in Pittsburgh*, 120.

55. O'Toole, *Branch Rickey in Pittsburgh*, 120.

56. O'Toole, *Branch Rickey in Pittsburgh*, 159.

57. O'Toole, *Branch Rickey in Pittsburgh*, 160.

58. Interview with Branch Barrett Rickey, Ohio Wesleyan University campus, Delaware OH, October 1999; Lardner, "The Old Emancipator," pt. 1, 85.

59. Leavy, *Sandy Koufax*, 53.

60. Koufax with Linn, *Koufax*, 60–61.

61. Rickey, "Goodby to Old Ideas."

62. Wagenheim, *Clemente!*, 7–8, emphasis in original.

63. Wagenheim, *Clemente!*, 42.

64. Unpublished 1964 essay by Branch Rickey, courtesy of Beth Louis (Rickey's granddaughter).

65. Interview, Dick Groat, July 2001.

66. Interview, Dick Groat, July 2001.

67. Interview, Dick Groat, July 2001.

68. Groat with Dascenzo, *Groat: I Hit and Ran*, 1.

69. Interview, Dick Groat, July 2001. Groat thought of Rickey's checkerboard warning when he witnessed Arnold Palmer playing a friendly game of golf with some friends on Groat's course. "Palmer was hitting the ball terribly on some of the last holes of my course," Groat recalls, "but then he finished birdie-par-birdie," winning bets from his friends. "Yes, never play golf with someone who knows the course as a pro," Groat advises.

70. Oliphant, *Praying for Gil Hodges*, 64–65.

71. O'Toole, *Branch Rickey in Pittsburgh*, 31.

72. *Total Baseball*, 108.

73. Sheean, "John Galbreath," 138.

74. O'Toole, *Branch Rickey in Pittsburgh*, 161.

75. Interview, Joe L. Brown, December 1999.

76. Bill Corum, "Rickey, the Man Nobody—but Nobody—Really Knows," *New York Journal-American*, January 29, 1956, 27-L.

77. O'Toole, *Branch Rickey in Pittsburgh*, 167.

25. Mr. Rickey Prepares to Do the Continental

1. Bragan as told to Guinn, *You Can't Hit the Ball with the Bat on Your Shoulder*, 220.

2. Polner, *Branch Rickey: A Biography*, 250.

3. Polner, *Branch Rickey: A Biography*, 251.

4. Conversation with Robin Roberts, New York City, January 1999.

5. Erskine, *Carl Erskine's Tales from the Dodger Dugout*, 134; phone interview with Carl Erskine, November 1998. See also a video presented to Ohio Wesleyan for an October 1999 honor ceremony for the Rickey family. Ohio Wesleyan University Beeghly Library, Delaware OH.

6. Branch Rickey, speech to the "One Hundred Percent Wrong Club," a black journalists' group, January 20, 1956, Atlanta, Branch Rickey Papers, Library of Congress, Washington DC. Also available at http://memory.loc.gov/ammem/jrhtml/branch.html.

7. Fox, "The Education of Branch Rickey."

8. Branch Rickey to Carl Rowan, April 10, 1958, Branch Rickey Papers, Library of Congress, Washington DC. See also Rickey, "How It Looks from Where I Sit."

9. E-mail to the author from Molly Eckler (Branch Rickey's granddaughter), May 2005.

10. Interview with Richard Moulton (Branch Rickey's grandnephew), Pittsburgh, July 2004.

11. Interview, Richard Moulton, July 2004.

12. Branham, "Of Thee I Sing," 642.

13. CD-ROM of Rickey's NAACP New York speech, November 22, 1957, National Baseball Hall of Fame, Cooperstown NY, in author's personal collection.

14. *New York Times*, November 23, 1957, 16.

15. Giles's indifferent comments can be found in the *New York Times*, February 1, 1958, 13, and March 5, 1958, 40. See also Havill, *The Last Mogul*, 99–100.

16. Mullin's cartoon is reproduced in Lowenfish, "A Tale of Many Cities," 71.

17. O'Toole, *Branch Rickey in Pittsburgh*, 153.

18. Al Abrams, "Sidelights on Sports," *Pittsburgh Post-Gazette*, January 8, 1959, 22, clipping in Branch Rickey Papers, Library of Congress, Washington DC.

19. Rickey with Riger, *The American Diamond*, 166.

20. *Total Baseball*, 108.

21. Memo of March 18, 1953, in Branch Rickey Papers, Library of Congress, Washington DC.

22. *Total Baseball*, 108.

23. Phone interview with Harold Rosenthal, November 1998.

24. Caro, *The Power Broker*, 1032; Fetter, *Taking on the Yankees*, 253.

25. John Lardner, *New York Times Magazine*, February 26, 1956.

26. Weiner, *Stadium Games*, 26–27; Buzzie Bavasi to Lee Lowenfish, October 8, 1998, author's personal collection.

27. Fetter, *Taking on the Yankees*, 268.

28. *Total Baseball*, 108.

29. *Total Baseball*, 108.

30. Richards with Cohane, "The American League Is Dying," 41.

31. Burk, *Much More than a Game*, 107, 125.

32. *New York Times*, March 11, 1958.

33. Quoted in Spink, *Sporting News*, May 21, 1958, 1.

34. Spink, *Sporting News*, May 21, 1958.

35. Terrell, "3rd League Cities Pin Hopes on This Man," 31.

36. Nicholas Pileggi, quoted in David Margolick's obituary for William Shea, *New York Times*, October 4, 1991, D16.

37. Lardner, "Third League Notes," 88.

38. *New York Herald Tribune*, August 19, 1959, sec. 3, 2.

39. Harold Rosenthal to Lee Lowenfish, November 25, 1999, in author's personal collection.

40. Terrell, "3rd League Cities Pin Hopes on This Man," 31.

41. Lowenfish and Lupien, *The Imperfect Diamond*, 187.

42. *New York Times*, May 22, 1959, 1.

43. Terrell, "3rd League Cities Pin Hopes on This Man," 31; see also Koppett, *The New York Mets*, 33.

44. Interview with Mrs. Ron (Jackie) Hunt about Joan Payson's gifts to Mets' families, New York City, August 1990.

45. Havill, *The Last Mogul*, xv–xvii.

46. Havill, *The Last Mogul*, 89.

47. Havill, *The Last Mogul*, 99–100.

48. Phone interview with Robert Howsam, May 2001.

49. For more on the fascinating figure of Edwin Carl Johnson, a conservative Democrat who was an early critic of both Joe McCarthyism and the war in Vietnam, see Howsam, *My Life in Sports*, 5–7, and a two-part series by Olga Curtis, *Denver Post Sunday Magazine*, February 18 and 25, 1968.

50. Titchener, *The George Kirksey Story*, 37, 49.

51. Titchener, *The George Kirksey Story*, 64.

52. Mann, "How to Buy a Ball Club for Peanuts," 25.

53. Titchener, *The George Kirksey Story*, 75–79; *Sporting News*, August 6, 1958, 6.

54. *New York Times*, August 28, 1958, 21; Weiner, *Stadium Games*, 31.

55. Weiner, *Stadium Games*, 42.

56. Michael E. Lomax, "The League That Never Was: The Continental League and the Birth of the Expansion Era," unpublished paper. I appreciate Professor Lomax's sharing this paper with me.

57. Branch Rickey memo to Continental League owners, July 27, 1959, Branch Rickey Papers, Library of Congress, Washington DC.

58. Buhite, "The Continental League and Its Western Carolina League Affiliate," 442.

59. *Organized Professional Team Sports*, Hearings of the Kefauver Subcommittee, 85th Congress, 1st session, July 1959, 148–56.

60. *Organized Professional Team Sports*, Hearings of the Kefauver Subcommittee, 156.

61. *Organized Professional Team Sports*, Hearings of the Kefauver Subcommittee, 161.

62. Lowe, *The Kid on the Sandlot*, 39.

26. The Continental Dance Card Goes Blank

1. *New York Herald Tribune*, August 19, 1959.

2. *New York Herald Tribune*, August 19, 1959.

3. *Sporting News*, August 26, 1959, 2.

4. *New York Herald Tribune*, August 19, 1959.

5. *Sporting News*, August 26, 1959, 2.

6. *New York Herald Tribune*, August 19, 1959.

7. Jimmy Cannon, *New York Journal-American*, August 19, 1959.

8. *Sporting News*, August 26, 1959, 2.

9. George Kirksey proposal, in Continental League box 39, Branch Rickey Papers, Library of Congress, Washington DC.

10. *New York Times*, August 19, 1959, 21.

11. Interview with Jack Bowen (Rex Bowen's son), Pittsburgh, July 2001.

12. E-mail to the author from Nancy Rickey Keltner (Branch Rickey Jr.'s daughter), May 2005.

13. Jack O'Brian, *New York Journal-American*, September 15, 1959, 21.

14. Interview with Carl Erskine, New York City, January 2001.

15. *Sporting News*, November 4, 1959.

16. Buhite, "The Continental League and Its Western Carolina League Affiliate," 436.

17. Arch Murray, *New York Post*, August 4, 1959, 72.

18. Walter O'Malley to Branch Rickey, November 30, 1959, Branch Rickey Papers, Library of Congress, Washington DC.

19. Branch Rickey to Walter O'Malley, December 6, 1959, Branch Rickey Papers, Library of Congress, Washington DC.

20. *New York Times*, December 10, 1959.

21. Phone interview with Craig Cullinan Jr., May 2001. For insight into the Chalkley-Hayward marriage, see LaGuardia and Arceri, *Red*.

22. *Sports Illustrated*, February 8, 1960, 26.

23. H. Lamar Hunt, letter to author, May 27, 2001.

24. Phone interview with Wheelock Whitney, May 2001.

25. Interview, Wheelock Whitney, May 2001.

26. Interview, Craig Cullinan Jr., August 2001.

27. Phone interview with Robert Howsam, February 2001.

28. *Sporting News*, February 17, 1960.

29. *Sporting News*, February 17, 1960; Buhite, "The Continental League and Its Western Carolina League Affiliate," 441.

30. Buhite, "The Continental League and Its Western Carolina Affiliate," 441.

31. New York *Times*, February 11, 1960.

32. Buhite, "The Continental League and Its Western Carolina League Affiliate," 444.

33. Buhite, "The Continental League and Its Western Carolina League Affiliate," 445, 451.

34. Phone interview with Charles Hurth Jr., March 2003; see also Gordon S. White, *New York Times*, April 7, 1960, 48.

35. *Newsweek*, May 16, 1960, 88.

36. *Organized Professional Team Sports*, Hearings, 86th Congress, 1st session, late July 1959, 171.

37. Burk, *Much More than a Game*, 125.

38. *Sporting News*, May 25, 1960.

39. *Sporting News*, May 25, 1960. See also Stanley Frank, "George Weiss: Boss of the Yankees," *Saturday Evening Post*, May 14, 1960.

40. Branch Rickey testimony, May 18, 1960, *Organized Professional Team Sports*, 86th Con-

gress, 2nd session, 65–66. St. Louis native Dickie Kerr, a five-foot-seven-inch pitcher, had won 2 games for the White Sox in that tainted World Series.

41. Branch Rickey testimony, May 18, 1960, 72

42. Branch Rickey testimony, May 18, 1960, 65, 69.

43. *Sporting News*, May 25, 1960.

44. Paul Porter, *Current Biography Yearbook*, 1975, 120; *Sporting News*, August 6, 1958, 6.

45. Titchener, *The George Kirksey Story*, 83–84.

46. *Sporting News*, August 5, 1959, 22; Lowe, *The Kid on the Sandlot*, 45.

47. Tom Wicker, *New York Times*, June 29, 1960, 36.

48. Branch Rickey memo, June 29, 1960, in Continental League boxes, Branch Rickey Papers, Library of Congress, Washington DC.

49. Lardner, "Third League Notes," 88.

50. Phone interview with Wheelock Whitney, May 2001.

51. Interview, Wheelock Whitney, May 2001; see also interview, Craig Cullinan, August 2001.

52. Leonard Shecter, *New York Post*, August 3, 1960, 57.

53. Miller, *The Baseball Business*, 83–84.

54. *New York Times* August 3, 1960; "Peace, It's Wonderful," 52.

55. Harold Rosenthal, *New York Herald Tribune*, August 3, 1960.

56. Leonard Shecter, *New York Post*, August 3, 1960, 57.

57. Branch Rickey to Wheelock Whitney, August 2, 1960, in Branch Rickey Papers, Library of Congress, Washington DC (emphasis in original). Also quoted in Weiner, *Stadium Games*, 49–51.

58. Memo to Charles Hurth, n.d. (probably early 1961), Branch Rickey Papers, Library of Congress, Washington DC.

59. E-mail to the author from Nancy Keltner (Branch Rickey Jr.'s daughter), May 2005.

60. *Sudbury (Ontario) Gazette*, July 28, 1961, clipping in Branch Rickey Papers, Library of Congress, Washington DC.

61. Phone interview with Charles Hurth Jr., November 2003.

62. Donald Grant to Branch Rickey, March 2, 1961, Branch Rickey Papers, Library of Congress, Washington DC. This letter informs Rickey that because he did not sign a contract offer extended in February, it has been withdrawn.

63. Interview, Charles Hurth Jr., November 2003; Mitchell, *The Amazing Mets*, 233.

27. Meet Me in St. Louis, Final Chorus

1. Robert Lipsyte, *New York Times*, July 24, 1962, 20.

2. E-mail to the author from John Branch Jakle, May 2005.

3. Jackie Robinson to Branch Rickey, December 12, 1959, Branch Rickey Papers, Library of Congress, Washington DC.

4. Branch Rickey to Jackie Robinson, April 4, 1965, Branch Rickey Papers, Library of Congress, Washington DC.

5. Frisch as told to Stockton, *Frank Frisch: The Fordham Flash*, 199.

6. Rampersad, *Jackie Robinson: A Biography*, 362.

7. Lipsyte, *New York Times*, July 24, 1962, 20.

8. *Sporting News*, August 4, 1962, 4.

9. Polner, *Branch Rickey: A Biography*, 265.

10. Hernon and Ganey, *Under the Influence*, 214.

11. Polner, *Branch Rickey: A Biography*, 263–65.

12. Neal Russo, *Sporting News*, October 6, 1962, 32.

13. Parrott, *The Lords of Baseball*, 18.

14. Neal Russo, *Sporting News*, November 10, 1962, 32.

15. Bob Broeg, *Sporting News*, November 10, 1962, 12.

16. Golenbock, *The Spirit of St. Louis*, 448; phone interview with Bing Devine, May 2001.

17. Interview with Dick Groat, Bolivar PA, July 2001.

18. Golenbock, *The Spirit of St. Louis*, 448; interview, Bing Devine, May 2001.

19. Graham Jr., "Branch Rickey Rides Again," 66, 68.

20. Graham Jr., "Branch Rickey Rides Again," 66 (emphasis in original).

21. Huhn, *The Sizzler*, 272.

22. Interview with Elizabeth Adams Louis, St. Louis, August 2000.

23. Interview, Elizabeth Adams Louis, August 2000.

24. Polner, *Branch Rickey: A Biography*, 269.

25. Branch Rickey, memo to August Busch, April 16, 1963, in Branch Rickey Papers, Library of Congress, Washington DC.

26. Tim McCarver, e-mail to the author, June 2005.

27. Branch Rickey to August Busch Jr., April 16, 1963, Branch Rickey Papers, Library of Congress, Washington DC.

28. *Delaware (Ohio) Gazette*, October 11, 1965, clipping in the Branch Rickey file, Ohio Wesleyan University Beeghly Library, Delaware OH.

29. Obituary for Houston Peterson, *New York Times*, May 20, 1981, A28.

30. Branch Rickey to Norman Vincent Peale, February 14, 1964, letter in possession of Elizabeth Adams Louis (Branch Rickey's granddaughter).

31. *Sporting News*, May 30, 1964, 34.

32. Golenbock, *The Spirit of St. Louis*, 444.

33. Interview, Dick Groat, July 2001.

34. Phone interview with George Vecsey, June 2002.

35. Phone interview with Bob Howsam, May 2001.

36. Interview with Branch Barrett Rickey, Ohio Wesleyan campus, Delaware OH, October 1999.

37. Rickey with Riger, *The American Diamond*, 3.

38. Rickey with Riger, *The American Diamond*, 10, 27.

39. Rickey with Riger, *The American Diamond*, 23.

40. Branch Rickey to Archibald Carey Jr., September 28, 1964, Branch Rickey Papers, Library of Congress, Washington DC.

41. "Remembering Mr. Rickey," 2004 fund-raising brochure, Ohio Wesleyan University, Delaware OH.

42. Interview with Robert Holm, Ohio Wesleyan campus, Delaware OH, October 1999.

43. Phone interview with Alan Cherry (Pepper Martin's son-in-law), McAlester OK, May 2002.

44. Barthel, *Pepper Martin*, 191, 216–17. See also valedictories to Pepper Martin written by Bob Broeg and Roy Stockton in the *St. Louis Post-Dispatch*, March 7, 1965, 2D.

45. Phone interview with Wheelock Whitney, May 2005.

46. Phil Pepe, *New York Daily News*, December 10, 1965.

47. Phone interview with Fran Drochelman (George and Kathleen Sisler's daughter), May 2005.

48. Norman Vincent Peale to Mary Iams Rickey, November 2, 1971, letter in possession of Beth Louis.

49. Phone interview with Portsmouth Murals Inc., May 2005.

50. Rickey with Riger, *The American Diamond*, 4.

51. Methodist hymn #76. I am indebted to Donald Hughes (Branch Rickey's grandson-in-law) for this reference.

Bibliography

All baseball statistics are drawn from two sources: *Total Baseball*, 6th edition (New York: Total Baseball, 1999), and *The Baseball Encyclopedia*, 7th edition (New York: Macmillan, 1990).

Adler, Rich. *Baseball at the University of Michigan.* Charleston SC: Arcadia, 2004.

Alexander, Charles. *Breaking the Slump.* New York: Columbia University Press, 2003.

———. *Rogers Hornsby: A Biography.* New York: Henry Holt, 1995.

Alexander, Jack. "Lew Wentz: Oklahoma Godfather." *Saturday Evening Post,* December 18, 1948.

———. "Missouri Dark Mule." *Saturday Evening Post,* October 8, 1938.

Allen, Lee. *The Giants and the Dodgers: The Fabulous Story of Baseball's Fiercest Feud.* New York: Putnam, 1964.

———. *The Hot Stove League.* 1955. Reprint, Kingston NY: Total Sports Illustrated, 2000.

———. *The National League Story: The Official History.* New York: Hill and Wang, 1961.

———. *100 Years of Baseball.* New York: Bartholomew House, 1950.

"The Amazing Larry MacPhail." *Newsweek,* June 24, 1940, 43.

Andersen, Donald Ray. "Branch Rickey and the St. Louis Cardinal Farm System: The Evolution of an Idea." PhD diss., University of Wisconsin, 1975.

Barber, Lylah. *Lylah: A Memoir.* Chapel Hill NC: Algonquin Books, 1985.

Barber, Red. *1947—When All Hell Broke Loose in Baseball.* Garden City NY: Doubleday, 1982.

———. *Walk in the Spirit.* New York: Dial, 1969.

Barney, Rex, with Norman L. Macht. *Rex Barney's Thank Youuuu for 50 Years in Baseball from Brooklyn to Baltimore.* Centreville MD: Tidewater, 1993.

Barry, John M. *Rising Tide: The Great Mississippi Flood of 1927 and How It Changed America.* New York: Simon and Schuster, 1997.

Barthel, Tom. *The Fierce Fun of Ducky Medwick.* Metuchen NJ: Scarecrow, 2003.

———. *Pepper Martin: A Baseball Biography.* Jeffersonville NC: McFarland, 2003.

Bavasi, Buzzie, with John Strege. *Off the Record.* Chicago: Contemporary Books, 1987.

Bell, Floyd L. "Branch Rickey: The Major League Manager Who Is Different." *Baseball,* April 1920, 646.

Bernstein, Sam. "George Sisler and the End of the National Commission." *National Pastime* 23 (2003): 92–96.

Biemiller, Carl L. "Florida's Baseball Riviera." *Holiday Magazine*, March 1955.

"The Birth of Methodism." *Newsweek*, June 6, 1938.

Boxerman, Burton A., and Benita W. Boxerman. *Ebbets to Veeck to Busch: Eight Owners Who Shaped Baseball.* Jefferson NC: McFarland, 2003.

"Boycott in Brooklyn." *Time*, May 31, 1948.

Boyle, Kevin. *Arc of Justice: A Saga of Race, Civil Rights, and Murder in the Jazz Age.* New York: Henry Holt, 2004.

Bragan, Bobby, as told to Jeff Guinn. *You Can't Hit the Ball with the Bat on Your Shoulder.* Fort Worth TX: The Summit Group, 1992.

Branham, Robert J. "'Of Thee I Sing': Contesting America." *American Quarterly* 48, no. 4 (December 1996): 623–52.

Broeg, Bob. *The 100 Greatest Moments in St. Louis Sports.* Columbia: University of Missouri Press, 2000.

———. *The Pilot Light and the Gashouse Gang.* St. Louis: Bethany, 1980.

———. *Redbirds! A Century of Cardinals Baseball.* St. Louis: River City, 1981.

Broeg, Bob, and William Miller. *Baseball from a Different Angle.* South Bend IN: Diamond Communications, 1988.

Bryson, Bill. "There's Nobody like 'Em." *Baseball*, May 1940, 540.

Buhite, Russell. "The Continental League and Its Western Carolina League Affiliate: Branch Rickey's Second Finest Hour." *North Carolina Historical Review*, October 2004, 426–60.

Burk, Robert F. *Much More than a Game: Players, Owners, and American Baseball since 1921.* Chapel Hill: University of North Carolina Press, 2001.

———. *Never Just a Game: Players, Owners, and American Baseball to 1920.* Chapel Hill: University of North Carolina Press, 1994.

Burley, Dan. "Negroes in the Major Leagues?" *Inter-Racial Review* 17, no. 7 (July 1944): 102–4.

Butterfield, Roger. "Brooklyn's Gentleman Bum." *Saturday Evening Post*, August 20, 1949.

Caro, Robert A. *The Power Broker: Robert Moses and the Fall of New York.* New York: Vintage, 1975.

Chalberg, Charles C. *Rickey and Robinson: The Preacher, the Player and America's Game.* Wheeling IL: Harlan Davidson, 2000.

Chamberlain, John. "Brains, Baseball, and Branch Rickey." *Harpers*, April 1948.

———. *Life with the Printed Word.* Chicago: Regnery Gateway, 1982.

Charnley, Mitchell V. *The Boy's Life of Herbert Hoover.* New York: Harper & Brothers, 1931.

Clark, Tom. *One Last Round for the Shuffler.* New York: Truck Books, 1979.

Cohane, Tim. "A Branch Grows in Brooklyn." *Look*, March 19, 1946.

———. *Bypaths to Glory.* New York: Doubleday, 1963.

Corum, Bill. *Off and Running.* Edited by Arthur Mann. New York: Holt, 1959.

Creamer, Robert W. *Baseball in 41.* New York: Viking, 1991.

Crepeau, Richard C. *Baseball: America's Diamond Mind, 1919–1941.* Lincoln: University of Nebraska Press, 2000. First published 1980 by University Presses of Florida.

Crichton, Kyle. "Comeback." *Collier's*, July 13, 1940.

Current Biography: Who's News and Why. New York: H-W-Wilson, 1941, 1943, 1945, 1954.

Daley, Arthur. "Baseball's Showmen—The Dodgers." *New York Times Magazine*, June 8, 1947.

D'Amore, Jonathan. *Rogers Hornsby.* Westport CT: Greenwood, 2004.

Davies, Richard O. *Defender of the Old Guard: John Bricker and American Politics.* Columbus: Ohio State University Press, 1993.

"Democrats Try to 'Steal' Missouri Governorship." *Life,* February 24, 1941.

Devaney, John. *The Greatest Cardinals of Them All.* New York: Putnam, 1968.

Dewey, Donald, and Acocella, Nicholas. *Biographical Dictionary of Baseball.* New York: Carroll and Graf, 1994.

Dexter, Charles. "The Mahatma and the Lip." *Baseball Digest,* February 1948.

Dilliard, Irving. "Missouri Has No Governor." *Nation,* February 15, 1941.

Dixon, Phil, with Patrick J. Hannigan. *The Negro Baseball Leagues, 1867–1955: A Photographic History.* Mattituck NY: Amereon House, 1992.

Dorinson, Joseph, and Joram Warmund, eds. *Jackie Robinson: Race, Sports, and the American Dream.* Armonk NY: Sharpe, 1998.

Durocher, Leo. *The Dodgers and Me.* Chicago: Ziff-Davis, 1948.

Durocher, Leo, with Ed Linn. *Nice Guys Finish Last.* New York: Simon and Schuster, 1975.

Eckler, John. "Baseball—Sport or Commerce?" *University of Chicago Law Review* (Fall 1949): 56–78.

Einstein, Izzy. *Prohibition Agent Number One.* New York: Frederick A. Stokes, 1932.

Eisenbath, Mike. *The St. Louis Cardinals Encyclopedia.* Philadelphia: Temple University Press, 2000.

Ellison, David L. *Healing Tuberculosis in the Woods: Medicine and Science at the End of the Nineteenth Century.* Westport CT: Greenwood, 1994.

Erskine, Carl. *Carl Erskine's Tales from the Dodger Dugout.* Champaign IL: Sports Publishing, 2000.

Eskenazi, Gerald. *The Lip: A Biography of Leo Durocher.* New York: William Morrow, 1993.

Evans, Billy. "The Somewhat Different Manager." *Harpers Weekly,* August 27, 1914.

Falkner, David. *Great Time Coming: Jackie Robinson from Baseball to Birmingham.* New York: Simon and Schuster, 1993.

Feldmann, Doug. *Dizzy and the Gas House Gang: The 1934 St. Louis Cardinals and Depression-era Baseball.* Jeffersonville NC: McFarland, 2000.

———. *September Streak: The 1935 Chicago Cubs Chase the Pennant.* Jefferson NC: McFarland, 2003.

Fetter, Henry D. "Robinson in 1947." In *Jackie Robinson: Race, Sports, and the American Dream,* ed. Joseph Dorinson and Joram Warmund, 183–92. Armonk NY: Sharpe, 1998.

———. *Taking On the Yankees: Winning and Losing in the Business of Baseball, 1903–2003.* New York: Norton, 2003.

Fitzgerald, Ed. "Dodger Deacon." *Sport,* November 1947, 59–69.

Fleming, Gordon H. *The Dizziest Season: The Gashouse Gang Chases the Pennant.* New York: William Morrow, 1984.

Fontenay, Charles. *Estes Kefauver: A Biography.* Knoxville: University of Tennessee Press, 1980.

Fox, Stephen. "The Education of Branch Rickey." *Civilization* (Magazine of the Library of Congress), September/October 1995, 52–57.

Frank, Stanley. "Big Bobo." *Colliers,* May 3, 1941.

Frisch, Frank. "Why Player Oddities Have Their Place in Baseball." *Baseball,* May 1926, 552.

————, as told to J. Roy Stockton. *Frank Frisch: The Fordham Flash.* Garden City NY: Doubleday, 1962.

Frommer, Harvey. *Rickey and Robinson: The Men Who Broke Baseball's Color Barrier.* New York: MacMillan, 1982.

"The 'Goat' of the Series." *Baseball,* December 1921, 604.

Goldman, Herbert G. *Jolson: The Legend Comes to Life.* New York: Oxford University Press, 1988.

Golenbock, Peter. *Bums: An Oral History of the Brooklyn Dodgers.* New York: Putnam, 1984.

————. "Men of Conscience." In *Jackie Robinson: Race, Sports, and the American Dream,* ed. Joseph Dorinson and Joram Warmund, 13-21. Armonk NY: Sharpe, 1998.

————. *The Spirit of St. Louis: A History of the St. Louis Cardinals and Browns.* New York: Avon Books, 2000.

Gough, David. *Burt Shotton, Dodgers Manager: A Baseball Biography.* Jeffersonville NC: McFarland, 1994.

Gould, James M. "Considering the Cardinals." *Baseball,* November 1928.

Graham, Frank. *The Brooklyn Dodgers: An Informal History.* 1945. Reprint, Carbondale: Southern Illinois University Press, 2002.

————. *The New York Giants: An Informal History.* 1944. Reprint, Carbondale: Southern Illinois University Press, 2002.

Graham, Frank, Jr. "Branch Rickey Rides Again." *Saturday Evening Post,* March 9, 1963.

————. *A Farewell to Heroes.* New York: Viking, 1981.

Granger, Lester. "No Short-cut to Democracy." *Common Ground,* Spring 1944.

Gregory, Robert. *Diz!: Dizzy Dean and Baseball during the Great Depression.* New York: Viking, 1992.

Griswold, J. B. "Rickey Starts in the Cellar Again." *American,* May 1951.

Groat, Dick, with Frank Dascenzo. *Groat: I Hit and Ran.* Durham NC: Sports Publishing, 1978.

Gunther, John. *Inside Asia.* New York: Harper, 1942.

Hallock, Grace T., and C. E. Turner. *Health Heroes: Edward Livingston Trudeau.* Boston: Heath, 1929.

Hanners, John. "Branch Rickey, College Football Coach." *Western Pennsylvania Historical Magazine* 70 (1987): 291–99.

Harris, Mark. "Branch Rickey Keeps His 40 Year Promise." *Negro Digest,* September 1947, 4–7.

Havill, Adrian. *The Last Mogul: The Unauthorized Biography of Jack Kent Cooke.* New York: St. Martin's, 1992.

Heinz, W. C. "The Rocky Road of Pistol Pete." In *The Best American Sports Writing of the Century,* ed. David Halberstam. Boston: Houghton Mifflin, 1999.

Hernon, Peter, and Terry Ganey. *Under The Influence: The Unauthorized Story of the Anheuser-Busch Dynasty.* New York: Simon and Schuster, 1991.

Hoke, Travis. "The Base in Baseball." *Esquire,* October 1935.

Holland, Gerald. "Mr. Rickey and the Game." In *The Best American Sports Writing of the Century,* ed. David Halberstam. Boston: Houghton Mifflin, 1999. Originally appeared in *Sports Illustrated,* March 7, 1955.

Holmes, Tommy. *Dodger Daze and Knights.* New York: David McKay, 1953.

Holtzman, Jerome, ed. *No Cheering in the Press Box*. Rev. ed. New York: Holt, 1995.

Holway, John. *The Complete Book of Baseball's Negro Leagues: The Other Half of Baseball History*. Fern Park FL: Hastings House, 2001.

Honig, Donald. *Baseball When the Grass Was Real: Baseball from the Twenties to the Forties Told by the Men Who Played It*. New York: Coward, McCann, and Geoheghan, 1975.

———. *The St. Louis Cardinals: An Illustrated History*. New York: Prentice Hall, 1991.

Hood, Robert. *The Gashouse Gang*. New York: William Morrow, 1976.

Hoover, Herbert. *On Growing Up: Letters to American Boys and Girls*. New York: Morrow, 1962.

Horwitz, Richard P., ed. *The American Studies Anthology*. Wilmington DE: SR Books, 2001.

Howsam, Robert Lee. *My Life in Sports*. Privately printed, 1999.

Hubbart, Henry Clyde. *Ohio Wesleyan's First Hundred Years*. Delaware: Ohio Wesleyan University, 1943.

Huhn, Rick. *The Sizzler: A Biography of George Sisler*. Columbia: University of Missouri Press, 2004.

"Introducing Branch Rickey." (Ohio Wesleyan University) *Bulletin* 37, no. 2 (March 1938), extra edition.

James, Bill. *The New Bill James Historical Abstract*. New York: Free Press, 2001.

"Just Chums." *Time*, March 3, 1941.

Kahn, Roger. *The Boys of Summer*. New York: Harper and Row, 1972.

Karst, Gene. "The Cardinals' First Publicity Man." In *Road Trips*, ed. Jim Charlton. Lincoln: University of Nebraska Press, 2004.

Karst, Gene, and Martin Jones. *Who's Who in Professional Baseball*. New York: Arlington House, 1973.

Kieran, John. "Big League Baseball," *Saturday Evening Post*, May 31, 1930.

Kiner, Ralph, with Joe Gergen. *Kiner's Korner: At Bat and on the Air*. New York: Arbor House, 1987.

King, Clyde, with Burton Rocks. *A King's Legacy: The Clyde King Story*. Lincolnwood IL: Masters Press, 1999.

Kirkendall, Richard S. *A History of Missouri: 1919–1953*. Vol. 5. Columbia: University of Missouri Press, 1986.

Koppett, Leonard. *The New York Mets*. New York: MacMillan, 1974.

Koufax, Sandy, with Ed Linn. *Koufax*. New York: Viking, 1966.

Lacy, Sam, with Moses J. Newson. *Fighting for Fairness: The Life Story of Hall of Fame Sportswriter Sam Lacy*. Centreville MD: Tidewater, 1998.

LaGuardia, Robert, and Gene Arceri. *Red: The Tempestuous Life of Susan Hayward*. New York, Macmillan, 1985.

Lamb, Chris. *Blackout: The Untold Story of Jackie Robinson's First Spring Training*. Lincoln: University of Nebraska Press, 2004.

Lanctot, Neil. *Negro League Baseball*. Philadelphia: University of Pennsylvania Press, 2004.

Lane, F. C. "The Speed of 'The Fordham Flash.'" *Baseball*, June 1930.

Langer, William L. *Gas and Flame in World War I*. New York: Knopf, 1965.

Lardner, John. "The Old Emancipator." Pt 1. *Newsweek*, April 2, 1956.

———. "The Old Emancipator." Pt 2. *Newsweek*, April 9, 1956.

———. "Reese and Robinson: The Team within a Team." *New York Times Magazine*, September 18, 1949.

———. "77 Is as 77 Does." *Newsweek*, August 31, 1959.

———. "That Was Baseball: The Crime of Shufflin' Phil Douglas." *New Yorker*, May 12, 1956.

———. "Third League Notes." *Newsweek*, July 20, 1959.

———. "Time for the Shotgun." *Newsweek*, November 9, 1959.

———. "Would It Still Be Brooklyn without the Dodgers?" *New York Times Magazine*, February 26, 1956.

Launius, Roger D. *Seasons in the Sun: The Story of Big League Baseball in Missouri*. Columbia: University of Missouri Press, 2002.

Leavy, Jane. *Sandy Koufax: A Lefty's Legacy*. New York: HarperCollins, 2002.

"Lew Wentz Bids for Championship Cardinals," *Newsweek*, November 24, 1934.

Lieb, Frederick. *The St. Louis Cardinals: The Story of a Great Baseball Club*. 1944. Reprint, Carbondale: Southern Illinois University Press, 2002.

"Life Goes to Dodgertown." *Life*, April 5, 1948.

Lincoln, C. E. "A Conversation with Clyde Sukeforth." *Baseball Research Journal* 16 (1987): 72–73.

Lipman, David. *Mr. Baseball: The Story of Branch Rickey*. New York: Putnam, 1966.

Lowe, Stephen R. *The Kid on the Sandlot: Congress and Professional Sports, 1910–1992*. Bowling Green OH: Bowling Green State University Popular Press, 1995.

Lowenfish, Lee. *The Imperfect Diamond: A History of Baseball's Labor Wars*. Rev. ed. New York: Da Capo, 1991.

———. "Sport, Race and the Baseball Business: The Jackie Robinson Story Revisited." *Arena Review* (Spring 1978): 2–16.

———. "A Tale of Many Cities: The Westward Expansion of Major League Baseball in the 1950s." *Journal of the West* (July 1978): 71–82.

———. "The Two Titans and the Mystery Man." In *Jackie Robinson: Race, Sports, and the American Dream*, ed. Joram Warmund and Joseph Dorinson, 165–78. Armonk NY: Sharpe, 1998.

———. "When All Heaven Rejoiced: Branch Rickey and the Breaking of the Color Line in Major League Baseball." *NINE* 11, no. 1 (Fall 2002): 1–15.

———. "World Series 2000 A.D." In *2000 World Series Official Program*. New York: Major League Baseball, 2000.

Lowenfish, Lee, and Tony Lupien. *The Imperfect Diamond: The Story of Baseball's Reserve System and the Men Who Fought to Change It*. New York: Stein and Day, 1980.

Lucas, John A., and Ronald A. Smith. *Saga of American Sport*. Philadelphia: Lea and Febinger, 1978.

Mack, Connie. *My 66 Years in the Big Leagues: The Great Story of America's National Game*. Philadelphia: Winston, 1950.

Maier, Joseph, and Richard W. Weatherhead. *Frank Tannenbaum: A Biographical Essay*. New York: University Seminars, Columbia University, 1974.

Mann, Arthur. "Bad Boy Bounces Back." *Collier's*, September 30, 1944.

———. *Baseball Confidential*. New York: McKay, 1951.

———. *Branch Rickey: American in Action*. Cambridge MA: Riverside Press/Houghton Mifflin, 1957.

———. "Has Rickey Failed in Pittsburgh?" *Sport*, June 1954.

———. "How to Buy a Ball Club for Peanuts." *Saturday Evening Post*, April 9, 1955.

————. *The Jackie Robinson Story.* New York: Harper's, 1956.

————. "The Life of Branch Rickey—I." *Look,* August 20, 1957.

————. "The Life of Branch Rickey—II." *Look,* September 3, 1957.

————. "The Life of Branch Rickey—III." *Look,* September 17, 1957.

————. "Say Jack Robinson." *Colliers,* March 2, 1946.

————. "The Truth about the Jackie Robinson Case—I." *Saturday Evening Post,* March 13, 1950.

————. "The Truth about the Jackie Robinson Case—II." *Saturday Evening Post,* May 20, 1950.

Maranville, Walter ("Rabbit"). *Run, Rabbit, Run: The Hilarious and Mostly True Tales of Rabbit Maranville.* Cleveland: Society for American Baseball Research, 1991.

Margolick, David. *Beyond Glory: Joe Louis vs. Max Schmeling and a World on the Brink.* New York: Knopf, 2005.

Markusen, David. *Roberto Clemente: The Great One.* Champaign IL: Sports Publishing, 1998.

Marshall, William. *Baseball's Pivotal Era, 1945–1951.* Lexington: University Press of Kentucky, 1999.

McCollister, John. *The Bucs: The Story of the Pittsburgh Pirates.* Lenexa KS: Addaz, 1998.

McCue, Andy. "Two out of Three Ain't Bad: Branch Rickey, Walter O'Malley, and the Man in the Middle of the Dodger Owners' Partnership." *NINE* 14, no. 1 (Fall 2005): 41–46.

————. "Walter O'Malley." Bioproject for the Society for American Baseball Research. http://bioproj.sabr.org/bioproj.cfm?a=v&v=l&bid=790&pid=16919.

McElvaine, Robert S. *Mario Cuomo: A Biography.* New York: Charles Scribner, 1988.

McGee, Bob. *The Greatest Ballpark Ever: Ebbets Field and the Story of the Brooklyn Dodgers.* New Brunswick NJ: Rutgers University Press, 2005.

McKelvey, G. Richard. *The MacPhails: Baseball's First Family of the Front Office.* Jeffersonville NC: McFarland, 2000.

Mead, William B. "Robert Hyland: Surgeon General of Baseball." *National Pastime* 22 (2002): 95–98.

————. *Two Spectacular Seasons: 1930 and 1931.* New York: Macmillan, 1992.

Meadows, Lee. "How Lee Meadows Rose Above All Handicaps to Become a Star." *Baseball,* December 1925.

"Methodism Warmed." *Time,* May 30, 1938.

Miller, James Edward. *The Baseball Business: Pursuing Pennants and Profits in Baltimore.* Chapel Hill: University of North Carolina Press, 1990.

Mitchell, Jerry. *The Amazing Mets.* New York: Grosset and Dunlap, 1970.

Monteleone, John. *Branch Rickey's Little Blue Book: Wit and Strategy from Baseball's Last Wise Man.* New York: Macmillan, 1995.

Mooney, Elizabeth. *In the Shadow of the White Plague: A Memoir.* New York: Crowell, 1979.

Moss, Robert A. "Burt Shotton: The Crucible of 1947." In *Jackie Robinson: Race, Sports, and the American Dream,* ed. Joseph Dorinson and Joram Warmund, 121–31. Armonk NY: Sharpe, 1998.

Murdock, Eugene C. *Ban Johnson: Czar of Baseball.* Westport CT: Greenwood, 1982.

Noguchi, Takuro. "The Residue of Design: How Branch Rickey Organized the St. Louis Cardinals." Bachelor's thesis, Brown University, May 2005.

Okkonen, Marc. *The Federal League of 1914–1915: Baseball's Third Major League.* Garrett Park MD: Society for American Baseball Research, 1989.

The Old Ball Game as Told by Mr. Branch Rickey. An Art Lieberman Production, 1965. DVD.

Oliphant, Thomas. *Praying for Gil Hodges: A Memoir of the 1955 World Series and One Family's Love of the Brooklyn Dodgers.* New York: Thomas Dunne Books/St. Martin's, 2005.

O'Toole, Andrew. *Branch Rickey in Pittsburgh.* Jeffersonville NC: McFarland, 2000.

Owen, M. "Mystery of the Missed Third Strike." *Colliers,* April 18, 1942, 19.

Parrott, Harold. *The Lords of Baseball.* 1976. Reprint, Atlanta: Longstreet, 2001.

"Peace, It's Wonderful." *Newsweek,* August 15, 1960.

Peale, Norman Vincent, ed. *Faith Made Them Champions.* Pleasantville NY: Guideposts, 1954.

Peary, Danny, ed. *Cult Baseball Players: The Greats, the Flakes, the Weird, and the Wonderful.* New York: Simon and Schuster, 1990.

Peterson, Houston, ed. *A Treasury of the World's Greatest Speeches.* New York: Simon and Schuster, 1954.

Pietrusza, David. *Judge and Jury: The Life and Times of Kenesaw Mountain Landis.* South Bend IN: Diamond Communications, 1998.

Polner, Murray. *Branch Rickey: A Biography.* New York: Atheneum, 1982.

Prince, Carl E. *Brooklyn's Dodgers: The Bums, the Borough, and the Best of Baseball, 1947–1957.* New York: Oxford University Press, 1996.

Rabinowitz, William Scott. "Thriving in Hard Times: The St. Louis Cardinals Make the Best of the Depression." *Gateway Heritage,* Summer 1988.

Rader, Benjamin G. *Baseball: A History of America's Game.* 2nd ed. Urbana: University of Illinois Press, 2002.

Rains, Rob. *The St. Louis Cardinals: The 100th Anniversary History.* New York: St. Martin's, 1992.

Rampersad, Arnold. *Jackie Robinson: A Biography.* New York: Knopf, 1997.

Reisler, Jim. *Black Writers/Black Baseball.* Jeffersonville NC: McFarland, 1994.

———, ed. *Guys, Dolls, and Curveballs: Damon Runyon on Baseball.* New York: Carroll and Graf, 2005.

Rice, Robert. "Thoughts on Baseball—I." *New Yorker,* May 27, 1950.

———. "Thoughts on Baseball—II." *New Yorker,* June 3, 1950.

Richards, Paul, with Tim Cohane. "The American League Is Dying." *Look,* February 17, 1959, 41–47.

Rickey, Branch. "Goodby to Old Ideas." *Life,* August 2, 1954.

———. "How It Looks from Where I Sit." *Look,* May 27, 1958.

———. *Recordings of Branch Rickey.* Anne Grimes [Folklore] Collection. Tape 56. Washington DC: Smithsonian Institution, n.d. Audiocassette.

———. "World Series 2000 A.D." *Colliers,* October 7, 1950.

Rickey, Branch, with Robert Riger. *The American Diamond: A Documentary of the Game of Baseball.* New York: Simon and Schuster, 1965.

Ritter, Lawrence S. *The Glory of Their Times: The Story of the Early Days of Baseball Told by the Men Who Played It.* New York: Morrow, 1984.

———. *Lost Ballparks: A Celebration of Baseball's Legendary Fields.* New York: Viking Studio Books, 1992.

Roberts, Milton. "Historically Speaking: Charles Follis." *Black Sports*, November 1975.

Robinson, Jackie. "Trouble Ahead Needn't Bother You." In *Faith Made Them Champions*, ed. Norman Vincent Peale. Carmel NY: Guideposts Associates, 1954.

——. "What's Wrong with the Negro Leagues." *Ebony*, June 1948, 16–18.

Robinson, Jackie, with Charles Dexter. *Baseball Has Done It*. 1964. Reprint, Brooklyn NY: 2004.

Robinson, Jackie, with Alfred Duckett. *I Never Had It Made: An Autobiography*. 1972. Reprint, New York: HarperCollins, 1995.

Robinson, Jackie, as told to Wendell Smith. *Jackie Robinson: My Own Story*. New York: Greenberg, 1948.

Robinson, Rachel, with Lee Daniels. *Jackie Robinson: An Intimate Portrait*. New York: Abrams, 1996.

Rodengen, Jeffrey L. *The Legend of Pfizer*. Ft. Lauderdale FL: Write Stuff, 1999.

Rodney, Lester. *Press Box Red: The Story of Lester Rodney, the Communist Who Helped Break the Color Line in American Sports*. Philadelphia: Temple University Press, 2003.

Roeder, Bill. *Jackie Robinson*. New York: Barnes, 1949.

Roper, Scott C., and Stephanie Abbot Roper. "'We're Going to Give It All We Have for This Grand Little Town': Baseball Integration and the 1946 Nashua Dodgers." *Historic New Hampshire* 53, no. 1-2 (Spring–Summer 1998): 3–18.

Rowan, Carl T., with Jackie Robinson. *Wait Till Next Year*. New York: Random House, 1960.

Ruck, Rob. *Sandlot Seasons: Sport in Black Pittsburgh*. Urbana: University of Illinois Press, 1987.

Rust, Art, Jr. *Get That Nigger off the Field! A Sparkling, Informal History of the Black Man in Baseball*. New York: Delacorte, 1976.

Safire, William, ed. *Lend Me Your Ears: Great Speeches in History*. New York: Norton, 1992.

Schwarz, Alan. *The Numbers Game: Baseball's Lifelong Fascination with Statistics*. New York: T. Dunne Books, 2004.

Seymour, Harold. *Baseball: The Golden Age*. New York: Oxford University Press, 1971.

Shaplen, Robert. "The Nine Lives of Leo Durocher" (three-part series). *Sports Illustrated*, May 23, May 30, and June 6, 1955.

Shapiro, Michael. *The Last Great Season, 1956*. New York: Simon and Schuster, 2003.

Shatzkin, Mike. *The Ballplayers*. New York: Macmillan, 1990.

Sheean, Robert. "John Galbreath: Buildings, Brood Mares, and Baseball." *Fortune*, July 1955, 114.

Sheed, Wilfrid. "And Now Playing Second Base for Brooklyn . . . Jackie Robinson." *Esquire*, December 1983.

——. *Baseball and Lesser Sports*. New York: HarperCollins, 1991.

Shotton, Burt. "The Batting Order." *Baseball*, June 1930.

Silber, Irwin. *Press Box Red: The Story of Lester Rodney, the Communist Who Helped Break the Color Line in American Sports*. Philadelphia: Temple University Press, 2003.

Simon, Tom, ed. *Deadball Stars of the National League*. Cleveland: Society for American Baseball Research, 2004.

Sisler, George. "Why I Enlisted in the Army." *Baseball*, March 1919, 265–67.

Skipper, John C. *Wicked Curve: The Life and Troubled Times of Grover Cleveland Alexander*. Jefferson NC: McFarland, 2006.

Smith, Curt. *America's Dizzy Dean.* St. Louis: Bethany, 1978.

Smith, Red. *Red Smith on Baseball: The Game's Greatest Writer on the Game's Greatest Years.* Chicago: Dee, 2000.

Smith, Richard Norton. *Thomas E. Dewey and His Times.* New York: Simon and Schuster, 1982.

Smith, Ronald A. "Robeson and Robinson." In *The Jackie Robinson Reader,* ed. Jules Tygiel, 169–88. New York: Dutton, 1997.

Snyder, Brad. *Beyond the Shadow of the Senators: The Untold Story of the Homestead Grays and the Integration of Baseball.* Chicago: Contemporary Books, 2003.

"The Specialist." *Time,* November 3, 1947.

Spink, J. G. Taylor. *Judge Landis and 25 Years of Baseball.* St. Louis: Sporting News Press, 1974.

Staten, Vince. *Ol' Diz: A Biography of Dizzy Dean.* New York: HarperCollins, 1992.

Steinberg, Steve. *Baseball in St. Louis, 1900–1925.* Charleston SC: Arcadia, 2004.

Stevens, John D. "As the Branch Is Bent: Rickey as College Coach at the University of Michigan." *NINE* 2, no. 2 (1994): 277–85.

Stockton, J. Roy. "A Brain Comes to Brooklyn." *Saturday Evening Post,* February 15, 1943.

———. "Double-whammy Doc." *Saturday Evening Post,* July 31, 1943.

———. *The Gashouse Gang and a Couple of Other Guys.* New York: Barnes, 1945.

———. "Me and My Public: What Happened to Dizzy Dean." *Saturday Evening Post,* September 12, 1936.

———. "Singing Sam, the Cut-rate Man." *Saturday Evening Post,* February 22, 1947, 17.

Sullivan, Neil J. *The Dodgers Move West.* New York: Oxford University Press, 1987.

Sweet, William Warren. *Religion on the American Frontier, 1783–1840.* Vol. 4, *The Methodists.* Chicago: University of Chicago Press, 1946.

Tannenbaum, Frank. *Slave and Citizen: The Negro in the Americas.* New York: Knopf, 1947.

Taylor, Robert. *Saranac: America's Magic Mountain.* Boston: Houghton Mifflin, 1986.

Taylor, Robert Lewis. "Borough Defender—I." *New Yorker,* July 12, 1941.

———. "Borough Defender—II." *New Yorker,* July 19, 1941.

Terrell, Roy. "3rd League Cities Pin Hopes on This Man." *Sports Illustrated,* July 20, 1959.

Thompson, Fresco, with Cy Rice. *Every Diamond Doesn't Sparkle.* New York: McKay, 1964.

Titchener, Campbell B. *The George Kirksey Story: Bringing Major League Baseball to Houston.* Austin TX: Eakin, 1989.

Tygiel, Jules. *Baseball's Great Experiment: Jackie Robinson and His Legacy.* New York: Oxford University Press, 1983.

———, ed. *The Jackie Robinson Reader.* New York: Dutton, 1997.

———. *Past Time: Baseball as History.* New York: Oxford University Press, 2000.

Urwin, E. C., and Douglas Wollen. *John Wesley, Christian Citizen: Selections from His Social Teaching.* London: Epworth, 1937.

Veeck, Bill with Ed Linn. *The Hustler's Handbook.* New York: Putnam, 1965.

Wagenheim, Kal. *Clemente!* New York: Praeger, 1973.

Ward, John J. "Here's an Outfielder Who Always Hustles." *Baseball,* June 1925.

———. "Lee Douthit, a Victim of World Series Perils." *Baseball,* January 1927.

Warfield, Don. *The Roaring Redhead: Larry MacPhail, Baseball's Great Innovator.* South Bend IN: Diamond Communications, 1987.

Bibliography

Weiner, Jay. *Stadium Games: Fifty Years of Big League Greed and Bush League Boondoggles.* Minneapolis: University of Minnesota Press, 2000.

Wesley, John. "Thoughts on Slavery." In E. C. Urwin and Douglas Wollen, *John Wesley, Christian Citizen: Selections from His Social Teaching.* London: Epworth, 1937.

White, G. Edward. *Creating the National Pastime: Baseball Transforms Itself, 1903–1953.* Princeton NJ: Princeton University Press, 1996.

Who's Who in America 1930–31. Chicago: Marquis Publications, 1931.

Wilber, Cynthia J. *For the Love of the Game: Baseball Memories from the Men Who Were There.* New York: William Morrow, 1992.

Williams, Joe. "Deacon Bill." *Colliers*, September 14, 1940.

Woodward, Stanley. "How to Build a Ball Club." *Argosy*, June 1950. Clipping in Branch Rickey Papers, Library of Congress, Washington DC.

Yablonsky, Lewis. *George Raft.* San Francisco: Mercury House, 1989.

Index

Black, William, 581

Blackburn, Ken, 559, 583, 586

black players: American League inclusion of, 433; and the civil rights movement, 538; increased signing of, 483; Giants and, 462; scouting of, 349–50, 354, 525

"Black Sox," 117, 129–30, 252, 294, 569

Blades, Ray, 158, 197, 291, 293, 296, 297, 301, 331

Blaik, Earl "Red," 537

Bloomington MN, 552

Boise ID, 53–54, 57

Bondy, Leo, 177

Bonham, Ernie, 317

bonuses, 506–7, 516, 556, 569. *See also* salaries

The Book of Common Prayer, 361

Bordaragay, Stanley "Frenchy," 294, 617n2

Bossert Hotel, 498

Bostic, Joe, 361–63

Boston Braves: (1941), 312; (1947), 427; (1948), 461; (1949), 468–69, 475; (1950), 492; and Babe Ruth, 241; and Eddie Stanky, 447; move to Milwaukee, 540; and players' union, 393; and Sam Jethroe, 483; and Scott Perry, 101; in World Series (1914), 81; in World Series (1948), 462

Boston Celtics, 529

Boston MA, 540, 541

Boston Red Sox: (1915), 81; (1918), 102; (1949), 475; dominance of, 540; Jackie Robinson tryout for, 363–64; and players' union, 393; sale of Babe Ruth, 302; in World Series (1916), 477; in World Series (1918), 115; in World Series (1946), 402

Bottomley, Jim, 141; and Cardinals (1923), 144–45, 148; and Cardinals (1924), 149; and Cardinals (1926), 157, 163; and Cardinals (1927), 179; and Cardinals (1928), 184; and Cardinals (1929), 192; and Cardinals (1930), 195, 197; and Cardinals (1931), 213–14; and Cardinals (1932), 221; and Cardinals (1933), 231; memories of, 3–4; recruitment of, 118–19; salary of, 150; signing of, 292; trade of, 220; and World Series (1930), 200

Boudreau, Lou, 428

Bowen, Rex, 113, 327–28, 338, 501, 515, 517, 560

Bowman, Bob, 296, 302–3

Boyer, Ken, 585, 588, 589, 596

Braddock, James, 355

Bradenton FL, 142, 144, 191, 208–9, 211, 236, 273–74

Bradley, Alva, 433, 451

Bragan, Bobby, 332, 335, 418–20, 534

Bramham, William, 283, 380–81, 422

Branca, Ralph: and Dodgers (1944), 342; and Dodgers (1946), 401; and Dodgers (1947), 432, 436, 438; and Dodgers (1948), 453–54, 462; and Dodgers (1949), 477; and Dodgers (1950), 482, 492; and Dodgers (1951), 508; marriage of, 630n20; salary of, 457; in tryout camp, 339

Branch Rickey: American in Action (Mann), 593

Branch Rickey's Little Blue Book (Monteleone), 8

Brant, Clyde, 19, 20

Breadon, Samuel: and attendance, 219, 233, 251–52, 266, 272; and Austin McHenry, 134; and Billy Southworth, 193, 301; and Branch Rickey's resignation, 148–51; business decisions of, 297–99; and Cardinals' financial situation (1932), 222; as Cardinals president, 119–24; and Charles Street, 194; at Charley Barrett's funeral, 293; Columbus Redbirds affiliation of, 206, 207; contract offers of, 139–40, 181, 225, 272, 309; and Cubs-Cardinals doubleheader (1931), 213; as "David Harum," 124; and discipline problems (1935), 265; and discipline problems (1937), 274, 276, 277; and Dizzy Dean's salary, 269; and Dizzy Dean's trade, 285–86; and exhibition games, 162–63, 243, 244; and farm system, 130, 155–56, 283; and football, 455; and Frank Frisch, 232–33; and Grover Cleveland Alexander, 192; and Hornsby-Rickey confrontation, 147; and Hyde Beer sponsorship, 324; and injuries, 294, 298; and Larry MacPhail, 234; and Marty Marion, 304; and Miguel Gonzalez, 288; at Minor League Baseball meeting (1930), 203; and Paul Derringer, 211; and pennant victory (1934), 251; and racial integration, 396, 430; and Ray Gillespie, 395; relationship with Branch Rickey, 133, 183, 291, 309; retirement of, 451; and Rogers Hornsby, 160–61, 170–73, 176–77, 180, 223; and Roy Stockton, 319; and sale rumors, 260–63; and spring training (1922), 132–33; and suspension of Dizzy Dean and Paul Dean, 246; and World Series (1928), 187; and World Series (1930), 200

Cold Spring Harbor Library
Cold Spring Harbor, NY 11724

4. Each borrower is responsible for all items checked out on
   his/her library card and for all fines accruing on the same.

DEMCO